228218

THE ECONOMIC DEVELOPMENT
OF JAPAN

THE ECONOMIC
DEVELOPMENT OF
JAPAN

Growth and Structural Change
1868-1938

BY WILLIAM W. LOCKWOOD

PRINCETON, NEW JERSEY

PRINCETON UNIVERSITY PRESS

1954

To My Father

PREFACE

"WRITING a book is an adventure," Sir Winston Churchill once said. "To begin with, it is a joy and an amusement. Then it becomes a mistress. And then it becomes a master. Then it becomes a tyrant and in the last phase, when you are reconciled to your servitude, you kill the monster."

This volume was begun several years ago as a modest inquiry into the international aspects of Japan's economic growth in modern times. It was to have two purposes. One was to show the importance to Japan of the international order which her militarists had done so much to destroy, and which would have to be recreated in its essentials if she were again to prosper. The other was to challenge a notion prevalent in books about Japan—the notion that her economic development since the Meiji Restoration had been confined mainly within the sphere of foreign trade and factory industry, that its benefits had been largely drained away in imperialist wars and *zaibatsu* profits, and that otherwise it had little substance. New evidence had lately become available, and new tools of economic analysis. It seemed that the nature and significance of Japan's entry into the world economy could now be given a fresh and more authentic interpretation.

In some degree, I trust, these purposes are served by the volume as it finally appears. Before it was completed, however, it had broadened into a study of the whole process of Japan's economic growth from 1868 to 1938. Initially I should hardly have dared undertake such a work, particularly in view of my limited access to the immense body of Japanese literature in the field. But Japan's expanding economic relations overseas were of course intimately associated with all aspects of her economic modernization and structural change. And the sources available failed to provide satisfactory answers, especially quantitative answers, to basic questions about this growth process. Step by step, therefore, I became involved in the harassing perplexities of Japanese statistics bearing on the expansion of national output, markets and technological change, capital formation, and other aspects of development. These matters in turn raised absorbing questions concerning the dynamics of growth, particularly the role of the State and the nature of Japanese business enterprise.

The resulting study, it is hoped, will help to illuminate the wider perspectives of Japan's remarkable industrialization over half a century. The first two chapters chronicle the history of the period, primarily for readers little acquainted with modern Japan. Chapter 3 attempts to establish the over-all dimensions of growth in the

economy—an impressive record of achievement. The remainder of
the volume takes up the chief elements in the development process,
and the conditions shaping the direction and rate of change. These
chapters call into question a number of opinions about Japan that
have long circulated with little challenge. Others they confirm. And
at still other points they are inconclusive, pointing to matters that
require more intensive study. Of the various shortcomings of the
analysis, I regret most keenly the fact that the impersonal statistics
which crowd its pages fail entirely to convey a sense of the human
aspirations, the personal leadership, the toil and learning and sacrifice which built the Japanese economy.

Japan's economic development after 1868 brought an unfolding
of productive powers thus far unique in the annals of Asia. A long
wave of expansion, sustained by the inflow of technology from the
West, persisted for nearly seventy years until shattered by a catastrophic war. The devastation of that war, and the new circumstances
to which it has given rise, justify treatment of the prewar decades as
a separate era. Yet both the achievements and the shortcomings
of this transition to industrialism have a continuing significance
for the Japanese today, as they painfully rebuild their economic
life.

The experience of Japan also contains lessons for nations of Asia
still only on the threshold of economic development. These lessons
have been too much neglected, in their constructive aspect, perhaps
because the well-known militaristic and plutocratic features of
prewar Japanese society suggest that Japan's pattern of growth
is more to be guarded against than emulated. With all the contrasts between Japan and her neighbors, they can learn more from
her in many fields than from any Western nation. It is hoped that
this volume will draw her experience more directly into the study
and planning of economic development in Asia—"the great un-
finished business of the Industrial Revolution."

Turning to more personal matters, I confront a long list of obligations to persons who have encouraged this study. For financial
assistance and working opportunity I owe much to the Rockefeller
Foundation, as well as to Princeton University, particularly its
University Research Committee and the Woodrow Wilson School of
Public and International Affairs. Here I must express my gratitude
especially to Dr. Joseph H. Willits and Mr. Roger F. Evans, of
the Foundation; and to Professor Dana G. Munro, Professor Harold
H. Sprout, and Dean J. Douglas Brown, of the University. Like
so many students of Far Eastern affairs over the past twenty years,
I am also greatly indebted to Mr. William L. Holland, of the Institute of Pacific Relations, both for his personal advice and for a

summer's research grant from the Institute. Others who have assisted in one way or another include Professors Abbott Payson Usher and Alexander Gerschenkron, of Harvard University; Professor Klaus Knorr, my colleague at Princeton; Sir George Sansom, of Columbia University; Mr. Harry Oshima, of the United Nations Secretariat; and, not least, Miss Dorothea Zyfers of the Woodrow Wilson School. The text of this volume further acknowledges, again inadequately, the many Japanese and Western scholars upon whose work I have drawn so freely.

WILLIAM W. LOCKWOOD

Woodrow Wilson School of Public
   and International Affairs
Princeton University
March 1954

CONTENTS

TABLES

CHARTS

THE ECONOMIC DEVELOPMENT
OF JAPAN

Crop areas taken from Edwin O. Reischauer, *The United States and Japan*, Cambridge: Harvard University Press, 1950, end-paper map.

CHAPTER 1

FOUNDATIONS OF INDUSTRIALISM: THE MEIJI ERA

The Restoration Background

THE speed with which Japan emerged from quasi feudalism to become a modern state with a large sector of its economy organized along industrial, capitalistic lines is in striking contrast to the centuries of evolutionary growth characterizing the process in the West.

In Europe capitalistic production had its origins in the late Middle Ages. In England, for example, it can be traced back to the growth of exports of wool and wool manufactures as early as the thirteenth and fourteenth centuries. Foreign trade stimulated the rise of the merchant-employer system of industry under the leadership of merchant guilds. Gradually there developed in Western Europe new modes of economic organization, e.g., wholesale trade, improvements in banking and transport, commercial accounting, the domestic system of manufacture and later the factory. These interrelated changes were associated with other expansive influences which slowly undermined the old, localistic order. Of primary importance was the widening of markets for staple manufactures. The growing requirements of armies and navies, the spread of colonization and conquest, the growth of population and cities—all played their part. So, too, did the progress of mechanical invention, especially in the utilization of iron and new sources of power. By the nineteenth century the factory, with its organization of labor and power machinery in a single coordinated process, was firmly established in England. More slowly it spread across the Continent, fostered by the growing power of the merchant-industrialist class allied with the new national states in their competitive struggle for supremacy.

By comparison, Japan as recently as the early nineteenth century remained in a stage of economic development hardly more advanced than that of Western Europe in the late Middle Ages. Of her 28 to 30 million people the overwhelming majority were unfree, poverty-stricken peasants. They lived mostly in self-sufficient rural villages. The foundation of the economy and chief source of wealth was the cultivation of rice, carried on by primitive methods little changed over the centuries.

This agrarian base supported an aristocratic ruling hierarchy of some 270 territorial lords (*daimyō*) and the warrior class (*samurai*). The former had long held feudal sway in their territorial fiefs, while acknowledging nominal allegiance to the emperor in Kyoto. Since 1603, however, they had been actually under the dominance of one of the great military families, the Tokugawa, at Edo (Tokyo). Some 40% or more of the peasants' produce was annually appropriated by the *daimyō* and the shogun (the hereditary Tokugawa dictator) for the support of themselves and a vast army of vassals and retainers numbering upwards of 2 million. The remainder barely sufficed to sustain the population at its existing level. An earlier growth in numbers, associated with an expansion of the cultivated area in the seventeenth century, had been arrested, despite the persistence of high fertility patterns. Thereafter a precarious equilibrium between population and food supply was maintained only by famine, disease, abortion, infanticide, i.e., by operation of all the Malthusian checks save war.

Accompanying the growth of cities in the seventeenth and eighteenth centuries, and fostered by the peace and unity of Tokugawa rule, was a considerable development of manufacturing, mining, and interregional trade. The home industry of farm households came to be supplemented by workshop production organized under clan monopolies or craft guilds.[1] But industrial output continued to be essentially handicraft in character. And the artisans and tradesmen remained an inferior class without political rights or social status. Manufacturing was dispersed through rural villages or concentrated in castle towns and centers like Edo and Osaka where it served the wants of the aristocrats. Trade was predominantly a movement of rice from country to city, mostly in payment of feudal dues. There was only limited exchange of industrial products. Mainly these were luxury items. Commerce remained crippled by manifold political restrictions and regulations, including an almost complete ban on foreign intercourse.[2] Through strict controls over

[1] After 1800 silk textiles, *sake*, rapeseed oil, cotton cloth, candles, seaweed, etc. were produced on an increasing scale in various regions of Japan for the commercial markets of Edo, Osaka, and Kyoto. By this time Edo already boasted a population of over 1 million. However, like other Asiatic cities of its time, it was a vast agglomeration of people rather than a highly specialized and coordinated organization of labor such as the urban metropolis of today presents. See Eijiro Honjo, *Social and Economic History of Japan*, Kyoto, 1935, pp. 75-76; also Takao Tsuchiya, *An Economic History of Japan*, Tokyo, 1937, pp. 175-86.

[2] In 1640 all foreign trade and foreign contacts were excluded from Japan except at Nagasaki, where a few Dutchmen and Chinese were allowed to remain under rigid supervision. The death penalty was prescribed for any Japanese attempting to leave or return to his country, and the construction of ocean-going vessels (i.e., those of more than 500-*koku* capacity) was forbidden. It is interesting to speculate on the different course which developments in Japan might have taken had the extensive foreign intercourse of the sixteenth century been allowed to expand, in-

travel and trade, as well as over freedom of occupation and enterprise, the Tokugawa regime sought to suppress the growth of any new forces which might threaten the feudal-agrarian foundations of the state.

"This late feudalism," writes E. Herbert Norman, "represents one of the most conscious attempts in history to freeze society in a rigid hierarchical mold."[3] Significantly, nevertheless, it served only to stunt and not to stifle the advances in technology and commerce which had received their first sharp impulse in the turbulent fifteenth and sixteenth centuries. Already by 1750 and even earlier the institutions of agrarian feudalism were heavily qualified. The economic disorder of the next 100 years itself testifies to this fact. Much of it can be attributed simply to the ineptness of an archaic military dictatorship in dealing with the resulting problems of population growth, currency, debt, and taxation. Only when Japan's industrialization in the twentieth century is seen as a projection of these earlier trends, now accelerated by the opening of the country to Western influence, can its speed and its technical achievements be understood.

The Decay of Feudalism. The modernization of Japan after 1868 has been likened to the bursting of a dam. It was the more violent because it brought the release of long-pent-up forces.

In part these pressures were economic in character. The latter half of the Tokugawa period, from the early eighteenth century onwards, resembled in certain respects the situation which had recurred periodically in the long history of Japan and other Oriental countries. Consumption requirements expanded beyond the inelastic limits of a backward and exploitative agrarian society, as a result of population growth and the insatiable demands of a parasitic ruling caste.[4] Production and distribution within the traditional framework also became subject to violent disturbances arising from the mismanagement of public finance. From 1750 on the Shogunate was in almost constant financial difficulty. It sought escape by heavier taxes, borrowing, and disorderly debasements of the currency. In lesser degree this was true of many *daimyō*, who tried in turn to solve their problems at the expense of the *samurai* and peasantry. These circumstances sharpened the struggle among con-

---

stead of being stifled, for the next 200 years. The commercial and capitalistic evolution of the old agrarian economy would certainly have been accelerated; on the other hand, Japan might not have succeeded as well as she did in escaping the imperialist controls which the Western powers fastened upon most other Far Eastern peoples during the eighteenth and nineteenth centuries.

[3] *Japan's Emergence as a Modern State,* New York, 1940, p. 12.

[4] See G. B. Sansom, *Japan, A Short Cultural History,* New York, 1943, p. 307; James Murdoch, *A History of Japan,* vol. III, London, 1926, pp. 201-07.

tending classes to either maintain or improve their positions. Alone they might have led to nothing more than a redistribution of political power along traditional lines. This time, however, new and revolutionary forces were at work within the country. The traditional institutions of Japanese feudalism were progressively undermined at the foundations by the slow growth of a commercial economy, and the rise of a new and ambitious class of merchants and townspeople.

As in Europe, the old self-contained barter economy, and the rigid pattern of class relations associated with it, gradually crumbled under these mercantile influences. The *samurai*, a *rentier* caste, became progressively impoverished and indebted to the merchants (*chōnin*) as their rice stipends proved inadequate to meet increasing money requirements. Attempts to extract larger revenues from the peasants only intensified the difficulties of the latter, who likewise found themselves exposed to the insecurity of a growing money economy. Currency debasement and crop variations brought wide fluctuations in the price of rice, the one crop that was the precarious base of the economy. To these uncertainties the manipulations of merchant speculators further contributed, now injuring the farmer and now the city consumer.

The *chōnin*, though expanding their wealth and influence at the expense of the *samurai*, chafed under multifarious feudal restrictions on initiative and opportunity. These included restrictions on the transfer of land, on foreign trade, on improvements in internal transport, and on the manufacture of certain goods. Most irksome was the subordinate social status to which they were confined by an arrogant military aristocracy. Progressive clans also sought to expand their revenues through promotion of new manufactures and of trade. Here developed a new breeding ground for mercantilist ambition. The energetic young *samurai*-bureaucrats who pioneered this development began to display a new spirit of capitalistic enterprise which could only find full expression through a break with the *ancien régime*.

To these difficulties and discontents were added a series of famines and natural disasters in the latter Tokugawa years. The misery of the peasants in certain areas drove increasing numbers off the land in flight to the cities. After 1750 the strain on the traditional structure was reflected at the base in a series of peasant rebellions.[5] At

[5] Hugh Borton, *Peasant Uprisings in Japan of the Tokugawa Period*, Tokyo, 1938. These rural insurrections, like the famines and natural catastrophes which incited them, are reminiscent of similar occurrences in Europe during the fourteenth century. See Henri Pirenne, *Economic and Social History of Mediaeval Europe*, New York, undated, pp. 195-201. While comparisons are difficult, it is probable that the Japanese peasantry were no worse off than the farming class of large parts of

the top there was a steady decay of the power of the Shogunate, and increasing defiance of its authority by the more independent clans. The whole process culminated in a crisis of public finance in the nineteenth century, reminiscent of that of Louis XVI on the eve of the French Revolution. All the authority of the *Bakufu* (the Shogunal regime), with its highly developed system of espionage and military repression, was unable finally to stave off collapse after 1850.[6]

Economic discontent was reinforced in turn by other factors in the last decades of the Tokugawas. Some were literary and religious in character. An intellectual renaissance led to a rediscovery of national traditions and a revival of Shintoism, with its glorification of the emperor, whose traditional prerogatives had been usurped by the shogun. Such movements were eagerly supported by dissident clans restive under the autocratic rule of Edo. It was the arrival of Western gunboats and traders, however, coinciding with the virtual bankruptcy of the Shogunate, which precipitated the crisis. The expansion of Russia in the north, the encroachments of Britain and other powers in China, finally the "apparition of Perry" and his warships—all these were watched with rising apprehension in Japan. They revived and intensified memories of European ambitions and predatory rivalries dating back to the sixteenth century, before the exclusionist edicts of Tokugawa Ieyasu and his suc-

---

Europe at various times, for example, in the eighteenth century. Kurt Singer, in his interesting annotations of Tsuchiya's *Economic History of Japan*, cited, points out that the Bordeaux farmer of this time paid taxes and feudal obligations no less extortionate than those paid by the Tokugawa farmer, and that such exactions also tended in France to increase as the nobility became involved in growing financial difficulties.

6 There are also parallels and common elements in the process of financial disorder and agrarian decay as it appeared in both China and Japan after 1800. However, the extent of economic deterioration in China seems to have been more serious than in Japan, and in any case the firm grip of the ruling class in the island empire precluded anything like the Taiping Rebellion.

Moreover, there seems to have been a basic difference in the nature of the disorders attacking the foundations of the State. The revolutionary change which took place in Japan after 1850, while equally stimulated by the intrusion of the West, was partly a response to expansive forces already latent within the Japanese economy. These were economically progressive in that they fostered the growth of industrial production, trade, and commercial capital, but their full expression required a reorganization of political institutions. In China the nineteenth century witnessed the reappearance of the familiar cycle of economic decline and dynastic upheaval. Except for disruptive influences from the West, this might have left unchallenged the basic pattern of an agrarian bureaucratic state. Japan seems to have been headed for some radical change in her institutions in any event. Only the tight seclusion policy of the Tokugawas prevented it from appearing some time before it did. This difference had a good deal to do, no doubt, with the contrasting response of the two societies to the impact of the West in the nineteenth century.

cessors. This time the conviction spread that a policy of passive isolation could lead only to disaster.

Effective power within the feudal clans had now passed largely from the control of the effete *daimyō*—"aimless nobodies," W. E. Griffis[7] calls them—into the hands of able young *samurai* of inferior rank. By various means these men had steadily acquired a growing knowledge of Western military science, practical arts, and history. In the new learning, and in expanding intercourse with the West, the more farsighted saw fresh possibilities for national rejuvenation under the aegis of the emperor, as well as new scope for personal enterprise and power. More and more it seemed that only through such a course of action was national survival possible. The obstacle was the Shogunate, which now found itself caught between the insistent demands of the foreign powers and the growing assertiveness of rebellious clans grouped around the throne.

Intense indignation was aroused in Kyoto circles by the treaties of the 1850's. In these the Shogun was forced to grant such privileges as limitation of customs duties and extraterritorial rights to the "hairy foreigners." No less rankling were the indemnities subsequently exacted in reprisal for incidents. The luckless *Bakufu* was now attacked as the betrayer of national interests and usurper of imperial prerogatives, as well as the cause of mounting economic distress. Already weakened by internal decay and financial ineptitude, which had brought it to the verge of insolvency, it was unable to stem the rising tide of revolt. In the early 1860's the forced residence of the *daimyō* at Edo, a powerful device of political control in earlier years, was abolished. "Like wild birds from an opened cage," they fled with all their retainers in the space of a week. Other reforms followed, but they were too little and too late. In 1867-68, after a brief military struggle, the western clans emerged victorious; the Shogunate fell. With it collapsed the whole structure of centralized feudalism.[8]

[7] The contemporary views of this shrewd American observer are of interest. Griffis arrived in Japan shortly after the Restoration and knew personally many of its leaders. Writing in 1875 (*The Mikado's Empire*, New York, 1894, pp. 292-93) he notes that "long before its abolition feudalism was ready for its grave." To explain its collapse solely by events after 1853 is like explaining the Civil War "by beginning at Sumter." Of the political and intellectual movements leading to the Restoration, Griffis writes as follows: "There existed, long before the advent of Perry, definite conceptions of the objects to be accomplished. These lay in the minds of earnest thinkers, to whom life under the dual system was a perpetual winter of discontent, like snow upon the hills. In due season the spring would have come that was to make the flood. The presence of Perry in the Bay of Yedo was like an untimely thaw, or a hot south-wind in February. The snow melted, the streams gathered. Like houses built upon the sand, the shōgunate and the feudal system were swept away."

[8] The situation is epitomized by the leading Western historian of Japan, G. B.

Restoration and Reform. Supported by the triumphant clansmen, a new boy emperor assumed the throne in 1868. In his Charter Oath he promised a series of reforms, including the famous pledge that "intellect and learning would be sought for throughout the world, in order to establish the foundations of Empire."

During the next decade sweeping reforms were undertaken by the new clan bureaucrats around the throne. Their central purpose was to strengthen and consolidate the new regime. In 1869 the clans were induced to surrender their land registers; in 1871 came the abolition of fiefs. A new structure of national administration and taxation arose on the ruins of the old territorial organization. As in France after 1789, feudal proprietary rights were swept away by decree. In Japan, however, government pensions (later commuted to national bonds) were issued to the feudal nobility in return for the surrender of their revenues. In addition the government assumed the debts of the *daimyō* to the merchants. This minimized resistance to the new regime and enabled many of the more enterprising aristocrats to metamorphose themselves into leading financiers of the new Japan.

Restrictions were abolished on freedom of movement and internal trade, freedom of cropping and property rights in land, and freedom of entry into new occupations. The land tax reform of 1873 created a unified revenue system in the form of a fixed money tax collected from landowners in proportion to the newly assessed value of their land. Through this device the State financed itself through the early, critical years. The result, however, was to fasten fresh burdens on the peasant which largely nullified his "emancipation" and threatened at times to bring on widespread rebellion. Other reforms, based on foreign study and the advice of foreign experts, were introduced in the Army and Navy; in education, law, and public health; and in police and civil administration. In industry and finance the Meiji statesmen assumed the lead in pioneering the new technology. They created a new fiscal system, banks and insurance companies, railways, steam shipping, postal and telegraph services, and factories. With driving energy the new regime bent itself to the task of building new foundations of national power

Sansom, in the following words: "The country was full of restless spirits, dissatisfied with their condition and thirsting for activity. There were nobles who wanted independence and foreign trade, to develop the resources of their domains; samurai who wanted opportunities to use their talents, whether as soldiers or as officials; merchants who wanted to break the monopolies of the guilds; scholars who wanted to draw knowledge from new springs; humble peasants and townsmen who wanted just a little freedom from tax and tyranny. Every force but conservatism was pressing from within at the closed doors: so that when a summons came from without they were flung wide open, and all these imprisoned energies were released." *Japan, A Short Cultural History*, New York: Appleton-Century-Crofts, 1943, p. 524.

which would be secure against opposition at home and potential threats from abroad.

The lead in the Restoration and subsequent reforms was taken by a group of able young *samurai*-bureaucrats. These came mainly from the powerful western clans—Choshu, Satsuma, Tosa, and Hizen. Their motives were a mixture of patriotism, fired by the dangers of the international situation, and ambition for personal advancement. They were supported by a few of the court nobles and by the Osaka and Kyoto merchants, whose financial aid in the revolt against the Shogun proved indispensable. By 1850, indeed, the line between the *chōnin* and the *samurai* had become increasingly blurred, both socially and economically, as the former acquired aristocratic privilege and the latter were driven into commercial pursuits. As a class, however, the merchants were still weak and politically dependent. Many were tied to the Shogun and the more conservative elements of the aristocracy by monopolistic privileges of trade and finance. Popular hostility toward the *ancien régime* was in fact directed partly at these exclusive privileges, which restricted the economic opportunity of independent journeymen, traders, and *samurai*.

In the transition to Meiji Japan, comparatively few of the wealthy *chōnin* had the enterprise and flexibility to adapt themselves to changed circumstances. The new industrialists, landlords, financiers, and public officials who emerged after 1868 to share political power with the military bureaucrats were largely recruited also from *samurai* ranks,[9] as well as from the more prosperous farmers and petty tradesmen. Thus the Meiji "Revolution" was not the story of a rising business class, which burst the bonds of feudalism to establish its supremacy in a mercantile state. Still less was it a democratic revolt transferring political power to representatives of the mass of peasants and workers.

The great Prince Hirobumi Ito, framer of the Constitution of 1889, later said of his task: "It was not the people who forcibly wrested constitutional privileges from the Crown as in other countries, but the new regime was to be conferred upon them as a volun-

---

[9] The ability and energetic ambition of many of these young *samurai* of the nineteenth century belies the reputation for indolence, brawling, and incompetence which this class in general has acquired. Numerically, however, it was only a small proportion of the nobility who rose to affluence and power under the new dispensation. Others became small landlords and businessmen, or minor officials. Large numbers disappeared into the ranks of common peasants, soldiers, and workers. In 1876 Griffis wrote as follows of the once great ruling family: "The Tokugawas, once princes and the gentry of the land, whose hands never touched other tools than pen and sword, now live in obscurity and poverty, and by thousands keep body and soul together by picking tea, making paper, or digging the mud of rice-fields they once owned, like the labourers they once despised." *op.cit.*, p. 296.

tary gift for the sake of their future prosperity."[10] This statement is rather euphemistic in its implications, both as to the role of the "people" in earlier revolutions of the West, and the power of the emperor in Japan. The French Revolution, for example, despite its slogans, was hardly what we would today call a democratic revolution in either its inception or its outcome. Its actual consequence was to complete the emancipation from feudal serfdom, to establish a unified nation-state, and to proclaim a new legal freedom and equality under the ascendant power of the middle class. So in Japan a political unification and legal emancipation now took place. Here, in contrast to France, the leadership came largely from the more able and independent members of the former ruling caste, who revived the ancient symbols of the throne as a weapon of power. Joined by similar elements from merchant and commoner ranks, they combined to form a new oligarchy securely in control of the apparatus of the modern state and armed with the techniques and resources of a developing capitalism.

Despite the shifts in the balance of forces within this oligarchy, which in later decades were considerable, and despite the underlying trend toward democracy which manifested itself particularly in the decade 1920-30, this constitution of power remained basically unaltered in prewar Japan.

With this dramatic series of events, Japan was now opened to the first tides of the Industrial Revolution, and the attendant growth of modern capitalism. But the development which followed was more than simply the absorption by the Japanese of the material drives and technology of the West. Its tempo reflected the release of indigenous forces long latent in Japan. Similarly, its progress continued to be shaped by national characteristics deeply rooted in Japan's ancient culture. It gave new expression to the traditional eagerness of this island people for foreign ideas, especially in the applied arts. It gained momentum from their traditional industry and skills, built up in the exacting tasks of rice culture and peasant handicrafts. It found cohesive strength in the amenability of the Japanese to disciplined organization under acknowledged leaders— beyond the family. "To work in a group is second nature to him," says Emil Lederer. Recalling the experience of other peoples,

10 "New Constitution—Reminiscences," in *Fifty Years of New Japan,* compiled by Count Shigenobu Okuma, London, 1909, vol. i, p. 128. Prince Yamagata, founder of the modern Japanese Army and a powerful figure in Japanese politics for forty years, expressed his views in the following words: "The origin of the new regime and the spirit of the Constitution are all against the introduction of party politics; if ever a party Government be formed our country would, I am sure, go the way of Spain or Greece." Quoted in Shimasa Idditti, *The Life of Marquis Shigenobu Okuma,* Tokyo, 1940, p. 323.

one also remarks with what comparative ease in Japan the old caste distinctions and guild controls of feudal days broke down in favor of a more rational organization of economic life within the national framework. Again, the imprint of centralized dictatorship under the Tokugawas, together with the smallness and cultural unity of the country, helped to spare the Japanese that long struggle to overcome town and territorial localisms which intervened in Europe between the breakup of feudalism and the formation of national states. (See below, Chapter 10.)

The very speed of the transition in Japan, however, and the manner of its accomplishment, gave a twist, a special emphasis, to what followed. Especially evident is the persistence of family patterns even in industrial organizations employing the most advanced technology; the firm grip of the ruling group directing national development toward the ends of state power and military expansion; and the formation, within this oligarchy, of great financial combines inheriting the traditions of clan and guild monopoly and dominating large-scale industry, trade, and finance from the very beginning. The liberalizing tendencies which elsewhere accompanied the growth of a broad middle class and an urban proletariat have not been absent in Japan. But they have labored under exceptional disabilities traceable to the peculiarities of Japan's historical development. Only in a general and imprecise fashion can one speak of the rise of capitalism in Japan, in the Western sense, and then only with reference to certain sectors and aspects of Japanese society.

The Meiji Framework

With the opening of the Meiji era there set in a feverish process of modernization. Japan was now exposed to a rising tide of Western influence. Foreign trade more than doubled in volume in the first decade after 1868. Young Japanese by the score went abroad to study Western science and technology, political institutions and economic organization. Foreign experts and foreign merchants arrived in increasing numbers. The young *samurai*-bureaucrats of the new Imperial regime embarked on a program of sweeping and autocratic national reforms. The dream of men like Okubo, Kido, Iwakura, and others was first to consolidate the power and authority of the new government against internal opposition; second, to build a strong national state able to defend and assert itself in the arena of world politics. These ambitions set the framework and tempo of national development during the next quarter century. They formed the natural basis for a close mercantilist alliance between the bureaucrats and the nascent class of financiers and industrialists.

Both the Meiji Restoration and the reforms which crowded in

its wake showed the remarkable capacity of the Japanese at critical points to produce vigorous leaders able to map out a long-term program and then to move decisively to put it in action. As H. F. MacNair once observed, Japanese history is replete with examples of this trait of leadership: the will to power, the plan, the patient wait for the strategic moment, then the bold, swift stroke. It appears in Ieyasu's ruthless measures after 1600 to stabilize the Tokugawa Shogunate on enduring foundations. It reappears in the cool calculation and decisive action of the Western clans when the moment came to overthrow the Shogun. It now led to an eager, discerning acceptance of the West by the young *samurai* reformers, which contrasted so strongly with the inertia and obscurantism of the scholar-bureaucrats of contemporary China when faced with the same challenge. Coupled with this trait of leadership is the *judō*-like tactic of biding time, bowing when necessary to superior force, and calculating the strategic moment for driving at a weak point in an opponent's armor. These qualities in combination have featured Japan's foreign policy through the modern period—most recently in the decision to plunge into war in 1941 and the philosophic acceptance of defeat and occupation in 1945.

In the early Meiji years the new government proceeded resolutely to demolish the crumbling structure of feudalism and assert its authority throughout the country. With the suppression of the Satsuma Rebellion in 1877, its political supremacy was finally established over the dissident clans. Political conflict, however, led to acute financial disorder through the seventies. Governmental expenditure far outran revenue, owing to heavy military outlays and the burden assumed when the clan debts were taken over and pensions were awarded the old aristocracy in return for cancellation of their feudal dues. Issues of government paper money invited currency depreciation. The latter was further aggravated, beginning in 1877, by the note issues of the new national banks.[11] These banks had been formed largely by ex-aristocrats with little banking experience but now possessed of capital in the form of national bonds turned over to them by the government when their pensions were commuted.

As in France a century earlier, large currency issues thus resulted from the financial demands upon the new regime and its inexperience in money matters. But here the parallel ends. The French upheaval and ensuing wars led to the total repudiation of the *assignats* in 1797. In Japan the disorder was checked before it got

[11] Government paper money in circulation rose from 24.0 million yen in 1868 to 79.7 million in 1873. By 1878 the total of government and national bank notes issued had reached 165.7 million yen—a sixfold increase in a decade. Tōyō Keizai Shimpō-sha, *Meiji Taishō Kokusei Sōran*, Tokyo, 1927, p. 132.

out of hand. After 1881 the government finances and the currency of the country were put on a stable basis under the skillful guidance of the new finance minister, Count Matsukata.[12] The depreciated paper of the preceding years was progressively retired in favor of convertible notes issued by the Bank of Japan, established in 1882. The banking system was reorganized, the national debt stabilized and refunded. Additional sources of revenue were developed to supplement the land tax. As a result the new financial regime was able to weather the Sino-Japanese war of 1894-95 with little difficulty. Following the abandonment of silver in favor of a gold standard in 1897, Japan's credit standing had improved to the point where she could borrow advantageously in foreign capital markets. (See Chapter 5.)

Pioneering of Industry and Trade. Meanwhile energetic steps were taken by the government to modernize the Army and Navy, to improve transport and communications, and to establish new industries. The first railroad was constructed from Tokyo to Yokohama with the aid of a small British loan in 1870-72. The first steamship built by the Japanese was the 104-ft., 60-h.p. *Chiyoda-gata,* completed in 1866 after four years of effort. Steamer service was inaugurated shortly thereafter between Yokohama and Nagasaki. It was rapidly extended with government subsidies and encouragement. By 1893 Japan had acquired her first 2,000 miles of operating railway, her first 100,000 tons of steam vessels (mostly purchased abroad), her first 4,000 miles of telegraph lines. Shipyards, arsenals, foundries, machine shops, and technical schools were established or modernized with the aid of imported equipment and the advice of foreign technicians. Also under state patronage, the first modern silk filature was opened in 1870 with a French expert as superintendent. Cotton spinning mills were built or reequipped with imported machinery, largely from England. Experimental factories were set up to produce cement, sugar, beer, glass, chemicals, and a variety of Western-type goods.[13] The mining of copper, coal, and precious metals was also energetically promoted. Mineral production increased sevenfold from 1876 to 1896;[14] in the latter year the consumption of coal reached 3.6 million tons. Nearly

[12] See Masayoshi Matsukata, *Report on the Adoption of the Gold Standard,* Tokyo, 1899. The best concise narrative in English of the economic events of this period, indeed of the whole prewar era in Japan, is G. C. Allen's *A Short Economic History of Japan,* London, 1946.

[13] "It can be said with truth that there was scarcely any important Japanese industry of the Western type during the latter decades of the nineteenth century which did not owe its establishment to State initiative." Allen, *op.cit.,* p. 30.

[14] According to the Nagoya index of mineral output. "Hompō Genshi Seisambutsu no Seisan Sūryō," in Nagoya Chamber of Commerce and Industry, *Nagoya Keizai Tōkei Geppō,* vol. VIII, no. 4, May 1936, p. 60.

half of the coal was consumed in factories, which already numbered 7,640 and employed 435,000 operatives.[15]

The government itself financed and operated many of these new ventures in the early years. Especially was this true of transport, mining, and engineering industries, where military needs were important. Later, as private initiative and experience developed, as the profits of government undertakings proved meager, and as the State needed funds for armament, it disposed of most of its industrial properties, often at bargain prices.[16] It thus assisted in founding a number of the great financial and industrial fortunes of later years. Strategic industries like iron and steel remained under close official supervision, however. They were sheltered from competition by tariffs and subsidies. In addition, the State retained a powerful voice in the over-all direction of industrial development through the activities of the official and semiofficial banks, and more indirectly through the close affiliations of the bureaucracy with big business.

The growth of foreign trade after 1868 was both a cause and a result of these expansionist influences. Imports in the early years consisted largely of Western manufactures, chiefly textiles, machinery and equipment, and other metal products. Factory-made yarn and cloth tended to displace handicraft products of domestic origin. This added to the distress already occasioned by the decline of town markets which had followed upon the loss of feudal income by the nobility and their retainers. As a result large numbers of artisans in traditional trades lost their livelihood. Only gradually were Western techniques assimilated in such industries as cotton manufacture and sugar refining to the point where domestic producers could withstand foreign competition. On the other hand, an increasing share of imports represented Western-type goods serving new wants—e.g., ships, petroleum products, woolen goods, railway equipment, munitions, and machinery. In the early years about half of the total came from Great Britain, whose nationals also predominated in the handling of trade. Import requirements, together with remittances for shipping, banking, and commercial services performed by foreign firms, imposed a heavy strain on Japan's balance of payments. From 1872 to 1881 gold and silver were ex-

---

15 Asahi Shimbun-sha, *Nippon Keizai Tōkei Sōkan*, Tokyo, 1930, pp. 960, 1222.

16 Officially the reasons for the curtailment of State enterprise were given as follows in the Regulations for the Transfer of Factories in 1880: "The factories established for encouraging industries are now well organized and business has become prosperous, so the Government will abandon its ownership (of factories) which ought to be run by the people." Yasuzo Horie, "An Outline of the Rise of Modern Capitalism in Japan," *Kyoto University Economic Review*, vol. xi, no. 1, July 1936, p. 262. At this time these enterprises included 3 shipyards, 51 merchant vessels, 5 munitions plants, 10 mines, and 52 factories.

For further discussion of State enterprise in this era see below, Chapter 10.

ported (net) to the amount of 71 million yen. (The yen averaged U.S. $0.94 in exchange value between 1874 and 1881.)

Among merchandise exports, raw silk occupied the leading position from the beginning of the Meiji era. A foreign demand also developed for Japanese tea, rice, copper, coal, marine products, and miscellaneous handicrafts such as pottery, paper, lacquer, and bronze. It was silk, however, which dominated the export trade from the outset. Production of raw silk expanded from 2.3 million pounds in 1868 to 10.2 million pounds in 1893. Exports of silk and silk manufactures constituted the bulk of this production. They accounted for as much as 42% of Japan's total exports abroad during this whole period. Under the stimulus of foreign demand, cocoon raising was improved, and the reeling process began to be taken out of the peasant household to be organized in workshops and factories employing mechanical power. Throughout the modern history of Japan this single raw material played a unique role. Until as late as 1930 it continued to be the chief source of foreign exchange to finance Japan's industrialization, as well as the chief source of rural income supplementing the proceeds of rice cultivation. (See Chapters 6 and 7.)

The Formative Stage. The dramatic character of events in Japan in the quarter century after 1868 often leads to an overestimate of the speed of her economic transformation. First steps are important, to be sure. It was during this formative stage that the foundations were laid for the building of the defense industries and for the steady expansion of the civilian economy in subsequent decades. New wants came into being, new techniques were slowly assimilated, and a new framework of government institutions and policy was established. As industry, trade, and finance assumed more capitalistic forms, the economy as a whole also began to display the cyclical alternation of expansion and contraction which characterized the capitalist economies of the West. The vagaries of currency and fiscal policy, coupled with variations in the foreign trade balance, brought an expansionist boom from 1877 to 1881, followed by a period of deflation and retrenchment in the eighties. This gave way in turn to a revival of prosperity at the end of the decade, which was further intensified by the Sino-Japanese war in 1894-95.[17]

As the nineteenth century drew to a close, Japan's business and political leaders were gripped by a fever of industrialization. Her commercial expansion was also beginning to attract the attention

---

[17] An admirable study of the "gestation" of Japanese capitalism in the late nineteenth century, and the appearance of the business cycle, will be found in Shigeto Tsuru, *The Development of Capitalism and Business Cycles in Japan*, unpublished MS, Widener Library, Harvard University.

of the outside world. Robert P. Porter, an American economist who visited the islands on behalf of the U.S. National Association of Manufacturers, was struck with the soaring industrial ambitions voiced by Japanese leaders in all walks of life. "Among public speakers are found not only officials whose special province is trade and agriculture, but even a naval officer of high rank has considered it not beneath his dignity to tell his countrymen that they can only become a great nation by development of trade, and that trade is as worthy of their best efforts as war."[18]

Actually, however, the basic economic occupations and mode of life of the common people remained substantially unchanged through the first twenty-five years of the Meiji era. Foreign trade did not expand beyond modest proportions in relation to the economy as a whole. Its importance lay mainly in the realm of technological borrowing—i.e., as a highroad for the introduction of new influences. (See Chapter 6.) Exports consisted almost wholly of agricultural, fishing, and mineral produce, supplemented by the handicraft wares of traditional industries. Modern-style factories were still limited in number and small in scale. In 1886, for example, the steam power used for industrial purposes totalled only 4,094 h.p., distributed through 217 plants.[19] Inland transport was still largely by hand-drawn cart and pack horse. Wide price disparities between interior regions reflected the continuing self-sufficiency of village life. The land tax, a heavy burden on small peasants, furnished over 90% of State tax revenues in the early seventies. Twenty years later it still accounted for as much as 60%.[20] Together with exorbitant rents and usurious debt charges, it continued for another generation or more to sluice off large amounts of agricultural income for the support of State enterprise and industrial investment.

Probably the most substantial additions to real national income during this period did not result directly from the growth of factory industry and foreign trade. They grew mainly out of general improvements in agriculture, handicrafts, and internal commerce following the removal of feudal restrictions and the unification of the country under a strong, central government. Freedom of movement and occupation, the abolition of clan tariff barriers and tolls, free transfer of property rights in land, the unification of the monetary and banking systems, the growth of population, steady improvements in agricultural methods, better transport—such new conditions and new forces brought a slow expansion of the internal

[18] *The Commerce and Industries of Japan,* Philadelphia: National Association of Manufacturers, 1898, p. 10.

[19] Yeijiro Ono, *The Industrial Transition in Japan,* Baltimore, 1890, p. 64.

[20] *Nippon Keizai Tōkei Sōkan,* cited, pp. 63-66.

market and a rise in productivity. For example, with little change in production techniques the cultivated area in rice is reported to have increased 7% from 1878-82 to 1888-92 while the average yield rose 21%. This resulted in a significant increase even in the rice crop, long the great staple of Japanese farming. A similar growth appeared in other agricultural output, in the extension of fishing activities, and in the mushrooming of numerous small handicraft industries scattered through the countryside. Capital accumulated from land rents and from small-scale trade and banking formed a growing pool of funds for the financing of land improvements, and of workshops, trading ventures, and the like.

The framework of large-scale enterprise was being laid in the seventies and eighties; but the bulk of the new economic activity in this gestation period was along more traditional lines which required no sharp break with the past. The continuing rural character of Japan is shown in the fact that places of under 10,000 population still accounted for an estimated 82% of the people in 1898. The new growth in population at this time was still being absorbed mainly in rural areas.[21] The redistribution of people toward the cities in new industrial and commercial occupations was only setting in at the turn of the century.

Rise of Modern Industry and Trade

The decade of the 1890's marked a turning point in the evolution of the Japanese economy. On the foundations laid in earlier Meiji years the outlines of an industrial system now began to take shape. The assimilation of machine technology, the accumulation of banking and industrial capital, the expansive influences of world prosperity and rising prices—all facilitated a rapid rise of industrial output. Especially was this true for textiles and other consumer goods. Two victorious wars, at an interval of a decade, gave additional impetus to the development of transport, banking, and strategic industries under the leadership of the State and the nascent *zaibatsu*. By 1914 Japanese industrial capitalism was still weak and rudimentary by comparison with the advanced economies of the West. But it had now emerged from its formative stage. The basic patterns were established which were to characterize it for the next quarter century.

War and Economic Expansion. The first war with China, 1894-95, grew out of the designs of Japan's military bureaucrats upon Korea; also, it is said, from their need at home for a "forward" foreign policy to distract and disperse the rising tide of parlia-

---

[21] Imperial Cabinet, Bureau of Statistics, *Nippon Teikoku Tōkei Nenkan*, no. 43, Tokyo, 1924, p. 28.

mentary obstruction which had emerged under the Constitution of 1889.[22] Politically the war reinforced the power and prestige of the oligarchy for another generation, winning unified support for Japan's aggressive entry into the arena of Far East imperialism. Economically, it exerted a stimulus no less immediate and far-reaching in its consequences. Arms expenditures accelerated the upswing in prices already under way. New banks and small industrial and trading concerns mushroomed under the recently promulgated Commercial and Banking Acts, of 1890 and 1893. Military requirements doubled the merchant marine in two years. A boom developed in a number of industries producing war supplies.

The brief military campaign resulted in a resounding victory on land and sea over the forces of the corrupt and decadent Manchu regime. From this Japan proceeded to wrest important advantages, despite the intervention of Russia, Germany, and France to prevent her from retaining the principal prize, the Liaotung Peninsula, which the luckless Li Hung-chang had been forced to cede in the peace negotiations. Under the treaty of Shimonoseki (and the subsequent convention retroceding the Liaotung Peninsula) an indemnity of £38.1 million was exacted from China. This provided Japan with a gold and sterling reserve with which she made the important shift to the gold standard in 1897.[23] By virtue of her newly won prestige she was also able to terminate the humiliating treaties of 1858 with the Western Powers. The new treaties ended extraterritorial privileges for foreigners in Japan. They also freed her from the limitation of her tariff to a 5% level under an agreement of 1866.

Achieving independence at home, Japan's leaders now embarked forthwith on a career of imperialist expansion in Asia. The familiar slogans of markets, national security, and imperial destiny found an immediate response in the quickened national consciousness and the commercial ambitions aroused by Japan's first triumph on the stage of world politics. The initial step, following the victory in China, was the acquisition of Formosa and the Pescadores, and of trading, navigation, and industrial rights in China. Obtaining these strategic assets, and redoubling her armament program, Japan now prepared in turn for the challenge to Russia in 1904. From the second conflict she again emerged with swollen territorial and strategic gains. She had won a paramount position in Korea and succeeded to czarist rights in South Manchuria. These commitments to empire assumed during the critical decade from 1895 to 1905,

[22] See W. W. McLaren, *A Political History of Japan during the Meiji Era, 1867-1912,* New York, 1916, chap. 9.

[23] For details see *Report on the Adoption of the Gold Standard in Japan,* cited, chaps. 3-6.

together with the political prestige and authority conferred upon the armed forces by victories in the field, were destined to exert a profound influence upon the subsequent course of Japan's development. They cast the mold for her domestic politics, as well as her relations with the rest of the world.

The economic impetus afforded by the Sino-Japanese War likewise carried over into the next decade. Now it was reinforced by similar stimuli on a larger scale during the war with Russia. Again a conflict of limited duration, fought on foreign soil, hastened the development of financial institutions, marine transport, and industrial technology, without itself imposing an insupportable drain on Japan's still meager reserves. The necessary financial resources were mobilized with the aid of an improved banking system, and at the price of continued, heavy taxation. The special banks of an official or semiofficial character set up in previous years now proved their value, for political as well as economic ends.[24] This time, too, Japan was able to supplement domestic loans and expanding tax receipts with substantial foreign borrowings. Basically, however, it was the steady underlying expansion of national productivity and wealth which made it possible for her to extend rapidly her military and overseas commitments during this period. Economic growth thus lent support to rising political ambitions.

Reliable over-all measures of this economic growth are lacking for the period before World War I. Data summarized in Chapter 3 suggest that total production and real income in Japan, allowing for the rise in prices, may have increased by 80 to 100% in the quar-

[24] These special banks were essentially government instrumentalities, supervised and in part financed by the State. (See Chapter 10.) They derived their importance from this favored position; also from the fact that, in the absence of a developed security market, the big public and private banks afforded the main channel for mobilizing public savings to finance the long- and short-term capital requirements of both the government and large-scale private enterprise.

Beside the Bank of Japan, concerned mainly with note issue and treasury operations, the principal special banks created during this period were as follows: the Yokohama Specie Bank (1880), the chief foreign exchange institution; the Hypothec Bank (1896) and its forty-six satellite prefectural Agricultural and Industrial Banks, making long-term loans on land and other immovable property; the Industrial Bank of Japan (1900), making similar loans on industrial securities and movable property; the Bank of Taiwan (1899) and the Bank of Chosen (1909), note-issuing banks engaged in financing the development of these colonies. Another agency, the Deposits Bureau of the Ministry of Finance, collected postal savings from myriads of small depositors and invested them in public and semipublic enterprises. In addition, there were large numbers of small private commercial banks, as well as the big city banks, most of which were key instruments of zaibatsu expansion and control.

The importance of the special banks is indicated in the fact that those named above, excluding the colonial banks, had paid-up capital and reserves aggregating 212 million yen at the end of 1913, as compared with 606 million for some 2,262 ordinary and savings banks.

ter century ending in 1914 (Table 12). Whatever the details, certainly the growth was substantial, and pervasive. Manufacturing, mining, and large-scale transportation advanced by leaps and bounds, agriculture and many of the service industries at a slower rate. Yet even farming and fishing expanded sufficiently to supply food for a 25% gain in population from 1894 to 1914, with some rise in dietary standards and only minor imports of foodstuffs.[25] This growth seems to have been achieved with little or no increase in the number of workers in these primary occupations. Virtually the entire increase in the number of gainfully employed was absorbed in industry, commerce, and the other services. As a result it appears that by 1914 no more than three out of five families in Japan were still earning their living mainly in farming, and a third of them had some supplementary occupation.[26] By comparison, the proportion runs above this in China, India, and most other Far Eastern countries even today.

It is important to observe, however, that the shift of employment to manufacturing and the service trades was able to proceed as it did only because primary production also expanded. Agriculture, fishing, and forestry provided the new industries with domestic raw materials and markets. They also furnished exports with which to pay for industrial materials and machinery. And they made it unnecessary to import large quantities of food to support growing city populations. Even the production of rice, staple crop for centuries, is estimated to have increased 30% from 1890-94 to 1910-14. It reached 249 million bushels a year in the latter period. Net imports also increased nearly fourfold, but still amounted to only 5.5% of total consumption.[27]

More and more the Japanese people were now specializing their economic activities to produce surpluses for sale in the commercial market. For example, mining and manufacturing (excluding tiny family workshops) expanded until they employed over 2 million

[25] The Nagoya index of Japanese food production actually shows a 65% rise in total food output from 1890-94 to 1910-14, but this is probably an exaggeration. "Hompō Genshi Seisambutsu no Seisan Sūryō," *Nagoya Keizai Tōkei Geppō*, vol. VIII, no. 4, May 1936, p. 58. Estimated "actual" population rose from 41.6 to 52.8 million. Imperial Cabinet, Bureau of Statistics, *Shōwa Go-nen Iko Waga Kuni no Jinkō*, Tokyo, 1930, pp. 3-5. Further discussion of production, population, and living standards will be found in Chapters 3 and 4. For a summary of the Nagoya index of primary production, see Tables 2 and 3, below.

[26] Occupational statistics for this period are admittedly poor. It is interesting to note, however, that the number of families registered in farming rose only from 5,359,065 in 1903 to 5,456,231 in 1914. They dropped from 64% to 57% of the total population. *Meiji Taishō Kokusei Sōran*, cited, p. 507. For the latter year Hijikata estimates that 60% of the gainfully employed were in agriculture. For further discussion see Chapter 9.

[27] *Nippon Keizai Tōkei Sōkan*, cited, p. 1197.

workers in 1913. These mines and factories produced commodities mainly for the growing home market, but also to a lesser extent for sale abroad. Allowing roughly for price changes, both Japan's imports and exports approximately doubled from 1889-93 to 1899-1903.[28] They doubled again in the ensuing decade. The expansion of exports provided foreign exchange which, supplemented by borrowings abroad, made it possible for Japan to buy a growing volume of foreign machinery, equipment, and raw materials to meet her industrial and military requirements. One index of industrial activity, coal consumption in industry and transport, rose from 2 million tons in 1893 to 15 million tons in 1913. Railway mileage more than tripled, while freight ton-mileage increased seventeenfold. Japan was still a third-rate industrial nation by world standards. But she was well embarked by this time on an industrial revolution, with substantial gains already apparent in national income and power.

Founding of Large-Scale Industry. This development presented two aspects, in part supplementary, in part antagonistic, to each other. One was the forced-draft expansion of large-scale banking, shipping, heavy industry, and colonial enterprise. The other was the more diversified and pervasive modernization of agriculture and traditional industries, and the appearance of Western-style factories producing consumer goods like textiles.

The first grew largely out of government initiative, subsidy, and protection. Here the aims of State policy joined with the interests of private financiers to build up enterprises essential to military preparedness and colonial development. The second likewise benefited immensely from various types of governmental aid in such fields as technical education, crop improvement, reclamation, bank credit, transport and other public utilities.[29] These benefits, however, were more indirect and more diffused throughout the economy (though in the case of technical education they accrued in the largest measure to the financier-industrialist-trader class, especially its more powerful members).[30] Here the expansion of output and trade grew out

[28] According to the indices of the Oriental Economist. See *The Foreign Trade of Japan: A Statistical Survey*, Tokyo, 1935, pp. 699-700.

[29] Technical education as a significant factor in Japan's industrialization probably receives less attention commonly than it deserves. T. Amano and M. Shiozawa point out that pre-Meiji Japan had no system of commercial education except the apprentice system. Formal learning was monopolized by the *samurai*. The development of technical and trade schools under both private and public auspices, along with the general spread of literacy, afforded an important stimulus to improvement in technology and organization after 1870. For certain details see "Commercial Education," by the above authors, in *Fifty Years of New Japan*, cited, vol. II, pp. 175ff.

[30] The incidence of government policy on the distribution of income is of course a complex field of inquiry. In addition to a preoccupation with strategic industries, it may be noted here simply that State policy in Japan reflected a consistent bias (1) in favor of industry as against agriculture, (2) in favor of exports to finance

of the development of specialization, of more modern techniques, of new circuits of exchange. It came about through the response of tens of thousands of entrepreneurs to new economic opportunities at home and abroad. (See Chapters 4 and 5.)

This latter sector of the economy was in the main competitive and small-scale in organization. Its production processes were technically simple; its capital requirements limited. By contrast the mining and metallurgical industries, shipping, and colonial enterprises like the sugar industry of Formosa were dominated from their inception by comparatively large financial groups. They worked in close association with the government and were most of them dependent on official support. Typically these industries required advanced industrial techniques and were capital-intensive in character.[31]

Of the large-scale, State-sponsored industries established in the years before World War I the most successful perhaps was the merchant marine. Japan had an ancient tradition of maritime enterprise, interrupted only by the exclusionist policy of the seventeenth and eighteenth centuries. The Meiji regime early recognized the strategic importance of shipping and ship construction. From 1870 on it extended official support. Progress was rapid after the fillip given by the Sino-Japanese War, which required the purchase and charter of a considerable amount of foreign tonnage. In 1896 the government undertook a general subsidy of ocean shipping. It thus abandoned its earlier, more selective favors to particular firms like the Nippon Yusen Kaisha, formed in 1885 through a merger of government and private interests and with a government-guaranteed dividend of 8%. In 1899 a differential subsidy in favor of Japanese-built ships was introduced to stimulate domestic construction.

As a result the Japanese merchant fleet (steam vessels) expanded to 1,500,000 tons in 1913. This represented a threefold increase over 1896. Half of Japan's overseas trade was now carried in Japanese bottoms, as against less than 10% before the war with China. The large Japanese firms were now in an increasingly strong bargaining position in the shipping conferences of the Far East. Within two generations they were to rise to a commanding position in the carrying trade of the region. By contrast, Japanese shipyards had yet acquired only limited capabilities. And they were still largely dependent on imported materials. But with the help of construction

---

Japan's external requirements, and (3) in favor of large propertied interests and employers, as reflected in discriminatory tax policy, hostility to trade unions, and the absence of protective legislation for factory workers. (See Chapter 10.)

[31] An up-to-date steel plant at the turn of the century required an investment of at least $28-$30 million. The requirement for a successful silk filature or cotton mill in Japan was tiny by comparison. Even the cotton spinning industry in Japan presented a gross investment of no more than $250,000 per factory in 1900.

subsidies they were now turning out ships at an average rate (1909-13) of about 100 steam vessels totalling 50,000 tons a year, in addition to the smaller types of warships. Overseas shipping, and the larger shipyards, remained in the hands of a few big companies. These continued to receive, after 1909, government support under the Ocean Service Subvention Act of that year. Government subsidies supplied most of the profits of the ocean shipping trade throughout this period. (See Chapters 7 and 10.)

Equally strategic in character, but more difficult to establish in Japan, were the metallurgical industries. Steps were taken early in the Meiji era to modernize and expand the mining industry. But the lack of mineral resources confined subsequent developments to small proportions except in two fields: copper and coal. Copper production expanded through the World War years; subsequently, here as in the case of oil, Japan became increasingly dependent on imports. Though a variety of other minerals registered large relative advances in output,[32] the actual amounts remained small except in the case of coal. In 1913, in fact, coal accounted for 71 million yen, half the total value of mineral production. Imports of foreign ores, metals (including semimanufactures), and other minerals already amounted to about 100 million yen, reflecting the growing demands of the machinery, equipment, and construction industries.

The principal requirement of the metal-working industries was of course iron and steel. Of total metal and mineral imports in 1913, pig iron constituted 10% and finished steel about one half. A Japanese iron and steel industry had been launched in 1901 when the government-owned Yawata Iron Works commenced operations. Several smaller plants were also built by private interests during the next decade. But severe handicaps were encountered in the technical difficulties of the process and the inadequacy of domestic supplies of ore and coking coal. By 1913 pig iron output had been pushed up to 243,000 tons and steel output to 255,000 tons. Yet the former still represented only one half and the latter one third of domestic consumption. The rest was supplied by imports. Costs were high, and the industry achieved even this limited development only by State sponsorship and subsidy. It is interesting to note, nevertheless, that growing production plus imports now provided steel supplies for domestic use at an annual rate of about 740,000 tons during the years 1911-13.[33]

In the machinery and equipment industries the modest success of the shipbuilding trade was fairly typical. After the nationalization

[32] The Nagoya index of total mineral production rose from 100 in 1893 to 285 in 1903 and 609 in 1913. "Hompō Genshi Seisambutsu no Seisan Sūryō," cited, p. 60.

[33] *Nippon Keizai Tōkei Sōkan,* cited, p. 1220.

of railways in 1906, the manufacture of railway equipment increased in response to government orders. The electrical equipment industry also advanced in the 1900's as new thermal and hydroelectric generating plants were built. On the whole, however, Japan remained dependent throughout this period on imports of vehicles, scientific instruments, and machinery, as well as finished steel. Had it not been for war and armament expenditures, and a national policy dedicated to the encouragement of strategic industries, this dependence would have been even greater.

Agriculture and the Traditional Industries. The founding of large-scale industry in Japan, because of its political support, its strategic implications, and the striking contrast it offered with traditional Japan, attracted a good deal of attention from the outside world. But it was the expansion of Japan's basic economy—agriculture and small-scale industry built on traditional foundations—which accounted for most of the growth of national productivity and income during this period.

Here and there a domestic occupation gave way to foreign competition as the Japanese economy became more closely linked with the outside world. One striking case was the decline of raw cotton production after 1887, despite the growing demands of Japanese spinners. With the removal of the duty on cotton in 1896 Japan accepted dependence on imports of Indian (and later, American) cotton. Cotton imports were handled by a few big importing firms, which maintained close relations with the spinners. The future growth of the cotton textile industry proceeded on this basis, and cotton virtually disappeared as a domestic crop. In the main, however, the history of different sectors of Japan's economy at this time is one of differential rates of expansion, with varying degrees of modernization in traditional occupations.

The growth of food production has already been noted. Probably it approached a 35-40% increase over the period 1894 to 1914. This growth is highly significant in view of the basic importance of agriculture in the national economy and the likelihood that the farm population increased little during this period. (See Chapter 3.) In part it represented a slow increase in the cultivated area. In part it resulted from more fertilizer, better credit facilities, double cropping and other more intensive methods of farming, paralleled by corresponding changes in coastal fishing. The basic organization of agriculture remained little altered. Some 55% of the cultivated area was still devoted to rice, produced chiefly by the hand labor of farm households on tiny plots of ground. Japan's 5.4 million farm families still cultivated farms averaging only 2.6 acres apiece. Many had a good deal less.

Land ownership was also dispersed in small holdings, except for the holdings of a few big proprietors. The commercialization of agriculture, however, and the burden of high taxes and interest charges on the small peasant, had brought a large increase in tenantry in the earlier Meiji years. Some 39% of the cultivating farmers owned no land by 1910. About 45% of farm acreage was tenanted. Tenants typically paid rents in kind, fixed by oral agreement and amounting to 45 to 60% of the crop on rice land. In addition they usually had to furnish their own farm implements, seed, and fertilizer.[34]

The crowding of people on a limited land area resulted in high rents and land values; it also perpetuated the low productivity of hand cultivation. Farm machinery was virtually unknown, of course. Over half the land was cropped without even the help of draft animals. Improvements in the lot of the small farmer were further limited by the shortage of credit. Interest rates still ran to 20% or more in the villages. Taxes likewise remained a heavy burden. Even with the introduction of business and income taxes to supplement the land tax in meeting the rising level of armament expenditures, the agricultural class continued to furnish the principal source of government revenue. In 1908 it was estimated that the farmer paid land, income, and business taxes amounting to 28% of his income, by comparison with 14% in the case of the merchant and industrialist.[35] Low farm income from all these causes impelled people toward the cities in search of better economic opportunity. There they exerted a persistent drag on wage levels in nonagricultural occupations. Despite the advances recorded above, P. Mayet's dictum of 1878 was to remain true for a long time to come: "The principal and most needed improvement in the system of Japan's National Economy is to be found in the direction of agriculture."[36]

Rice and other food crops continued to provide the principal

[34] The system of tenantry in Japan exhibited certain unique features which are often misunderstood. As indicated above, it combined certain features of capitalistic tenantry as practiced, for example, in England with other features carried over from the old days. See S. Kawada, "Tenant Systems in Japan and Corea," *Kyoto University Economic Review*, vol. 1, no. 1, July 1926, pp. 38ff. In prewar Japan almost all rents were fixed rents, not share rents, but as late as 1943 the rent on 66% of all tenanted farm land was paid in kind. That on another 13% was fixed in kind but paid in money at current prices. Supreme Commander for the Allied Powers, GHQ, Natural Resources Section Report No. 101, *Japanese Agricultural Land Statistics*, Tokyo, 1943, p. 42.

[35] Ushisaburo Kobayashi, *War and Armament Taxes of Japan*, New York, 1922, pp. 98-99.

[36] *Agricultural Insurance*, London, 1893, p. 243. Had the early reforms proposed to the Japanese government by this able German adviser been adopted, two main barriers to rural progress—heavy taxes and the lack of farm credit—cc·ld long since have been substantially reduced.

means of farm livelihood. To an increasing degree, however, agriculture was now being supplemented by alternative sources of income from industry and ancillary services. This came about in a variety of ways. One, of course, was the migration of members of farm families to the cities in search of jobs—as in the case of recruiting of farm girls by the spinning mills. Another was the spread of new industrial demands and employment opportunities to small towns and through the countryside, especially in the vicinity of the larger cities. (See Chapter 9.) In some cases there developed an expanding domestic or foreign market for traditional Japanese handicrafts—native-style paper, pottery, luxury fabrics, etc.—with little resulting change in production techniques. In others, new industries were introduced, e.g., those producing Western-style paper, beer, bicycles, and cement. Or a substantial change took place in traditional methods, such as the introduction of power looms in the export branch of the textile trades.[37]

Growth of the Textile Trades. The rise of the silk industry was the most conspicuous instance of the adaptation and growth of a traditional industry in response to foreign demand. World silk demand continued to expand in the years before World War I. Japan rapidly acquired a dominant position in the market. Her output of raw silk grew from 7.5 million pounds annually in 1889-93 to 27.9 million pounds in 1909-13. Exporting three quarters of this product in the latter period, Japan had already passed China and her European competitors. She was now supplying half the requirements of the United States, the world's principal consumer. In addition, a small trade in silk fabrics was maintained. This languished after 1898 in the face of rising tariffs in the United States and elsewhere, but exports of silk fabrics (mainly habutai) still led cotton cloth exports until 1913.

The expansion of silk production and improvement in quality were accomplished through technical advances in both cocoon raising and the reeling industry. In cocoon production one half the gain in output through these two decades resulted from the spread of double cropping—the introduction of a summer-autumn crop. More scientific methods of egg production and silkworm feeding also improved and standardized the quality of cocoons. This period, moreover, witnessed a growth in the average size of filatures, and the extensive replacement of hand reeling by machine methods. By 1913, 76% of the raw silk produced was filature silk; the hand reel persisted mainly in the supply of silk to domestic weavers.

[37] For an excellent account of such developments in a number of industries and regions of Japan, see John E. Orchard, *Japan's Economic Position*, New York, 1930.

The silk industry as a whole, however, continued to be essentially small-scale and rural in character, except for the larger filatures and big export houses. Nearly one third of the farm households of the country derived some supplementary income from the raising of cocoons.[38] In 1913 there were still 284,869 hand-reeling establishments in the countryside, in addition to 4,701 machine-reeling filatures. Weaving likewise remained a peasant occupation to a large extent. The chief element in production costs, from silkworm to fabric, was labor. Much of the capital even was accumulated from local sources, though increasingly the working capital of the filatures and commission merchants came to be provided directly or indirectly by large exporters and city banks.[39]

The second large industry to develop during this period, cotton textiles, was likewise built on traditional foundations. In this case, however, the technical transformation under the impact of Western influence was more radical, especially in the spinning branch.

It is a familiar fact that the cotton textile industry has been the pioneer of the industrial revolution the world around. Japan was no exception. The factors which led to its rapid assimilation and growth in Japan were no different than those which have operated elsewhere, notably in Asia: a large consumer market ready at hand; the adaptability of handicraft skills and of unskilled, low-wage labor to the operation of power machinery for weaving and spinning; the limited capital requirements of textile mills; the availability of cheap raw cotton; and a climate sufficiently humid for spinning. The twenty years before World War I saw the firm establishment of the factory system in cotton textiles in Japan. By 1913 the Japanese industry was securely in control of the home market. In addition, it had already commenced that overseas expansion which was to raise it to a front rank position in the world's cotton goods trade during the next generation.

Like other Japanese industries, the cotton mill industry achieved its first substantial growth after 1890. Prior to this time machine-spun yarns from abroad had made heavy inroads in the Japanese market, traditionally supplied by the coarse hand-spun product of peasant households.[40] Meanwhile the introduction of factory spin-

---

[38] *Nippon Teikoku Tōkei Nenkan*, cited, no. 38, 1920, p. 80.

[39] "Thus, although the great silk industry might seem to be rooted in the old economy of the countryside, it was nourished by streams flowing from the terrain where the great Japanese merchant houses and foreign financiers had their homes." Allen, *op.cit.*, p. 64.

[40] "When European cotton yarns were first brought over into Japan, nobody was able to identify the materials used because of their fineness and people thought that the stuff was a mixture of silk and cotton." Teijiro Uyeda and Tokijiro Minoguchi, *Small Scale Industries of Japan: The Cotton Industry*, Tokyo: Japanese Council, Institute of Pacific Relations, 1936, p. 3. In Japan, as a century earlier in the West,

ning in Japan proceeded only slowly despite government patronage. In the nineties progress was accelerated. By 1899 the industry boasted some eighty-three mills with 1,170,000 spindles and an output of 355 million pounds of yarn.[41] The larger firms, organized in the Japan Cotton Spinners' Association, had also begun to modernize the weaving industry with power looms imported for use in specialized weaving sheds attached to their spinning mills.

Domestic factory yarn now rapidly replaced Indian yarn in the Japanese market. Aided by an epidemic in Bombay, which temporarily disrupted Indian exports in 1896, the Japanese spinners also gained a substantial foothold in the China market for coarse yarns. India's textile industry, however, still greatly exceeded that of Japan in size. The Chinese industry was yet in its infancy, though beginning to embark on a similar process of growth. For many years China, together with India, was to remain the principal international market for cotton goods from Lancashire and its newer competitors. In all three countries the process of spinning was modernized far more swiftly than weaving. The latter continued mainly on a workshop, hand-loom basis.

The Japanese spinning industry continued its expansion through the 1900's. By 1913 it had doubled again, with capacity now at 2.4 million spindles and a yarn production of 672 million pounds. Along with this growth in production had come an increase in the size of plants, and a slow improvement in their ability to spin finer yarns. Their competitive position abroad was further improved by the better marketing and credit facilities and the closer integration of the industry, especially in its export branch.[42] Capital costs, in-

---

machinery made it possible to produce for mass consumption goods of a quality formerly confined to luxuries.

[41] Japan, Department of Agriculture and Commerce, *Twenty-second Statistical Report of the Department of Agriculture and Commerce*, Tokyo, 1907, p. 182.

[42] Such integration was fostered by the handling of cotton imports by a few big importing houses, the advantageous arrangements between the Japan Cotton Spinners' Association and the Nippon Yusen Kaisha on shipments of Indian cotton, and the entry of the big spinners into the weaving trade. Another feature was the Japan Cotton Export Guild, an export cartel formed in 1906 to capture the Manchurian cotton goods market from American competitors. The cartel's members included four big companies which controlled 73% of the looms of concerns affiliated with the JCSA. Sales were managed exclusively by Mitsui Bussan, the big Mitsui trading firm.

The inroads made upon United States cotton cloth exports to North China are reflected in the following distribution of China's imports of cotton cloth:

		PERCENTAGE FROM:		
ANNUAL AVERAGE	TOTAL IMPORTS (HK. TAELS)	*United Kingdom and Hongkong*	*United States*	*Japan*
1902-04	68.0	66.2	25.0	2.9
1911-13	95.5	64.6	9.0	16.9

cluding the costs of imported British machinery, were still relatively
high, but were offset by day-and-night operation in two shifts. Output per spindle was therefore two or three times as large as in Western countries. Concurrently the weaving trades also increased the
scale and efficiency of their operations as the power loom and factory
system slowly made their way. From 1894 to 1913 the number of
weavers and weaving establishments declined by one third; yet the
production of fabrics woven from cotton, silk, hemp, and other fibers
approximately doubled. However, weaving remained essentially a
cottage industry. At the end of this period there were still nearly
400,000 independent and piecework establishments. They averaged
only 1.5 workers per plant. Even in cotton weaving, where the big
cotton spinners extended their activities, the number of power looms
did not exceed 50,000.[43]

In Japan as elsewhere the textile industries relied mainly on low-
wage female labor. In the weaving sheds and silk filatures, largely
rural industries, nine out of ten workers were women. Even in the
cotton spinning mills over 80% of the operatives were females. One
out of four was under sixteen years of age. These girls were recruited
on contract from peasant homes, often reluctantly. They were housed
and fed in company dormitories which blended the factory system
of the West with the paternalism and strict discipline of traditional
Japan. Wages were low, even by Japanese standards. Labor efficiency was equally so. Japanese spinning and weaving mills required about four times as many operatives as American mills of
similar size and equipment.[44] There were no factory laws.[45] Any organization of workers to bargain collectively or strike was effectively
forbidden under the Police Regulations of 1900. Except in a few
model mills, conditions of life and work generally exhibited the
poverty, the crowding, the lack of worker protection which characterized the introduction of the industrial system in the West
early in the nineteenth century. In Japan as in England the factory
system in its first stages relied mainly on the labor of women, who
were more amenable to the discipline of factory work and also less
able to protect themselves from industrial abuses.

The coming of age of the Japanese cotton industry is reflected in

[43] Data from *Nippon Keizai Tōkei Sōkan*, cited, pp. 744-45, and *Statistical Reports
of the Department of Agriculture and Commerce*, cited, passim.

[44] For studies of Japanese and comparable American mills at this time see United
States Tariff Board, *Cotton Manufactures*, H.R. Doc. 643, 62d Congress, 2d session,
Washington, 1912, pp. 519-27; also United States Tariff Commission, *The Japanese
Cotton Industry and Trade*, Washington, 1921, pp. 88-132.

[45] The first factory act in Japan was passed in 1911, after thirty years of discussion
during which the Cotton Spinners' Association and other employer groups successfully opposed any action. It was not enforced until 1916, and then only partially.
See Chapter 10.

its growing strength in international competition during this period. Imports of both cotton yarn and piece goods into Japan no longer figured significantly in the domestic market. Exports grew steadily. At first they consisted mainly of coarse cotton yarns (20-count and below), sold in China and to a lesser extent in Korea for hand-loom weaving. By 1913 Japan already supplied a quarter of the world exports of yarn, sharing the large Chinese market with India.[46] China still imported two thirds of her yarn requirements, though her own spinning industry was now becoming mechanized and re-established as a factory industry. By 1913 she too had nearly a million spindles, a quarter of them owned by Japanese companies.[47] A growing share of Japanese exports now began to take the form of cotton cloth. It was mainly gray shirtings and sheetings, drills, and other coarse and heavy goods. Totalling 412 million linear yards in 1913, these likewise found their principal market in China. Here they had largely ousted American exporters from the field, as noted above.[48] They also offered increasing competition to the products of Lancashire, long dominant in the China import trade.

By 1913 Japan was already exporting to foreign countries and Korea about half of the cotton processed by her cotton mills. Some 30% of the output of her spindles was exported directly as yarn, as compared with over 40% in 1900. The remainder was processed by the Japanese weaving trade. But perhaps as much as 20% (by value) was subsequently sold abroad as cotton cloth. Another 10% was exported in the form of knit goods and other manufactures.[49] A rough comparison of 1913 with 1900 yields the following conclusions: spinning mill output rose 150%—from 268 to 672 million pounds; something over one half of this increase represented an increase in exports of yarn and cloth; less than 10% went into replacing former imports into Japan; the balance, about one third, apparently reflected a net expansion of the domestic market for cotton yarn and its manufactures. (Hand-spun yarn had virtually disappeared from the market by the turn of the century.)

Thus the early growth of the cotton industry took place in response to an expansion of the market at home as well as abroad. It was in the export branch of the industry that technical progress was most rapid. But the importance of the foreign market in the

[46] *The Japanese Cotton Industry and Trade*, cited, p. 22.

[47] H. D. Fong, *Cotton Industry and Trade in China*, Tientsin, 1932, vol. 1, p. 8.

[48] For details see W. A. Graham Clark, *Cotton Goods in Japan and Their Competition in the Manchurian Market*, U.S. Department of Commerce, Special Agent Series, no. 86, Washington, 1914.

[49] *The Japanese Cotton Industry and Trade*, cited, p. 21. These estimates are only approximate, for they take no account of changes in stocks.

rise of the industry, great as it was, appears to have been less than is often supposed.

In cotton consumption Japan now ranked sixth in the world. Some 60% of her raw cotton came from India in the years 1910-13, another 25% from the United States. Though the Japanese industry could still boast only one third the spindleage of Indian mills, it was now forging ahead more rapidly.[50] Together with India, Japan had ousted Britain from the yarn market of China. In addition, she was already supplying about 15% of China's imports of cotton piece goods, having captured much of the market for coarse goods from American exporters.

Yet the widespread expansion of Japanese goods to more distant markets still seems remote. Exports of broad goods (20's and over) were still confined to a few coarse and heavy types. Sixty percent of Japan's yarns were 20's or less.[51] The finishing industry was undeveloped. Reliance on British machinery made costs of mill construction relatively great, while labor costs were much higher than wage comparisons suggest. As yet Japan still presented no serious challenge to Lancashire in world markets. The latter's exports of cotton cloth were nearly thirty times those of Japan in 1910-13, and still constituted two thirds of world trade in this field.[52]

Within Japan, however, the cotton industry ranked second only to silk in importance. These two far overshadowed other industries, both in employment and value of output. Woolen, hemp, and muslin manufactures had also developed on a modest scale, but they remained largely dependent on Army orders and government protection. The structure of Japanese industry at this time was probably about as follows: In all manufacturing industries (excluding construction) there were something over 3.5 million persons occupied wholly or part-time in 1913. This was still less than one seventh of the country's total labor force. Probably one in three such persons

[50] The same technical and geographic factors operated to develop the industry in both countries, and in China. Yet the Indian industry lagged progressively behind, despite its earlier start. One reason was that the Bombay mills were largely in the hands of "managing agents," who were apt to be more interested in speculative company promotions and quick commercial profits than in long-term industrial development. By contrast, the Japanese entrepreneurs were aggressive in making technical improvements and in building a close-knit, integrated system of production and trade. In addition the Japanese mills benefited from government patronage, especially in transport, banking, and tariffs. The Indian industry was long handicapped by duties on machinery imports and by lack of protection against competing goods from Lancashire. See The Royal Institute of International Affairs, *Notes on the Textile Industry in Lancashire, India, China and Japan*, London, 1933, pp. 8, 55-56; P. S. Lokanathan, *Industrial Organization in India*, London, 1935, chaps. 1, 9.

[51] *Nippon Keizai Tōkei Sōkan*, cited, p. 743.

[52] *The Japanese Cotton Industry and Trade*, cited, p. 23. The first comparison is in linear yards, the second in pounds.

was a small employer, or an independent who engaged neither hired nor family labor in significant amounts. Excluding these proprietors would leave 2.0-2.5 million wage and family workers. According to S. Uyehara, who puts the number at about 2 million, textiles alone employed 40% of these workers, largely women and girls.[53]

Most of the remaining industrial employment was found in traditional trades even less affected by modernization. For example, three occupations—the making of Japanese paper, braids, and mats —accounted for another 40%. About half of the total of 2 million employees were in factories with less than five operatives. The newer, larger-scale industries like the metallurgical, machinery, and chemical still contributed only a small fraction of industrial income and employment. Japanese industry remained at this time predominantly small-scale in organization, its roots in the traditional skills of old Japan, its markets mainly the consumer needs of people still living close to the traditional poverty line of the Orient.

The preponderance of the cotton and silk industries is almost equally striking in Japan's foreign trade. As already noted, both imports and exports expanded rapidly throughout the Meiji era, playing a key role in the whole process of economic development. For the most part this was trade with foreign countries, not Japan's own colonies. Even in 1913 exports to Formosa and Korea were only 13% of other exports; imports from them only 9%. Of total shipments overseas, raw silk constituted 30% and silk manufactures another 7%. Cotton goods of all types added a further 20%. Thus silk and cotton together provided nearly three fifths of Japan's exports.[54]

This textile trade was highly specialized by regions. China (with Hongkong and the Kwantung Leased Territory) took three quarters of Japan's cotton goods exports to all countries, including Korea. The United States took two thirds of her raw silk. On the import side, raw cotton from India and the United States accounted for a third of the value of all foreign purchases. Another third was divided evenly between foodstuffs, and metals and manufactures. The remainder represented miscellaneous raw materials and equipment for Japanese industries, purchased in a wide range of markets. Already well established, in short, was the pattern of Japanese trade which was to persist for another twenty years, until, in the thirties,

[53] *The Industry and Trade of Japan*, London, 1926, pp. 43-47.

[54] Silk was far more important, actually, in the growth of Japanese national income than this comparison would suggest, for at least half of the proceeds of cotton goods exports went to pay for imports of raw cotton embodied in these exports. By contrast, the entire proceeds of silk exports were available to finance imports for domestic consumption. See Chapter 7.

dislocations set in motion by the world depression and the war in China brought radical changes.[55]

It was this underlying growth of Japan's agriculture and other basic industries, most of them consumer goods industries built on ancient foundations, which enabled the island empire to support her growing population and expanding political commitments during this period. Through a steady process of modernization they produced the rising national income which supported large State budgets for armament and colonial development. They provided the exports to pay for much of the heavy import of munitions, machinery, and other essentials for strategic industries. Despite these charges upon the national dividend, they were the means by which Japan carried herself through the first stages of economic development and emerged from her agrarian-feudal background to take on the aspects of a modern industrial power.

What actual improvements came about in the material well-being of the Japanese population during this early period is difficult to determine. Some advance in living standards is evidenced in the decline of mortality rates, in increased per capita consumption of food and clothing supplies, and in the growth of public services of various kinds—especially in the cities. Most of the rise in total national income, however, seems to have been absorbed in supporting the growing population. Capital formation and arms expenditure absorbed additional amounts of the increment. Kokichi Morimoto, on the basis of fragmentary family budget studies in 1913, concludes as follows: "The mode of living—housing, food, clothing, and other factors of living—has not made noteworthy improvement. The mass of the people live in just the same way as they did during the feudal régime."[56] This verdict appears to be too sweeping. (See below, pages 143ff.) But it points to the formidable obstacles, both social and technological, which stood in the way of real improvements in the lot of the peasant and worker, despite the notable growth in the scale and productivity of the Japanese economy.

War Finance and Foreign Borrowing. How much of the gain in national income was devoted to the two wars of this period and the related colonial and strategic enterprise of the intervening years is also problematical. (See below, pages 290ff.) The greater share must actually have gone to support Japan's growing population at a somewhat improved level of living. Of the remainder the larger portion was employed in private and State investment of an essentially productive character—land reclamation, urban develop-

[55] Table 34, below, gives the regional distribution of Japan's overseas trade in 1893, 1913, and 1936.

[56] *The Standard of Living in Japan,* Baltimore, 1918, p. 12.

ment, roads, railways, public utility and industrial construction, and the provision of working capital for commerce and industry. Evidence in support of these general conclusions will be found in later chapters of this book, especially 3 and 5.

A glance at government finances during this period, however, will show the strain imposed by heavy expenditures for war and armament. Mainly as a result of the Sino-Japanese War, and of growing armament and colonial enterprise which followed in its wake, the expenditures of the national government tripled from 1893 to 1903. They reached 289 million yen in the latter year—no small sum for the time. Again, they more than doubled in the course of the Russo-Japanese War. With the Army and Navy now expanded, and with new commitments in Korea, they remained from 1909 to 1913 just under 600 million yen.[57]

To finance this burden taxes were progressively boosted. Care was taken at the same time to see that they fell mainly on small peasants, merchants, industrialists, and others in the lower- and middle-income classes.[58] Additional revenue was sought by the organization of government monopolies in salt, tobacco, and camphor. The indemnity of 360 million yen secured from China in 1895 was also largely used to finance an interwar program of armament expansion. These resources proved inadequate, however, and resort was had to extensive borrowing. The national debt rose from 235 million yen in 1893 to 539 million in 1903. It then soared to 2,592 million yen ($1,300 million) in 1913, as a result of large war bond issues and the nationalization of the railways in 1906.[59]

A leading authority, Ushisaburo Kobayashi, makes an interesting estimate of the uses to which the Japanese government had put the funds raised by its loans outstanding on March 31, 1913 (2,744 million yen).[60] He finds that war and armament took 1,518 million (55%); railways and public works, 797 million (29%); Formosan and Korean development, 80 million (2.9%); and financial readjustment, etc., 345 million (13%). In other words, more than half of the proceeds of these loans went directly into war and armament. Nearly 50% of the government's entire budget in 1913 was devoted

---

[57] The expenditure and debt figures in this and the following paragraphs are for fiscal years ending March 31 of the year indicated. Japan, Department of Finance, *Financial and Economic Annual of Japan*, Tokyo, annual. The value of the yen during this period was about $0.498, or 2s.

[58] For a detailed study of tax policy through this period, see *War and Armament Taxes of Japan*, cited, and for a briefer examination, Chapter 10, below.

[59] Tōyō Keizai Shimpō-sha, *Meiji Taishō Zaisei Shōran*, Tokyo, 1927, p. 608.

[60] *War and Armament Loans of Japan*, New York, 1922, pp. 89, 94–95. To the total usually cited, Kobayashi adds 250 million yen for paper money and unfunded loans outstanding. He designates these figures as referring to the end of the fiscal year 1911/12; actually they correspond with official totals for March 31, 1913.

to the Army and Navy, military pensions, and war debt service.

The immediate burden of these large military outlays was mitigated in some degree by foreign loans. In fact, the "extraordinary" military expenditures charged to the war with Russia (1,730 million yen) were largely balanced by borrowings in London and Paris. Before the war (i.e., in 1903) the outstanding total of Japan's national loans issued abroad amounted to only 98 million yen. By the end of 1913 it had climbed to 1,525 million, representing over half the swollen national debt. (Table 20.) Other public and corporate securities issued or purchased abroad added another 445 million. Direct foreign investment in business enterprise in Japan amounted to about 70 million. All told, Japan's total foreign indebtedness now stood at approximately 2 billion yen. Her net indebtedness, deducting her own assets abroad, was approximately 1,350 million yen, or $650 million. (For sources and further details see Chapter 5.)

These foreign borrowings played a critical role in the financial and political history of the period. Indeed, it is only in this period that foreign capital assumes much significance in Japanese expansion. As already described, the country was undergoing a process of general economic growth, accelerated by heavy military spending at home and abroad. The result was a heavy strain on the capital resources of the country, and a growing deficit in the balance of payments on current account. From 1904 to 1913 the merchandise exports of the Japanese Empire fell short of paying for imports by 707 million yen. Current invisible items, notably debt service and governmental payments, widened the gap by another 436 million yen. This large deficit was financed by capital imports.[61]

Foreign loans, however, were more than a passive, balancing factor which enabled Japan to augment her own resources temporarily with an increment from abroad. They had an inflationary effect within the country. This was the more pronounced because they were used in part to accumulate gold reserves held either at home or in London. Against these reserves the Bank of Japan increased its note circulation. From 1900 to 1913 the Bank's note issue nearly doubled, and wholesale prices in Japan drifted upwards

---

[61] See Table 21, below; adapted from figures compiled by Margaret S. Gordon in E. B. Schumpeter, ed., *The Industrialization of Japan and Manchukuo, 1930-1940*, New York, 1940, p. 866. There are no data on invisible transactions between Japan Proper and the colonies during this period. Hence all references here to Japan's balance of international payments relate to the Japanese Empire as a whole. However, the great bulk of the Empire's transactions with foreign countries are those of Japan Proper. Official foreign trade statistics are believed to undervalue exports and overvalue imports in some degree. This may lead to exaggerated estimates of capital inflow, which is a residual in the balance. (See Chapter 5, below.)

more rapidly than in the United States or Great Britain.[62] Expanding money incomes and rising prices tended to make the trade deficit even larger. This necessitated still more loans to support the exchange, and these in turn further increased service charges on the mounting debt.

Once this inflationary cycle got under way it was difficult to check. The Bank of Japan had no effective control over the money market. In any case its policy was subordinated to the fiscal requirements of the Treasury. Expenditures for the production of armaments and other strategic undertakings expressed a national policy inflexibly pursued, and amounted to a fixed charge on the economy. From 1910 to 1913 Japan lost over 20% of her gold holdings, despite continued borrowing abroad.[63] A financial crisis was approaching.

Then, just as Japan seemed near the end of her rope, the entire prospect was suddenly altered. War broke out in Europe. By 1915 orders began to pour in for Japanese goods, for her shipping and other services. Almost overnight the country began to be embarrassed by a surfeit of riches in its international accounts. A boom developed in trade and industry which brought unprecedented financial prosperity—while it lasted. In its wake, as we shall see, it left a series of problems which were to plague Japan for a decade.

[62] See S. Y. Furuya, *Japan's Foreign Exchange and Her Balance of International Payments*, New York, 1928, pp. 48-52; also Junnosuke Inouye, *Problems of the Japanese Exchange, 1914-1926*, London, 1931, pp. 73-80.

[63] *Meiji Taishō Kokusei Sōran*, p. 139.

CHAPTER 2

JAPAN'S ECONOMY IN
TRANSITION

The War Boom, 1914-19

THE outbreak of hostilities in Europe had the initial result of increasing the strain on Japan's international accounts. For her foreign trade and debt operations had always been financed largely in London. Now the dislocation of the British money market precipitated an immediate crisis. But this was short-lived; soon events began to take a new turn. The Allies commenced to place large orders in Japan for munitions and other manufactures. Neutral countries, especially those of the Far East, turned to Japan for goods formerly supplied by the industrial nations now belligerents. Though technically at war herself after 1915, Japan's military operations were insignificant in extent. Thus her industry was in a position to take full advantage of the fabulous trade opportunities that developed. Her merchant marine likewise fell heir to an expanding share of the world's carrying trade.

Japanese exports proceeded to increase by leaps and bounds. Especially was this true of finished manufactures in growing variety. A boom developed in Japan's leading prewar markets, China and the United States. Soon it appeared also in new and more distant markets throughout the world. Cotton goods exports nearly doubled in amount. Exports of cotton cloth rose from 412 million linear yards in 1913 to 1,174 million in 1918, a 185% increase.

For the first time Japanese textiles won a firm foothold in India, the Dutch East Indies, and other countries of Southeast Asia and Oceania.[1] Most of the increased shipments took the form of staple gray shirtings, sheetings, drills, and twills. But new and more diversified types—bleached, dyed, and printed cloths of finer weaves —now appeared in growing quantities. Booming exports and industrial expansion in turn stepped up Japan's requirements for materials and equipment from abroad. This was especially true of American raw cotton, metals, and machinery. However, imports now fell short of exports by a wide and growing margin, hampered as they were by wartime controls in the supplying countries. The result for Japan was a huge export surplus—something totally new in her experience.

[1] A detailed study of this wartime trade expansion will be found in the U.S. Tariff Commission's *Japanese Cotton Industry and Trade*, Washington, 1921, and *Japan: Trade during the War*, Washington, 1919.

In merchandise trade alone Japan and her colonies piled up an export balance of nearly 1.2 billion yen in trade with foreign countries between 1914 and 1919. Soaring freight rates, plus a well-nigh limitless demand for Japanese shipping, swelled still further the country's balance on current account. The merchant fleet suffered little from submarine warfare, and rose from 1,577,025 gross registered tons in 1914 to 2,840,650 in 1919.[2] It now carried over 80% of Japan's own foreign trade as compared with 57% in 1914. In addition it entered the tramp business on more distant ocean routes. Thus the net shipping income of the Empire rose from 41.2 million yen in 1914 to 381.4 million yen in 1919.[3] Mainly for this reason Japan's invisible accounts showed a surplus of 1,800 million yen over the six-year period. With the merchandise balance added in, the Empire accumulated on current account through these years the enormous net sum of 3,035 million yen (about $1,500 million). This contrasted with a deficit of 549 million yen in the preceding six years. By the end of 1919 her foreign assets exceeded her outstanding debts by 1,300 million yen, whereas in 1913 she had been a net debtor by nearly the same large sum. (See below, Table 21 and pages 258-59.)

Inflation and Industrial Progress. The dazzling world demand for Japanese goods and services had effects within the country which might be expected. Money incomes rose, note issue and bank credit expanded. Industry and trade embarked on a period of unprecedented prosperity. By 1919 Japan was in the grip of an accelerating price inflation. Profits soared to fabulous levels. New plants mushroomed, and commodity and security markets became the scene of feverish speculative activity.

In part this prosperity was fictitious. Wholesale commodity prices rose nearly 150% from 1914 to 1919. The values of agricultural land and industrial capital were written up even more rapidly. Exports and imports both tripled in value from 1913 to 1919, but their actual volume rose only by one quarter. Industrial production (in plants with five or more operatives) increased from 1,371 million yen in 1914 to 6,738 million yen in 1919 (Table 10); agricultural output rose from about 1,700 million to 4,083 million yen; the paid-up capital and reserves of all Japanese companies soared from 2,676 million to 7,615 million yen. All these values, too, reflected the rapid depreciation of the currency.[4]

[2] Japan, Imperial Cabinet, Bureau of Statistics, *Nippon Teikoku Tōkei Nenkan*, no. 43, Tokyo, 1924, pp. 218-19.

[3] Oriental Economist, *The Foreign Trade of Japan: A Statistical Survey*, Tokyo, 1935, pp. 448-49, 690-91.

[4] The figures are from the following sources: wholesale prices from Bank of Japan, *Economic Statistics of Japan, 1931*, Tokyo, 1932, p. 102; foreign trade from

Nevertheless, Japan reaped substantial gains from the war boom in national output, in industrial capacity, and in technical experience. From 1914 to 1919 the Nagoya index of physical output rose 16% in agriculture and 29% in mining.[5] Railway freight and passenger traffic doubled. Foreign and domestic shipping cargoes entering Japanese ports increased 20%. The number of factory workers rose from 1,187,249 to 2,024,870, accompanied by a parallel increase in machinery installed in factory industry. (See Chapters 3 and 4.) Manufacturing output is estimated to have risen as much as 78% in total volume.[6] Especially significant for the future was the high level of construction activity; also the growth from small beginnings of the newer engineering and chemical industries. The older, more conservative industries like cotton spinning took advantage of enormous wartime profits to retire their funded debt, write off sums to depreciation, and build up their financial reserves.[7]

Some of the plants and industries which started operations during the war years failed to survive the postwar deflation and the resumption of world trade on a more normal basis. Others continued in operation only by virtue of government protection and subsidy. Also, as we shall see, the overcapitalization of Japanese industry at wartime price levels left in its wake a series of banking and exchange disorders which plagued the country for a decade. By almost any standard, however, the war years witnessed a significant advance in Japan's productive capacity, foreign trade position, and technical maturity.

Gains of this character seem to have been more important than any immediate rise in the standard of living. The evidence on changes

---

The Foreign Trade of Japan: A Statistical Survey, cited, p. 698; industrial output from Yasuji Koide, "Hompō Sangyō Kōzō no Hendō ni Kansuru Shiryō," *Nagoya Keizai Tōkei Geppō*, vol. VIII, no. 9, October 1936, p. 9: agricultural output from Asahi Shimbun-sha, *Nippon Keizai Tōkei Sōkan*, Tokyo, 1930, p. 684, and S. Hijikata, *Kokumin Shotoku no Kōsei*, Tokyo, 1933, p. 389; company capitalization from *Nippon Teikoku Tōkei Nenkan*, cited, no. 43, pp. 180-81.

[5] "Hompō Genshi Seisambutsu no Seisan Sūryō," *Nagoya Keizai Tōkei Geppō*, vol. VIII, no. 4, May 1936, p. 60. See below, Table 3.

[6] Nagoya Commercial College, *Hompō Seisan Sūryō Shisū Sōran*, Nagoya, 1933, p. 30. A description of this index is given below, in the notes to Table 8.

[7] The gross earnings of firms belonging to the Japan Cotton Spinners' Association were actually 98% on their total capital investment in 1919. The production of yarn had increased only moderately from prewar levels but yarn prices increased fourfold, for Japan was unable to manufacture spinning machinery herself or to procure much abroad. This gave the Japanese industry strong financial resources with which to undertake rationalization measures in the postwar decade. Lancashire, by contrast, became heavily burdened with fixed debt and high-cost equipment as a result of wartime expansion, a circumstance which subsequently imposed a severe handicap in meeting the postwar challenge of Japanese competition. See *The Japanese Cotton Industry and Trade*, cited, pp. 54-60; also Teijiro Uyeda and Tokijiro Minoguchi, *Small-Scale Industries of Japan: The Cotton Industry*, Tokyo: Japanese Council, Institute of Pacific Relations, 1936, pp. 20-24.

in consumption is admittedly scanty for this period. A 6% growth in population from 1914 to 1919 absorbed part of the increased production of consumer goods; in addition, the evidence indicates a 13% rise in per capita food supply from home production and imports, as well as some diversification and improvement in diet, clothing, and minor items in family budgets.[8] It is significant, however, that Uyeda's index of real industrial wages remains virtually stationary through the war years.[9] The rising cost of living bore heavily on the urban population. It became the cause of spreading social discontent which culminated in serious rioting during 1918. With prices and profits soaring, a large share of the increment of income accrued to the more well-to-do classes in the form of rents, dividends, interest, and corporate savings. This was associated, both as cause and effect, with the high level of savings and investment which is characteristic of such boom conditions. (See Chapter 5.) While the changing components of national income cannot be satisfactorily measured at this time, an unusually large share of the gain in income appears to have gone into capital formation. This took the form both of improvements and enlargements in Japan's domestic plant, equipment, and inventories, and of the huge credit balances built up abroad.

Meantime these foreign balances accumulating from exports and shipping services created a difficult financial problem for the authorities. As already noted, they aggregated over 3 billion yen from 1914 to 1919. Some of the proceeds were brought home in the form of gold. After September 1917, however, and until June 1919, the United States, now the world's money market, applied an embargo on gold exports. As a result Japanese exchange bankers were hardpressed to finance exporters in Japan. The proceeds of their export bills could not be matched with import bills. These proceeds tended to pile up in New York in immobilized and depreciating funds.[10] In the absence of a discount market, the problem was met largely by yen advances from the central bank and government purchase of

---

[8] See E. F. Penrose's index of food production and imports in *Food Supply and Raw Materials in Japan*, Chicago, 1930, p. 73; also consumption data assembled by Teijiro .Uyeda and Tosuke Inokuchi in *Cost of Living and Real Wages in Japan, 1914-1936*, Tokyo: Japan Council, Institute of Pacific Relations, 1936, appendix, and by Kokichi Morimoto in *The Efficiency Standard of Living in Japan*, Tokyo: Japan Council, Institute of Pacific Relations, 1931, chap. 7.

[9] *op.cit.*, p. 23. From 1919 to 1923, however, the index rose 50% as a result of the fall of living costs in the postwar deflation. See below, pages 143-44.

[10] Despite the government's efforts to peg the exchange, the Yokohama Specie Bank's official rate on New York rose from an average of $0.495 per yen in 1913 to an all-time high of $0.521 at the end of 1918. For details on the wartime exchange difficulties of Japan see Junnosuke Inouye, *Problems of the Japanese Exchange, 1914-1926*, London, 1939, chap. 1; also S. Y. Furuya, *Japan's Foreign Exchange and Her Balance of International Payments*, New York, 1928, chap. 3.

foreign currency balances. This had further inflationary effects in Japan.

Unhappily, the opportunity to employ these surplus foreign credits in retiring a large share of Japan's foreign debt was lost. The government was reluctant to float domestic loans for this purpose. In the end only a small amount was redeemed. Nor were the funds employed overseas in prudent long-term investment. Short-term war loans were extended to the British, French, and Russian governments in the amount of 518 million yen (net). But these were repaid soon after the war, except for 240 million yen loaned to the czarist regime which went into default. Some 336 million yen (net) was "invested" by Japanese interests in China.[11] Most of this represented the notorious Nishihara loans, which were political in character and soon defaulted.

The greater part of the exchange proceeds of Japan's wartime boom were allowed simply to accumulate in short-term foreign credits and specie balances. At the end of 1919 Japan's specie holdings at home and abroad totalled 2,045 million yen, as compared with only 376 million yen at the end of 1913. Most of this hoard, as we shall see, was to be dissipated in attempts to cope with the exchange difficulties of the postwar years.

The Postwar Decade: Economic Growth

The armistice of November 1918 signalized the approaching end of Japan's war boom. As in other countries, economic activity was maintained at a high level for another year under the influence of a continuing spiral of inflation. The break in Japan came in March 1920, heralding the world-wide collapse a few months later. There followed a period of deflation and readjustment. From this financial crisis Japan recovered rather more quickly than most countries, owing to the liberal credit and subsidy policies of the government. With the return to "normalcy," however, she now faced again the problem of finding peacetime economic opportunities for her rapidly growing millions, a problem temporarily obscured in the flush of war prosperity.

The postwar decade registered only modest progress toward this long-term goal, though it did witness the consolidation and extension of the industrial advance of the war period. It was, first of all, a decade of marked financial instability. The inflated cost structure of the war years remained to complicate postwar adjustment, in Japan as elsewhere. Before much headway had been made in this direction the great earthquake of 1923 dealt a shattering blow.

[11] H. G. Moulton, *Japan, An Economic and Financial Appraisal*, Washington 1931, pp. 514-15.

Some 100,000 lives were lost in the fires which swept great cities like Tokyo and Yokohama. Property destruction was estimated at 3.1 to 5.5 billion yen. A reconstruction boom developed in the wake of the catastrophe, but this led into a banking crisis in 1927. Certain sectors of the economy—notably the silk industry—shared in world prosperity induced by boom conditions in the United States. Others failed to do so. The gains were spotty and irregular, and economic opportunity hardly kept pace with the large number of new job seekers pouring into the labor market each year as the population grew. Japan was now reaping some of the disadvantages as well as the advantages of industrialism—dependence upon an unstable world economy, growing class conflicts and social strains, and all the difficulties that go with the maintenance of growth and equilibrium in an industrializing economy.

Meanwhile the rise of an urban proletariat and a middle class brought liberalizing and democratic trends in Japanese society. They appeared in education, in the press, and notably in politics. Through the growing power of the Diet, the business classes—especially big business—now gained influential representation in the formation of national policy. During these interwar years Japan achieved the fullest expression of constitutional democracy she had ever known, heavily qualified as it was by a still powerful feudal heritage. Social issues such as the factory standards, the protection of the tenant farmer, and birth control came into the foreground of public discussion with an articulateness and insistency never witnessed in earlier decades.

Confronted with major decisions in the field of economic policy, however, the party governments of the twenties were inclined to vacillate and compromise. Perhaps it was for the very reason that national politics now represented more adequately the diversity of interests and classes in Japan. In this respect the situation in Japan was not unique. But here the issues were peculiarly urgent, as subsequent events showed all too clearly. When the great depression descended in 1930-31, an acute crisis set in. The history of the thirties, in both its military and economic aspects, was in some degree a delayed response to the pressures building up in the preceding decade.

Trade and Economic Growth. Before examining these difficulties, we may note more explicitly the economic growth which was in fact achieved in a number of fields. These gains have often been obscured by apologists seeking to justify Japan's subsequent military aggression on grounds of economic necessity. In fact, they were not inconsiderable.

In agriculture, to be sure, progress was comparatively slight, except in sericulture. And farming remained basic to the whole economy, still occupying half the working population in 1930.[12] The total area under cultivation remained virtually unchanged from 1920 to 1930; so also did the farm population.[13] This meant that the entire gain in employment for Japan's expanding numbers took place in nonagricultural pursuits. Among those who remained on the farm, the cultivation of rice continued to be the chief occupation and source of income. In contrast to the earlier decades, rice production in Japan showed little upward trend in the twenties, despite increased application of fertilizer and other efforts to increase yields. Partly this reflected the principle of diminishing returns, and partly a trend toward greater diversification in farming. There was a marked increase in the production of wheat, cocoons, fruits, vegetables, and animal foodstuffs. As a result, total food production (including that of fish) expanded 35% from 1910-14 to 1925-29.[14] Growth now proceeded at a diminishing rate, however. It no longer satisfied the slowly rising dietary standards of Japan's expanding population. The gap was filled by increasing imports of overseas food, especially rice from Korea. By 1930 net imports of foreign and colonial foodstuffs (deducting food exports) supplied about 15% of Japan's total food consumption.[15]

In industrial products as well as food Japan's foreign trade gained in importance during the postwar decade. Unfortunately it was subject to wide swings, which lent a sense of insecurity to the whole economy. In this it reflected the ups and downs of world prices, as well as the vagaries of Japanese exchange policy. Following the postwar slump both imports and exports recovered in the early twenties. In 1925 they reached peaks of 2,573 and 2,306 million yen, respectively.[16] After that a gradual decline set in, as world raw material prices began their downward drift and the yen appreciated in value. Meantime the volume of trade continued to expand; for example, silk shipments were fairly well maintained in total yen value until 1929 by virtue of a steady increase in the amount sold in the United States.

[12] Imperial Cabinet, Bureau of Statistics, *Shōwa Go-nen Kokusei Chōsa Hōkoku*, vol. 2: *Shokugyō Oyobi Sangyō*, Tokyo, 1935, pp. 2-3.

[13] The cultivated area actually declined from 6,033,000 to 5,987,000 hectares during the decade. While the total Japanese labor force increased from 27.3 to 29.6 million, according to the census, the number of people principally occupied in farming dropped from 14.3 to 14.1 million. *Nippon Teikoku Tōkei Nenkan*, cited, no. 57, p. 32. The redirection of employment as a result of industrialization is examined below in Chapter 9.

[14] According to the Nagoya index. "Hompō Genshi Seisambutsu no Seisan Sūryō," cited, p. 58.

[15] Further details on agricultural production will be found below in Chapter 3, and on food imports in Chapter 7.

[16] The yen was now worth $0.41, or 1s. 8d.

Some idea of the over-all growth of Japan's trade with foreign countries, Korea, and Formosa in these years may be gained from the following comparisons: In 1929 the value of both exports and imports had more than tripled the 1913 figures. About a third of this increase represented higher prices, which now averaged 50% above the 1913 level. Thus the volume of imports and exports had approximately doubled through the war and postwar decade. (Table 26, below.) Japan's economy meantime had become increasingly integrated in the world economy—agriculture mainly through silk exports and rice imports, and industry and finance through a growing complex of commercial and banking relationships. Japanese industry was now importing a large proportion of its requirements in raw materials and semimanufactures. Merchandise imports from foreign countries and from the colonies amounted to about 20% of Japan's national income. Exports took almost as high a percentage of her total output of goods and services, and as much as 25 to 35% of her manufacturing output. These over-all ratios, however, hardly suggest the vital dependence of the whole economy on overseas commerce, as detailed in Chapters 6 and 7.

Raw silk and cotton textiles continued to dominate Japan's export trade by a wide margin. Despite a decline in silk prices by one third from 1925 to 1929, exports of raw silk still came to 784 million yen in the latter year. This represented 36% of Japan's commodity sales abroad. Almost the entire amount was sold to hosiery and broad goods mills in the United States, making the American market by far the largest for Japanese exports. The expansion of the silk trade, which tripled in volume from 1913 to 1929, was made possible by the continuous extension and improvement of cocoon production and silk reeling. At the end of the twenties, two in every five farm households were engaged in the supply of cocoons as a supplementary occupation.[17] The earnings of peasant girls in silk filatures provided another important source of cash income for the rural population.

Of Japanese exports to foreign countries other than raw silk, one half consisted of textile products of other varieties. Textiles of all kinds made up two thirds of Japan's total exports of 2,149 million yen in 1929. In other words, her earning power in foreign trade was still confined largely to this complex of industries. Next to silk, cotton piece goods were the largest item, amounting to 1,791 million sq. yds. valued at 413 million yen. Cloth exports had quadrupled from 1913 to 1920; they doubled again from 1920 to 1929. India now had replaced China as the largest foreign market for Japanese cloth. Here

17 Tōyō Keizai Shimpō-sha, *Keizai Nenkan*, no. 16, Tokyo, 1932, p. 182.

Japanese exporters had made heavy inroads in the trade formerly monopolized by Lancashire, although India herself was now supplying half her own requirements in mill cloth. By the end of 1929 Japan boasted 6.5 million spindles, two and a half times her 1913 spindleage. In consumption of raw cotton she was exceeded only by the United States and Great Britain. Her cloth exports— 1,781 million sq. yds. in 1929—were now about half the exports of Lancashire.[18]

With the expansion of capacity in the cotton industry came improvements in business organization, equipment, and technical skills. These were associated with a growth in the average size of firms and plants, increasing control by the big spinners over the weaving branch of the industry, and close integration of cotton imports with the manufacturing and export business. Technical progress was particularly marked after 1927. The deflationary monetary policy inaugurated by the government stimulated a rationalization movement in Japanese industry and forced the introduction of many technical improvements neglected during the war and early postwar years. This movement carried over into the depression and contributed to the spectacular growth in exports in the early thirties. Many small firms were squeezed out. The larger plants were reequipped with more modern, automatic equipment, particularly high-draft ring spindles and automatic looms. The result was a rapid rise in output per worker and a marked reduction in labor costs. The latter, of course, was reinforced after 1929 by the fall of wages in the depression.

Industrial Diversification. Similar gains in production capacity and in technical maturity were recorded in other lines of industrial activity. Though textiles continued to hold the first place, Japanese factory industry grew steadily in the range and variety of other manufactures during the twenties.

This was reflected in production and trade at the time, and even more in the industrial boom which followed the depreciation of the yen in 1931. The chemical and machinery industries, for example, assumed a new importance; the processing of foodstuffs retained a leading place; and the production of such industrial essentials as cement and electric power tripled in the decade ending in 1929. Symptomatic of Japan's technical progress through these years is the fact that the capacity of electric motors installed in Japanese factories rose from 1,063,000 h.p. in 1919 to 2,301,000 h.p. in 1928.[19]

[18] International Labour Office, *The World Textile Industry*, Geneva, 1937, vol. II, part 1, pp. 22, 40, 124.

[19] The figures are for private and government factories. Ministry of Commerce and Industry, *Kōjō Tōkeihyō* (1930), Tokyo, 1932, pp. 283-84; *The Statistics of the Department of Commerce and Industry, 1925*, cited, pp. 52-53.

Manufacturing output increased 70% in the meantime, even though factory employment remained at about 2 million workers.[20] (See Chapters 3 and 4.)

By contrast the mining industries lagged behind in this development. Here Japan became increasingly dependent on foreign supplies, as further expansion of production from her own limited reserves tended to bring rising costs. From 1919 to 1929 the output of metals rose only 16% and that of coal 10%.[21] Domestic producers were able to maintain profits only with the aid of tariffs and restriction schemes engineered by the large interests which dominated these fields.[22] Imports of ferrous and nonferrous metals and minerals from the United States and from adjacent countries of Asia therefore grew steadily in amount. The resulting dependence of the Japanese home islands on overseas supplies is best expressed by the percentages that imports from foreign and colonial sources were of apparent domestic consumption (imports plus domestic production minus exports). Combining supplies in both raw and processed forms, these percentages were as follows in 1930: iron and steel materials, 85%; petroleum, 79%; lead, 93%; zinc, 69%; tin, 74%; aluminum, 100%. (See below, Table 33.)

The metallurgical industries expanded through this period, processing both domestic and imported materials. As they developed, imports shifted gradually from metals in the more advanced stages of processing to ores and concentrates. Steel production, for example, reached 2,034,000 tons in 1929. This was eight times the output of 1913. Yet the steel industry, long dominated by the State-controlled Yawata Iron Works, still failed to meet the country's requirements, either in quantitative or qualitative terms. Especially was this true of high-grade steel products. In 1930 over one third of the processed iron and steel materials consumed in Japan were still being imported in the form of pig iron, scrap, and steel products. As a source of income and employment the metallurgical industries also failed to grow to a major place in the Japanese economy. In terms of value added by manufacture, privately owned plants produced only 191 million yen in 1929. This was less than the

20 The Nagoya index of manufacturing production rose from 287 to 492 (1905= 100). *Hompō Seisan Sūryō Shisū Sōran,* cited, p. 30.

21 "Hompō Genshi Seisambutsu no Seisan Sūryō," cited, pp. 53-57.

22 Coal production in the twenties remained at about double the level of 1909-13. In 1925-29 Japan produced 33 million tons annually, 2.5% of the world output. In addition, she was now drawing coking coal from Manchuria and North China. Big advances were also made in the utilization of coal. In 1914, for example, it took 2.11 tons of coal to produce 1,000 kw. of electric power; in 1932 only 0.7 ton. (International Labour Office, *The World Coal Mining Industry,* Geneva, 1938, vol. 1, p. 99.) This development of fuel supplies supported the increasing mechanization of industry and transport noted above.

net-value product of the ceramics industry and only one quarter of textile output, even disregarding the large output of pottery and textile fabrics by plants with less than five workers.[23]

The machinery and equipment industries likewise fell short of meeting the growing demands of Japanese industry, especially for machinery of the more advanced and complicated types. Here, however, Japan's growing technical maturity in the engineering field was evidenced in her increasing ability to manufacture electrical apparatus, railway equipment, bicycles, and industrial machinery of relatively simple and standard designs. By 1929 this category of factory production stood second only to textiles, with net product value at 519 million yen. In electrical equipment, for example, Japanese plants were now able to supply most of the domestic market efficiently and economically, and were beginning to engage in active competition overseas.

The general growth of manufacturing capacity in Japan, both in scale and in technical achievement, brought a marked shift in the character of imports. Finished manufactures were purchased abroad during the years 1925-29 in aggregate amounts little greater than before World War I, despite the growth of Japanese consumption. By contrast raw materials and semimanufactures, taken as groups, were now imported from foreign countries in quantities more than double those of 1913. (See below, Table 30.) Throughout the whole range of manufactures there was a general tendency for domestic industries to take over the less complicated processes of machine production. Accordingly, imports tended to be concentrated on growing amounts of unprocessed materials, together with the more advanced types of machinery and equipment which Japan could not yet turn out in competition with the United States, Britain, Germany, or smaller European competitors. After 1925 unprocessed industrial materials comprised over 50% of the value of total imports from foreign countries. Thirty years earlier they had been only 25%. Tariffs and other forms of indirect protection played a part in this shift. Yet basically it reflected the coming of age of Japanese industry.

Imports played an essential role both in providing for the consumer necessities of the people and in expanding and maintaining capital plant and equipment. As previously noted, about one sixth of Japan's food supplies now came from her colonies and from foreign countries. The rise in per capita consumption since 1914 had been made possible only by increasing imports. All the principal

---

[23] "Hompō Sangyō Kōzō no Hendō ni Kansuru Shiryō," cited, p. 49. For a more extensive discussion of the relative importance of various industries at this time see Chapter 9.

clothing fibers except silk, which was too expensive for daily use, likewise came from abroad in the form of cotton, wool, and rayon materials. Japan also continued to borrow Western technology in the form of machinery imports. Such purchases were essential to the continued growth of industry—far more than their money values would suggest. (See Chapter 6.) Moreover, the metal materials manufactured into vehicles, machinery, and other capital goods were largely of overseas origin. Foreign trade was indispensable for the growth of real capital in industry and transport, as well as for food and clothing supplies for the people.

In financing her overseas requirements, however, Japan relied mainly on her own financial resources after 1913. Imports of producer goods, wholly or partly manufactured, were paid for mainly by exports of consumer goods, rather than by foreign borrowings, over the period 1914-29. A few industries, notably electric utilities, attracted some foreign capital—mostly American—in the twenties. A number of small investments in Japanese plants by American and European concerns took the form of supplying patents, technical personnel, and specialized equipment, as in the Ford and General Motors assembly plants. But direct foreign investment in Japanese business enterprise was hardly more than 200 million yen ($100 million) at the end of 1929. In addition 579 million yen of Japanese corporate securities were now held abroad. Of the latter sum, however, 340 million yen represented the securities of electric power companies, mostly dollar bonds issued in the twenties. All but 12 million yen of the remainder was capital borrowed by the South Manchuria and Oriental Development companies for their activities in Manchuria and Korea. By way of comparison, the paid-up capital and reserves of Japanese industrial, mining, trading, and transportation companies totalled 16,410 million yen—twenty times the amount of foreign investment in Japanese business.

Aside from electric utilities, therefore, foreign investment in business enterprise in Japan was rather insignificant in amount. It took the forms mainly of purchases of corporate bonds and debentures, and of certain direct undertakings by American equipment and concerns. In this respect Japanese business retained the independence from foreign control which it had enjoyed from early days. Foreign investment in Japan's public debt was a good deal larger, to be sure. At the end of 1929 it totalled 1,724 million yen. Interestingly enough, however, this was almost identical with the value of Japanese national and local bonds held abroad in 1913. Total loan indebtedness abroad, public and private, stood at only 2,304 million yen (face value) at the end of 1929, as compared with 1,970 million yen in 1913. Meanwhile Japanese investments abroad, outside the colonies, had come to be valued at upwards of 2,500 million yen or $1,250 million. (See Chapter 5.)

So far as net capital movements in and out of Japan Proper are concerned, the principal changes from 1913 to 1929 were, first, the piling up of huge short-term credits overseas during the flush years of World War I and, second, their subsequent liquidation to finance the trade deficits of the postwar years. By this means the rate of private domestic investment and public borrowing was sustained through the twenties at a level well above new savings from current income. Meanwhile the country moved increasingly into a creditor position in relation to China and the colonies. But this took place in considerable measure through the reinvestment of business profits abroad. In contrast to the earlier period 1896-1913, when the net inflow of capital into Japan approached 1.6 billion yen, the next twenty years witnessed a substantial balancing of imports and exports of goods and services in the aggregate. She was neither a net lender nor a net borrower on any scale.[24]

The Empire as Asset and Liability. As Japan's requirements for food and raw materials increased, her expanding overseas empire began to take on economic significance. It now comprised southern Sakhalin (Karafuto) to the north, Korea and the Kwantung Leased Territory on the continent, and Formosa and the mandated islands of the Pacific (Nanyo) to the south—altogether a territory of 115,000 square miles with a population of 27.3 million (1930). Under the sponsorship of the government, Japanese capital undertook the active development of the resources of these regions along lines serving the requirements of the metropolitan country. By 1929 there were some 1.2 million Japanese nationals resident in the empire overseas, nearly half of them in Korea. Most of them were engaged in business, government, and professional services.[25]

Foreign trade and investment in these colonial areas were largely monopolized by Japanese firms. This was done through open and disguised preferences, some of them official and others arising from the dominant position of Japanese nationals in the economic life of the colonies. The Empire was developed to supply the home islands with growing amounts of food and a few raw materials. Most important, Korea and Formosa furnished Japan in the late twenties with about four fifths of her rice imports, two thirds of her imports of sugar, and lesser amounts of oil-bearing materials, minerals, lum-

[24] The above estimates are taken from Chapter 5, where a more detailed résumé of Japan's borrowing and lending experience is given.

[25] *Nippon Teikoku Tōkei Nenkan*, cited, no. 57, pp. 8-9. By comparison there were only about 500,000 Japanese resident in foreign countries, over 40% of them in the United States.

ber, etc. Phosphates began to come from the Pacific island mandate, while Karafuto produced lumber and pulp, fish products, and some coal. The colonies also provided a modest export market for Japanese manufactures. In 1930, for example, they absorbed about 20% of Japan's industrial exports and about 10% of her exports of textile manufactures. (See Table 28.) Altogether her colonial trade, most of it with Korea and Formosa, came to nearly one quarter of her total overseas trade in 1928-30. Imports from the entire Empire averaged about 580 million yen annually, exports about 475 million. (This includes the trade with Karafuto and Nanyo, but not that with the Kwantung Leased Territory, most of which was actually trade with Northeast China through the Port of Dairen.)

Since Japanese manufactures had a preferred position in the colonies, the home islands were enabled to pay for imports of food and other materials from these regions more readily than if political control had been lacking. Moreover, thanks to Japanese enterprise and control, these areas developed food and raw material surpluses geared to Japan's needs, surpluses which might not otherwise have become available, at least on such favorable terms. Her foreign trade requirements were also eased somewhat by the foreign exchange accruing from reexports of colonial products like camphor and sugar.

A good deal of this trade, however, would probably have grown up even in the absence of political control, owing to geographic and economic circumstances. A part of it, too, was uneconomic in character. For example, tariff preferences directed sugar purchases to Formosa which might have been made more cheaply elsewhere, thus restricting sugar consumption in Japan. Indeed, a high proportion of colonial trade in a country's external commerce tells little of the economic value of the country; it may reflect economic losses rather than gains. In some degree this was true of Japan. Probably the chief significance of her colonial establishment from a national standpoint lay in the strategic realm.[26] It gave the Japanese government political control over enlarged food resources, created a ring of defensive barriers around the home islands, and afforded a series of steppingstones for further imperialist expansion in East Asia.

Much the same broad conclusion may be drawn regarding the economic value at this time of Japan's political foothold in Manchuria. Here Japanese companies, notably the semiofficial South Manchuria Railway, expanded their activities under the protection

[26] That establishment also strengthened the economic and political position within Japan of the big banks and industrial concerns which dominated large-scale enterprise in the colonies. For example, the four big companies which owned most of the sugar refineries in Japan also controlled 80% of refining capacity in Formosa.

of the Railway Zone and Leased Territory secured from Russia following the war in 1904-05. By 1930 some 1.7 billion yen of Japanese capital had been invested in a variety of enterprises, mostly railways, public utilities, and mining. (See below, page 535.) As in Korea, the exploitation of Manchurian iron resources had already acquired some importance for the Japanese steel industry, though full-scale development was not undertaken until the seizure of all Manchuria in 1931-32 and its development as a war base. Also, the port of Dairen had become a large entrepôt for trade with Manchuria and North China. It was here on the mainland, of course, that Japan's politico-economic ambitions came into sharp conflict with rising Chinese nationalism and ultimately precipitated the Sino-Japanese War.

Some idea of the relative preponderance of Japan Proper in the economic life of the Empire can be gained from national income statistics. The national income of the home islands in 1930 was 10,239 million yen, according to Table 38, below. The Japan Economic Federation places the net income of the colonies, leased territories, and mandates at 1,369 million yen in the same year.[27] The latter's method of calculation is dubious, and the resulting figure is certainly an underestimate. Even allowing for a generous margin of error in both estimates, however, it is likely that per capita income in the overseas territories was little more than one third of that in Japan Proper. With productivity and purchasing power at this low level, it is not surprising that these regions failed to bulk larger in the external trade of Japan, despite her assiduous efforts to increase their importance.

An economic balance sheet of the results for Japan of political control over this overseas empire is impossible to construct, even for the period before 1930. What benefits would have accrued to Japan from economic relations with these countries had they remained independent of Japanese rule? Would the resources invested there have otherwise been available for other uses, or were they created in response to the opportunity? If the former, to what use would they have been put? Such questions are unanswerable in any bookkeeping fashion. But it is certain that colonial enterprise occupied a subordinate place in Japanese economic development during the first three decades of the twentieth century. And it is likely that whatever contributions were made to Japan's national income and industrial development by political control over these areas were more than offset, even at the time, by the costs of the military outlays, developmental subsidies, and tariff preferences through which she acquired

[27] *National Income of Japan, 1930-1939*, Tokyo, 1939, pp. 5, 95.

and developed her empire. In Korea alone, for example, the Japanese government is said to have spent 651 million yen upon "defense" and development from 1907 to 1931.[28] In any event, the direct gains and losses for Japan in dollars and cents are of quite secondary importance, even in economic terms, by comparison with the fateful consequences which ultimately flowed from her policy of imperialist expansion in the Pacific.[29]

Foreign v. Domestic Market. From the foregoing account it is clear, first, that Japan continued during the period 1914-29 the process of industrial growth which set in at the turn of the century, and second, that industrial progress was associated with a parallel expansion of foreign trade.

In some industrializing countries the rise of factory industry has been achieved in considerable measure by the creation of tariff-protected industries, with a resulting reduction of foreign trade. Under these circumstances an expansion of industrial output may or may not represent an increase in national production and income, whatever its other benefits. By contrast, the rise of Japanese industry was accompanied by, and was dependent upon, an expansion of imports and exports from the beginning. It was chiefly in the limited category of strategic—especially metal-working—industries that tariffs and subsidies played an important and continuing role. In the main Japan's industrial growth was concentrated in the light industries, notably cotton goods. In textiles, and in a wide range of miscellaneous consumer goods, natural advantages soon enabled Japanese producers to stand on their own feet in international competition with comparatively little direct aid from the State. Contrary to a widespread impression, there are few instances in modern history when so substantial an industrial development has taken place within three decades with as little direct government subsidy and protection as in Japan from 1900 to 1930. This is not to deny that the State exercised decisive leadership in the earlier decades, and continued to exert a pervasive influence. (See Chapter 10.)

Despite the prominence of overseas trade, it is also worth noting again that the Japanese home market continued actually to absorb the bulk of the goods and services produced by the Japanese economy. Here also a prevailing impression runs contrary to the fact. This domestic absorption was necessarily true of a wide range of services and industries like the construction trades whose output was by nature nonexportable. It was almost equally true of agriculture, excepting sericulture. And even in industry, the major part of the

28 Estimate of K. Takahashi, quoted by Andrew Grajdanzev in *Modern Korea*, New York, 1944, p. 211.
29 These questions are considered further in Chapter 10.

output of Japan's factories and workshops, perhaps 65 to 75%, was produced for home consumption. (See below, Chapter 7.) Indeed, if we accept the available estimates, the value of total exports and imports seems to have increased little in relation to total national income over the period from 1914 to 1930. The ratio of exports to net national product rose only from 15% to 18%. (Table 27.) Foreign trade expanded severalfold, but so also did the production of goods and services for the domestic market.

However, Japan's poverty in natural resources and her continuing need for machinery and other specialized manufactures from overseas exerted a constant pressure for the expansion of exports to pay for imports. The pressure for exports of industrial manufactures was held in check for a while by the phenomenal American demand for Japanese raw silk, essentially an agricultural product. When silk prices began their downward descent after 1925, this intensified both the necessity and the opportunity for other industries to expand in foreign markets.

In the first instance, of course, the extension of foreign trade in these years resulted from the strivings of businessmen for profits. Basically, however, it reflected the wider search for economic opportunity on the part of a rapidly growing population. As we have seen, nonagricultural opportunities failed to expand sufficiently in the postwar years to take people off the land, in addition to absorbing the annual increase in the number of job seekers. While the output of industry and ancillary trades and services was increasing steadily, in good part this was due to a rise in output per worker rather than in the number of jobs. Workers engaged principally in manufacturing employment increased only from 5,139,000 in 1920 to 5,876,000 in 1930. (Table 40, below.) Employment in agriculture, as noted above, actually remained stationary at a figure a little over 14,000,000. With population increasing nearly a million a year in the late twenties, the result was intense competition in the industrial labor market and the crowding of workers into commerce and the services.

Meantime agriculture on the whole retained its primitive organization and techniques. It was comparatively unaffected by the social and technological changes so apparent in urban areas. As already observed, the principal growth after 1920 took place elsewhere. The governments of the time continued to encourage scientific improvements in crop methods, which brought a slow increase in output. They also came to the rescue of the farmer with financial subsidies and price stabilization efforts in periods of acute distress. But they showed little disposition to correct the obvious social inequities in agriculture, e.g., to undertake any thoroughgoing reconstruction as regards the fragmentation of land, the conditions of tenantry, or the burden of taxation and debt.

Any real program to raise per capita productivity in agriculture by enlarging and mechanizing Japanese farms, indeed, faced the dilemma that displaced workers would intensify economic pressure in nonagricultural employment. The same issue, in different form, was also presented by increasing imports of colonial rice. Here Japan found herself with the problem typical of many industrializing countries. The interests of industry and the urban classes favored cheap food from overseas; moreover, it was illogical to attempt to develop the colonies and then exclude their produce. The interests of the Japanese farmer, however, argued for restriction. And this was supported by military considerations: the peasant was regarded as the backbone of the nation. The controversy which developed over this issue was reminiscent of the celebrated debate in Germany between Adolph Wagner and Lujo Brentano on the virtues of the *Industriestaat* late in the nineteenth century.[30] In the end the government chose a middle course through this dilemma. It permitted growing quantities of Korean and Formosan rice to be imported. It protected both the colonial and the home producer with a tariff of 1 yen per 100 *kin* (132 lbs.) on foreign rice. And it attempted further to balance the interests of producers and consumers by establishing maximum and minimum prices in the Japanese rice market.[31]

The Postwar Decade: Economic Instability

While this was the underlying situation in Japan—and one which bred a good deal of pessimism at the time regarding her economic future—there were actually wide variations from year to year in the fortunes of agriculture and industry. Indeed, a notable characteristic of the postwar period was the financial instability which marked all of it and which culminated in the acute crisis at the end of the decade. This is not the place to trace the troubled monetary history of these years in detail. Yet some understanding of the movement of prices and exchange, and the factors at work, is essential to an understanding of this period.

[30] There are striking parallels between Japan's economic position in 1930 and Germany's position in 1880. Both had rapidly growing populations, becoming steadily more urbanized and industrialized and more dependent on foreign trade. See Emil Lederer, "Japan in World Economics," *Social Research*, vol. 4, no. 1, February 1937, pp. 1-32.

[31] Under the Rice Control Act of 1921. For a study of this stabilization program see Seiichi Tobata, "The Japanese Rice Control," in *Commodity Control in the Pacific Area*, ed. W. L. Holland, Stanford University Press, 1935, pp. 157-97. In November 1930, the tariff on foreign rice was raised to 2 yen per 100 *kin*.

Instability of Farm Prices. First it should be observed that increasing integration in the world's economy had brought a growing
sensitivity on the part of Japanese prices and incomes to the tides
of world prosperity and depression. Owing to the predominance of
the American market for Japanese exports, Japan was especially
influenced by the postwar boom which developed in the United
States; equally by the crash which followed.

Moreover, the growing commercialization of the Japanese economy meant that dislocations at one point were transmitted to other
parts much more pervasively and speedily than in the earlier days
of localism and self-sufficiency. Japan's working population was
now producing largely for the market, as a result of the transformation of the previous half century. This meant that they had become
involved in the network of financial relations characteristic of a
capitalistic economy. Even in agriculture this was true, for not less
than 60% of the average farmer's produce was now sold for cash.[32]
On the proceeds of such sales he depended for income to meet such
expenses as fertilizer purchases, debt charges, and taxes. He also
had to pay in money for a growing fraction of his food and other
items of family consumption.

Yet it was in agriculture that the price swings of the postwar
period were especially pronounced. The efforts of the government to
stabilize the prices of leading staples met with only limited success.
The price of rice, for example, taking the Tokyo average for 1914
as 100, rose to 274 in 1920. Following the crash of March 1920 it
dropped by more than one half within a twelve-month period. Re-
covering to 257 in 1925, it again began to decline in succeeding
years. By 1931 it had sunk to 114. Raw silk was even more unstable.
From a postwar high of 222 in 1925, it dropped to 151 in 1929. By
1931 it had plummeted to 67. Meanwhile the farmer's operating
expenses and his cost of living failed to decline in proportion.[33] As
his standard of living was meager at best, such fluctuations meant

[32] Official surveys in 1933 indicated that about 63% of the farmer's agricultural
income, 93% of his other income from subsidiary sources, and 64% of his total income were in cash. Even in the case of rice, about 55% of the total crop was sold
in the market during the years 1925-29. Tobata, *op.cit.*, p. 165. Many writers have
exaggerated the degree of family self-sufficiency in the peasant economies of the
Orient, even in advance of any significant industrialization. R. H. Tawney cites
evidence to show that in China at this time farmers typically sold over half of their
crops on the market, and purchased more than one quarter of the goods they consumed. *Land and Labour in China*, London, 1932, pp. 54-55.

[33] This is especially true of production costs in agriculture during a period of
rapid price changes. Costs are incurred through the growing season and bear no
necessary relation to the selling price of the crop after the harvest. The ratio of
the index of agricultural prices to the index of prices of industrial products consumed by Japanese farmers fell from 100 in 1925 to 73 in 1931. Mitsubishi Economic
Research Bureau, *Japanese Trade and Industry*, London, 1936, p. 170.

the difference between solvency and bankruptcy. After 1929 the burden of farm debt, taxes, and rents became progressively heavier and was a principal factor in spreading political unrest through the countryside. In 1930 it absorbed two thirds of the net income produced in Japanese agriculture.[34]

This instability of farm prices was the more marked because of certain characteristics of primary production. These characteristics were by no means peculiar to Japanese agriculture. Nor were they of recent appearance in Japan. But they were of notable significance in the functioning of the Japanese economy at this time because of the continuing importance of agriculture.

For one thing, rice yields are heavily dependent on the weather, being easily affected by droughts and typhoons. The records of wide variations in rice crops and prices go back to Tokugawa times and earlier. They are all the greater in Japan because the country is small and climatic changes are apt to be fairly uniform over much of the crop area. The years after World War I witnessed first a series of abundant harvests in the years 1919, 1920, and 1922; then a fairly steady run of crops in the middle twenties, followed by large harvests from 1927 to 1931. The latter drove prices down to ruinous levels.

Equally important, agricultural production is generally insensitive to a fall in prices, being a matter mainly of the labor of the farmer and his family. Both rice and silk tended to be characterized by inelasticity of supply in response to falling prices, especially as alternative occupations to attract labor from the farms were largely lacking. Indeed, in the case of silk, it would appear that declining prices served for some years to increase cocoon production as the farmer sought to maintain his aggregate income. From 1925 to 1931 cocoon prices declined by more than two thirds, but output rose 25%.

Exchange and Banking Disorders. In addition to these special factors in agriculture, there were other financial circumstances of the postwar years which contributed to the difficulties of the Japanese economy at this time. In industry the World War boom left a heritage of inflated capital values and high operating costs. Coupled with the monetary policy pursued by the government, this introduced an element of chronic maladjustment and financial uncertainty both within Japanese industry and banking and in their relations over-

[34] Agricultural net product was 1,883 million yen, according to the Cabinet Bureau of Statistics. Interest, taxes, and rent are estimated to have amounted to 1,259 million yen. More than half of the latter amount is believed to have been paid over to absentee landlords, banks, the government, and other recipients not directly engaged in agriculture. U.S. Department of State, *National Income of Japan*, Washington, 1945, pp. 161, 171.

seas. Though these circumstances did not prevent a substantial growth of industry in size and maturity, they did bring periodic interruptions and setbacks. In the end they reinforced the Great Depression which came with the collapse of world prosperity at the close of the decade.

In retrospect, these financial disorders appear to have been due, first, to the failure of the business community and the government in the early twenties to stabilize Japanese prices, costs, and exchange rates at a level which would maintain equilibrium in the Japanese balance of payments. Through most of this period it seems likely that the yen was overvalued in foreign currencies.[35] The early postwar years, 1920-22, were characterized by a huge deficit on current account. Exports declined more sharply than imports, and ship earnings dropped by two thirds from 1918 to 1921 as world trade returned to a more normal, peacetime basis. This deficit was further increased by large imports for reconstruction purposes after the earthquake in 1923. The yen was maintained in the neighborhood of its prewar dollar parity only by using up most of Japan's huge short-term credits and specie balances remaining abroad at the end of 1920.[36] After 1924 the situation improved as the yen was allowed to fall for a time to a level around $0.40. Exports promptly rose in 1925 to an all-time high. But they slumped again when the yen recovered nearly to parity ($0.4985) late in 1926. Concurrently prices in Japan dropped steeply, precipitating a banking crisis.

The bank panic of 1927 brought into prominence a second and related source of financial difficulty. Basically this was a weakness in Japanese banking structure and practices, especially a reluctance to liquidate wartime values which had persisted in business and official circles ever since the slump in 1920. At that time the Bank of Japan had rushed to the aid of banks and business with liberal loans. The government likewise lent its support to commodity markets. Recovery was rapid, but as a result Japan entered the postwar era with internal costs and prices high relative to international prices. This situation, together with the earthquake of 1923, and the policy

---

[35] See Furuya, *op.cit.*, chaps. 4, 5.

[36] With the removal of the United States embargo on gold exports in June 1919, Japan brought home a part of her foreign specie balances. At the end of 1920, 1,116 million yen of specie was held at home by the government and Bank of Japan and 1,062 million abroad. The foreign balance was rapidly drawn down in subsequent years to finance import surpluses, so that by the end of 1924 only 326 million yen was left. Domestic holdings remained virtually intact through the twenties, but were drawn upon heavily in 1930-31 during Japan's brief and ill-fated attempt to remove the gold embargo and return to the gold standard. Annual figures for Japan's specie holdings from 1871 to 1929 are given in *Nippon Keizai Tōkei Sōkan*, cited, p. 347.

of pegging the yen at the expense of the country's foreign balances, accounted for the enormous import deficits of these years.

In addition, the banks were heavily burdened with frozen assets still carried on their books at inflated values. In 1922, when a minor bank crisis occurred, and again on a larger scale after the earthquake, the central bank and the government once more adopted a liberal lending policy. They continued for some time thereafter the credits extended. A write-off of bad debts and reorganization of capital structures were thus further delayed. In 1927 matters finally came to a head. A number of banks crashed, among them the Bank of Formosa and one of the five largest private banks. A general moratorium had to be invoked. Subsequently many banks and many trading and industrial concerns were liquidated, reorganized, or absorbed by competitors better able to weather the strain.[37]

Concentration of Controls. The financial disorder of this period appears to have been traceable in some degree to the power and independence of Japan's great business combines, the *zaibatsu*. At the same time it tended to concentrate economic control still further in their hands. The *zaibatsu* held an important position in Japanese banking and finance, but their interests in early postwar years were still predominantly industrial. G. C. Allen, a close student of this period, concludes that these interests led them to resist the deflationary policy which seems to have been called for on technical, financial grounds.[38] Their opposition was the more effective because of their influence with the Diet and the bureaucracy, and their comparative independence from central bank control. Yet the government authorities, with few exceptions, appear to have shared with business circles a persistent bias in favor of cheap money and liberal lending through most of the period after 1868. (See below, pages 512ff.)

These great family combines grew steadily in size and power during the war and postwar years. Already dominant in the more modern sectors of the Japanese economy, they now extended their control indirectly over an increasing share of small-scale commerce and manufacturing. Through an intricate, pyramided structure of intercorporate, personal, and political ties, the larger combines, notably Mitsui and Mitsubishi, developed into huge agglomerations

[37] The weaknesses of Japanese banking organization and practices at this time are discussed in Mitsutaro Araki's *Financial System in Japan*, Tokyo: Japan Council, Institute of Pacific Relations, 1933, pp. 23-31. Araki remarks that Japanese financial crises (before 1933) were due to "the excessive profit-making activities of banks." But he also blames the government. "In fact . . . the Government, misled by the beautiful name of restitutions given to banks, promised them implicitly that it would help them should they fail, and . . . thus armed by Government promise of economic aid, they rushed into profit-making activities."

[38] *A Short Economic History of Modern Japan*, London, 1946, p. 94.

of heterogeneous enterprise—trading, shipping, banking, insurance, real estate, mining, manufacturing, and colonial undertakings. As described in Chapter 4, this concentration of control had been facilitated from the beginning by close association with the military oligarchy and the civil bureaucracy; also by the complete absence of antitrust laws and other public restraints on the exercise and perpetuation of monopolistic power such as developed in the United States and England with the growth of the corporate device. Now it was accelerated by postwar financial difficulties like the bank crisis of 1927. These eliminated thousands of smaller and weaker concerns which were less well equipped than the *zaibatsu* companies to take losses, cut costs, and readjust to the new situation.

The decade of the twenties witnessed a large reduction in the number of small banks. While aggregate bank deposits increased by one quarter from 1920 to 1929, the number of banks declined from 2,041 to 1,008.[39] Financial power came to be centered increasingly in a handful of great private banks and trust companies, along with semiofficial institutions like the Bank of Japan, Industrial Bank, and Yokohama Specie Bank, in which the former also had influential representation. These private banks with their numerous branches were largely owned or controlled by the *zaibatsu*. Their key position in the Japanese economy was enhanced by the typically close relations between commercial banks and industrial concerns in Japan. The absence of a capital market for public issues made the banks the chief external source of private capital for business firms. The *zaibatsu* banks were also relatively free from bank inspection and other forms of government regulation.[40] Tied in as they were with all sorts of affiliated concerns, they were powerful instruments for eliminating and absorbing their smaller competitors and those of their sister companies. Thus they served steadily to extend the dominion of the family partnerships or holding companies at the top of the combines.

Probably no other modern industrial society organized on the basis of private property has offered a comparable display of the unrestrained "power of bigness," employing all the devices of monopolistic control. The single qualification—and an important one —would seem to be the comparative rarity of actual market monopolies in individual products. Usually two or more of the giant com-

39 *Nippon Teikoku Tōkei Nenkan*, cited, no. 50, 1931, p. 138.

40 Despite the banking standards prescribed by Japanese law, the principal *zaibatsu* banks were not inspected at all from 1928 to 1935, and their books were examined only once from 1928 to 1945. The law vested wide discretion in the minister of finance, who in prewar years commonly had personal *zaibatsu* affiliations. U.S. Department of State, *Report of the Mission on Japanese Combines*, Washington, 1946, part 1, pp. 53-56.

bines were found in more or less active rivalry with each other and sometimes with a host of small producers. The same combines, however, tended to dominate a number of fields of industry and trade. This situation of oligopoly probably encouraged the maintenance of prices and profits above the level to which they would have been reduced by a more atomistic type of competition. As a group, in any case, the *zaibatsu* and their satellites dominated the more modern sector of the Japanese economy. With controls ramifying outwards from their nuclei of great financial, industrial, and trading concerns, they presented the most extreme contrast to the small-scale pattern of organization which persisted in agriculture and even in a large proportion of Japanese manufacturing and commerce. (See Chapter 4.)

The institution of the *zaibatsu* contributed greatly to the rapid accumulation of capital and modernization of technology which underlay Japan's industrial development. It enabled Japan to reap certain economies of large-scale organization, even where the production unit remained small; it placed the direction of large sectors of the economy in the hands of able technicians and executives employed by the combines; it afforded a device by which industrial investment was accelerated through the ploughing back of huge profits accruing to the owners.

On the other hand, if the concentration of control in Japanese industry and finance was progressive in these technical aspects, its social aspects were less admirable. It was one of the factors perpetuating inequalities of income and opportunity in modern Japan almost as wide as those of feudal times. It carried over into modern industry the tradition of hierarchical status and authoritarian control which was inimical to political and social democracy. By hampering the pervasive growth of independence and individual initiative in economic life it reinforced other circumstances militating against the emergence of a broad and sturdy middle class, or a vigorous trade union movement. And in politics the plutocratic alliance of the *zaibatsu* and the political parties contributed eventually to the defeat and discrediting of parliamentary government after 1930.

It is widely assumed today that the introduction of modern technology to raise the productive power of "backward" peoples will itself bring democracy and peace. Japan's experience hardly supports this thesis—even over a span of fifty years. For she acquired modern industrialism without a corresponding growth of liberal movements such as have emerged in countries with a more democratic tradition to harness this power in pursuit of welfare goals. The latter trend was by no means absent in the prewar years, to be sure. In the twenties especially, Japanese liberalism asserted itself with increasing vigor despite the heritage of authoritarian government so firmly entrenched in the Constitution of 1889. However, its power base remained essentially weak, and its programs compromised by the interests of the business oligarchy. In the end it proved inadequate to withstand the resurgence of the military after 1931. For this there are many reasons, including the impact of the forces let loose in the outside world by the Great Depression. But one major explanation is to be found in the realm of economic organization. Here both tradition and circumstance combined to concentrate controls over wide sectors of industry, commerce, and finance, and prevented the creation of a firm economic foundation for political and social democracy.

The growth of combines and cartels after World War I also gave rise to structural changes in the Japanese economy which contributed to the financial maladjustments of the period. Specifically, it weakened the forces of domestic and international competition in certain sectors of the economy where previously they had been dominant. As in other industrial nations, this evolution brought with it a certain loss of flexibility, an increasing element of rigidity in the determination of prices and adaptation of resources to changing conditions. Attempts at monopolistic price controls and restraints on output, though often attended with little success, were now observable in industries like paper, cement, copper, coal, dyestuffs, and chemical fertilizer. They were made more feasible than before by increasing freedom from foreign competition in the Japanese market, especially after the tariff was revised upwards in 1926. And they were rendered more attractive by inflated capitalizations and productive capacities left in the wake of World War I. It would be easy to exaggerate this structural change in the Japanese economy before 1930. Yet one can see in the twenties the beginnings of a process which was to develop much more fully in the succeeding decade under the stimulus of the depression, the devaluation of the yen, and later the requirements of a war economy. (See Chapter 10.)

Collapse of the Yen. In concluding this narrative of the twenties, it remains only to record the events which brought the decade to a dramatic close. With the advantage of hindsight it is possible to see the onset, as far back as 1926, of the deflationary pressures which were to reach a climax in the world depression of 1929-32. Following the bank crisis of 1927, however, the Japanese economy seemed financially in a sounder position than before. Manufacturing and trading activity was buoyed up in the two succeeding years by easy money conditions and by prosperity abroad, especially in the United States. Industrial production rose 23% from 1926 to 1929, and exports almost in proportion.

The Minseito government which assumed office in 1929 thereupon determined, under the leadership of its finance minister, the vigorous Mr. J. Inouye, that greater exchange stability and prestige should be sought through returning to the gold standard at the old parity. It prepared itself to undertake whatever measures of retrenchment were necessary to this end. Accordingly, government expenditures were cut, and industry was encouraged to cut costs through rationalization measures. In January 1930 the gold embargo was lifted.

The moment could hardly have been more inopportune for stabilization along orthodox lines. The return to gold would doubtless have called for some deflation in any event, as Japanese domestic prices were still relatively high. But now world commodity prices had already begun their steep descent from postwar levels. This greatly intensified the deflationary strain in Japan. Wholesale prices, having already declined 20% from the end of 1925 to the end of 1929, proceeded to drop another 20% in the next twelve months.[41] Agricultural staples, notably rice and silk, fell even more precipitately under the influences of shrinking monetary demand and a series of bumper crops.

As previously observed, the impact upon the rural population was calamitous. From 1925 to 1930, according to surveys of the Department of Agriculture and Forestry, gross income per agricultural household declined 40 to 45%. Net income after deducting working expenses shrank by one half or more. The farmer's cost of living meantime declined only 26%. Thus his real income, meager in the best of times, was reduced by something like one third.[42]

In Japan's balance of payments the repercussions were also serious. With the removal of the gold embargo early in 1930 gold exports were resumed. They far exceeded Mr. Inouye's expectations.[43] The bottom dropped out of the export market as the value of exports declined 50% from 1929 to 1931, again mainly as a result of the collapse of prices. The Minseito government nevertheless strug-

---

[41] The relative severity of the decline in Japan is indicated in the following indices of wholesale prices (1913 = 100, except for India, where 1914 = 100):

	Japan (*Tokyo*)	India (*Calcutta*)	United States (*BLS*)	United Kingdom (Statist)
1925	202	159	148	160
1929	166	141	137	134
1931	116	96	105	98

Figures from *Statistical Yearbook of the League of Nations, 1934/35*, Geneva, 1935, pp. 227-29.

[42] *Japanese Trade and Industry*, cited, pp. 171-72. At most these figures are only approximations, but they illustrate the forces at work.

[43] M. Takita, "Japan's Gold Embargo Lifted and Reimposed," in Oita Commercial College, *Research Department Bulletin*, December 1932, p. 29.

gled on with its "no loan" policy. Increasingly it incurred the enmity of the Army over its opposition to military expenditure. At the same time it lost popular favor as the plight of the country went from bad to worse.

In September 1931, England abandoned the gold standard, and the Kwantung Army launched its attack in Manchuria. The one event created fresh difficulties in the export trade, and started a flight from the yen in which the authorities fought a losing rearguard action against the speculators. The other spelled the doom of political liberalism and financial orthodoxy at home. In December the government of Premier Wakatsuki was swept out of office. The gold embargo was reapplied, and the yen fell precipitously. Early in February military fanatics murdered Mr. Inouye, the architect of the ill-times policy of deflation and one of the ablest leaders of the now demoralized Minseito. Ironically he paid with his life not so much for the damaging economic consequences of deflation as for his courageous opposition to Army expansionism on the continent. The two factors were associated together, however, in the ascendancy of the military and the discrediting of party government.

Trade, Armament, Industrial
Expansion, 1930-38

The decade of the thirties was dominated by two sets of forces now placed in motion. One was the great boom in industrial exports which followed upon the collapse of the yen. This gave fresh impetus to the growth and diversification of Japanese manufacturing and trade, while presenting the world with acute problems of commercial dislocation and rivalry in the markets where Japan's export drive was concentrated. The second was the recrudescence of Japanese militarism, culminating finally in the Pacific war.

For a time the Japanese economy was able to sustain both courses of development, contradictory as they were. The twofold demands placed upon it drew hitherto idle resources into employment, and revealed an unsuspected potential in technological advance and production achievements. Initially, indeed, the expansion of peacetime trade and industry supported and reinforced imperialist aggression by building up national income and industrial strength to unprecedented levels. In the end it was destroyed by the militarism which it fed. For the mounting ambitions of Japan's military leaders finally wrecked her civilian economy after 1936, just as they had suppressed and discredited the liberalism which had accompanied the growth of that economy in earlier years.

Invasion of World Markets. The most conspicuous feature of the early thirties in Japan, so far as the rest of the world was concerned, was the boom in Japanese exports after 1931. The immediate stimulus came from the swift depreciation of the currency. From U.S. $0.494 in November 1931 the value of the yen plummeted to $0.207 a year later. With the devaluation of the dollar in 1933, it recovered to the neighborhood of $0.30 (or 1s. 2d.). Here it remained until 1939.

The bounty thus conferred upon Japanese exports—in part a correction of the previous overvaluation—brought a soaring advance in shipments of Japanese goods all over the world. From 1930 to 1936 exports to foreign countries increased from 1,435 to 2,641 million yen. Their physical volume increased even more rapidly than their value. For export prices (in yen) dropped 24% in 1931, and despite currency depreciation had failed to return to their 1930 level by 1936. The volume of exports nearly doubled in six years. Meanwhile sales to the colonies (Korea and Formosa) advanced even more rapidly, so that total overseas exports, valued at 1930 prices, rose by 104%.[44]

Textile manufactures, long dominant in Japan's export trade, again led the way in this new penetration of world markets. But there were conspicuous shifts within this category, as well as a decline in its relative importance. Raw silk failed notably to share in the recovery. Hard times in the United States, coupled with rising competition from synthetic fibers, exerted a severe drag on any revival of silk prices. Shipments continued at a high level, but their yen value was only half what it had been a decade earlier.

By contrast, Japanese cotton goods spread rapidly through foreign markets; the production and exports of rayon textiles both mounted steeply for the first time; and Japanese woolens also won a substantial foothold abroad. By 1936 Japan had become the world's premier exporter of cotton piece goods. Sales reached 2,710 million square yards valued at 473 million yen. Textile yarns, fabrics, and clothing as a group now provided 1,570 million yen of exports, or 58% of total exports to foreign countries. Before the displacement of silk, however, they had supplied nearly three quarters. Although now more diversified, and more advanced in manufacture, they were also more dependent on imported materials (cotton, wool, rayon pulp). Taken together, therefore, they yielded less to the country per yen of exports than in the heyday of Japan's great staple, raw silk.

[44] U.S. Department of State, *The Place of Foreign Trade in the Japanese Economy*, Washington, 1946, vol. II, pp. 24, 33. This invaluable study integrates the statistics of foreign and colonial trade, giving a detailed analysis of Japan's trade dependence during the prewar decade.

The trend toward export diversification was also reflected in the rapid expansion of nontextile exports, likewise consumer goods for the most part. Among them were toys, pottery, brushes, hat braids, rubber tires and shoes, electric lamps, canned fish, and miscellaneous manufactures of wood, paper, and celluloid too numerous to mention. Cheap Japanese wares of these varied kinds soon became a familiar sight through the bazaars of the Far East and on Woolworth counters in the United States. Metals and machinery also began to rise to prominence in the export trade, stimulated especially by large capital construction programs in Manchuria. In 1936 such exports reached 354 million yen, of which about one half represented machinery, vehicles, and scientific instruments. Only in cheap metalwares, bicycles, and the simpler types of machinery and electrical equipment, however, could Japan yet compete in the open market.

Meanwhile the export boom, and the domestic revival which accompanied it, brought a steady rise in imports. Purchases from foreign countries advanced from 1,542 million yen in 1930 to 2,753 million yen in 1936. The import price index rose 31%, so that the actual volume of imports increased about one third. Most of this increase was in imports of cotton, wool, rayon pulp, petroleum, iron and steel materials, and nonferrous metals. Raw materials now comprised nearly two thirds of all imports from foreign countries— about the same share as that held by manufactures in the export trade. Although the Japanese engineering industries made rapid strides in technical proficiency, the large expansion in plant capacity taking place in Japan induced heavy purchases of machinery and vehicles. Mainly they came from the United States. Imports also continued to provide some 10 to 15% of the country's net requirements of food and fertilizer, after deducting exports. They were divided about equally between foreign countries and the Japanese colonies, the share of the latter being maintained by preferential tariffs at a high level.

This expansion of imports and exports was accompanied by significant changes in the regional distribution of Japan's trade. Whereas the United States took 42% (by value) of her exports in 1926, its share had declined to 22% in 1936, owing to the fall in silk prices. Meanwhile exports of manufactures to China, India, and other countries of Asia increased; they found a growing market in Europe, especially in Britain; and they invaded new markets throughout Africa, South America, and Oceania. Asia alone now took as much as 63% of all Japanese exports, if Korea and Formosa are included along with foreign countries. (Table 34.)

Certain countries, particularly the United Kingdom, felt keenly the pressure of Japanese competition. Others found new markets for raw materials and equipment in Japan which could only in part be said to have replaced former markets elsewhere. This was especially true of the United States. She now supplied large quantities of cotton, petroleum products, iron and steel, machinery, copper, and lumber to Japanese industries engaged in the manufacture of consumer goods, munitions, and plant equipment. By 1936, in fact, Japan was absorbing half of all United States exports to Asia—or as much as the whole continent of South America.[45]

The balance of trade with the United States, long heavily in Japan's favor, now reversed itself. A credit balance of 167 million yen in 1927 was converted into a deficit of 244 million yen in 1936. (Table 35, below.) Simultaneously Japan's former deficit in trade with Asia changed to a large credit balance. The facility of this change underlines the important fact that Japan was only able to build up her prewar foreign trade to such heights by capitalizing on the world's multilateral trading system. This enabled her thus to buy and sell according to economic advantage, offsetting bilateral balances in the world money market. Paradoxically, it might be added, Japan now bought more from the United States because she could now sell less. The decline of the once great silk market had set in motion a train of events which brought a drastic reorientation of her trading relations all over the world. (For a fuller analysis of Japan's dependence on overseas trade, see below, Chapters 6 and 7.)

The flooding of Japanese goods into foreign markets after 1931 brought frantic outcries in the West. Most other countries, including Japan's major industrial competitors, were struggling in the slough of depression. This was, indeed, one of the reasons for the ready appeal of Japanese manufactures. Their cheapness enabled them in some degree to tap levels of consumer demand below the reach of higher-priced European and American goods. But they also cut deeply into established markets, especially those of Lancashire. And elsewhere, as in the United States, though they remained small in volume, their unsettling effects spread uncertainty and alarm just when governments were attempting to put a floor under prices and wages, or at least to reserve shrunken markets for home producers. Antagonism was further increased by the political reaction to the Japanese Army's concurrent invasion of China. Only in China itself, however, did popular boycott reach substantial proportions. This was countered by steady Japanese encroachments upon China's territorial and administrative integrity in the north.

[45] See the author's *Trade and Trade Rivalry between the United States and Japan*, New York: American Council, Institute of Pacific Relations, 1936.

Almost everywhere else, after 1932, tariffs were raised or quotas established against Japanese goods. Probably they were most effective, and least justified, in the colonial markets of Asia and Africa controlled by the other industrial powers. Where Japan happened to buy more than she sold, as in Australia and India, she was not without bargaining power to defend her export interests. In the case of India, for example, she was able to conclude an agreement in 1934 providing for the purchase of 1 million bales of Indian cotton against the sale of 325 million yards of Japanese cotton piece goods in the Indian market.[46] And in some cases she was able to mitigate foreign restrictions by imposing voluntary controls through her own export guilds, or through temporary "gentleman's agreements" limiting shipments. (See below, Chapter 10.) But the rise of trade barriers aroused fear and resentment among the Japanese. Despite the spectacular expansion of trade actually achieved, and Japan's obvious economic interest in supporting the kind of world trading system which would permit its continuation, her militarists were quick to make propaganda out of the situation. It was now easier to summon economic arguments to support a drive toward the illusory goal of self-sufficient empire.

In retrospect, the near hysteria aroused abroad by the Japanese "trade menace" seems to have had little justification. At its peak Japan's total export trade was less than 4% of world exports. Moreover, the expansion of the thirties did not represent some new and unlimited competitive power suddenly acquired by Japanese industry. Nor could it be attributed simply to low-wage Oriental labor, against which the higher-standard countries were helpless to compete. Japanese labor had always been miserably paid, judged by Western standards. The new circumstances which now strengthened its competitive ability in certain lines were the marked gains in technical efficiency and business organization achieved through the decade 1926-36 and the violent dislocation of costs, prices, and exchange rates precipitated by the Great Depression. It was the concentrated impact of Japan's export drive, both in time and in particular types of manufactures, which created the problem.

Currency depreciation in the Japanese case seems to have had unusually acute and prolonged effects through these years. The matter is too complex to examine here. But the reasons are associated with certain characteristics of Japan's economic structure, as well as the circumstances of world depression. Many Japanese exports, including cotton textiles, required imported raw materials for their manufacture. In 1936, for example, these "dependent industry" ex-

[46] Tokyo Association for Liberty of Trading, *Trade Agreements between Japan and Some Other Countries*, Tokyo, 1937, pp. 26ff.

ports comprised 60% of all exports to foreign countries and colonies. Nearly 40% of their value represented imported materials.[47] As compared with raw silk, which they now tended to replace, they had to be exported to a much larger total value before they would yield an equivalent amount of foreign exchange to finance imports for home consumption.

The rise in export costs which might have been expected to follow from the depreciation of the yen in 1931-32 was retarded by several factors. Huge stocks of cotton were purchased by the Japanese at rock-bottom prices in the early years for subsequent use. This delayed for a time the effect of currency depreciation upon production costs in the cotton industry. Labor costs in export industries were also held down by extensive rationalization of production processes and business organization, and even more by the acute depression which gripped Japanese agriculture. Average wage rates in industry remained virtually stationary from 1931 to 1937. Far less than in England was the worker's standard of living dependent on imports. Except in clothing, therefore, the Japanese cost of living failed to rise significantly in direct response to the fall of the yen. Finally, many branches of the export trades were fiercely competitive, being crowded with small industrialists and merchants. The benefits of depreciation appear to have been passed on in large degree to the foreign consumer in the form of lower prices. Under conditions of world-wide depression, the overseas demand for these cheap manufactures, whether in high- or low-income countries, seems to have been highly elastic.

For these reasons, too, Japan's net gains from this trade boom were less substantial than the trade figures themselves might suggest. The years 1930-36 saw a marked deterioration in the terms of trade, both with foreign countries and with the colonies. By 1936 the ratio of export to import prices was only 74% of 1930. (See Table 26, below.)' The ratio had become even more unfavorable if we compare the prices of "originated exports" (the quantum of domestic production embodied in exports, after allowing for imported materials used) with the prices of imports retained for home consumption and investment. This exchange ratio had dropped to 65%. Thus 50% more Japanese production had now to be exported to pay for a given value of retained imports. Although the volume of exports nearly doubled, retained imports increased only 27% in the six-year period.[48] Only in part was this loss offset by technical

[47] *The Place of Foreign Trade in the Japanese Economy*, cited, vol. i, pp. 30, 32.

[48] *ibid.*, pp. 12, 20, 32. About one quarter of Japan's total imports at this time were used in exports, or offset by exports of comparable types. The balance was available for home consumption and investment.

gains reducing the amount of capital and labor embodied in exports.

Reflation and Armament. Meanwhile, at home, other policies reinforced the expansion of industry. No country, in fact, pursued a more successful policy of rapid industrial recovery after 1931—or one which ultimately ended in greater disaster.

The ill-timed retrenchment program of Mr. Inouye was now abandoned in favor of monetary expansion. Under the direction of the veteran finance minister, Korekiyo Takahashi, rising armament expenditures were met by deficit financing—"red ink bonds," as they were called. This steadily enlarged the monetary supply. The Army had launched its Manchurian enterprise and reestablished its grip on the levers of power in Tokyo. Increasing sums were now demanded for war operations, and for military and naval expansion. On top of this was the huge program launched to develop the basic resources of the new puppet state of Manchukuo.

The requirements of the armed forces were skillfully met by Mr. Takahashi through the flotation of government loans and encouragement of credit expansion at low interest rates. From 1930-31 to 1936-37 national government expenditures in the general account rose from 1,558 million to 2,282 million yen—nearly a 50% increase. Four fifths of this increase went to the Army and Navy. Tax revenues increased comparatively little, and from 1932 to 1938 there was an inflationary gap of 600-800 million yen each year, covered by borrowing.[49] Interest rates declined, while the national debt nearly doubled. It rose from 6 billion to over 10 billion yen. This was still a relatively modest sum, however, absorbed by the banking system without undue strain. Wholesale prices at the end of 1936 stood only 33% above 1930. The cost of living had advanced even less. Although the note issue of the Bank of Japan had risen 30%, bank loans and discounts outstanding remained at about the same level.

Reflation at home thus reinforced the stimulus of yen depreciation abroad, without cancelling its effects. Under this double impetus Japanese industry forged rapidly ahead. Mining output rose 34% from 1930 to 1936; manufacturing, 63%.[50] Meanwhile wage rates recovered only slowly from their depression lows in most industries. Average real wage rates, which had risen as much as 50% from 1914 to 1926, showed little net advance over the next decade. (See below, page 144.) The gain which came from the fall in living costs during the depression was largely cancelled by the upward drift of

[49] Bank of Japan, *Economic Statistics of Japan, 1950*, Tokyo, 1950, pp. 146-47.

[50] According to the index of industrial production of the Economic and Scientific Section, GHQ, Supreme Commander for the Allied Powers, Tokyo. *Economic Statistics of Japan*, cited 1949, p. 231.

prices from 1932 to 1936. Such benefits as accrued to workers from the industrial boom thus came largely in the form of wider employment opportunities, particularly for males in industry.[51] Business profits reached peak levels, however. They provided huge sums for the expansion and reequipment of Japan's major industries.[52]

The progress of different sectors of Japanese industry was nevertheless uneven. All of. the textile trades except raw silk made substantial advances in their scale of production, equipment, and organization. Among the big cotton firms, for example, the spread of automatic power looms and high-draft spinning brought marked increases in output per worker. The smaller weavers specializing in diversified cotton, rayon, and silk piece goods for foreign and domestic markets likewise improved their equipment and capabilities through these years. Especially significant for the future was the growth of the rayon and staple fiber industry. Here costs fell rapidly as the output of rayon yarn was increased from 17,000 tons in 1930 to 125,000 tons in 1936. The production of textile manufactures of all types expanded 25% in this six-year period. It rose nearly 50% in the decade 1926-36. (See Table 8.)

It was chiefly the metallurgical, machinery, and chemical industries, however, which mushroomed under the stimulus of armament spending and industrial construction. Consumer goods production in Japanese industry advanced only 33% from 1930 to 1936. By contrast, the output of producer goods jumped 83%.[53] In the machinery trades, where production was valued at 1,609 million yen in the latter year, Japan could now supply virtually all her own requirements except in the more specialized and advanced types of machinery, power plant, and metalworking equipment. The expanding output of fuel and basic materials—coal, steel, cement, and electricity, for example—likewise reflected her growing industrial capacity. Soda ash, caustic soda, dyestuffs, and other basic chemicals advanced two- and threefold in production, some items even more.

The structure of Japanese industry continued through this period to exhibit the evolutionary tendencies observable in the previous

---

[51] These general conclusions are verified in substance by wage and employment data published by the Bank of Japan and Ministry of Commerce and Industry, as well as indices of retail prices and the cost of living prepared by T. Uyeda, the Bank of Japan, and the newspaper *Asahi* for various years. Different indices, however, give somewhat different results. The best estimate of real wage trends from 1914 to 1933 is that of T. Uyeda and T. Inoguchi in *Cost of Living and Real Wages in Japan, 1914-1936*, Tokyo: Japan Council, Institute of Pacific Relations, 1936.

[52] Manufacturing corporations averaged profits of 11% on net worth in 1936, according to a Mitsubishi survey. Some 37% of these profits were reinvested as corporate savings. Mitsubishi Economic Research Bureau, *Monthly Circular*, no. 171, January 1938, p. 15.

[53] *Oriental Economist*, vol. VI, no. 10, October 1939, p. 692.

decade. Throughout manufacturing there was a growth in the scale and efficiency of factory production, despite the persistence of the small plant of less than 100 workers as the typical establishment in all but a few lines. The great firms and combines which had always dominated heavy industry increased their preponderance. They were joined now by several newer financial groups which rose to prominence through association with the Army and Navy in the expansion of munitions production. In foreign trade, the closer integration of the processes of importing, exporting, production, shipping, and finance contributed to Japan's commercial successes, especially in cotton goods markets.

At home the depression of 1930-31 gave a marked impetus to the formation of cartels. These were now legally sanctioned and encouraged by the government under the Major Industries Control Law and Industrial Association Law of 1931. Government intervention and control was also extended in several key industries, notably iron and steel, electric power, and shipping. In the main, however, the cartel movement proved largely ineffectual until after 1936, when the State began to foster it more actively as an instrument of national policy in the transition to war economy. Except in Manchuria, where industrial development under the aegis of the Army followed the pattern of state capitalism from the beginning, Japanese industry preserved its predominantly private and uncontrolled character until the eve of World War II.[54]

In marked contrast to the flush of industrial prosperity was the situation which prevailed in Japanese agriculture. Here, as previously observed, the depression fell with crushing impact. At prices prevailing in 1930-31 a large section of the Japanese farming class was insolvent, burdened as it was with heavy taxes, high rents, and a farm debt of 5-6 billion yen. Agricultural output increased comparatively little in the years which followed. And it was 1935 before farm prices climbed back to their predepression parity with the prices of industrial goods purchased by the peasant. In the meantime agricultural distress bred social unrest through the countryside, affecting also the Army, which drew most of its recruits from farm families. This failed, however, to induce large-scale relief expenditures, in preference to armament, despite the ascendancy of military leadership in Tokyo. The government did appropriate considerable sums in the effort to stabilize rice and silk prices. It also

[54] G. C. Allen's chapters in *The Industrialization of Japan and Manchukuo, 1930-1940*, ed. E. B. Schumpeter, New York, 1940, give an admirable account of the structure and organization of Japanese industry at this time. On the development of cartels see also Keizo Fujita, "Cartels and Their Conflicts in Japan," *Journal of the Osaka University of Commerce*, no. III, December 1935, pp. 65-109. We return to these matters again in Chapters 4 and 10.

experimented with the readjustment of farm debts, the relief of tenancy, the control of fertilizer prices, and even the encouragement of emigration to Manchukuo. But these were all makeshifts which hardly touched the fundamentals of the problem. (See Chapter 10.)

More significant was the acceleration of the long-term drift from agriculture into industrial and urban occupations. As before, this failed to reduce the farm population. But it did take care of the increased numbers seeking gainful employment. Factory employment alone increased from 1,886,000 in 1930 to 2,876,000 in 1936. By the latter date one in every three Japanese lived in a city of 30,000 or more; one in four in a city of over 100,000. Mining, manufacturing, and construction taken together now afforded the chief occupation for about a quarter of the entire working population, and a considerably larger fraction of all able-bodied males. They provided as much as 40% of the national net product, at price levels prevailing in 1936.

Manufacturing alone, including handicraft as well as factory industry, accounted for 5 billion yen, nearly a third of the total national income. In factory industry, net product was valued at 3.6 billion yen. Here the traditional supremacy of the textile trades was now challenged by the chemical and machinery industries. At the comparatively high prices and rates of earnings prevailing in 1936, these newer groups each far surpassed the textile industries in net value of output. (See Table 39, below.) The most rapid growth thus took place in heavy industries which, while serving civilian uses, were also crucial in the military realm. Significant for the latter purpose, too, was the fact that another large complex, that of iron and steel and other basic industries, was now being established under Japanese political control in Manchuria.

The net growth of the Japanese economy during this period may be summarized as follows:[55] From 1930 to 1936 Japan's net national product, at 1930 prices, increased from 10.2 billion to 15.8 billion yen. Real net *income* rose less substantially, however, as a result of the adverse shift in the barter terms of trade following the depreciation of the yen in 1931. From 1930 to 1936 the average price of exports to foreign countries and colonies dropped 5%, while import

[55] This summary is supported broadly by statistical evidence compiled in various studies by the U.S. Department of State, particularly *National Income of Japan* and *The Place of Foreign Trade in the Japanese Economy*, cited; also by the gross national product estimates of the postwar Japanese Economic Stabilization Board, the income estimates in Y. Yamada, *Nihon Kokumin Shotoku Suikei Shiryō*, Tokyo, 1951, and related data in two reports of the U.S. Strategic Bombing Survey, *The Effects of Strategic Bombing on the Japanese Economy*, Washington, 1946, and *The Japanese Wartime Standard of Living and Utilization of Manpower*, Washington, 1947.

prices rose 29%. As already mentioned, Japan thus had to ship larger amounts of goods abroad to pay for her 1936 imports than would have been required had the terms of trade remained unchanged. These additional exports absorbed about one fifth of the gain in real national product. Net income therefore increased only about 4.3 billion yen at 1930 prices—still an impressive advance.[56]

Part of the 40% gain in real income from 1930 to 1936 represented increased civilian consumption. But the greater share probably took the form of additions to capital assets and military supply, especially the former. In 1930 military expenditure was still relatively small. Net investment, including changes in stocks of goods as well as in durable assets, may well have been negative. By 1936 direct military expenditures were running close to 1 billion yen (1930 prices). Net private and governmental investment was on the order of 2 billion yen. Thus at least 20% of the national income was now being withheld from civilian consumption for one purpose or the other. The greater part of this 3 billion yen, however, was still being ploughed back into plants, equipment, and business inventories in Japan Proper, most of them civilian or civilian-military in character.[57] Net investment in Manchuria, North China, and elsewhere abroad probably did not yet exceed 250-350 million yen.

Meanwhile real civilian consumption in Japan rose about 20% from 1930 to 1936. The total output of consumer goods actually increased more than this. But part of it went into exports, where it was exchanged against imports on less favorable terms than before. At the same time the population grew from 64.5 million to 70.2 million, or 9%. Consumption of goods and services per capita therefore advanced only 10% or so.

Food standards remained more or less unchanged in the aggregate. Imports of foodstuffs for domestic use actually increased one third, but this was little more than enough to support the growing population at existing levels of diet. The principal gains came in other types of consumption, which now comprised over half of consumer expenditures. Per capita use of clothing materials increased one third. Other basic materials going into civilian consumption show a somewhat similar growth. Most of this advance came from more effective utilization of home resources, rather than greater per capita imports for domestic use. The latter continued, however, to play a vital role in sustaining the whole Japanese economy.

[56] *The Place of Foreign Trade in the Economy of Japan*, cited, vol. i, pp. 23-26. I have used slightly different income estimates than are quoted in this report, but without materially affecting the argument.

[57] This estimate receives some corroboration from the gross national product figures of Tables 22 and 36, below.

In the light of the above summary, this dramatic period in Japan's economic growth can be seen in its true perspective. Essentially it continued the trends observable in previous decades. It did not signify merely a boom in armaments and *zaibatsu* profits without gains to the general civilian economy, as some critics have alleged. Nor, on the other hand, did it bring sweeping advances in the material well-being of the population as a whole. Such gains as were achieved were distributed unevenly through the country. They accrued largely to the urban population, thus accelerating the drift to the city so long in evidence. Being heavily concentrated among well-to-do groups who owned and managed the great industries, banks, and trading houses, they probably increased somewhat the gross inequalities of income and wealth which characterized the whole course of Japan's prewar development. From these higher income classes, and the corporations they controlled, came much of the savings which permitted large investments in the creation of new productive capacity as well as rising military expenditure.

Since the period bridged a great world depression, it was no small achievement even to maintain the country's living standards, especially as the population was now growing at the rate of a million a year. These standards were now the highest in the Far East, and well above those of the previous generation in Japan. Rising employment opportunities had only been sustained, it is true, by accepting less favorable terms of exchange on world markets. These terms had deteriorated with the decline of the silk trade, and their improvement was now hampered by spreading restrictions on Japanese goods. The Japanese could nevertheless look with satisfaction on the progress of the decade ending in 1936. It had witnessed a substantial growth in the scale and maturity of industry and trade through a period in which many other countries, particularly those more abundantly blessed with raw materials, were mired in depression.

Road to War. The rise of foreign barriers to Japanese manufactures was an ominous portent of a future which boded ill for Japan. No country had a greater stake in multilateral trading relations which would enable it to buy and sell according to economic advantage all over the world. Her economic expansion over half a century had been built upon this opportunity. By 1936 Japan depended upon overseas sources, foreign or colonial, for 20% of her net supply of rice and beans, 35% of her fats and oils, 60 to 80% of her iron and steel materials, 90% of her superphosphate fertilizer, and 100% of her cotton, wool, and rubber. Many of her most vital needs could only be satisfied advantageously in markets quite beyond the range of political control on the most foolhardy military

estimate. And if liberalism in world economic policies was everywhere now in retreat, Japan herself had to accept a full measure
of responsibility. For it was she who had assaulted the principle of
collective security in 1931 by her seizure of Manchuria. And her
subsequent trade invasion of world markets proceeded in such headlong fashion as was bound to invite a protective reaction.

Under these circumstances the task of statesmanship in Japan
was at least to make a prudent calculation of the main chance as between supporting and tearing down the world structure which had
served her economic needs so well, and to weigh this against other
national interests at stake. As late as 1936 it seemed that the issue
was still open. Indeed, business and popular sentiment in the spring
of the year was strongly expressed in favor of a political settlement in China. Here Army intrigues in the North were seriously
damaging legitimate trade and arousing growing political hostility
in the Western world as well as among the Chinese.

Economic considerations were secondary, however, in the minds
of military leaders who were now in the ascendancy. Probably they
were grossly misunderstood as well; but in any case they were subordinate to the political and imperial ambitions of Japan's modern
samurai. As it turned out, the die was cast in favor of renewed aggression in China.

The renewal of hostilities in 1937 required fresh military outlays
on a greatly expanded scale. The government deficit financed by
borrowing jumped from 605 million yen in 1937 to 1,298 million in
1939 and 2,406 million in 1941. By this time, however, Japanese
resources were near full employment. Accelerated war spending
quickly brought mounting inflation. Almost at once a crisis was
precipitated in the foreign exchange market. Drastic controls had to
be imposed to restrict normal imports and divert exchange resources
progressively to oil, steel, and other strategic materials. Continued expansion of war industries, both in Japan and on the continent, led
also to a spreading network of controls over domestic production and
investment to channel materials and labor away from civilian supply. The result was progressive dislocation of the whole structure
of peacetime industry and trade.[58]

Meanwhile political events marched step by step, with the in-
exorability of a Greek tragedy, toward the outbreak of general war
in the Pacific. By 1940 Japan was already on a war footing, with
17% of her national output devoted directly or indirectly to war
purposes. In foreign policy she had now committed herself to a
course of imperialist expansion from which there could be no turn-

[58] See Jerome B. Cohen, *Japan's Economy in War and Reconstruction*, Minneap-
olis, 1949, chap. 1; also the reports of the U.S. Strategic Bombing Survey, cited.

ing back without disastrous consequences for the ambitions and fortunes of the leaders now in the saddle. With the attack on Pearl Harbor, her military extremists embarked on a reckless gamble which ended in destroying the very empire it was to aggrandize. In so doing they mortgaged the economic future of their people for a generation, beside spreading ruin through the rest of the Far East.

The events of the late thirties thus brought to a close an era in modern Japanese history. In the economic realm this era wrought a transformation in the old Japan under the impact of the new forces of trade and technology. The process by which this came about is important to an understanding of the industrial Japan of today. Even more, it has a broad significance in the light of the general movement now under way throughout Asia to modernize economic life and lift the level of productive power and material well-being. To a more analytical study of this process of growth and structural change we shall now turn our attention.

CHAPTER 3

THE SCALE OF ECONOMIC GROWTH

The Transition to Industrialism

THE narrative sketch of the preceding chapters testifies to the persistent and cumulative advance of Japan over half a century or more in modernizing wide areas of economic life and integrating them with the structure of world production and trade.

Almost every aspect of Japanese society responded in varying degrees to the new forces at work. However, it was in the economic realm, and such related fields as national defense and public health, that the changes were most profound. Characteristically, Japan assimilated the applied arts of the West more readily than the spirit and social ideals of Western culture. The spinning wheel and the *samurai* sword gave way more rapidly than traditional ideas concerning the status of women, or the role of the fighting man in the state.[1] An early translator of Mill's essay "On Liberty" had great difficulty, "because of the lack of proper words in the Japanese vocabulary."[2] And even in economic life the transformation proceeded unevenly. Everywhere the new jostled the old. A peasant might be seen riding along in an electric tram while lighting his pipe with flint and tinder, remarks one observer. Throughout Japan one found—still finds—those bewildering contrasts, side by side, epitomizing the conflict and adjustment between the eighteenth and twentieth centuries. It is this very fact, indeed, which makes generalization difficult, and which gives rise to the contradictory interpretations found in the literature on modern Japan.

[1] "Into no branch of State activity did foreign influence more quickly, more completely, or more effectively enter than into the art of war. The adoption by us of a Western military system and of military engineering was, in fact, a most fertile marriage of the newest invention in technology with the martial spirit of long training." Inazo Nitobe, "The Influence of the West," in *Fifty Years of New Japan*, compiled by Count Shigenobu Okuma, London, 1909, vol. II, p. 469.

Thorstein Veblen once referred to this prior assimilation of the military arts as "Japan's opportunity." By this he meant the opportunity granted her military-minded rulers to employ modern technology to pursue traditional aims of military expansion before the gradual infiltration of ideas of democracy, popular education, and commercial interdependence, also inevitable accompaniments of industrialism, undermined old feudal values. In ascribing modern Japanese imperialism exclusively to "the spirit of old Japan," however, Veblen seems to have underestimated the extent to which industrialism and political nationalism imported from abroad were reinforcing rather than dissipating the impulses to national aggrandizement. "The Opportunity of Japan," in *Essays in Our Changing Order*, New York, 1934, pp. 248-66.

[2] Nitobe, *op.cit.*, vol. II, p. 469.

Nevertheless, the changes at work were pervasive and profound. If they were most pronounced in the cities, and especially in the superstructure of large-scale banking, transport, and industry, they were by no means confined to these spheres. Much remained of the simple, largely precapitalistic economy of Tokugawa days, especially in the countryside. But increasingly this was giving way to a fundamental reorganization and expansion of the country's productive resources along the lines pioneered by the West a century or more before. From being "a peasant-handicraft society with Western adjuncts," Japan was now emerging as "an industrialized society with survivals of peasant-handicraft institutions and feudal forms."[3]

Japan at the Midpoint. By the end of the twenties the first difficult stages of this transition may be said to have been completed. The processes of modernization and growth had extended in varying degrees to all sectors of the economy: to agriculture as well as industry, to small-scale trades as well as factory industry, and to the home market as well as foreign commerce. In economic maturity and productive power Japan was still far behind her advanced industrial competitors in the West. Yet she now invited comparison in many respects, no longer with her Asiatic neighbors, but with a number of Western nations that tradition and circumstance might seem to have endowed with far superior advantages.

One significant index of economic development is the amount of energy of all types utilized by a nation in productive activity. Primitive peoples are forced to rely mainly on human muscle, sun and wind, and animal power. The struggle to improve material well-being is in good part a struggle to create the kind of production system which can harness increasing amounts of energy derived from fuels and falling water. Even a small tractor has a work output ten times that of a horse or buffalo and 100 times that of a man. In measuring energy utilization it is best to eliminate the requirements for heating houses and other buildings in various climates and to compare energy consumed in production, processing, and transport. Here the U.S. Department of State has made some interesting calculations of the prewar world situation, combining all forms of energy in terms of their equivalent in kilowatt-hours of electricity. Per capita consumption of energy from all sources, animate and inanimate, for productive purposes (as defined above) is estimated in Table 1 for a number of countries in 1937.

The position of prewar Japan was still quite inferior to that of Western Europe and the United States. But equally it was far

[3] Nathaniel Peffer, *Prerequisites to Peace in the Far East*, New York, 1940, p. 79.

above that of most of Latin America, Africa, and the rest of Asia. What the figure may have been in the Japan of 1867 we can only conjecture. However, a clue to the transformation over seventy years may be found in the situation in other countries of Asia more recently. India, for example, was able to utilize only 0.5 unit of inanimate energy from coal, oil, falling water, and other sources in 1937 for every single unit of animate energy (mainly human labor).

Table 1. *Energy Consumption per Capita for Productive Purposes in Japan and Selected Countries, 1937*[a]

(electricity equivalent in kilowatt-hours for all energy sources)

	Per Capita Use	Ratio of Inanimate to All Sources
United States	6,996	97.6
United Kingdom	5,553	97.9
Germany	3,461	96.2
Australia	2,971	91.3
USSR	1,380	88.2
Japan	*1,251*	*91.0*
Poland	961	82.6
Brazil	450	56.6
India	289	35.4
Egypt	242	36.0
Netherlands Indies	197	30.9
China (excluding Manchuria and Jehol)	164	21.2

[a] U.S. Department of State, *Energy Resources of the World*, Washington, 1949, table 51. "Including the animate and inanimate energy used in production, processing and transportation, but excluding the energy used in domestic, commercial and public establishments, a small part of the energy used in farming and the energy lost and stored. The fuels consumed in overseas bunkers have been allocated on the basis of merchant fleet tonnages rather than of loading points."

For Japan the ratio was 10/1, or twenty times as high. These figures themselves can have no great precision, nor do they take account of other productive resources like land and mineral wealth. But clearly the Japanese had progressed a long way from their old subsistence economy, despite the fact that more than twice as many people were now crowded on their islands as in Tokugawa times.

Associated with this rise in productive power are other evidences of a socio-economic character which testify to the intermediate position Japan had reached by 1937 in the scale of world economic development. In life expectancy, for example, the Japanese were now halfway between the "elite" nations of the West and those mass populations of Asia still ridden with grinding poverty, malnutrition, and disease. Infant mortality in Japan had fallen until in the prewar decade it compared favorably with the situation in Eastern Europe. It was at least 30 to 50% better than the rate still prevailing in most other Asiatic countries. In simple literacy the Japanese had also gained a favored position, thanks to years of compulsory primary education. More generally, in her consumption of a number of standard goods and services Japan ranked alongside Italy, far below the countries of the West with the highest standards but well above most of the rest of Asia and the Middle East. (See below, page 148.) Finally, her formidable Army and Navy, and the war she was about to undertake, are further evidence of the economic "surplus" which could now be produced and withheld from civilian needs in the interest of national power and aggrandizement.

This midposition in the scale of economic development is also evidenced by Japan's trading relations with the world toward the end of the prewar era. Here one might describe her as "facing two ways," as in so many other aspects of her national life. Thanks to the progress of industrialization she now imported more than any other Asiatic nation from the non-Asiatic world. Yet she was also the chief center of intraregional trade within the Orient. She traded heavily with both East and West, but along rather different lines.

On the one hand, to the United States, the Dominions, and Europe she sold a variety of semimanufactures, especially raw silk, together with other simple types of crude manufactures also embodying large amounts of cheap labor. Her chief competitive advantage lay in having labor that worked at much lower wages than her Western competitors paid, plus better technical skills and business organization than were found among her Oriental competitors. On the other hand, she had now also become a large exporter to other parts of Asia of textiles and other consumer manufactures, and even some machinery. Here she was well ahead of other Far Eastern nations in machine techniques and labor productivity. Yet she still enjoyed far more abundant supplies of low-paid skills than were found in the West, together with greater facility in adapting to Asiatic markets where tastes and purchasing power more nearly resembled those in her own home market. Her import trade reflects the same duality: large purchases of raw materials from all over the world, and continued dependence on the United States and Western Europe for industrial equipment of the more advanced and specialized types.

Historically these shifting lines of competitive advantage were the outward reflection of the process of industrialization (and its limitations) at home. At the stage reached during the interwar period it made it peculiarly difficult to fit Japan into the usual classification of trading nations as agricultural, industrial, etc.[4]

All such international comparisons as the foregoing are necessarily imprecise. And they must be interpreted in the light of various conditioning factors. They do support the conclusion, however, that the Meiji "Renovation" set in motion a genuine economic revolution. Whatever its limitations in the political realm, and its uneven progress everywhere, it did initiate a fundamental reorganization of large sectors of the Japanese economy. The resulting growth of Japan's productive powers in ensuing decades went ahead with cumulative momentum.

This chapter is concerned primarily with only one aspect of Japan's experience, albeit a central one. Its purpose is to assemble evidence bearing on the rate and magnitude of growth in the Japanese economy through the prewar decades. Only incidentally does it touch on the processes by which this growth took place: the expansion of population and resources; the acquisition of new skills; the mechanisms of capital formation; the redirection of demand and employment; the strategic role of foreign trade; etc. These are all major facets and will be treated later. For the moment they are largely left aside in order to focus on the net result in terms of a growing output of goods and services. First the main components of the economy are examined, after which an effort is made to summarize the over-all increase in national income as related to population and standards of consumption.

Most people will accept as one fundamental test of economic progress a greater per capita flow of goods and services in relation to the expenditure of human effort, provided they serve the felt needs of the community. There are other tests as well—the degree of equality among classes, the conservation or waste of human and material resources, the stability of an economic system, and the capabilities or propensities it creates for waging war or preserving the peace. Any broader social accounting must likewise take account of all the strains and dislocations attending the industrialization process. In the face of the challenge of poverty throughout Asia today, however, no problem is more paramount than that of raising the productive power of great masses of people. The case of Japan in this regard is so far unique, and it is instructive. It is important to see what the Japanese achieved, and how they achieved it, without losing sight of those human costs and social injustices which so qualified their successes in the technical realm.

Limitations of Economic Statistics. Our first question, then, concerns the rate of physical growth in the Japanese economy, measured

4 See Chapters 6 and 7.

in terms of its output of goods and services. Important as it is, this question is impossible to answer in any precise fashion. The reasons are worth noting in brief, since they complicate many important issues of fact concerning the economic development of Japan. An understanding of them will perhaps make the reader more tolerant of the obvious deficiencies in the analysis which follows. It should also caution him to allow a generous margin of error in the broad statistical judgments presented.

In the first place, no matter how accurate the basic data, certain technical limitations are inherent in any summary measure which, by its nature, must strike an average for quite divergent tendencies in various lines of economic activity over long periods of time. This applies, for example, to indices of the volume of production or trade, where the constituent products themselves undergo divergent changes in character and relative importance, as well as in price. Even with the best of statistics, what does it mean to say that machinery output tripled in fifteen years, or that exports increased 150%, if meanwhile the whole composition of production or exports radically changed?

Despite the intrinsic limitation of index numbers as an expression of average change—or, more accurately, of the whole concept of "average" in such cases—this chapter makes extensive use of the best of such measurements available for Japan. Short of an exhaustive chronicle, which would lose one in a forest of trees, there is no other way to proceed. Yet these measurements should be understood for what they are. At best they give only a shorthand expression of a general trend which is not very meaningful except as it is supported by and interpreted with the more concrete information detailed in this study. The longer the period of comparison, the less representative of anything the index numbers become.

In the second place, quite aside from this technical difficulty, one encounters major inadequacies in the basic facts concerning Japan's economic growth. These arise out of the scope and the method of collecting economic statistics in Japan; also the manner of their processing and publication. Much of Japan's economic life, for one thing, has remained largely precapitalistic in spirit and mode of organization down to recent times. To cite one illustration, 35 to 45% of the commodities entering into the household expenditures of Japanese farm families were self-supplied in the years 1921-31.[5] Among millions of small, family-type industrialists and tradesmen,

[5] Estimate of the Imperial Agricultural Survey, quoted by Shiro Kawada in "The Income and Living Conditions of the Agrarian Population of Japan," *Journal of the Osaka University of Commerce*, no. 4, December 1936, p. 18.

as well as farmers and fishermen, practices of accounting are still rudimentary where they exist at all.[6]

Where such conditions prevail, the collection of reliable statistics on production, income, and costs presents formidable problems to the central statistical agencies. Until recent years, moreover, such agencies, whether public or private, were comparatively undeveloped in Japan. Staffs were largely untrained and funds were limited. This restricted both the volume and the reliability of economic data. It is certain, for example, that many series of production, population, employment, etc. reflect in their upward trend not only actual growth but also more complete enumeration from the earlier to the later years.[7] Finally, two further problems arise. There is reason to suspect that statistical reporting in Japan has not been free from bias and distortion of a more calculated variety, arising from motives of tax evasion or considerations of local and national prestige.[8] And the failure in many cases to have essential

[6] Japanese economic development again illustrates Max Weber's familiar thesis stressing the spread of rationalistic business accounting as a cardinal feature of the rise of capitalistic industry and trade. A significant story is told of a Mr. Shimono, long a prominent accountant in modern Tokyo. When a young student at the Tokyo Commercial College early in the Meiji period he was advised by the College Director to read Pixley's *Duties of Auditors*, and "to introduce the accountancy system to this country." He read the book and duly reported back that it was of no interest; the system was not worth importing into Japan! Nevertheless, modern accounting practices were gradually introduced, receiving a powerful impetus from the Nitto scandal of 1909, when the Japan Sugar Company failed owing to fraudulent practices, and several prominent politicians were found guilty of bribery. Prof. Koji Usui likens this incident to the "South Sea Bubble" affair which led to reforms in English accounting standards. "The Past and Present of the Accountancy Profession in Japan," Oita Commercial College *Research Department Bulletin*, December 1932, pp. 3-4. Today, however, even among the big banks and corporations in Japan, accounting practices fall far short of modern standards, particularly in financial statements put out for tax purposes or public consumption.

[7] J. W. Robertson Scott, who travelled widely in rural Japan during 1915-20 ventured the opinion that cereal output was underestimated and cocoon production overestimated. "Roughly, the statistics [for rice] show a production 15% less than the actual crops. Formerly the underestimation was 20%." He attributed this to the practice in older times of basing taxes on grain yield. *The Foundations of Japan*, London, 1922, pp. 86-87, 404. The possibility of error was heightened by the fact that until 1929 statistics of land use and crop production were collected locally by untrained individuals who relied heavily on personal estimates by the farmers or themselves. See R. Nagasawa, "The Method of Statistical Investigation Concerning Agricultural Production in Japan," *Bulletin de l'Institut International de Statistique*, vol. xxv, part 2, Tokyo, 1931, pp. 151ff. Lest this seem unduly discouraging, however, it might be noted that the United States censuses of the nineteenth century, and probably more recent ones, are believed to contain errors of underenumeration in various economic series amounting to 10% or more.

[8] I know of no substantial evidence of deliberate falsification of national statistics prior to 1937. It is commonly suspected, however, that the reports of individual establishments were not free from error, for the reasons mentioned, and that both locally and nationally the desire to make a good showing tended to impart an upward bias to statistics bearing on the strength of the economy and on its public credit.

After the outbreak of Sino-Japanese hostilities, the enveloping war atmosphere

details and explanations accompany published data creates a series of pitfalls and exasperating puzzles which baffle even the most experienced student.

One American economist, as he confessed to the writer, was so discouraged by the gaps, discrepancies, and arithmetic errors in Japanese economic information that he deserted the field in favor of the greater precision and certainty of research upon the American economy. On this argument perhaps one should quit the study of economics altogether, for, in F. W. Taussig's phrase, it abounds in "loose ends and rough edges." Despite the above limitations, the fact is that Japan has been well endowed with economic statistics compared with any other Far Eastern country. Especially is this true of the period since 1920.[9] The study of Japan, therefore, can often throw light not only on the experience of that country but indirectly on analogous phenomena in other parts of East Asia as well. The deficiencies mentioned argue for discriminating judgment, and against precise measurements in most fields. In production data, for example, the margin of error may run as high as 20%, even after World War I. There are also large gaps which can probably never be filled. This need not prevent us, however, from forming reliable judgments as to the general direction of economic growth and the processes by which it came about.

Natural Resource Industries

Growth of Production. In the extractive industries, first of all, Japanese production statistics are fairly abundant, especially since about 1905. Here also we have comprehensive indices of the physical volume of production prepared at Nagoya Commercial College for the years 1878 to 1934.[10] With the figures for the earlier years

---

led to the progressive withdrawal and distortion of all sorts of information, on subjects ranging from bauxite imports to the birth rate. This reached its climax in the war years. Ultimately the policy of suppression and falsification was disastrous, for, by concealing the true state of affairs in Japan's collapsing economy, it prolonged the war and intensified the hardships visited upon the people.

9 Public concern over economic and social issues after World War i led to the growth of private research agencies and the improvement of government statistical services. In the next decade were launched the first extensive inquiries into population, agriculture, industrial conditions, family budgets, and national income and wealth.

10 These valuable studies were begun under the supervision of E. F. Penrose and carried forward by Y. Koide and other Japanese statisticians at Nagoya. The series in Table 2 represents a revision and extension of an earlier study published by Penrose in *Food Supply and Raw Materials in Japan*, Chicago, 1930. Previous editions of Penrose's work were published in Japan by the Institute of Pacific Relations (1929), and, under the title "Agricultural and Mineral Production in Japan," in *Bulletin de l'Institut International de Statistique*, vol. xxv, part 2, Tokyo, 1931, pp. 221-82.

omitted, because of their unreliability, the summary Nagoya series for food and raw materials are presented in Table 2. For agriculture, fishing, forestry, livestock and mining, they are found in Table 3.

Table 2. *Population, Cultivated Land, Food and Raw Material Production in Japan Proper, 1875-1939*

ANNUAL AVERAGE	POPULATION[a] Number (millions)	Index	CULTIVATED LAND[b] Hectares (thousands)	Index	FOOD PRODUCTION INDEX[c]	RAW MATERIAL PRODUCTION INDEX[c]
1875-79	35.9	71	—	—	—	—
1885-89	38.8	77	—	—	(57)	(22)
1895-99	42.2	83	—	—	67	48
1905-09	47.5	94	5,398	95	85	78
1910-14	50.6	100	5,695	100	100	100
1915-19	54.0	107	5,912	104	115	134
1920-24	57.6	114	6,051	106	125	140
1925-29	61.3	121	5,992	105	135	169
1930-34	66.3	131	5,936	104	145	175
1935-39	71.2	141	6,031	106	161[d]	205[e]

a Pre-1920 figures are those of "*de facto*" population, i.e., statistics of registered population as corrected by the Imperial Cabinet Bureau of Statistics and published in *Shōwa Go-nen Ikō Waga Kuni no Jinkō*, Tokyo, 1930, pp. 3-5. Census estimates for 1920-37 are from the Bureau's *Nippon Teikoku Tōkei Nenkan*, no. 58, Tokyo, 1939, p. 6.

b *Nippon Teikoku Tōkei Nenkan*, cited, passim. The first annual census of cultivated land was taken in 1903, and showed a total of 5,224,000 hectares. Earlier, in 1877, some 4,096,000 hectares of paddy and upland fields were registered under the new land tax. These figures are not sufficiently comparable, however, to permit any conclusions to be drawn concerning the growth in the interval.

c A recombination of the constituent items of the Nagoya indices of primary production for 1885-1934 from Table 3, with weights proportional to the gross value of output of each item in 1929-33. As noted in Table 3, these indices are less representative of the period before 1905 than of the years thereafter, and probably have a degree of upward bias throughout the pre-1905 period. For 1875-79 the Nagoya food index is 30 on a 1910-14 base, and the raw material index 12. These figures are regarded as too unreliable for inclusion here.

d The 1936-38 average of the production indices of the Ministry of Agriculture and Forestry for agricultural crops, livestock, and fishing, combined with the Nagoya weights (above) and linked with the Nagoya index in 1925-29. *Oriental Economist*, vol. vii, no. 7, July 1940, p. 414.

e The Nagoya index is projected to 1936-38 with the following data: the forestry production index of the Ministry of Agriculture and Forestry (see above); the mineral production index of the *Oriental Economist*, Tōyō Keizai Shimpō-sha, *Keizai Nenkan* (1940), Tokyo, 1940, p. 3; the production of cocoons, tea, and tobacco from *Nippon Teikoku Tōkei Nenkan*, cited, no. 58, 1939.

These indices can be taken as broadly indicative of the expansion of physical output in Japan Proper, especially after the turn of the century.[11] In using them, however, one should bear in mind the

11 Throughout this study, except in foreign trade statistics, the term Japan Proper refers to the four main islands of Japan (Hokkaido, Honshu, Shikoku, Kyushu),

Table 3. *Growth of Physical Volume of Primary Production
in Japan Proper, 1885-1938*[a]
(indices; 1910-14 = 100)

Annual Average	Agriculture[b]	Fisheries[c]	Pastoral and Dairy Industries[d]	Forestry	Mining	Total Primary Production[e]
1885-89	(55)	—	—	—	10	(44)
1895-99	69	41	50	—	28	60
1905-09	88	54	78	100	68	82
1910-14	100	100	100	100	100	100
1915-19	118	149	125	131	138	121
1920-24	120	225	162	135	133	130
1925-29	129	299	210	136	157	145
1930-34	134	343	277	149	166	150
1936-38	149	402	304	197	237	178

a For the period 1885-1934 these indices are based on annual indices prepared at Nagoya Commercial College and published in "Hompō Genshi Seisambutsu no Seisan Sūryō," Nagoya Chamber of Commerce and Industry, *Nagoya Keizai Tōkei Geppō*, vol. viii, no. 4, May 1936, Supplement, p. 60. For each of the extractive industries, the index is a geometric mean of production relatives for all items having a value exceeding 1 million yen in the years 1929-33, weighted by annual average value of output in this period. In the above table these indices are shifted from 1921-25 to 1910-14 as 100.

The Nagoya indices are the most comprehensive and continuous series available for Japan. They are less representative of the period before 1905 than of the years thereafter, however. Production data are lacking on a number of items in the early decades. Where they exist they may be subject to an upward bias through more inclusive reporting. Also, the use of 1929-33 value weights imparts some degree of upward bias throughout the period. It emphasizes more heavily the items which grew rapidly than would a set of weights based on production values in an earlier period. For example, cotton production had virtually disappeared by 1929, so that its rapid decline from 1887 to 1910 does not influence the agricultural index as it should.

The 1936-38 indices are those of the Ministry of Agriculture and Forestry for agricultural, fisheries, pastoral, and forestry production and of the *Oriental Economist* for mineral output. *Oriental Economist*, vol. vii, no. 7, July 1940, p. 414; Tōyō Keizai Shimpō-sha, *Keizai Nenkan* (1940), Tokyo, 1940, p. 3. These indices are spliced to the Nagoya series for earlier years, shifted to a 1910-14 base. It might be added that the mining index prepared by the Economic and Scientific Section, GHQ, Supreme Commander for the Allied Powers, Tokyo, agrees with the above index in showing a 43% rise from 1930-34 to 1936-38.

b Before 1905 there are no data on production of vegetables, fruits, or a number of the lesser industrial, tuber, and root crops. Included in the earlier indices, however, is the bulk of agricultural output, consisting of cereals, beans, potatoes, mulberries (silk cocoons), and other industrial crops.

c Total aquatic production, including that of products like seaweed and that from pelagic fisheries outside home waters.

d Before 1895 few livestock statistics are available, and not until 1905 are poultry and dairy products included.

e The five constituent indices are combined with weights proportional to net value of output in 1930. The average for 1885-89 includes the Nagoya index for pastoral production (28 on a 1910-14 base), which is not shown here for the reason mentioned in note d.

together with three small island chains—the Kuriles (Chishima), Bonins (Ogasawara), and Loochoos (Ryukyu)—and numerous smaller adjacent islands. Prewar foreign trade statistics also include southern Sakhalin (Karafuto) as a part of Japan Proper after 1904.

likelihood that they exaggerate the rate of gain in some degree, for reasons mentioned in the notes to Table 3.

The growth of primary production in Japan deserves close attention. Often Japan's economic development is described mainly in terms of industrial development, more particularly in terms of the rise of factory industry. The corollary, stated or implied, is that the extractive industries failed to share largely in this growth, because of Japan's limited natural resources and technical backwardness in agriculture. Yet it will be observed in Tables 2 and 3 that food and raw material production rose persistently and rapidly through this period. It outdistanced the growth of population by a wide margin.

Expansion was particularly marked during the decades before 1920. From the eighties on, under the stimulus of expanding markets, steady progress was made in enlarging the capacity of the extractive industries. This took many forms—applying modern methods in exploiting the country's mineral resources, especially coal; building up forestry reserves to provide sustained yields on a much larger scale; improving fishing boats and gear so as to utilize more intensively the rich resources of the nearby seas; extending the cultivated farm area through irrigation, drainage, and the settlement of Hokkaido, the northern frontier island; raising acreage yields by double cropping, better fertilizer, consolidation of strips, and other improvements in farming methods. A few products like cotton and indigo declined in production, as cheaper sources of supply or substitutes became available from abroad. But they were the exception. For the most part the story was one of differential rates of growth in response to expanding and shifting demands.

During the twenty-five years before World War I the total production of food and industrial materials doubled, according to the Nagoya index. (Table 3.) Even if the increase was in reality no more than a half or two thirds, the achievement was significant. For the entire Meiji period it was still greater. (The index itself actually advances from 16 in 1873 to 74 in 1911, but a good deal of the gain probably reflects the upward weight bias of the index, more complete reporting of crops, and perhaps also local pride in making a good showing.) Clearly expansion was already under way in the eighties. And from 1885-89 to 1910-14 even rice, the staple crop intensively cultivated for centuries, is estimated officially to have increased 40% in output, mainly through a 25% gain in yield per acre. Comparable increases are recorded in other crops like wheat and barley. Much steeper rises occur in the case of silk cocoons, tobacco, coal, and metals. It is fruitless to attempt any close measurement of the aggregate growth through these years. But there is every reason to believe it was substantial.[12]

The net value product of these natural resource industries grew more slowly than their gross output, for physical growth was achieved partly by proportionately greater outlays for fertilizer, land maintenance, etc. Yet it must have accounted directly for much of the gain in national income and wealth before 1914. It could hardly have been otherwise in view of the preponderance of agriculture at the time. This growth in primary production contributed largely to the support of the increase in population from 1873 to 1911, estimated at 40%, and a modest improvement in its material well-being. It also provided a major share of the savings and tax revenues which laid the foundations of industrial and military expansion during the Meiji period.

Nor did growth in the extractive industries cease after 1914. From 1910-14 to 1930-34 the Nagoya series show a gain of 45% in food production and 75% in the output of raw materials. The average annual increase in the former was 1.9%; in the latter, 2.8%. For food and raw materials in combination the aggregate growth over this twenty-year period was just 50% (Table 3) as contrasted with a 34% rise in the country's population (Table 2). Still further advances were recorded up to the eve of World War II, under the stimulus of the trade and armament boom of the thirties.

By this time, however, the great initial gains which come from relatively simple improvements in the traditional methods of an Oriental peasant economy had been realized. The cultivated area approached its limits; indeed, it declined slightly after 1920. Further gains in output depended on increasingly heavy applications of fertilizer. From 1912 to 1939 the area in farm crops increased only 4.4%, but the consumption of nitrogen fertilizer rose 163%, phos-

---

[12] Using official production statistics, Bruce F. Johnston has computed an index of the combined output (in caloric equivalent) of six major food crops making up the bulk of Japanese agricultural production during the period 1880 to 1920. ("Agricultural Productivity and Economic Development in Japan," *Journal of Political Economy*, vol. LIX, no. 6, December 1951, p. 499.) His food crop index follows closely the Nagoya index for agricultural foodstuffs, although lagging behind the index for all agricultural output.

	Six Food Crops (Johnston)	All Agricultural Foodstuffs (Nagoya)	All Agricultural Products (Nagoya)
1881-90	100	100	100
1891-1900	127	125	132
1901-10	146	149	165
1911-20	177	183	215

phoric acid 148%, and potash 129%.[13] Mining companies now found
it progressively more difficult to continue expanding production in
the face of competition from foreign supplies. The output of copper, silver, and crude oil actually receded from its wartime peaks.
And fishing fleets had to extend the range of their operations with
more expensive equipment and a larger scale of organization. A
more determined program of public investment, particularly in agriculture, could certainly have raised production above the plateau
where it now stood. The Japanese village was still starved for credit.
(See Chapter 5.) But further advances in most lines of primary
production were to be had only with proportionately heavier outlays
of capital and labor. In certain products these advances ceased
altogether; in others they continued only with the aid of higher
tariffs and subsidies. Thus the rate of growth in the extractive
industries as a group showed a tendency to taper off. Japan's potentialities for further expansion of income and employment came
to center mainly in industry, commerce, and other service occupations.[14]

To detail the history of these various extractive industries and
their individual significance is impossible here. So long as Japan had
access to overseas supplies of food and raw materials through external trade, it was economically less important that she produce
any particular items than that her limited resources be applied so
as to maximize her total output most efficiently in relation to domestic and foreign demands. It may nevertheless be worth while to
call attention to two industries whose contribution to national development is hardly expressed by the mere value of their output.
One is the fishing industry, the other coal mining.

"*Coal and Fish.*" It may be said of Japan that, like England, she
is "built on coal and surrounded by fish." The Japanese eat more
fish than any other large nation in the world. Marine products
actually supply four fifths of the protein in their diet. As a by-employment of farm families living along the shore, fishing provides
this protein supply with a relatively small investment of capital or
labor withheld from other productive uses. From ancient times the
lack of extensive pasture land and of stock farming in the crowded
home islands has thus been compensated by easy access to the sea.

Through the Meiji decades fishing activity continued to be confined principally to coastal waters. Here it was carried on largely by

[13] Supreme Commander for the Allied Powers, GHQ, Natural Resources Section,
Report No. 93, *Fertilizer Practices in Japan,* Tokyo, 1947, p. 43.

[14] This is not contradicted by the substantial gains recorded in the production of
many domestic materials from 1936 to 1944. For the most part these were achieved
as a measure of war economy, and replaced cheaper and better supplies from abroad
at the expense of real national income.

methods practiced from time immemorial. Only slowly were techniques modernized, and then chiefly by installing power engines and somewhat better gear in small fishing craft. After 1910 came the development of large-scale commercial operations by big concerns organized to exploit more distant seas. The total fisheries catch more than tripled from 1910-14 to 1930-34, according to the Nagoya index. While the figures are incomplete for the earlier years, it is clear that an increasing share represented the far-flung operations of trawlers and "floating factory" vessels in Soviet waters, throughout the Yellow Sea area, and among the South Sea Islands. In 1923 these offshore and overseas operations already provided 19% of Japan's total catch. By 1938 their share had risen to 38%.[15] The overseas fishing industry was oriented largely toward the growing foreign market for canned fish. Its protection and advancement now ranked among the important issues in economic foreign policy. Yet over 90% of the catch of the Japanese fisheries as a whole continued to be consumed at home, where it provided a vital part of the national food supply. (See Chapter 7.)

Japan's most important mineral resource, on the other hand, is her extensive deposits of coal. While hardly in a class with the reserves of China, the United States, Britain, or even Poland, they were ample for her prewar needs except in anthracite and coking varieties. Moreover, they are located within easy reach of her big industrial cities. Japan might have been able to meet her fuel needs more largely by importing foreign coal as well as oil, taking advantage of cheap water transport. And in fact, as her metallurgical industries developed, she did become heavily dependent on coking and blending coals from North China, beside importing petroleum supplies from the United States and Southeast Asia. For the bulk of her coal requirements, however, she would certainly have had difficulty in finding adequate overseas supplies at tidewater, either in her own colonies or elsewhere in the Far East. Her own substantial reserves of medium- and low-grade bituminous coal were essential to her rapid industrial growth, especially the great Chikuho fields of Kyushu.[16]

15 Supreme Commander for the Allied Powers, GHQ, Natural Resources Section, Report No. 95, *Japanese Fisheries Production, 1908-46*, Tokyo, 1947, p. 8.

16 To say that Japan's coal reserves have been largely adequate for her past requirements does not mean that they will provide for her future. U.S. experts estimated in 1952 that she might be expected to double her prewar energy consumption by 1975, through a threefold growth in industrial output. If she can also double her hydroelectric power, a reasonable assumption, this still leaves a coal requirement of 70 to 80 million tons a year, including virtually all of her metallurgical coking coal. Her peak output in prewar years was 57 million tons. At that time she imported only 7 to 10 million tons at the most, and this largely from China and Sakhalin, areas now beyond her political control. Here is a graphic illustration of

Coal production in Japan passed the 5-million-ton mark in 1897; the 20-million-ton mark in 1913; and the 40-million-ton mark in 1936. (See Table 31, below.) Meanwhile, consumption at home grew even more rapidly. Imports regularly exceeded exports after 1927. They would have reached even larger proportions had not domestic producers been able to secure government assistance and to restrict shipments from Manchuria. Not only was coal used in growing quantities but it was made steadily more efficient as a fuel. Elsewhere (page 47) it is remarked that the amount of coal required to produce 1,000 kw. of electric power was reduced from 2.11 tons in 1914 to 0.7 tons in 1932. Meanwhile the coal requirement per ton of steel declined from 3.5 tons in the early days to less than 2 tons. It is ironical that such technical progress in the utilization of fuel was not accompanied by any comparable effort to improve the welfare of the coal miner himself. Accident and sickness rates and general conditions of work remained shockingly bad, even by Japanese standards. Production costs, too, remained high, although this did not prevent steady expansion except when the big producers combined to restrict output.

For an economy shifting from a vegetable to a mineral basis this growing extraction of energy from inanimate sources is fundamental. In Japan, as we have seen, the per capita use of energy in all forms advanced through the prewar decades to a point where the Japanese now stood midway between the advanced industrial nations of the West and the rest of Asia. The annual input of inanimate energy into manufacturing and mining has been estimated at about the equivalent of 10,000 kw-h. of electricity per worker in 1936. This is equal to 6 tons of coal, or nearly seventy times the yearly work output of a man. (See below, page 181.) Most of this energy was actually derived from coal; indeed, coal furnished directly about one half of all the fuel and power consumed in Japan during 1936. (Table 4.) In addition, it supplied the energy source for a quarter of Japan's growing supplies of electric power, the remainder coming from hydroelectric plants. If we exclude fuel wood, used largely for domestic cooking and heating, more than two thirds of Japan's entire fuel and power economy still rested on coal. About 90% of it was produced at home. Consumption in Japan was still less than 10% of consumption in the United States, but it was over a third of the total for all of Asia (excluding the USSR). Thus the money value of coal output, only 300 million yen in 1936, is a poor measure of its role in Japanese industrialization.

Japan's increasing dependence on overseas materials as a result of industrialization and population growth. See President's Materials Policy Commission, *Resources for Freedom*, vol. III: *The Outlook for Energy Resources*, Washington, 1952, p. 30.

Table 4. *Fuel and Power Consumption in Japan Proper,*
by Nature and Uses, 1936[a]

Total Consumption in Japan Proper	Total	Coal	Electricity	Fuel Wood	Oil	Gas
Amount (millions of kw-h. electricity equivalent)	128,149	65,830	27,354	23,814	10,094	1,057
Percent from each source	100.0	51.4	21.3	18.6	7.9	0.8
Percentage distribution of energy sources in:						
Manufacturing and mining	100.0	71.2	25.0	0.5	2.5	0.8
Domestic, commercial, public, and agricultural purposes	100.0	23.4	18.5	55.7	1.0	1.4
Domestic transport	100.0	71.7	4.8	—	23.5	—
International shipping	100.0	84.0	—	—	16.0	—

a Adapted from U.S. Department of State, *Energy Resources of the World*, Washington, 1949, tables 44–49. All fuels and power are combined and compared in terms of kilowatt-hours electricity equivalent, after deducting losses (estimated at 80%) in the conversion of fuels to heat and power. These conversion rates are based on world standards not strictly applicable to Japan.
Of 44.9 million metric tons of coal available for use in Japan during 1936, 25.4 million were used in industry or stored; 5.9 million went into domestic, commercial, public, and agricultural uses; 5.8 million were converted to electricity, gas, or oil; 4.0 million were used by railways and domestic shipping; and 3.9 million went into bunkers for overseas shipping. *ibid.*, table 1.

Primary Production and Foreign Trade. Farm crops accounted for the great bulk of the aggregate growth in Japan's primary production through the prewar decades, measured in money values. The fishing, mining, forestry, and livestock industries expanded more rapidly; but they remained relatively small in value of output. Japan's 5.6 million peasant families, cultivating their tiny plots, still contributed over 70% of the net value of total food and raw material production in 1930.

Even with its slower rate of growth, gross agricultural output appears to have at least doubled in the fifty years after 1885-89. (Table 3.) Mainly this came about by increasing output per farmer and per acre on lands already under cultivation. The cultivated area probably increased no more than 25%, if that. After the turn of the century it grew 15%, while the number of farm families remained virtually stationary.[17] Official crop statistics indicate that

17 In 1903, the first year in which annual statistics were collected, a total of 5,359,000 farm families cultivated 5,224,000 hectares of land. Tōyō Keizai Shimpō-sha, *Meiji Taishō Kokusei Sōran*, Tokyo, 1927, p. 507. In 1935, 5,611,000 families cultivated 6,009,000 hectares. *Nippon Teikoku Tōkei Nenkan*, no. 58, Tokyo, 1939, pp. 65, 67.

meanwhile rice yields per acre increased by one third, from 1894-1900 to 1931-40, while yields of wheat, tea, and barley doubled.[18] Crop yields as a whole probably rose at least 50%; in fact the indices record a 65% gain. (Tables 2 and 3.)

Cereals remained the staple farm product, with rice leading all other crops by a wide margin. Rice tariffs and subsidies, national dietary habits (including the preference of Japanese for their own varieties of rice), and the efficiency of rice culture as a means of extracting food energy from limited amounts of land—all combined to keep over half of all cultivated land in rice production. After 1914, however, the rice crop showed little upward tendency. The subsequent gain in the country's rice supplies came mainly from the colonies, Korea and Formosa. Increasingly, the growth of domestic farm output was centered in vegetables, tubers, and industrial crops.

The most conspicuous development in nonfood crops was, of course, the rise of the silk cocoon industry. The growing demand for silk, mainly from the United States, led to an eightfold increase in cocoon output from 1880 to 1930. Even with the collapse of silk prices after 1925, cocoons contributed 17% of gross agricultural output from 1929 to 1933.[19] They were still a poor second to rice, which provided 52%. Like the coal and fishing industries, however, sericulture played a crucial role hardly expressed in mere output values.

Silk furnished a precious margin of money income for great numbers of peasant families—the more so as mulberries could be grown on land ill suited to food production and the rearing of silkworms required chiefly seasonal family labor. In foreign trade it provided Japan's premier export for over sixty years. Raw silk alone brought in more than one third of her entire commodity export earnings in foreign markets through most of the years from 1870 to 1930. Nor is even this a measure of its value, since unlike so many of her manufactured exports it required no imported materials. Probably the raw silk trade financed no less than 40% of Japan's entire imports of foreign machinery and raw materials utilized domestically over this period. It only yielded its supremacy as synthetic fibers made progressive inroads in the American market after 1930. That the lowly silkworn should play such a massive role in Japanese industrialization is truly astonishing.

18 Supreme Commander for the Allied Powers, GHQ, Natural Resources Section, Report No. 108, *Crop Statistics for Japan, 1876-1946*, Tokyo, 1948, pp. 16, 20, 24. Tea statistics were revised in a later report, NRS No. 125, *Tea in Japan*, Tokyo, 1949, p. 47.

19 "Hompō Genshi Seisambutsu no Seisan Sūryō," cited, pp. 2, 16. The silkworm industry is classified here in agriculture, rather than livestock.

Mention of raw silk, and earlier of cotton, draws attention to the powerful influence of foreign trade on the rate and direction of development in Japan's extractive industries. While we return to this point in Chapters 6 and 7, two further observations may be made briefly here.

The great bulk of Japanese primary production, including raw materials as well as food, continued to be sold in the home market for domestic purposes. It is true that a foreign market quickly arose after 1868 for such products as tea, copper, coal, and cocoons in the form of silk. Through the nineteenth century, indeed, the proceeds of primary exports were a major means of financing Japan's overseas requirements. Later, as industry developed, domestic raw materials diminished in relative importance, but they still furnished much of the net value embodied in exports, notably of silk products, and of certain foodstuffs and miscellaneous manufactures. Even so, the home market furnished the principal demand for the output of the extractive industries as a whole throughout the period. The growth of production reflected mainly a growth in domestic consumption, not the expansion of Japan's export trade.[20]

The second point concerns imports of food and materials in their supplementary and competitive aspect. After 1900 Japan became increasingly dependent on colonial foodstuffs, and still more on industrial materials purchased from foreign countries. In a few cases, like those of cotton, soybeans, and copper, imports displaced domestic production in the sense that the latter actually declined. In others, like those of sugar, rice, and coal, they at least retarded the growth of home output through providing better and cheaper sources of supply abroad. On the whole, however, imports were of such a character, especially in the case of industrial materials, that they tended to supplement rather than displace domestic production. Since the latter also continued to grow, the total supply

20 It is worth stressing that Japan's small exports of her own primary products (raw or processed), relative to the exports of other Asiatic countries, have been a function not merely of comparative poverty in many natural resources but of a growing home demand.

Through the prewar decades she exported two thirds or more of her cocoons (as silk), and from two thirds to one half of her tea. Like tea, coal and copper were also exported heavily before World War I, but overseas markets declined thereafter in relative importance as domestic requirements grew. During the interwar period Japan shifted to an import basis in both minerals. Shipments of primary products of all types, in raw or processed form, reached their all-time peak in 1927-36. Yet exports to foreign countries and colonies took only 7% of Japanese food output (in calories)—largely fish, sugar, and flour—and were greatly overbalanced by imports. In lumber and pulp the ratio was only 6%, even with Karafuto production regarded as domestic, while in most minerals, of course, the country was heavily dependent on foreign supplies. (See Chapter 7.)

of primary products utilized in Japan increased in response to the combined gain from both internal and external sources.

The *net* supply of such products available for domestic consumption increased less rapidly than the sum of imports and domestic output. For an important share of imports from foreign countries and colonies—at least 25% in 1930—were reprocessed for export as manufactured goods. (See below, Tables 28 and 32.) Cotton is the leading example; 505,000 tons were imported in 1930 as against 237,000 tons exported in the form of yarn, cloth, etc. Also, as observed above, domestically produced materials like silk continued to be exported. On balance, however, *net imports* of materials for domestic use were greater in value than the domestic materials embodied in raw and processed *exports*. In this sense, the total supply of food and raw materials available for domestic utilization (excluding exports) rose even more rapidly, relative to population, than the indices of domestic production—assuming they are accurate—would indicate. Imports, in other words, were adding a growing margin for domestic consumption and capital formation.

Primary Production and Industrial Progress. The growth of primary production was interrelated with industrialization and urbanization at every point.

As industry developed, it offered a widening market for the food and raw material surpluses of the countryside. It also contributed to fuller exploitation of Japan's natural resources by facilitating improvements in transport, credit, and production techniques. On the other hand, the increasing productivity of the primary industries created a growing home market for manufactures and services, especially as incomes rose beyond the level which afforded a bare subsistence.[21] Through the circuits of exchange which developed, moreover, it provided a large share of the food and raw materials to sustain industrial growth. As described above, it did this either directly from domestic output, or indirectly through exports of agricultural, mineral, and fishery products. The latter helped to pay for machinery and industrial materials required from abroad in increasing amounts.

Close functional interdependence between the extractive and nonextractive industries is characteristic of any economy undergoing all-round development. Rarely if ever has any country achieved substantial industrial development without an earlier, or a parallel, expansion of its agricultural and other primary industries. This is

[21] Not only did purchasing power grow, but a larger proportion, after a certain point, was devoted to the output of manufacturing and service industries in the form of more and better clothing and housing, education, travel, health services, and other amenities. See Chapter 8.

true notably of a "new" country, but also of an already densely settled region where modernization gives a fresh impetus to population growth. If its manufacturing industries must look abroad in the main for raw materials and markets to sustain their growth, if its farmers are unable to produce a growing food surplus to feed the cities, its industrial progress is apt to be slow.

Japan was no exception in this regard. In view of her limited soil and subsoil resources, however, she was fortunate in two respects. First, she was an island nation, with a relatively small population, a good location for trade with both the East and the West, and excellent sea communications both internally and externally.[22] Second, she passed through the early stages of industrialization in an era when world primary production was generally expanding. Her requirements, except in cotton, did not bulk large in world markets. She was able to buy in the cheapest market, wherever it might be, and payments were readily cleared through the multilateral arrangements which prevailed in world trade. These circumstances minimized the effect which her expanding demand for foreign food and raw materials would otherwise have had on the terms at which these commodities were exchanged for her own manufactures.

For these reasons alone, it will probably be more difficult today for big and also densely populated countries like China and India to achieve a comparable rate of industrialization. Their impact on world markets—especially in food supplies—might be far greater. Also, Japan was able to reduce the net cost of imports (1) by cheap water transport; (2) by developing colonial sources of certain foodstuffs which she was able to purchase on relatively favorable terms; and (3) by using secondary grades of many materials—short-staple cotton, reclaimed rubber, etc. These materials might be poor by Western standards, but they satisfied the demands of her domestic and foreign markets at the time for low-grade manufactures. This also lightened the load of her import requirements.

Even so, Japan's problem in financing her overseas needs imposed a heavy and continuous burden, especially as it was complicated at times by large outlays abroad for war purposes. It was handled as well as it was only because she was able, despite physical and social handicaps in agriculture, to increase her own food and raw material production perhaps as much as 200% in the course of five decades. (Table 3.) In considering the lessons of Japan's experience for other Far Eastern countries, this point is fundamental.

Interdependence between the growth of the extractive industries and the growth of the processing and service industries was thus a

[22] For a more general discussion of these factors in the dynamics of Japanese economic development, see Chapter 10.

condition of Japanese economic development no less than of that of most other countries. However, the balance among these industries and their relative rates of growth naturally vary widely among countries. One decisive factor lies in differences in natural endowments. Japan's complement of resources, together with the world trading opportunities which developed, worked strongly in favor of industrialization from an early date. But the pattern of development can also be strongly influenced by institutional factors. Again in the case of Japan political structure and national policy entered the balance to weight the scales against agriculture and in favor of the rising industrial and commercial classes. The extractive industries were so preponderant in Meiji Japan that they necessarily were the source of much of the income and wealth which went into industrial growth and military expansion. This tendency was further reinforced by the policies of the State and the interests of those groups which have held the dominant power in modern Japan.

To elaborate this aspect of Japanese history in detail would carry us far afield. In good part it centers on the institutional arrangements controlling the distribution of agricultural income, on the one hand, and the direction of private investment and State spending on the other. (See Chapter 10.) Heavy farm taxation provided the chief means through which the Meiji governments financed their heavy military outlays and development programs through the early decades. It was the farmers also who ultimately footed most of the bill for the huge loans through which the State commuted the feudal pensions of 400,000 *samurai* families in the seventies and staked many of them to a fresh start as bankers and businessmen. The new land tax of 1873 was fixed at 3% on land values assessed at 8.5 times the crop yield as determined at the time.[23] This tax is said to have appropriated 33% of the total crop at the outset—nearly as much as the share appropriated by the feudal lord under the Tokugawas. It provided 94% of the government's tax revenue at this time, and over half until almost the turn of the century.

In 1877 the land tax was cut to $2\frac{1}{2}\%$ on assessed land values. Also its yield was further reduced by the inflation of prices then under way. This lowered the proportion of the crop represented in the tax, which was paid in money at a fixed rate. But the benefits of the reduction accrued only to landowners who paid the tax, and particularly to the owners of tenanted land (already nearly a third of

[23] P. Mayet, the able agricultural expert employed by the government at the time, estimated the land tax in 1878 at 30% of net income on investment in land. This was two to seven times the rates prevailing in European countries at the time. *Agricultural Insurance*, London, 1893, p. 230.

the cultivated area), who collected their rents largely in the form of fixed amounts of produce paid over in kind. The more well-to-do landlords thus secured additional revenue for moneylending or new commercial and industrial ventures. For the small cultivator, however, such gains were likely to be offset by the disabilities suffered as he entered the money economy—lack of credit, the vagaries of prices, too little land.

No doubt the agricultural classes as a whole benefited from the rise of agricultural productivity which took place through the Meiji period. But masses of less successful peasants were driven into tenantry and debt in the first twenty-five years, especially when the price of rice fell calamitously in the eighties. In subsequent decades escape from this condition was made difficult—for many, impossible —by the high price of land, high rents, and the high cost of credit. Japan thus repeated the earlier experience of many European countries, but with less justification. For the social ills attending the unregulated commercialization of agriculture were now well recognized and the remedies were ready at hand had the country's rulers chosen to adopt them.[24]

The mounting surplus of farm population had to find employment increasingly outside agriculture. Those families which remained on the farm also sought supplementary income, either through part-time employment in local industries, or through putting their reluctant daughters into the textile factories of the towns and cities. High rents, interest on farm debt, and government taxes channelled a large share of agricultural income into the possession of financial institutions, city landlords, and the State treasury. This also drew an increasing share of the country's food supply off the farm and into the cities to support the rising urban population. Thus labor and income were steadily siphoned off the farm to provide the human and material resources for industrial and commercial expansion.

These pressures upon the Japanese peasant are reminiscent of those experienced by the English yeoman a century or more before, when he found himself dispossessed by the enclosure movement and the disappearance of common rights which accompanied the rise of capitalistic farming. In Japan, however, the new forces at work failed to produce any revolutionary change in the technology of agriculture, as in eighteenth century England. Topography, the nature of rice culture, the superabundance of farm labor, the social background of the peasant—all worked to perpetuate the small farm operated with family labor. On the other hand, these circumstances

[24] See, for example, Mayet's proposals, in *ibid.*, for a system of agricultural insurance, rural credit, and tax relief. Agricultural policy is discussed further in Chapter 10.

did not prevent a substantial growth in production, as we have seen. This growth, together with a pattern of income distribution which turned large streams of agricultural income into nonagricultural uses, brought a marked expansion in the surpluses of food and materials available from domestic production to satisfy the rising demands of industry.[25]

Perhaps total income and wealth in Japan would have grown more rapidly had national policy been directed more vigorously to improving the lot of the agrarian class.[26] Poverty and insecurity tended to deprive the peasant of both the means and the incentive for rapid gains in efficiency. Certainly such a policy could have produced significant changes in the direction of greater economic equality and political democracy. It appears that Japan's land and sea resources were nevertheless exploited with increasing success, and on a scale such that the exploitation played a vital role in the country's industrial transformation. The limits imposed by nature made it inevitable, however, that a growing population could only find economic relief in the long run as new opportunities were created in manufacturing and the services. If the growth in primary production failed to bring a more substantial gain to the farmer, the fisherman, or the miner who continued in these pursuits, this reflected the intense pressure of population upon employment opportunities, with its accompanying social and economic inequities. These circumstances put the mass of people at a constant disadvantage in their struggle to increase their output per capita and retain a larger share of the fruits of their labors.

Manufacturing and Services

When one leaves the field of primary production and turns to

25 In 1930, as noted in Chapter 2, out of net agricultural income totalling 1,883 million yen, taxes took 336 million; rent to absentee landlords, 173 million; and interest charges paid to persons outside agriculture, 173 million.

26 Particularly through greater investment in technical education, capital improvements in agriculture, and the provision of cheap credit and marketing safeguards for the small farmer. It cannot be denied, however, that the only ultimate solution for Japanese agriculture lay—still lies—in opening up alternative occupations for the agrarian population. In this respect the bias of State policy was sound. It should also be said that critics often overlook the measures of agricultural relief which the government did undertake after World War I, especially the efforts to stabilize rice prices and moderate the competition of colonial rice.

In the realm of fiscal policy, direct taxation continued to discriminate heavily against the agriculturist. This came to be offset, however, by the mounting burden of consumption taxes, which bore heavily (and regressively) on the city population. See Hioye Ouchi, "Tax Burden on Salaried Men and Farmers as Revealed by the Official Survey of Their Livings," *Bulletin de l'Institut International de Statistique*, vol. xxv, part 2, Tokyo, 1931, pp. 372-92. By modern Western standards, the outstanding characteristic of the Japanese tax system as a whole was not its unequal incidence on different occupations but its leniency in taxing high incomes, especially incomes from dividends and profits. See below, Chapter 10.

other major sectors of the Japanese economy it becomes more difficult to present any summary evidence of the aggregate growth over several decades.

This is true of "secondary" industry—manufacturing, construction, and public utilities.[27] Still more is it true of many commodity-handling and other services, sometimes called "tertiary" industries—i.e., transport, communications, trade, finance, government, and the professions. Throughout most of these fields production is less homogeneous and standardized than are agricultural crops or minerals. It is apt to change widely in character over periods of time. And for many of the services there is no yardstick of measurement at all except for unstable money values. Moreover, Japanese statistics are particularly deficient in the realm of handicraft industry and the small-scale trades, where they exist at all.

In some branches of secondary and tertiary industry, nevertheless, one can estimate at least roughly the magnitude of growth in modern times. Several such indices are presented in Table 5. They include manufacturing production; the two chief agencies of long-distance transport—railways and shipping; foreign trade; and clearing of bank bills (deflated).

The relative rates of advance depicted in Table 5 conform to one's expectations. Most spectacular is the rise of manufacturing activity. This index climbs steadily from 69 in 1905-09 to 377 in 1930-34, a more than fourfold increase in twenty-five years. Such long-term comparisons are not very meaningful, because of the great changes which took place meanwhile in the character and composition of manufacturing. Clearly, however, the advance of Japanese industry far outdistanced the growth of primary production in this period. The latter failed even to double in this quarter century. (Table 3.) In between are the indices for overseas trade and for transport, reflecting the combined influence of both types of commodity production. Here the gains are on the order of a two- to fourfold increase. If data were available on the other service trades—merchandising, finance, the amusements, etc.—one suspects they would tend also as a group to show these intermediate rates of growth. The index of clearings of bills (deflated for commodity price changes) is a rather unsatisfactory measure of the volume of commercial transactions, but it does point to the growth of activity in this field.

[27] Mining is sometimes classified with secondary rather than primary production, owing to its large-scale capitalistic organization, and its close relationship with the metallurgical and machinery industries. In the case of Japan, however, these latter industries are less reliant on domestic raw materials than a good many other industries. Moreover, a special interest attaches to the distinction between industries engaged in exploiting natural resources, taken together, and those whose net value product is created mainly by processing such materials, whether domestic or imported, or by providing nonmaterial services.

Table 5. *Growth of Manufacturing Production, Transport,*
and Commerce of Japan Proper, 1885-1938
(indices; 1910-14 = 100)

ANNUAL AVERAGE	MANUFAC- TURING PRODUCTION[a]	TRANSPORT		OVERSEAS TRADE[d]		BANK CLEARINGS (DEFLATED)[e]
		Railway Freight Traffic[b]	*Merchant Ship* Tonnage[c]	*Volume of* Imports	*Volume of* Exports	
1885-89	—	2	19	16	16	—
1895-99	37	24	38	46	31	—
1905-09	69	68	78	87	61	74
1910-14	100	100	100	100	100	100
1915-19	160	161	142	124	168	251
1920-24	217	218	213	190	142	344
1925-29	313	277	227	242	217	421
1930-34	377	256	238	277	327	443
1935-38	600	354	263	347	505	424

a Source and details are given in Table 8, below.

b Tons of freight carried by government and private railways. The 1910-14 annual average was 35,372,000 metric tons. Data for 1885-1925 from Asahi Shimbun-sha, *Nippon Keizai Tōkei Sōkan*, Tokyo, 1930, pp. 807, 818; for years thereafter from Ministry of Finance, *Statistical Year-Book of Finance and Economy of Japan, 1948*, Tokyo, 1948, pp. 707, 709.

c Gross tonnage of all steam, motor, and sailing vessels, unregistered and registered in Japan Proper. Japanese junks measured in *koku* capacity are converted to gross tons at 10 *koku* = 1 ton. The 1910-14 annual average was 2,226,000 tons. Data for 1885-99 from *Nippon Keizai Tōkei Sōkan*, cited, pp. 835-36; for 1905-37 from Imperial Cabinet, Bureau of Statistics, *Nippon Teikoku Tōkei Nenkan*, Tokyo, passim, and Prime Minister's Office, Statistics Bureau, *Japan Statistical Year-Book, 1949*, Tokyo, 1949, p. 436. This series is of limited significance as it lumps together ships of all types from ocean liners to 5-ton junks. Waterborne traffic in Japanese ports during the limited period 1913-27 is given below, page 108.

d See Table 26, below.

e Value of bills cleared at all clearing houses, deflated by the Bank of Japan index of wholesale prices. Tōyō Keizai Shimpō-sha, *Meiji Taishō Kokusei Sōran*, Tokyo, 1927, p. 81; *Nippon Teikoku Tōkei Nenkan*, cited, passim. Before 1905 the clearing of bills increases with great rapidity but this indicates chiefly the initial organization of clearing houses in the main cities.

The Shifting Center of Gravity. By the mid-thirties this shift in the Japanese economy had reached the point where secondary industry—manufacturing, in the broad sense—contributed nearly one third of Japan's total national income. The whole range of service trades, taken together, provided nearly half, and the extractive industries hardly more than one fifth.

Anticipating Chapter 9, we may note briefly the 1930 distribution of net income produced and labor force among these broad categories in the table on the next page.

At this midpoint in Japan's industrial transition, agriculture still afforded the principal occupation of 14.1 million people, nearly half the labor force. The figure is problematical when it comes to interpretation as a measure of employment, since many part-time

	NET PRODUCT, 1930[a] Value (millions of yen)	Percent	LABOR FORCE, 1930[b] Number of Persons	Percent
Total	*10,239*	*100.0*	*29,620*	*100.0*
Agriculture, forestry, fishing, mining	2,108	20.5	15,014	50.7
Manufacturing and construction	3,268	31.9	5,876	19.8
Services	4,863	47.6	8,659	29.3

[a] Estimates of the Imperial Cabinet, Bureau of Statistics, as revised and published in U.S. Department of State, *National Income of Japan*, Washington, 1945, p. 86, with further minor modifications by the author. (See below, Table 38). The figures purport to represent income produced in Japan Proper, including self-supplied commodities of marketable variety. They are calculated mainly by the gross-value-minus-cost method, and are net of depreciation, depletion, and most business taxes.

[b] Basic data from Imperial Cabinet, Bureau of Statistics, *Shōwa Go-nen Kokusei Chōsa Saishū Hōkokusho*, Tokyo, 1938, table 47 (industrial classification). Certain categories of the census have been shifted here and recombined to arrive at a classification roughly consistent with that used in the net product estimates. (See below, Table 41).

family workers are included. Nevertheless, a pronounced shift away from farming as the foundation of national economic life had clearly taken place over the previous half century. It now produced no more than 20% of Japanese national income at prevailing prices. While one is uncertain what comparable figures for 1870 or 1900 would show—the estimates are of dubious accuracy (see below)—there is no doubt as to the displacement of agriculture from its traditional supremacy by industry and related services. This shift was only accelerated in the decade 1930-40, despite the recovery of farm prices from their low level in 1930.

These differential rates of growth in major sectors of the Japanese economy involved many problems of structural change which cannot be examined here. One aspect may be mentioned, however, because of its particular relevance to the hopes of other Far Eastern countries now on the threshold of industrialization. Even Japan's rapid rate of industrialization failed evidently to reduce the actual farm population after the turn of the century. Some 5,359,000 farm families were recorded in 1903, when an annual count was begun. There were 5,575,000 families in 1937, three decades later. The actual increase may have been greater, though perhaps at the same time the peasant population became less wholly occupied in agricultural pursuits. In any case, it was no small achievement at least to prevent a sizable growth in the number of farm families while the country's total population was swelling from 46 to 71 millions. (See below, Chapter 9, for further details.)

Economic planners in other densely settled Asiatic regions would do well to bear in mind Japan's apparent inability to take people off the farm in large numbers, despite a spectacular rate of industrialization. If the figures are correct, she only managed to enlarge the average farm 10 to 15% by a corresponding addition to the cultivated area. It remained hardly more than 2½ acres. Her neighbors all have greater potentialities for adding to farm lands, but Japan's experience seems to create a presumption that they will be unable to move large numbers of people out of agriculture, unless they are more successful than the Japanese in controlling population growth. Countries like China could easily experience a considerable increase in agricultural population, not a reduction, even with a quite successful industrial advance.

One other observation from later chapters may be anticipated because of its general significance for the process of growth depicted here. Table 5 presents an index of overseas (foreign and colonial) trade which shows an upward geometric progression almost uninterrupted for fifty years. The volume of exports doubles every decade on the average. Imports also advance at about the same rate until the thirties. Meantime, of course, both changed radically in character. In 1878-82 exports were about equally divided in value between raw products and manufactures (including semimanufactures); imports were over 75% manufactures. (Table 29.) By 1935-38 exports to foreign countries were 85% manufactures, and imports 62% raw products. (The inclusion of colonial trade would raise the latter percentage still higher.) Japanese industries now drew their materials from all over the world. Their products likewise served far-flung markets, both in Asia and the West.

This rapid growth of overseas trade was associated at every point with the course of Japan's economic modernization and expansion. Initially, a swelling stream of imports formed a broad highway over which new ideas, skills, and tools poured in from the West. Export opportunities quickly appeared to stimulate new techniques of production and marketing and to create new pools of business savings and enterprise. As the years passed, access to world markets enabled the Japanese to build an industrial economy heavily dependent on food, materials, and equipment which they could secure more cheaply abroad than at home, paying for them with those products in which they were able to develop a competitive advantage in one market or another.

Yet it was the home market again which continued to absorb the bulk of the output of the secondary and tertiary industries, as well as primary production. This was necessarily true of the construction industry and a wide range of services—the professions, government, internal transport, and merchandising, catering, etc. Even the shipping industry, important as it was to Japan's foreign commerce and balance of payments, remained largely a home industry so far as actual cargo tonnage was concerned. Of all water-borne cargoes entering and clearing Japanese ports in Japanese vessels during 1930-37, 83% (by weight) were in coastwise and interisland trade. In manufacturing industry as a whole, no more than 25 to 35% of total production (by value) was sold abroad in foreign and Empire markets during the peak decade 1928-37. And one third of these exports came from two industries, silk and cotton goods, which bulked far larger in the export trade than in the manufacturing economy. (See below, Chapter 7.)

In quantitative terms, therefore, the expansion of Japanese industry and service trades represented mainly a growth in the output of consumption and capital goods marketed within the expanding exchange circuits of the domestic economy. Without foreign trade, to be sure, the Japanese economy would have borne little resemblance to what it had now become. But its vital significance lay in the manner in which it tied into these circuits, and nourished them with overseas resources, rather than in its bulk share of the web of activities which now constituted the livelihood of 70 million Japanese.

Transport and the Growth of the Market. No single industry played a more essential role than transportation in Japan's economic growth. Specialization by regions and occupations within the islands, the exchange of goods overseas, and the whole growth in the scale and productivity of the economy depended upon improved access to wider markets.

In Tokugawa days not only was foreign trade almost wholly interdicted, but internal trade was crabbed and confined by bad transport, along with official barriers and restriction. Land transportation was mainly by bearer, horse, or oxcart. Horses were mainly for the nobility and the military; cart traffic was limited; even the wheelbarrow was little used. There were few highways worthy of the name, and they were used chiefly for travel and posts.[28] Bulk cargoes like the feudal rice taxes moved principally by sea. But junk navigation was slow and uncertain, the construction of large vessels being forbidden by the Shogunate. In the 1860's it still took 30 to 40 days to go from Tokyo to Kyushu, a distance of 600 miles. And on the best highways, even as late as 1884, the cost of transport doubled the price of a bushel of rice in twenty miles. In Germany, by way of contrast, grain could now be hauled 100 miles on turnpikes or 400 miles by rail before its cost was similarly increased.

[28] Robert B. Hall, "Tokaido: Road and Region," *The Geographical Review,* vol. xxvii, no. 3, July 1937, pp. 353-77.

"On the poorer roads of Japan," remarks J. J. Rein at this time, "rice does not bear a transportation of five miles."[29]

In Japan, as in eighteenth century Europe, the industrial revolution brought with it a revolution in transport and communications. One of the first acts of the Meiji reformers was to build a railway from Tokyo to Yokohama.[30] The rapid extension of the rail net until it spread through the home islands was a prime objective of the authorities. Like Moltke, they sought it for strategic as well as economic reasons. In contrast to the Western countries, whose early railroads were often built in short stretches by local interests, Japan thus gained the economies of a national system almost at the outset. No less important for these sea-girt islands was the building of a merchant marine, first by the purchase of steam tonnage abroad and then by state-encouraged construction at home. (See Chapters 7 and 10.)

Better transport of both types, together with the creation of a modern system of postal, telephone, and telegraph communications, played a crucial part in unifying the national market and linking it with the outside world.[31] First it facilitated a geographic extension of the internal and external market by lowering the cost of moving goods and people. Then it sustained the further development of the market as rising productivity steadily widened the opportunities for profitable exchange. In one generation, from 1888 to 1913, freight traffic on Japan's spreading railways rose from 848,000 tons to 40,600,000 tons. For water-borne commerce no comparable figures were collected at this time. While its growth was less spectacular, the total tonnage of all merchant vessels over 5 tons increased from 494,000 gross tons to 2,400,000 gross tons. Moreover, 60% of the total in the earlier year represented slow sailing junks of traditional design. They averaged only 17 tons apiece. In 1913 60% was comprised of steamships averaging 500 tons.[32]

[29] *The Industries of Japan*, New York, 1889, p. 17. In parts of China today it is estimated that transport costs will double the price of wheat in fifty miles.

[30] With some exaggeration, Rein remarks that Commodore Perry impressed the Japanese more with miniature railway and telegraph exhibits which he brought along than with his "stately squadrons." *ibid.*, p. 511.

[31] Even such a commonplace thing as the rise of postal traffic to large proportions was symptomatic and wholly new. In old Japan, prior to the organization of a government postal service in 1871, letters were exchanged on a limited basis through private postal guilds. In 1872 the new postal system carried only 2.5 million items; in 1882 the number passed 100 million; and in 1904, 1,000 million. For an early history of the postal service see the Department of Communications' *A Short Sketch of the Progress of the Postal Service in Japan*, Tokyo, 1892.

[32] While laying emphasis on the importance of improved transport, one should not overstress this factor. The main limitations on the domestic market in Tokugawa Japan, as in the Middle Ages of Europe and in preindustrial Asia today, were social, not geographic. Many handicraft wares produced in ancient Japan could not

Railways and steamships have become the conspicuous, modern types of transport in modern Japan. Yet it would be misleading to confine attention solely to them. Back of their expansion lay a pervasive modernization of local traffic by more economical means, including simply the spread of wheeled vehicles. Today the horsecart and the ricksha may seem archaic. In Meiji Japan their appearance in large numbers was revolutionary. For a modern analogy one might cite the mountainous province of Kweichow in Southwest China, where as recently as twenty years ago there were virtually no roads or wheeled traffic. Through the nineteenth century, indeed, the economic gains from railway construction in Japan were overshadowed in their immediate economic importance by the benefits from the local building of narrow, dirt roads, the introduction of the ricksha,[33] and the growing use of carts. Table 6 shows a fourfold increase from 1877 to 1897 in the number of registered carts

Table 6. *Number of Carts, Motor Vehicles, and Bicycles Registered in Japan Proper, 1877-1937*[a]

	1877	*1897*	*1917*	*1937*
Horsecarts	782	86,596	216,574	307,889
Oxcarts	1,786	16,430	35,362	111,146
Other goods-carts, human- or animal-drawn	158,240	1,225,923	1,936,406	1,519,334
Rickshas	136,761	200,690	113,274	15,376
Bicycles	—	—	1,073,444	7,878,463
Motor vehicles	—	—	3,856	128,735

a Data for 1877-1917 from Asahi Shimbun-sha, *Nippon Keizai Tōkei Sōkan*, Tokyo, 1930, p. 833; for 1937 from Imperial Cabinet, Bureau of Statistics, *Nippon Teikoku Tōkei Nenkan*, no. 58, Tokyo, 1939, p. 214.

pulled by horses, oxen, or men. Partly this represents more complete registration for tax purposes; but it must also reflect an extensive growth and improvement in short-haul transportation. Increasing mobility, achieved mainly by simple, even traditional, techniques, was of great importance in reducing local price differentials, in mov-

be marketed in the immediate neighborhood, but only some distance away in Yedo and other cities where the wealthy nobility and merchants congregated. Only with the general rise of productivity and purchasing power could Japan develop a mass market for industrial goods, regardless of transport costs. Moreover, even today she lacks such a market for many manufactures in wide use, owing to marked consumer preference for individuality in style and design.

33 The ricksha was introduced in the 1870's for narrow, undeveloped roads. After 1900 its numbers began to decline as bicycles came to be widely used. By 1930 there was a bicycle for every ten people in Japan.

ing people to cities in search of new occupations, and in facilitating the growth and diversification of production.[34]

In later years the pack horse and the cart gave way increasingly to the railway and the truck, just as sailing vessels multipled less rapidly than steam. Similarly, water transport as a whole failed to keep pace with the railways as a carrier of domestic freight. From 1913 to 1927 coastal shipping increased 50% in cargo tonnage.[35] Railway freight traffic rose nearly 150%. In other words, the latter grew three times as rapidly. Yet Japan's resources for water transport continued to be of great significance, in domestic as well as foreign trade. Bulk commodities like Kyushu coal continued to move by boat to a considerable extent.[36] Nearly 80% of the total water-borne cargo entering and clearing Japanese ports still represented coastal and interisland traffic. (See page 350.) Taken together, rail and water freight traffic had approximately doubled since 1913. This may perhaps be taken as a fairly good index of the over-all growth in Japanese commodity production for the market over the intervening years.[37]

One of the most significant accompaniments of Japanese industrialization, then, was this increasing mobility of goods and people.

[34] Better transport was essential to the growth of urban populations. To cite one simple example, when the vegetable supply of a Japanese city had to be brought in by wheelbarrow, the supply area was confined to a radius of about 12 kms. When carts came into general use in Meiji times the limit was extended to 20 kms. Later, trucks pushed the limit to 40 kms., and, in addition, the growth of long-distance transport and marketing arrangements began to bring in supplies from distant districts. Y. Yagi, "Horizontal and Vertical Differentiations in the Agricultural Production of Japan," *Kyoto University Economic Review*, vol. ix, no. 1, July 1934, pp. 41-48.

[35] *Nippon Keizai Tōkei Sōkan*, cited, p. 1233, gives intra-Empire cargo entering and clearing Japanese ports as follows (in millions of long tons):

1913	60.5
1915-19 (average)	59.6
1920-24 (average)	69.1
1927	91.7

Traffic with the colonies is believed to comprise little more than 5% of these totals. With Korea it is entirely excluded during the years 1913-19. The balance is coastal and interisland trade.

[36] Like England and unlike China, Japan possesses the great advantage of large coal deposits located at tidewater. In the thirties about half the coal consumed in Japan moved by water. (*Oriental Economist*, vol. iii, no. 6, June 1936, p. 403.) Water-borne cargoes of all types carried by steam vessels in foreign and domestic commerce, and by auxiliary sailing ships in coastal trade, averaged 110 million metric tons in the fiscal years 1930-36. By comparison, all the railways of Japan carried only 79 million tons a year. (Bank of Japan, *Economic Statistics of Japan, 1950*, Tokyo, 1950, p. 75.)

[37] Because of its mountains, its poor road net and its good sea communications, Japan has never developed extensive motor transport. Domestic production of motor vehicles was also of little consequence until after 1935, when government protection and tax favors were increased for military reasons. See U.S. Strategic Bombing Survey, *Japanese Motor Vehicle Industry*, Washington, 1946.

Chapter 9 underlines its essential role in the adaptation of resources to new demands and production techniques. Its external aspect, the growth of overseas shipping and foreign commerce, is well known. Less fully appreciated is the corresponding advance which took place in internal mobility. Without it the spectacular growth of cities would have been impossible. Perhaps the point may be clinched by a final comparison of railway traffic in Japan with that in two other countries, both of them continental regions more dependent on land transport than Japan. Rail traffic in 1937 was as great in Japan as in France, a country nearly 50% larger in area. It was four fifths as great as in India, a country ten times the size of Japan.[38] No single feature of Japan's industrial revolution was more striking than this factor of movement.

Rise of Manufacturing Industry. We turn now to the growth of manufacturing production. This was of special significance for the rest of the world because of its close relationship with foreign trade. Here again, searching for measurements of over-all growth, one confronts the difficulty already mentioned in the case of transportation. For private plants large enough to be classified as factories the data are relatively complete in recent decades. For government-owned factories they are more limited. And for workshop industry, i.e., small establishments employing less than five operatives, production statistics were virtually nonexistent prior to 1939 except in a few major branches.

State-owned factories produced largely for the special requirements of the Army and Navy. The chief exception was the Imperial Iron Works, the largest iron and steel concern in Japan.[39] Other enterprises retained through the prewar period included the various arms and powder plants of the great Tokyo and Osaka arsenals;

[38] A rough comparison of all rail traffic, based on actual freight movement plus passenger traffic converted to freight equivalent in proportion to receipts. The figures are as follows for 1937:

	Area (thousands of sq. kms.)	*Rail Activity* (millions of ton-kms. freight equivalent)
Japan	382	46.9
France	551	46.9
India	4,079	57.7

Railway estimates are from U.S. Department of State, *Energy Resources of the World*, Washington, 1949, p. 9.

[39] The Imperial Iron Works at Yawata, organized by the government in 1896, produced at least 60% of the pig iron and nearly half of the steel of Japan Proper until 1933. In 1934 it was merged with six private companies to form the Japan Iron Manufacturing Company. The government retained a controlling interest, but thereafter the official manufacturing statistics apparently classify the entire enterprise in the category of private industry.

the dockyards and machine shops of the Yokosuka, Kure, Sasebo, and Maisuru Naval Stations; the factories of the Tobacco Monopoly; wool and clothing plants for the armed forces; and miscellaneous smaller establishments. In the infancy of Japanese industry, State enterprise was of considerable importance. As described earlier, many of the initial pilot plants in various industries owed their establishment to government initiative and operation. Especially was this true in metallurgy, machinery manufacture, and shipbuilding—all of first-class importance to the military. Even after the government withdrew largely from the field of industrial enterprise in the eighties, Army arsenals and Navy dockyards continued to foster improved technology in the engineering trades.

Quantitatively, however, with the growth of private capitalism State-owned enterprise became relatively unimportant, despite the size of the military establishment in Japan. By 1914 government plants employed only 12% of the total number of factory workers. Through the next twenty-five years their share was rarely more than 8%. In 1933, for example, only 188,000 out of 2,301,000 factory operatives were employed in State-owned enterprise.[40] Nearly half of them were engaged in turning out machinery, vehicles, and instruments mainly for the armed forces. Apart from their technological contributions in specialized fields, and the preponderance of the Yawata works in iron and steel manufacture, government plants had long since ceased to figure importantly in the civilian economy, except to compete for labor, capital, and materials on a limited scale.[41]

The myriads of tiny establishments comprising workshop industry on the other hand, continued to account for a major sector of manufacturing activity. Only slowly did they yield to factory competition. In fact, one of the striking aspects of Japanese industrialization has been the strength and staying power of the small industrialist, especially where he has been fitted into a framework of large-scale organization providing him with better marketing ar-

---

[40] Ministry of Commerce and Industry, *Kōjō Tōkeihyō* (1936), Tokyo, 1938, p. 970.

[41] The history of the Army and Navy industries through the Meiji period is set forth in detail in Ushisaburo Kobayashi's *Military Industries of Japan*, New York, 1922. Useful as is his account, Kobayashi grossly exaggerates their importance. He concludes with the extravagant statement that "most of the achievements which raised the Japanese industries, especially the manufacturing industry, as high as their present position at one bound within fifty years after the Restoration, are due to no other than the military industry" (p. 259). His own data hardly bear this out for the early period; and by 1913 his figures show that these industries employed only 75,000 workers, operated machinery with a total capacity of only 140,000 h.p., and spent only about 75 million yen on materials, wages, etc. (pp. 118-20, 156-57, 212). For comparisons with Japanese factory industry as a whole, see below, Table 10.

The role of the State in the ownership and development of industrial enterprise is discussed at greater length in Chapter 10.

rangements, credit, and cheap electric power. Here it may be recorded that as late as 1930 plants of less than five operatives still furnished 30% of the net product of all manufacturing establishments in Japan. (Table 38.)

Small-scale industry was even more important in terms of employment. Census data on Japan's industrial labor force in 1930 give the following distribution of the nearly 6 million men, women, and children (out of 29.6 million gainfully employed) who reported their chief occupation to be some branch of manufacturing or construction (thousands of persons) :[42]

	Total Persons	Independents and Employers	"Shokuin" (Managerial and Technical Workers)	Other Wage and Family Workers
Total	*5,876*	*1,662*	*173*	*4,041*
Manufacturing	*4,913*	*1,218*	*152*	*3,543*
Government factories	152	—	9	143
Private factories, five or more operatives	1,983	40	136	1,807
Private establishments, less than five operatives	2,778	1,178	7	1,593
Construction	*963*	*444*	*21*	*498*

[42] *National Income of Japan*, cited, p. 128. Factory labor force is the number of persons on year-end payrolls (*Kōjō Tōkeihyō* [1930], cited, p. 12), with the addition of an estimated 40,000 entrepreneurs and 57,000 unemployed workers. Other data are from the October 1930 census (Imperial Cabinet, Bureau of Statistics, *Shōwa Go-nen Kokusei Chōsa Hōkoku: Shokugyō Oyobi Sangyō*, Tokyo, 1935).

Figures for plants of less than five operatives are residuals, arrived at by deducting all other categories from the decennial census totals for industry. This method is open to objection, although used here with more refinements than have been employed by Prof. T. Uyeda and others. For several reasons it exaggerates the importance of small plants. First, factory statistics exclude several minor industries regardless of their scale, for example, newspaper and magazine publishing, movie production, and salt making. Second, factory unemployment, figured at 3% in accordance with the census estimate for manufacturing, is probably an underestimate. These errors increase by so much the small-industry totals in the above table. Third, and most important, is the vagueness of the census inquiry. Persons were asked in October 1930 what their "principal" occupation was, or, if out of work, what their last occupation was. The industrial total therefore includes all persons who regarded themselves as having their chief occupation in industry, even if unemployed at the time or only engaged part-time. (It omits persons whose chief occupation was elsewhere, even if they had subsidiary employment in industry.) By contrast, the annual factory census simply tabulated all employees on plant payrolls at the end of the year.

In an interesting article on "Small-Scale Industry in Japan" (*Quarterly Journal*

It appears that 2,778,000 persons, over half of those recorded as belonging to the manufacturing labor force in 1930, reported themselves as occupied (or last occupied) in establishments of less than five workers.[43] Here were over 1 million tiny shops, each engaging less than three persons on the average, many of them family members. As explained in the note to the table, there is some exaggeration in the figures, especially as a measure of actual employment. Many of these persons were engaged only part-time, and some not at all at the time of the census. In the aggregate, however, there is no question of the significant role still played by the small industrialists. They produced many of the native-style consumption goods still important in Japanese life—foodstuffs, household wares, and clothing. They also turned out a large share of the woven textiles and other consumer goods sold abroad.

To discuss the growth of industry without reference to the masses of workshops which crowd the side streets of Japanese cities and give employment to many a rural village is to leave out a considerable

---

of Economics, vol. ix, no. 4, August 1947, pp. 577-604), Edwin P. Reubens has questioned this method of estimating labor in plants of less than five operatives. He doubts that small industry declined absolutely or relatively during the thirties; yet when the factory census was finally extended in 1939 to include these small plants it reported only 1,283,901 persons gainfully occupied in them. He concludes that the 1930 figure could not have been as much as twice the 1939 figure.

Even granting that small-scale industry failed to decline relatively in the thirties— a doubtful point—a wide discrepancy is to be expected between the factory and decennial censuses, in view of the way they were compiled. The same discrepancy appears in the figures for 1940, when the decennial census reports over a million more people in manufacturing than the annual factory census. Moreover, it is not unlikely that the factory census in 1939 and thereafter failed to record large numbers of tiny enterprises scattered through the country. In the absence of better evidence to the contrary, I am inclined to accept the 1930 figures given above as broadly representative of the labor force (in terms of chief occupation), and to discount substantially the figures for small-scale industry as a measure of actual employment.

Table 16, below, uses slightly different figures and gives more details on labor force by size of plant.

[43] The phrase "plants of five workers or more" or "plants of less than five workers" is used in this study to indicate the distinction between "factories" and smaller manufacturing establishments. This shorthand expression is not strictly accurate, for reasons which may be made clear at this point. Actually, the factory census before 1929 defines a factory as an establishment *normally* employing five or more "operatives" (*shokkō*); thereafter a plant *equipped to employ* five or more. Moreover, the term "operatives" does not include the entire labor force, or even all employees. Besides entrepreneur-workers, it leaves out managerial, clerical, and technical staff (*shokuin*), and "other employees"—janitors, cooks, guards, etc. Thus a plant might employ five workers of all types and still not be classified as a factory. The discrepancy is not serious, however; in 1930 the factory census lists 1,885,518 workers, of whom 1,683,563 are operatives; 132,276, *shokuin*; and 69,679, other employees. Wherever possible I have used the more inclusive categories of statistics. The term "gainfully employed" refers to entrepreneurs, independents, and employees; the term "workers" refers to salaried, wage, and family employees; and the terms "worker" and "operative" are used interchangeably in speaking of the size of establishments classified as factories.

sector of the industrial economy. Moreover, estimates of the growth of industry based on factory production alone are bound to be misleading. The latter expanded more rapidly than small-scale manufacturing, and to some extent at its expense. Shoes and socks, for example, were once made in the home; now they became products of the factory. (Further discussion of the scale of Japanese industry is reserved for Chapter 4.)

With these distinctions in mind let us examine certain evidence concerning the growth of manufacturing production as a whole. As described in Chapter 1, the foundations of modern Japanese industry were laid in the eighties and nineties—the first quarter century of the Meiji era. Thereafter expansion was rapid and continuous. Already by 1914 nearly a million persons—mostly women and girls—were employed in factories of ten or more workers, and perhaps 1.5 million or more in smaller workshops and home industries. Table 7 gives several indications of this growth: (1) The increase in private

Table 7. *Growth of Private Factory Industry, Pig Iron Supply, and Production of Raw Silk and Cotton Yarn in Japan Proper, 1884-1914*[a]

	Number of Factories[b]	Number of Factory Operatives[b] (thousands)	Factory Consumption of Coal (thousands of metric tons)	Production of Raw Silk (thousands of pounds)	Production of Cotton Yarn (thousands of 400-lb. bales)	Net Supply of Pig Iron[c] (thousands of metric tons)
1884	—	—	147[d]	5,947	13	18
1889	—	—	367	7,167	67	24
1894	5,985	381	1,093	11,505	292	55
1899	6,699	423	2,615	15,835	757	48
1904	9,234	526	3,705	16,511	695	133
1909	15,426	692	4,319	23,998	1,025	283
1914	17,062	854	8,359	31,056	1,666	474

a Data on factories and factory operatives from Japan, Imperial Cabinet, Bureau of Statistics, *Rōdō Tōkei Yōran* (1930), Tokyo, 1930, p. 15, and *Statistical Reports of the Department of Agriculture and Commerce*, annual. Other series from Asahi Shimbun-sha, *Nipon Keizai Tōkei Sōkan*, Tokyo, 1930, as follows: raw silk, p. 1205; cotton yarn, p. 1213; pig iron, p. 1220; coal, p. 1222.

b Before 1909 includes only plants employing ten or more factory operatives; thereafter, plants employing ten or more operatives and "laborers" (cooks, guards, etc.). The 1909 and 1914 figures are therefore not strictly comparable with those for earlier years. Although often cited as including government factories, it appears from the official reports that the latter are excluded from the above figures. In 1914 there were 102 such plants employing 37,000 operatives.

c Production plus imports minus exports. Includes a small amount of steel in 1884. Exports before 1914 are disregarded, being insignificant in amount.

d In 1886.

factories of ten or more operatives (the only category for which statistics were collected at the time) ; (2) the growth of the silk and cotton industries which pioneered Japan's industrial advance; and (3) the increasing mechanization and expansion of manufacturing production in general as reflected in the rapid rise in consumption of coal and pig iron for industrial purposes.[44]

More broadly, the growth of manufacturing activity as a whole is portrayed in Table 8. Here is summarized the best available index of Japanese manufacturing production for the years 1895 to 1929, the index constructed at the Nagoya Commercial College. This is extended through 1938 by splicing on an index prepared after the war at General Headquarters, Supreme Commander for the Allied Powers, Tokyo. As described in the notes appended to Table 8, the Nagoya index is broadly based on a number of industries. It appears to represent, in some degree, though less adequately, the growing production of workshop industry and government plants as well as private factories.

The index of Table 8 almost certainly overstates the growth of manufacturing production in the aggregate. Especially is this true before 1905, and to a lesser extent from 1905 to 1929. It must therefore be interpreted with caution. The further back one goes, the less abundant and reliable are Japanese production statistics; the more the likelihood that a good deal of home and workshop output was omitted, thus exaggerating the subsequent increase; the less satisfactory the methods used to combine the various output series in the over-all index. Moreover, no simple measure, however well constructed, can give very meaningful expression to the divergent rates of growth and the extensive changes in the character and quality of goods produced in the scores of industries making up the whole complex of Japanese manufacturing.

Despite these reservations one does find here significant evidence of the rise of manufacturing output during the late Meiji decades spanning the wars with China and Russia. Even if the Nagoya index is heavily discounted, it would probably be safe to say that industrial production (excluding mining and construction) at least doubled in the twenty years after 1893. Not reflected in any such quantitative measure, of course, is the marked improvement in the quality of many Japanese manufactures during this period.

After 1905 the trend of aggregate production can be judged

[44] The rise in factory consumption of coal, rapid as it was, understates the effective increase in fuel and power derived from coal. Steady improvements were made through this period in the amount of energy extracted per ton of coal; and, in addition, factories purchased thermo-electric power from independent power companies in growing amounts.

Table 8. *Growth of Physical Volume of Manufacturing Production in Japan Proper, 1895-1938*[a]

(indices; 1910-14 = 100)

Annual Average	Textiles	Metals and Machinery	Chemicals and Ceramics	Wood Products	Food Products	Electricity and Gas	Other[b]	All Manufacturing
1895-99	41	25	—	—	80	—	49	(37)
1900-1904	50	33	—	56	88	10	90	(48)
1905-09	70	61	53	91	85	27	126	69
1910-14	100	100	100	100	100	100	100	100
1915-19	152	162	186	142	123	198	248	160
1920-24	185	244	252	441[c]	170	356	190	217
1925-29	270	355	453	570	193	653	260	313
1930-34[d]	352	410	643	601	186	1,002	—	377
1935-38[d]	416	920	1,255	1,018	190	1,517	—	600

a For the years 1895-1929, production indices of the Bureau of Industrial Research, Nagoya Commercial College, published in *Hompō Seisan Sūryō Shisū Sōran* (1894-1931), Nagoya, 1933; for 1895-1918, Series I; for 1919-29, Series II (p. 41). Here the Nagoya series are presented with 1910-14 as 100, and projected through 1930-38 with the aid of the index of industrial production prepared at General Headquarters, Supreme Commander for the Allied Powers, Tokyo. (See note d.)

The Nagoya indices are weighted geometric averages of various production series numbering 20 in 1895, 41 or more in 1905 and thereafter, and 51 from 1919 on. The individual production relatives making up each of the seven subgroups are combined with weights representing average gross value of production in 1926-28. Included are all items having an annual gross value of over 10 million yen at this time. The aggregate index is constructed by combining the subgroups with weights based on estimated total wage payments in each group during 1927.

The characteristics of this index are worthy of brief description. First, it represents more than private factory production. In some degree, at least, it appears to reflect also the output of small workshop establishments having less than five operatives, and government as well as private factories. For example, it includes such products of small-scale industry as straw mats, *sake*, tea, and salt so far as they could be estimated. It also includes the iron and steel output of the State-operated Yawata Iron Works. The lack of production statistics for many finished products, especially in workshop industries, is compensated partially by employing annual estimates of raw material consumption in Japan (based on production and imports) to measure the output of such items as textile piece goods, machinery and metal manufactures, and wood and rubber products.

For the years 1895-98 the index is confined to a few products, mainly cotton, silk, and wool yarns and piece goods; metals and machinery; and major foodstuffs like sugar, fish products, alcoholic liquors, soy, tea, and salt. In 1899-1904 electricity, wood products, straw mats, and leather goods are added. After 1905 the index is extended to include ceramics, paper, sulfuric acid, rubber goods, vegetable and mineral oils—all under "chemicals"—and wheat flour, hemp, and tobacco products. Gas production is added in 1911, fertilizers in 1914, and after 1919 the following: rayon, coke, celluloid, bean paste, and ice, each in its respective group. After 1904, therefore, the index is fairly consistent, though probably still subject to the upward bias resulting from more complete reporting of production amounts in the later years.

Like most indices of physical volume, the Nagoya series contains various biases arising from its method of construction. The use of weights based on production values in 1926-28, near the end of the period, naturally enlarges the influence upon the totals of those products like electricity and metal manufactures which became relatively important through expanding at a rate above the average. Value weights from an earlier period would have given greater weight to textiles and other industries which expanded less rapidly. The resulting upward bias in the group and aggregate indices is reinforced by the fact that factory in dustry is probably better represented than workshop industry, and grew more rapidly.

On the other hand, being based on physical quantities of goods, and often raw materials consumed rather than finished products, the index fails to reflect qualitative improvements in manufacturing. Raw cotton consumption, for example, does not measure "growth" in terms of finer counts of yarns or better weaves and finishes.

Other elements of distortion are latent in the weighting system employed. As noted above the lack of data made it necessary to use gross production values and wage payments, rather than the more satisfactory measure of net value added by manufacture. By comparison with the latter, weighting individual series by gross product values to compute subgroup totals tends to overstress commodities for which raw material costs bulk large and gross- to net-product ratios are high. More importantly, the use of total wage bills to weight the subgroups in arriving at the aggregate index overweights industries where labor costs are high in relation to net product. This includes textiles and wood products, for example, where the wage/net product ratio tends to run up to 35 to 60% or more. Conversely, wage weights understress industries where the wage costs are relatively unimportant, as in electric power and factory processed foodstuffs. Here the wage/net-product ratios are less than 5% and 10% respectively As the industries with high wage/net-product ratios generally grew less rapidly, and those with low ratios more rapidly, the effect is to impart a downward tendency in the aggregate index. This may offset in some degree the upward bias of late-period weights mentioned above

These methodological features of the Nagoya index, together with the inaccuracies inherent in the underlying production data, make the series at best a rough measure of the growth of manufactures, especially in the earlier years. Long-term comparisons are not very meaning ful, and probably exaggerate the growth in most industries. Nevertheless, it is the best index— Indeed, the only one—available for the entire period 1894-1931. A comparable rise in in dustrial output from 1913 to 1931 is shown by Rolf Wagenführ's index for Japan, published in "Die Industriewirtschaft," Institut für Konjunkturforschung, *Vierteljahrshefte zur Kon junkturforschung*, vol. XXXI, 1933, p. 67. A similar trend (with wider annual fluctuations) dur ing 1919-31 is also indicated by other indices published by the *Oriental Economist*, th Mitsubishi Economic Research Bureau, *Diamond*, and *Keizai Jihō*. See Yasuji Koide, "Hompe Getsuji Seisan Shisū no Sōkan," *Sekai Keizai Tōkei Sōsho*, no. 8, September 1934, pp. 1-16.

ᵇ Being confined to only two unrelated industries—straw mats and leather goods—this category has little significance except to extend further the scope of the aggregate index.

ᶜ The sudden jump in the index of wood products during the early postwar years is due entirely to a sharp increase in imports of wood, a major component. As these imports were mainly American cedar, fir, pine, etc., for construction purposes, they appear to exercise an undue influence on the index of wood manufactures as a whole, which could hardly have tripled in five years.

ᵈ Spliced with the Nagoya series in 1930-31, to give a projection through 1930-38, I have used the indices of industrial production prepared by the Economic and Scientific Section GHQ, Supreme Commander for the Allied Powers, Tokyo (Bank of Japan, *Economic Statistic of Japan, 1949*, Tokyo, 1949, p. 231). Each index is an arithmetic average of relatives (1932 36 = 100), weighted with value added by manufacture in 1936. To secure indices comparable with the Nagoya classes, pairs of SCAP series are combined here with weights as follows chemicals, 13.4, and ceramics, 3.5; ferrous metals, 13.0, and machinery, 18.6. Also the "al manufacturing" index given here combines the SCAP series for manufacturing and for publi utilities, with weights of 74.0 and 17.4 respectively.

with somewhat more assurance. A fairly steady rise takes place over the next thirty years. The index itself follows an almost straight line of geometric progression to 1938. Its upward and downward swings around the central tendency are suprisingly small in view of the pronounced booms and depressions which characterized these years. From the turn of the century the index advances for four decades at an average annual rate of almost 7.5%.

Very likely the actual growth of manufacturing output was not this rapid. Yet if sustained at anything over 5% a year during this long period the achievement is still impressive. It is equalled in the annals of few important industrial nations, if any, during this period. Japan's rate of expansion was more than double that in world manufacturing as a whole, as estimated by the League of Nations (Table 9). The latter's index of world manufacturing output rises 3.5% a year from 1876-80 to 1935-38. For the last thirty years the rate is only 2.8% annually. By comparison the Japanese advance was probably at least twice as rapid.

A comparison of the curves for a number of countries shows further that Japan's relative gain upon the other industrial nations was achieved mainly in two periods: the years of World War I, when

Table 9. *Growth of Manufacturing Activity in Japan, the World, and Selected Countries, 1876-1938*[a]
(indices; 1913 = 100)

Annual Average	World	Japan[b]	United States	United Kingdom	India[c]
1876-80	25	—	17	50	—
1881-85	30	—	24	57	—
1886-90	37	—	32	61	—
1891-95	43	—	38	65	—
1896-1900	54	35	45	74	54
1901-05	67	48	66	77	69
1906-10	80	64	79	83	85
1911-13	94	93	92	93	97
1921-25	103	205	129	76	122
1926-30	139	297	160	92	146
1931-35	128	410	118	92	175
1936-38	185	631	167	122	230

a Except for Japan, data are as given in League of Nations, *Industrialization and Foreign Trade*, Geneva, 1945, Annex, tables I and II. National indices relate to manufacturing activity, excluding mining, construction, and gas and electricity production. The world index is an arithmetic average of national indices (twenty-nine countries in the later decades), weighted so far as possible by net value of production, 1925-29, and corrected for the estimated growth of manufacturing in countries where indices are not available. Weights for the countries shown here are as follows: U.S., 42.5%; U.K., 9.5%; Japan, 2.5%; India, 1.2% (p. 128).

b Index of manufacturing production as given in Table 8, above, except for the difference in years averaged. This index conforms to the definition of manufacturing activity adopted by the League of Nations, except that gas and electricity are included. It differs somewhat from the Japanese index employed by the League, however, being based on a somewhat more comprehensive version of the Nagoya index before 1931, and thereafter on the index prepared at GHQ, Supreme Commander for the Allied Powers, Tokyo.

c For 1896-1932 the Indian index is confined to large-scale production of cotton, wool, and jute manufactures, paper products, beer, iron, and steel. For 1932-38 it represents only cotton consumption and the production of jute manufactures, steel ingots, pig iron, cement, and paper.

she seized the opportunity afforded by her virtual noncombatant status to forge ahead commercially and industrially; and the world depression of 1931-35, when her industry again spurted ahead under the impetus of monetary expansion and exchange depreciation. For most of the other leading countries these two periods were years of retarded growth or actual decline.

The League study of *Industrialization and Foreign Trade* also presents an interesting estimate of the distribution of the world's manufacturing production among various countries.[45] The criterion employed is the net product value added in the process of manufacture during the years 1925-29. The United States, for example, is given a weight of 42.5%; Germany, 11.5%; and the United Kingdom, 9.5%. Japan is far below these levels, her output being estimated at only 2.5% of the world's total. For reasons which we shall not enter into here, this figure is probably too low.[46] Even at this level, however, the League statisticians conclude that in 1926-29 Japan accounted for one fourth of all the manufacturing production of the "economically young areas"—Latin America, Oceania, Southeast Europe, Africa, and Asia (excluding the USSR).[47] The only other Asiatic nation which had undergone appreciable industrialization at this time was India. As indicated in Table 9, however, India's progress under British rule lagged far behind that of Japan during the first three decades of the twentieth century. At the end of the period she was no match in either the scale or the technical maturity of factory industry.

Any general measure of manufacturing growth is apt to conceal wide variations among individual industries. This is evident in Table 8, where the production record of six major components of Japanese industry is depicted. The differences among the series are what one might expect. The steepest curves of development are found among the producer goods industries as a group. These are the industries which were new—or nonexistent—in 1900. Most rapid is the advance in gas and electric power, the modern energy sources which were basic to industrial progress. Next came the metallurgical and chemical industries. Here, as observed earlier, government subsidy and armament expenditure fostered rapid growth, along with

---

[45] Pp. 127-29.

[46] To compare the net value of industrial production among countries with differing price levels is a complicated matter. In Chapter 4 I have attempted a rough comparison of factory production in Japan with that of the United States, the United Kingdom, and Germany during 1934-37. This yields ratios not very dissimilar from those given above. However, if *total* manufacturing production could be compared, including the output of plants with less than five workers, the Japanese figure would probably be increased by 40% or so.

[47] P. 13.

the expanding needs of transport, agriculture, and industry in general. Particularly noteworthy is the upward surge of the heavy industries in the years 1930-38, under the stimulus of large programs of capital construction and armament.

On the other hand, the older consumer industries advance more slowly. The processing of food, of clothing materials, and of wood, bamboo, and straw manufactures was already well developed at the turn of the century. These industrial pursuits, at a more primitive level of technology, had long served the basic necessities of the people. Their expansion in modern times is therefore less spectacular in character. Even so, the growth of the textile industries in serving the domestic and foreign market is nearly as rapid as the general average for all industry. Textiles, along with metals and machinery, form the two largest components of Japanese industry. Together they are given a weight of as much as 70% in the Nagoya index, and over 50% in the SCAP Headquarters index for the years after 1930. Naturally, therefore, the aggregate index follows closely their upward curves, rising somewhat more rapidly than the former and more slowly than the latter.[48]

The Factory System and Labor Efficiency. The bare statistics of manufacturing output recited above tell little of the actual processes by which industrial growth came about. Behind these curves of expansion lies a complex interaction of forces: the growth of population in urbanized, industrial employment; the extension of markets enlarging the circuits of exchange both at home and abroad; the accumulation of capital in new and diversified forms of plant, inventories, and equipment; the introduction of new technological skills and modes of business organization.

These factors of organization, skills, and resources receive further consideration in the chapters which follow. Here we need only supplement the record of physical expansion with a brief record of the growth of the factory system after the turn of the century. For of

[48] The Nagoya index tends to overweight textiles relative to metals and machinery in one respect, and to underweight them in another. As described in Table 8, note a, each group influences the aggregate index in proportion to wages paid in 1927. But net value added by manufacture (a more satisfactory weighting system) is lower relative to wage costs in textiles than in metals and machinery. In 1929, for example, the ratio was 2.7 in the former and 3.4 in the latter. (Yasuji Koide, "Hompō Sangyō Kōzō no Hendo ni Kansuru Shiryō," Nagoya Chamber of Commerce, *Nagoya Keizai Tōkei Geppō*, vol. VIII, no. 9, October 1936, p. 491.) Wage weights thus give textiles more influence upon the combined index than they deserve, and tend to retard its advance.

On the other hand, this is partially compensated by the use of late-period weights. Metals and machinery grew more rapidly than textiles through this forty-year period, so that 1927 weights assign greater importance to these industries than, say, weights based on their relative size in 1914. How far these counteracting biases offset each other cannot easily be determined.

course it was only the spread of specialization and machine production on a growing scale—of the factory—which made possible the rapid advances recorded above. In Table 10 the outlines of this development after 1909 are summarized.[49]

Table 10. *Growth of Factory Industry in Japan Proper,*
1909-38[a]

| | | MACHINERY CAPACITY[b] | | | GROSS VALUE |
| | NUMBER OF FACTORIES | (THOUSANDS OF HORSEPOWER) | | NUMBER OF WORKERS[c] | OF PRODUCTION[d] (MILLIONS OF |
	Total	*Equipped with Power Machinery*	*Prime Movers*	*Electric Motors*	(THOUSANDS)	YEN)
1909	32,390	9,155	—	—	1,012	781
1914	31,859	14,578	537	279	1,187	1,371
1919	44,087	26,947	719	992	2,025	6,738
1924	48,394	37,141	877	1,440	1,977	6,625
1929	60,275	48,555	695	2,600[e]	2,384	7,994
1934	80,880	68,806	972	3,730	2,580	9,758
1938	113,205	98,723	1,461[f]	6,290[f]	3,718	20,101

a Except as detailed in notes b and d, these are year-end figures covering all private and publicly owned factories other than a few local-government enterprises. Before 1929 private factories are defined as manufacturing establishments (including gas and electricity plants) normally employing five or more "operatives" (*shokkō*); thereafter, as establishments equipped to employ five or more. Factories owned by local-government authorities were of negligible importance; in 1929 they comprised only 137 plants employing 7,066 workers.

Much confusion is found in tables of Japanese factory statistics, owing to the inadequate or misleading descriptions often given in official publications. After a good deal of cross-checking I believe the above series are reasonably consistent and inclusive. The data have come mainly from the following sources: Ministry (Department) of Commerce and Industry, *Kōjō Tōkeihyō* (1930-36), and *The Statistics of the Department of Commerce and Industry, 1924-28*; Ministry of Finance, *Statistical Year-Book of Finance and Economy of Japan, 1948*; Prime Minister's Office, *Statistical Abstract of Japan, 1950*; Imperial Cabinet, Bureau of Statistics, *Nippon Teikoku Tōkei Nenkan*, annual; Supreme Commander for the Allied Powers, GHQ, *Number of Establishments, Employment, and Value of Products in Manufacturing Industries in Japan, 1929-1942*, Tokyo, 1947; Asahi Shimbun-sha, *Nippon Keizai Tōkei Sōkan*, Tokyo, 1930; and Yasuji Koide, "Hompō Sangyō Kōzō no Hendō ni Kansuru Shiryō," *Nagoya Keizai Tōkei Geppō*, vol. viii, no. 9, October 1936, pp. 1-65.

b Capacity of prime movers and electric motors installed in factories as defined in note a, except that the gas and electric industries are excluded here. Prime movers include mainly steam engines and turbines, whether operating or idle at year-end, beside smaller amounts of capacity in water turbines and wheels, and internal combustion engines. Some of these prime movers were used to drive machinery directly; others to generate electricity in plants not classified in the electrical industry subgroup and therefore included here. Thus the total for prime movers cannot be added to the total for electric motors without some duplication, although official reports do this constantly. For the years prior to 1931 I have been unable either to eliminate this duplication directly, or, alternatively, to estimate the amount of horsepower capacity in prime movers operated by the electric power industry itself to generate electricity for factory use. (The unwary student should perhaps be warned that the electrical industry subgroup reported in factory statistics [*Kōjō Tōkeihyō*] does not include the en-

49 Only after 1909 were statistics collected on a more or less standardized and comprehensive basis for industrial establishments of five or more operatives.

tire electric power industry.) However, duplication between factory prime movers and electric motors is considerably reduced by omitting the electric industry subgroup, as is done in the above table. On the other hand, the above series do not reflect the great increase in electric power generated in public utility plants and employed for factory lighting, electrolysis, heat treatment, and processes other than driving machinery. Moreover, there may have been a shift in the enumeration method in 1929, which casts doubt on any comparison between the years before and after.

c All employees, including factory operatives (*shokkō*), supervisory staff, technicians, clerical workers, guards, cooks, etc. Probably the figures include everyone on year-end payrolls, whether or not in actual attendance on December 31.

d Annual output of private factories only. Except in 1909 the estimated value of gas and electricity production is added to official factory totals, which exclude the output of this industrial group except for by-products of gas plants. For 1914-34 estimates are from Koide, *op.cit.*, p. 9; for 1938 gas output is valued at 0.73 sen per cubic meter and electricity at 1.9 sen per kilowatt-hour. Gross production values contain a good deal of duplication of products, since intermediate as well as finished products are reported. Although it means little in this connection, the reader may wish to know that the yen had an exchange value approximately as follows in U.S. cents: 1909-19, 50; 1924, 42; 1929, 46; 1934 and 1938, 29.

e An estimate based on the number of electric motors and on electricity consumption in 1929 compared with the years immediately preceding and following. The official figure is actually 4,673,000 h.p. in 1929, but this is incredible. It is more than double the figures for 1927 and 1928, and 50% above 1932 and 1933. In effect, I have merely smoothed out the trend through the years 1924-34, but, as remarked in note a, there may actually have been a permanent change in census methods falsifying any comparison of electric motors before and after 1929.

f In 1937.

The growth of manufacturing production in plants of five or more operatives—at least a sevenfold increase from 1909 to 1938, judging by the index in Table 8—took place through several related developments. These included (1) a 250% increase in the number of factories and factory workers, with little change in the average number of workers per plant;[50] (2) a rise of over 100% in output per plant (deflated for price changes), resulting from greater mechanization and other improvements; and (3) a corresponding advance in output per worker.

The gain in labor efficiency cannot be measured accurately in

50 It is surprising to find so little growth in the average number of workers per plant, considering the expansion of factory output over this period. The change in the distribution of employment between small, medium, and large factories was relatively slight.

SIZE OF PLANT	PERCENTAGE OF PRIVATE FACTORIES		PERCENTAGE OF FACTORY OPERATIVES	
	1909	*1934*	*1909*	*1934*
5-9 operatives	52.1	56.5	13.5	11.8
10-99 operatives	44.3	39.7	43.0	36.9
100 or more operatives	3.6	3.8	43.5	51.3

Source: "Hompō Sangyō Kōzō no Hendō ni Kansuru Shiryō," cited, pp. 4, 18.

In 1934, in addition to the above, there were over a million workshops employing less than five operatives. These tiny establishments still employed almost as many persons in manufacturing activity, at least part-time, as all factories put together.

Further discussion of the scale of Japanese industry will be found in Chapter 4.

the absence of more accurate data on production and man-hours of employment. Some indication of the change is given, however, by comparing the index of total manufacturing output in Table 8 with an index of year-end factory employment as defined in Table 10. The results are as follows (1910-14 = 100) :[51]

	Number of Factory Workers	Manufacturing Output	Output per Worker
1910-14	100	100	100
1915-19	150	160	107
1920-24	190	217	124
1925-29	190	313	165
1930-34	196	377	192
1935-38	228	600	263

Employment in factory industry, both public and private, more than doubled over this twenty-five-year period. From 1.1 million wage and salaried workers of all types in 1910-14 it grew to 2.6 million in 1935-38. Meanwhile the volume of production in these establishments of five or more operatives certainly increased no *less* rapidly than that reported in manufacturing industry as a whole, including small workshops. The indices suggest, accordingly, that the gain in gross output per capita was something over 150%. So far as physical outputs can be compared over this long span of time, one concludes that on the average a factory worker in Japan produced annually well over twice as much at the end of the period as at the beginning. Regular hours of work were reduced 10% or more during the interval, so that production per man-hour may have risen somewhat more rapidly. However, too little is known about actual hours of work, including part-time and overtime labor, to be certain at this point.[52]

[51] Prior to 1920 employment in private factories of five or more operatives was reported only for 1909, 1914, and 1919. From these figures I have made estimates for 1910-14 and 1915-19 by reference to the employment trend in establishments of ten or more operatives during the intervening years. The indices of employment and output are not exactly comparable, for, as explained in Table 8, the latter is not necessarily confined to factory production, but includes production in certain workshop industries. Moreover, the employment figures include all persons on the payroll on December 31 of each year, while the production index purports to measure activity throughout the year. The latter discrepancy, however, is minimized by the use of five-year averages.

[52] By way of comparison, physical output per manufacturing wage earner in the United States increased 55% from 1914 to 1937, and output per wage-earner-hour 109%. Solomon Fabricant, *The Relation between Factory Employment and Output since 1899*, New York: National Bureau of Economic Research, 1941, p. 37. This represents, of course, a far more careful and accurate measurement than the figures for Japan given above.

As labor efficiency increased, the gain in product per worker seems to have been widely shared. Some of it accrued to the worker himself in the form of higher wages; some of it went to the capitalist as interest and profits on the growing amounts of capital invested per worker; and a good deal was passed on to the consumer, either at home or abroad, in the form of reduced prices (in relation to money incomes) or better quality. From evidence examined below (page 144) it appears that the real daily wage of the average factory wage earner advanced by about two thirds from 1914 to 1937. To this extent he himself shared in the benefits.

This advance in the productivity of factory labor is not surprising in view of the improvements currently taking place in industrial organization and methods. Most important, the ratio between workers and capital equipment was steadily becoming more favorable. The actual change here is difficult to measure, for industrial capital takes many different forms not readily summarized and compared. One useful indicator, however, is the capacity of industrial establishments to harness inanimate energy to the driving of machinery. As an index of capital, this rests on the hypothesis that motive capacity, expressed in horsepower or kilowatts, measures roughly the amount of machinery and equipment in use, while the amount of equipment in turn is associated with building space and other forms of industrial capital.[53]

Table 10 presents two series of figures testifying to the mechanization of industry in prewar Japan. One is the horsepower of prime movers installed in all factories private and public, except those establishments classified as gas and electricity undertakings. (The latter are excluded since they supplied power not only for industrial use but also for household lighting, tramways, etc.) Prime movers are machines for transforming natural sources of energy—falling water, wind, and fuel of all sorts—into mechanical energy. This first series of figures tells very little, however, for Japanese factories at this time were securing more and more of their power in the form of electric energy generated in public utility plants. The prime-mover statistics therefore record only the motive capacity retained in factories to drive machinery directly, or to generate electric

[53] Actually the relationship between motive power and total industrial capital is only a loose one, particularly where power machinery is replacing hand machinery, or where there is a rapid growth in chemical and metalworking industries using large amounts of equipment for heating, cooling, separation, electrolysis, etc. Also, the efficiency of power machinery is apt to vary in relation to its energy input, and its amount is not necessarily correlated very closely with building space, or with transport equipment upon which a factory depends but which is outside the plant. See "Motive Power in European Industry," United Nations, *Economic Bulletin for Europe*, vol. 3, no. 1, first quarter, 1951, pp. 24-25.

power for use within the same establishment. Most of it was in the form of steam engines and turbines.

The second series, the horsepower of electric motors installed in factories, is the more significant one. It soars from 279,000 h.p. in 1914 to 6,290,000 h.p. in 1937—more than a twenty-fold increase.[54] Unfortunately a single total for motive capacity applied to factory industry cannot be secured merely by adding these two series together, although this is done in *Kōjō Tōkeihyō* and other official publications. One reason is that electric motors do not necessarily require generating capacity in prime movers on a one-for-one basis. As power machinery becomes more plentiful and more specialized, an increasing share is likely to be held in reserve or to be used only part-time in particular operations. The capacity of installed motors probably increased more rapidly, therefore, than the capacity and output of prime movers generating electricity to serve them. Another complication arises from the fact that the prime movers tabulated in Table 10 were employed for various uses, and some of them generated electric power to run motors within the same factory establishment. So far as the latter was true, one cannot add prime movers and electric motors without exaggerating the net amount of power equipment. In the mid-thirties Japanese factories, excluding the gas and electricity subgroup, supplied about 20% of their own electricity requirements. For the earlier years, however, no such information is available. Nor do we know the capacity of prime movers directly driving machinery, the amount of power used for heating and lighting, the loss of energy in transmission, or other complexities of the matter.

The opinion may be ventured, nevertheless, that the total net capacity of power equipment installed in public and private factories (other than gas and electricity undertakings) to operate machinery increased something like 400 to 500% from 1914 to 1935-38. Meanwhile the number of workers tripled. Per worker, the amount of power machinery in Japanese factories perhaps doubled. In 1936 the net capacity of prime movers and electric motors reckoned in this fashion was a little over 5 million h.p., or 1.69 per worker.[55] This

[54] As noted in Table 10, there is a jump in the official figure for 1929 which is inexplicable, and suggests a shift in the basis of compilation exaggerating the actual increase over preceding years.

[55] The nature of this 1936 estimate should be made explicit. *Kōjō Tōkeihyō*, 1936 (tables 7 and 21) reports 1,084,000 h.p. of prime movers (operating and idle) and 5,025,000 h.p. of electric motors installed in private and public factories, excluding gas and electricity undertakings, at the end of 1936. Table 14 further reports that private factories, again excluding the gas and electricity subgroup, supplied 21.5% of their own electric power requirements for all purposes in 1936. On the assumption that this also represents the share of electric motors driven with self-supplied power in private and public factories, 78.5% of the capacity of electric motors, e.g.,

per capita figure, incidentally, is about one third of the corresponding figure for American manufacturing in 1939, which was 4.8 h.p. per worker. (See below, page 180.)

The motive power actually required to operate factory machinery in 1936 was somewhat less than 5 million h.p., as electric motors do not ordinarily need prime movers of equivalent rated capacity to provide the power, even allowing for energy lost in transmission. On the other hand, a good deal of motive capacity was now employed in public utilities and factories to generate electricity for factory heat and light, electrolysis, chemical reaction, and other industrial purposes beside operating machinery. Here the increase in energy consumption in prewar Japan must have been even more rapid, for the chemical and metalworking industries use large amounts of power in this way, and they grew more rapidly than industry as a whole. A more accurate measure of inanimate energy applied to manufacturing processes, directly or indirectly, would thus include the power furnished for such purposes by electricity supply undertakings as well from generators located in manufacturing establishments. If this is reckoned in by allocating public utility generating capacity to factory use on the basis of the share of electric power supply consumed in factory industry, there may well have been an increase of 150% or more per capita in the total horsepower of prime movers installed and allocated in this sense for all factory requirements. Unless I have misinterpreted the official statistics, this figure also came to nearly 5 million h.p. in 1936, or 1.6. per worker.[56]

3,945,000 h.p., is added to the capacity of prime movers. The net total is thus 5,029,000 h.p. To add prime movers and motors in this fashion yields a rather ambiguous result, however, for reasons noted elsewhere in this discussion.

[56] Total consumption of electricity in 1936 is reported at 21,095 million kw-h. in Ministry of Finance, *Statistical Year-Book of Finance and Economy of Japan, 1948,* pp. 696-97. This table is believed to refer only to power generated by electricity supply undertakings. It is so interpreted for 1937 and thereafter in the *Statistical Year Book of the World Power Conference,* no. 4, London, 1948, table 19A. *Kōjō Tōkeihyō,* 1936, cited, table 14, puts at 10,427 million kw-h. the amount of non-self-supplied power consumed by all factory establishments excluding the gas and electricity industry. On the assumption that this power came from electricity supply undertakings, factories thus accounted for 49.4% of the consumption of power generated by electric utilities. Applying this percentage to the installed kilowatt capacity of the latter, and converting kilowatts to horsepower at the ratio 1/1.34, we may say that motive capacity rated at 3,837,000 h.p. was devoted to supplying power to factory establishments. Added to the 1,084,000 h.p. of prime movers installed in factories (excluding the gas and electricity subgroup) this means 4,921,000 h.p., or 1.65 h.p. per worker, available in this sense for all factory purposes. Other sources give somewhat different figures for power consumption in manufacturing, but they lead to substantially similar conclusions. One finds accordingly some confirmation here of the calculation of factory power equipment given above, despite the ambiguity of Japanese statistics in this whole field.

The progress of mechanization after 1914 was continuous, though somewhat erratic. The boom years of World War I brought a rapid expansion of industrial production and exports, as Japan moved into markets suddenly vacated by her European competitors. Her industries were still largely dependent on foreign machinery, however. This was difficult to procure under conditions of war. The supply of turbines, for example, was virtually cut off. Accordingly manufacturing output was expanded quite as much by simply adding to the labor force as by mechanization. In fact, production per worker appears to have risen very little from 1914 to 1919.

The rationalization movement of the twenties fostered a marked increase in power-driven machinery and other equipment utilizing Japan's growing supplies of electric power. Laborsaving improvements were encouraged by the failure of wages to decline from wartime peaks in proportion to prices, and by the rise in labor standards and labor efficiency. The dwindling profit margins of the post-1929 depression added a further incentive. Meanwhile the big electric utilities expanded rapidly with the aid of American capital and technical assistance. At the end of 1919 the generating capacity of all public and private plants in Japan Proper was only 1,133,243 kw.; in 1929 it was 4,193,623 kw.; and in 1934, 5,491,947 kw. With the industrial demands of the thirties it grew to 7,166,495 kw. at the end of 1937. Hydro plants accounted for 3,959,402 kw., or 55%; thermal plants for the remainder.[57] In a normal year, however, about 75% of Japan's electricity supply actually came from water power. Steam plants were apt to be held in reserve against a shortage of water.

At the close of this interwar period nine out of ten Japanese homes were wired for electric lighting, at least on a modest scale. Indeed, all of Japan's 11,500 towns and villages were said to have lighting facilities in some degree, except for 199 small hamlets in remote corners of the nation. Yet two thirds or more of the country's power supply actually went into mining and manufacturing. Industrial consumption of electricity tripled from 1926 to 1936. The chemical industry was the largest consumer, followed by metallurgy, mining, and textiles.[58]

[57] *Nippon Teikoku Tōkei Nenkan*, cited, passim. This is the most inclusive of the varying estimates quoted in different sources. In 1937 some 85% of Japan's generating capacity was found in public utility enterprises, some of which also had a controlling interest in electric railways. The balance was operated by factories, railways, and government establishments for their own requirements.

[58] According to the Electric Bureau, Ministry of Communications, the consumption of electric power (self-supplied and purchased from public utilities) in mining and manufacturing rose from 3,681 million kw-h. in 1926 to 13,366 million kw-h. in 1936. *The Japan-Manchoukuo Year Book, 1939*, p. 407. Somewhat higher figures

The electrification of industry thus enabled the Japanese to capitalize handsomely on their abundant natural sources of energy in the form of falling water and coal. It also facilitated a wide dispersal of manufacturing in small plants scattered through the towns and countryside. The result was to make it a good deal easier, both socially and economically, to bring into industrial employment Japan's great reservoir of cheap farm labor, and to hasten the modernization of techniques outside the main industrial centers.

If the productivity of Japanese factory labor more than doubled from 1910-14 to 1935-38, the instrument of this advance was this corresponding increase in power machinery and the installations required to house and operate it. The growth and modernization of capital equipment, reflected in the above statistics of motive power, brought a revolutionary advance in energy harnessed per worker, and made possible a far larger scale of production. In addition to mechanization, and the use of electric power in the chemical and metalworking industries for electrolysis, heat treatment, etc., other related changes contributed to the growing effectiveness of labor. Within industry itself both management and workers gained in experience and personal efficiency. Materials like cocoon silk, staple cotton, and raw steel were improved in quality and uniformity. Such auxiliary services as shipping and marketing were rationalized to keep pace with the requirements of large-scale production. In short, manufacturing progress was dependent on progress in other sectors as well.

Despite these advances Japan remained far behind the leading manufacturing nations of the West in the scale and efficiency of her industry. This was true of most of the big factory trades, and even more of the tiny workshops which still bulked so large in her industrial economy. Such comparisons, however, may be deferred more conveniently to the next chapter.

Other Service Occupations. The remaining field of economic activity to be mentioned includes the service industries, other than transportation. Here are found a wide range of occupations rendering all sorts of services which have little in common save that their product is nonmaterial. In Japan, as in other developing countries, the commodity-handling services, e.g., retail and wholesale trade, have become increasingly detached from commodity production itself. They afford independent employment and income to a substantial share of the working population. Of growing importance, too, have been other service industries like banking, the private professions,

---

for 1930 and thereafter are given in *Statistical Year-Book of Finance and Economy of Japan, 1948*, cited, pp. 694-95.

and commercial recreation. Not least in significance, of course, have been the activities of national and local government agencies.

These services are many of them apt to be slighted in accounts of Japan's industrialization. For one thing, they do not attract attention by entering into international competition, being largely nonexportable. Also, a large share of them are traditional trades still carried on with little modernization of skills and equipment. This makes it easier to conclude that they form a congeries of minor, relatively unproductive activities which gave employment to hosts of people but contributed little in the aggregate to the growth of the country's income and wealth. Yet to pass over them would be to ignore a segment of the Japanese economy which occupied close to 30% of the civilian labor force in the prewar decade and produced 40 to 45% of the country's income as estimated in the national income accounts. (See Chapter 9.)

Among these "tertiary" industries are a number which were directly essential to the growth of commodity production and distribution. Here, beside various kinds of land and water transportation, is most of the merchandising and financial world, as well as professions like engineering, law, and accounting. Other activities less closely associated with commodity output likewise reflected the increasing urbanization of living conditions and the decline of the self-sufficient family economy; also the rise in living standards which made for a more than proportionate growth of expenditure on amenities beyond the basic needs of food, clothing, and shelter. These trends created a growing demand for teachers and doctors. They shifted people increasingly into rented dwellings. They provided new commercial opportunities for theaters, restaurants, barbershops, artists, and *geisha*. They enlarged both the requirement and the means for personal travel and domestic service. Finally, the responsibilities of the State grew steadily in scale and complexity, as industrialism advanced and with it Japan's ambitions as a world power.

Unfortunately it is impossible to provide any summary measure of long-term growth which will cover adequately this miscellaneous field of productive effort. At any rate, it has yet to be done in any very persuasive fashion. For many individual occupations evidence is not difficult to assemble. One can find it in banking and insurance statistics; in the spread of educational institutions; in government payrolls; in the income tax returns of various trades and professions; in the municipal statistics of warehousing, retailing, and the other urban services of cities like Tokyo or Osaka. And, of course, there are data on railways, shipping, and communications, some of which were cited earlier. Yet for most of these occupations, even estimates of employment are quite unreliable before 1920. Any measure of income or product is still more speculative.

As an indication of the general tendency to growth, attention may be called to certain historical estimates of income produced in the service industries, prepared by Prof. Yuzo Yamada. For the services as a group they are summarized below in Table 12. They show total net product (at 1928-32 prices) rising from 1,421 million yen in 1883-87 to 6,483 million yen in 1933-37. This is more than a threefold increase in fifty years—a somewhat slower rate of growth than Yamada records for the entire national income. The estimate itself is highly questionable, however. It cannot be trusted either as regards (a) the price deflator (wholesale commodity prices), or (b) the figures on total employment and income per worker which are multiplied together to get total service incomes. Somewhat more reliable are Yamada's estimates after 1918, when income produced (at 1928-32 prices) in commerce, communications, public service, and the professions rises from 3,034 million yen in 1918-22 to 6,453 million yen in 1933-37.[59]

Historical changes in the labor force employed in service occupations one might expect to be estimated more plausibly. Beginning in 1920, decennial censuses enumerate the working population in detail by principal occupation. Prior to that time the figures most commonly cited are those of S. Hijikata, used by Professor Yamada in the income estimate cited above. Table 11 gives his estimate for 1880 and 1900, together with the census figures for 1920 and 1930.

The census figures for 1920 and 1930 probably come fairly close to the mark in distributing people by their principal occupation. As a measure of employment they are subject to more qualification. They fail to record the amount of part-time employment, or the labor contributed to an occupation by persons for whom it was a subsidiary employment. Neither is necessarily a constant percentage. Hijikata's pre-1920 estimates, however, are much more open to doubt. They almost certainly understate the number of people in commerce and transport in the early years, and they progress in each category by regular (sometimes rising) increments from year to year. This is most implausible, to put it mildly.[60]

59 *Nihon Kokumin Shotoku Suikei Shiryō*, Tokyo, 1951, p. 130. For a revision of Yamada's estimates giving a much higher rate of growth in service incomes, see below, note 66.

60 For example, the number recorded by Hijikata in commerce increases about 50,000 every year from 1876 to 1920, when it equals the census figure. In the professions there is a regular increment of 18,000 to 20,000, and in industry about 100,000 every year. I am indebted to Harry Oshima, of the United Nations Secretariat, for pointing this out. While I have not had access to Hijikata's original publication, it seems likely that he began with certain estimates of the size and distribution of the working population in the 1870's, and then extrapolated the

Table 11. *Hijikata and Census Estimates of Labor Force in Service Occupations of Japan Proper, 1880-1930*[a]

	1880	1900	1920	1930
	NUMBER OF PERSONS IN THOUSANDS			
Total gainfully occupied	*19,872*	*25,308*	*27,268*	*29,620*
Total occupied principally in services, excluding domestics[b]	*1,934*	*3,616*	*5,667*	*7,630*
Commerce, catering, finance, etc.	1,154	2,171	3,188	4,478
Transport and communications	123	395	1,037	1,108
Private professions and public services	657	1,050	1,442	2,044
	PERCENT			
Ratio of service occupations, above, to total gainfully occupied[b]	9.7	14.3	20.8	25.8

a The 1880 and 1900 estimates are S. Hijikata's, published in *Shakai Seisaka Jihō*, September 1929, and quoted here from Yamada, *Nihon Kokumin Shotoku Suikei Shiryō*, Tokyo, 1951, p. 152. Official census data (occupational classification) for 1920 are from Imperial Cabinet, Bureau of Statistics, *Rōdō Tōkei Yōran* (1930), Tokyo, 1930, pp. 3-4, and for 1930 from the same bureau's *Kokusei Chōsa Saishū Hōkokusho* (1930), Tokyo, 1938, pp. 202-03. The census occupational distribution is used here rather than its distribution by industries. It classifies people according to their reported chief occupation (carpenter, salesman, etc.), or, if unoccupied, by their most recent type of employment. The 1920 census total in the occupational classification is increased here by the addition of 642,000 domestics (derived from the industrial classification) to make it more nearly comparable with the 1930 total. The distribution of the working population by *industry* in 1920, 1930, and 1940 is given below in Table 40, and in greater detail for 1930 in Table 41.

b Also excludes any service personnel classified in an undefined miscellaneous category amounting to 4% or less of the total labor force in each year.

It is reasonable to conclude, nevertheless, as this table suggests, that Japan's economic development brought a large rise in employment (and product) in the service occupations. The figures themselves indicate a threefold increase from 1880 to 1930, with an advance from 10% to 25% in the proportion of the labor force finding its chief occupation in these tertiary employments. Whether or not the pre-1920 figures are worth much, one may reasonably infer that there was already in progress the trend revealed by the later interwar censuses.

From 1920 to 1930 a gain of 2.4 million occurred in the total

changes to the 1920 census more or less evenly over the intervening years. Similar estimates for early Meiji years appear elsewhere; for example, figures for 1873 and 1876 are quoted in E. B. Schumpeter, ed., *The Industrialization of Japan and Manchukuo, 1930-1940*, New York, 1940, p. 65. It is possible, of course, that Hijikata's base-line data for the early years are better than his extrapolations.

number of people who reported themselves gainfully occupied (though they might have been wholly or partly unemployed on the date of the census). The bulk of the increase appears to have been absorbed in the service occupations. In private education, medicine, law, and religion the number rose from 622,000 to 752,000; in civilian government administration (excluding State-owned enterprise) from 335,000 to 436,000; in hotel and restaurant employment from 714,000 to 1,161,000; and in trade from 2,108,000 to 3,255,000. The decade of the thirties, with its industrial boom, considerably modified this trend. The 1940 census registered the principal gains in manufacturing and the armed forces. The civilian labor force increased 3.1 million over 1930, but civilian services (industrial classification, excluding domestics) absorbed only 828,000, as against 2,300,000 drawn into industry. (See below, Table 40.) Yet the secular drift of civilian employment away from the extractive industries was only accelerated. (For further discussion, see below, Chapter 9.)

In this expansion Colin Clark finds verification of the fact that economic progress, in Japan as elsewhere, has induced a progressive shift of resources out of the primary industries and into the services as well as manufacturing.[61] No doubt this is true. As evidence of such progress, however, labor force figures like those above must be used with caution. For economic growth meant specialization of functions. And increasingly such services as transport, selling, and finance, once performed extensively by farmers or handicraft workers as subsidiary functions, now came to be separated out as specialized occupations. Once a farmer might borrow from another farmer; now he was more likely to borrow from a bank or cooperative society. Once he might transport and market his own product, if he did not consume it himself; now an increasing share was marketed at a distance and handled by merchants, banks, and railways. Once food processing and amusements were largely confined to the home; now they developed as large commercial occupations. Thus, institutional groupings like transport and trade tend to gain in relative importance in the occupational statistics more rapidly than the actual functions themselves. The growth in the former exaggerates the growth in the latter.

There is a second reason why the rise of employment in the services is a less satisfactory index of economic progress in Japan than

[61] *The Conditions of Economic Progress,* cited, p. 122. "Studying economic progress in relation to the economic structure of different countries, we find a very firmly established generalization that a high average level of real income per head is always associated with a high proportion of the working population engaged in tertiary industries" (pp. 6-7).

in most Western countries. For in part it simply reflected the pressure upon limited employment opportunities in other fields. Population growth was pushing large numbers of people into food peddling, ricksha pulling, domestic service, and other stopgap occupations for want of any more skilled and permanent employment. Clark finds the share of total employment offered by the service industries "inexplicably high" in prewar Japan by comparison with other industrial countries.[62] Also, his figures on the United States, Great Britain, and other countries show income per occupied worker to be rather large in this field compared with manufacturing, while in Japan it is not. Clark was working with limited materials on Japan, and his calculations are open to question on a number of counts. Even so, it would not be surprising if per capita productivity in a large share of the Japanese service trades, relative to other industries, was considerably lower than in most Western countries, owing to the expanding number of workers forced into unskilled and low-paid services in the absence of suitable alternatives.

The recorded shift of employment to the services, therefore, cannot be taken entirely as a sign of growth and maturity. In such occupations as retail commerce, it helped to preserve the primitive organization, the underemployment, and low per capita output long characteristic of these trades throughout the Orient.

National Income and Living Standards

What summary conclusions may be drawn concerning the rate of expansion in the Japanese economy, considered as a whole?

The best criterion is the over-all growth in net national product, i.e., the annual flow of goods and services produced in Japan for consumption and new investment, after allowance for materials, fuel, and capital assets used up in the process of production. This measures the objective income of labor and capital employed in economic activity, except for changes in the terms on which exports are exchanged for imports, and certain other qualifications. In practice, of course, any quantitative expression of such income has to be confined to that part which can be measured in money. This rules out significant elements in economic welfare (e.g., job security), and raises troublesome questions on the borderline between goods and services sold for money and others which are self-supplied within the family or by the community through its government.

To arrive at any satisfactory measure of real product is a difficult undertaking, particularly in a country still passing through the early stages of industrialism and capitalism. It is impossible at best to give any very meaningful expression to "average" changes

[62] *ibid.*, pp. 182, 342.

in various categories of activity over a long period of time. Both the components and the techniques of production underwent radical changes in prewar Japan. There were also wide fluctuations in prices, as well as differences from one locality to another in the level and movement of prices. These must be allowed for in some fashion to arrive at real values of net output. Moreover, the gaps and deficiencies in Japanese statistics are so serious, especially before 1920, that one has to resort to crude techniques of estimation which permit a very wide range of error at best. Some will question, indeed, whether the concepts of national income measurement have much applicability where economic activity is still so largely carried on within the household, where the functions of commodity production and various services are often so intermingled in the livelihood of families and individuals, and where even commercial markets for goods, labor, and capital are as localized as they were in Meiji Japan.[63]

It is interesting, nevertheless, to see what conclusions emerge from Japanese investigations in this field. By far the most comprehensive inquiry yet published is that of Prof. Yuzo Yamada, of Hitotsubashi University, in *Nihon Kokumin Shotoku Suikei Shiryō*, Tokyo, 1951.[64] Drawing on previous studies, and utilizing such data

[63] See Harry Oshima, "The Price System and National Income and Product," *The Review of Economic Statistics*, vol. xxxiii, no. 3, August 1951, pp. 248-54.

[64] In 1930 the first systematic official investigation of national income was conducted by the Imperial Cabinet Bureau of Statistics, and published in *Shōwa Go-nen Kokumin Shotoku Chōsa Hōkoku*, Tokyo, 1933. The CBS estimate for 1930 was revised and projected through the years 1931-39 by the U.S. Office of Strategic Services, and the results published by the U.S. Department of State in *National Income of Japan*, Washington, 1945. Other estimates for the thirties have been made by the Japanese Economic Stabilization Board, the Japan Economic Federation, the *Oriental Economist*, the Mitsubishi Economic Research Bureau, and several individuals.

For pre-1930 years Yamada's inquiry is by far the most extensive, though much more limited in scope and reliability than the CBS estimate for 1930. Previously the only investigation utilizing extensive data over a period of years was S. Hijikata's *Kokumin Shotoku no Kōsei*, Tokyo, 1933, covering the period 1919 and thereafter. With much more limited information Hijikata also computed annual income totals for the years 1900-1918 (pp. 389-90). His figures are below those of Yamada's, especially in the earlier years, and show a more rapid rate of growth.

Other independent estimates are either scattered single-year computations like those of T. Nakamura (1900), C. V. Sale (1907), and Colin Clark (1887, 1897, 1908) or annual series computed mainly from income tax returns. In this latter category are Shiomi's estimates of "national income" for 1903-19 (*Archiv für Sozialwissenschaft und Sozialpolitik*, vol. liii, 1925, pp. 141-85) and a CBS series for 1887-1925 (see K. Mori in *Bulletin de l'Institut International de Statistique*, vol. xxi, part 2, pp. 179-204). Shiomi's figures are confined to taxable income, a changing fraction of total income. The CBS likewise uses this very unreliable basis for extrapolating back through the years a 1925 income estimate, with the result that it heavily understates national income in the earlier decades.

Similarly untrustworthy are the annual estimates of F. Barret for 1900-1934 in *L'Evolution du Capitalism Japonais*, vol. iii, Paris, 1946. Barret's data are grossly

as are available, Yamada presents a series of detailed estimates covering the entire period from 1875 to 1949.

Growth of National Product (Yamada Estimates). Yamada's summary estimates of national product in Japan, at constant prices, are given in Table 12 for the years 1883 to 1937. The author himself acknowledges their provisional character. Without entering here upon a long critique, we may note several of the chief questions.[65] In so doing I should like to pay tribute to Professor Yamada's valiant effort to grapple with the problem and advance the frontier of historical national income studies in his country.

First, the use of a general price index of commodities at wholesale to eliminate changes in the value of money is quite unsatisfactory for all of these series, especially service incomes. (See Table 12, note a.) Since wholesale commodity prices in city markets doubtless rose more rapidly from 1885 to 1920 than the general buying power of the yen depreciated, one broad tendency is to minimize unduly the growth in real output through this earlier period. Conversely, wholesale prices fell somewhat more sharply from 1920 to 1930, so that this deflator exaggerates the actual expansion of net product during the twenties. Even in the commodity sectors one questions how adequately Tokyo prices reflect changes in regional and local markets.

Second, a considerable amount of unrecorded output produced and consumed within the peasant household economy is probably omitted, particularly in the early years. This includes fish, seaweed, and vegetables; charcoal and other forest products; clothing and household utensils of wood and straw; fertilizer; buildings; land improvements; etc. On this score Yamada's figure for commodity output during the eighties at current yen values possibly should be raised by 10%, perhaps more.

Third, net product in each commodity sector rests on estimated ratios of net to gross income which are less trustworthy the further back they are carried.

Fourth, no allowance can be made for sweeping changes in the quality of many goods and services brought about by industrialization. On this score there is probably considerable unrecorded gain in the later decades with the improvement of skills and methods made possible by science, machinery, and large-scale organization.

Finally, the whole computation of service incomes before 1920 (as

inadequate, his concepts are confused, and obvious errors and omissions cast doubt on his whole computation.

[65] I am indebted to an unpublished memorandum by Harry Oshima, of the United Nations Secretariat, for an appraisal of the Yamada figures on these and a number of additional points.

well as workshop production) ·rests on a shaky foundation. It consists in multiplying estimated per capita income in this sector by employment, both of them calculated from quite inadequate data. As remarked earlier (page 129), estimates of labor force in pre-1920 Japan, and still more of employment, are of dubious reliability

Table 12. *Yamada Estimates of Net National Product of Japan Proper, 1883-1937 (in 1928-32 Prices)*[a]

| Annual Average | Aggregate Net Product (millions of yen) | | | | Per Capita Net Product (yen) | |
	Total	Agriculture, Forestry, Fishing, and Mining[b]	Manufacturing[b] (and Construction)	Services[c]	Per Capita, Total Population	Per Capita, Gainfully Occupied
1883-87	2,854	920[d]	513	1,421	74	132
1893-97	4,114	1,410[d]	877	1,827	98	170
1903-07[e]	4,584	1,921	967[f]	1,696	98	175
1908-12	5,593	2,218	1,283	2,092	112	208
1913-17	6,344	2,310	1,748	2,286	119	233
1918-22	8,085	2,768	2,283	2,750	144	297
1923-27	10,247	2,654	3,085	4,568	171	360
1928-32	11,931	2,672	3,927	5,334	186	402
1933-37	14,926	3,141	5,329	6,483	216	475

a Net product estimates are from Yuzo Yamada, *Nihon Kokumin Shotoku Suikei Shiryō,* Tokyo, 1951, p. 130, except that per capita product (total population) is calculated here from "*de facto*" population figures (above, Table 2). To compute net product in manufacturing and services, Yamada places extensive reliance on estimates of gainfully occupied persons before 1920 by S. Hijikata and thereafter on decennial national censuses. (See his Appendix Table I.) For the serious deficiency of these figures as a measure of actual employment see above, page 129; also Chapter 9 below.

Yamada's concept is net income produced within Japan, without correction for the net balance of investment income and labor earnings remitted between Japan and overseas areas. Current yen values are converted to values at 1928-32 annual average prices by means of a simple average of wholesale commodity prices only. (Appendix Table II.) Throughout most of the period he used a Bank of Japan index which is an unweighted arithmetic average of monthly price relatives for fifty-odd commodities in Tokyo. This poorly constructed deflator is ill suited to each category of output, and especially services, both because of the selection of commodities it comprises and because Tokyo prices are apt to deviate from prices in other parts of the country, notably rural areas. A cost-of-living index would probably be better, though still unsatisfactory; in any case it is not available except for the later years.

b Income produced in the commodity sectors is computed largely by applying net income ratios to gross product estimates. It is intended to represent net product at market prices, including indirect taxes. Rather crude assumptions are made; for example, an unvarying net/gross ratio of 40% is applied to factory output prior to 1930, despite the great changes in industrial structure. (Pp. 48-49, 126-27.) In workshop industry the ratio is put at 60% before 1900 and 55% thereafter. Gross product in these small plants from 1896 to 1933 is estimated by multiplying estimated employment here by 40% of gross product per worker in factory industry (the 1930 ratio). From 1886 to 1894 it is assumed to be one and one half times total factory gross product. (Pp. 48-54.) In agriculture, a fluctuating net/gross ratio is computed.

It rises from 82% in 1883-87 to 88% in 1893-97, and then declines to 70% in 1933-37, reflecting mainly heavier expenditure for commercial fertilizer (pp. 28-29). Probably a considerable quantity of farm produce, wood fuel, and handicraft manufactures, as well as fishery and mineral output, is omitted in the earlier decades, thus exaggerating the real rate of long-term growth. (See note d.)

c Lacking sales and income figures for many of the service trades before 1930, Yamada begins with average net income per gainfully occupied person in all such trades in 1930 (650 yen), and extrapolates this figure through the years before 1919 by a geometric average of changes in wholesale commodity prices and wages. The resulting series is multiplied by estimated employment in these trades to get net product aggregates (pp. 58-60, 114-18, 124-30). From 1919 on, reliance is placed largely on more direct evidence of incomes. The logic of the former method is certainly open to question, and the employment figures are no less problematical. (See note a, above.) Income from services shows an improbable rise in relation to other incomes during the twenties, probably because of these statistical difficulties.

d Fishery and mining output is omitted altogether in these earlier years. Its inclusion would raise the figure for agriculture, etc. to over 1,000 million yen in 1883-87, and to 1,500 million yen or more in 1893-97. The total and per capita product series in these years would accordingly each be increased by at least 4%.

e It is very implausible that net output should have increased only 10% in manufacturing from 1893-97 to 1903-07, and in services actually declined.

f Given erroneously in Yamada's final tables (pp. 128-30) as 767 million yen. (See pp. 126-27.)

owing to the lack of accurate census figures, and the large but unrecorded amount of part-time employment (e.g., of farmers' wives) in agriculture, household industry, etc.

For these reasons no precise significance can be attached to the figures of Table 12. Yet they do support, and are supported by, the other evidences of physical growth cited in the foregoing pages. In a rough fashion they can be taken to represent the persistent tendency to expansion which characterized the Japanese economy over this half century after 1885. The aggregate product series is probably closer to the truth than its component series, for the reason that some of the errors and biases in the latter tend to cancel each other. The direction and rate of change of the aggregate series are something like what one would expect from many known facts: the increase in population, the rapid accumulation of capital, the application of science and machinery to the productive process in many industries, the gain in fuel and power consumption, the expansion of buying power in home and foreign markets, the slow rise in living standards, and the building up of armament and war potential. All of these developments, taken together, testify to some such sustained growth in aggregate product and income as is depicted here.

In the light of this supporting evidence, certain broad conclusions may be stated with reasonable assurance.

Japan's productive powers increased rapidly and continuously in the seventy years following the Meiji Restoration. The aggregate increase, as suggested here, was fourfold from 1885 to 1935. This is an annual rate of nearly 3.3%. According to Yamada's figures, real income produced within the country nearly doubled in the quarter century before 1910. It then doubled again during World War I and the postwar decade. In the boom of the thirties the index climbs another 50%.[66]

While the statistics themselves are open to question, for all the reasons stated above, it is not implausible that the over-all expansion of Japanese output approached some such magnitude as this. As would be expected, the total product series falls in between the slower advance of primary production and the more rapid gains in manufacturing and large-scale transport. As would be expected, too, the net value of output in primary production gains more slowly after 1910 than the physical output series of Table 3. Gross production increases were achieved only by heavier use of fertilizer and of other intermediate products in fishing and mining.

Meanwhile the population of the country rose from 39 million in 1885 to 69 million in 1935. Yamada's figures therefore imply a per capita increase of 150 to 200% in net output. One hesitates to put much faith in the estimates of gainful employment for reasons already stated. Per worker, however, it might be safe to say that industrialization brought a cumulative gain of at least 200% in average net product over fifty years. Yamada's index itself actually advances at a rate of 2.6% a year. (All such calculations, even with accurate statistics, are subject to the qualifications mentioned earlier

[66] Certain revisions of Yamada's estimates by his Hitotsubashi University colleagues Shigeto Tsuru, Kazushi Ohkawa, and others have come to my attention too late for scrutiny here. In their latest version they are summarized in Ohkawa's "A Note on 'Long Term Changes in the National Product of Japan,'" *The Annals of the Hitotsubashi Academy*, vol. III, no. 2, April 1953, pp. 164-78.

Ohkawa's revision suggests that Yamada understated rather than overstated the growth of national product in Japan over fifty years. Aggregate net product in the goods sector is not radically changed. When deflated for price changes it is 13% above Yamada's figure for 1883-87; thereafter it is 5 to 15% below because of consistently lower estimates for manufacturing. The principal change is a more rapid rise in service incomes, beginning from much lower levels. While some revision in this direction is plausible, and the new mode of computation is more logical, the resulting estimate for the services is still very questionable in its basic data and assumptions.

The new series show a more substantial rise in national product than does Table 12, largely because of the new services estimate. Deflated to 1928-32 values by an index of wholesale prices, Ohkawa's figures are as follows in millions of yen (pp. 176-77):

| | NET NATIONAL PRODUCT | | | NET NATIONAL PRODUCT | |
	Total	*Services*		*Total*	*Services*
1883-87	1,784	548	1918-22	7,087	2,851
1893-97	2,845	850	1923-27	9,081	4,314
1903-07	3,886	1,292	1928-32	12,089	6,151
1908-12	4,813	1,736	1933-37	14,564	6,990
1913-17	5,554	2,051			

as to the meaning of any such summary expression of myriads of divergent changes.) Most of the increase in aggregate output, in other words, is attributable to the rise in the unit efficiency of labor, not merely to the greater input of labor. To this point we return again in Chapter 4.

It is interesting that Yamada's data show no tendency for the rate of expansion in national income to taper off over the fifty-year period. This is true even if the boom of the thirties is discounted so as to allow for the deterioration which took place in the terms of international trade. The persistency and continuity of economic growth in prewar Japan suggests that her achievement in this respect is to be compared with that of Western industrial nations in their earlier (and most recent) periods of growth, rather than in their experience between the two World Wars. Despite the contrast in objective circumstances, the analogy is rather with Britain from 1810 to 1860, or the United States and Germany during the next half century, when great lands and resources were being opened up to exploitation and settlement.

Japan's good fortune in escaping the ravages of the first European war—even profiting handsomely from it—and her success in freeing herself quickly from the constrictions of the Great Depression, have much to do with her rather impressive showing in any international comparisons of secular growth in income, trade, and production since 1900. Her rapid expansion from 1914 to 1936, while the Western industrial world wrestled with war dislocations and unemployment, had extensive repercussions both upon the world balance of power and upon industrial competition in world markets. The decade of the forties, and perhaps that of the fifties, is another story. For the first time in their modern history, the Japanese involved themselves in a military struggle which dealt shattering blows to their domestic economy, and helped destroy the foundations of international trade upon which they had built their prosperity.

Income and Consumption. If these statistics of growth are anywhere near the truth, this half century of industrialization brought a marked reduction of the pressure of population upon resources in Japan, by comparison with anything known previously in Japanese history.

Much confusion has been displayed over this question of population pressure in Japan. The term is an ambiguous one. Sometimes it is used in the psychological sense to refer to the degree of well-being, of satisfaction or dissatisfaction, which a people find in their existing plane of living or in their anticipations of the future. In these subjective terms, it becomes impossible to measure. But it is not less important for that reason. Whatever their past or present condition, a people may become increasingly discontented with what they have, or may fear they are about to lose it. Or they may become resentful that others have still more. Paradoxically, the grievances within modern society have grown with its comfort. Only in this way can one explain how so many Japanese allowed themselves to be persuaded that economic necessities drove them to war in the years 1937-41, at the very climax of a period of prosperity unprecedented in their history.

In objective terms, however, population pressure has no meaning except as measured by the existing plane of living—the actual consumption of goods and services. It is a matter of the size of incomes, their distribution, and their stability. In the broadest sense it includes the supply of free and social services (e.g., education and medical care), the amount of leisure, and the working conditions of the population. It cannot be expressed as a mathematical ratio between people and land. Still less is it correlated with national dependency or self-sufficiency in food supply. It is a function of all the geographic, social, and technical circumstances affecting the production of goods and services and their distribution in consumption and other uses.

Japan has remained heavily overpopulated throughout modern times, so far as economic welfare is concerned. Had there been fewer people, income per capita would have been higher, and probably more evenly distributed. (See Chapters 4 and 5.) Equally, however the pressure of population was being gradually relieved by the growth of income and wealth per person. This process went forward steadily with only temporary setbacks, until war destroyed the civilian economy after 1938 and produced an "overpopulation" crisis of first-rate magnitude.

Any definitive measurements of the rise in Japanese living standards after 1868 would require prolonged investigation. If this is the most important aspect of economic history, it is also the most difficult. Since 1926 Japan has had an excellent record of family budget studies, better than many Western countries.[67] One such study is examined at length in Chapter 8. Prior to that time, however, materials are fragmentary. One is forced to rely on wage statistics, on estimates of net national "disappearance" of a few staple commodities, or on the inconclusive testimony of individual observers whose personal acquaintance with Japanese life extends over a long span of years.

On the face of it, the meager livelihood of the masses of people

[67] Convenient summaries of these investigations will be found in the files of the *International Labour Review* during the prewar decade.

in Japan at the end of the prewar era, even the dire poverty of
millions of tenant farmers and unskilled workers, seems to challenge
the evidence offered above as to the expansion of national output.
How could a growth of such apparent magnitude have left most of
the population so close to the minimum of subsistence, as Westerners would regard it?

In considering this question, one must understand that only a
fraction of the growth in aggregate Japanese output went directly
into raising the plane of living of the mass of peasants and urban
workers from traditional, preindustrial levels. For this there are
several reasons. Some apply with special force to the case of Japan,
but mostly they are inherent in the problem of developing any
"backward area."

First, the increase in population operated as a heavy drag on the
rise in living standards. In fifty years the Japanese population
nearly doubled. This alone meant that a good deal of the net gain
in total production was absorbed simply in feeding, clothing, and
housing a greater number of people.[68] From evidence presented below, in Chapter 8, one may conclude that even in the later years as
much as half or more of Japan's total national income, and 75%
of the income of most households, had to be devoted to meeting these
basic wants of the swollen population in a very meager fashion.

Second, per capita changes in net product do not result in
equivalent changes in real income if exports no longer exchange
against imports on the same terms. For part of the national product
is not used at home, but exported in payment for imports, which
are the real income.[69] If the terms of exchange move unfavorably to
a country, real income in the form of consumption and net additions
to capital will fail to rise as much as output expands. This was true
of prewar Japan after 1928. In 1935-39 the import price index
stood at about the same level as in 1928-29, whereas the export
price level had dropped 30%. Here was one reason why the industrial boom of 1931-38 failed to bring larger benefits in consumption.
Japan lost a billion yen a year of real income (at 1930 prices)
from 1934 to 1938 through exporting as much as she did at the
prices then prevailing, by comparison with what she would have
enjoyed had she been able to purchase her 1934-38 imports at the

---

[68] The number of "consumer units" actually increased less than the total population, for the percentage of children increased. Also population growth itself may
have stimulated the growth of total production in some degree. (See below, Chapter 4.) However, these qualifications hardly affect the main argument. Offsetting
them is the fact that a high dependency ratio meant a high ratio of unproductive
persons in the population.

[69] Strictly speaking, it is the imports retained for domestic use, and not processed
for reexport, which constitute real income.

1930 terms of exchange. In other words, while net national product is estimated to have risen from 10 billion yen in 1930 to 16 billion in 1936 (at 1930 prices), 20% or so of this gain yielded no corresponding gain in real income to the country. (See above, pages 73-74.)

Third, some of the rise even in per capita income was more apparent than real during the prewar decades. For it represented goods and services which were required for urbanization and industrialization but did not actually increase real consumption from its earlier level. As cities grew, food and raw materials had to be hauled longer distances. As market organization became more elaborate, complicated structures of merchandising and finance had to be created. As industrialization proceeded, the needs for government services multiplied. All such activities gave employment and produced income in the national accounts. But they themselves did not directly raise living standards; in Simon Kuznets' phrase, they yielded only "intermediate" production. From a social viewpoint they are more properly reckoned as the costs rather than the gains of modern economic organization. This is quite aside from the point that some of the most serious human costs of industrialization fall entirely outside national income accounting—e.g., the disease and accident rates produced by city slums and poor factory standards.

Fourth, prewar Japan presented a picture of extremes of wealth and poverty. The broad base of the income pyramid comprised the great mass of peasants and urban workers whose family incomes in 1930 still fell below 800 yen. Numbering 10.6 out of Japan's 12.6 million families in that year, they received only half of the country's household income. At the top some 24,000 well-to-do families with incomes over 10,000 yen appropriated over 10% of aggregate family income. (See Table 23, below.)

Whether income and wealth were more or less unevenly distributed in 1880 than in 1930 we do not know. The destruction of feudal privilege after 1867 was soon followed by the creation of a new plutocracy on the foundations of the new capitalistic order. Attempts to measure the subsequent shifts in income distribution from tax statistics, using Pareto's formula, are not convincing, owing to the deficiencies in the statistics and in the formula itself. However, it is evident that the stock of productive wealth grew rapidly; that returns on property, relative to labor, remained high; and that a large share of property income tended to be concentrated in the upper tail of the income distribution curve. This does not mean that the wealthy, propertied class swallowed up all the gains of economic development, leaving the rest of the population where it was. Rent, interest, and profits together comprised only 25 to 30% of the national income in the thirties (excluding the property income accruing to entrepreneurs jointly with their income on labor). But a small segment of the population were able to appropriate far more than their per capita share of the aggregate growth in income. Large groups and regions of the country—the mass of the people— were at a marked disadvantage in sharing the fruits of economic progress. (See Chapter 5.)

Fifth, the Japanese economy was a dynamic one characterized by a high rate of savings and investment, compared with that of other Far Eastern countries. This meant that a significant part of annual net product—possibly 15% or more in the later boom years—was withheld from consumption and applied in building up the plant, equipment, and inventories of the country. (See Chapter 5.) Whether the share of income withheld from consumption for purposes of investment tended to grow as industrialization proceeded is now known; probably it did. Also a growing share of *gross* production went into replacing the wear and tear and depreciation of existing capital assets, as industry became steadily more capitalistic, and as agricultural yields were forced upward by heavier doses of fertilizer and careful preservation of the land. Through this process the production of consumer goods steadily increased. But the resources applied to capital formation were not immediately available for consumption purposes.

Finally, one must allow for the drain on living standards imposed by the costs of war, armament, colonies, and strategic industries. In what periods, and to what degree, these outlays may have been justified on political and military grounds need not be argued here. In economic terms, however, such expenditures, and the whole emphasis in national policy which they reflected, represented in the main a diversion of resources away from the production of goods and services for civilian use. To be sure, their net effect is sometimes exaggerated so far as the period before 1937 is concerned. Deficit financing of military expenditures from 1867 to 1893, and in each of Japan's three succeeding wars, tended to expand money incomes and productive activity. To some degree it "paid for itself," in the sense that it stimulated the fuller and more efficient utilization of resources. In the interwar periods, moreover, direct and indirect outlays for military purposes probably rarely exceeded 10% of national income. During war years, however, the burden ran much higher. And even in "normal" times, the military establishment was consistently an item of top priority in the national budget, absorbing 35 to 50% of national government expenditures from the Sino-Japanese War on. This severely handicapped expenditures for education, rural development, and other programs of social welfare which were sorely lacking in Japan and which only the government could undertake. (See below, pages 290-92.)

Rise in Consumption Levels. These various circumstances meant that only a part of the aggregate growth in income produced in Japan was actually available for raising the living plane of the population from the levels which prevailed in the early decades.

That the rise in consumption levels was substantial, nevertheless, there can be no doubt. For one thing, the mere disappearance of famines and epidemics on a great scale, as well as earlier practices of infanticide, is itself strong evidence. A Japanese male born in 1935, from the mortality experience of that year, could expect to live at least ten years longer than his grandfather born in the eighties.[70] He could hope to live twenty years longer than a Chinese boy of the same age. Medical science can now reduce the incidence of many diseases without great improvements in the standard of life in other respects. In the era here under review mortality was more closely related to levels of consumption and income. If Japan's standards of nutrition, housing, and medical care were still grossly inadequate, she had nevertheless attained by this time an enviable position in Asia. Mortality had dropped to the point where she was now to be classed with France, Spain, and Eastern European countries having "middle" death rates of 15 to 19. She no longer stood with most Asiatic countries, where the rate ran to 30 or more.[71]

Other evidence of improvement in the well-being of great masses of people in Japan may be found in national wage statistics. These statistics relate largely to industrial workers. Even here they are too unreliable to give more than a crude approximation of the change which took place, especially before 1914. They are worth examining, nevertheless, as they testify to the broad tendency of economic growth.

The best available index numbers of the average daily earnings of Japanese industrial workers, and their buying power, are pieced together and summarized in the following table (1914 = 100):[72]

[70] The official statistics of the Meiji era actually show a rise in the death rate. Rejecting these figures as spurious, because they are based on incomplete population registers, Irene B. Taeuber and Frank W. Notestein project as a "reasonable inference" a level of Japanese mortality in the 1880's at about the rate prevailing in Korea in 1926-30. "The Changing Fertility of the Japanese," *Population Studies*, vol. I, no. 1, June 1947, p. 10. The life expectancy of males at birth rose from 42.06 in 1921-25 to 46.92 in 1935-36. The latter was about the level in France, Germany, and Italy just before World War I. Irene B. Taeuber and Edwin G. Beal, "The Dynamics of Population in Japan," in *Demographic Studies of Selected Areas of Rapid Growth*, New York, 1944, pp. 16-17.

[71] "Food, Income and Mortality," *Population Index*, vol. 13, no. 2, April 1947, pp. 100-101.

[72] For the years prior to 1914 I have merely averaged daily earnings in twenty-

	Money Wages	Cost of Living	Real Wages
1895-99	(50)	(69)	(73)
1905-09	(84)	(91)	(92)
1914	100	100	100
1915-19	142	142	101
1920-24	302	212	141
1925-29	317	204	155
1930-34	284	163	174
1935-39	312	189	166

Real wage rates—the purchasing power of the average daily earnings of employed industrial workers—would appear from these statistics to have risen about 33% between the years 1897 and 1914. No great reliance can be placed on the data for this early period, as the wage information is scanty and the cost of living is expressed merely by certain commodity prices at wholesale. Retail prices certainly advanced less rapidly than wholesale commodity prices, however. If the two measures given here are at all representative, the buying power of industrial wages did not increase by less than one third, though this may seem a modest gain, considering that the worker's needs were also increased by urbanization and factory life.

More accurate is the estimate beginning in 1914. Over the next twenty to twenty-five years it would appear that real wage rates advanced 65 to 75% on the average in Japanese industry. Most of the rise occurred in the decade 1914-23, through the fact that money wages failed to decline after World War I in proportion to the fall in prices. The same phenomenon occurred again in the de-

---

seven to forty industrial (largely handicraft) and service occupations, and deflated them by a wholesale price index based on fifteen staple commodities. Data are from *Nippon Teikoku Tōkei Sōkan*, cited, pp. 939, 1108. Hijikata's wage index (Yamada, *op.cit.*, p. 154) shows money wages rising from 1885-89 to 1914 only 20% more than wholesale prices.

After 1914 the data are better. Money wages from 1914 to 1925 are represented above by the index of the Ministry of Commerce and Industry. This is based on the daily earnings of twenty-eight or more grades of skilled industrial workers in the factories (and a few handicrafts) of thirteen large cities in Japan. Included are all money wages and allowances, as well as payments in kind. Linked with this index in 1926 is the more reliable index of the Bank of Japan for factory industry. This is computed from the monthly wage bill (including all allowances except bonuses) in factories of forty to fifty workers or more, divided by total man-hours worked during the month. Thus it reflects not only changes in wage rates but also shifts in employment from one industry or type of labor to another. Uyeda's cost of living index for Tokyo industrial workers (*op.cit.*, p. 22) is used for the years 1914-33, and thereafter the index of the *Asahi Shimbun* for thirteen cities. Both of them employ weights derived from a 1926-27 family budget survey, and include services as well as commodities.

pression of 1929-32, but this gain was partly cancelled out during the inflationary boom which followed. While industrial employment revived after 1932, the depressed condition of Japanese agriculture retarded wage increases in industry. A growing share of manufacturing output went into plant expansion, armament, and payment for imports. Total manufacturing payrolls are of course a product of both wage rates and employment. In the twenty-five years after 1914 the buying power of aggregate payrolls in factory industry probably rose fivefold. In all manufacturing, including small workshops, it must have increased by something like 150%.

One would conclude from the above table that the average industrial worker in Japan was able to buy at least twice as much with his daily earnings in 1937 as he could have afforded in 1897. There was no "average worker," needless to say; and this limits the usefulness of any calculation which lumps together all men and women of various grades and skills employed in various branches of industry. Moreover, consumer needs and spending habits tended to change, so that any cost of living measure of this sort is an abstraction, too. Certainly the index does not measure welfare, which takes in other values as well. And some part of the rise, as previously remarked, represents the additional requirements of urban living, not an advance in well-being. Nevertheless, one finds here some corroboration of the slow improvement in the material position of the Japanese worker through the process of industrialization. In agriculture the advance was slower, especially in the more remote prefectures of the country; in particular industries it was more rapid.

As one would expect, the statistics suggest that the rise in real wages over half a century lagged far behind the rise in total national output, which now had to support a much larger population. For other reasons already mentioned the gain also falls somewhat short of the estimated rise in per capita product. In short, the relationship between the estimates in this respect is a reasonable one, which lends somewhat greater credibility to them both.[73]

Still more direct evidence of the advance in Japanese living levels can be found in the consumption per capita of staple foods, clothing, and other measurable items in family budgets. This, of course, must be judged against the traditional background of extreme poverty for all but the privileged few; also in terms of the

[73] Yamada, *op.cit.*, pp. 94-95, estimates the money value of per capita consumption in Japan from 1887 on. Deflated by the above cost-of-living index, his series shows the following rise (1914 = 100): 1895-99, 54; 1925-29, 132; 1935-39, 146. There is a twofold gain in forty years. Prior to 1930, however, Yamada concedes that his figures are very unreliable. Per capita consumption is merely extrapolated back from 1930 by reference to estimates of nontaxable money income per capita at the average ratio prevailing in 1925 and 1930.

frugality and simplicity of Japanese consumption habits down to the present day.

The food intake of the average Japanese appears to have risen appreciably in the forty or fifty years ending in 1930. It also became more diversified, especially among the urban classes. Rice consumption per capita seems to have risen about 25%.[74] In part this meant more calories, in part the preferred substitution of rice for barley, which is itself an index of a rise in income. At the end of this period the average Japanese was eating about a pound of rice a day, still depending on this staple for over half his diet, excluding fish, meat, and sugar. The intake of fats and proteins in the form of fish products increased more rapidly; official data—which should probably be discounted—record nearly a twofold gain in fish consumption per capita during the first three decades of the twentieth century.[75] There were also substantial increases in a good many lesser items—in sugar and salt, in wheat, soybeans, and fruit, and (on a very small scale) in meat and dairy products.

Food production and imports, according to E. F. Penrose's index, show a 20% increase in per capita food supply from 1910-12 to 1925-27 (disregarding exports, which were of minor importance).[76] This modest rise was made possible only by increasing imports from overseas. Similarly, growing imports of cotton and wool brought a concurrent rise of 40% or more in the domestic use of all clothing fibers per person.[77] Other diverse improvements in welfare now also became evident: the widespread use of electric lighting, which replaced the kerosene lamp, itself an earlier innovation; the

[74] Wen Yuh Swen and Carl L. Alsberg, *Japan as a Producer and Importer of Wheat*, Wheat Studies of the Food Research Institute, Stanford University, vol. VI, no. 8, July 1930, p. 377.

[75] John E. Orchard, *Japan's Economic Position*, New York, 1930, p. 18.

[76] *Food Supply and Raw Materials in Japan*, cited, p. 73. "On balance," says Penrose in another study, "the evidence points to increased per capita consumption of food, agricultural, fishery, and mineral products." *Population Theories and Their Application*, Stanford University, 1934, p. 122. For details on the rising consumption of food and other items in the period after 1914 see Kokichi Morimoto, *The Efficiency Standard of Living in Japan*, Tokyo: Japanese Council of the Institute of Pacific Relations, 1939; Egerton C. Grey, *The Food of Japan*, Geneva: League of Nations, 1928; and Teijiro Uyeda and Tosuke Inokuchi, *Cost of Living and Real Wages in Japan, 1914-1936*, Tokyo: Japanese Council of the Institute of Pacific Relations, 1936.

[77] Consumption of cotton goods in 1910-13 seems to have run around 140,000 metric tons a year in yarn equivalent. By 1930 it had reached 240,000 tons—a rise from 6 lbs. to 8 lbs. per capita. (Table 33.) Home consumption of the four clothing fibers—cotton, wool, silk, and rayon—increased from 150-160,000 tons to nearly 290,000 tons. (Yarn output minus exports plus imports of yarns and fabrics, with a correction in 1930 for changes in stocks.) Meanwhile the population rose from 51 to 64 million. Japanese consumption was still well below that of the more prosperous Western countries, but above that of most of Asia and the Near East. International Labour Office, *The World Textile Industry*, Geneva, 1937, vol. I, p. 168.

increase in postal traffic, railway passenger travel, buses, and bicycles; the tiled roof of the more prosperous farmer; the wool clothing and leather shoes now seen among middle-class men and boys; the spread of literacy and expansion of book and newspaper sales; the cheap Western-type gadgets of which the Japanese seem so fond.

During the decade after 1926, increased consumption of food and clothing materials just about kept pace with the growth of population, now at its full tide. Per capita intake of food remained at about 2,300 calories per day. Consumption of clothing materials averaged around 10 lbs. per year, rising slightly over the period. Such further gains as were recorded in living standards, before the wartime deterioration set in, seem mainly to have accrued in housing and household equipment; in travel, recreation, and education; and in other amenities which become attainable as a people rise from the subsistence level.

Finally, indirect evidence of the historical rise in Japanese consumption levels may be sought in international comparisons with Far Eastern nations which are still in the early stages of economic development. It is perhaps a fair presumption that the plane of living in early Meiji times was at best no higher than that of most other Asiatic peoples today, judged by some of the major indicators more or less common to all cultures. To be sure, such comparisons are difficult to make even under present-day conditions. Monetary comparisons are particularly elusive and ambiguous. And even limited tests of more "objective" nature become entangled in differences in cultural values and physical requirements. Yet testimony of this sort to the relatively favorable position attained by the Japanese in modern times may at least increase confidence in the more direct evidence of material improvements wrought by industrialization.

M. K. Bennett has made the most inclusive attempt to compare prewar consumption levels internationally by a series of non-monetary measures.[78] He selects sixteen indicators for thirty-one countries during the years 1934-38. They give a partial and admittedly crude basis for ranking these countries in their consumption of food, medical services, housing and clothing materials, education, recreation, mechanized transport, and communication. (Correctives are applied for climate, number of livestock units, and use of energy in manufacturing.) Each country is rated on each indicator in terms of the ratio of its per capita consumption to that of the leading country. These percentage relatives are then weighted after a

[78] "International Disparities in Consumption Levels," *American Economic Review*, vol. XLI, no. 4, September 1951, pp. 632-49.

fashion and combined to arrive at the country's ranking with respect to its general consumption level.

The position of Japan is interesting. In mechanical transport, telephones, and movies, she utilized less than 20% of the per capita services enjoyed by the leading Western nation, though more than any of her Asiatic neighbors. On the other hand, she exceeded 60% of the per capita standard of the leading nation in a number of more significant consumption measures: caloric diet, physicians per 1,000 population, availability of textile fibers, and school attendance. In combined score she ranked tenth among the thirty-one nations— well below half a dozen Western countries, about even with Italy and Cuba, and well above the Middle East and the rest of Asia. Her comparative position was as follows in the weighted aggregate of percentages (*ibid.*, p. 648):

United States	100	Philippines	22
United Kingdom	77	Egypt	18
Czechoslovakia	45	India	17
Japan	*38*	China	14
USSR	31	Netherlands Indies	12

The limitations of this computation are obvious. Bennett himself warns against attaching any precise significance to the aggregate scores. The indicators selected tend to be weighted against certain indigenous values of traditional Asiatic societies, and they take no account of the important factor of income distribution. It is inconceivable, however, that Japan could have attained this position unless her economic growth over seventy years had led to a substantial rise in consumption levels for her expanding population, beside providing for steady capital accumulation and a large military establishment.

For most of the Japanese people, nevertheless, the prewar plane of living remained far below the minimum requirements of health, comfort, and security, even by Japanese standards. On an income of 3 yen a day—the average earnings of an urban worker family in 1935-36—over a third of family expenditures still went for a simple diet of boiled rice, soybean soup, pickled radishes, and a few vegetables, and now and then some fish. The mass of small farmers managed to eke out an even more meager existence only by unremitting seasonal toil on the part of the whole family. The bare necessities of existence were leavened by only a few comforts, mostly of the traditional variety. If the peasant had won some security from great natural calamities and the harsh political oppression of feudal times, he was now exposed to the vicissitudes of a money economy and the demands of the landlord and moneylender. Standards of sanitation, education, and housing were still needlessly low, in the city as in the country. In factory legislation and social security services Japan lagged far behind modern democratic practice. Nor was this offset by the much advertised paternalism of the Japanese employer. The poor conditions of life and work in the great cities still took their toll in excessively high mortality among women of childbearing age; also among adult young men. Historically, these seem to be the implacable costs of industrialism in its raw, early stages. But there was now far less justification for such conditions in Tokyo and Osaka than, say, in Bombay or Shanghai.

These all too obvious facts of Japanese life have attracted widespread attention in the West, especially as they appeared to be directly contributory to the rapid inroads which Japan's export industries were able to make in prewar markets for textiles and other cheap manufactures. Often they have been allowed to obscure entirely the substantial advances in economic welfare achieved over preceding decades. For example, the following glib assertions by the editors of *Fortune* in 1936 are fairly typical: "Elsewhere in the world the industrial revolution has meant a general rise in the standard of living which has meant in turn a general increase in wage scales. . . . In Japan the industrial revolution has not meant a general rise in the standard of living. The agricultural half of the population, always too numerous to live fatly upon Japan's limited farmlands, has long been habituated to an existence of extreme frugality and has long possessed a communal life making that frugality endurable. Partly by government policy, partly by social habit, and partly by the sheer weight of its own numbers, it has been held not far above the level it knew three or four hundred years before the revolution. . . . The consequence is that Japan, outwardly industrialized maintains inwardly the life of a simple agrarian country. The further consequence is that her industrialization is an industrialization which must sell its goods abroad since her domestic market is incapable of buying her industrial products. The industrial workers of Japan live on one economic level while their goods sell on another."[79]

The sudden impact of Japanese competition in world markets in the thirties was attributable mainly to short-term dislocations of prices, wages, and exchange rates sketched briefly in Chapter 2. Basically, however, it was the rise of industrial efficiency in Japan which accounted for her growing strength in international competition, not any permanence or fixity in the Japanese standard of living. The living standard of the industrial worker, it is true, was based

[79] *Fortune*, vol. xiv, no. 3, September 1936, pp. 116, 118.

ultimately on that of the countryside. The peasant farm remained the great reservoir of low-wage labor and social conservatism. Yet even here, despite the backwardness of agriculture and the tenacity of the old social pattern, gradual changes were in process. Shiro Kawada, President of Osaka University of Commerce, while deploring the relatively low living standard of the peasant, wrote as follows in 1936: "It is hardly possible to deny that the agrarian standard of life has been raised to a much higher level than obtained formerly, for agricultural communities have had their share in the general increase in wealth experienced in the capitalistic age. As a matter of fact there is a considerable gap between the modern standard of rural life and that of the feudalistic period, or even between the present standard and that of the periods preceding the Sino-Japanese War and the Russo-Japanese War."[80]

There can be no doubt that the great expansion of Japan's productive powers had raised the general level of economic well-being appreciably above that of Commodore Perry's day, despite a doubling of the population. Japan had also emerged on the world stage as an aggressive, front-rank military power, soon to make a spectacular bid for dominion over East Asia. This also reflected the technical achievements of industrialization, as well as the social stresses, the insecurities, and the restless ambitions which all too frequently accompany the progress of modern industrialism.

[80] "The Income and Living Standards of the Agrarian Population in Japan," *Journal of the Osaka University of Commerce*, no. 4, December 1936, p. 13.

CHAPTER 4

TECHNOLOGY

FROM a description of the growth of Japan's productive powers after 1868 we turn now to a more analytical study of certain essential features of the growth process. Once that process was set in motion in Japan, it went forward with cumulative momentum and almost uninterruptedly for three generations. Evidently it was not confined to any single sector or aspect of economic life, but was an all-round affair characterizing the whole range of economic activity in varying degrees. Yet there is nothing inevitable or inexorable about the process of economic development, as shown by the resistances it encountered at numerous points in Japan, and its still more qualified progress in most other countries of Asia. If its main components can be established in the Japanese case, with their intricate interrelations, this may serve to illuminate not only the Japanese experience, but also the opportunities and problems faced by other nations emerging from similar backgrounds.

Of capital importance to Japan was her opening to contacts with the outside world, and her eager grasp of the opportunities which appeared. What followed within the country, indeed, can be described in large measure as a long wave of response to those impulses from abroad. One must be wary of assigning too much importance to the international aspect, however. Other countries similarly exposed, and sometimes with far more foreign assistance, have often failed to respond in the same degree. Also, the process of change and growth spread far beyond those sectors of economic life involved more or less directly in foreign trade. And at every point it was conditioned by the country's social and political traditions, as well as its natural endowment. These inherited circumstances influenced the rate and direction of developments in the domestic economy, which reacted in turn on its trading and financial relations abroad.

The economic history of Japan, as of all nations, thus reveals a complex interaction of physical resources, human aptitudes and ambitions, and the external opportunities afforded by the world of its time. No one of these factors can be assigned an exclusive or even predominant role. The historian's task is to search below the narrative of events, as set forth in Chapters 1 and 2, and beyond the statistical evidences of growth set forth in Chapter 3, to discover the forces at work. The chapters which follow examine the principal economic and technical conditions of that growth.

We begin with the central feature of the whole process, advancing labor efficiency. In this chapter, under the general heading of "Technology," the secular rise in productivity is considered in relation to population growth, changes in production technique, the widening of markets, and new forms of industrial organization. From this broad survey certain aspects are selected for more extended analysis. Chapter 5 deals further with the accumulation of capital through the institutions of savings and investment. Chapters 6 and 7 stress the role of overseas trade as a catalyst, feeder, and outlet for industrial expansion. Chapters 8 and 9 describe structural changes in the demand for and employment of resources as the condition and consequence of economic growth. A final chapter takes up more elusive issues respecting the underlying dynamics of Japan's economic development, particularly the role of the State in relation to economic enterprise.

Population and Economic Growth

One striking feature of Japanese economic development has been of course the sudden impulse to population increase. This appeared almost at once after 1868 and has persisted with little abatement down to the present day. Industrialization produced a demographic revolution of major proportions.

Like Germany in the seventeenth and eighteenth centuries, the Japan of latter Tokugawa times (1720-1850) seems to have had virtually a stationary population.[1] A population of 28 to 30 millions pressed close to the limits of subsistence afforded by the simple rice economy of her coastal plains and mountain valleys, with its restricted commerce and handicrafts, and the burdensome exactions of a feudal aristocracy. Further increase was checked by famine, earthquake, and flood, by malnutrition and disease, and by the widespread practice of abortion and infanticide.[2]

With the opening of the country to modern influences, this balance of births and deaths was dramatically overthrown. There set in a rapid growth in numbers which doubled the population in fifty to sixty years. (Table 2.) Thus the spurt of population brought on earlier in Western Europe by the Industrial Revolution was repeated here. In Japan, however, population growth took place under circumstances seemingly far less auspicious for surmounting its perils. First, the Japanese islands were a region already heavily populated in relation to their resources in land and minerals. Second,

---

[1] "Owing to the terrible sufferings of the seventeenth century the total German population in 1800 was perhaps no greater than it had been in 1600." J. H. Clapham, *The Economic Development of France and Germany, 1815-1914*, Cambridge, England, 1923, p. 32.

[2] Eijiro Honjo, *The Social and Economic History of Japan*, Kyoto, 1935, chap. 5.

their people now entered a world where the safety valve of emigration on a large scale was to be denied the yellow man. Third, the alternative of industrializing and modernizing economic life to care for growing numbers at a rising standard had to be begun from a level of productivity and incomes probably well below that enjoyed through much of Western Europe for centuries. The economic "surplus" thus available for investment in land, equipment, and education was comparatively meager except as greater restraint and self-denial were accepted by the masses.

One comparison alone is suggestive. The population of the United Kingdom also doubled between 1800 and 1860; that of Germany between 1830 and 1905. Until the Industrial Revolution, however, the normal density of population in Europe was only 100 persons per square mile. In England around 1600 it was actually about 88 persons. During the next two centuries it doubled, but still it was only 164 in 1800, though the country was even now becoming dependent on imported food.[3] Already in Japan at the time of the Meiji Restoration there were around 225 persons per square mile. By 1935 the figure had reached 469—in a chain of islands so mountainous that little more than 15% of the area can be regarded as cultivable. The contrast in the objective circumstances under which the Industrial Revolution with its accompanying demographic revolution has been approached by the sparsely peopled lands of the West and populous Asiatic nations like Japan suggests a difference not merely in degree, but almost in kind.

The dynamics of population growth in Japan need not detain us here, except to observe that in its essentials it followed the pattern already made familiar in the West.[4] Contrary to earlier interpretations, it is now believed that the Japan of 1868 shared the high fertility and mortality rates common to most preindustrial societies. As modernization proceeded, these rates underwent a marked decline, with the death rate falling earlier and more rapidly in response to improvements in food supply, sanitation, and medical care.[5]

A drop in fertility is also evident in more recent decades, mainly as a result of later marriages. The birth rate, however, was more

[3] Abbott Payson Usher, *An Introduction to the Industrial History of England,* Boston, 1920, pp. 89-90.

[4] A detailed reexamination of Japan's demographic experience in modern times is in preparation by Irene B. Taeuber, under the auspices of the Office of Population Research, Princeton University. I attempt nothing more here than to restate a few familiar facts.

[5] Official campaigns against abortion and infanticide may also have had some effect. See Ryoichi Ishii, *Population Pressure and Economic Life in Japan,* Chicago, 1937, pp. 31-37.

deeply rooted in the traditional cultural pattern of the Japanese peasant. It responded less readily than the death rate to the new influences. Significantly, one finds clear evidence of fertility control among married couples toward the end of the prewar era, but only in the larger cities.[6] And falling reproduction rates had failed as yet to slacken the rate of natural increase appreciably, because of the concomitant decline in mortality among females before and during the childbearing ages.

The net result was a growth in the total Japanese population from about 35 million in 1875 to 69 million in 1935.[7] Toward the close of the period the expansion was at full tide, adding nearly a million persons to the population every year.

This increase in numbers greatly influenced the rate and direction of Japan's economic development, including her relations with the outside world. Complex problems arise, however, when one tries to disentangle the demographic factor from other forces at work, to say just how it operated, and to what effect. For the consequences of a swarming population extended not merely to objective matters like the wage rate or the dependency ratio; they also include more subtle influences upon personal and family psychology, class relations, and national policy. The strains it imposed upon the social fabric and the fears it engendered regarding national food supplies contributed heavily to Japan's career of military expansionism. It had certain inevitable consequences in both economics and politics. But it had others which more intelligent leadership might have averted, or which occurred only because its significance was misinterpreted to serve special ends.

One obvious result of population growth was to double the number of claimants on the Japanese national income. This limited the popular gains from any given expansion of income, first by reducing the per capita share, and second by fostering greater inequalities in its distribution. Before concluding that greater numbers of people meant only more mouths to feed, however, one must ask whether the national dividend in goods and services was increased at the same time in greater or less proportion. For another consequence was to swell the aggregate supply of Japan's greatest productive asset, her manpower. The most significant economic is-

[6] See Irene B. Taeuber and Edwin G. Beal, Jr., "The Dynamics of Population in Japan," in Milbank Memorial Fund, *Demographic Studies of Selected Areas of Rapid Growth*, New York, 1944, pp. 22-32.

[7] At the end of the Tokugawa era the Japanese population is believed to have been around 30 million. For 1875 a none too reliable estimate by the Imperial Cabinet, Bureau of Statistics, puts the "actual" population at 35.6 million. *Shōwa Go-nen Ikō Waga Kuni no Jinkō*, Tokyo, 1930, pp. 3-5. Beginning in 1920 there are comparatively accurate estimates based on periodic census enumerations.

sue concerning the influence of a growing population upon economic development would appear to center around its effects upon consumption and distribution as compared with its effects upon the productive energies and capacities of the people.

Growth of the Labor Force. Whether the Japanese labor force or the actual amount of gainful employment grew more or less rapidly than the total population after 1868 we do not really know from reliable statistics. These concepts are difficult to define and apply even in a highly commercialized economy with advanced census techniques. For Japan any answer is complicated by the lack of a national census prior to 1920; by the wide prevalence of joint and part-time occupations; and by the immense but declining amount of productive labor devoted by farmers, industrial workers, and their families to goods and services for home consumption. Here, as elsewhere, the proportion of the population available for gainful employment has varied in response to changing circumstances. Shifts in the age distribution of the people altered the percentage found in the working ages. Slow modifications took place in social attitudes toward the employment of women and children, as well as in their gainful opportunities. Other changes resulted from the rise in per capita incomes, the relative decline of agriculture, and the new requirements of urban, industrial life.

The 1935 census showed 31.4 million people gainfully occupied in Japan, out of a total population of 69.2 millions. In the preceding fifteen years their number had risen some 4.1 millions, or 15.2%. But their ratio to the total population dropped from 48.7% in 1920 to 45.3% in 1935. For earlier decades such figures as are available show a still higher percentage of the people gainfully employed. For example, one Japanese authority puts the number at 19.9 million in 1880, or 55.3% of the total registered population.[8] These early estimates are unfortunately quite problematical.

[8] Estimate of S. Hijikata, published in *Shakai Seisaka Jihō*, September 1929, and quoted here from Yuzo Yamada, *Nihon Kokumin Shotoku Suikei Shiryō*, Tokyo, 1951, p. 152. The general tendency of Hijikata's annual labor force totals before 1920, linked with estimates thereafter from the official census, is indicated in the following:

Year	Total Population (thousands)	Gainfully Occupied (thousands)	Percent
1880	35,929	19,872	55.3
1900	44,826	25,308	56.5
1920	55,963	27,261	48.7
1935	69,254	31,400	45.3

The pre-1920 population estimates here are uncorrected registration figures. They are less accurate than the corrected series in Table 2, but are used here because they

Moreover, even were the statistics accurate, they would fail to measure changes in total man-years or man-hours, owing especially to shifts in the relative amount of part-time employment.

Despite these uncertainties, it is likely that the Japanese labor force did grow more slowly than the population. In other words, the ratio of dependents to workers tended to increase. For one thing, the proportion of the population under fifteen increased in the latter decades by virtue of the sharp decline in infant mortality. In 1884 the proportion was put officially at 31.6%; in 1930 at 36.6%.[9] At the same time educational standards improved, while minimum age laws also restricted child labor somewhat in factories and mines.

Apart from legislation, the growing technical maturity of Japanese industry itself tended slowly to discourage the employment of women, children, and older workers in certain trades. The lag of farm employment after 1920, as well as the transfer of industrial work from the household to the factory, limited the growth of employment opportunities for family dependents at home. Indeed, the census figures show an absolute decline from 1920 to 1930 in the number of gainfully occupied persons, both male and female, under fifteen and over sixty. Even the number of women in the more productive ages between fifteen and fifty-nine who were reported gainfully occupied increased only slightly. Their proportion to the total population in these age groups fell from 57.5 to 52.8% in a single decade.[10]

These figures do not prove much, it is true. The term "gainfully occupied" in the Japanese census can mean anything from a ten-hour day in a factory to spare-time assistance to a farmer or shopkeeper by his children, wife, or aged parents.[11] Furthermore, it is not

---

are believed to be those on which the Hijikata series for the working population is built. For further discussion of these figures, see Chapter 9.

[9] Tōyō Keizai Shimpō-sha, *Meiji Taishō Kokusei Sōran*, Tokyo, 1927, p. 636; Imperial Cabinet, Bureau of Statistics, *Shōwa Go-nen Kokusei Chōsa Saishū Hōkokusho*, Tokyo, 1938, pp. 202-03. The relative youth of the Japanese population in the later year explains the deceptively low ratio of workers per 1,000 population. At 46.0% in 1930 this was higher than the corresponding figure for the United States (39.8%) but about the same as that for the United Kingdom. If we compare populations aged fifteen and over, more than 90% of the men were gainfully employed in both Japan and Britain, but the percentage of women was 51.9% in the former as against only 34.9% in the latter. Ishii, *op.cit.*, pp. 82-84.

[10] *Shōwa Go-nen Kokusei Chōsa Saishū Hōkokusho*, cited, pp. 110, 113.

[11] It also includes some persons totally unemployed at the time of the census. However, the 1930 census reports only 320,000 unemployed, or 1.1% of the total number of persons "gainfully occupied." As 1930 was a year of business recession, this probably reflects a good deal of underreporting of unemployment. But it also indicates the tendency in Japan for persons losing their jobs in the cities to return to the rural family or to take up some relatively unremunerative, part-time employment in the traditional trades. In using the census figures to measure employment the more serious difficulty is this large, indeterminate, and fluctuating amount of part-time employment. See below, pages 463-64.

unlikely that underreporting of family labor on the farm and in the home tended to increase in the later years as such employment became less "respectable." Nevertheless, one would expect some such trend as living standards improved, as education spread, and as a decline set in in the relative amount of employment opportunity afforded by farming and home industry.[12] Other industrializing countries have likewise reported a fall in the proportion of women gainfully occupied—for example, Italy, Belgium, and Austria during the period 1900-1920.[13]

Possibly the Japanese labor force as a whole grew by no more than 65 to 75% from 1875 to 1935, while the population doubled. The published estimates suggest some such conclusion. Even this represents a large expansion of labor power. Moreover, the expansion was greatest in the most productive ages toward the end of the period. After 1920 the population in the age groups fifteen to sixty-four was increasing more than 500,000 a year, with about three out of four (men and women) desirous of some sort of gainful employment.

Emigration to the colonies and foreign countries siphoned off a small stream from this growing pool of manpower. But those who went overseas in search of civilian employment were mainly young men qualified for business, professional, and clerical work. They helped to relieve population pressure not so much by reducing the number of job-seekers at home as by developing markets and materials for Japanese industry. They also remitted home some of their profits and wages earned abroad. As for peasant emigration, most of the areas of the world favorable to agricultural settlement were closed to Japanese. Such northern regions as Sakhalin and Manchuria offered the farmer-emigrant little but isolation and hardship. By 1936 there were only 1.7 million Japanese civilians residing in the whole colonial empire, and hardly 1 million in foreign countries.[14] Manchuria had attracted less than 600,000, despite the colonization efforts of the government.

12 See, for example, Prof. T. Uyeda's comments in *Occupational Changes in Japan,* Tokyo Association for Liberty of Trading, 1934, pp. 9ff.

13 Marguerite Thibert, "The Economic Depression and the Employment of Women: I," *International Labour Review,* vol. xxvii, no. 4, April 1933, pp. 447-48.

14 The number of Japanese civilians resident overseas grew by migration and natural increase as follows, according to the official yearbook *Nippon Teikoku Tōkei Nenkan:*

Year	Japanese in Empire Areas (Including Kwantung Leased Territory and S. Manchuria Ry. Zone)	Japanese in Foreign Countries	Total Japanese Resident Abroad
1920	792,260	560,272	1,352,532
1936	1,673,277	997,115	2,670,392

Only briefly in the late thirties, when the Japanese Army began in earnest to construct its "Greater East Asia Coprosperity Sphere," did the removal of productive manpower from the domestic labor force either by military conscription or by emigration overseas reach substantial proportions.[15] Earlier the Empire had offered marginal opportunities to a few thousand venturous individuals every year. Even this was partially offset, so far as the *total* labor supply was concerned, by the influx of Korean workers to fill low-paid jobs in Japanese mines and industries. By 1930 there were already 385,000 Koreans resident in Japan, and a decade later almost a million.

It was at home, in Japan Proper, that the rapidly growing population in the productive ages had to find its livelihood in the main. Here the job frontier was predominantly an industrial and an urban one. No unfilled lands beckoned for colonization, except to a limited extent in the northern island of Hokkaido. Japan's entire cultivated area may have increased by one third or more from 1877 to 1937. But after 1900, when the figures become more accurate, the increase was only 15%. (See Table 2.) In this latter period the number of agricultural families increased no more than 5%, even including those engaged in farming as a supplementary occupation.[16] Almost the whole of the gain in the working population after the turn of the century had to be absorbed in nonagricultural pursuits, unless farming was to become even more overcrowded than it was.

Population growth thus transformed the country's labor force, not only by swelling its size but by requiring great numbers of people to seek new occupations and ways of living. Its most spectacular outward feature was the mushroom growth of cities after the turn of the century. Annual streams of migrants applied relentless pressure on city job markets, exceeded only by the pressure of the rural population on the land, from which young, able-bodied men and girls sought escape. By 1920 two out of three Japanese still lived in places of 10,000 or less; but thereafter growth took place mainly in urban areas, and especially in the great metropolitan centers of Tokyo, Osaka, Nagoya, Kyoto, and Yokohama. The growth of population and industrialization reacted upon each other to thrust increasing numbers of people into a milieu requiring patterns of family organization, economic behavior, and social outlook radically different from those of traditional Japan. On the other

---

[15] Asahi Shimbun-sha, *Nippon Keizai Tōkei Sōkan*, Tokyo, 1930, p. 688; Imperial Cabinet, Bureau of Statistics, *Nippon Teikoku Tōkei Nenkan*, cited, no. 58, Tokyo, 1939, p. 67.

[16] Concerning developments in this period see below, pages 464ff.

hand, the superabundance of manpower at cheap, unskilled levels operated itself to retard the acquisition of new skills and new values, which are implicit in the shift from peasant agriculture to industrial capitalism. The mode of industrial life into which the Japanese worker was projected by the conflicting pulls and pressures of the transition are sometimes expressed, not inaptly, in the term "urban peasant."

In Chapter 9 some further attention is given to the changes which resulted in the distribution of the labor force. There, also, certain aspects of the process of structural change are emphasized, especially the unusual degree of occupational, social, and geographic mobility displayed by the Japanese in responding to new economic opportunities.

Here we shall continue only with one broad question. If the growth of population was itself a result of the industrialization process, did it also furnish a major stimulant? Was the rapid increase in numbers after 1868 itself one of the dynamic factors in Japan's economic development? More specifically, what would have happened had the gap between high fertility and declining mortality been sufficiently narrowed by the practice of family limitation so that in the prewar decades the population advanced only to 50 million, say, rather than 70 million?

Population and Industrial Efficiency. Not infrequently one encounters the argument that rapid population increase was one of the chief expansive forces in the over-all growth of the Japanese economy. This argument takes various forms. Economists have maintained that a sustained and rapid increase in a country's population can sometimes exert a generally stimulating effect upon production, by itself enlarging the demand for goods and services and encouraging the fuller and more efficient utilization of resources. Sociologists also have suggested that it may create a psychic milieu conducive to greater personal industry and frugality, a more aggressive search for economic opportunity, and more flexible processes of social change than would otherwise prevail.

In the case of Japanese industrialization an even more direct causative role is often assigned to the demographic factor. It is sometimes said that the growth of the labor force beyond the limited absorptive capacities of agriculture *forced* Japan to industrialize. At the same time it facilitated the process by giving her industries the competitive advantage in international competition of an almost inexhaustible supply of low-paid workers. Because labor was so plentiful, and wages so low, the domestic accumulation of industrial capital out of profits was rapid, while abroad Japanese manufacturers were able to capture large markets for their cheap wares. The rapid rise of capitalistic industry, and especially its success in foreign trade, are ascribed in no small measure to Japan's expanding reservoir of low-wage labor.[17]

One obvious difficulty with such arguments is that economic growth on a comparable scale has failed to take place in many other countries of Asia whose populations also increased rapidly and were no less necessitous. The difference between Java and Japan, for example, is hardly to be explained on demographic grounds.

No doubt the mere pressure of numbers in Japan operated in some respects to break down traditional modes of peasant life and outlook which stood in the way of industrialization. But in other respects it served to perpetuate them, as it has throughout Asia. One questions whether any gains on this score could have offset the manifest disadvantages of overpopulation in terms of the more objective conditions of economic progress. Those types of energy and capacity which count in economic development were probably not greatly stimulated by the marginal increment of 15 to 25 million people who crowded the Japanese islands and had somehow to be supported. Quite possibly, even the aggregate scale of Japan's economic growth, as well as the share of her resources which came to be devoted to nonagricultural pursuits, could have advanced no less rapidly had her population increased more slowly and her manpower been less abundant—and with far greater benefits to the mass of her people. The reasons may be worth elaborating, since this issue is of such importance in other Asiatic countries with ambitions to industrialize.

Put in the simplest terms, population increase was a deterrent to Japanese industrialization insofar as it retarded the rise in per capita incomes. No country industrializes rapidly merely because it has great masses of poverty-stricken people in search of industrial employment. For one thing, a market is lacking. At the subsistence level families must spend their incomes almost wholly on food and other bare necessities produced mainly in the extractive occupations. (See Chapter 8.) The simplest food requirements are apt to absorb 60 to 70% of family budgets. Only as incomes rise can demands in the form of consumption and investment outlays be directed increasingly toward a wider variety of manufactures and services, thus supporting industrial diversification.

Nor is the logic of industrial expansion built upon the foreign market different in the main. A smaller population in the Japanese

[17] Although by no means confined to Marxist writers, this thesis is elaborated by F. Barret in *L'Evolution du Capitalisme Japonais*, vol. III, Paris, 1946. Barret goes so far as to pin the responsibility for population growth itself on the Japanese capitalists. They deliberately discouraged birth control and emigration, he says, in order to create a limitless supply of industrial labor forced to work at starvation wages. (Pp. 221ff.)

islands would not require such large imports of overseas rice and other living necessities. But if it made possible higher per capita incomes, one would expect larger demands for other consumer goods and services from abroad, or for the materials and equipment entering into their domestic production. There is no reason to assume that the aggregate demand for imports to be utilized in Japan would have grown less rapidly under these conditions. It was this demand which furnished foreign countries in turn with the bulk of their yen funds used to purchase Japanese industrial exports.[18]

Evidently the issue turns mainly on how population increase affected the ratio of gainfully occupied workers to their family dependents, and the efficiency of the labor force in the broad sense. The increasing dependency ratio in Japan as an economic burden—35% or more of the population under age fifteen—has already been noted. The "effectiveness of labor"—to borrow Taussig's term—is a function of the capacities and aptitudes of the working population at various levels of skills, the efficiency of economic organization, and the amount and quality of capital resources. These are the factors which are decisive for industrial progress, and they operate no less in a country's external relations than in its internal development. Lionel Robbins observes that the Industrial Revolution came more rapidly in England than elsewhere, and at an earlier date, not because labor was relatively plentiful but because it was scarce.[19] British manufacturers accordingly were induced to turn to machinery as a substitute. The United States more recently has gained great industrial markets abroad despite her still higher wage level and her dearth of unskilled labor.[20] Similarly, Japan, in both her

[18] This argument passes over many influences upon the composition and direction of foreign trade arising from variations in the distribution of income, savings ratios, capital transfers and other elements in the balance of payments, etc. Perhaps the chief qualification of significance here relates to the share of Japanese overseas trade which took the form of processing imported materials for reexport. Trade of this type is less dependent on the level of income than is the exchange of exports for imports destined directly or indirectly for home consumption. Its importance for Japan, especially in cotton textiles, is discussed in Chapters 6 and 7.

[19] "The Dynamics of Capitalism," *Economica*, vol. vi, no. 16, March 1926, pp. 37-38. Professor Lillian Knowles summarizes the circumstances in Britain in terms which might also be applied in good part to Japan a century later: "The coming of machinery in the textiles was due to a growing demand at home, large markets abroad, a scarcity of hands which made it necessary to employ mechanical devices if those markets were to be filled, large accumulations of capital which enabled men to try experiments, the knowledge of how to cater for markets in every part of the globe, freedom to take advantage of those markets and political security to enjoy the fruits of enterprise." *The Industrial and Commercial Revolutions in Great Britain during the Nineteenth Century*, London, 1933, pp. 28-29.

[20] Technological advances in the high-wage exporting industries of the United States can create problems for European competitors not unlike those created by Japan. Ironically, *The Statist* in 1949 reported that in Britain "textile men in their

trading relations with her Asiatic neighbors and those with the West, offers abundant evidence that low wages do not necessarily mean low competitive costs, or vice versa.

Despite the abundance of workers seeking employment in Japan, there has always been a shortage of labor in the grades and skills necessary to industrialization. This has been true especially of technical and organizing abilities at the higher level. As a result these skills have commanded a high premium over the general wage level. But even industrial labor of suitable grades is a matter of a certain general level of education, of technical experience, and of willingness to accept the terms and conditions of factory life. Its supply in Japan has never been readily elastic over short periods. This difficulty plagued her war mobilization and industrial expansion as recently as World War II. Earlier, in the Meiji period, it was a constant drag on industrial progress. Everywhere the turnover of labor was high. Rural workers, especially men, entered the factory only with great reluctance and in response to various recruiting pressures and inducements. This was one reason—the chief reason—why factories were established in rural areas, and commonly with a dormitory system which provided accommodations (and confinement) for young girls off the farm.[21]

Because of population growth, it is true, millions of workers could only improve their livelihood by replacing or supplementing agricultural pursuits with newer types of employment. Equally, however, the crowded labor market exerted a persistent drag on advances in health and physical efficiency, in the general level of education, and in the acquisition of technical skills. Sheer numbers of job-seekers in an already densely settled country do not necessarily give an expansive, dynamic impulse to industrialization. Far more significant is the capacity to acquire and apply the techniques of science and machinery. The same thing holds true of competitive ability in international markets. In an undeveloped country already densely populated on the land, a further growth in numbers is apt to retard rather than advance this end. Such was evidently the case in Japan.

---

wilder moments have spoken of the U.S.A. as the 'new Japan' among their competitors!" Vol. cxlix, no. 3701, February 12, 1949, p. 170.

[21] It should be noted that most of the traditional handicraft industries of Japan underwent no violent contraction after 1868 forcing large numbers of craftsmen to search for other employment. Nor did the introduction of capitalism bring with it a revolutionary reorganization of agriculture driving masses of peasants off the land. However, the revision of the land tax in 1873 on the basis of cash payments, and the price fluctuations of the period (see above, pages 98-100) did cause many small farmers to lose their land and to seek other means of family livelihood. See Yasuzo Horie, "An Outline of the Rise of Modern Capitalism," *Kyoto University Economic Review*, vol. xi, no. 1, July 1936, pp. 108-09.

Aside from these broad social effects, population increase may sometimes lead to improvements in economic efficiency through enlarging the demand for goods and services produced under conditions of increasing return. In Japan it undoubtedly broadened the market for many staple goods and services. Among the latter no doubt were some which could best be produced by industries built and operated in large units serving very wide markets. This was probably true, for example, in railway passenger service and electric lighting, both extensively used by the general public. The mere growth of numbers here may have had an expansive effect on economic development through making possible more efficient techniques of production.

This influence can easily be exaggerated, however. Except in sparsely settled countries, external and internal economies arising from an increasing scale of output are less likely to be found in simple necessities like food and clothing than in more advanced manufactures, especially durable goods. Throughout this period Japan remained overpopulated in the sense that, other things being equal, fewer people would have meant higher per capita incomes and a more even distribution of wealth. If this is so, the growth of population probably reduced rather than increased the potential benefits of large-scale production of commodities and services. In other words, it restricted those very markets (e.g., consumers' durable goods) where they were potentially most important. Certainly no gains on this score could have offset the obvious disadvantages of dwarf farms, of relentless competition for industrial employment, and the sponge-like absorption of workers in commerce and similarly low-paid occupations.[22]

Population and Capital. This leads to a further question as to the effects of population growth upon the per capita endowment of Japanese workers in natural resources, plant, and equipment. Whether Japan's economic growth has been hastened or retarded by the increase in numbers of people hinges in good part on its effects upon capital formation. For the creation of new capital goods is important both as a dynamic factor in maintaining employment of existing resources at a high level, and as a condition of technical progress.

From the standpoint first of Japan's requirements for capital, the increase in population clearly intensified the pressure upon land, mineral deposits, and other natural resources incapable of rapid

[22] "The larger the population, the less important will the advantages of large-scale production become, and the more important will be the fact that there is little capital and land to use with each worker, so that at some point output per head would be reduced by a further growth of numbers." J. E. Meade, *An Introduction to Economic Analysis and Policy*, New York, 1938, p. 285.

expansion. A slower rate of growth would have made it easier to reduce the rural population, to enlarge the average farm, and to raise production and income per farm family. Such industries as fishing and coal mining would not have needed to be carried so far into the stage of diminishing returns involving more and more investment per unit of output. A smaller share of new, man-made capital assets would have sufficed to supply the physical needs of the smaller population for food, housing, and other living necessities. In Britain, J. M. Keynes once estimated that as much as one half of the total increment in home capital from 1860 to 1913 went into caring for a 50% increase in population.[23] More recently, in studies of the economic development of "backward" areas, it has been concluded that a 1% increase in population requires savings of from 2 to 5% of the national income merely to provide the capital necessary to maintain the standard of living at its existing level.[24] The Japanese population doubled in sixty years, growing at an average rate of 1.2% per annum. Had the curve flattened out more quickly, a larger proportion of any *given* stock of capital could have been devoted to raising production and income per head.

Historically, however, the stock of capital assets is not "given," except insofar as it consists of unalterable natural resources. Its size and composition depend upon a variety of factors governing the savings-investment process and the amount and types of real capital created by investment activity. The interaction of these factors will influence the growth of total production, and the proportion which takes the form of new capital assets. It is appropriate, therefore, to ask how the secular growth of the Japanese population affected the utilization of existing resources, and to what extent it may itself have stimulated the formation of new capital.

Any answers to these questions must be quite speculative. There are grounds for arguing that the rapid increase in population after 1868 stimulated the fuller utilization of Japan's labor supply and other resources at the existing level of technology. For a high level of economic activity required that new investment in producing capital goods be maintained in sufficient amounts to balance the savings generated by rising incomes as the economy expanded. The inducement to invest depended in turn on the level of profit expectations and the terms on which funds were available.[25] With population expanding rapidly and moving to the cities in large numbers,

[23] "Some Economic Consequences of a Declining Population," *The Eugenics Review*, vol. xxix, no. 1, April 1937, p. 15.

[24] United Nations, Department of Economic Affairs, *Measures for the Economic Development of Under-developed Countries*, New York, 1951, p. 47.

[25] Or the value placed upon leisure by the farmer or artisan who improved his land, buildings, and tools in his spare time.

investment incentives were sustained by the demand for greater productive capacity in transportation, food supply, housing, and other necessities. This raised profit opportunities and employment in these industries, and had a generally stimulating effect on economic activity. Especially was this true as subsistence needs like food and clothing directed investment into more or less familiar channels. Here timorous, inexperienced entrepreneurs could find a comparatively certain and predictable demand, and overestimates in particular industries were more easily corrected as population grew.[26]

It was characteristic of these decades in Japan that depressions tended to be short and sharp. They were followed by relatively long periods of upswing.[27] One stimulus may have been the growth of population, through its effect in creating a greater historical marginal propensity to consume (a higher share of successive increments of income devoted to consumption) than would otherwise have prevailed. This would have helped to ensure that the inducement to invest remained strong relative to the disposition to save, and that investment and savings were balanced at steadily rising levels of income. Paradoxically, it could even have made for a greater expansion of Japan's total capital assets than would have occurred had a slower rate of population increase created a higher savings ratio through raising per capita incomes more rapidly.

All this is true only if dynamic growth could not have been maintained equally with a population which advanced more slowly. It is doubtful, however, that a much slower increase in numbers would have invited difficulties through raising the historical propensity to save or weakening the incentives to investment. Given the stimuli arising from other circumstances of the time, independent of the population factor, "stagnation" could hardly have been a serious problem.

A more stable population might have increased the share of income which the masses of people desired to save, through permitting family incomes to rise more rapidly from the subsistence level. But it would probably also have encouraged a more even distribution of income throughout the population. This would have had the opposite effect upon the rate of savings. For a large part of Japanese savings

---

[26] This point regarding the effects of population growth in the United States is made by William Fellner, who is otherwise skeptical concerning its influence on the consumption function. See his *Monetary Policies and Full Employment*, Berkeley, 1946, pp. 55-73.

[27] Overcapacity appeared rather generally in a number of industries during the twenties, but this was attributable to the abnormal expansion and financial maladjustments created by the war boom of 1914-19. It retarded only temporarily the continuing process of growth. See Chapters 2 and 3.

came from the well-to-do class, whose property incomes—rent, interest, and profits—were maintained at a high level, relative to wage rates, by the unfavorable ratio of population to land and other resources. (See Chapter 5.) Especially if these two factors had tended to counterbalance each other, a slower rate of population growth might actually have made little change in the share of income devoted to consumption.[28] New demands for investment goods would have arisen more rapidly in industries and services catering to higher consumer incomes. They would have grown more slowly in those providing rice, cheap cotton clothing, and other living necessities. Profits from the former type of investment might have been less predictable, and errors of judgment less easily corrected. But much of the new investment was of this character anyway, and proceeded at a rapid rate.

In any event, other inducements to invest would have remained strong under the circumstances of this period even if a slower increase in population had weakened the stimulus from this quarter. Wide investment opportunities were created by the rapid advance in the industrial arts which followed upon the opening of the country to Western influence and trade. The new political freedom and legal security of the commercial classes after the Restoration also reduced the traditional preference for hoarding wealth in the form of money, land, or other existing assets. This made funds available for industrial investment on more favorable terms. The government also gave active assistance through its fiscal and banking policies. If income per capita had risen more rapidly, and been more evenly distributed, this would itself have accelerated the "deepening" of investment through more capitalistic modes of production. For it would have hastened the acquisition of the necessary technological skills through advancing the general level of education and technical training.

Whether, as a result of all these influences, Japan's total stock of capital would have grown more or less rapidly with a slower rate of population growth is problematical. But clearly both her natural resources and man-made assets could have been devoted more largely to the requirements of technical progress and higher standards of living. They would not have been absorbed so heavily in merely supporting greater masses of people on the poverty line.[29]

[28] It is worth noting that Simon Kuznets' figures for national product, consumer outlay, and capital formation in the United States from 1880 to 1930 fail to support the notion that population growth raises significantly the ratio of aggregate consumption to income. *National Product since 1869*, New York, 1946, pp. 106, 119.

[29] The nature of real capital in Japan and the factors affecting its accumulation are discussed more fully in Chapter 5.

To return to the starting point of this discussion, it is doubtful that Japan's rise as an industrial power, or her whole process of economic development, can be regarded as having been stimulated or advanced by rapid population growth in any significant fashion. Whether viewed from the standpoint of markets, of technology, or of capital accumulation, it appears to have been a decided deterrent to economic progress—certainly in per capita terms. The persistence of a high birth rate despite the steady decline in mortality increased the dependent child population just when the Japanese economy could ill afford the burden. It imposed a heavy drag on improvements in the skills and equipment of the labor force. It hastened the exhaustion of natural resources at home, and required huge industrial exports abroad merely to feed and clothe greater numbers. Probably it failed even to benefit the long-run interests of the propertied class; certainly it robbed the people as a whole of much of the potential gain from economic progress in terms of material well-being and personal freedom.

One finds difficulty, indeed, in discovering any social value, other than that of military manpower, which was served by the excessive growth of population in prewar Japan. It is even arguable that the country's total national income and wealth would have risen more rapidly had population been held down more nearly to the optimum size. This point is indeterminate, and unimportant except perhaps in terms of national prestige and power. In any event, Japan's experience casts doubt on any idea that population increase is an expansive stimulant to economic development in a country already densely settled in relation to its natural resources. Other factors clearly preponderated in bringing about the growth of Japan's productive powers, and despite her swarming numbers rather than because of them.

Productivity, Markets, Technical Progress

The foregoing paragraphs emphasize again the distinction which must be drawn between two different measures of economic advance. One is the size and growth of total national income and wealth. The other is the ratio of the national aggregate to the number of producers and consumers, i.e., the per capita level.

Aggregate size may often be more important for purposes of national security. It may also count heavily in international bargaining where sheer weight is a factor. Aside from considerations of national power, however, economic progress in welfare terms depends in the main on the level of per capita production, together with the way in which income, wealth, and leisure are distributed among the people. In fact, even military security in modern times is a function of output per worker in no small degree. Recent history is full of examples of nations with large populations, and therefore vast totals of income and wealth, which have been at the mercy of smaller countries more heavily industrialized and able accordingly to mobilize a larger percentage of manpower and resources of the kind necessary to wage war. One need look no further than Japan herself, first in her invasion of China, and second in her ultimate defeat at the hands of the Allies.[30]

Secular Rise in Productivity. The scale of aggregate growth in the Japanese economy over half a century was portrayed in Chapter 3. The more significant point as to the advance in productivity is less readily established, owing to the lack of reliable data on the labor force. Plainly, however, the bulk of the secular growth in national income is not attributable to an increase merely in the working population. It resulted also from a sustained rise in the unit efficiency of labor.

Yamada's estimates of total national product (Table 12) suggest at least a 50% over-all advance in output per gainfully occupied person from 1885 to 1910. During the next twenty-five years the figure increases still more rapidly—over 100%. Through the fifty-year period 1885-1935 it grows from 132 yen to 475 yen of net product per worker (at 1928-32 prices). The average geometric rate of increase is 2.6% a year.

These estimates of output per head are of dubious accuracy, for reasons already given. Yet they at least show the direction of change in the Japanese economy as a whole, and something of its order of magnitude. Whether actual hours of work also declined through the period, bringing added gains in leisure, is difficult to judge. They were shortened in factories, mines, and large-scale transport. However, peasant families may well have found fuller year-round employment through the spread of subsidiary occupations. In any case, our only measure of total work input is a crude annual estimate of the working population, some occupied full-time, others part-time, and a few actually idle.

Despite these obscurities, it is of interest to measure the "productivity increment" indicated by Yamada's figures. As defined by Frederick C. Mills,[31] this is the margin of total output added by

---

30 The fallacy that Asia's immense populations, because of their prospective growth, constitute in themselves a potential military menace to the West runs through Warren S. Thompson's otherwise valuable *Population and Peace in the Pacific*, Chicago, 1946. It seems more probable that China's and India's military potential will be weakened by population growth, not strengthened, compared to what it otherwise would be.

31 "The Role of Productivity in Economic Growth," *American Economic Review*, vol. XLII, no. 2, May 1952, p. 546.

technological advance from one period to another. For any period it is the increment in aggregate product over and above what the work input of the period would have produced had its productivity per unit remained unchanged from the earlier period. If we assume that the Japanese work input is measured crudely by the Hijikata-census estimates of the occupied population, Yamada's national product figures[32] yield the following calculation of the productivity increment from decade to decade in annual averages (values at 1928-32 prices):

ANNUAL AVERAGE	TOTAL NET PRODUCT (MILLIONS OF YEN)	GAINFULLY OCCUPIED POPULATION (THOUSANDS)	PRODUCT PER CAPITA (YEN)	INCREMENT IN TOTAL PRODUCT ATTRIBUTABLE TO:	
				Increase in Working Force[a] *(millions of yen)*	*Increase in per Capita Product*[b] *(millions of yen)*
1888-97	3,821	23,637	162	—	—
1898-1907	4,645	25,749	180	342	482
1908-17	5,968	27,070	220	239	1,084
1918-27	9,166	27,851	329	172[c]	3,026[c]
1928-37	13,428	30,510	440	875	3,387

a For each decade, the increase in the number of gainfully occupied multiplied by product per capita in the preceding decade.

b For each decade, the increase in per capita product multiplied by the total number of gainfully occupied.

c A discrepancy between the Hijikata and census labor force figures, pre- and post-1919, leads almost certainly to an underestimate of the relative growth in the working population from 1908-17 to 1918-27. This exaggerates the apparent productivity increment, even for this decade of rapid technological progress.

In each successive decade a part of the gain in national output is attributable to the growth of the working population alone, in the sense that output could have increased modestly even if the unit efficiency of labor had not improved at all. Increasingly, however, it is productivity advances resulting from technical and other changes which account for most of the actual increment in the total production of goods and services. Over the forty years, if we add the average annual increments from decade to decade, as given by the Yamada estimates, more than 80% of the total gain is associated with increases in unit efficiency. Less than 20% is attributable to increases in the working population. Actually this distinction is somewhat unreal. Changes in productivity and in labor input are not independent of each other, as Professor Mills points out in the

32 *Nihon Kokumin Shotoku Suikei Shiryō*, cited, p. 130.

case of the United States. Yet one finds here added confirmation of
the basic importance in Japan's economic growth of accumulating
capital resources, science and education, power machinery, improved
business organization, and all the other factors which steadily advanced the productivity ratio. This is true even if the 80/20 ratio
is heavily discounted, as resting on very problematical statistical
estimates.

Even in agriculture, physical output of food and raw materials at
least doubled from 1885 to 1935. The production index of Table 3
actually triples, though reasons were given in Chapter 3 to doubt
its accuracy. Yamada's net product total also advances from 920
million to 2,445 million yen, at 1928-32 prices, even after the deduction of fertilizer and other relevant expenses from gross values.[33]
Meanwhile, as stated in Chapter 3, the cultivated area grew no more
than 25% or so; the number of farm workers probably increased
still less, if at all; and the actual labor input may even have declined. The data are so uncertain as to discourage any measurements of increasing output per worker, but there can be little doubt
that it was substantial.[34]

Most of the efficiency gain in Japanese farming was achieved
through rather simple scientific improvements, better irrigation,
and more fertilizer. Almost no mechanization took place (see below,
pages 193-96), and the average farm increased only slightly in size.
In the production of silk cocoons, the most important subsidiary
occupation of the Japanese peasant, the spread of double cropping
and improved breeding methods brought a 100% increase in output
per sericultural family from 1905 to 1926. In the fishing industry,
where fairly complete figures are available only after 1923, the
next fifteen years witnessed a 66% gain in the tonnage of the catch,
despite a slight reduction in the number of people and fishing vessels
employed. Here, in contrast to sericulture, increased efficiency was
associated with the rise of big concerns engaged in exploiting deep-
sea fisheries through large-scale, capitalistic operations.[35]

[33] *ibid.*, p. 130. Yamada's figures probably exaggerate the rate of growth in agriculture, mainly because of the underreporting of farm output in the early years.
Also, he derives net from gross value of output with coefficients which rest on very
slender information for the early period. Deductible expenses are figured at 18%
of gross output in 1883-87, and 30% during 1933-37 (pp. 28-29).

[34] Hijikata puts the total Japanese labor force at 21.5 million people in 1885,
of whom 16.3 million were in agriculture. *ibid.*, p. 152. In the 1930 census there were
29.6 million gainfully employed, of whom 14.1 million gave agriculture as their
chief occupation. Imperial Cabinet, Bureau of Statistics, *Shōwa Go-nen Kokusei
Chōsa Hōkoku*, vol. 2, Tokyo, 1935, p. 240. More accurate data show the number of
farm households increasing slowly after 1900: from 5.4 million in 1903 to 5.6 million
in 1930. *Meiji Taishō Kokusei Soran*, cited, p. 507; *Nippon Teikoku Tōkei Nenkan*,
cited, no. 55, p. 3.

[35] Supreme Commander for the Allied Powers, GHQ, Natural Resources Section,

In manufacturing the productivity of Japanese labor advanced much more rapidly than in agriculture. Certain statistics highlighting this advance were summarized in Chapter 3. If one may generalize concerning the whole range of factory industries (plants of five or more operatives) it appears that output per man-year increased after 1910 at an average rate which served to double it in twenty to twenty-five years. The production and employment indices given on page 122 actually show a rise in physical output per factory worker from 100 in 1910-14 to 263 in 1935-38. In the earlier years there may have been some underreporting of factory output; but its influence on the index tends to be offset by the fact that the index also includes some of the production of small workshops, which generally grew less rapidly than factory production. Moreover, no account is taken of qualitative improvement in products.

A similar rate of gain in gross product per capita is suggested by more inclusive census figures on the labor force in all manufacturing, including workshop industry. From 1920 to 1940 the number of people who gave manufacturing (excluding construction) as their principal occupation increased from 4.3 million to 7.6 million.[36] Meanwhile manufacturing output rose some 200%, as measured by the summary index of Table 8. Earlier I have questioned the accuracy and meaning of this production index; and it should further be recalled that the census figures include some persons employed only part-time, and others not at all at the time of the inquiry. Nevertheless, one finds here some additional support for the conclusion that the average tendency in Japanese manufacturing was for gross output per worker to double during the interwar period. As a matter of fact, Yamada's calculation of net value of product per manufacturing worker, at 1928-32 prices, rises from 444 yen in 1918-22 to 944 yen in 1938-42.[37]

Particularly in factory industry one would expect to find marked gains in labor efficiency from improvements known to have taken place in industrial equipment and techniques. One outstanding aspect was the increasing use of inanimate energy to mechanize production processes. The statistics of factory motive capacity were cited in Chapter 3 as a rough indicator of the substitution of mechanical for human energy. Table 10 shows an increase in prime

---

Report No. 95, *Japanese Fisheries Production, 1908-46*, Tokyo, 1947, pp. 8, 30-31. While the total number of fishing vessels declined from 365,000 in 1923 to 356,000 in 1938, the number equipped with engines rose from 9,068 to 68,155. Powered vessels over 50 tons increased from 134 to 927. Prime Minister's Office, Statistics Bureau, *Japan Statistical Yearbook, 1949*, Tokyo, 1949, pp. 244-45.

36 *Japan Statistical Yearbook, 1949*, cited, tables 37, 38.

37 *op.cit.*, p. 130.

movers installed in Japanese factories (public and private, excluding the gas and electric industries) from 537,000 h.p. in 1914 to 1,461,000 in 1937. Installed electric motors jumped from 279,000 to 6,290,000 h.p. Meanwhile the number of workers in factories, similarly defined, grew only from 1,182,000 to 3,365,000. All told, the amount of power machinery per worker installed in factory industry probably doubled. Adding in the electric power used for purposes other than driving machinery brings the total gain in utilization of mechanical power to 150% or more per worker.

In small workshops the unit efficiency of labor increased more slowly than in factory industry. Yet here too there were significant advances—especially better overhead arrangements for marketing and finance. One also finds evidence in many specific trades of improvements in the arrangement and equipment of production processes. Often these took the form of greater subdivision and specialization of operations, both between workers and between establishments, making it more economical to introduce simple improvements in tools and machinery. It is well known that the increasing availability of electric power to the small Japanese industrialist encouraged the mechanization of operations like weaving, even in quite small plants, and increased their competitive efficiency.

Naturally there were wide variations in technological progress from one industry to another, and from year to year. To examine them in detail is hardly necessary here. One case in particular may be mentioned, however, because of its world-wide consequences. Cotton spinning, once it was well established in Japan as a factory industry, showed comparatively little gain in labor efficiency in most of its processes from 1913 to 1926. Beginning about this time, however, narrowing profit margins put severe pressure on management to cut costs and improve production methods. An additional incentive and opportunity to increase labor efficiency came with the shortening of spindle hours which followed the abolition of night work for women and children after 1929. Between 1926 and 1931 the production of cotton yarn held to a level of about 2.6 million bales. Meanwhile, the number of spinning mill operatives dropped from 183,000 to 122,000, even though finer yarns were being produced and hours of work were cut from 9.8 to 8.5 per day. Labor-saving economies in the large weaving plants attached to spinning mills were even greater, thanks to the introduction of the automatic loom. Here physical output per worker doubled from 1926 to 1931.[38]

[38] Teijiro Uyeda and Tokijiro Minoguchi, *Small-Scale Industries of Japan: The Cotton Industry*, Tokyo, 1936, p. 22ff. See also International Labour Office, *The World Textile Industry, Economic and Social Problems*, Geneva, 1937, vol. i, chaps. 8, 12, 13.

Japan's spectacular invasion of world cotton goods markets after 1931 owed a good deal to other factors of business rationalization, exchange depreciation, and falling wages. If we compare 1934 with 1914, however, the significant new element in her competitive position was the technical progress of her cotton industry rather than low wages or exchange manipulation.

The Japanese mining industry probably fell into an intermediate position between agriculture and manufacturing as regards advances in labor efficiency. It was developed on a capitalistic basis, and increasingly so. But the law of diminishing returns imposed progressive limits as output increased. Yamada's estimate of net value of output per worker, at 1928-32 prices, advances only from 534 yen in 1898-1902 to 1,070 yen in 1933-37.[39]

In coal mines, to cite the principal branch of mining, physical output per man-day rose from 0.38 ton in 1897-99 to 0.57 ton in 1925-29. It then jumped to 0.761 ton in the next five years. This is a doubling in thirty-five years, as shown in the following table:[40]

	Total Coal Production (thousands of metric tons)	Man-Days of Mining Labor (thousands)	Coal Output per Man-Day (metric tons)
1897-99	6,255	16,448	0.381
1900-1904	9,434	20,263	0.465
1910-14	19,313	38,592	0.500
1920-24	28,445	64,953	0.438
1925-29	32,906	57,905	0.568
1930-34	31,173	40,987	0.761

It is characteristic of the industrial history of this period that Japanese coal was not only mined more efficiently; it was also employed with increasing effectiveness as fuel. In 1914, 2.11 metric tons of coal were required to produce 1,000 kw. of thermal electric power; in 1932, only 0.7 ton. Locomotive consumption of coal on Japanese railways was reduced from 70.8 kg. per 100 ton-km. of traction in 1914 to 40.1 kg. in 1922. The steel industry in its early days required 3.5 tons of coal to produce a ton of steel. By the thirties the requirement had been cut to less than 2 tons.[41]

In contrast to coal mining, most of the service trades in Japan do not lend themselves readily to productivity measurements. No ac-

[39] op.cit., p. 130.

[40] Statistics of the Mining Bureau, as reported in the Financial and Economic Annual of Japan, cited, passim.

[41] Estimates of K. Furuta, quoted in International Labour Office, The World Coal-Mining Industry, Geneva, 1938, vol. II, pp. 99-100.

curate data on labor input exist over any long period of time. Nor is the output of nonmaterial services easily recorded and compared from one year to another. Who can measure the "output" of a cabinet minister or a trained nurse? At one extreme were the myriads of Japanese men, women, and children who eked out a living as shop-keepers, peddlers, cart-pullers, boatmen, domestic servants, etc. Here equipment and skills remained comparatively simple, or at any rate traditional. No radical changes occurred either in the scale of or-ganization or in techniques. At the other extreme were the few serv-ice industries like large-scale shipping, railway transport, and elec-trical communications which were organized from the beginning in a highly capitalistic fashion.

Wherever the Industrial Revolution has arrived, long-distance transport is one of the most spectacular cases of saving labor on a massive scale. The transformation it wrought in Japan is char-acterized in Chapter 3, and in Chapter 9 we return again to its effects. Even the ricksha, the cart, and the bicycle multiply the muscles of man severalfold. Still more significant for Japan was the replacement of sailing junks of 10 to 50 tons with steam vessels of 500 tons or more. Short of the airplane, however, the railway is "the most revolutionary instrument in history." Elsewhere (pages 478-79) it is questioned whether the total amount of labor devoted to transporting goods and people in Japan increased at all over fifty years, despite the tremendous growth in freight and passenger move-ment. To illustrate the point, it is remarked that an able-bodied man armed with nothing more than a pole can carry 100 lbs. 20 miles a day, or 320 ton-miles a year, at best. By comparison, the Japanese State Railways handled 33,000 ton-miles of freight per employee in 1930, beside 61,000 passenger-miles of traffic. To reckon in the labor expended in producing the railways and their fuel would not radi-cally reduce the contrast.

Much of this gain in transport efficiency, measured in human effort, naturally occurred in the initial shift to steam and steel dur-ing the Meiji years. Further improvements continued through sub-sequent decades, however. From 1914 to 1934, for example, if freight and passenger traffic are combined with weights based on gross re-ceipts in 1920-24, traffic per employee on the Imperial Railways rises 70%. Better transportation in turn brought productivity gains in all other branches of the economy. For it provided efficient means for concentrating and distributing goods and people at points where they could best be utilized.

These evidences of rising labor efficiency are selective, of course. Even if pursued a good deal further, one would hesitate to affirm any definite conclusions regarding the over-all change which occurred during the first half century of Japan's economic modernization. They do lend some credence, however, to the general impression which emerges from the rough calculations of national product and labor force given earlier. So far as it is possible to measure and sum up the diversified and shifting output of the Japanese economy over the fifty or sixty years before World War II, the record suggests something like a 200 to 250% increase in the annual net-value product per worker. The average rate of gain, in other words, lay in between the slower advance in agriculture and the nonmechanized services and the faster one in large-scale manufacturing and transport.

With all the uncertainties of this statistical conclusion, Japan's technical achievement throughout large areas of her economic life is impressive by any standard. And it was fundamental to her emergence as one of the world's great trading nations in the later decades. While the volume of a country's international trade is determined by a number of factors, none is more decisive than the general level of productivity in its economy. Another determinant is the degree to which its complement of resources encourages specialization in world markets. In this regard, too, Japan's deficiency in natural wealth fostered the growth of international dependence. A lack of certain natural resources, however, will not itself induce a large volume of trade; quite the contrary. If we have been at pains to examine the rise of production and labor efficiency in Japan it is partly to establish this basic point. Commercial expansion overseas was paralleled by a rapid growth of productive powers throughout the Japanese economy. The two developments stood in a close and mutually dependent relationship to each other.

A second observation is equally pertinent. Despite rapid progress, the Japanese economy as a whole remained exceedingly backward in organization and production technique, judged by modern standards. All comparisons between Japan and the West with respect to per capita productivity were still heavily to the disadvantage of the former.[42] In every sphere the more productive use of manpower was held back by its very abundance, and by the shortage of capital and advanced mechanical and organizing skills. Even rather simple improvements which would greatly have increased labor efficiency were still uneconomical. Hence the paradox that labor seemed to the Westerner to be so heavily underemployed, yet such "wastefulness"

---

[42] The technical backwardness and weakness of the Japanese economy in the thirties were graphically set forth by Freda Utley in *Japan's Feet of Clay*, New York, 1937. However, Miss Utley's indignation over the injustices and inequalities of Japanese society led her to neglect rather unsympathetically the progress of preceding decades, as well as grossly to underestimate Japan's war potential in the years immediately ahead.

was necessary in the sense that a reduction in manpower without corresponding advances in technique would force a decline in production.[43]

Labor Efficiency in Japan and the West. The disparity in labor
productivity between Japan and the more advanced, industrial nations was perhaps greatest in farming. Here efforts to raise the
efficiency of labor encountered the most severe resistance from the
pressure of population on the land, the scarcity of capital, and the
other social and technical characteristics of small-scale, peasant
agriculture.[44]

Productivity was also conspicuously low among millions of workers in commerce and the other small-scale services, most of them
grossly wasteful of manpower if judged by Western standards. Low
productivity was even characteristic of coal mining, despite the
progress cited above. Here physical output per man-hour in 1925-
29 was only one ninth as great as in the United States, with its
richer coal deposits, its advanced mechanization, and its better working conditions.[45] And it was evident in the more efficient branches of
large-scale factory industry. For example, the large spinning-weav-

[43] Even—or especially—in the "overpopulated" field of agriculture. This con-
tradicts the notion that Far Eastern countries have a limitless reserve of farm
labor which might be taken off the farm and put to work in factories without
substantial changes in agricultural technique, or a fall in agricultural production.
In Japan this was strikingly evidenced during World War II. Conscription and
industrial demands reduced the agricultural labor force by 874,000 in the year
1944/45. The U.S. Strategic Bombing Survey reports as follows: "The decline in
Japanese agricultural production between 1941 and 1945 was considerably influenced
by a shortage of able-bodied farm labor. This manpower shortage contributed to
the reduction of land under cultivation . . . and resulted in the use of less efficient
farm labor, mainly women and older members of the farming households. . . .
Agriculture, the least mechanized field of Japan's economy, was least able to afford
a loss of manpower." *The Japanese Wartime Standard of Living and Utilization of
Manpower*, Washington, 1947, pp. 9-10.

[44] Colin Clark gives the following comparison of males employed in agriculture
per 1,000 hectares of arable and pasture land around 1930: Argentina, 7; the United
States, 25; Holland, 235; Japan, 868. *The Conditions of Economic Progress*, London,
1940, p. 246. Clark presents many ingenious comparisons of productivity in primary,
secondary, and tertiary industries among a number of countries. Those relating to
Japan contain such a high margin of error, however, that it has seemed better here
to rely on more accurate if more limited illustrations.

[45] The soft coal miner in the United States averaged 4.2 metric tons per day in
1925-29, as compared with the 0.57-ton output of the Japanese miner given above.
U.S. Department of the Interior, *Minerals Yearbook* (1936), Washington, 1936,
p. 563. Moreover, he worked only a little over eight hours a day, while Japanese
miners put in nine and a half hours, including overtime. (The only data on actual
hours in Japan during this period are for October 1927, as reported in the Census
of Labor.) The latter received wages only a little above subsistence, they suffered
from accident and sickness rates which were excessively high, and their living
and working conditions were among the worst in Japan. Yet the price of coal
in Japan was twice what it was in the United States. For other international comparisons in this industry, see *The World Coal-Mining Industry*, cited above.

ing mills of the cotton industry still employed at least twice as many workers as an American mill producing the same output in the early thirties.[46] Yet compared to most Japanese industries these cotton mills were now extensively equipped with modern, automatic machinery. As noted above, they had doubled their output per worker from 1926 to 1931. Here the gap was narrower perhaps than in any other industry. Its rapid reduction, without a corresponding rise in relative wage rates, was a principal factor in Japan's inroads on world textile markets during these years.

The best way to place Japanese industry as a whole in its proper perspective at this time is to compare Japan and other leading industrial nations with respect to net product in factory industry (i.e., "value added by manufacture," after the costs of raw materials, fuel, and power are deducted from gross value of product). This is attempted in Table 13, with the aid of census data assembled by L. Rostas on the United Kingdom, Germany, and the United States. In a rough fashion the output of each country is revalued at British prices so as to afford a more or less common basis for comparison.

The results are interesting. Allowing for the fact that the estimates are for different years,[47] and that the conversion to British prices is crude, we find that the *total* net output of factory industry in Japan was probably less than one quarter of that in Britain or Germany. It was less than one twelfth of the output of American manufacturing. Japan was still far from the front rank of industrial powers, as her subsequent war experience was to show.

In part this was simply due to the fact that the whole industrial establishment was smaller. Britain and Germany had more than twice as many factory workers. The United States had three to four times as many. A comparison of total manufacturing production rather than factory production would be more favorable to Japan

[46] The Fuji Gas Spinning Company made a study of ring-spinning of cotton yarns up to 40 count in several countries during 1932. It found Japanese mills employing 6.1 workers per 1,000 spindles, as compared with a figure of 3.4 in the United States and 4.0 in the United Kingdom. International Labour Office, *The World Textile Industry*, Geneva, 1937, vol. 1, pp. 207-10.

In spinning finer yarns and in weaving, Japanese labor efficiency was relatively lower. However, if the above figures are correct, they reveal a relative gain in efficiency as a result of the belated abolition of night work for women and children and greater mechanization in the years immediately preceding. A decade earlier the U.S. Tariff Commission had found Japanese spinning-weaving mills employing 3.6 times as much labor as comparable American mills. *The Japanese Cotton Industry and Trade*, Washington, 1921, pp. 100-103. In the middle twenties J. E. Orchard estimated the Japanese labor requirement in spinning at more than three times the requirement in the United States, and in the case of weaving at seven times. *Japan's Economic Position*, New York, 1930, pp. 367-75.

[47] Japanese industrial production rose 10% from 1934 to 1935. Tōyō Keizai Shimpōsha, *Keizai Nenkan* (1940), Tokyo, 1940, p. 2.

Table 13. *Net Value of Production, Employment, and Net Product per Worker in the Factory Industry of Japan, the United Kingdom, Germany, and the United States, 1934-37*[a]

	Total Net Product of Factory Industry (millions of pounds sterling)	Number of Factory Workers (millions)	Net Product per Factory Worker (pounds sterling)
Japan (1934)	235-285	2.3	105-125
United Kingdom (1935)	1,182	4.5	263
Germany (1936)	1,505	5.1	295
United States (1935)	3,786	7.2	526
United States (1937)	5,096	8.6	593

[a] Data for the United Kingdom (excluding Northern Ireland), Germany, and the United States are from censuses of production as compiled by L. Rostas and converted to pound sterling values at British prices. "Industrial Production, Productivity and Distribution in Britain, Germany and the United States," *Economic Journal*, vol. LIII, no. 209, April 1943, pp. 39-43. Industrial production of all types is included, except for mining, construction, and public utilities. In the United Kingdom all firms employing ten or more workers are enumerated, in Germany all firms employing five or more, in the United States all plants whose product was valued at $5,000 or more. Costs of raw materials, fuel, power, etc. are deducted from gross output to arrive at net product.

The Japanese data conform approximately to the same definition of manufacturing. "Factories" comprise all plants equipped to employ five or more operatives, including government owned plants but excluding gas and electricity production. The number of workers is the 1934 year-end total of factory operatives and "other" workers (Ministry of Commerce and Industry, *Kōjō Tōkeihyō* [1936], pp. 12-13) adjusted to an average for the year by the employment index of the Bank of Japan.

Net product in Japanese factory industry as defined above is calculated as follows: (1) For private factories, it is derived from gross product by deducting (a) raw material, fuel and power expenses as given by Yasuji Koide in "Hompō Sangyō Kōzō no Hendō ni Kansuru Shiryō," *Nagoya Keizai Tōkei Geppō*, vol. VIII, no. 9, October 1936, p. 59; and (b) other expenses reckoned at 2.5% of gross product on the basis of 1930 data from the Cabinet Bureau of Statistics' national income study. This gives a net value product of 2,577 million yen for private factories employing 2,130,000 workers. (2) The net product estimate for government owned plants is that of the U.S. Department of State (*National Income of Japan*, Washington, 1945, p. 46), which is extrapolated in turn from the figure for 1930 given by the Cabinet Bureau of Statistics. (3) The resulting total, 2,836 million yen, is revalued at British prices by applying yen/sterling price ratios tabulated by Colin Clark (*The Conditions of Economic Progress*, London, 1940, p. 122) for various industrial goods to the net value products of the major Japanese industries. This conversion rate, 10 to 12 yen per pound should be recomputed with more adequate data for an accurate measure. However, it is closer to the truth than the official exchange rate of 17 yen per pound in 1934, and will serve our purpose here

in this respect, for it would take into account the large output of plants of less than five operatives. In the Western countries these were of minor significance. In Japan their net product in 1934 is estimated at 1,136 million yen, or 42% of factory output.[48] Even if we add them in, however, manufacturing production in the United States was still probably *ten* times as great.

[48] U.S. Department of State, *National Income of Japan*, Washington, 1945, p. 48.

The Japanese total also reflects a lower level of output per wage earner. Net product per worker in England and Germany was at least twice what it was in Japan, even in factory industry. In the United States it was four or five times as great. (Table 13.)

If allowance were made for the longer hours worked in Japan, the superiority of the West in labor efficiency would appear even greater. Factory workers averaged 61.8 hours of actual work per week in Japan during 1934; in the United States they worked only 38.6 hours in 1937.[49] And the gap would be widened still further if one took account of workshop industry in Japan, where productivity was typically even lower. Workshop and factory industry together employed about as many workers in Japan as in Britain and Germany, but total manufacturing output was much smaller.

This disparity in the effectiveness of labor, even in factory trades, calls for some further explanation. Many factors enter into the difference: the efficiency of large-scale business organization, the level of mechanical skills and aptitudes, the structure of demand, etc. But the fundamental disadvantage of the Japanese worker, which underlay most other differences as well, was the relative scarcity of capital. Japanese wage rates were relatively low, of course; capital costs high. Since most products can be turned out with varying combinations of labor and equipment, it paid Japanese manufacturers to economize capital at the expense of labor. Relative to their Western competitors they employed many more workers and ran their machinery longer hours to produce goods comparable in amount and quality. Inevitably this meant a low level of output per worker in factory industry, and a still lower one in the small-scale workshop trades.

Actually to measure this comparative disadvantage of the Japanese worker in capital equipment is difficult to do, except in particular industrial operations. Comparisons applying to industry as a whole are complicated by the lack of a quantitative unit with which to measure industrial capital in different forms and in different countries. One significant indicator already discussed in Chapter 3, however, is the amount of motive power used to operate machinery. For any country this can be expressed in standard units—horsepower or kilowatts. A large share of the capital assets of manufacturing industry consist either of power machinery itself, or of buildings and other equipment necessitated by the use of mechanical

[49] The U.S. figure is from U.S. Department of Commerce, *Statistical Abstract of the United States, 1941*, p. 368. Japanese hours are estimated from comprehensive data from the 1933 Census of Labour, adjusted to 1934 by the Cabinet Bureau of Statistics reports on large factories. See *International Labour Review*, vol. xxxix, no. 4, April 1939, pp. 496ff.

energy in manufacturing processes. The amount of such machinery and equipment is the most important determinant of per capita output.

In Japan, as detailed in Chapter 3, rapid advances took place in the mechanization of factory production after 1914. Some of the power was furnished by prime movers like steam turbines and engines used to drive machinery directly. The bulk of it, however, came to consist of electricity supplied by Japan's growing capacity to generate electric power, both hydro and thermal. While no very accurate estimate can be made, it appears that the power machinery installed in Japanese factories (excluding gas and electricity undertakings) had increased to about 1.7 h.p. per worker in 1936. Similar data for a number of countries are given for about the same time in a study prepared by the United Nations Economic Commission for Europe. Horsepower per employed worker in factory industry was roughly as follows in five countries which may be selected for comparison with Japan:[50]

	Horsepower per Worker		*Horsepower per Worker*
United States (1939)	4.8	*Japan (1936)*	*1.7*
United Kingdom (1930)	2.4	Italy (average 1937-40)	2.1
Germany (1933)	2.4	Czechoslovakia (1930)	1.4

The average factory worker in Japan might now be equipped with twice as much power machinery as a generation earlier, but he still made use of only about one third as much as the average industrial worker in the United States before the war. By comparison with workers in Britain and Germany, too, he was still at a marked disadvantage. Moreover, these comparisons of horsepower,

[50] Data for all countries except Japan are from "Motive Power in European Industry," *Economic Bulletin for Europe*, vol. 3, no. 1, first quarter, October 1951, pp. 24-40. As in the case of Japan they relate to all manufacturing industries except the construction, water, gas, and electricity industries. The Japanese figure is estimated motive capacity in all government and private factories equipped to employ five or more operatives, divided by the total number of wage and salaried workers (2,981,000). Minor differences in census coverage of the other countries probably do not materially affect the comparison.

The ECE employed various methods for estimating industrial motive power in different countries. For Japan I have followed the method used for the United States: the capacity of prime movers installed in manufacturing establishments is added to the capacity of electric motors driven with electricity furnished from outside. The nature of the calculation, including its various assumptions and ambiguities, is explained above, pages 123-25. The total for all factories consisted of 1,084,000 h.p. of prime movers and 3,945,000 h.p. of electric motors (operating and idle).

even if reasonably accurate, do not take account of differences in the efficiency of machinery in relation to driving power. Nor do they measure differences in other forms of industrial capital—equipment, buildings, and stocks—which are not directly associated with mechanical operations. It would be surprising if the contrast between Japanese industry and British and American industry was not greater than is suggested by these figures, even though plants of less than five operatives are excluded. A decade earlier it certainly was. And, of course, a large sector of handicraft industry omitted here was still close to the handicraft stage. But the rapid electrification and mechanization of industry had undoubtedly narrowed the gap, in both large and small establishments. In one decade, 1930-39, total energy consumption in Japan is said to have risen 70%.[51]

Some corroboration of this international comparison is found in the U.S. Department of State's *Energy Resources of the World*, Washington, 1949. Here the consumption of fuel and power of all types and for all purposes in manufacturing and mining is compiled for a number of countries in 1937. When coal, fuelwood, oil, and all other energy sources are converted to their energy equivalent in kilowatt-hours of electricity, the figures are as follows:[52]

Energy Consumption per Person Employed in Manufacturing and Mining, 1937		*Energy Consumption per Person Employed in Manufacturing and Mining, 1937*	
United States	34,449	*Japan (1936)*	*10,077*
United Kingdom	18,173	Australia	9,466
USSR	11,312	Chile	7,469
Germany	10,858	Turkey	1,837

The work output of one man ordinarily does not exceed 150 kw-h. a year in energy equivalent. By contrast, a ton of coal yields 1,680 kw-h. at 20% efficiency. If the above figures are correct, therefore, the average industrial worker in Japan by 1936 was being aided with inanimate energy equal to 67 man-years of work, or 6 tons of coal. Actual coal consumption in industry was over 4 tons per worker, and accounted for 71% of the inanimate energy used. (Electricity provided most of the remainder.) By comparison, the energy used per person in American manufacturing and mining was more than three times the Japanese figure. It was equivalent to 230 man-years or 20

[51] President's Materials Policy Commission, *Resources for Freedom*, vol. III: *The Outlook for Energy Resources*, Washington, 1952, p. 30.

[52] Page 8. Table 47 summarizes the amounts of fuel and power of various types used in industry, as compiled in preceding tables.

tons of coal in 1937. Again the estimate for Japan may seem surprisingly high; yet it rests on an employment figure as high as 5.9 million persons. Mining and factory industry actually employed only 3.4 million in 1936, so that a large allowance is made here for persons in workshop industry, many of them using little or no power equipment, and many employed only part-time.

At best these comparisons of motive power and energy consumption are only suggestive of the range of difference between Japan and the other countries. They tend to support the early comparison of net output per factory worker, nevertheless, just as they testify to its primary cause. A large sector of Japanese industry had become mechanized by this time beyond any resemblance to the silk weaver's shed, the hand forge, or the wooden-boat yard. Technologically it had left still further behind the world in which peasant agriculture still remained, where human muscle was the principal source of power. Yet a significant gap still separated the typical manufacturing process in Japan from the even more capitalistic modes of production now prevalent among the industrial nations of the West. Even in cotton spinning, where Japanese mills were now equipped with large amounts of high-speed, automatic machinery, nearly twice as many workers per 1,000 spindles were still employed as in a typical American mill.

A second difference between Japan and the more advanced manufacturing nations reinforced the difference in output per capita arising from the comparative scarcity of capital equipment and related disadvantages in particular industries. This is found in the structure of Japanese industry. Not only was its aggregate scale smaller, as noted above, but various industries and products differed in relative importance. The contrast in this respect also helps to explain both the smaller degree of over-all mechanization, and the lower productivity of labor in the comparisons given above for factory industry as a whole.

Japanese factory industry was specialized more heavily in products and processes where, for technical reasons, the employment of large amounts of labor in the lower grades is relatively more suitable, as compared with expensive equipment and the more advanced technical and managerial skills. The textile, clothing, wood, and leather industries, for example, tend to be relatively labor-intensive in this sense. By contrast, net output per worker is higher as a rule in the machinery, chemical, paper and printing, and food processing industries. These are organized on a larger scale and employ more machinery and equipment per unit of output.[53] Any

[53] Valued at market prices, net output per worker in the Japanese metal and machinery industries was four times the corresponding figure in textile manufacture

country where the labor-intensive industries predominate will of course tend to show a lower average output per worker, even if the relative scale of labor and capital costs is no different.

Except for the smaller aggregate size of Japanese factory industry, which limited the economies of mass production in a good many industries, such structural differences no longer appear at first glance to be very significant in the middle thirties. Table 14 illustrates the point. It shows the proportionate importance, judged by net value added by manufacture, of five major groupings of factory industry in Japan, and in the United Kingdom, Germany, and the United States. These figures seem to indicate that by 1934 Japanese industry had become diversified to the point where it paralleled the structure of industry in the other countries. Judged by net value product, it was no longer heavily concentrated in textiles, or even in nondurable consumer goods in general.

The comparison is deceptive, however. Net output is valued and distributed among the various categories in Table 14 at the prices prevailing in each country. But the price ratios of different products may differ substantially from one country to another. Specifically, in the case of Japan, such products as machinery and metal products were generally higher in price, relative to textiles, for example, than in Western countries. This reflected relatively high costs of production, higher tariffs, and probably greater elements of monopoly in industrial organization.

If Japanese factory output were revalued at identical prices, item by item, the metalworking industries would be considerably reduced in importance, relative to their importance in Britain or the United States. Probably this is true of the heavy industries as a group. As these are generally capital-intensive industries with relatively higher output per worker, the effect would also be to reduce average output per factory worker in Japan, as compared with the other countries. It was a rough calculation of this sort which was embodied in Table 13.

In terms of a uniform scale of prices, in other words, Japanese manufacturing was still weighted on the side of the consumer goods, notably textiles. It was more heavily concentrated in labor-intensive industries than industrial production in the other countries. This is corroborated by statistics of employment. In 1934, 41.0% of all factory labor in Japan was engaged in textile manufacture, as com-

---

during 1934. Partly, no doubt, this was attributable to tariffs and monopolistic pricing in the former trades. But a marked disparity would doubtless have existed even under identical competitive conditions, owing to differences in the technical requirements of production. Generally speaking, relative variations in output per head among different industries tend to follow a similar pattern in all industrialized countries.

Table 14. *Structure of Factory Production in Japan, the United Kingdom, Germany, and the United States: Distribution of Net Product Value by Industrial Groups, 1934-37*[a]
(percentages)

	Japan (1934)	U.K. (1935)	Germany (1936)	U.S.A. (1937)
All factories	100.0	100.0	100.0	100.0
Metals, machinery and vehicles	36.3	33.4	40.3	38.3
Chemicals, paper and printing	22.2	16.9	15.6	20.0
Textiles and clothing	15.1	20.2	15.0	13.5
Food, drink, tobacco	15.4	17.0	14.0	14.6
Other	11.0	12.3	15.1	13.6

[a] Data for the United Kingdom, Germany, and the United States are from L. Rostas, "Industrial Production, Productivity and Distribution in Britain, Germany, and the United States," *Economic Journal*, vol. LIII, no. 209, April 1943, p. 44; for Japan, from Yasuji Koide, "Hompō Sangyō Kōzō no Hendō ni Kansuru Shiryō," *Nagoya Keizai Tōkei Geppō*, vol. VIII no. 9, October 1936, p. 59. For definitions of factories see Table 13, above, note a. The groupings used here, the second rather illogical, have been adopted in order to minimize the difficulty arising from discrepancies in census classifications. Certain minor inconsistencies remain, but are not serious.

pared with only 20.5% in Britain (1935) and 13.4% in the United States (1937). Here capital investment per worker was comparatively low in most branches of production, price competition was keen, and four out of five workers were women.[54]

A more detailed analysis by commodities would show also that the demand for Japanese manufactures *within* each broad category of Table 14 was such that a greater share of production was directed toward particular products and processes which required larger amounts of labor per unit of output. One thinks, for example, of raw silk as compared with rayon yarn, of bicycles as compared with automobiles, or of flashlights and small motors as compared with big generators. Abroad it was in such lines that Japan still found her chief advantage in competition with the West. At home, too, the scale of production organization was limited by the comparative poverty of the Japanese market, in terms of aggregate size; also by the Japanese attachment to individuality and variety of design in household goods. These factors retarded the advance of mechanized, mass production methods, and made for a higher ratio of labor to capital than in the manufacturing industries of the West.

The structure of demand, therefore, combined with the relative

[54] In industry as a whole women comprised 44% of all factory workers in Japan (1934, private and government plants); 37% in the United Kingdom (1935); 28% in Germany (1936); and 22% in the United States (1929, all persons employed in manufacturing). *Kōjō Tōkeihyō* (1936), cited, pp. 14, 970; L. Rostas, "Industrial Production, Productivity and Distribution in Britain, Germany, and the United States," *Economic Journal*, vol. LIII, no. 209, April 1943, p. 44.

abundance of labor to hold physical output per worker in Japan well below the level achieved in the more advanced industrial countries. In a broad sense, both circumstances testify to the scarcity of capital, the lag in technology, and the persistent drag on productivity and incomes exercised by an unfavorable ratio between population and resources.

For a true perspective, then, one must appreciate the limitations as well as the achievements of the Japanese record. The former do not necessarily detract from the latter. Indeed they only emphasize the exceedingly primitive state of Japan's pre-industrial economy, which furnished the background and starting point for modernization. With all the qualifications which must be made, the changes of 1868 to 1938, in terms of the organization of wealth-producing activities, were more profound than those of the previous millennium.

The processes by which this change took place in Japan are the subject of this book. If correctly understood, they can throw a good deal of light on the essential conditions of economic progress for other Asiatic nations today—indeed, for any undeveloped country. Stated in general terms, most of them are almost truisms, in that they are common to the past experience of all industrializing nations. Yet they are often glossed over in plans and proposals put forward today for attacking the problem of poverty in Asia. Thus they deserve constant reiteration.

Technology and the Market. Among the conditions of economic development, one thinks first of changes in production technology. These proceeded unevenly in various sectors of the economy, as we have seen. The most conspicuous feature was the harnessing of mechanical energy to industrial pursuits, which brought a sustained rise in labor efficiency. By the end of the prewar period the engineering and power industries, together with imports of metals and machinery, had grown to major significance in the economic life of the country. Even though more than half of the working population was still occupied in peasant agriculture and other handicraft trades, the Japanese now stood midway in energy consumption between the advanced industrial nations of the West and the rest of Asia.

Initially, power machinery and the techniques required to put it to use were almost wholly an importation from the West. Through the Meiji era, indeed, the strategic function of foreign trade for Japan was as a channel and stimulus for the inflow of modern equipment and the technical knowledge to put it to use. (See Chapter 6.) Not until later did overseas markets and raw materials begin to assume a large importance quantitatively in economic life. Then it was only as a result of the growth of population and productivity stimulated by persistent technological advance. It is impossible here to describe the process of technical change in its complex ramifications; curiously, little study seems yet to have been devoted to this critical phase of Japanese economic history. However, two further observations of a general character may help to place it in perspective.

The first is simply the reminder that the rise of productivity involved much more than the acquisition of machinery and a corps of technicians to supervise its use. If it meant no more than this, the Industrial Revolution would have spread through Asia much more rapidly than it has. The change in the industrial arts was actually secondary in one sense. It rested upon much broader changes in economic life, including especially the growth of the market. For the use of power equipment in production becomes profitable only as it becomes possible to move out of the sphere of self-sufficient economic activity. It requires railways and banks and an efficient medium of exchange. It signifies the rise of an economy in which labor and capital are combined and concentrated in various specialized ways, with the resulting surpluses exchanged against each other in widely organized markets. To place it in the foreground runs the risk of obscuring other conditions of economic progress which are less visible but no less essential.

In Japan the beginnings of a trend toward regional and occupational specialization, linked with simple improvements in production, are clearly discernible in the last century of Tokugawa rule and even before. As noted in Chapter 1, the expansionist pressures thus generated had a good deal to do with the eventual overthrow of the Shogunate. Indeed, it was mounting ambition on the part of clan bureaucrats, merchants, and craftsmen to extend such innovations, and widespread discontent with the obstacles imposed by feudalism, that hastened the collapse of the *ancien régime*.

The new freedom and leadership after 1868 ushered in a rapid forward movement. The introduction of machinery and science went forward hand in hand with progressive division of labor. The latter brought the disintegration of the traditional processes of nonagricultural production, and their reintegration under capitalistic forms of organization. As regions and occupations became more specialized they were linked together in expanding circuits of exchange. With the extension of the market, and the growing mobility of labor and capital, it became both possible and profitable to subdivide production operations. This led to better tools, machinery, and business methods. The latter served to raise productivity and incomes, and further expanded the market.[55]

[55] Regional and craft specialization was by no means unknown in pre-Meiji

In all this Japan did no more than move at an accelerated rate along a path of experience already pioneered in the West. In England the factory system evolved over two centuries or more; in Japan it was established in fifty years, or even less. The main difference, of course, was that the techniques of machine production and large-scale organization were already highly developed by the nations which led the Industrial Revolution. As rapidly as they could be assimilated in Japan they afforded a decisive profit advantage over the traditional modes of economic organization, especially in certain branches of manufacturing and transport. The introduction of machine-spun yarn into Japan, for example, immediately put hand-spun cotton at a hopeless disadvantage, both in quality and price. Also, pre-factory industry was less highly elaborated in Japan before 1868. There was less resistance from custom and from legislative and gild restrictions favoring the old as against the new.

The domestic market for industrial goods was now freed from feudal sumptuary restraints and internal toll barriers. It was increasingly commercialized, especially after the land tax reform required peasants to sell more of their crops to raise cash for tax payments.[56] And as income rose it also became slowly but increasingly a market for goods of wide consumption. Especially was this true among the growing urban classes.[57] No longer was the demand confined largely to a few simple products for local use, or to luxury goods consumed by a parasitic feudal aristocracy. This greatly enlarged its scope. And, what is of equal significance, consumer demand was now being directed increasingly toward standardized commodities more suitable for factory production. The latter was a slow process, resisted by the Japanese love for variety and artistry in decoration and design. Even today many industries serving primarily domestic requirements for native-style clothing, utensils, and furnishings remain on an individualized small-scale basis, however large their output may be in the aggregate. For many products very widely used, there is still no "national market" of the highly

---

Japan. As in all preindustrial societies, however, it was mainly a specialization by products, rather than by processes coordinated in a unified production operation. Similarly Tokugawa Japan had its great cities; but these were vast agglomerations of tiny commercial and handicraft establishments, lorded over by the feudal nobility and their retainers. They were not the highly organized and integrated metropolitan communities of the modern world.

[56] Yasuzo Horie, "The Development of the Domestic Market in the Early Years of Meiji," *Kyoto University Economic Review*, vol. xv, no. 1, January 1940, pp. 48-49.

[57] In 1895 only 12% of the Japanese lived in places of over 10,000 population. Forty years later the proportion had grown to 46%. One in every four now lived in a city of over 100,000. The rural population (in places of less than 10,000) actually remained stationary after 1920, the entire increase in the country's total population being absorbed thereafter in the larger towns and cities.

standardized American type. It was the export industries producing silk, cotton goods, chinaware, and other manufactures for Western consumption which led the way in standardization.[58] Characteristically, therefore, it was the export branches of these industries which tended to be on a larger scale and more capitalistic in organization. In certain other industries, however, the reverse was true, as described in Chapter 7.

The growth of the market was also stimulated after 1880 by the heavy expenditures of the State for armaments, transport, communications, and supporting industries. These outlays were significant in economic terms chiefly because they were concentrated upon the metal, machinery, and shipbuilding industries, rather than because of their actual bulk. They helped materially to launch new enterprises in these fields and to get them over their first technological hurdles. In addition, government expenditures at home had a general expansionist effect on domestic industry and trade insofar as they were financed by credit creation or taxing agricultural incomes which would not otherwise have been spent in the market. An important share was actually devoted to purchasing arms and ships abroad. This also stimulated domestic production by encouraging the export of various commodities in payment.[59]

Historically, then, the development of technology and the development of the market proceeded simultaneously, each reinforcing the other. Each was fostered by the new freedom of occupation, security of property, and stimulus to business enterprise afforded by the political institutions and objectives of the Meiji government. Technical, economic, and political changes were intertwined. The one progressed with the others, and where there was a lag in the requisite economic and social conditions, as in agriculture, there was a corresponding lag in technological innovations. The condition for a

---

[58] Sometimes export standardization meant deterioration in quality, sometimes substantial improvement. The cheap Japanese pottery and textiles which came to be sold in large quantities abroad were far below the standard of traditional craftsmanship in Japan. On the other hand, in the raw silk trade the demands of Western silk manufacturers for better quality and uniformity exerted steady pressure on Japanese reelers and exporters to raise standards. See, for example, the negotiations between Japanese export associations, the government and American and European importers which are detailed in the *Thirty-fourth Annual Report of the Silk Association of America*, New York, 1906. Silk importers abroad gradually persuaded the Japanese that inferior silks damaged the reputation of good silks, and that inaccuracy in the invoiced weight of silk bales was a serious deterrent to purchases. Japan soon outdistanced China in supplying the American silk market. This was not because of any natural advantages, but because her silk industry, with the aid of the government, was more successful in dealing with the problem of quality and uniformity.

[59] The broad relations between the growth of national income and the changing pattern of national expenditures are examined in greater detail in Chapter 8.

revolution in production methods was a corresponding revolution in the other spheres as well.

Foreign trade, of course, played an essential role in the growth of the market from an early date in the modern period. For instance, the match industry developed in response to market opportunities in China; the modern silk industry was the creation of the American market; tea, coal, and copper all found important outlets abroad. There was nothing novel in this except in the history of Japan herself. Nor was it, as is sometimes alleged, any necessity peculiar to the capitalistic form of organization.[60] The international market has been predominant in the economic development of other areas as far back as the Middle Ages, and even in that of the ancient Mediterranean world, long before the advent of modern capitalism. In the industrial growth of an undeveloped country, it is precisely in this early phase that exports may be of special importance, as the history of England's textile and wrought iron industries well shows.

Particularly where a country has good sea communications, it is apt to be easier to overcome the territorial limitations of the market externally than its social and economic limitations at home. Japan is a conspicuous case of maritime expansion, but one which is by no means unusual. Much more unique, indeed, was the long isolation of pre-Meiji Japan from the foreign contacts which an island nation might be expected to develop. For the Tokugawa interdiction of trade and intercourse not only walled off knowledge of the West; it also checked the stimulus which elsewhere a lively export trade has exerted on indigenous developments in industrial organization. Even in Japan's modern history it is doubtful if exports have played as crucial a role in the growth of factory industry as in the classic case of Britain. In any case it is worth noting that the domestic market for Japanese manufactures, as well as other commodities and services, has remained far greater in size throughout the modern period. It expanded *pari passu* with the growth of overseas trade.

Japan's actual dependence on export markets in prewar years is examined at length in Chapter 7. While the details may be left for consideration there, the conclusions may be anticipated briefly

[60] F. Barret makes an elaborate attempt to apply the Marxist-Leninist thesis to Japan in his work cited above. The growth of Japan's foreign trade, in his view, represented nothing more than a contradiction between the productive power of Japanese capitalism, on the one hand, and the lack of buying power among the masses, on the other. Since the Japanese trusts kept the people so impoverished, they could only dispose of their growing output in foreign markets, or dissipate it in war and conquest. (Pp. 371-90.) Anyone who has the patience to wade through Barret's voluminous statistical "evidence" will find it no more convincing that his theoretical propositions.

at this point. Few products from her extractive industries ever found a market abroad in significant amounts, either in raw or processed form. The outstanding exceptions were silk and tea, and in the earlier decades coal and copper. During the interwar years, when foreign trade reached its largest dimensions, foreign and colonial markets took less than 4% of most Japanese farm products, 3% of forestry products, and only 7% of the fishing catch. In minerals and foodstuffs generally the country became a heavy importer on balance. The reason for these low export ratios was not simply Japan's poverty in natural resources; her extractive industries grew substantially, as we have seen. It was also her growing home market, which came to absorb all that and more than could be produced by her farms, forests, fisheries, and mines. Among the service trades, too, only one—shipping—was heavily dependent on foreign trade, for obvious reasons. In manufacturing industry, on the other hand, the export share reached 25 to 35% of total output in the decade 1927-36, thanks mainly to raw silk and cotton textiles. Here opportunities for Japanese goods abroad, both in the West and throughout Asia, enabled her to finance her heavy import requirement, beside contributing importantly to technological advances in her manufacturing capacity.

For the Japanese economy as a whole, it would appear from statistics given in Chapter 7 that overseas markets at their prewar peak absorbed no more than 20% of the net value of goods and services produced in the country. (Table 27.) This is a substantial share, strategic to Japan's whole economic existence because of the food and materials it brought in return. Circuits of overseas exchange tied into domestic economic activity at almost every point. Yet it remains true that the growth of the market even for manufactures was in the main the growth of purchasing power at home. Quantitatively, at least, the world market has attracted attention out of proportion to its importance for Japan as a source of expanding demand.

A good deal of attention has centered likewise on the efforts of the Japanese government to foster the export trade after 1868. This was, indeed, a cardinal object of state policy, assiduously pursued for strategic as well as economic reasons. Much more significant economically, however, especially in the early decades, were the measures taken to unify and consolidate the domestic market. Along with political unification, these included a number of steps already recounted in Chapter 1: the abolition of clan tariff barriers and other feudal restrictions on internal freedom of movement and enterprise; the creation of railways, communications, and commodity exchanges; the spread of technical education; the drafting of a code of commercial laws; the establishment of a national currency and banking system; etc. More broadly, they involved the reduction of restrictions of all sorts—political, economic, and psychological—on the mobility of goods, labor, and capital within the national boundaries. The history of modern Japan in this regard also repeats the history of all modern, industrializing nations. It differs mainly in the speed with which the process went forward, once undertaken.[61]

The chauvinist and warlike manifestations of Japanese nationalism in recent years have tended to dim the memory of this earlier, constructive phase. It is worth recalling, therefore, that nationalism fulfilled this historic mission here, as elsewhere. The economic and technical progress of Japan has been due in no small measure to the fact that a firm and durable framework of national unity was achieved at an early date. The small size of the country, its excellent inland sea communications, its racial and cultural homogeneity, its success in warding off foreign domination, the caliber of its political leadership—all played their part. To see the basic importance of internal unity and order one has only to look at China, where, for various reasons including notably the aggression of Japan herself, its fulfillment was so long delayed.

Technology and Capital. The second general observation to be made regarding technological progress in Japan is to caution against the tendency to think of such progress mainly in terms of the introduction of power machinery organized in large complexes and therefore requiring large units of capital investment.

This did take place in Japan from an early date. It was conspicuous in railway transport, shipping, electric power, and the metal and engineering trades. It was also evident in certain consumer goods industries like cotton yarn and flour. On the other hand, it was notably lacking in agriculture. And generally in Japan, as in most newly industrializing countries, the process was at once simpler and more complex.

One may recall that in the Industrial Revolution of Western Europe the great inventions of the eighteenth century were preceded by a long evolution of small-scale technical improvements in the earlier forms of production, especially domestic industry. In the

---

[61] This had broad social as well as economic consequences. Fifty years after the Restoration, Prof. Sakutaro Fujioka wrote as follows: "Formerly, by glancing at the accoutrements of a procession, one could tell what *daimyo's* it was, and likewise the *samurai* belonging to each *daimyo* had their own peculiar language and manners. But the introduction of the telegraph and telephone, the steamer and railway has contracted ten thousand miles to ten steps, and these facilities, assisted by the general diffusion of knowledge among the people, are yearly lessening the distance between districts, and bridging the gulf between city and country." *Fifty Years of New Japan,* compiled by Count Shigenobu Okuma, London, 1909, vol. II, p. 452.

Far East today, and particularly in Japan, the whole process has been telescoped. All stages of technological maturity and complexity tend to develop side by side in the greatest variety. But it is always easier to introduce these innovations which do not break radically with the past. They generally require no large accumulations of capital or advanced technical skills. And in the aggregate such lesser adaptations and improvements were of immense importance in Japan.

The spread of wheeled vehicles of any sort in transportation, the use of imported kerosene to lengthen the working day in peasant homes, the small power loom in the cottage, the gas engine in the fishing boat, better methods of collecting and spreading fertilizer, improvements in the farmer's hoe and the silk-reeler's basin—such changes in an Oriental economy are not less significant because unspectacular by modern standards. So, too, with regard to the introduction of simple forms of accounting, or the rise of postal communications, commodity exchanges, and bank credit. Even such a simple thing as more adequate warehousing may increase food supplies substantially.[62] The advance of productivity in Japanese agriculture, in many services, and even in a large share of manufacturing industry proceeded mainly by the cumulative spread of such modest innovations through millions of small establishments.

Partly, of course, this is a matter of the difficulty of any people in readily assimilating science and technology in their more complex forms. The limiting factors may include certain physical conditions of production, as in farming Japan's terraced mountainsides. More widely they are found in patterns of social organization which are resistant to change; in habits of mind which can only be modified slowly by education and experience; and in a pervasive shortage of capital, which has tended to make economic in Japan certain techniques and equipment long since discarded as obsolete in wealthier countries. In this general sense the industrialization of any country tends to follow the "line of least resistance." Such resistance in Japan was broken down and the frontiers advanced with unusual rapidity, except in agriculture and the traditional service trades. Even so, it would be a mistake to think that economic development consisted, or could consist, mainly of the introduction of great factories, power plants, and transportation systems.

Such large enterprises were necessary to full-scale industrialization. It was here that the State and the *zaibatsu* played a key role. But these enterprises were made possible, and derived much of their

---

[62] Indian authorities estimate today that the loss of grain in India through decay and infestation amounts to at least 3% of the annual crop. In China some 5 to 10% of farm crops are said to spoil before they reach the consumer.

utility, from less dramatic but more pervasive changes in traditional Japanese economic life. In certain instances—for example, steel and shipbuilding—they were supported only at the expense of other industries through a continuous process of State subsidy. In other industries like textiles and ceramics the large, capitalistic establishment was closely tied in with numbers of smaller, less mechanized enterprises. The latter supplied raw materials and services, or handled certain stages of manufacture. Similarly the growth of import requirements and of export capacity in foreign trade represented in no small degree the extension of small-scale production. These small firms employed comparatively simple techniques of production and small investments of capital, but were integrated increasingly within a framework of large-scale marketing, transportation, and finance. One asset of great significance already commented upon was the wide distribution of electric power. This facilitated a good deal of mechanization, even where (apart from the power generation itself) the units of investment and management remained small. Japan's progress in industrialization owes much to her comparative success in combining large and small enterprise in intricate patterns of cooperation—a point to which we shall return again.

A steady growth of savings and investment in new forms of capital goods was essential to the whole process of modernization, of course. In Chapter 5 the factors influencing its rate are discussed at some length. To what extent the availability of new capital can be called *the* decisive factor in increasing productivity, however, is not clear. The Japanese experience certainly argues for its importance. Yet it also demonstrates the possibility of substantial advances from traditional levels of output in many activities even in the absence of large outlays for plant and equipment.

The gains in Japanese agricultural output, notably, were achieved mainly by better use of existing resources of land and labor. Marked increases in productivity per acre and per worker resulted from new methods of seed selection, weeding, disease control, crop storage, and animal breeding; from ready improvements in tools; and from the consolidation of land holdings.[63] Such improvements as these required only modest amounts of new capital in comparatively simple forms. They entailed no radical reorganization of farming practices. They were pioneered by a network of government agricultural experiment stations, supported by the agricultural departments of

[63] In regions where scattered plots belonging to a single farmer were consolidated in a single, compact holding, it is said that the resulting elimination of boundary lines made it possible to increase the cultivated area by as much as 15%. The Japan Year Book Office, *The Japan Year Book* (1906), Tokyo, 1905, p. 177. In this sense much of the technical innovation in Japanese agriculture was capital-saving— i.e., it economized land.

the universities. Relative to her cultivated area, and perhaps her agricultural income as well, prewar Japan came to spend more on agricultural research than even the United States.[64] Other gains resulted from the shift to more remunerative crops; for instance, from cotton to mulberries. Still others, like better marketing or intensive fertilization to make possible double cropping and higher yields, necessitated mainly an increase in working capital. (It was the shortage of such capital, as much as anything else, which drove the peasant into debt and often lost him his land.)

By such technical advances as these, plus better irrigation and drainage, the law of diminishing returns in Japanese agriculture was postponed in its effects for several generations.[65] From 1894-1900 to 1931-40, average rice yields per acre increased by one third, according to official statistics cited in Chapter 3 (pages 93-94). The yields of wheat, tea, and barley doubled, while crop yields as a whole rose at least 50%, judged by the Nagoya indices (Tables 2 and 3). This took place for the most part on land already closely cultivated for centuries, it should be noted, although not without increasingly heavy doses of fertilizer every year.

To expand agricultural output on this scale required a growth of agricultural capital, to be sure. Most of the growth, however, took the form of improvements in land and buildings, or of working capital to finance outlays for fertilizer, seed, etc. Fixed capital improvements were made chiefly through employing local labor on public works, or through the peasant's use of his spare time to build up the productivity of his own farm. The latter proceeded mainly by small increments of labor, supplemented by the investment of such money savings as the farmer might painstakingly accumulate. In good part it represented the sacrifice of family leisure rather than of income for consumption.

The average farm family, cultivating two and a half acres, utilized capital other than land amounting to only 1,038 yen as late as 1930. Of this sum, buildings accounted for over one half, leav-

---

[64] Supreme Commander for the Allied Powers, GHQ, Natural Resources Section, Report No. 59, *The Agricultural Experiment Stations of Japan*, Tokyo, 1946, p. 21.

[65] J. W. Robertson Scott gives many interesting illustrations from his travels in rural Japan during 1915-19. In one village, for example, he tells of a progressive headman who persuaded a group of farmers to keep accurate accounts of their farm operations. These showed that the cultivation of their land required only a fraction of their time (generally in Japan no more than 200 days a year); also that much labor was wasted in cultivating irregular and scattered strips. Accurate knowledge of these facts stimulated the readjustment of land holdings, better drainage to economize manure, and a search for more secondary employment to fill in idle hours. Village income was increased, and the labor required to farm one *tan* of rice land was reduced from twenty-three ten-hour days to sixteen or seventeen, as a result of more efficient cultivation and irrigation. *Foundations of Japan*, London, 1922, pp. 231-32.

ing a meager 500 yen for farm animals, tools, working capital, etc.[66]

Power machinery was almost nonexistent on the Japanese farm. In 1937 there were only 187,813 power-operated machines owned by farmers in all Japan, plus 59,047 available from rental agencies. This is one to every twenty-two families. Nearly two thirds of them were small kerosene- or gasoline-operated units averaging only 2.9 h.p. Even this small amount of mechanization represents a marked advance over the years immediately preceding. Stimulated by the prosperity and growing labor shortage of the thirties the number of farm machines had tripled since 1927. In Okayama a small 350-lb. tractor was even being put into use on a limited scale. Despite such advances, however, the total capacity of all power-operated equipment available for farming in Japan was still only 623,000 h.p. in 1937. This was no more than 0.11 h.p. per farm household. And virtually all of it was used in pumping water or processing grain; the actual cultivation of crops continued to be done almost exclusively by hand.[67] Assistance even from draft animals was limited. Only 2 million out of 5.6 million farm households kept either cattle or horses. The total number was hardly more than one draft animal to every two farms.

It is well known that Japanese agriculture was neglected and discriminated against, in matters of taxation and public expenditures, in favor of industrial and military expansion. (See Chapter

[66] This is a national average computed from an estimate of aggregate capital invested in Japanese agriculture. Shiroshi Nasu, *Aspects of Japanese Agriculture*, New York: Institute of Pacific Relations, 1941, p. 152. Estimates of "productive" capital in Japanese farming are complicated by the difficulty of distinguishing producers' from consumers' capital in the case of buildings, cash, etc. A sample survey of the Ministry of Agriculture and Forestry, covering 279 farm families in 1937, most of them operating 3- to 4-acre farms, gives the following family assets in yen (*Japan Statistical Year-Book 1949*, cited, pp. 222-23):

	Owner-Operator	Part-Owner	Tenant
Total family assets	10,736	9,010	7,748
Land	6,063	5,981	4,996
Owned	(5,839)	(3,005)	(154)
Rented	(224)	(2,976)	(4,842)
Cash and liquid assets	1,235	840	583
Other family property	3,438	2,189	2,169
Net worth	10,125	5,363	2,372

[67] The above figures are from "Mechanization of Japanese Farms," *Oriental Economist*, vol. VI, no. 8, August 1939, pp. 514-18; and Kinichi Yoshioka, "Agricultural Machinery Making Industry Shows Great Strides," *Contemporary Opinions*, no. 309, December 14, 1939, pp. 4-6. The "great strides" consisted in a growth of the agricultural machinery industry from 2,555 workers and an output of 4.4 million yen in 1929 to 6,553 workers and an output (at inflated prices) of 14.2 million yen in 1937. By this time, however, the industry was already being squeezed out of the market for materials and labor by the armament boom.

10.) The agricultural community also remained the center of social conservatism, burdened with a high rate of population growth, and a system of land ownership and credit which was inefficient as well as oppressive. Land was subdivided uneconomically into tiny parcels, half of it cultivated under a tenancy system which often tended to discourage capital improvements and other types of modernization because it failed to give the cultivator assured, long-term tenure. If the gains in productivity were nevertheless as significant as they appear to have been, this suggests how great are the possibilities for increasing the efficiency of the traditional modes of agriculture everywhere in the Far East. These potentialities seem to be large even with comparatively small outlays of capital per worker, provided other circumstances are not too unfavorable to development.[68]

In the field of industrial production, large-scale investments of capital in the form of buildings, machinery, and equipment obviously played a more decisive role. But here also there were wide variations from one industry to another, and commonly within a single industry, as regards the size of the typical plant, the amount of capital per worker, and the relationship between increasing capital outlays and gains in labor efficiency.

Coal mining, mentioned above, was a case where the investment of large sums in plant and equipment brought only moderate advances in productivity. Probably this was true in general of the mining industries, where more intensive exploitation of the country's limited deposits met with rising costs. At the other extreme, the silk industry progressed rapidly with only modest demands upon Japan's resources, either in man-made capital or in land and labor diverted from other uses. In Nagano Prefecture, for example, output per man-hour in silk reeling doubled between 1874 and 1913 as the process was transferred from home to factory.[69]

---

[68] The discussion of Japanese farming in this study, both here and in other chapters, does not pretend to be a full assessment of the position of agriculture in modern Japan, or of the effects of industrialization on the livelihood of the peasant. The latter involves not merely the growth of production, but equally the distribution of income from agricultural pursuits. As briefly observed, this was heavily to the disadvantage of the small cultivator.

In addition, the question of stability of farm livelihood is of immense importance. The great famines of Tokugawa Japan were now eliminated by improvements in transport, marketing, and control of water supply. Plant and animal disease were also brought under increasing control; Robertson Scott notes that the sericulturist need no longer fear the loss of his silkworm harvest from disease every five years or so, as formerly. (*op.cit.*, p. 158.) However, the peasant was now subject increasingly to the vicissitudes of the market for cash crops, often aggravated by vagaries in the weather. The ups and downs of farm prices were a constant source of insecurity. Periodically they plunged the farming class into disaster. (See above, pages 56ff.) This insecurity, combined with the lack of reserves in the form of savings or cheap credit, was a major factor in the growth of tenantry and debt.

[69] Shuichi Harada, *Labour Conditions in Japan*, New York, 1928, p. 174.

Silk filatures grew mainly from small establishments with an average investment of only 1,500 yen per plant in the early days.[70] They were financed largely with local capital and operated with local water power. Thus the scale of investment was small; costs involved little beside the outlay for cocoons and labor.[71] Even as regards land and labor, the diversion of resources for alternative employments was slight by comparison with the gains in income. The seasonal labor required for cocoon rearing and silk reeling fitted in well with crop requirements. It provided valuable supplementary earnings for millions of underemployed farm women. The land required for mulberries was also limited in extent. It consisted largely of upland areas in the more mountainous prefectures less well suited to food production. Finally, the transport costs for this high-value product were comparatively small.

In a manufacturing industry, typically, one finds within certain limits a direct relationship between per capita output and the mechanization and size of the plant. In textile weaving, for example, the following table from an Indian source illustrates the relations which also prevailed in Japan:[72]

	Capital Invest-ment per Worker (rupees)	Net Product per Worker (rupees)	Ratio of Capital to Product per Worker	Workers per Rs. 1,000 of Capital
Modern, large-scale factory	1,200	650	1.9	0.8
Power loom, small-scale	300	200	1.5	3.3
Automatic loom, cottage	90	80	1.1	11.1
Hand loom, cottage	35	45	0.8	28.6

These figures portray the familiar principle that the more mechanized and capitalistic process tends to be characterized by a rela-

[70] Yeijiro Ono, *The Industrial Transition in Japan*, Baltimore, 1890, p. 58.

[71] In later decades the silk-reeling industry came to be organized and mechanized on a larger scale, under the pressure of demand for a more uniform product of high quality. It also was financed increasingly with capital supplied by city merchants and banks. However, an abundance of cheap and dextrous female labor remained the basis of its competitive strength. In the early thirties, labor still constituted 60% of the production cost of cocoons, other than mulberry leaves. In the added expenses of reeling, 45% went for labor and "provisions," another 9% for commissions. Mitsubishi Economic Research Bureau, *Japanese Industry and Trade*, London, 1936, pp. 256-61.

[72] S. K. Iyengar, "Industrialization and Agriculture, Postwar Planning," *Economic Journal*, vol. LIV, no. 214, June-September 1944, pp. 189-205. The last column, computed from the first, differs slightly from Iyengar's figures.

tively high product per worker (and low ratio of wages to net product). The big textile mill equipped with a good deal of power machinery employs fewer workers per unit of investment, while mechanization greatly increases their productivity.[73] Beyond a certain point, however, such gains are no longer great enough to offset the added costs of capital and other expenses of production, including managerial talent of the requisite experience and skill in large-scale enterprise. In practice, this point varies widely from industry to industry, and within an industry from country to country. The determinants include the technical conditions of production, the costs of capital, and the supply and price of labor of the necessary grades.

In Japan, by comparison with more advanced industrial nations, these circumstances have been such that it has been profitable to economize capital and the higher-grade managerial and technical skills at the expense of the more plentiful grades of labor. Earlier in this chapter the point was discussed at some length. To cite one more illustration, the average Japanese sawmill runs on 25 h.p.; it cuts no more in one day than an American mill will cut in an hour.[74] In short, machine-made products are "copied with hand labor," in the sense that the typical combination of the productive factors is weighted more heavily in favor of human energy. This fact has made for a much lower output per worker than in the West. Yet clearly, in the context of Japan's resources, it has been the economical way to proceed in building the foundations of modern industry.

If Japan's experience teaches any single lesson regarding the process of economic development in Asia, it is the cumulative importance of myriads of relatively simple improvements in technology which do not depart radically from tradition or require large units of new investment. The big, modern establishment with its concen-

[73] For purposes of brevity here, we are treating together two aspects of mechanized production which are not necessarily directly related to each other: the size of the plant and the degree of mechanization. One of the characteristics of certain Japanese industries, indeed, was their adoption of machinery and electric power without any radical increase in the number of workers per plant. Generally speaking, however, the transition from handicraft to machine production entails some growth in the average-size plant, as well as the scale of organization in banking, transport, and other auxiliary services.

Increasing per capita productivity also tends to accompany a growth in the size and integration of an industry as a whole, as distinguished from the plant. This makes it possible for firms to specialize in various aspects of the production process, and encourages the development of specialized transport, marketing, and supply agencies which enable fewer workers to turn out more product.

[74] "Little thought is given to production-line methods, and labor-saving devices are non-existent." Supreme Commander for the Allied Powers, GHQ, Natural Resources Section, Report No. 32, *Lumber Production in Japan*, Tokyo, 1946, p. 14.

tration of capital in advanced forms of technology was essential in many fields, of course. It provided the framework of economic growth in the form of railways and steam shipping, coal and electric power, the metallurgical industries, banking and insurance. It enlarged the opportunities in foreign trade; it was indispensable to the building of industrial war potential. Much of the real substance of Japanese economic growth, however, is found in the more modest types of improvements which were more easily and pervasively adopted, more economical in cost, and often more productive of immediate returns in income. For any poor country beginning to industrialize, one of the crucial problems is to introduce and spread such innovations as widely as possible.

These technological aspects of growth lead naturally into further questions concerning economic organization and enterprise. Innovation is "getting a new thing done"; it requires a doer. The spirit and structure of the enterprise system is fundamental to all other developments in an economy such as we have been reviewing. The remainder of this chapter therefore characterizes somewhat more fully the structure of private ownership and control which prevailed in prewar Japan. It will lay some factual basis for the more interpretive judgments reserved for the concluding chapter on "The State and Economic Enterprise."

Technology and Enterprise

The most casual acquaintance with Japanese economic life is sufficient to reveal a tremendous diversity in the organization of production and marketing structures, and equally in patterns of business ownership and control.

The forms of enterprise in prewar days ranged all the way from the giant *zaibatsu* combines which dominated the heavy industries to myriads of small farmers, petty tradesmen, and handicraftsmen whose outlook and modes of activity were essentially precapitalistic. Even within single industries like the cotton and machinery trades these contrasting patterns developed side by side. Certain products or processes were still left to independent workshops; other branches of the market were served by small plants coordinated and financed by wholesale merchants. Still others were dominated by large factories, many of them linked horizontally or vertically with other enterprises owned by the big trusts.

A large share of Japanese enterprise came to be organized on the joint-stock principle—that great invention only fully developed in the West during the past century. In Japan, as elsewhere, this made it possible to pool savings under unified direction far beyond the limits of family and personal acquaintance, and to separate the

functions of savings, risk taking, and management. It was a technological innovation fully as significant as the introduction of power
machinery, and indispensable to it. Yet other areas of economic
activity continued to be organized in terms of the individual proprietorship, and even joint-stock enterprise was suffused with the
spirit of the Japanese family system.

This diversity in structure is found in every industrial country
to a considerable degree. It arises naturally from differences in the
physical and technical conditions of production in various industries,
and in the nature of their capital resources and markets. In Japan
it was accentuated by other circumstances: her late start and rapid
progress in industrialization; the duality which persisted between
traditional and Western-style demands; the encouragements given
by the State to large-scale organization in certain industries; the
crowding of population on a limited farming area; and other social
factors making for inequalities in access to capital and opportunity,
with corresponding lags and leads in the process of modernization.

The patterns of business organization which emerged in almost
bewildering array led in turn to an equal diversity in the play of
forces determining prices, output, and technology. This greatly
complicates any attempt to arrive at summary judgments as to how
Japanese capitalism really functioned. One may say that the modern
Japanese economy was developed mainly by private enterprise,
operating within a framework imposed by social tradition and a
good deal of conscious political manipulation. But terms like
capitalism and private enterprise do not tell us much. They can
cover a great variety of ways of organizing productive resources to
meet the demands of a community. Too often in the case of Japan
there is a tendency to apply easy labels, derived from Western
experience. They may only obscure the complexity of the facts.

One of the most important questions to be faced, nevertheless,
concerns the system of enterprise and controls which shaped the
course of Japan's prewar economic development. For the processes
of growth—new products and methods of producing them, growing
pools of capital and skills, widening markets at home and abroad,
etc.—were not mechanistic forces blindly impersonal in their impulse and direction. They were an expression of human energies
latent in great masses of people. They worked toward a set of goals
reflecting the not always consistent aspirations of these people and
their leaders. And they were controlled by institutional values which
were deeply rooted in the past but underwent progressive modification under the new influences at work. How the function of initiative
and responsibility in this historic process was organized had everything to do with the rate and direction of economic growth.

Certain larger aspects of the enterprise system in modern Japan are left to Chapter 10. There the role of the State is examined, and an attempt is made to weigh various influences which gave drive and substance to economic development. Other chapters call attention to particular phases relating more particularly to the dynamics of capital formation, foreign trade, and other structural changes in economic life. Here it may suffice to describe certain dominant features of business organization, especially Japan's unique blend of large-scale and small-scale enterprise, which was such a conspicuous aspect of her growth and technical modernization. Attention is focussed mainly on the later years, but much that is said is applicable as well to the earlier decades.

The Small Establishment. First, one should recall the continuing importance of the small plant as the technical unit of Japanese production. The establishment of less than fifty workers, even less than five workers, has displayed marked powers of survival in competition with larger, more capitalistic establishments right down to the present day.

In agriculture the single-family farm, either owner-operated or -tenanted, has remained the dominant form of organization. Through the prewar decades rice and other crops continued to be produced largely with the hand labor of 5 million peasant families cultivating holdings which averaged only 2.5 acres. Most of the service occupations, too, except for the public services, banking, and large-scale transport, were crowded with independent workers or small businessmen assisted by their families and perhaps a few wage employees. This was true of retail and wholesale trade, for example, of construction and local transport, of amusements, and of the professions.

In manufacturing, as in mining and long-distance transport, the small establishment gradually lost ground. The reasons are obvious. A larger scale of production became more feasible as capital and technical experience accumulated. It also became more efficient with the widening of markets for standardized types of products. Significantly it appeared more prominently in the export branch of a number of consumer goods industries than in those industries producing for the home market. At home variety of style and design were more important, and the small producer had more ready access to the market. Finally, the average size of the manufacturing establishment was raised in the later years by a growing importance of the metalworking, chemical, and electric power industries. Here technical considerations favored the large unit from the beginning. By 1934 plants of 500 operatives or more had gained in the textile and metallurgical fields until they accounted for over half of the gross output and employment of all plants in these industries classified as factories (normally employing five or more operatives).

Even in factory industry, however, the small plant continued to demonstrate its competitive strength as the technical unit. As shown in Table 15, establishments of less than 100 workers still contributed over one third of total private factory production (gross value) in 1934. They employed about one half of all factory operatives, having maintained their share since 1919, and accounted for over one half of factory machine capacity. During the next decade a substantial change in the industrial pattern was brought about by the armament boom, and the measures of regimentation imposed by war governments. In Japan, as elsewhere, the exigencies of war con-

Table 15. *Private Factories in Japan Proper: Percentage Distribution of Number, Employment, Motive Capacity, and Production, by Size of Plant, 1919, 1934*[a]
(percentages)

| | FACTORIES | | OPERATIVES[b] | | MOTIVE CAPACITY[c] (HORSE-POWER) | GROSS VALUE OF OUTPUT |
	1919	1934	1919	1934	1934	1934
All private factory industry	100.0	100.0	100.0	100.0	100.0	100.0
5-9 operatives	45.8	56.5	8.5	11.8	14.2	6.9
10-99 operatives	49.1	39.7	35.9	36.9	46.2	29.8
100-499 operatives	4.3	3.1	23.5	22.0	⎱ 39.6	25.1
500 or more operatives	0.8	0.7	32.1	29.3	⎰	38.2
Textile industries	100.0	100.0	100.0	100.0	100.0	100.0
5-9 operatives	38.2	47.4	5.4	7.2	3.7	4.5
10-99 operatives	54.4	45.8	31.8	31.8	15.7	23.9
100-499 operatives	6.0	5.4	24.4	26.4	⎱ 80.6	20.3
500 or more operatives	1.4	1.4	38.4	34.7	⎰	51.2
Metallurgical industries	100.0	100.0	100.0	100.0	100.0	100.0
5-9 operatives	49.0	51.5	11.0	10.6	1.3	3.3
10-99 operatives	46.7	45.7	37.7	39.7	9.0	22.0
100-499 operatives	3.6	2.2	22.6	16.2	⎱ 89.7	17.0
500 or more operatives	0.7	0.6	28.7	33.5	⎰	57.8

a Yasuji Koide, "Hompō Sangyō Kōzō no Hendō ni Kansuru Shiryō," *Nagoya Keizai Tōkei Geppō*, vol. VIII, no. 9, October 1936, pp. 4, 18-19, 24-25, 58-59.

b Excludes supervisory, technical and clerical personnel, guards, messengers, etc.

c Instilled capacity of prime movers and electric motors. The ambiguity of this concept is criticized in Table 10, above, and the discussion attendant to it. However, the figures as given here will at least suggest the large proportion of mechanical energy utilized in small- and medium-size plants.

ferred advantages on the large enterprise. Significantly, however, small- and medium-size factories tended on the whole to maintain their relative position through the thirties, clustering as subsidiary establishments around the great arms plants.[75]

In manufacturing as a whole the small workshop remained even more important then the above figures would suggest. For this included over a million tiny household establishments too small to be classified as factories. More than half of them were nothing but one-man shops ("independents") engaged in some sort of industrial activity. Although gradually declining in relative importance, these small plants with less than five operatives still contributed a quarter or more of Japanese industrial output during the early thirties. In 1930 their net product (value added by manufacture) is estimated at 832 million yen. This was 30% of the product of all manufacturing industry, public and private. (See below, Table 38.)

Employment figures are more problematical. The 1930 census indicates, however, that private manufacturing establishments of less than five operatives afforded the principal field of employment for over 2.5 million persons, including entrepreneurs, their family members, and hired workers. One tabulation from this source was given in Chapter 3 (pages 111-12). From the official statistics one arrives also at the estimate in Table 16 of labor force in private manufacturing in 1930 by size of establishments (excluding the building trades and government factories).

After a half century of industrial development, industrial workplaces too small to be classified as "factories" (five operatives or more)[76] still afforded upwards of 50% of all manufacturing employment in Japan, even when allowance is made for the fact that many workers were only engaged part-time, and that some were unemployed at the time of the census. By comparison, factories of over 100 workers still furnished no more than 50% of industrial production, and no more than one third, perhaps as little as a quarter, of industrial employment. In 1930 there were 2,500 private factories in this class; but there were 60,000 smaller establishments employing five to ninety-nine workers, and a million or more still smaller establishments engaging less than five persons.

From these small industrial plants came most of the traditional necessities and luxuries of the people—foodstuffs, straw mats, footgear, silk fabrics, pottery, lacquerware, etc. They had also sprung up in other, newer trades producing for the foreign or domestic market such Western-style manufactures as bicycles, rubber shoes

[75] See Edwin P. Reubens, "Small-Scale Industry in Japan," *Quarterly Journal of Economics*, vol. IX, August 1947, pp. 577-604.
[76] See Chapter 3, note 43.

Table 16. *Labor Force of Private Manufacturing Industry in Japan Proper, by Size of Establishment, 1930*[a]

SIZE OF ESTABLISHMENT	NUMBER OF ESTABLISHMENTS	PERSONS ENGAGED (PRINCIPAL OCCUPATION)	
		Number	*Percent*
Total	*1,240,038*	*4,759,921*	*100.0*
Independents	665,533	665,533	14.0
1-4 operatives	512,271	2,106,650	44.3
5-99 operatives	59,643	988,465	20.8
100-499 operatives	2,178	504,512	10.6
500 or more operatives	413	494,761	10.4

a The number of establishments of five or more operatives is the factory census figure (Ministry of Commerce and Industry, *Kōjō Tōkeihyō* [1930], Tokyo, 1932, table 4). The number of independents (one-man establishments employing neither family nor hired labor) is from the decennial census (Imperial Cabinet, Bureau of Statistics, *Shōwa Go-nen Kokusei Chōsa Saishū Hōkokusho*, Tokyo, 1938, table 41). The number of establishments of one to four operatives is the census total of employers, minus 40,000 estimated to own plants employing five or more operatives. (The remainder of the factories were owned by joint-stock companies and partnerships not defined as employers by the census.) The actual number of plants of one to four operatives was somewhat higher, as some employers owned more than one.

The number of persons occupied in the different categories is estimated as follows: (1) for plants of 100 or more operatives, factory employment at the end of the year plus unemployed workers estimated by the census as 3.3% for all industry; (2) for plants of five to ninety-nine operatives, the same as above, with the addition of 40,000 entrepreneurs operating factories assumed to be in this class; (3) for plants of one to four operatives, a residual figure derived by subtracting the other classes (and government factories) from the census total for all persons gainfully occupied in manufacturing (industrial classification, *ibid.*, table 47). Excluded throughout are persons gainfully occupied in construction (962,722) and in 152 government plants (153,348).

This method of estimation tends to exaggerate the importance of plants of less than five operatives, especially since so many people in this category worked only part-time. The reasons are set forth in note 42 to Chapter 3, above, where a similar tabulation is given using slightly different figures and including government factories. The conclusion given there may be repeated here: The census figures may be taken as broadly representative of the size and distribution of the labor force (in terms of chief occupation), but must be discounted substantially as a measure of actual employment.

and toys, electric lamps, and machine parts. In major industries like textiles and pottery they mushroomed along with the larger factories, either specializing in particular types of goods, or serving as feeder and finishing plants for the big enterprises. Osaka's 211,500 workers in 1932, for example, were distributed among as many as 31,800 industrial plants. Some 80% of these establishments in Japan's premier industrial city had less than five employees.[77] The same situation prevailed in Nagoya, likewise a center of textiles, foodstuffs, chemicals, and metal manufactures.

77 "Commerce and Industry of Osaka," *Commercial Japan*, vol. 12, October 1935, p. 55.

The importance of household production in several industries throughout the country is indicated in the following percentages (1932) :[78]

	EMPLOYMENT IN PLANTS OF:		VALUE OF OUTPUT IN PLANTS OF:	
	Less than five operatives	*Five or more operatives*	*Less than five operatives*	*Five or more operatives*
Cotton fabrics	48.2%	51.8%	31.1%	68.9%
Silk fabrics and mixtures	66.2	33.8	57.4	42.6
Porcelain	56.9	43.1	62.3	37.7
Wooden wares	84.9	15.1	58.5	41.5
Lacquer wares	95.6	4.4	95.0	5.0

If all establishments of less than 100 operatives are considered together, we find that plants of this size contributed 45 to 50% of the gross output of Japanese manufacturing in 1934.[79] Of the total amount of gainful employment in industry, they accounted for not less than 65%, and probably more. This is a conservative estimate which allows for a large amount of part-time employment in small-scale industry.[80] It may be contrasted with the corresponding figure for the United States. Here only 29% of all manufacturing wage earners were employed in plants of 100 workers or less in 1935.[81]

[78] Nagoya Chamber of Commerce and Industry, *Industrial and Labour Conditions in Japan*, Nagoya, 1934, pp. 12-14. Employment and output in plants of less than five operatives are residuals obtained by deducting the totals for factories (plants equipped to employ five or more operatives), as given by the Ministry of Commerce and Industry in *Kōjō Tōkeihyō*, from the totals for all plants, as given in *Shōkōshō Tōkeihyō*. Unfortunately the "all industry" returns of the latter are published for only a few industries.

[79] Factory output was valued at 9,390 million yen in 1934. Ministry of Commerce and Industry, *Kōjō Tōkeihyō* (1934), Tokyo, 1936, p. 732. For home industry, gross output is estimated by the method employed by the Japan Economic Federation in *National Income of Japan, 1930-1939*, Tokyo, 1940, pp. 66-69. The Cabinet Bureau of Statistics' ratio of home to factory output in 1930 (27%) is extrapolated by reference to the share of the former in five branches of industry where data for 1934 are available. This puts home industry output at 20 to 25% of total factory production.

[80] From certain municipal data and other evidence it is reasonable to conclude that the number of persons in establishments of less than five operatives was not less in 1934 than in 1930, the estimate above for the latter year being 2.8 million. Even if we cut this in half, to allow for part-time work and for possible overestimate of the number of persons actually employed, the result when combined with employment in factories of less than 100 operatives gives the total share of plants of this size as 65% of total industrial employment.

[81] *Statistical Abstract of the United States, 1940*, cited, p. 803. This U.S. figure is not strictly comparable, since it is confined to wage earners and excludes the gas and electric industry as well as all manufacturing plants with an annual out-

Thus Japanese manufactures were still being produced mainly by plants of less than 100 workers, except where large-scale methods conferred a decisive advantage. The latter cases included the basic metals, heavy engineering equipment, gas and electricity, foreign-style paper, cotton and rayon yarn, flour, sugar, cement, beer, glass, dyestuffs, and chemical fertilizers. On the other hand, woven and knit fabrics of all types, many wood, straw, and celluloid products, porcelain and enamelled ware, brushes, rubber and leather goods, and most other consumer goods continued to come largely from the small workshops and medium-size factories which crowded the cities and dotted the rural landscape.[82] Likewise, Japan's principal exports of manufactures, except for raw silk, cotton yarn, and sugar, were the products of medium- and small-scale factories.

As Uyeda, Allen, and others have shown, the small plant of five to fifty workers can hardly be described as a "feudal survival," lingering on until the large factory should give the *coup de grâce.* In many trades, including a number of export trades, it was admirably suited to Japan's complement of capital resources and skills. It could also be flexibly adapted and specialized to serve the varied market for Japanese manufactures at home, and changing demands from abroad. In certain fields it actually displayed a growing competitive superiority before the war. Relatively small independent weavers, for example, expanded their market more rapidly than their big competitors from 1931 to 1937. Specializing in individual fabrics and designs, they were able to improve their relative position as Japan's export opportunities shifted progressively toward cotton and rayon goods of wider diversity and finer quality. Gradually Japanese industry as a whole was becoming organized on a larger scale, as one would expect. Yet the wide dispersion of manufacturing among small work places survived even the pressures of the armament boom and war mobilization after 1938. It remains a striking characteristic to this day.

Small-Scale Enterprise. One must distinguish, of course, between the technical unit of production—for example, a factory or a shop—and the business or enterprise unit. The latter is a more elusive concept, for it involves the location of decision-making responsibility for a business enterprise. In almost any field, particularly manufacturing industry, this function is apt to be more narrowly concentrated than

put of less than $5,000. These differences, however, do not alter the comparison significantly.

[82] Excellent brief studies of a number of these small-scale trades will be found in Teijiro Uyeda's *The Small Industries of Japan,* New York, 1938. See also John E. Orchard, *Japan's Economic Position,* New York, 1930; and chaps. 13-16 by G. C. Allen in E. B. Schumpeter, ed., *The Industrialization of Japan and Manchukuo, 1930-1940,* New York, 1940.

the number of production establishments itself might suggest. Thus
the plant is not to be confused with the firm, still less with the combine of which the firm may be a part. In joint-stock enterprise,
moreover, the elements of ownership, investment risk, and managerial
decision can be separated or combined in the most diverse ways. To
locate entrepreneurial responsibility in any inclusive sense becomes
a complicated matter.

So much is heard of the great combine networks of prewar Japan,
with their pyramids of concentrated control, that it may be well to
begin by stressing the wide diffusion of entrepreneurial responsibility which has persisted through the major part of Japan's economic life. The census figures of 1920-40 distributing the working
population by industrial status are of interest here. Though they
suggest a more atomistic structure than actually prevailed in the
prewar years, they are highly significant. The pattern revealed by
the census of 1930, for example, may be taken as representative of
the situation after fifty to sixty years of economic modernization and
growth. It reflects one of the cardinal features of that growth.

Out of 29,619,640 Japanese gainfully occupied in 1930, 6,149,944
reported themselves to the census as "employers."[83] In other words,
over 6,000,000 people operated businesses which were not incorporated as juristic persons, but which employed some additional wage
or family labor. Agriculture and fishing alone absorbed 4,393,000.
But there were 1,757,000 in nonagricultural pursuits as well. Another 3,395,845 people were "independents," who made a living on
their own in one way or another with no hired labor or family helpers.
Thus almost one third of the working population were still classed
as entrepreneurs in some sense, so far as their principal occupation
was concerned.

Table 17 gives an interesting breakdown of the Japanese figures
published by the U.S. Department of State. Between the two broad
categories of agricultural and nonagricultural occupations, the
working population is divided about equally. Within each category,
in turn, about one third are classified as entrepreneurs. The remainder were wage earners and family workers, except for 800,000
managerial, technical, and professional persons and the 230,000 in
the armed forces.

Most entrepreneurs, it will be noted, are classified as "small" in
Table 17. This includes all farmers working less than 7.35 acres of

[83] Imperial Cabinet, Bureau of Statistics, *Shōwa Go-nen Kokusei Chōsa Saishū
Hōkokusho*, Tokyo, 1938, table 41, p. 202. An employer is defined as a person who
is "assisted, whether by an employee or a member of his own family, in transacting
his own business." Corporation executives are not employers; nor are persons who
only employ domestic servants.

Table 17. *Gainfully Occupied Population of Japan Proper, by Industrial Status, 1930*[a]

	AGRICULTURE AND FISHING		ALL OTHER (INDUSTRY, TRANS- PORT, SERVICES)		TOTAL	
	Number (thousands)	*Per- cent*	*Number (thousands)*	*Per- cent*	*Number (thousands)*	*Per- cent*
Total, gainfully occupied	*14,687*	*100.0*	*14,933*	*100.0*	*29,620*	*100.0*
Entrepreneurs[b]	*5,239*	*35.7*	*4,307*	*28.9*	*9,546*	*32.2*
Large	391	2.7	704	4.7	1,095	3.7
Small	4,848	33.0	3,603	24.2	8,451	28.5
Employed workers	*9,448*	*64.3*	*10,626*	*71.2*	*20,074*	*67.8*
Managerial[c]	2	—	817	5.5	819	2.7
Wage earners[d]	745	5.1	7,586	50.8	8,331	28.2
Family workers	8,701	59.2	1,993	13.4	10,694	36.1
Armed forces	—	—	230	1.5	230	0.8

a Data are from the Japanese census of 1930 and other sources, as compiled by the U.S. Office of Strategic Services and published by the Department of State in *National Income of Japan*, Washington, 1945, p. 194. "All Other" comprises mining, manufacturing, transport, communications, commerce, government, private professions, and domestic service. Persons are classified according to chief occupation, whether full- or part-time.

Figures include unemployed persons classified in the trades where they were last employed. The census showed only 319,813 persons unemployed in October 1930, but unofficial estimates run two or three times as high.

b Employers plus independents, as given by the 1930 census, whose businesses were not legalized as juristic persons. This excludes all corporation officials. "Large" entrepreneurs are defined as follows: in farming, those operating over 3 *cho* (7.35 acres) of land; in factory industry (establishments normally employing five or more operatives), all entrepreneurs; elséwhere, employers and independents having a net income, as reported for the business profits tax, of 400 yen or more. "Small" entrepreneurs comprise all other employers and independents, including all home industrialists, classified in accordance with principal occupation as reported by the census.

c Includes corporation officials down through department heads, and all technicians, engineers, doctors, dentists, teachers, priests, and other professionals requiring a "higher school" education or better.

d A residual, after deducting other categories from the total.

land (4.8 million). In nonagricultural trades it includes some 3.6 million small merchants, industrialists, tradesmen, and other employers or independents whose net income was reported for tax purposes as no more than 400 yen in 1930.[84] Trade and home industry (plants of less than five operatives) each accounted for around 1.2 million. The remaining third were widely scattered through the construction trades, catering and amusements, local transportation, and minor services.

Here we find added confirmation of the family pattern of Japa-

84 This 400-yen limit was hardly $200 at current rates of yen-dollar exchange, but represented something more than $200 would have bought generally in the United States at the time.

nese agriculture. Some 36% of the people principally engaged in
farming were farm operators, either owners or tenants. The remainder were mostly members of their families; wage labor was
negligible in amount. By contrast, industry and the service trades
as a whole now recruited their labor on a wage basis. Yet one in three
persons in these nonagricultural pursuits, taken together, was also
an entrepreneur in some degree. In construction, workshop industry,
and commerce the ratio was as high as one in two. In all manufacturing and nonrail transport it was one in four. By contrast, mining
had developed from the beginning on a large-scale, capitalistic
basis. It now showed a ratio of one unincorporated employer and
independent to every thirty workers. Similarly in factory industry
the ratio now stood at one to fifty.

The persistence of small, unincorporated business is further
revealed by comparing the census figures of Table 17 with statistics
of Japanese "companies." Under the prewar Commercial Code
the latter include principally joint-stock companies (*kabushiki
kaisha*), limited partnerships (*goshi kaisha*), and unlimited partnerships (*gomei kaisha*). Even in 1900, after revision of the Commercial Code, only 8,598 such private concerns had been organized
in all fields, excluding finance. Their paid-in capital and reserves
were reported at 880 million yen. By 1930 the number had risen
to 51,910, with paid-in capital and reserves of 16,837 million yen.
(Joint-stock companies now accounted for about 40% of the total
number and 80% of the capital; they represented around 4 million
individual shareholdings.) Yet all but 1,150 of these 51,910 companies were in fields other than agriculture and fishing. By comparison even "large" entrepreneurs in agriculture and fishing numbered 391,000, and in nonagricultural occupations 704,000. The
individual proprietor accounted for a much smaller share of total
capital and production, of course. Even so, the corporate form of
organization, while it now dominated large-scale industry and trade,
had yet to take over major sectors of the Japanese economy.[85]

[85] The number of companies in Japan Proper classified by types and fields increased as follows from 1900 to 1930:

	UNLIMITED PARTNERSHIPS		LIMITED PARTNERSHIPS		JOINT-STOCK COMPANIES		TOTAL	
	1900	1930	1900	1930	1900	1930	1900	1930
Total	*784*	*8,525*	*3,560*	*23,995*	*4,254*	*19,390*	*8,598*	*51,910*
Agriculture and fishing	14	232	125	425	81	493	220	1,150
Industry, including mining	274	2,813	1,271	8,651	1,009	7,117	2,554	18,581
Commerce	455	5,172	1,828	13,645	2,914	8,874	5,197	27,691
Transportation	41	308	336	1,274	250	2,906	627	4,488

Data are from Japan, Department of Finance, *Financial and Economic Annual of*

Just what is meant here by "entrepreneur" should be understood. To the American or European the term connotes a degree of independence and middle-class well-being associated with owning and controlling one's own business. In Japanese society this is found among the "large" entrepreneurs and some of the smaller ones— substantial peasant proprietors and town merchants, small factory owners, independent doctors and lawyers, etc. These classes contributed importantly to Japanese economic development through venturing their savings and energies in new and productive activity. Along with managerial and professional personnel in the salaried category, they carried through the innovations in technology and organization.

Also classified as entrepreneurs in Table 17, however, are vast numbers of smaller businessmen whose economic status was no higher than that of the male factory hand, and who might have even less in the way of capital resources or modern skills. In agriculture, for example, there were millions of tenant farm-operators near the bottom of the Japanese income scale. Other entrepreneurial groups included such independent craftsmen as the carpenter, the fisherman, the barber, and the matmaker, together with less skilled independent workmen—e.g., ricksha- and cart-pullers—who were little more than day laborers. Taxable earnings in 1930 averaged only about 1 yen per day among the 168,000 "small" entrepreneurs in transportation and the 1,214,000 in wholesale and retail trade. While the labor performed in these services played its part in Japan's economic growth, its unit efficiency necessarily remained low. There was little scope at such levels for entrepreneurial initiative in technical innovation. Nor was there much incentive so long as the growth of population crowded such occupations with masses of people unable to find a better livelihood elsewhere.

Even in industry the independence of the small businessman was likely to be more apparent than real. Often he secured his raw materials, his credit, and his market from a merchant or a large industrialist whose financial resources and knowledge of market conditions far exceeded his own. Small plants producing for the national or foreign market in particular were dominated by the great banks and industrial and trading corporations through a network of financial and commercial relationships. To cite one instance, the Mitsui interests built up an investment of 150 million yen in wholesale and retail commerce before the war. Much of it was handled through a single great trading company, Mitsui Bussan, which was backed by the powerful Mitsui Bank, and had affiliates and offices

Japan, passim. "Joint-Stock Companies" in 1930 include forty-one joint-stock limited partnerships.

all over the world. Similar enterprises were developed by other combines, e.g., Mitsubishi, Okura, Sumitomo, and Yasuda. These big
trading companies were heavily engaged in domestic as well as foreign activity, making loans to small producers either directly or
indirectly through local merchants and banks, and acquiring rights
to the disposal of their product in one way or another. While there
were thousands of medium-size trading companies of all sorts, and
hosts of still smaller merchants, the larger concerns were financially
able to exercise far-reaching influence over the sphere of small-scale
production as well as that of marketing. The small fellow at the
bottom of the pyramid, whether industrialist or merchant, might be
reduced virtually to the status of a wage worker, squeezed between
the price he paid for his credit and supplies and the price he could
get for his product.

Yet equally it was this larger framework of finance and distribution which gave competitive strength and resilience to the whole system of small-scale production. The small producer was able to reach
out to wider markets beyond the neighborhood only by virtue of the
entrepreneurial risk taking, the improved quality standards, and
the contacts which were thus afforded. If the system was exploitative
in the sense that financial resources and business acumen were on the
side of the large capitalist, it nevertheless represented a skillful
utilization of Japan's limited capital resources and technical experience to employ a large and expanding population in productive
pursuits.

So varied were the industrial and commercial arrangements in
this vast sector of the Japanese economy that it is difficult to generalize regarding the response of prices and production to changing
market conditions. Where the small craftsman merely served his
immediate neighborhood, the concept of a market for labor or capital
or the finished product has only the most localized meaning. This
remained true of a large segment of economic life. In the trades
supplying wider markets, on the other hand, it is obvious that effective business influence over credit and prices was concentrated
much more narrowly than the wide diffusion of ownership might lead
one to suppose. But even here, despite the marked advantages enjoyed by the big buyers and suppliers, one finds comparatively little evidence of centralized coordination of the market for the
products of small-scale production. The prevailing organization
tended to remain quite atomistic in structure.

In agriculture, it is true, the government stepped in after 1917,
both to encourage the formation of cooperatives and to attempt to
stabilize the price of rice. Later in the interwar period it began to
experiment—none too successfully—with the organization of associa-

tions of small industrialists and traders, particularly to relieve cut-throat competition in the export field. The intensity of competition which persisted in the small-scale trades is attested, however, by the difficulties encountered in all such efforts to control output or to regulate prices, wages, and working conditions. (See Chapter 10.)

Sellers' competition tended to be ruthless wherever numerous small industrialists supplied a common market. Individually the little man could exert no influence on price. He had to adjust himself as best he could to the over-all conditions of demand and supply. Entry of new producers was comparatively easy; typically it required only a modicum of capital and technical experience. Hard times took effect in extensive underemployment, or in the sweating of labor at substandard wages. Disadvantages of size, location, or equipment could often be offset by lower wages or poorer working conditions, especially where the employer relied on family labor. Such conditions were inherent in the abundance of labor, and in the comparative freedom of the small producer, within the limits of his resources, to conduct his own business, risking his tiny savings or negotiating a small loan, engaging his labor and arranging the production process, and seeking such outlets for his product as his local horizon afforded.

When one speaks of the enterprise system in prewar Japan, therefore, full allowance must be made for a wide diffusion of ownership and entrepreneurial initiative through a great part of the Japanese economy. Equal emphasis must be placed on the structure of overhead controls which concentrated major innovations and decisions shaping the direction of national development in the hands of the government and the *zaibatsu*. Yet it was the opportunities which arose for the expansion of small enterprise, and the adaptation of small businessmen to these opportunities, which explains Japan's economic growth in considerable degree. If the dynamics of economic expansion owed much to the Meiji bureaucrat and the Mitsui executive, its substance came in no small measure from the responses and capacities of the small peasant, trader, and industrialist.

This question of the potentialities of the small enterprise is of immense importance in the future industrialization of other Far Eastern countries. The virtues of decentralized, small-scale industry are not unmixed with social evils, of course. Here one is apt to find the longest hours, the most unsanitary working conditions, the most severe exploitation of children—often by their own parents. The system frequently enables the big capitalist to load commercial risks on the small entrepreneur, who is least able to bear them. Likewise well known are its disadvantages in terms of marketing and production efficiency, as well as economic planning and control. Particularly as a transitional stage, however, and even thereafter, it has much to recommend it wherever technical conditions do not rule it out. By comparison with large-scale industry, it economizes on the need for large units of capital investment and for those technical and managerial skills which are most difficult to acquire, while spreading incentives to capital formation and modest technical innovations among masses of small producers. It can more easily be dispersed to take advantage of local materials, markets, and pools of underemployed labor. Especially is this true where a broad framework of education, bank credit, electric power, and distribution facilities is provided, as in the Japanese case. Nowhere else, unless in certain basic public improvements in land, are the immediate returns per unit of investment likely to be more immediate.

In any densely populated, capital-poor country, economic growth can hardly make significant headway without capitalizing in one way or another on the enterprise and energies latent in the small businessman. With all of the twentieth century technology now at hand, this presumption still holds. The Japanese experience with both small and large-scale organization deserves more study than it has yet received—particularly the ways in which the two were combined and integrated.

The difference between Japanese and Indian industrialization, for example, is particularly instructive as regards the contrasting relations between modern and traditional industries. Factory enterprise developed more rapidly in Japan than in India after 1900; but it appears to have been much less destructive of cottage and workshop industry. To a far greater degree the Japanese succeeded in modernizing the production technique of the small establishment. More important, they strengthened it with external economies introduced by large-scale organization in the supply of raw materials, working capital, and markets. The whole process of industrialization was more rapid and more pervasive as a result, and some of its social dislocations were moderated.

The reasons for this difference are too complex to examine here. They comprise all those factors which served in Japan to alleviate, though not to prevent, the profound dualism observable everywhere in Asia where modern capitalistic enterprise has developed in conflict with traditional modes of economic life. One suspects that the mere geographic compactness of Japan and its island character had a good deal to do with the difference. Here it was far easier than in continental India or China to diffuse new ideas and skills through the countryside; to draw a large proportion of the people into new, urban occupations; and to create easy, efficient ties between rural industries on the one hand and the factories, banks, and merchants of the cities on the other. Here, too, a national network of electric power could be more readily created through cheap water transport of coal and the development of dispersed hydroelectric resources. Contrasting social traditions also made for decisive differences; in Japan there seems to have been a more eager and flexible response to the introduction of capitalistic incentives and industrial discipline among millions of small businessmen and workers.

Finally, the Englishman as a foreign entrepreneur in India, like the Dutchman in Java and the American in the Philippines, found it both more difficult and less profitable to adapt to new purposes the traditional fabric of industrial organization. The Japanese business-man was working in his own country and among his own people. And his activities were subject to the surveillance and control of a government which, while not unduly preoccupied with the interest of the small fellow—to put it mildly—was a regime independent of foreign domination and concerned with Japan's own autonomous development.

The Great Combines. At the other pole from the family farm and workshop were the towering combines which dominated the large-scale industry and commerce of prewar Japan. The one, like the other, was a sign of Japan's late entry on the path of industrialism; but it also reflected her ambition to acquire the sinews of national power as rapidly as possible. Political pretension thus reinforced economic circumstance to develop in combination such extremes of economic organization as few countries in history have displayed side by side.

The pattern of small enterprise in most fields was dictated by Japan's poverty in capital, as well as in advanced technical and entrepreneurial skills. A national framework of banking and trans-port could hardly be created on this basis, however. Nor was it adequate for the heavy industries essential to military strength—mining, metallurgy, machinery, and chemicals. From the beginning they required large units of investment in capitalistic establishments operated on a large scale. As described in Chapters 1 and 10, such enterprises were launched early in the Meiji period by the State and various financial magnates, acting in conjunction. Although the State soon withdrew from active participation all but a few selected fields, especially banking, railways, and steel, it continued to lavish patronage on the few families and groups able to command the necessary capital and technical experience. Out of this situation grew the great financial aggregations known as the *zaibatsu* (money cliques). With the advantages gained in the early years, they were able to develop far-flung networks of business enterprise which maintained their predominance in large-scale finance and industry for sixty years.

One can list ten to twenty *zaibatsu* in prewar Japan, depending on the scope of the definition. Four were outstanding, however, until their preeminence was challenged by the new war-created combines of the thirties. There were Mitsui, Mitsubishi, Sumitomo, and Yasuda. Others were important in restricted fields: Furukawa in copper and electric power; Shibusawa in banking and engineering; Kawasaki in shipbuilding, locomotives, and steel products; Asano in cement and steel; Okura and Kuhara in mining and engineering; etc. The Big Four were distinguished not only by their size but also by the spread of their interests through industry, commerce, and banking. Especially strategic were their powerful banks, which in turn gave them tremendous influence throughout Japanese economic life.

Each of the Big Four combines remained a family enterprise in some degree. The exact pattern of control varied from one to another. The Sumitomo interests were almost entirely owned and directed by the single head of the family. The Mitsubishi combine was controlled by two Iwasaki families, with common policy responsibility vested alternately by custom in the eldest son first of one family, then of the other. The eleven branches of the Mitsui family acted as a unit in accordance with formal household rules, last revised in 1900. They held 90% of their wealth collectively. Policies were decided through a family council presided over by the head of the elder son's family. While the *zaibatsu* families invested largely in equities, and thus retained ownership control over immense properties, their practice increasingly was to vest managerial responsibility in hired executives (*bantō*). These men were carefully selected, trained, and rewarded for their skill and clanlike loyalty to the house.

Internally the devices employed to concentrate control below the family level were the familiar techniques of Western corporate practice, reinforced by the Japanese penchant for disciplined, group action. Each combine was dominated by a closely owned holding company. Here the bulk of the house fortune was usually concentrated, though the family might invest directly in operating enterprises as well. Control was then extended through a network of subsidiaries and affiliates by intercorporate stockholdings, interlocking directorates, management agreements, and loans from the combine bank. This gave a degree of cohesion and unity which might extend even to companies only 10 to 20% of whose stock was actually held by the combine. Supplementing the more formal instruments of control was of course the tremendous financial power latent in the hands of the executives at the top levels.

The House of Mitsui was the largest and most powerful of these financial aggregations. Unlike the Mitsubishi and Yasuda combines, which first gained importance in post-Restoration shipping and banking respectively, the Mitsuis were important bankers and traders as early as the seventeenth century. They played a leading role in financing the Restoration movement and the governments which followed. Like the other houses, they received numerous privileges in return which enabled them steadily to expand the scope of their activities. From commerce and banking they went into mining and lumbering. In subsequent decades the great family holding company, Mitsui Gomei, the Mitsui Bank, Mitsui Bussan (trading), and Mitsui Kozan (mining) extended their interests into textiles, shipping, warehousing, sugar, metals and machinery, and scores of other branches of industry. Whereas Yasuda remained first and foremost a banking combine, and Mitsubishi and Sumitomo were preeminent especially in the mining and equipment industries, Mitsui branched out in all directions, both at home and abroad. By 1937 the House was said to own properties with a market value of 1,635 million yen ($470 million), giving control over a business empire many times this size.[86]

The Mitsui empire in 1945, on the eve of its dissolution, is depicted in Chart 1, on pages 218-219, based on postwar American investigations. The eleven branches of the family jointly held wealth now amounting to some 600 million yen in the paid-in value of securities. Most of it was in the shares of the holding company, now Mitsui Honsha, and other top companies. The Honsha in turn controlled dozens of subsidiaries, as did Mitsui Bussan, Mitsui Mining, Oriental Cotton Trading, etc. Some Mitsui interest held over 10% of the stock of about 90 companies. When their subsidiaries in turn are added the number reached about 300 to 350. The leading 80 companies of the combine, where Mitsui control averaged 50%, had over 3 billion yen of paid-in capital. While there is some intercorporate duplication here, the actual control extended much further. For example, Mitsui Bussan, with a paid-in capital of only 100 million yen, had assets of 6,400 million yen in 1945. The paid-in capital of all acknowledged Mitsui companies amounted to 5.7% of the paid-in capital of all Japanese corporations in 1944, according to a Mitsui report.[87]

[86] Oland D. Russell, *The House of Mitsui*, Boston, 1939, p. 4.

[87] The facts in this paragraph are taken from the U.S. Department of State, *Report of the Mission on Japanese Combines*, part 1, Washington, 1946, pp. 106-18. This postwar investigation is a mine of information on the *zaibatsu*, and is exten-

The other combines likewise employed the device of intercorporate stockholding to pyramid business controls on a scale without parallel in the history of Western industrial nations. In this phase of business technology the Japanese were apt students. Yasuda Hozensha, the holding company of the Yasuda combine, valued its assets at only 140 million yen at the end of 1944; its own capital was only 30 million. Yet through its stockholdings in Yasuda subsidiaries, especially financial institutions, it "directly controlled assets in excess of forty billion yen in banking enterprises and two billion yen in other enterprises."[88] Sumitomo Honsha was itself a great mining operator, but in 1945 it also had investments of 326 million yen in 123 other companies and over 30 industries. Its 18 admitted subsidiaries had assets of 13.9 billion yen.[89] Mitsubishi's importance in the Japanese economy can be illustrated by citing its share in the control of various spheres of activity in 1944: shipping and shipbuilding, 25%; coal and metals, 15%; warehousing, 16%; bank loans, 16% (March 1945); electrical equipment, 21 to 35%; flour milling, 50%; sheet glass, 59%; sugar, 35%; cotton textiles, 15%.[90]

All such estimates of *zaibatsu* "control" are necessarily partial, and they can be misleading unless one is careful to note the fields to which they are restricted. They show nevertheless the tremendous concentration of entrepreneurial control in major sectors of prewar Japanese industry, finance, and commerce. Even if the seventeen leading combines are defined so as to include only companies in which they held 25% or more of the stock, their aggregate paid-in capital was nearly one fifth (18%) of the paid-in capital of all Japanese joint-stock companies in 1935.[91] Even greater was the concentration of control in the banking, insurance, and trust business. This grew steadily with the failure and absorption of hundreds of small banks during the twenties. On the eve of World War II, the seven big private banks of the country—each with assets exceeding 1.5 billion yen ($350 million)—held nearly 60% of the total assets and the deposits of "ordinary" (private, commercial) banks. To-

---

sively drawn upon here. Though its statistics relate primarily to the late war years, its analysis appears to be applicable in large part to the earlier history of the combines. For an excellent picture of big business in Japan during the interwar period see also the writings of G. C. Allen, especially "The Concentration of Economic Control in Japan," *Economic Journal*, vol. XLVII, June, 1937, pp. 271-86, and chaps. 12-22 in Schumpeter, ed., *op.cit.*, New York, 1940.

[88] *Report of the Mission on Japanese Combines*, cited, p. 174. This estimate is based on the assets of only the principal subsidiaries controlled by the Hozensha, and does not include companies controlled by these subsidiaries. The 1945 figures reflect the wartime inflation of prices, which greatly expanded the assets of Yasuda's financial institutions.

[89] *ibid.*, p. 134.

[90] Estimates quoted in *ibid.*, p. 133.

[91] *ibid.*, p. 7.

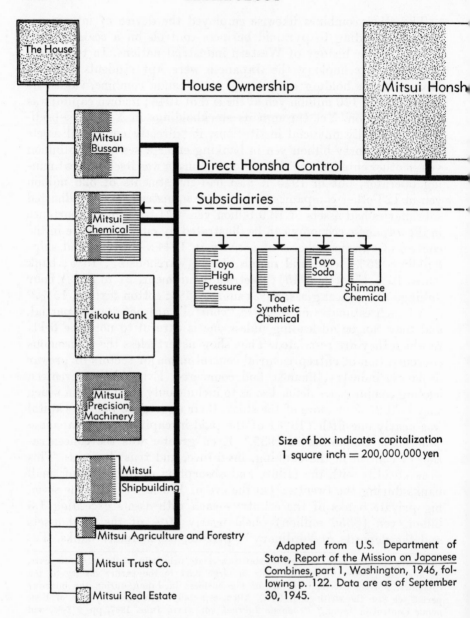

House Ownership

Mitsui Honsha

Direct Honsha Control

Subsidiaries

The House

Mitsui Bussan

Mitsui Chemical

Teikoku Bank

Mitsui Precision Machinery

Mitsui Shipbuilding

Mitsui Agriculture and Forestry

Mitsui Trust Co.

Mitsui Real Estate

Toyo High Pressure

Toa Synthetic Chemical

Toyo Soda

Shimane Chemical

Size of box indicates capitalization
1 square inch = 200,000,000 yen

Adapted from U.S. Department of State, Report of the Mission on Japanese Combines, part 1, Washington, 1946, following p. 122. Data are as of September 30, 1945.

Chart 1

Selected Mitsui Companies

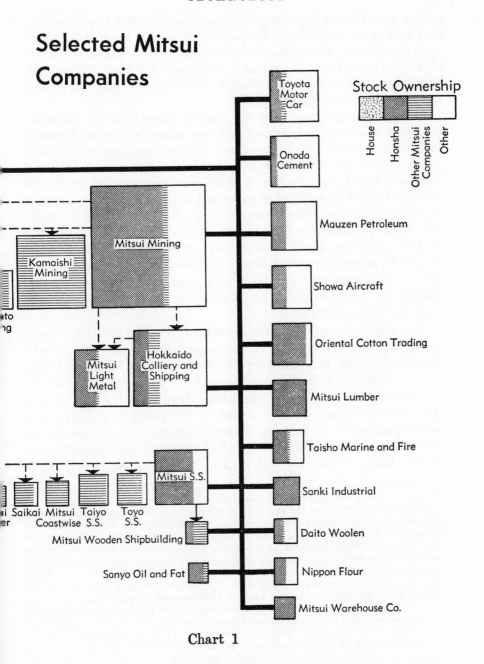

Chart 1

gether with the six leading government banks, they accounted for over half of the capital and deposits of *all* banks. Four of the seven were the Mitsui, Mitsubishi, Sumitomo, and Yasuda Banks. In the others the lesser *zaibatsu* were also prominent: the First (Shibusawa, Furukawa, Kawasaki); the Sanwa (Yamaguchi, Konoike); and the One Hundredth (Kawasaki).[92]

Many factors entered into the historic growth of the Japanese combines. Some were social and political, others of a more economic and technical character. In a real sense the *zaibatsu* carried over into modern times, but with a new tempo of innovation, the traditions of merchant guild organization, and of clan monopoly in trade and manufacture. The spirit of hierarchical organization, of leadership, subordination, and group teamwork, found fresh expression in the new world of corporate finance and industry. The ancient practice of primogeniture, another aspect of family relationship, likewise helped to perpetuate great family fortunes under unified and continuous management, especially as it was sometimes qualified to permit the family headship to pass by the eldest son where he was unfit for responsibility.[93]

The political and legal framework of post-Restoration Japan, partly because it grew out of the same background, was likewise congenial to the concentration of control in big business. Public policy in this realm is discussed more fully in Chapter 10, but requires brief mention here. Completely absent was the suspicion of concentrated business power rooted in the political philosophy of modern America or Britain. Throughout the prewar decades no anti-trust or fair-trade laws worthy of the name were placed on the statute books.[94] Company and banking laws were notoriously lax in

[92] Headquarters, U.S. Army Service Forces, *Civil Affairs Handbook, Japan, Section 5: Money and Banking,* Washington, 1944, pp. 12-13, 53.

[93] Although the terms of the law are not always a reliable guide to practice, prewar Japanese law reflected the spirit of family solidarity—"the family state"—and operated to preserve it against corrosive influences. The head of a "house" had the legal duty to support members of the house, who in turn had certain obligations to him. Under the law, for example, they could not choose a place of residence or a spouse without his consent. Legally the eldest son normally succeeded to the headship. He could not be deprived, by will or otherwise, of more than half of the estate. Also, the Inheritance Tax Law of 1905 permitted higher exemptions and lower tax rates where succession was to the headship of the house, and not merely to the property of a member. Such legal safeguards helped to preserve family holdings from being dispersed. They also facilitated collective management of the personal holdings of family members as in the great combines. See *Report of the Mission on Japanese Combines,* cited, part 1, pp. 34-35.

[94] A League of Nations report summarized the situation in Japan as follows in 1927, using information supplied by the Japanese government: "Japan has no particular legislation forbidding or establishing control over trusts and cartels. The judicature has not concerned itself with this question." *Review of Legislation on Cartels and Trusts,* Geneva, 1927, p. 46. Later, in 1931, the Major Industries Control

their safeguards for the small investor or the consumer. The Japanese tax system by modern standards was likewise very lenient in its treatment of large property incomes, especially before 1920. Particularly where political influence could be exerted on the tax collector the systematic evasion of business and personal income taxes was commonplace.

More positively, Japanese governments looked to the *zaibatsu* for aid and assistance in financing public budgets, in building foreign trade and colonial enterprise, and in creating the heavy industries required by the Army and the Navy. Especially where strategic interests were involved the political authorities were disposed to afford maximum opportunity for entrepreneurial initiative, at least by certain "chosen instruments," and to seek to minimize the risk deterrents by quasi-monopolistic grants and subsidies. The combines, as they grew in power, came in turn to exercise pervasive influence in the government itself. They contracted close family and business affiliations with leading bureaucrats. They financed the major political parties. Their top executives moved in and out of official agencies like the Bank of Japan or the Ministry of Commerce. And they operated as virtual partners of the government in developing the semiofficial institutions like the Yokohama Specie Bank, the South Manchuria Railway, and other "national policy companies" at home and abroad. (See Chapter 10.)

All these political perquisites and connections worked to the advantage of the great financial houses, making it the more difficult after 1900 for any upstart to challenge their supremacy. The first real opportunity only arose in the thirties on the wave of Japan's armament-building and overseas expansion. Now the older, more conservative combines took alarm at the recklessness of the militarists. Although they ultimately supported the war effort, indeed played a leading role, they were inclined to be skeptical of the long-run profits to be gained, for example, out of the Kwantung Army's plans for industrializing Manchuria. The unprecedented scale of Japan's inflationary war expansion, as well as this cautious attitude on the part of the groups like Mitsui, served to bring to the fore a number of new combines such as Nakajima (aircraft) and Nissan (Manchurian development). Again the political and military aspect of *zaibatsu* enterprise was underlined.

Given this political setting, and the general shortage of capital

---

Law included a provision empowering the authorities to curb the abuse of monopolistic power achieved through cartel agreements. The main purpose of the law, however, was to foster such agreements, not to restrain them, and the policing power was little used in practice. "Industrial Control Law in Operation," *Oriental Economist*, vol. 1, no. 3, 1934, p. 14.

and experience for large-scale industry, the big combines enjoyed unusual opportunities for employing familiar business devices to concentrate power. Their prestige enabled them to hire the best business and engineering talent of the country. Their size and diversified interests made possible certain economies in management, in research, in the pooling of risks from new undertakings, and in integrated industrial and commercial operations. Their great trading companies gave their manufacturing affiliates efficient channels of buying and selling. These companies also furnished instruments for aggressive pressure on independent competitors, and for controlling great numbers of small producers and merchants. Wherever cartels or control associations were formed, the combine networks were sure to be in a leading position. Their cooperation was essential to success.

Most important as an instrument of expansion was *zaibatsu* control of bank credit. Big banks and trust companies were securely tied into each major combine by intercorporate stockholding, interlocking directorates, and the "interrelated solvency" of these institutions and their combine affiliates. They held the deposits of affiliated companies (as well as individual depositors) and were at the same time their chief source of capital. They were also powerful instruments for extending control over competitors, customers, and suppliers. Such banking connections were especially important in a country where a wide public securities market was lacking, where corporations were prone to pay out most of their earnings in dividends, and where individual savings took the form mainly of bank deposits. The financial institutions of Japan, concentrated as they were in the hands of the government and big business, were the major source of capital for modern industry, chiefly in the form of loans or debenture purchases.[95] Characteristically, therefore, the growth of combine industry was closely associated with the growing power of the *zaibatsu* banks (and their affiliations with semi-official banks). U.S. investigators of the system summarized this key feature in these words: "Where some industrial and commercial enterprises have access to capital far more readily than their competitors, the hardship to the latter is almost insurmountable."[96]

[95] A study of 669 companies whose shares were traded on the Tokyo Stock Exchange in 1933 confirms this statement. Though corporate savings were now a major source of industrial capital, the greater part continued to come from bank loans and debenture issues, the latter also purchased largely by financial institutions. The restricted share market is further evidenced by the fact that the average number of shares per shareholder in these companies was 125. a figure much higher than the comparable one for the United States. Industrial Bank of Japan, *Survey of Japanese Finance and Industry*, vol. i, no. 1, June 1949, p. 2.

[96] *Report of the Mission on Japanese Combines*, cited, part 1, p. 53.

Structure of Large-Scale Industry. This sketch of the combine networks leads naturally to questions of economic structure and market behavior in the industries where they operated. Here one must be cautious about generalization, because of complex variations from industry to industry and the lack of information on actual market practices.

One characteristic of large-scale enterprise in prewar Japan is striking. Despite the concentration of control evidenced in giant combines, there were few cases of outright monopoly by a single seller of a product or group of allied products. Obvious exceptions were the government railways and electrical communications, and the official monopolies on salt, tobacco, and camphor. In private industry, however, even with the lack of legal restraints upon monopoly and "unfair" practices, the exceptions seem to have been rare. One was the Oji Paper Company, which for many years controlled 75% or more of the output of foreign-style paper. Other instances could doubtless be cited in markets for particular types of industrial goods, e.g., machinery and equipment, where there was considerable product differentiation. Each combine tended in some degree to specialize, as described above. Generally speaking, nevertheless, it seems to have been difficult for any single firm or combine to secure and maintain a position so monopolistic that ready substitutes could not be found in either domestic production or imports. Mitsui and Mitsubishi each grew to giant size because of the variety of industrial and commercial enterprise brought within its control, and not because of its specialized domination of a single market. In other words, the combination movement in Japan followed a pattern distinctly different from that in the United States at the turn of the century. Here such trusts as U.S. Steel, Standard Oil, American Tobacco, American Sugar Refining, and United Shoe Machinery came to control 65% to 95% of the capital and output in their respective fields.

Far more prevalent in Japanese large-scale enterprise was the condition of oligopoly (fewness of sellers). Owing to the importance of the small industries in manufacturing as a whole, oligopoly was much less pervasive in prewar Japan that in the industrial markets of the United States. But it was the rule in Japanese mining and metallurgy. It was also characteristic of heavy chemicals and machinery, of shipping and shipbuilding, and of a few types of manufactured foodstuffs, like sugar and flour, produced by highly capitalistic methods. Whether it became more or less prevalent in manufacturing as Japanese capitalism "matured" is hard to say. The capital goods industries requiring large-scale methods developed on this pattern from the time when they were first organized by financial magnates under the patronage of the Meiji governments. After 1900 it was characteristic that with certain variations, more or less the same group of combines, each with its far-flung interests, tended to preponderate throughout the heavy industries.

The structure of large-scale enterprise, as it stood in the middle thirties, has been well described by G. C. Allen in *The Industrialization of Japan and Manchukuo*, cited above. In the steel industry, Nippon Seitetsu, newly formed by a merger of the government's Yawata Iron Works with six private concerns, accounted for nearly all of the pig iron and 52% of the raw steel produced in Japan and Korea during 1934. The Japanese copper industry was controlled by the Mitsubishi, Nissan, Furukawa, Fujita, and Sumitomo interests. Five or six *zaibatsu*-affiliated companies likewise dominated other fields of mining and metallurgy, usually with a close vertical integration of mines, smelters, and refineries. In coal mining there were 110 firms, but Mitsubishi and Mitsui controlled 50% of the capital. These two combines likewise built half the merchant ship tonnage launched in Japan during 1935. Similarly two to six industrial groups controlled factories responsible for 70% or more of the production of rayon, dyestuffs, refined sugar, flour, cement, and sheet glass in Japan.

In still other industries the big interests shared the market, or rather a complex of markets, with small enterprise. A well-known case is that of the cotton industry. Only the cotton import business was heavily concentrated. Here three big firms led by a Mitsui company handled 40% of the trade, and twelve firms accounted for 80%. In cotton spinning at the end of 1932 there were seventy-one concerns, six of which owned half of Japan's total spindleage. The weaving trade, on the other hand, was divided between the weaving sheds attached to the large spinning mills and innumerable small weavers each specializing in a narrow range of fabrics. The big firms together accounted for only about a quarter of the production and a half of the exports of cotton fabrics.[97]

Another instance was the electric lamp industry. Here the large, mechanized factories of the Tokyo Electric Light Company long dominated the Japanese market, owing to the fact that it held the tungsten filament patent through affiliation with the General Electric Company. This patent expired in 1927. Thereafter eleven independent concerns of medium size developed to supply the bulk of the home demand for standard house lamps, buying parts and ma-

[97] Teijiro Uyeda and Tokijiro Minoguchi, *Small-Scale Industries of Japan: The Cotton Industry*, Tokyo: Japanese Council, Institute of Pacific Relations, 1936, pp. 13ff. For a note on the highly effective cartel in the spinning industry see below, pages 230-31.

terials from numerous small manufacturers. Meanwhile there were some 2,000 smaller establishments, most of them family workshops concentrated in the crowded living quarters of Tokyo workers. Primitively equipped and chaotically organized, these "town" manufacturers specialized in miniature bulbs such as found their way (via merchant employers and exporters) to the counters of 5-and-10 cent stores in the United States.[98]

A third industry, the pottery trades, is described by Allen as "an epitome of modern Japanese industrial organization."[99] Various branches of the market were served by all forms of enterprise reproducing simultaneously the stages of industrial evolution in the West from the seventeenth to the twentieth centuries. They ranged from the artist-craftsmen of Kyoto, through small plants specializing in ordinary table and ornamental ware and coordinated by merchant entrepreneurs, to the large factories turning out industrial porcelain and lavatory equipment by highly mechanized factory processes.

It is easy to see why these industries and others like them present a wide array of production and marketing structures. The basic determinants were the variety of Japanese manufactures and markets, and the adaptability of different industrial forms to their peculiar requirements, as influenced by the scarcity of capital and of advanced entrepreneurial and engineering skills. Earlier it was remarked that the small plant and the small firm were well suited to supply most of the home market for consumer manufactures, especially as the Japanese never developed a standardized national market even for widely used personal and household effects. In the export trade, too, with the conspicuous exception of raw silk, Japanese goods tended to be quite diversified. They catered flexibly to a wide range of consumer tastes. Where economic and technical conditions called for large-scale, capitalistic processes, however, the big combines preponderated as a group. Their command over capital, their ability to hire the best technical talent, and their role as agents of State policy gave them decisive advantages in this realm.

Less evident is the reason for the prevalence of oligopoly as opposed to single-seller monopoly in the heavy industries. Particularly in a country where the market for many products of heavy industry was so limited, and where legal restraints were lacking, the contrary might be expected. One factor was possibly the interest of the armed forces and civilian bureaucracy in preserving a degree of

[98] Teijiro Uyeda and Tosuke Inokuchi, *Small-Scale Industries of Japan: The Electric Lamp Industry*, Tokyo: Japanese Council, Institute of Pacific Relations, 1936, pp. 5ff.

[99] Schumpeter, ed., *op.cit.*, pp. 536ff.

rivalry among the big producers and importers of metals and machinery. Competition offered certain safeguards to technical progress. It also weakened the grip of any single business group upon the key industries and hence upon political power. Another factor was the rivalry among the various cliques of the Army and Navy, the bureaucracy, and the political parties themselves. Each had its own personal and financial connections among the *zaibatsu*, which tended at least to disperse government contracts and other favors around the inner circle. The early affiliations of Mitsui with Count Kaoru Inouye and of Mitsubishi with Marquis Shigenobu Okuma are cases in point.

More important perhaps was a technical limitation. Once Japanese industrialization got well under way, the market for most types of industrial goods probably soon grew beyond the point where complete monopolization of any single category could have afforded any real economies of large-scale production or distribution, given the existing level of technology and managerial skills. In other words, the optimum-size operating concern, and still more the plant, fell far short of satisfying the demand. Whatever advantages accrued from grouping a number of operating companies within a single holding-company empire could apparently be realized more effectively by combining a variety of types of enterprise rather than specializing in single markets. Under these circumstances the pattern of oligarchy which characterized Japanese politics tended to assert itself in big business as well. It was easier, safer, and evidently more lucrative in the end to accept a division of the market rather than for any single combine to attempt to wrest the market from the others.

The economies—or diseconomies—of the Japanese trusts are still little understood. To what extent was this clustering of all sorts of miscellaneous undertakings under unified ownership and control conducive to economic or engineering efficiency? Doubtless the answer would vary from combine to combine, and industry to industry. Integration, both horizontal and vertical, undoubtedly afforded certain economies of the usual variety. They would be expected in research and development, in marketing efficiency, in making the best use of managerial and technical talent. And many of the combine affiliates certainly pioneered in technological advance. In the case of Japan, as in that of the United States, however, one wonders if efficiency in mass production has not accrued more largely through intraplant than through interplant economies.[100] Especially where

[100] Temporary National Economic Committee, *Relative Efficiency of Large, Medium-Sized, and Small Business*, 76th Congress, Senate Committee Print, *Investigation of Concentration of Economic Power*, Monograph No. 13, Washington, 1941, p. 96.

the pyramided superstructure of ownership and control was extended indiscriminately over scores of light and heavy industries, trade, banking, real estate, and even forestry—as in the Mitsui trust, for example[101]—the advantages appear to have lain in good part in sheer financial size and bargaining power. The power of bigness tended to be cumulative in its effects except for the limiting human element, e.g., the increasing complexity of internal management.

From a social standpoint one point in particular deserves further study, as it has a general significance for the problem of economic development. In the early stages of industrialization, the national market for such industries as metallurgy, equipment, and power is limited. There may accordingly be economic advantages in concentrating production in the hands of a few firms in order to approach more rapidly the optimum scale of operations. Even more, big private combines like the Japanese, or alternatively State enterprise, may offer certain social gains arising from "combined investment." One difficulty facing any country on the threshold of industrialization is the fact that a venture in any single big enterprise may be attractive only if the simultaneous development of other industries is undertaken. Investment to build an electric power industry, for example, is encouraged by the simultaneous development of electric light and equipment industries. But the individual promoter looking at the power enterprise as a single venture may be deterred from going ahead by uncertainty as to whether these complementary industries will in fact develop and thus make profitable what would otherwise be a dubious undertaking. If complementary enterprises are joined in a single program of development —whether at the hands of the government or of a private group— this reduces the risk estimates all around. It makes it more likely that interrelated innovations will proceed simultaneously, each creating the profit expectations of the other. When a combine (or the State as investor) can thus expect to capture part of the gains which accrue outside any single industry, a deterrent to that single investment may be removed.[102]

101 A partial list of Mitsui activities includes the banking, trust, insurance, and securities business; forestry and tea and rubber plantations; mining and processing of coal, bauxite, salt, lead, zinc, gold, sulphur, mica, copper, and other minerals; real estate and general contracting; shipbuilding and marine transport; buying, selling, importing, exporting, and warehousing of commodities; spinning and weaving of silk, cotton, rayon, wool, and hemp; manufacture of human and animal foodstuffs, tobacco, beer, coke, dyes, pharmaceuticals, petroleum products, fertilizers and other chemicals, porcelain, pottery, brick, machine tools, mining and industrial machinery of many types, railway equipment, automobiles, radios, electric furnaces, cement, iron and steel, rubber goods, and aircraft.

102 See P. N. Rosenstein-Rodan, "Problems of Industrialization of Eastern and

The channelling of investment into large-scale Japanese industry through the big financial groups may well have accelerated the country's industrial development in this respect. The large combines, with their far-flung interests in manufacturing and trade, in shipping and shipbuilding, in mining and metalworking, in fuel and power, were able to anticipate more certain returns from new undertakings in particular industries by virtue of their parallel activities in related fields. Especially in the early stages their very size and diversification probably helped Japan over the hurdle of the small market, which offers an obstacle to certain major innovations in any newly industrializing country.

The *zaibatsu* may thus have fulfilled in some degree a function which elsewhere in the modern world is being assumed increasingly by State investment. If so, the growth and diversification of the Japanese economy under private auspices was thereby hastened. Whether this continued to be true after 1920 is more problematical. Also, whether it was necessary or desirable that such extravagant rewards be lavished on the big capitalists is quite another matter.

Competition v. Collusion. In the realm of market behavior, the size and diversity of *zaibatsu* interests had still other consequences. Little is known of the actual forces determining the price and output decisions of their operating subsidiaries. But their domestic activities took place for the most part in markets where there were a few big domestic sellers, and sometimes equally few buyers. This meant that any single firm enjoyed a wide area of administrative discretion. Also its decisions as to prices, output, or investment were bound to be influenced by the response which it anticipated from its major competitors. Under such conditions there inevitably are powerful incentives to collusion among major concerns, either express or tacit, and efforts to force compliance by lesser rivals. Thus, if single-seller monopolies were uncommon in Japan, and if inter-combine rivalries were keen, this does not mean that markets where the big trusts dominated were competitive in reality.

The sense of mutual interdependence among big business rivals in a market is apt to be characteristic of oligopolistic industries. In prewar Japan it may well have been heightened by two circumstances emphasized by Eleanor M. Hadley.[103] One was the fact that more or less the same combines tended to face each other in a number of markets, but with each one enjoying varying degrees of strength from one market to another. This meant that a combine competitively

South-Eastern Europe," *Economic Journal*, vol. LIII, no. 210-11, June-September 1943, pp. 205-07.

[103] In a paper read before the Far Eastern Association, New Haven, April 5, 1949.

strong in one field might nevertheless be deterred from cutting prices, or otherwise taking advantage of its strength, because of fear of retaliation in another field where its position was weaker in relation to the same rival combines. Collusive action across a broad range of markets would thereby be encouraged, provided a second condition prevailed. The operating concerns within each combine would have to be centrally controlled and directed.

From evidence gathered in postwar Japan, Miss Hadley believes that the combines did achieve a high degree of control over their operating affiliates. The top holding companies sought to keep a firm grip on major questions of policy throughout their major subsidiaries. This was done by various devices: ownership of shares; interlocking appointments of key personnel; central sales agencies; banking pressure; and sometimes written contracts specifically restricting the autonomy of subsidiary concerns with respect to personnel, investment, and operating policies.

The coordination of policies within the single combine may thus have fostered coordination among rival combines in setting prices, regulating output, and maximizing profits. To what extent this actually took place it is extremely difficult to know. Within the typical combine there were strong tendencies to decentralization and managerial independence. Indeed, this was the very thing that the controls mentioned above were designed to combat. Managerial responsibility came to be centered increasingly in the hands of professional executives. Operating within a clanlike hierarchy of loyalties they nevertheless had strong personal and professional incentives to carry on their individual responsibilities with a large measure of autonomy.[104] Among the combines, too, there was a

[104] The following comment by the British Shipping Committee in the late thirties is interesting, if inconclusive (*British Shipping in the Orient*, London: H.M. Stationery Office, 1939, p. 74):

"233. The policy of the Zaibatsu appears to be that each of the many concerns controlled should maintain its position as an independent entity and work for its own profit. We have been assured, for instance, that a Mitsui producing or trading firm would not hesitate to put even a foreign shipping company into competition with Mitsui vessels if the foreign country offered better terms. None the less, it is obvious that in the main the whole group of companies financially controlled by a family interest will normally play into the hands of one another.

"234. Under this system there is scope for competition between one Zaibatsu and another, and such competition has undoubtedly made itself felt among the great shipping companies, as for instance between the N.Y.K. (controlled by Mitsubishi) and the O.S.K. (controlled by Sumitomo). Of late the Government has used its influence and the powers which it has taken under the Shipping Routes Control Law . . . to moderate such internal rivalry in order to prevent uneconomic competition."

In explaining the inroads of Japanese shipping competition, the British Committee cited as "an important source of strength" the fact that in Japan, by contrast with Britain, the ship-owner was apt to be controlled by the same interests which

good deal of evidence of dog-eat-dog rivalry. While this did not necessarily make for competition in the economist's meaning of the term, it hardly bespeaks cordial and trustful relations.

Increasingly after World War I, it is true, concerted efforts were made to organize cartels, associations, and agreements of one sort or another in the large-scale industries like copper, coal, and fertilizers. Their purpose was to fix prices, restrict output, follow a joint sales policy, or otherwise engage in practices in restraint of trade. Such measures were stimulated by inflated production capacity and capital values created by the war boom and the temporary cutting off of foreign competition during 1914-19. In few cases, however, were they really effective so long as they relied merely on voluntary agreement.

Only after 1931, when the government itself got behind the combination movement more actively, did cartelization on a national scale extend to many industries. Even then such agreements tended to prove weak in practice until the State finally gave them legal force in the interest of greater coordination and control of the economy. In 1931 when the Major Industries Control Law was passed to authorize the enforcement of industrial agreements in designated industries, only 24 voluntary cartels were in existence. Most of them were inactive. By May 1935, there were 25 "compulsory" agreements, and 14 voluntary ones, beside 80 "industrial associations" mainly concerned with relieving cutthroat competition in the small-scale export trades. Even the semicompulsory cartels were restricted as a rule to a limited purpose. Often they were severely crippled by the refusal of powerful firms to cooperate.[105] The full cartelization of major industries came only as a part of the strait jacket of war mobilization after 1937. (For further discussion of government policy in this sphere, see Chapter 10.)

It can be argued that the very absence of strong cartels is itself evidence of widespread collusion by more informal means. If one was effective, why bother with the other? The most successful, long-lived cartel was found in cotton spinning, where control was less heavily concentrated in a few combines than in most other large-scale industries.[106] Yet it testifies to considerable independence of

---

originated and financed much of his business. It noted as a major exception, however, the cotton textile industry, where much of the trade originated with independent firms.

[105] Keizo Fujita, "Cartels and Their Conflicts in Japan," *Journal of the Osaka University of Commerce*, no. 3, December 1935, pp. 65-109.

[106] The general secretary of the powerful Japanese Cotton Spinners' Association once enumerated the factors responsible for progress in his industry. In typical Japanese fashion, he put "sincere effort by managements" at the head of his list. Then came capital, research, improved efficiency, etc., and finally "firm solidarity

action that efforts to pursue monopolistic practices by express con-
tractual arrangement should meet with so much resistance. Professor Fujita, in the article cited above, emphasizes the intercompany
struggles which went on in such cartels as cement and phosphoric
acid. He lists numerous reasons why powerful interests often refused to cooperate in industrial agreements: confidence in their
superior financial resources or production techniques, clique rivalries, prejudice and ignorance, the desire to guard business secrets,
dissatisfaction with cartel prices or quotas. These factors would
operate in informal as well as formal undertakings to weaken the
sense of interdependence which is the basis of joint action. The path
of collusion was thus beset with difficulties. This remained true despite the absence of antitrust and unfair practice laws, the presence
of a strong tradition of corporate activity to advance mutual
interests, and, after 1931, official support of the combination
movement.

Evidently, then, the enterprise system in this realm of Japanese
business was a rather indeterminate blend of sharp jealousy and
mutual solidarity, of rugged individualism and collusive action. If
rivalries were keen, they yet operated in a setting characterized by
a propensity among the rivals to cooperate in abating the rigors of
the free market.

There is a striking parallel, as already mentioned, between
Japanese politics and big business as regards the structure of
power and the behavior of dominant groups. The concentration of
political power never led to totalitarian dictatorship. Instead the
various cliques represented in the ruling oligarchy vied with each
other for prestige and influence around the emperor, while combining—except for extremists—to defend their common interests
in the fundamental structure. Similarly, the business cliques con-

between mills and self-sacrificing cooperation to safeguard the common interest."
Seitaro Kamisaka, *The Cotton Industry of Japan*, Osaka, 1934, p. 6.

This trade association is of special significance, since it dominated the cotton-
spinning industry from the beginning. Its functions included (1) the encouragement
of technical improvements, (2) regulation of competition for workers, (3) representation of the spinners in negotiations at home and abroad over markets, credit
facilities, freight rates, taxes, etc., and (4) production control exercised on eleven
different occasions between 1890 and 1936. (Limitation of yarn output was apt to
run into difficulties, as it tended to bring an increase in spindleage.) In addition, the
Association conferred a great advantage on its members through a unique monopoly of shipping space for raw cotton imported from India. Beginning in 1893 it was
able to impose contracts on Japanese and foreign shipping firms by which the latter
agreed to ship Indian cotton only for the account of its members, and, further, to
grant a rebate to the Association on all such shipments. This arrangement afforded
a source of income to the Association and gave its members a strangle hold on the
spinning of cotton in Japan. In 1936 its sixty members controlled 97.8% of Japan's
total spindleage, 31.5% being controlled by the "Big Three"—Toyo, Dai Nippon, and
Kanegafuchi.

tended among themselves in the market for power and profits, but recognized their mutual interdependence in a broad area of joint interest. The entry of newcomers into large-scale industry was made difficult by ownership of mineral resources, patent control, international agreements, and all the advantages of size, financial strength, and contacts enjoyed by those already dominant in the field. It is significant that a new group of *zaibatsu* rose to prominence only after 1931 when new armament industries mushroomed, first in Manchuria under the aegis of the Kwantung Army and later in Japan itself.

Economic Consequences of the Zaibatsu. Any full appraisal of the economic consequences of the *zaibatsu* must take into account an extremely broad range of value judgments. So much has been said of the social evils latent in monopolistic aggregations of wealth and financial power that it is easy to overlook other considerations. Market structure and business practice must be judged in part at least by their effects on long-run economic development. Beyond the size of profits is the question of how they are used. And the ultimate test of efficiency is not any particular structure of enterprise, but whether wide scope is allowed for initiative, whether steady improvements take place in products and processes, whether output grows and diversifies with increasing maturity and falling costs, whether the system works for or against economic stability and the wise use of resources.

In these terms one approaches with diffidence any summary verdict on the Japanese enterprise system as it developed after 1868. Moreover, the judgments applicable to 1890 or 1910 are not necessarily valid in 1930 or 1950.

Looking back at the broad history of the prewar era, one cannot fail to be impressed with the constructive role of the Japanese combines in technical progress, especially in the earlier decades. The *zaibatsu* were not merely political wire-pullers, or financial manipulators, or even *rentier* investors. They performed an essential function in large-scale enterprise which could otherwise have been performed only by the State, and not necessarily with greater public benefit. If they reaped fabulous gains, as they did, they continued to plough back the larger share in entrepreneurial investment in new and expanding activity. The new is always uncertain, and, as Joseph Schumpeter remarks, some degree of market power to ward off competition is apt to be the condition of successful innovation, especially where large outlays are at stake.

Very likely the concentration of control was "excessive" in various fields, even taking efficiency alone as the criterion. Yet the combines were able to risk major undertakings of a "combined" character because they were large, and to gain substantial profits from new products and new processes even if rival firms subsequently copied them. By virtue of their resources they were able to command and train the best business and engineering talent to staff their companies. Their operating companies pioneered many of the major innovations in banking, large-scale industry, and trade, capitalizing on the freedom and support extended by a solicitous government. In so doing they built a new framework within which their top executives reigned as oligarchs, but where millions of small businessmen also found new opportunities for productive activity. A good deal of *zaibatsu* activity itself, it is true, was centered in strategic industries which increased the national power of Japan more than her national income in goods and services. As emphasized elsewhere in this study, much of the real substance of her economic growth actually took place in other sectors of economic life which remained dominated by small business. Yet the two types of enterprise developed in mutual interdependence, despite their differences in organization and purpose, and the currents of technological advance generated in the one flowed over into the other.

Fortunately for Japan, the dangers of restriction and stagnation latent in monopolistic concentrations of power were held somewhat in check by one circumstance. This was the country's continuing dependence on imported materials and machinery, which made for vigorous competition in many domestic markets. Japan was forced to import all of her cotton, silk, wool, rubber, and aluminum; most of her iron, lead, zinc, tin, and petroleum; and large amounts of machinery, machine tools, vehicles, and equipment. Moreover, the combines with their numerous affiliates were apt to be heavy importers as well as domestic producers. Where this was true, they had a consumer interest in high quality and low price; perhaps also a merchant's and shipper's interest in a large trading volume. The force of international competition could be moderated by tariffs, government buying, and subsidy. Sometimes it was entirely excluded. Through a very wide range of producers' goods, however, it could not be eliminated without blockading the road to industrial expansion.

Dependence on overseas materials thus served to restrain monopolistic practices which in other countries have sometimes grown up on the basis of concentrated control of minerals and other basic industries, shielded by high tariffs. The once great German complex of Lorraine iron and Ruhr coal comes to mind. In this respect (as well as others) Japan's natural poverty was not without its compensations. Moreover, she exported up to 25 to 35% of her manufactures to foreign and colonial markets. (See Chapter 7.) Here competition was usually keen, especially where numerous small firms shared the market. In such industries—mainly consumer goods —competition in the export branch introduced complications in any effort to monopolize the domestic branch, until centralized co-ordination became a military necessity in the late thirties. It is significant that war mobilization was accompanied finally by the virtual destruction of normal foreign trade relations. Only in this way was it possible to build up numerous cartelized and subsidized industries whose costs and prices bore no relation to those of comparable industries abroad.

Against the technical achievements of the *zaibatsu* as capitalists and innovators in prewar Japan must be set the more repugnant social and political features of the system. If these aspects have not been dwelt upon here, it is not to minimize their significance. Extreme inequalities of wealth and income characterized Japanese capitalism from the beginning. (See Chapter 5.) Under different forms this perpetuated the inequality of status and opportunity which runs so deeply in Japanese history and tradition. The actual concentration of economic power went even beyond the concentration of property ownership, through the wide ramifications of economic and political influence exercised by financial magnates.

Aside from the obvious evils of gross disparity between the wealth of the few and the poverty of the many, there were other social consequences of profound significance.

The existence of great aggregates of financial power, reinforced by political influence, tended from early times to discourage the growth of a sturdy middle class, i.e., a broad class of independent businessmen endowed with sufficient capital and freedom of opportunity so that they could develop medium-size, modern enterprise efficiently and on their own. Equally, the power of the *zaibatsu* concerns in the labor market, where they were careful to maintain a common front, helped to stifle the growth of a vigorous trade union movement. There were other obstacles to trade unionism, to be sure—the pressure of population, the prevalence of female labor in factory industry, the wide dispersion of small enterprise throughout the countryside, the lack of experience in democratic, mass organization. But the weakness of collective bargaining, even at its height in the twenties, and especially Japan's lagging progress in factory and social legislation, must be attributed in large measure to the intense opposition, led by business interests, which greeted every proposal for advance in these fields. Whatever the business rivalries of big firms, here they closed ranks and presented a solid front.[107] In the political realm, as well, the existence of concentrated business power retarded the growth of democratic movements at home, while providing a pliant instrument for military aggression abroad.

In retrospect these political and social considerations seem overriding, especially after 1920. By comparison, as Japanese capitalism matured, the technical justification for great aggregations of financial power became steadily less convincing. Indeed, in certain instances the big trusts probably tended to become retrogressive. This is difficult for an outsider to judge; but there is some evidence that entrepreneurial initiative and the full exercise of managerial skills in productive channels were not infrequently restricted by tight overhead controls by owners whose financial interest did not necessarily coincide with economic efficiency in social terms. Collusive restraints in markets dominated by the combines in the later years may well have blunted the spur to cost-saving innovations, making for a lag in technology no longer necessitated by any continuing handicap in capital and skills.

In any event, it was the broad considerations cited above which dictated the Allied undertaking, under American leadership, to dissolve "excessive" concentrations of economic power in Japan after World War II. Whatever the net outcome proves to be—a problematical question—the attempt at reform was not mere quixotic meddling by foreign busybodies. On the contrary, it was conceived in response to a need for democratic changes in Japanese economic structure long recognized by thoughtful, modern-minded observers of prewar Japan, including many liberal Japanese themselves.

[107] See the account of employers' organizations in the report of the International Labour Office, *Industrial Labour in Japan*, Geneva, 1933, chap. 2. Even so cautious an international body as the ILO has this to say of the Japan Cotton Spinners' Association: "Although an economic organization, the Association has always actively opposed any proposed social legislation which was believed to be adverse to industrial interests. The position it took up as regards the Factory Act before its enactment in 1911, and its attitude towards the proposed Trade Union Bill, may be considered as characteristic" (p. 83).

CHAPTER 5

CAPITAL

THE creation of capital in massive amounts and radically new forms is evident in the whole record of Japanese technological advance sketched in the preceding chapter. These two processes, coordinated in new patterns of economic enterprise, were the essential conditions of Japan's prewar economic growth. Through their cumulative interaction economic life was progressively reorganized to achieve a rising level of productivity and income, despite the relentless growth of population. The difficulties of other Asiatic countries today in financing development on a comparable scale adds fresh interest to the experience of the Japanese. How did they do it?

Capital accumulation is related in two ways to the level of production in a country, and hence its plane of living.

The first has come to be recognized as a matter of concern particularly in advanced industrial nations during recent years. Investment plays a strategic role in fluctuations of employment, incomes, and prices. Given a certain income-consumption pattern, existing resources will be fully utilized only if new investment (and government spending) is forthcoming in amounts sufficient to balance the amounts of income which the community is disposed to refrain from consuming at the level of incomes generated by full employment. If it exceeds this amount, on the other hand, it creates inflationary pressures which may have undesirable effects.

The second function of capital accumulation, of course, is to improve the stock of tools and material resources which man can use to make his labor more productive. Only as new capital assets are accumulated in increasing amounts or more efficient forms is it possible to enlarge productive capacity so that a growing population can be sustained at a rising level of income and material well-being. Where an economy is growing at a moderate rate, experience indicates that some 10% or more of national income is likely to go into the creation of new capital assets.

In underdeveloped areas both problems have been present in greater or less degree.[1] It is the second, however, the problem of intro-

[1] "The weakness of the inducement to invest has been at all times the key to the economic problem. Today the explanation of the weakness of this inducement may chiefly lie in the extent of existing accumulations; whereas, formerly, risks and hazards of all kinds may have played a larger part. But the result is the same. The desire of the individual to augment his personal wealth by abstaining from consumption has usually been stronger than the inducement to the entrepreneur to

ducing more capitalistic modes of production, which is the key to economic progress in these regions today. The word "underdevelopment" itself signifies a lack of income-producing wealth, and a primitive state of the industrial arts. No country can undertake economic development on a large scale without contriving in some way to multiply its stock of productive capital in the form of land improvements, developed mineral deposits, transport systems, industrial plant, and the like. This it may do partly by borrowing or securing donations abroad. Mainly, however, the job must be done at home. Indeed foreign aid itself is likely to be ineffective unless it supports and reinforces the direction of home resources into capital formation on an increasing scale. How to finance the process, how to make savings eventuate efficiently in real capital assets, what priorities to assign among the latter—these are among the crucial issues in any program of modernization and growth.

As regards Japan's whole experience in this field, a good deal has already been said in preceding chapters about the interrelations of capital, enterprise, and technical progress. One major aspect, the role of the State, is reserved for more extended discussion in Chapter 10. The over-all, quantitative aspects of capital accumulation should obviously be the subject of the present chapter. At the outset, however, it must be said that in no other phase of Japan's prewar development is one more handicapped by the lack of comprehensive measurements carrying back over several decades. This bars any inclusive analysis built up on statistical aggregates of savings, consumption, and investment such as have been constructed in recent years for more highly developed economies.

The place to begin may be with a picture of the real capital accumulated in Japan over a half century of industrialization. This will lead us in turn to certain social factors which appear to have fostered a rapid rate of accumulation throughout this period. The chapter concludes, then, with further reflections on the dynamics of the investment process.

Growth of Real Capital

Capital Requirements of Industrialization. The nature of the real capital required for industrialization is sometimes obscured by preoccupation with the financial mechanisms of savings and investment. Or it is thought of largely in terms of factory buildings and machinery required by manufacturing industry itself. In Chapter 4, indeed, a good deal was said about the increase and im-

---

augment the national wealth by employing labour on the construction of durable assets." J. M. Keynes, *The General Theory of Employment, Interest and Money,* New York: Harcourt, Brace, 1936, p. 348.

provement in the equipment of Japanese industry and transport as the means of harnessing mechanical energy to the production process. Nothing was more fundamental to growth. Yet, in terms of the capital problem, this needs to be put in the perspective of the total wealth structure of the country, in order to provide some quantitative bearings.

Ideally one should be able to place, side by side, comparable estimates of Japan's capital stock in 1880, say, and 1930, to discover the main fields of expansion. Unfortunately the statistical records do not allow such comparisons. For the year 1930, however, a rather careful census of national wealth was conducted by the Imperial Cabinet Bureau of Statistics. (Table 18.) This is worth examining for the light it throws on the components of real capital in Japan at this midpoint in her industrial transition.

The total physical assets of Japan were valued at 110 billion yen, on this reckoning.[2] This is ten times the national income produced in that year, which was 10.2 billion yen according to the best estimate. (See below, Table 38.) One might have expected a higher ratio of income to wealth, judging by estimates for other countries.[3] The problematical character of both computations, however, makes it hardly worth while to pursue such comparisons. It is especially difficult to value national wealth in any accurate and meaningful way.

Despite this uncertainty, Table 18 serves to illustrate a few general characteristics of Japan's prewar endowment in capital assets:

1. Most of the national wealth of modern Japan has remained in the hands of private owners. Of the 1930 total, 110 billion yen, the property of the national and local governments was valued at 18.5 billion yen, or 16.9%. Nearly 40% of this was lands and forests, the balance being chiefly public buildings, ships, and the Imperial Railways. Over four fifths of the national capital as given here was thus privately owned, a proportion similar to that in the United States.[4] The exceptions were the public forests, transport, communi-

---

[2] To this total of 110 billion yen, the Bureau of Statistics added an item of 191.6 million yen representing the estimated net balance of Japanese-owned assets in foreign countries over assets in Japan owned by residents of foreign countries. It was unable, however, to make a similar estimate of the balance of claims and obligations between Japan and her colonies. For this reason, and because we are mainly interested in real capital in Japan, we have disregarded the foreign credit balance. Table 18, therefore, is a census of physical assets in Japan Proper, irrespective of ownership nationality.

[3] See Joseph J. Spengler, "Economic Factors in the Development of Densely Populated Areas," *Proceedings of the American Philosophical Society*, vol. 95, no. 1, February 1951, p. 27.

[4] Government-owned property in the United States comprised $56 billion in 1935, or about 15% of national wealth. National Resources Committee, *The Structure of the American Economy*, part 1, Washington, 1939, pp. 375, 377.

Table 18. *National Wealth of Japan Proper, 1930*[a]

	Value (millions of yen)	Percent
Total national wealth	*109,996*	*100.0*
Natural resources	*54,298*	*49.4*
Land	41,091	37.4
Paddy and upland fields (taxable)[b]	(16,200)	(14.7)
Residential land and factory sites (taxable)[b]	(14,582)	(13.2)
Mines	6,500	5.9
Trees[c]	6,707	6.1
Buildings	*22,843*	*20.8*
Stocks of goods	*18,847*	*17.1*
Household chattels	12,473	11.3
Other	6,374	5.8
Transport and communication facilities	*7,343*	*6.7*
Railways	3,598	3.2
Shipping	2,060	1.9
Harbors, canals, bridges	826	0.8
Vehicles	660	0.6
Telephone and telegraph	199	0.2
Other machinery and equipment	*4,067*	*3.7*
Electricity, gas, and water supply	2,258	2.1
Industrial machinery and tools	1,809	1.6
Cattle and poultry	*346*	*0.3*
Miscellaneous	*2,251*	*2.1*

a Year-end estimates from Imperial Cabinet, Bureau of Statistics, *Nippon Teikoku Tōkei Nenkan*, no. 53, Tokyo, 1934, p. 384. See also Saburo Shiomi, "On the National Wealth of Japan in the Year 1930," *Kyoto University Economic Review*, vol. IX, no. 1, July 1934, pp. 16-32. Land and trees are valued at 1930 market prices; mines at estimated value of deposits; railways and public works at cost of construction, minus wear and tear; other items generally at reproduction cost, with allowance for depreciation. The official categories are regrouped here, and one item, balance of international claims and obligations, is omitted. (See note 2, this chapter.)

b Shiroshi Nasu, *Aspects of Japanese Agriculture*, New York: Institute of Pacific Relations, 1941, p. 15.

c This includes timber trees, mulberry trees, bamboo, firewood, and tea plants. Shiomi, *op.cit.*, p. 19. Evidently it does not include forest lands.

cations, education, and certain other services inherently public in character.

2. An important share of national wealth consisted of goods intended directly for consumption. These included residential dwellings, furniture, other household goods, and a part of business inventories. The distinction between producers' and consumers' capital is difficult to draw with precision, especially where, as in Japan, so many residential dwellings were also places of business. However, about half the buildings (by value) were classified as dwellings; and

about two thirds of the stocks of goods were household property. These two categories add up to 44% of the total wealth of the country, excluding natural resources.

In a country where capital needs sorely to be economized for purposes of economic development, it is clearly desirable to channel accumulations largely into forms of wealth which are most productive in increasing per capita income still further. Without extensive coercion, however, any people are likely to devote a considerable share directly to consumer goods, even with such strong inducements to invest in income-yielding producer goods as existed in Japan. And, of course, better housing in particular is one of the conditions of economic progress as well as one of its benefits.

3. Another significant feature of Table 18 is the high proportion of improved natural resources to other forms of real capital. Land (valued at market price) is by far the largest component of national capital. It totals 49% in 1930, if we accept these figures.

This tends to be true in all countries, to be sure. But the case of Japan is particularly interesting in view of her rapid movement toward a pattern of industrialization based on raw materials imported from abroad. The rise of such imports was a response to the growing inadequacy of Japan's agricultural land, mining deposits, and forests to sustain the growing population at a rising level of production and income. The structure of the Japanese economy came to depend increasingly on foreign natural resources to supplement her own. Among her own capital assets of all types, however, land still comprised the chief form of productive wealth by a wide margin. This testifies to the continuing importance of agriculture, as well as the scale of urban development. It reflects intense competition for the use of a limited amount of urban and farm land, reinforced by the continuing social prestige of land ownership. The market price of agricultural land in Japan tended to be consistently higher than the landlord's revenue capitalized (after taxes) at the market rate of interest on most other kinds of investment.[5]

Western economists argued for a century or more as to how land should be classified as a factor of production. Formerly the practice was to distinguish it from man-made capital as being a free

[5] Shiroshi Nasu, *Aspects of Japanese Agriculture*, New York: Institute of Pacific Relations, 1941, pp. 129-31. See also Masao Kambe, "Rising Tendency of Land Values in Japan: Its Effects, Causes and Some Control Measures," *Bulletin de l'Institut International de Statistique*, vol. xxv, part 2, Tokyo, 1931, pp. 205-10. Total rent on taxable paddy and upland fields, priced at 16,200 million yen in Table 18, was 1,243 million yen at the end of 1930. Imperial Cabinet, Bureau of Statistics, *Nippon Teikoku Tōkei Nenkan*, no. 58, Tokyo, 1939, pp. 4-5. Taxes took 30 to 40% at this time, so that the landlord's return was around 5% of the market price of land on this crude calculation.

gift of nature, which never wears out although equally it cannot be readily increased in amount. Such distinctions run into difficulties, however, and nowhere more than in Asia. In the traditional agrarian societies of the Orient, with their intensive agriculture, gross capital formation has taken the form largely of public and private activities devoted to maintaining and improving the land. "More than in any country, not excepting Holland," says R. H. Tawney, "land in China is an article manufactured by man." Agricultural productivity throughout monsoon Asia, and equally in the arid North, depends heavily on man-made dykes, canals, wells, and other aids to irrigation, drainage, and transport. Without constant care the high-yield values of land will deteriorate more quickly than many other forms of durable capital.

To digress for a moment, we have here one of the economic bases for bureaucratic rule over Oriental peasant societies. If political feudalism gave way in China 2,000 years ago to the imperial bureaucratic state, staffed with a corps of educated, appointive officials, it was in part for this reason. K. A. Wittfogel explains this type of Oriental state as one peculiarly adapted to performing the key function of building public works in plains and alluvial valleys like those of China.[6] The subsequent rise and fall of Chinese dynasties, like the growth and decay of Mesopotamian societies, were linked with cycles of care and neglect of the land. Their importance in modern China is no less apparent. Civil disorder and political neglect have brought catastrophic floods, soil erosion, and declines in agricultural productivity.

In Japan large-scale agricultural public works have been of less economic and political significance than in China, owing to physiographic differences between the two countries. Irrigation works themselves were valued at only 250 million yen in the 1930 census, even though virtually all the country's domestic rice is grown on irrigated paddy fields, and reservoirs supply 20% of the water. In the absence of great continental plains and river systems, the problems of water control in mountainous Japan have been smaller in scale of management. Soil fertility could be maintained more easily by efforts of the family, the village, or the manor, adapted to the local need. Transport is likewise over shorter distances, and with the advantage of inland sea communications. Here probably lies the key to many of the historic contrasts between the two societies. Particularly it helps to explain the long persistence of feudalism in Japan, despite efforts as early as the seventh century to adopt the

6 "The Foundations and Stages of Chinese Economic History," *Zeitschrift für Sozialforschung*, vol. 4, no. 1, 1935, pp. 26-58.

Chinese system of land tenure, national taxation, and centralized bureaucratic administration.

However this may be, the difference between Japan and China in this regard is only one of scale. A leading historian, describing extensive reclamation projects in ninth century Japan, writes that "riparian works were regarded as one of the most important affairs of the state as well as of the manorial lord."[7] And in modern as well as ancient Japan much farm land has been "created" in the sense that immense human effort has been devoted to draining it, irrigating it, repairing the damage wrought by floods and storms, and otherwise keeping it cultivable. If urban land, in Japan as in most countries, owes much of its value to man-made improvements, so too do the farm lands of her coastal plains and mountain valleys. Their productivity is sustained only by constant repair of irrigation systems, and also large applications of fertilizer year after year. Experiments conducted on plots of land planted to rice, wheat, and barley show that average yields drop as much as 50% or more where no fertilizer is applied, as compared with the yield of fully fertilized plots.[8] In terms of its economic value, agricultural land so intensively cultivated "wears out" with great rapidity. Heavy outlays of labor and working capital are required annually to maintain current yields.

Ricardo's phrase—"the original and indestructible powers of the soil"—is thus singularly inappropriate here. The maintenance and improvement of land have been one of the major components of gross capital formation in Japan. Elsewhere in Asia where industrialization is less rapid, they are likely to be even more significant in economic development.[9]

4. Also of interest in Table 18 is the fact that buildings comprised as much as 40% of Japan's capital assets, if natural resources are excluded. As a component of producers' capital, building structures (omitting residential dwellings, which comprised one half) far outweigh machinery and equipment in value. In fact, machinery alone is a relatively small component of capital even in most manufacturing industries.

[7] Takao Tsuchiya, *An Economic History of Japan*, Tokyo, 1937, p. 70.

[8] Supreme Commander for the Allied Powers, GHQ, Natural Resources Section, Report No. 86, *Field Experiments with Fertilizers in Japan*, Tokyo, 1947, pp. 13-18; also NRS Report No. 93, *Fertilizer Practices in Japan*, Tokyo, 1947.

[9] "The general disposition of many economists to think of land as not producible," remarks Robert R. Doane, "is largely due to the fact that it has been regarded more from a physical than an economic point of view." *The Anatomy of American Wealth*, New York, 1940, p. 117. Doane cites an estimate of the Federal Trade Commission distinguishing between the values of "land" and "improvements in land" in the United States in 1922. This showed 60.7% of the value of taxable real property as attributable to "land" and 39.3% to "improvements" (p. 184).

This underlines still further the importance of construction activity as a means of creating real capital, as distinguished from producing or importing machinery and equipment. Not only buildings, but also land improvements, and much of the capital value of railways, roads, and port facilities, are created mainly by "laying brick upon brick and moving tons of earth from one place to another."[10] Even in the cost of hydroelectric plants in prewar Japan, equipment amounted to only 20%. In the United States, where producers' durable equipment is relatively much more important, construction accounted for 50% of all net capital formation from 1914 to 1933.[11]

It is fortunate for undeveloped regions like the Far East that this is so. For it means that from a quantitative standpoint the chief resources required for a major share of capital growth and maintenance are domestic labor and building materials. Only a small part of the real capital needed for industrialization can by its nature be imported from abroad. This is apt to be a highly strategic portion in the sense that certain essential machinery and materials cannot be manufactured in the industrializing country. Foreign loans can also facilitate the whole process of capital investment even if—as has commonly been the case—they are used to finance the importation of food and other consumer goods, rather than machinery. They make it easier to turn domestic resources to the construction of capital goods without the strain on present living standards which might otherwise be imposed. The composition of Japan's capital, however, bears out the general truth that the real capital assets required in various forms for economic growth must be largely produced at home.

The problem is mainly one of providing the necessary framework of finance, technological advance, and personal or political incentives to bring this about. In Japan, as in other densely populated and undeveloped areas, much capital formation took place with comparatively little actual sacrifice of consumption, either directly or indirectly. Building construction, as well as improvements in land, transport facilities, and public works, was carried on largely with labor equipped with only the simplest hand tools. To produce materials like structural steel and cement required considerable outlays in machinery, but the construction industry itself was hardly mechanized at all. Even as late as 1937, the 44 biggest civilian contractors in Japan together owned only 467 trucks, 26 tractors,

---

[10] Norman S. Buchanan, *International Investment and Domestic Welfare*, New York, 1945, p. 18. Thomas D. Cabot writes that in Central America "the United Fruit Company has moved more dirt in building its banana farms than was moved in building the Panama Canal." *Land Use and Its Relation to Foreign Trade*, New York: Middle America Information Bureau, 1948, p. 5.

[11] Simon Kuznets, *National Product since 1869*, New York, 1946, pp. 115, 118.

and 9 steam shovels, though they employed 40,000 workers.[12] More-over, the labor required to improve land and build most types of structures could be found largely in the traditional skills. Much of it was performed in spare time, or by workers who would otherwise have added comparatively little to the flow of current goods and services for consumption.

5. Finally, the various forms of Japanese capital assets itemized in Table 18 were characterized by wide differences in mobility and variability. Land is fixed in location, and relatively inelastic in sup-ply, though still capable of varying uses in accordance with chang-ing needs. Plant structures and equipment are more mobile except in short periods of time. Even so, any pronounced shift in the compo-sition of this type of capital can occur only through replacement over a period of years.[13] The greatest mobility and variability, of course, are found in stocks of raw materials and finished goods. Ex-cluding household property and coins and bullion, stocks in the pipelines of the system of production—business inventories—were valued at 5.4 billion yen in Japan at the end of 1930. This repre-sented as much as 17%, or one sixth, of all producers' capital other than natural resources, as estimated here.

As markets broaden, and the division of labor becomes pro-gressively more elaborate, an economy is apt to require increasing inventories of goods in various stages of manufacture. In Japan, to judge by estimates of the Cabinet Bureau of Statistics, such in-ventories at the end of 1924 bore the following relation to gross production in that year: agriculture, 70%; mining, 20%; fishing, 20%; manufacturing (except food processing), 50%.[14] It was also figured that 20% of annual imports at this time were being re-tained in stock.

How indispensable this component of national capital is has been shown in the experience of countries which have been denuded of current inventories by war or depression. For example, Japan's ever present need for imported materials was still further enlarged dur-ing the occupation years by the necessity of restocking empty pipe-lines. Even in normal times a substantial share of the growing capital requirements of an expanding economy are apt to take the form of increasing stores of processed and semiprocessed goods in

---

[12] U.S. Strategic Bombing Survey, *The Japanese Construction Industry*, Wash-ington, 1946, pp. 36-41.

[13] The actual rate of replacement is determined not merely by the physical wearing out of capital goods, but also by other factors affecting obsolescence. A greater speed of technical innovation and a relative abundance of capital make for a far higher rate of obsolescence in industrial equipment in the United States than in Japan.

[14] K. Mori, "The Estimate of the National Wealth and Income of Japan Proper," *Bulletin de l'Institut International de Statistique*, vol. xxv, part 2, Tokyo, 1931, pp. 184-85.

factories, warehouses, and shops. In the United States, for example, net additions to business inventories accounted for 20% of net capital formation from 1899 to 1928.[15]

In summary, Table 18 serves to indicate the diverse forms of real capital accumulated over several decades of industrialization and economic growth. Mostly it was private wealth. A very large share still took the form of greatly improved natural resources. Of the remainder, residential dwellings and household chattels accounted for as much as 40%, the rest being distributed among public and business buildings, transport and communication facilities, public utilities, and industrial machinery. Despite the importance of Japanese industry by this time as a source of employment and income, and the essential character of the transport system, the actual capital assets of all types in these fields do not bulk large in the national aggregate. Of those assets which yielded income in significant amounts, however, they were a considerably larger share, and of course they were highly strategic in the development process.

Expanding Resources: The Meiji Period. To describe the processes by which this fund of national wealth was enlarged and made more productive would be to repeat much that is said elsewhere in this book. It would also take one into the detailed financial history of Japan, which is sketched only briefly in Chapters 1 and 2. Here just a few broad characteristics will be noted.

Perhaps the first point to emphasize is the rising demand for new capital assets created by the forces of modernization and growth set in motion after the Restoration. The whole conjuncture of circumstances after 1868 was such as to make for a high rate of anticipated return on new income-producing wealth in various forms, and to call forth a growing stream of investment expenditure.

Some early investment was "capital-saving," in Japan as elsewhere. Land could be economized, for example, by better irrigation, by investing more working capital in fertilizer, or by consolidating scattered farm strips so as to eliminate the ditches and paths around each tiny patch. The technical innovations which raised crop yields made it possible nearly to double agricultural output with probably no more than a 25% increase in the cultivated area. Moreover, better transport and storage, by widening the range of markets, could economize on the stocks of food previously required to maintain a given standard of life. But technical progress in a traditional society undertaking modernization more generally requires a change in "capital technique" entailing more roundabout, capitalistic modes of production. A greater stock of capital, i.e., greater intensity of investment, is the condition of replacing the hand loom with the

[15] Kuznets, *op.cit.*, p. 118.

power loom, the forge with the rolling mill, the sampan with the steamer, or the musket with the machine gun. The process of industrialization requires greater amounts of capital per worker, while also bringing revolutionary improvements in its efficiency.

Such new demands for capital in Meiji Japan, initiated and sustained by a long wave of technological change, were reinforced by other expansive forces. One was the upsurge of population. To maintain even the existing plane of living for growing numbers required a corresponding increase in the stock of productive resources. As people flocked to the towns and cities in nonagricultural employment, moreover, they created new demands for housing, transportation, and urban public services. While the total registered population grew from 42.0 million in 1893 to 55.1 million in 1913, the number residing in communities of over 10,000 increased from 6.7 to 15.2 million.[16] Throughout Asia in recent decades residential construction has been a major component of capital formation, and all estimates of national wealth in Japan since 1905, excluding natural resources, value buildings at 25% or more of the total. Another set of requirements of the highest political priority was associated with the building of the Imperial Army and Navy, and the two successful wars which they waged around the turn of the century. Government investment and investment subsidy were directed to this end in considerable degree. Finally, the slow gain in consumption standards among the people added new demands for productive plant, either to supply goods and services directly, or to turn out export goods to pay for imports from abroad.

A major part of new private investment during the early decades must have gone, first of all, into simple advances in farming, especially the extension and improvement of agricultural land. Hand in hand with this growth of agricultural capital went similar changes in fishing, home, and workshop industries, and in marketing structures. Only fragmentary statistics can be assembled to indicate the actual process of expansion in these sectors. For it was largely in the realm of unincorporated enterprise, and even such basic changes as the increase in arable land are not recorded accurately. Investment of this sort was carried on by individual proprietors with little more than family labor and their own slender resources, supplemented by the local moneylender or bank. Yet substantial gains in production could be achieved, as described in Chapter 4, with relatively modest outlays of capital, provided they were intelligently directed and cumulative in their effect. The greater share came from small increments of saving by the peasant or small businessman, or represented the investment of family labor previously employed to

16 *Nippon Teikoku Tōkei Nenkan*, cited, no. 38, 1920, p. 28.

little advantage. No government guarantees were involved, and very little in the way of government funds.

If the total wealth of Meiji Japan grew as much as appears to have been the case, it must have come in good part from this combination of small-scale accumulation and modest technical innovation spreading through the more or less traditional occupations which still engaged the bulk of the working population.

The more strategic sectors of early investment were doubtless the dramatic, large-scale undertakings which created the framework of national government, finance, transport, education, and defense. Such structural changes provided the setting for the immediate advances in agriculture and small-scale business. Without them the stimulus of political security, wider markets, and new skills and techniques would have been lacking. They also set the stage for large-scale industrialization after the turn of the century. Other types of investment, strategic out of all proportion to their size, were the pioneering outlays for the first factories, machine shops, and technical schools through which the Japanese began to acquire the secrets of modern science and machinery. Here, as is so often pointed out, the State played a critical role, drawing on its taxing and borrowing powers to provide funds for the purpose. It reached abroad for the new techniques, shouldered the initial risks, and lavished rewards on those who followed—particularly where the urgent concerns of national defense were at stake.

Much attention has been paid to the industrial and military enterprise of the Meiji governments. Less conspicuous was State activity in the construction of roads, irrigation and drainage systems, warehouses, port facilities, etc. Probably this type of capital formation was a good deal more productive of immediate returns in real income and better living standards than State-sponsored industrial investment.[17] Certainly it was technically much easier to accomplish, being largely a matter of mobilizing local labor. Almost from the beginning, however, it was starved by the demands of armament, so far as the central government was concerned. Judged by the standard of national development programs today, its outlays were surprisingly small. Between 1876 and 1882, for example, only 45 million yen ($40 million) of official funds was spent on public works of the above type, one half of it supplied by prefectures, towns, and villages.[18] This was hardly 10% of tax revenues. Even so it is worthy

---

[17] Better rural roads and warehouses, for example, make an almost immediate contribution to the food supply of an undeveloped Asiatic country. For they make it possible not only to pool supplies over a wider area, but also to reduce the loss of grain from decay and infestation in storage. Such losses can easily run up to 5 to 10%, even in normal years.

[18] P. Mayet, *Agricultural Insurance*, London, 1893, p. 183.

of note that as the current revenues of prefectural, city, town, and village governments increased, a considerable share began to be spent on local improvements. Public works and public utilities likewise accounted for the bulk of local government loans, which had risen to 306 million yen by 1913.[19] These various public investments were financed mainly out of taxes, directly or indirectly, particularly the land tax, which provided the bulk of national and local revenue in this early period. (See Chapter 10.)

More catalytic and cumulative in their long-term effects were the contributions of the State to the growth of private investment. The new national regime was hard-pressed in its early years. It had to finance its own administrative requirements, build the new Army and Navy, and suppress the Satsuma Rebellion of 1877. Its own fiscal needs led it immediately to encourage the spread of deposit and note-issue banking; even then it had to resort extensively to the printing press. At the same time it strained its public credit to create, almost at one stroke, a huge fund of liquid capital in private hands. This came about through the decision to commute the feudal pensions of 400,000 aristocrats, the final stage in the political compromise by which Japanese feudalism, in McLaren's words, was "partly driven and partly lured to its own destruction."

Under the pension capitalization scheme of 1876 some 210 million yen of public bonds and cash were issued. By the same method the government likewise paid off old clan debts of 41 million yen to merchants and moneylenders. These public bonds were secured in effect by taxes to be paid mainly by the peasant. They promptly fell to a discount. And much of the purchasing power they represented was probably dissipated in consumption. The more enterprising *daimyō, samurai,* and *chōnin,* however, were endowed with funds to venture in new banking and business enterprise, some of which brought gains in both productive wealth and entrepreneurial talent.

The ensuing inflation of 1877-81 further enlarged the pool of investment funds, albeit at the expense of tax revenues. Rice prices advanced rapidly, presenting a windfall gain in income to landlords whose rents were fixed in kind while their taxes were fixed in money. New banks, small industries, and trading firms mushroomed. Agricultural land was steadily improved and put to more efficient use. Many small business ventures were swept away in the depression of 1881-85, when the whole currency and banking system was reorganized on a more stable basis by the able statesman-financier Count Matsukata. Through these first two decades of turbulent

19 Tōyō Keizai Shimpō-sha, *Meiji Taishō Zaisei Shōran,* Tokyo, 1927, pp. 625-27.

finance, however, a good deal of income, mostly from agriculture, must have found its way by one means or another into investment in new enterprise.

After 1882 the State receded into the background as an entrepreneur. Thereafter it confined its own industrial undertakings within Japan to a few strategic industries, notably iron and steel. (The chief exception was the nationalization of the trunk railways in 1906-09, when the government purchased 2,800 miles of lines from seventeen companies at a price of 476 million yen.) It continued, on the other hand, to pursue policies and practices calculated to stimulate private investment. Some were pervasive in their effects: a broad framework of legal security; freedom of enterprise; technical research and education; encouragement to the joint-stock form of organization; the creation of big banking institutions to channel funds into private industry and trade; overseas borrowing to help provide for its own needs (1897-1913); a fiscal policy which relied heavily upon taxes on real estate and consumption, and dealt leniently with incomes from business enterprise, especially in the upper income brackets. Other encouragements to investment were more selective. Such was the case with tax rebates, subsidies, and lucrative purchase contracts given to industries like steel and ship-building which carried a high military priority. (For a more extended discussion of the role of the State, see Chapter 10.)

The credit system of modern Japan began to take shape in the eighties. Of key importance was the creation of a group of official or quasi-official banks, side by side with the growing private banks. The Yokohama Specie Bank (1880) became the chief foreign exchange bank of the country, the Bank of Japan (1882) the central bank of note issue and fiscal agent of the government. The Hypothec Bank (1896) was established as the central organ of forty-seven prefectural Agricultural and Industrial Banks to make long-term, low-interest loans on immovable property. The Industrial Bank of Japan (1900) specialized in financing large-scale industry and public undertakings like the South Manchuria Railway Company, borrowing considerable sums of foreign capital for its operations. Other colonial enterprise was undertaken by the official Bank of Taiwan (1899), the Oriental Development Company (1908), and the Bank of Chosen (1909). Finally, mention should be made of the Deposits Bureau of the Ministry of Finance, into which was attracted a large stream of small-scale postal savings for investment in government bonds and semiofficial undertakings.

The special banks in effect were partnership ventures on the part of the government and leading financial interests. As a group they secured their funds mainly from private sources (and the Imperial

Household). But they were closely controlled by the State, which did not hesitate to use them as instruments of national policy. They played a large part in mobilizing resources for the introduction of modern techniques in commerce and industry, as well as for financing military and colonial enterprise overseas. In 1913 they accounted for 28% of the paid-up capital and reserves of all banks in Japan. By 1933 their share had risen to one third. Here, and in the realm of fiscal policy, were the levers by which capital formation continued to be influenced and channelled according to the priorities of the State. (See below, pages 512ff.)

As in all undeveloped countries, the building of a national system of transport and communications made heavy demands on Japan's resources for capital investment—in her case, prior to 1914. In that year, for example, the sum invested in the Imperial Railways stood at 1,007 million yen, slightly more than the total paid-up capital and reserves of all industrial companies. The introduction of the railway and the steamship in turn set in motion a whole wave of technical innovations which created further opportunities for profitable investment in other fields. Fortunately for Japan, the demands of land transport itself must have been proportionately less than in continental countries, owing to the excellence of her interior sea communications. Even so, the growth of transport requirements and the shift from men as beasts of burden to wheeled vehicles increasingly powered by machinery must have absorbed a considerable share of the new capital formed through the Meiji period. According to a 1913 official estimate, railways, shipping, and other vehicles were valued at about 1,800 million yen.[20]

More onerous, and less productive economically, was the burden imposed on Japan's new financial system by two wars fought near the turn of the century, and the accompanying rise in expenditures on armaments, colonies, and strategic industries. During the conflict with China in 1894-95 the Army and Navy spent 200.5 million yen. Half of it was raised by public loans. Ten years later the Russo-Japanese War cost another 1,730 million yen, two thirds or so of a year's national income at the time. This sum, too, was financed by public borrowings to the extent of over 80%.[21] In addition, large arms expansion programs were vigorously pursued before and after each conflict. These programs likewise exceeded current revenues and enlarged still further the scope of deficit financing. The national debt, leaving aside the part incurred in nationalizing the railways, rose from 235 million yen in 1893 to almost 2 billion yen in 1913.

---

[20] Mori, *op.cit.*, p. 199.

[21] On the financing of the two wars, see Ushisaburo Kobayashi, *War and Armament Loans of Japan*, New York, 1922, pp. 40-42, 61-86.

As described in Chapter 1, some 1.5 billion yen of the latter total was devoted to war and armament outlays.[22]

To have financed these expenditures entirely out of Japanese taxation and savings would have put a severe strain on the national economy. It would certainly have required much more coercive restraints on consumption, in the form of inflation, taxation, and other direct controls. This is the more true as the period 1893-1913 was also a period of extensive private capital formation for industrial and commercial purposes. (For example, the paid-up capital of all concerns juristically organized as joint-stock companies and partnerships grew from 398 million yen at the end of 1896 to 1,983 million in 1913.) Annual tax revenues increased from 105 to 660 million yen in the twenty years, including fiscal monopoly profits, which were a form of consumption tax. (See Chapter 10.) But they failed by a wide margin to cover government expenditure.

Private saving was also growing apace, along with taxes, and was turning toward those forms which made it more readily available for investment in government and corporate securities, either directly, or indirectly through the banks. This is shown in Table 19, a partial estimate of gross private savings by decades from 1893. (Yamada's annual data show a rise in personal liquid savings from 74 million yen in 1896 to 384 million yen in 1913.) Actual gross savings were much larger than Table 19 indicates. For the figures here relate only to (a) the increase in private holdings (by nonfinancial institutions) of securities, bank deposits, etc., and (b) undistributed company profits as reported for tax purposes. Particularly they leave out much of the savings of unincorporated proprietors and other persons represented in net additions to their equity in improved land, buildings, equipment, and inventories. This has been a large component of the real savings of Japanese farmers and the hosts of small industrialists and tradesmen.

[22] The following figures testify to the expanding fiscal operations of the national government:

	1893-94	1903-04	1913-14
	MILLIONS OF YEN		
Tax revenue	70	146	369
Expenditure	85	250	574
Public debt (year-end)	235	539	2,592
National income (estimated)	1,380	2,575	4,556
	INDEX NUMBERS		
Wholesale price index (year-end)	100	156	200

Tax, expenditure, and debt figures are from *Meiji Taishō Zaisei Shōran*, cited, pp. 2, 4, 608. The national income estimate and price index are from Yuzo Yamada, *Nihon Kokumin Shotoku Suikei Shiryō*, Tokyo, 1951, pp. 114-17, 154, and refer to the calendar year 1893, etc.

Table 19. *Partial Estimate of Gross Private Savings
in Japan Proper, 1893-1937* (Yamada)[a]
(annual averages in millions of yen)

		PERSONAL LIQUID SAVINGS		UNDISTRIBUTED	GROSS
		Cash and	Other	COMPANY	PRIVATE
		Current Bank	Deposits and		
	Securities	Deposits	Savings	PROFITS	SAVINGS
1893-1902	45	22	36	—	103
1903-12	139	46	110	20	315
1913-22	579	180	723	36	1,518
1923-32	561	—22	720	4	1,263
1933-37	860	280	1,760	455	3,355

a Data from Yuzo Yamada, *Nihon Kokumin Shotoku Suikei Shiryō*, Tokyo, 1951, pp. 102-05, 114-115, 120-21. The various components include average year-end changes in the following: "Securities": all public debt, corporate shares, and debentures held outside financial institutions; "Cash and Current Bank Deposits": current deposits, transfer savings, and currency owned by other than financial institutions; "Other Deposits and Savings": postal savings, savings through credit and mutual credit associations, funds in trust, and all bank deposits (except in the Bank of Japan), excluding current deposits and deposits of government and financial institutions; "Undistributed Company Profits": net company profits minus dividends and corporation taxes.

Yamada's figures are labelled "partial" here for the following reasons: Not included are such forms of gross private saving as net acquisition by unincorporated proprietors and other persons of real property net of depreciation, e.g., buildings and equipment; changes in personal indebtedness; and corporate savings in the form of depreciation charges and capital outlays charged to current expense. Nor is any adjustment made for accidental damage to capital assets, which at times is quite large in Japanese agriculture.

Despite the nation's growing resources, government spending and private investment through these years went well beyond the amounts of income which the Japanese either paid in taxes or would otherwise have withheld from consumption voluntarily and made available by orderly, noninflationary processes. Japan's own productive capacity, given the existing level of technology and the limited mobility still found in the savings-investment flow, was inadequate to satisfy the requirements of both war and industrial expansion on the scale now being pursued, without serious disruptive consequences.

It was at this juncture that Japan turned to Western money markets. She proceeded to borrow heavily on the credit of the government. Extensive loan flotations between 1896 and 1913, amounting in all to almost 2 billion yen ($1 billion), made it possible to finance a large excess of imports over exports through the period. By this means the total real resources at the disposal of the nation for consumption, investment, and government purposes were augmented, even though return interest and amortization payments abroad quickly began to cut down the net annual yield from further borrowings. As the government did virtually all the borrowing, and at comparatively low rates, it was able to meet its own financial needs more economically than at home. Meanwhile it freed the domestic capital market for private borrowers. Most important, perhaps, assistance was provided at one of the chief bottlenecks to national expansion, i.e., the need for large imports of military and industrial equipment and materials from overseas.

Since this was the one prewar period when Japan imported foreign capital on a large scale, it may be appropriate at this point to examine the episode a little more fully.

The Balance of Payments and Foreign Borrowing. Today it seems rather curious that the Japanese should have borrowed so little overseas through most of the era 1868 to 1938, relying instead on their own resources. Elsewhere capital imports have served industrializing nations in a variety of ways. Sometimes they have paid for purchases of machinery and technical know-how, or have furnished currency reserves, or offset the servicing of previous borrowings. More often the foreign buying power they provide has been used generally to enlarge the total volume of resources currently available, so that large investment or war-spending programs could be undertaken without undue strain on the financial mechanisms and consumption standards of a country.

In the case of Japan one type of capital inflow, foreign business investment, has played a strategic role in helping to transfer to Japanese equipment industries the advanced engineering techniques of the West. This point is discussed in Chapter 6, along with the broader aspects of technological borrowing. From a financial standpoint, however, direct foreign investment in Japan has never been significant in the aggregate, in relation to either business capital or the balance of payments. And it was much more than offset throughout the prewar decades by Japanese business investment overseas, in the colonies and elsewhere. Such large-scale borrowing from the West as took place was by the government itself, or its quasi-official banks and development corporations. It was largely portfolio borrowing from private investors abroad, and it was confined mainly to the period 1899 to 1913.

Prior to 1897, the deterrents to the flow of Western capital into Japan were found on both sides. The Japanese were wary of financial imperialism, seeing it in operation among their Asiatic neighbors. In any case Japan was not a very inviting opportunity, for either the European *rentier* investor or the European businessman. Two small loans were issued in 1870 and 1873. Paying 9% and 7%, they yielded only 30 million yen. No more foreign capital entered the country for twenty-five years, except for small sums invested by foreign trading firms.[23] Japan was drawing heavily on the West, but for knowledge and purchased equipment, not financial loans. She paid for her merchandise imports through 1895 with the proceeds of her silk and other exports. The small surplus which accrued was used to retire the above loans on maturity and to cover other outlays like military expenditures abroad. The chief items (net) in her international current accounts from 1873 to 1895 are summarized in Table 21, below.

With the prestige won in her quick victory over China, and the adoption of the gold standard in 1897, the Japanese government moved into a position where it could more advantageously seek financial aid overseas as it needed. The China war itself yielded an indemnity of 360 million yen, payable in sterling. However, this failed to meet the needs of the expansionist programs now set in motion. From 1897 to 1903 domestic bonds amounting to 93 million yen were marketed abroad, and a £10 million loan floated in London at a net interest of only 4.4%. Borrowing began in earnest with the outbreak of war with Russia. Thirteen sterling and franc loans were made by the national government between 1904 and 1913, aggregating £145 million and Fr. 650 million. Smaller sums were also raised by Japanese municipalities and corporations—the latter being mainly the semi-official South Manchuria Railway, the Industrial Bank of Japan, and the Oriental Development Company.[24]

The steep rise in the country's foreign debt as a result of these operations is shown in Table 20.

Japan's gross foreign indebtedness growing out of security purchases abroad at face value rose from 467,000 yen in 1896 to 1,970 million yen at the end of 1913. As these securities were sold at an average discount of about 10% (including commissions),[25] they yielded about 1,775 million yen. The war indemnity, paid over in 1896-98, added 360 million yen; Japan's slice of the subsequent Boxer indemnity, another 24 million. Meanwhile direct business investments by foreigners in Japan probably increased by 50 million

[23] Harold G. Moulton, *Japan, An Economic and Financial Appraisal*, Washington, 1931, pp. 490-97.

[24] Statistical details of Japan's prewar foreign borrowings are readily found in various government publications, for example, Ministry of Finance, *Statistical Year-Book of Finance and Economy of Japan, 1948*, opposite p. 324, and the Ministry's prewar *Financial and Economic Annual of Japan*, annual. The best discussions in English of Japan's foreign borrowing experience are in Moulton's work cited above; Margaret S. Gordon's study in E. B. Schumpeter, ed., *The Industrialization of Japan and Manchukuo, 1930-1940*, New York, 1940; the book by the former minister of finance Junnosuke Inouye, *Problems of the Japanese Foreign Exchange, 1914-1926*, London, 1931; and particularly a forthcoming study of foreign capital in Japan by Edwin P. Reubens, of Cornell University.

[25] Moulton, *op.cit.*, p. 507.

Table 20. *Outstanding Foreign Loan Indebtedness of Japan Proper, 1896-1934*[a]

YEAR-END	TOTAL FOREIGN LOAN INDEBTEDNESS	FOREIGN-CURRENCY BONDS AND DEBENTURES OUTSTANDING		DOMESTIC ISSUES SOLD ABROAD
		National	*Municipal and* Corporate	
1896	—	—	—	—
1904	421	312	4	105
1913	1,970	1,525	344	101
1919	1,722	1,311	313	98
1929	2,304	1,447	711	146
1934	2,041	1,408	583	50

a Adapted from Harold G. Moulton, *Japan, An Economic and Financial Appraisal*, Washington, 1931, pp. 494-95, except that 1934 figures are from Mitsubishi Economic Research Bureau, *Japanese Trade and Industry*, London, 1936, p. 83. See also Oriental Economist, *The Foreign Trade of Japan, A Statistical Survey*, Tokyo, 1935, p. 696. Estimated sales of domestic bonds abroad do not include home issues of municipalities, or, in 1934, any such issues of corporate debentures. Nor do they allow for extensive repatriation of foreign currency bonds into the hands of Japanese nationals, as discussed in the text. The conversion of foreign issues into Japanese currency, after the yen depreciation of 1931-32, remains at the earlier rates: pound sterling, 9.763 yen; U.S. dollar, 2.006 yen; franc, 0.387 yen.

yen or so. Total receipts from all these sources were therefore about 2,200 million yen. On the other hand, part of the loan and indemnity proceeds were left abroad as short-term assets, largely specie holdings. Such holdings at the end of 1913 were 227 million yen higher than in 1899.[26] Also, Japanese capital went abroad for foreign long-term investment (mostly in China) in the amount of 300 to 350 million yen.[27] Thus the net inflow of capital in the form of loans, indemnities, and investments from 1896 through 1913 was on the order of 1,600 million yen ($800 million) or more. The figures are necessarily inexact, but they leave no doubt that Japan borrowed heavily abroad at this critical turning point in her modern history.

The significance of this foreign borrowing has already been indicated. For Japan the twenty years before World War I were

26 *ibid.*, p. 539.

27 C. F. Remer's careful study of *Foreign Investments in China*, New York, 1933, values Japanese investments in China in 1914 at U.S. $219.6 million, or about 440 million yen (p. 446). Direct business investment comprised 385 million yen, and loans to the Chinese government and corporations the remainder. An earlier estimate by the Bank of Japan puts the Japanese total at 365 million yen. (Moulton, *op.cit.*, pp. 508-09.) Both estimates include 90 to 100 million yen for properties of the South Manchuria Railway taken over from Russia without international payment. To its China figure the Bank of Japan adds 96 million yen for Japanese investments in Hawaii, the United States, and other foreign countries. Presuming that the 1914 estimates for both China and elsewhere include some assets created through the reinvestment of profits abroad, one may conclude that the actual export of capital from Japan to foreign countries to be offset against the inflow recorded above was probably 300 to 350 million yen. This leaves out investments in Formosa and Korea.

years of rapid economic expansion. In particular, military expenditure and private capital formation strained the capacity of the country to mobilize resources over and above its requirements for civilian consumption.[28] Evidence of the strain is seen in the steady rise of commodity prices, which doubled from 1893 to 1913. Foreign borrowing itself contributed to the increase in spending, especially as the Bank of Japan enlarged its note issue against the specie holdings acquired. But it also served to relieve the pressure at critical points, and thus to accelerate the expansion process.

Most of the borrowing, first of all, had as its immediate purpose financing the deficits in the national budget incurred primarily for military expenditure. The government's current outlays were covered mainly by taxes, it is true. But foreign loans added a significant margin, especially in the war years. Of the entire national debt, 2,600 million yen in 1913, foreign holdings of government bonds comprised 1,600 million yen. The State thus met its fiscal needs without monopolizing the domestic capital market, and did so mostly at interest rates no higher than $4\frac{1}{2}$ to 5%. It was also helped directly in making sizable military expenditures abroad.

For the country as a whole, capital imports served to augment the real resources at its disposal through the large excess of commodity imports which they permitted. Table 21 shows an Empire deficit of 1,083 million yen on current account from 1904 through 1913. Probably it was 400 to 500 million yen in the preceding eight years. This is not far from the direct estimate of 1,600 million yen of net capital inflow. It is only about $2\frac{1}{2}$% of Japan's total national income through these years, as estimated by Yamada.[29] Against the inflow, moreover, must be set the rising obligation of interest payments abroad. Table 21 shows that these payments already amounted to 637 million yen in 1904-13, or over 60% of the net capital imports of the decade. During the war years of heaviest borrowing, however, the temporary gain was much larger. And generally through the period, foreign borrowing enabled private domestic investment and the government deficit to exceed savings by a considerable sum. It is significant that personal liquid savings, as estimated in Table 19, increased no more than 300 million yen a year from 1903 to 1912. By comparison with this estimate, admittedly an incomplete one, foreign holdings of Japanese securities grew as much as 178 million yen a year.

[28] For example, in 1906-07, on the heels of a war costing 1,800 million yen, some 311 new companies were floated calling for a capital investment of over 400 million yen in cotton mills, electric railways, shipping, mining, etc. *The Japan Year Book, 1906*, p. 227.

[29] *Nihon Kokumin Shotoku Suikei Shiryō*, cited, pp. 114-17.

Table 21. *Balance of Current International Payments of the Japanese Empire, 1873-1936*[a]

(millions of yen)

	1873-95	1896-1903	1904-13	1914-19	1920-29	1930-36
Net balance of current transactions and gold			−1,083	2,431	−2,272	1,302
Merchandise trade[b]	30	−355	−707	1,198	−4,216	−538
Invisibles			−436	1,838	1,897	1,032
Interest and dividends	−25	−41	−637	−314	−603	−665
Income on undertakings and services abroad			274	441	1,094	1,049
Freight receipts			252	1,357	1,424	968
Government payments abroad			−330	166	−344	−660
Other			4	187	326	340
Gold[b]	72	−62	60	−604	−452	808

a Data for 1904-36 compiled by Margaret S. Gordon in E. B. Schumpeter, ed., *The Industrialization of Japan and Manchukuo, 1930-1940*, New York, 1940, pp. 866, 875, 880, table III. Figures on trade, interest, and specie, 1873-1903, from Harold G. Moulton, *Japan, An Economic and Financial Appraisal*, Washington, 1931, pp. 496-501. All statistics relate to the Empire, including Japan Proper and Sakhalin, Korea, Formosa, and Nanyo (as each was assimilated).

The dollar value of the yen declined from U.S. 102 cents in 1874 to 51 cents in 1895; it fluctuated around 49.5 cents from 1896 to 1919; through the decade 1920-29 it averaged 46.4 cents; and after 1931 it dropped to 28 to 29 cents, averaging 34.1 cents during the years 1930-36.

b All specie movements prior to 1904 are included with gold; thereafter specie other than gold is included with merchandise trade. Exports of gold, like other commodities, are a credit item; imports a debit item.

Commodity exports are believed to have been consistently undervalued in prewar Japan, thus exaggerating the trade deficit (or understating the surplus). Mrs. Gordon concludes (p. 916) that the error in the later years may have run to 100 to 200 million yen a year. Before 1914 it was smaller. Junnosuke Inouye says (*Problems of the Japanese Foreign Exchange, 1914-1926*, London, 1931, p. 205) that exporters' declarations undervalued true f.o.b. export values by 4%, according to the Department of Finance.

The loans were not tied to specific imports of capital goods for the most part. They served mainly to enlarge the general pool of foreign exchange resources on which Japanese importers could draw—with certain priorities dictated, no doubt, by the government and its special banks. Yet the small amounts of consumer goods in the import tables of these years show that the savings institutions, consumption habits, and tax burdens of the time were such that the proceeds of the loans were spent mainly on materials and equipment for industrialization and armament. There does not appear to have been even much indirect "leakage" on finished consumer goods through the multiplied effects of investment spending on national income. Nor did rising incomes at home prevent exports from tripling in volume between 1900 and 1913. (Probably they did contribute to the failure of exports to grow from 1904 to 1908.)[30]

Viewing the Japanese case in retrospect, one may conclude that it was a rather successful case of foreign borrowing, in the sense that a large flow of private *rentier* capital from abroad was attracted, largely on government credit. It was utilized to tide the country over a difficult financial period, without introducing the political frictions or foreign controls which have often attended external borrowing elsewhere. The interest charges piled up were to prove a burden in subsequent years, especially since the windfall surpluses which were soon to appear, in the war years 1914-19, were not used to retire the debt. They were a diminishing burden, however, as the country's productive capacity and foreign trade steadily increased.

Just what contribution was made by this borrowing episode to Japan's actual economic development is more difficult to determine. It was war and armament more than anything else which created the need, and absorbed the bulk of the funds placed at the government's disposal. Except as the military expenditure of the time can be shown to have enlarged the nation's capacity to gain something more than armies, warships, and territory flying the Rising Sun, the foreign borrowing must be regarded as a chapter in Japan's military expansion more than anything else. It may be, nevertheless, that the war spending of these years, with its still limited scale and successful military outcome, so stimulated the general advance of industrialization that it more than paid for itself in the end. (See below, pages 291ff.)

From Debtor to Creditor. The remainder of Japan's prewar borrowing experience may be briefly summarized. Already on the eve of World War I her foreign indebtedness had reached its all-time peak. Her foreign bond obligations stood at 1,970 million yen. To this sum the assets of foreign business enterprise in the country probably added no more than 70 million yen.[31] Meanwhile Japanese assets abroad comprised specie holdings of 246 million yen and long-term investments estimated at 536 million yen. (See above.) Of the

---

[30] *The Foreign Trade of Japan, A Statistical Survey,* cited, p. 698.

[31] Moulton puts direct foreign investments in Japan at 100 million yen in 1913, capitalizing at 8% the outgo on "Foreign undertakings and services." (*op.cit.,* p. 507.) Mrs. Gordon (Schumpeter, ed., *op.cit.,* p. 922) cuts it to the above figure of 70 million yen, since this outgo includes personal remittances as well as business profits.

latter, the properties of the South Manchuria Railway alone accounted for 231 million yen. With these offsets, net foreign indebtedness was reduced to 1,250 to 1,300 million yen in 1914—about $650 million.

The war years 1914-19 brought a sudden reversal in this debtor position. Overnight Japan became a creditor of large proportions, as the boom in exports and shipping piled up huge balances abroad. Domestic capital formation also took place on a considerable scale. Yet the inflated volume of savings (9,000 million yen in the categories given in Table 19) was sufficient to support this capital export in addition. The accumulation of short-term balances, together with loans to the British, French, and Russian governments, momentarily gave the nation a net creditor position of 1,350 to 1,400 million yen at the end of 1919. The position was an abnormal one, however. It was soon liquidated. Britain and France repaid their war debts, and specie holdings abroad were virtually used up in supporting the overvalued yen and financing the heavy trade deficits of the twenties. From 1920 to 1929 Allied loan obligations were reduced by 317 million yen and foreign specie balances by at least 1,229 million yen.[32]

Other two-way capital movements took place through the twenties. The Japanese government itself floated several sterling and dollar loans, mostly for refunding purposes. Smaller issues were also placed abroad by electric utilities, banks, and municipalities.[33] The figures given earlier (Table 20) put total foreign loan indebtedness at 2,304 million yen in 1929 and 2,041 million in 1934. Concurrently, foreign business investment in Japan increased by 100 million yen or so in the postwar decade, and Japanese capital exports outside the Empire by two or three times this sum. The net movement of capital, however, is obscured by large unrecorded flows of short-term funds back and forth, and by uncertainty as to real deficit on trade and invisible account. If export declarations undervalued exports by at least 4% (see Table 21, note b) the reported Empire deficit of 2,772 million yen on current account actually scales down to no more than 2,000 million yen. This is not much more than the return of wartime funds invested in Allied loans and foreign specie balances.

Over the twenty-year period 1914-34, considered as a whole, it appears that Japan was a *lender* rather than a borrower overseas.

[32] Moulton, *op.cit.*, pp. 516-21. The government ceased publication of foreign specie balances at the end of 1928, when only 114 million yen remained.

[33] See Yasuzo Horie, "Foreign Capital and the Japanese Capitalism after the World War I," *Kyoto University Economic Review,* vol. xx, no. 1, April 1950, pp. 38-59.

The credit surpluses accumulated during 1914-19 were largely dissipated in the postwar decade, but were succeeded by new overseas investments, particularly in Manchuria. Even the net foreign borrowing of the twenties (disregarding Japanese investment in the colonies) was slight in relation to the country's own capital resources or its trading operations overseas. Foreign capital now entering Japan was significant chiefly in relation to the technological borrowing which accompanied Western business investment in Japan. Exports of Japanese capital served on the other hand to carry Japanese business enterprise to the colonies and China, and to extend concurrently the nation's political influence and control in East Asia. On balance Japan did not repeat the borrowing episode of 1897-1913. Indeed, the thirties witnessed an outpouring of funds into the development of Manchuria, Korea, and Formosa. (See Chapter 10.)

By 1934 Japan's gross foreign indebtedness probably stood at little more than 1,500 million yen. Year-end figures (Table 20) place the total of Japanese bonds and debentures nominally held abroad at 2,041 million yen—about the same as in 1913. However, many of these securities actually had now been repurchased by Japanese nationals. The repatriated share is estimated at one third in 1934, and no less than one half by 1937.[34] These estimates are probably on the low side. An allowance of 150 to 200 million yen for direct foreign investment in Japan[35] gives us about 1,500 million yen ($750 million) as the gross total of claims and assets held in Japan by nonresidents of the Empire at the end of 1934—less than in 1913. (Short-term bank balances are excluded from this total, and Japanese foreign-currency bonds are valued at pre-1931 exchange rates.)

Japan's own overseas assets far exceeded her obligations by this time. Investments outside the Japanese colonies by individuals and

[34] The 1934 year-end estimate is from *Japanese Trade and Industry*, cited, p. 83. The 1937 figure is the Finance Ministry's estimate quoted in Foreign Affairs Association of Japan, *Japan's Finance and Industry*, Tokyo, 1937?, p. 5. In private correspondence an official of the Yokohama Specie Bank estimated in 1936 that 40 to 80% of Japan's $360 million of dollar bonds outstanding had been repatriated.

[35] Moulton uses remittance figures from the balance of payments to arrive at an estimate of 245 million yen for direct foreign investment in Japan at the end of 1929. (*op.cit.*, p. 524.) In adopting a lower figure here I have been influenced by the facts that foreign business investment in Japan was mainly American, and that direct American investments (those carrying with them a significant degree of control over management) were only U.S. $60.7 million at the end of 1929 and U.S. $46.7 million at the end of 1936. For the nature of these investments see U.S. Department of Commerce, *American Direct Investments in Foreign Countries—1936*, Washington, 1938, p. 16. At the end of 1941 foreign capital paid up in Japanese companies totalled only 106 million yen. (Horie, *op.cit.*, pp. 55-56.) The total paid-up capital of all Japanese companies was 30,453 million yen.

firms domiciled in Japan Proper probably approached 2,500 million yen in value in 1931. They were largely in China, and especially Manchuria.[36] During the years 1932-34 new Japanese investment in Manchuria is put at 520 million yen.[37] While there was also some new investment elsewhere, the balance of payments data suggest that a good deal of liquidation took place too. It would probably be safe to say that long-term foreign assets owned in Japan totalled around 3,000 million yen in value at the end of 1934.

In addition, Japanese banks and business concerns had now built up substantial holdings in Korea and Formosa, and lesser invest-ments in Sakhalin and the Mandated Islands. Without searching the literature at length, I have found little basis for estimating such holdings, especially properties owned by institutions and persons domiciled in Japan Proper. They seem to have defied any compre-hensive census, so intricate were the financial relations between the home islands and the overseas territories. From stray bits of evidence one suspects that they approached in scale the Manchurian invest-ment, 1,800 to 2,000 million yen in 1934, but this is little more than guesswork.

It is clear, in any event, that Japan was now a creditor nation by a considerable margin, in the sense that the valuation placed upon the overseas assets of residents of the home islands was several times the claims of nonresidents on the wealth of Japan Proper. This had probably been true ever since 1918, if colonial investment is reckoned

[36] Japanese investments in China had a value of 2,274 million yen at the end of 1930, according to C. F. Remer's authoritative study, already cited, p. 548. They comprised (in millions of yen): direct business investment in Manchuria, 1,100; business investment elsewhere in China, 648; secured loans and railway and com-munications obligations of the Chinese government, 248; unsecured government loans, 200; investment in Chinese corporations, 77. Firm estimates of Japanese assets out-side China are lacking. Inouye (*op.cit.*, app. x) puts Japanese capital in Southeast Asia at 134 million yen in 1924. A 1927 study of the Ministry of Commerce and Industry (Remer, *op.cit.*, p. 448) reports overseas investments of 110 million yen by eighty-nine leading Japanese companies, exclusive of loans, and outside the fields of shipping, finance, and insurance. The Mitsubishi Economic Research Bureau (*op.cit.*, p. 92) makes a statement regarding Japanese capital in China which implies that foreign investment elsewhere stood at about 300 million yen in 1931. On this slender evidence, and allowing for the fact that Remer's China figures include some assets of Japanese resident in China, I conclude that total foreign investment in 1931 was on the order of 2,500 million yen. This is somewhat above the estimate of 2,209 million yen of foreign assets included in the 1930 census of national wealth by the Cabinet Bureau of Statistics.

[37] Annual estimates of the Japanese government's Bureau of Manchoukuo Affairs for 1932-39 are given in "Japan's Manchoukuo Investments," *Oriental Economist*, vol. VII, no. 3, March 1940, pp. 152-54. While the figures omit additions to corporate reserves, they appear to include some investment by companies and individuals domiciled in Manchuria. The period of heavy investment in Yen Bloc territories, inspired by goals of military self-sufficiency, only began in 1934. From 1935 through 1939 another 2,534 million yen was sunk in Manchuria, according to the Bureau's figures.

in. Leaving the colonies aside, long-term foreign assets owned in Japan were valued at about 3,000 million yen at the end of 1934, as compared with counterobligations of no more than 1,500 million yen.

These debtor-creditor accounts, it should be pointed out, are no gauge of the annual remittances of interest, dividends, and profits to and from Japan. Actually outpayments from the Empire to foreign countries for this purpose still exceeded inpayments by a small margin after 1930, according to balance of payments figures. Nor is such a census of assets any measure of the earlier movement of capital in and out of the country. As it happens, Japan's debt obligations did represent actual capital imports in large part. Absorbed mainly from 1897 to 1913, they augmented the real resources at the disposal of the economy. By contrast, Japanese assets overseas were largely entrepreneur investments which had increased in value partly through the reinvestment of profits, the appreciation of capital values, and even military seizure as in the case of the South Manchuria Railway. Remer states (*op.cit.*, p. 550) that Japanese investments in China valued at 2,274 million yen in 1931 had been created with actual remittances from the home islands of no more than 1,200 million yen. This is hardly more than 50% of the total.

The actual export of capital from prewar Japan was thus more modest than the growing margin of external assets over obligations might suggest. Net capital outflow assumed large proportions only in two war periods, 1914-19 and 1934-39—both of them abnormal and short-lived in duration. Prior to 1934 a slow growth was taking place in Japanese business enterprise and investment in East Asia; yet it remained concentrated chiefly in China, Korea, and Formosa, where it owed much to political influence and government patronage. Such overseas business enterprise was significant in relation to Japanese trade and imperialism. On balance, however, it actually drew little wealth produced in Japan Proper into external investment, until the Empire development schemes of the late thirties. A much greater drain on resources for domestic investment was imposed by military expenditure in support of the expanding Empire, together with related financial outlays for colonial subsidy and political intrigue in China. If Japan imported little capital from abroad after 1913, neither did she devote sums to capital export which were very significant in the total scale of national savings and investment.

Capital Formation, 1913-38. To return to the broader aspects of capital, the war years 1914-19 greatly accelerated the formation of capital in Japan from domestic sources, by comparison with the earlier period. The expansion of foreign trade and industry was associated with an unprecedented increase in savings. Part of these savings went into the foreign credits mentioned above, and the remainder into domestic investment.

New investment in agricultural capital may well have slackened from this time on. The farmer was hard-pressed to compete with industry for credit, and the government never made a determined effort to step up agricultural output by large-scale public outlays. In industry and transport, on the other hand, the war boom raised investment activity to a high level. Thereafter it slumped, as inflationary prosperity gave way to years of deflation and financial disorder. Probably domestic capital formation remained at a relatively low level through the twenties; meanwhile disinvestment abroad was reflected in the large import deficits of these years. (Tables 19 and 21, above.) This is one reason why industrial wage rates rose 50% in buying power from 1915-19 to 1925-29, the one period in prewar Japan when they moved rapidly upward, thanks to the falling cost of living. (See above, page 144.)

The most significant gains in productive capacity during the postwar decade were technological improvements in capital efficiency, which proceeded apace. In Japanese industry, as contrasted with agriculture, they were especially marked from 1926 to 1931, under the pressure of falling prices and dwindling profit margins. (See Chapters 2 and 4.) They set the stage in turn for the upsurge of production and new capital formation in the thirties. Again the financial statistics show a renewed expansion of savings and investment, turning increasingly to military purposes as war mobilization gripped the economy. By 1937 corporate profits and new capital issues had nearly doubled the levels of 1929. The output of the equipment industries grew more or less in proportion. Meanwhile real wage rates failed to share appreciably in the advance.[38]

While many details in support of these general statements can be produced, and appear elsewhere in this volume, we are not much better off in this period than the earlier one when it comes to measuring aggregate capital formation. Three sets of data may be briefly considered.

One direct approach to the growth of Japanese capital is through successive estimates of national wealth. There were seven such estimates between 1905 and 1935. The Cabinet Bureau of Statistics, on publishing the 1930 census (Table 18), attempted to revise the earlier totals for 1913, 1919, and 1924 on a comparable basis. When this series is deflated crudely for price changes, with the 1935 estimate added, it shows a geometric rate of increase in national

---

[38] The gains of the depression years were largely cancelled by the subsequent rise of living costs.

wealth of 3.8% a year from 1913 to 1935—higher during 1913-19 and 1930-35, lower during the twenties. The estimates are so questionable in their meaning, accuracy, and consistency, however, that one must reject them as quite unreliable for the purpose in view.[39]

A second approach to the measurement of capital formation is through financial statistics indicating the growth of savings. Gross private savings consist of corporate savings in the form of undistributed company profits, depreciation charges, and other capital outlays charged to current expense, plus the personal savings of individuals and unincorporated proprietors, i.e., their surplus of income over and above consumption expenditure and taxes. In the aggregate such savings are equal, by definition, to gross investment plus the government deficit (or minus the government surplus).

Certain partial estimates of gross private savings in Japan were given in Table 19, based on data compiled by Yamada. They are computed by adding up year-end changes in holdings of cash, deposits, securities, etc. by individuals and companies other than financial institutions, with the further addition of undistributed company profits. Private savings thus estimated may be compared with Yamada's estimates of national income in five-year annual averages as follows (in millions of yen) :[40]

	Gross Private Savings (partial estimate)	National Income	Savings÷Income
1913-17	804	4,964	16.2
1918-22	2,230	11,882	18.8
1923-27	1,328	13,804	9.6
1928-32	1,196	12,184	9.8
1933-37	3,355	15,509	21.6

As one would expect, the savings ratio is high during World War I, much lower during 1923-32, and rises steeply in the boom of the thirties. For the entire twenty-five-year period it averages 15.3%.[41]

[39] Figures for 1913-30 will be found in S. Shiomi, "On the National Wealth of Japan in the Year 1930," *Kyoto University Economic Review*, vol. IX, no. 1, July 1934, p. 25; the 1935 estimate is reprinted in Prime Minister's Office, Statistics Bureau, *Japan Statistical Year-Book, 1949*, Tokyo, 1949, pp. 782-83. Details of the 1924 census, together with earlier estimates, are given in K. Mori, "The Estimate of the National Wealth and Income of Japan Proper," *Bulletin de l'Institut International de Statistique*, vol. xxv, part 2, pp. 179-204; also S. Shiomi, "On Japan's National Wealth and Income," *Kyoto University Economic Review*, vol. IV, no. 1, July 1929, pp. 28-46.

[40] For details as to these estimates, see above, Tables 12 and 19.

[41] Similar estimates of "savings," usually more ambiguous in character, were published by Japanese economists and the Ministry of Finance in the thirties; see, for

One should not read more into these figures than they warrant. They do not give a true estimate of gross savings unless numerous omissions and probable duplications happen to cancel out. They leave out entirely certain components of real saving—for example, the farmer's improvements in his own land, the small proprietor's acquisition of real property net of depreciation, the capital outlays of companies charged to depreciation and current expense.[42] They also fail to reflect accidental damage to capital assets, as in the 1923 earthquake. Moreover, even if accurately computed, gross savings are not to be equated with investment. They may be balanced partly with deficit spending by the government, whose expenditure may or may not contain elements of investment. The steep increase of 1933-37, particularly, was associated with large government deficits financed by "red-ink" bonds. About all that can be said, without much more detailed inquiry, is that a large-scale process of savings and investment was now being conducted through the financial institutions of Japan to cover the capital requirements of private business and the budgetary needs of the government.

A third method of gauging capital formation is through national expenditure accounts. Estimates of the main components in Japan during the years 1930 and thereafter have been published by the postwar Economic Stabilization Board. Table 22 gives a summary of the figures for 1930-38, with such details of the investment accounts as are available.

Capital formation is represented in Table 22 principally by private domestic investment expenditure on residential dwellings, producers' plant, and inventory increases. Such outlays are given as only 6.2% of gross national expenditure in the depression years 1930-32. They increase to 11.3% in the recovery period 1933-35, and then rise to 18.7% in the three years that follow. (The formation of new capital would have been of smaller proportions, for gross investment by definition includes depreciation charges and other allowances for business consumption of durable goods.) Another indeterminate share of capital expenditure is that portion of

---

example, S. Hijikata, "Saikin Waga Kuni Kokumin Shotoku," *Keizai-gaku Ronshū*, vol. viii, July 1938, pp. 810-29.

[42] Corporate balance sheets in Japan are a poor guide to changes in corporate assets, particularly those accounts which are prepared with an eye on the tax collector. In Japanese business practice profits and reserves are often put ahead of depreciation. Large amounts may be charged off to depreciation in good times but little or nothing when business is poor. The U.S. Department of State's *Report of the Mission on Japanese Combines*, Washington, 1946, remarks that "the financial statements submitted to Japanese stockholders are curiosities in obscurity and evasion." (Part i, p. 26.) Even in the United States, with its more rigorous accounting standards, inaccurate valuation practices make it difficult to estimate invested capital from the balance sheets of corporations.

Table 22. *Investment Expenditure in Relation to Gross*
National Expenditure in Japan Proper, 1930-38
(Economic Stabilization Board)[a]

| | ANNUAL AVERAGE | | |
| | (MILLIONS OF YEN) | | |
	1930-32	*1933-35*	*1936-38*
Gross national expenditure	*12,339*	*15,038*	*22,364*
Personal consumption expenditure	*9,372*	*10,483*	*12,797*
Government expenditure on goods			
and services	*1,838*	*2,487*	*4,772*
Gross private domestic investment	*763*	*1,745*	*4,181*
Residential construction	274	327	409
Producers' plant and equipment	69	445	2,117
Net change in business inventories	420	973	1,654
Net foreign investment	*366*	*320*	*615*

[a] Adapted from Y. Yamada, *Nihon Kokumin Shotoku Suikei Shiryō*, Tokyo, 1951, pp. 21, 106.

government outlays going into capital creation and maintenance.
Finally, net lending to the rest of the world—the balance of current
receipts over payments on account of trade and invisible transactions
—ran between 2 and 3% of gross national expenditure as given
here.

These figures, like the savings estimates of Table 19, indicate
an investment process of substantial proportions in the thirties.
As statistical estimates, however, they too rest on incomplete and
uncertain data. Residential construction is believed to omit farm
dwellings as well as other dwellings used partly for business purposes. There can hardly be any firm basis for estimating gross
investment on the part of great masses of small farmers and businessmen. Evidently it is not included at all in the case of finance, transport, communications, and professional services. Nor did accounting
practice meet the requirement for such estimates even in the world
of corporate industry and trade, as noted above. I have not had the
opportunity to examine the Stabilization Board's calculations in
detail; more adequate knowledge of its methods might modify these
doubts. Yet it is difficult to believe that such estimates for the prewar
years can serve as the basis for any firm statistical judgment concerning the actual volume of capital formation in relation to income
and consumption.

It is regrettable that a phase of Japan's economic development so
significant as the growth of income-producing wealth should remain so obscure in statistical terms. Here is a field where fresh investigation would probably add considerably to understanding. Yet
the facts of capital formation are elusive in all countries, as are the

very concepts themselves.[43] Even where the financial data are fairly complete, there remains the problem of allowing for qualitative improvements. Advances in capital technique are often more important in raising productivity than merely duplicating existing equipment. Multiplying. kerosene lamps and sailing vessels is not to be compared with introducing the electric light and the marine engine. This aspect of capital, discussed in Chapter 4, is certainly no less significant than the quantitative measurements under discussion here.

Moreover, in Japan, as throughout Asia, the problem of measuring capital formation is greatly complicated by the persistence of small, unincorporated enterprise through large sectors of the economy. Upwards of half of Japanese economic life was still organized on this principle as late as 1930. It characterized not only agriculture but much of the field of manufacturing and services as well. Even with the decline of industrial handicrafts and progressive adoption of the juristic form of the company and partnership, the stock of capital in the hands of unincorporated firms and individuals must have grown substantially in the aggregate through the prewar decades. It continued to comprise a major portion of the national capital, even if we exclude land.

Most of this unincorporated investment proceeded through the accretion of small units. A good deal took place without resort to financial institutions except perhaps the local moneylender. Capital accounting was rudimentary where it existed at all. In rural Japan productive assets might be created simply by employing local labor directly in improvements in land, buildings, simple agricultural or industrial tools and vehicles, or forestry and fishery resources. A farmer uses his spare time to convert a hillside to irrigated paddy fields; a village reclaims a coastal strip by building a dyke; small traders and industrialists invest bits of savings in equipment and working capital; myriads of home-owners use their own labor and earnings to build new houses, which may also be places of business. In good times land may be improved, tools and machinery purchased, buildings constructed, and materials accumulated on a considerable scale. In hard times the entrepreneur draws heavily on his capital by curtailing his stock of goods or allowing his land, buildings, or tools to deteriorate. He may also borrow for consumption purposes. Rarely can the individual himself calculate his net investment or disinvestment, much less any central statistical agency.

This rather tedious review of capital measurements thus yields

[43] "The tedious and intractable problems of measuring real national income are child's play in comparison with the difficulties of measuring real national capital." Colin Clark, *The Conditions of Economic Progress*, London, 1940, p. 374.

only meager results. More significant indicators of capital growth are found in the upward curves of production traced in Chapter 3, and the technological changes sketched in Chapter 4. Yet such fragmentary data as can be assembled on national wealth, savings, and investment do support the other evidences of accumulation. The volume of investment appears to have been raised and sustained at levels sufficient to increase the national income at a rate seldom achieved elsewhere over a similarly long span of time. That this took place in a country where per capita income remained low, judged by Western standards, and without primary reliance on taxation and public investment, is further reason to examine more closely into the circumstances which brought it about.

Savings and Capital

The Rate of Saving. Let it be repeated, first of all, that if Japan's stock of income-producing wealth grew steadily through the prewar era it was primarily because the incentives to invest in newly produced capital assets were raised and sustained at a high level. These investment demands were associated in turn with a long wave of technical innovation set in motion by the opening of the country to Western contact, and with resulting changes like population growth. Combining as they did the factory, the railway and the battleship, power machinery and modern chemistry, the joint-stock principle and the world-wide market, they opened up revolutionary opportunities to expand national power and to reap personal rewards from the acquisition of new producer capital goods.

The growth in productive capacity which took place was the more continuous in Japan because, as Edwin P. Reubens points out, she could draw steady infusions from the world's existing reservoir of technology, rather than having to advance the frontier of knowledge in surges of fresh invention. No less important, the opportunities at hand were reinforced and made effective by a new framework of national security, political ambition, and credit expansion. In this climate of incentives, innovation and imitation worked with cumulative effect to enlarge the country's capital stock and improve its efficiency—albeit unevenly in various sectors of economic life.

The essential point to begin with, then, is that both market forces and political drives were so organized in prewar Japan as to afford strong inducements to apply a substantial margin of the nation's resources to capital formation. If this is true, it follows that one may not merely observe how meager is the margin of savings in a poor and undeveloped country and conclude that here is the great obstacle to economic progress. The decisive difference between Japan and most of her Asiatic neighbors during the period under consideration was not so much a greater disposition to save on the part of the Japanese as it was the more effective inducements to a high rate of investment in productive enterprise. Everywhere the process of capital formation has in some degree this bootstrap character.

On the other hand, one should not underestimate the importance for efficient capital accumulation of those psychological impulses and social and political arrangements which govern habits of spending and saving. Some savings are essentially voluntary, in the sense that people will refrain by so much from spending their incomes on consumer goods and services even if consumption is not restricted by price inflation, by direct government controls, or by taxation in excess of government expenditure on consumer goods and transfer payments. Additional amounts can be mobilized only by employing these more restrictive and coercive measures. If direct controls and taxation are the means, however, the government will require strong popular support or harsh measures of compulsion to carry the process very far. Even then it may defeat its own ends by deadening private incentives to saving and enterprise, unless it is prepared to resort extensively to State capitalism. The latter in turn brings its own special problems. Alternatively, when resources are appropriated for capital formation (or armament) by inflationary finance, there is always the danger of distorting the economy so as to cripple its over-all productivity. The postwar world has been plagued with the misuse of resources and maldistribution of income resulting from persistent inflation. Politically, socially, and economically, therefore, it makes a good deal of difference by what method savings are mobilized to finance economic development.

Particularly, countries which are already densely populated and which are embarking upon the early stages of economic development are confronted with major problems in accumulating a large volume of savings by orderly and mainly voluntary means. Unless this can be successfully accomplished, any large program of capital construction is apt to have disruptive inflationary consequences. Or it may impose such deprivations on people as only a totalitarian government armed with the most oppressive police regime can enforce. This is the more true as such countries, in contrast to highly industrialized nations, are less adequately equipped with the machinery and skills necessary to mobilize large investment resources efficiently by collective action.

Foreign borrowing may relieve the strain temporarily, as in Japan from 1904 to 1913. In this respect, there is a significant connection today between the amount of financial and technical assistance granted by the West to the economic development of Asia, on the one hand, and the prospects of liberalism in these countries, on the other. But even under the most favorable circumstances the actual capital contribution from outside is apt to be quantitatively small in relation to the total requirement, however strategic it is in other respects.

The experience of Japan in this whole aspect of internal development is therefore of more than historical interest.

Plainly, in the early stages, private enterprise fell far short of meeting the ambitious programs blueprinted by the Meiji leaders. The government did not hesitate to use the weapons of taxation, public loans, and currency inflation to accumulate large funds and to employ them in laying the foundations of industrialization and defense. These funds came directly or indirectly for the most part from the peasant, who thus bore the chief burden. Yet the great bulk of new investment resources came not from the coffers of the State, but increasingly from personal and business savings. The critical function of the new government was to establish and maintain the framework of political order and legal security essential to this purpose. Beyond this it soon came to adopt a philosophy which restricted its role in capital accumulation mainly to investment of a strategic character, to its foreign borrowing operations described earlier, and to the more pervasive and persistent stimulus applied to private capital accumulation by its fiscal and banking policies.[44]

We are led, therefore, to consider more closely what circumstances influenced the amounts of personal and corporate income made available for private capital formation. The question has both short- and long-term aspects.

The actual ratio of savings to national income must have varied widely from year to year, of course. In the agricultural sector a chief determinant was the harvest, and the varying requirement of maintaining the productivity of land. As industrialization got under way, wide swings came to be associated more and more with the booms and depressions of the business cycle, which were influenced in turn by similar movements abroad. Year-to-year changes in prices and money income; expectations of future movements in prices, exchange, inventories; fluctuations in interest rates; government fiscal policy and corporate practice—such factors as these naturally affected savings. Underlying the play of such forces, however, were certain basic institutional arrangements which determined the disposition of the community to withhold income from consumption and free resources for investment. It is this underlying propensity, technically known as the consumption function, which is more particularly under discussion here.

[44] See Chapter 10.

When a country is undeveloped, and densely populated in relation to its technical capacity to exploit its resources, most of its productive powers are absorbed in providing the current essentials of life. Little margin is left to take care of the future. This has been true of all the traditional economies of the East, including preindustrial Japan. Moreover, a growth of population such as took place in Japan after 1868, to the extent that it holds down per capita income, also restricts the proportion of income which can be diverted from consumption.[45]

Other factors beside the average level of income also influence the propensity to consume, of course. Together they include the whole set of institutional arrangements and psychological incentives which determine the thrift habits of people in various income classes and occupations; also the tax and spending policies of the government as they affect consumer outlay and savings. As regards disposable income (income after net payments to government), the degree of equality or inequality in the distribution of income is likely to make an important difference. Well-to-do families do not necessarily save a larger share of their income than families more moderately placed. But they have a greater ability to save, and if they have also the necessary incentives, a concentration of disposable income in the higher brackets is apt to reduce the aggregate share devoted to consumption below the level that would otherwise prevail. How the income and expenditure patterns of Japan were shaped in these respects had evidently a good deal to do with the course of economic development.

Inequality of Income. One can only guess what the curve of income distribution during the early Meiji period was. The events attending the Restoration undoubtedly had a certain levelling influence, in that they destroyed the great feudal incomes of the ruling class. On the other hand, the nobility were pensioned off, not wholly expropriated, and their clan debts to the merchants were shouldered by the government. These obligations, as subsequently commuted by the State, together with mercantile wealth carried over from the old days, provided the start for a new aristocracy of wealth to be erected on the foundations of the new capitalistic order. The new regime was therefore characterized in all probability by a fairly high degree of inequality from its early days, so far as the upper tail of the income distribution curve was concerned. This tendency

45 Not only does population growth retard the rise of income per head in already densely settled countries, but it also increases the percentage of the population in the dependent ages. Today most of Asia has 35 to 45% of its people under the age of fifteen. In Japan the figure was around 36% during the interwar years, and probably higher during the earlier decades.

was only reinforced by the regressive tax policies of the government, the favors lavished on successful financiers and industrial magnates, and the opportunities for large speculative gains in the years that followed.

Attempts to measure the historical tendency toward concentration and dispersion of personal incomes in Japan have necessarily been based on income tax data. For various reasons the latter are an uncertain guide.[46] A more reliable single-year estimate, for 1930, was prepared by the U.S. Office of Strategic Services from Japanese statistics. It can probably be taken as broadly representative of the interwar period. The figures are given in Table 23.

Table 23. *Household Income in Japan Proper,*
by Income Classes, 1930[a]

INCOME BRACKET (YEN)	HOUSEHOLDS Number	Percent	AGGREGATE INCOME Amount (millions of yen)	Percent
Total	*12,600,276*	*100.0*	*8,740*	*100.0*
Over 1,000,000	19	—	32	0.4
50,000 - 1,000,000	1,739	—	276	3.2
10,000 - 50,000	22,674	0.2	596	6.8
3,000 - 10,000	145,360	1.2	1,010	11.6
1,200 - 3,000	723,141	5.7	1,542	17.6
800 - 1,200	1,087,343	8.6	1,096	12.5
400 - 800	3,500,000	27.8	2,142	24.5
200 - 400	4,888,000	38.8	1,711	19.6
0 - 200	2,232,000	17.7	335	3.8

a U.S. Department of State, *National Income of Japan*, Washington, 1945, p. 233. In the construction of this estimate the procedure was as follows: For incomes above 1,200 yen, which were subject to the Class C income tax in 1930, figures published by the Japanese Cabinet Bureau of Statistics in connection with its 1930 study of national income were used. The CBS evidently corrected statutory tax incomes in various brackets to allow for deductions for earned income and dependents, tax exemption of 40% of dividend income and virtually all interest received, and other nontaxable income. The number of households in each bracket was then estimated in the American study from Japanese household tax statistics. For incomes below 1,200 yen, a national distribution was computed from 1931 data on income distribution in Kumamoto, a representative city, and from 1933 data on 203 agricultural villages.

The authors of this study conclude that it contains "a wide margin of error." The total is 1.1 billion yen short of total income received by individuals (9.8 billion yen), as given in their national income estimate for 1930. The latter may be an exaggeration, and the former may well understate household incomes in the higher brackets.

[46] The principal work on the changing distribution of Japanese incomes over a period of years has been done by Prof. Saburo Shiomi. His results are found in "Die Entwicklung des Volkseinkommens in Japan in den Jahren 1903-1919," *Archiv für Sozialwissenschaft und Sozialpolitik*, vol. 53, 1925, pp. 141-85, and numerous studies summarized in English in the *Kyoto University Economic Review*.

Shiomi's measurements, using Pareto's formula, fail to show incomes to be more unequally distributed in prewar Japan than in Britain, Germany, or the United

In approximate terms we find that over half of Japan's 12.6 million households received incomes below 400 yen in 1930. These incomes accounted for about a quarter of aggregate household income. The second quarter went to 28% of the families in the 400-800-yen range. The remaining half accrued to the most prosperous 16% of the nation. Over 10% was actually appropriated by the 0.2% of the people at the apex of the pyramid. The great mass of the population, therefore, was below the 1,000-yen level, while some 1,739 families enjoyed incomes of 50,000 yen or more. The true income distribution was probably even more concentrated than these figures indicate. For this household distribution does not include corporate savings, which accrued mainly to the well-to-do class. Probably, too, incomes in the upper brackets are understated.[47]

The distribution of incomes in an economy is a principal determinant of the demand for various goods and services. It therefore largely influences the use of productive resources. In foreign trade, to cite one aspect, the prevailing inequality in Japan was reflected in the small amounts of Western-type consumer goods imported for mass consumption. This meant in turn that a high proportion of foreign exchange earnings (or borrowings) were available for financing imports of producer goods. More generally throughout the economy it probably encouraged a lower propensity to consume and facilitated a higher rate of saving. It therefore fundamentally influenced the economic development of the country, its internal as well as external aspects. And, needless to add, the ex-

---

States. (See Clark, *op.cit.*, p. 425.) His Pareto coefficients run from 1.89 in 1903-14 to 1.66 in 1930. However, the Japanese personal income tax statistics, upon which he was forced to rely, understate incomes in the higher brackets. In the successive tax laws beginning in 1887 interest and dividends were largely exempt from the personal income (Class C) tax until the 1920 revision. Even then only 60% of dividends became taxable. These and other deductions, together with nonreporting of incomes, cast doubt on any measure of income dispersion based on statutory incomes, even in the upper tail of the distribution. In addition, the distribution of taxable incomes is not representative of the distribution pattern found within the broad mass of incomes below the exemption point (1,200 yen in 1930). For Japan this is clearly demonstrated by Hayakawa in the article cited in note 47, below.

[47] Confirmation of the extreme skewness of income distribution shown here is found in another study of the distribution of Japanese households by income brackets in 1932, by Miyoji Hayakawa, "The Application of Pareto's Law of Income to Japanese Data," *Econometrica*, vol. 19, no. 2, April 1951, pp. 174-83. In summary form his frequency distribution of 13.9 million households is as follows: above 3,000 yen, 1.9%; 800 to 3,000 yen, 10.9%; 400 to 800 yen, 37.3%; below 400 yen, 49.9%. The Pareto coefficient for incomes above 1,000 yen (subject to Class C income tax) is 1.56; for all incomes it is 1.41. Hayakawa's frequency distribution is constructed by methods generally similar to those employed in Table 23, but his data are less accurate, at least in the upper income brackets. For incomes over 1,000 yen he uses uncorrected statutory tax incomes, and below that the pattern found in a 1932 investigation of households in 108 communes in Hokkaido.

treme skewness of the income curve presented a social problem of profound significance.[48]

Property Incomes v. Labor Incomes. The chief cause of this inequality in incomes in prewar Japan was the size and concentration of property incomes, relative to incomes from labor.

National income in 1930—to take this year again—can be divided into the following shares of income paid out (including business savings): (1) entrepreneurial incomes, 2.8 billion yen (28%); (2) other labor incomes (chiefly wages and salaries), 4.3 billion yen (42%); and (3) other property incomes, 3.0 billion yen (30%). The estimates on which these percentages are based are as follows:[49]

	Agriculture and Fishing	Mining and Industry	Services	Total
		(*millions of yen*)		
Total income, 1930	*1,719*	*3,144*	*5,330*	*10,193*
Entrepreneurial incomes	*583*	*744*	*1,522*	*2,848*
Other labor incomes	*201*	*1,605*	*2,502*	*4,308*
Other property incomes	*936*	*795*	*1,306*	*3,037*
Interest	463	260	479	1,202
Corporate profits	8	408	431	847
Rents and royalties	465	127	396	988

[48] "The problem of poverty and the problem of great fortunes are the problems of the lower and upper limits of this income (frequency) curve. But the problem of great fortunes is only part of the larger problem of the general skewness of the curve, the problem, that is, of the extremely small average differences in the incomes of persons in the lower part of the income range and the unduly rapid increase of these average differences as the view is shifted to successively higher income groups. . . . The most serious aspect of the distribution of property and incomes in this and other countries is not the presence of a larger or smaller degree of 'concentration,' but the general distortion of the whole income scheme, reflecting as it undoubtedly does the presence of a high degree of inequality in the distribution of opportunity." Allyn A. Young, *Economic Problems New and Old*, Boston: Houghton Mifflin, 1927, pp. 102-03.

[49] Adapted from *National Income of Japan*, cited, sect. C. These estimates by the U.S. Office of Strategic Services are necessarily crude and various residuals remain undistributed, despite extensive use of official national income data, S. Hijikata's pioneer study of factor payments (*Kokumin Shotoku no Kosei*, Tokyo, 1933), and other statistics. Excluded from the table are 621 million yen of corporate and business taxes, including national and local taxes on agriculture; also 356 million yen of returns on government-owned enterprise, chiefly railways, electrical communications, and factories. Entrepreneurial incomes comprise the business savings and withdrawals of 5,239,000 farmers and fishermen, and 4,307,000 other businessmen whose enterprises were not organized as juristic persons. Imputed wages for family labor are included in this category in the case of agriculture. They are classified as labor income in industry, and largely so elsewhere. Labor incomes also include wage bonuses and other allowances and perquisites, except that bonuses to high corporation officials (64 million yen) are entered with corporate profits. Rents include residential rents of 270 million yen actually paid out.

Interest, corporate profits, and rent thus came to nearly one third of national income paid out (plus business savings) in 1930. Some additional return on property is contained in entrepreneurial incomes, for such incomes are a joint yield on the labor and capital of the farmer, the businessman, and the independent professional. It is of interest to note figures for the United States, although they admit of no precise comparisons. Here property incomes averaged only 20% of aggregate income payments from 1924 to 1933. Entrepreneurial income or withdrawals were 17%, and wages and salaries as much as 63%.[50]

The large share of national income going to property-owners was attributable partly to the growth over fifty years in the aggregate stock of capital productively employed. But it also reflected the fact that the return on these resources, relative to labor, continued to be high in Japan as compared with countries more abundantly endowed. Thus farm rents in prewar Japan commonly ran to 50 to 60% of the rice crop on paddy land, and somewhat less than that on upland fields. Even disregarding the property income of the cultivating owner, payments of agricultural rent on tenanted land and interest on farmer's debts probably amounted to one third or more of total net income in agriculture through the interwar years. In a system of private ownership left to the play of market forces, this is the natural result of a highly unfavorable ratio of population to land and other capital assets. In Japan, too, other factors of monopoly and government policy probably raised even further the

[50] Simon Kuznets, *Uses of National Income in Peace and War*, New York: National Bureau of Economic Research, 1942, p. 38.

Other figures of Japanese national income by distributive shares have been published by the Economic Stabilization Board for 1930 and annually thereafter. They differ somewhat in concepts and basic data from the estimate given above. As quoted in Bank of Japan, *Economic Statistics of Japan, 1951*, pp. 367-68, the ESB estimates give the following threefold division of national income over the period 1930-36 (with net income from abroad and surplus of government enterprises excluded to make the total more comparable with that of the table above):

	NATIONAL INCOME, 1930-36 AVERAGE	
	Millions of Yen	Percent
Total income	13,614	100.0
Proprietors' income	4,968	36.5
Other labor income (employees)	5,461	40.1
Other property income	3,185	23.4

It should be noted that proprietors' income here apparently includes not only self-supplied consumption, but also the income of all unpaid family workers, and, in agriculture, forestry, and fisheries, the wages of employees as well. Labor income in the form of tips and payments in kind is probably understated also. On the other hand, certain elements of property income may be grossly underestimated. Statistics of corporate profits have been notoriously unreliable in Japan, being based on tax returns.

share of income appropriated by the owners of industrial and financial capital.

In Japanese industry the high dividend rates and heavy corporate savings of big concerns in good years are sometimes contrasted with the prevailing rate of wages to show the unequal distribution of the proceeds. More representative of the actual distribution of industrial income in Japan, as compared with other countries, is the share of wages in the total net output of factory industry, i.e., in value added by manufacture. Again, as in Chapter 4, certain data assembled by L. Rostas for Britain, Germany, and the United States[51] may be placed alongside figures for Japan which are roughly comparable. The result is as follows:[52]

	Average Actual Ratio of Wages to Net Product in Factory Industry	Average Ratio of Wages to Net Product when Industry Ratios Are Weighted by Net Output in British Industries
Japan, 1934	27.4	29.1
United Kingdom, 1935	44.3	44.3
Germany, 1936	32.0	31.0
United States, 1937	40.2	41.0

This comparison calls for brief explanation. One might suppose from the relatively large number of workers employed by Japanese factories that the total wage bill would also comprise a large fraction of net value added by manufacture. In the textile industries this was true. Here wages in 1934 amounted to 50% of net product after the costs of raw materials, fuel, and power were deducted from gross value of output.[53] In food processing, however, to cite the other extreme, the wage bill was only 10% of net product. Wide variations

[51] "Industrial Productivity, Production and Distribution in Britain, Germany, and the United States," *Economic Journal*, vol. LIII, no. 209, April 1943, p. 52.

[52] Definitions of scope, details of sources, etc. will be found in Table 13, above. It should be noted that wages exclude salaries, which amounted to 20 to 25% of the wage bill in Japan. They also exclude other labor income in the form of entrepreneurial withdrawals from unincorporated enterprises. Net output is gross value of production minus the costs of raw materials, fuel, and power. Discrepancies among the countries make the comparison only approximate. In weighting wage/net-output ratios in Japanese industries by British net output in the same industries (column 2), certain rough adjustments were made to allow for differences in census classifications.

[53] Yasuji Koide, "Hompō Sangyō Kōzō no Hendō ni Kansuru Shiryō," *Nagoya Keizai Tōkei Geppō*, vol. VIII, no. 9, October 1936, p. 59. Koide's figures are from *Kōjō Tōkeihyō*, the census of manufactures, but with an additional cost deduction for gas and electricity consumption.

such as this reflect corresponding variations in the importance of salaries, depreciation, taxes, interest payments, and other costs, as well as in profits. They are characteristic of all countries, and will distort any direct comparison of average wage/net-output ratios between countries *having a different balance of industries.*

To reduce the influence of this structural difference, the wage/net-output ratio of each industry in Japan, Germany, and the United States is weighted in the above table, column 2, in accordance with the importance of that industry in Britain as judged by its relative net product.

Thus in Japan, assuming a distribution of production similar to that in Britain, 29% of the net proceeds of manufacturing, as defined above, would have gone into factory wages at the level of costs and prices prevailing in 1934. In Nazi Germany the figure is close enough to the Japanese for the difference to be explainable merely on grounds of year-to-year variations. But in Britain and America, the percentage of wages was appreciably higher, around 40%. Some part of the difference may have resulted from relatively higher salary payments in Japan (including not only salaries themselves but managerial bonuses paid out of corporate profits and enterpreneurial incomes properly chargeable to managerial functions). Salaries are not included here as wages. Certainly it was not higher taxes, for the tax burden was lighter in Japan. Mainly it must have represented the comparatively large claim of property incomes—profits, interest, and rent—on the proceeds of industry.[54]

Property incomes were not only a large share of national income in Japan; they were also highly concentrated at the upper end of the income scale. This is the main reason for the gross inequality found in the distribution of personal incomes.

In agriculture, to be sure, a large share of the productive wealth was distributed in small parcels among millions of farm families. There was even a slight tendency after World War I for an increasing dispersion of land ownership in Japan (excluding Hokkaido and Okinawa). Even so, only 56% of the cultivated land in Japan was owned by 4,765,000 households with holdings of 7.35 acres or less in 1935. Most of the remainder was held by 377,000 families with 7.35 to 12.25 acres. Moreover, many small farms were actually mortgaged to banks and moneylenders. And at the top of

---

[54] There are no data on long-term changes in the distribution of national income between labor and capital. The difficulty of distributing the large income of independent entrepreneurs on this basis alone makes any such calculation virtually impossible. The statistical evidence presented above is not conclusive even for the limited period 1930 to 1936, but it does suggest the general pattern that prevailed through the twenties and thirties.

the scale were a handful of big landlords, 3,415 in all. Together they owned 4.7% of the nation's cultivated land.[55]

More massive in scale was the concentrated ownership of modern industry, banks, and trading firms by the great *zaibatsu* families (including the Imperial Household) with their immense fortunes. This concentration of property income was further reinforced by the high salaries and bonuses paid to the upper managerial class who operated the properties of the big combines. Below this relatively small group, and ranging down into the lower income brackets, were some 4 million medium-size and small entrepreneurs engaged in industrial and service occupations. (See Table 17, above.) Their incomes, like those of small owner-farmers, represented a combined return upon their labor and capital. For most of them, however, it was mainly a labor income. Six out of seven were industrialists employing less than five operatives, or other entrepreneurs reporting net incomes of less than 400 yen in 1930.

At the base of the pyramid, finally, stood the wage-earning class. In common with tenant farmers and many small independents of comparable status, it had virtually no property income. By way of illustration, the chief savings institution of this class was the postal savings system, the poor man's bank. Yet industrial wage earners had aggregate deposits of only 12 million yen in 1913 and 138 million in 1930. These brought a return of only 500,000 yen in the first year and 6,000,000 in the latter—a negligible income for this large segment of the population. While family incomes under 3,000 yen—this included 75% of the population—were overwhelmingly labor earnings, those over 3,000 yen were preponderantly a return on property in the aggregate.

The actual magnitude of *zaibatsu* wealth I have not attempted to determine. To do so from published data is a difficult undertaking at best. Oland D. Russell cites a Japanese estimate putting the total fortune of the House of Mitsui at 1,635 million yen in 1937.[56] Very likely the aggregate wealth of the Big Four, including the other great family empires represented in Mitsubishi, Sumitomo, and Yasuda, was more than double this amount. Next in line were a score or more of lesser combines. Together with the Imperial Household, these family groups account for the few hundred households at the top of the income pyramid depicted in Table 23.

The interesting and unique feature of these great family fortunes lay not alone in their size, but in two other characteristics already emphasized in the account of *zaibatsu* enterprise in Chapter 4. The

[55] *Japanese Agricultural Land Statistics*, cited, pp. 30, 56.

[56] *The House of Mitsui*, Boston, 1939, p. 4. This was equivalent to $470 million at the prevailing exchange rate, and a good deal more in actual buying power.

House of Mitsui furnishes a notable example, as described by the U.S. Mission on Japanese Combines.

First, over 90% of the total wealth of the eleven family branches of Mitsui (excluding art works and family real estate) was held collectively in November 1945. It was jointly controlled by a family council, presided over by the head of the elder son's family. Second, over 90% of this joint wealth represented *equity* holdings in Mitsui Honsha (the top holding company) and other banks and business concerns. The Honsha in turn had 75 to 90% of its funds invested in such a way as to control numerous subsidiaries, each in turn with its own smaller subsidiaries ramifying throughout the entire Japanese economy.

Through this network of interlocking controls the active power of decision over business savings and investment in the hands of the managers of the combine went far beyond the relatively small share of business assets actually owned by the House. This was characteristic of each of the Big Four, and of the lesser trusts which grew up in the later decades. Thus the inequalities of wealth and power which characterized the ancient feudal system, with its territorial magnates, were now superseded by corresponding inequalities in the new regime of private property and corporate business enterprise.[57]

Under these conditions, as capitalism developed in Japan, the upper income groups were responsible for a major portion of the savings invested in corporate business enterprise. This came about either through their refraining from spending a large portion of their personal incomes, or through their decisions to reinvest the earnings of firms they controlled. One estimate puts the *average* income of the thirty-one families represented in Mitsui, Mitsubishi, Sumitomo, and Yasuda at about 8 million yen in 1937, including corporate savings accruing to them. The total income of the 100 leading families (excluding the Imperial Household) is estimated at 348 million yen, or 2% of the entire national income.[58]

[57] Takao Tsuchiya estimates that the annual rice yield of the later Tokugawa period was "well over 30 million *koku*." (*An Economic History of Japan*, Tokyo, 1937, p. 223. Of this amount, 4.2 million *koku* came from lands directly controlled by the shogun, and 2.6 million from the lands of his retainers. The lands of the other *daimyō* yielded 22.5 million *koku*. The Shogunate collected 40 to 50% of the total yield of its land in taxes, in addition to numerous other taxes and levies. The exactions of the *daimyō* were proportionate. While the nobility supported their retainers with these revenues, the average *samurai* was little better off than many peasants. The lot of the common people is summed up in the famous adage of the times that the ruling class should govern in such a way that the peasants "had just enough to keep alive on and no more."

[58] *National Income of Japan*, cited, p. 208. "The incomes derived from a monopolistic situation often have provided the financial power which has been used to further the concentration of industrial control. Such increases in the power of

By contrast, if the national income of that year had been equally divided among Japan's 13.4 million families, each household would still have had less than 1,400 yen, or 3 yen a day. Even at this level of income, family budget studies show that the requirements of food, clothing, housing, and a few amenities left comparatively little for savings. (See Chapter 8.) Such productive capital as the mass of peasants, workers, and small businessmen were actually able to acquire over the years came from the laborious accumulation of small surpluses of money income, or from labor applied directly to improvements in land, buildings, and equipment. The pattern of Japanese savings resembled in this respect that of all countries displaying wide inequalities in the distribution of income and wealth.[59] In modern business enterprise, however, there are few parallels to the concentration of property income and control achieved in prewar Japan.

Other Determinants of Savings. A high degree of inequality in incomes does not itself ensure that upper income groups will refrain from attempting to consume their incomes, except at the level of great fortunes. The matter is essentially one of consumer habits and preferences, so far as the voluntary disposal of income is concerned. It involves individual or family choice between material comforts and social satisfactions in the present and other values which lie largely in the future. For most people the latter center around provision for future security. But for the more well-to-do they also include considerations of power, prestige, and institutional loyalties. Even among families modestly placed, consumer spending may be heavily influenced by social prestige and social obligation. Historically, too, broad shifts in the consumption function might be expected as changes take place in living habits (e.g., urbanization), in what

---

monopoly have in turn made it possible to sustain a level of profits sufficiently high to perpetuate and augment these incomes. In this way the relationship between the concentration of income and industrial monopoly has tended to be interacting and cumulative. The inheritance of these great fortunes operates to continue the concentration of income. The perpetuation of large fortunes, however derived, is a potent factor in diminishing equality of opportunity and, therefore, results in a greater degree of inequality in the distribution of income than would otherwise be the case." Temporary National Economic Committee, *Concentration and Composition of Individual Incomes, 1918-1937*, Senate Committee Print, *Investigation of Concentration of Economic Power*, Monograph No. 4, Washington, 1940, p. 1. This statement, made with reference to the United States, is certainly applicable to prewar Japan.

[59] "In all studies of family expenditures in relation to current income the pattern of savings exhibits the same general characteristics. From average dissavings in the lowest income brackets there is a progression to rapidly increasing average net savings in the highest income brackets." Dorothy S. Brady and Rose D. Friedman, "Savings and the Income Distribution," in National Bureau of Economic Research, *Studies in Income and Wealth, Volume Ten*, New York, 1947, p. 250.

a people come to regard as a decent or respectable standard of living, in their evaluation of the risks of and gains from hoarding or investment, in their age distribution, and in their expectations of the future.

Except for isolated family budget studies, no satisfactory data are available on consumers' outlay in relation to income in prewar Japan over a period of years.

One might suppose that the substantial growth in per capita income which occurred in Japan after 1880 brought with it a still more rapid growth of savings, even assuming no change in the distribution of income. Indirect evidence on this point might seem to be afforded by the spending habits of families at different levels of income at any given time. In Chapter 8, for example, a study of family income and expenditure of Japanese farmers, wage earners, and salaried workers in 1926-27 is analyzed. (Table 37.) It appears that the mass of the people, comprising upwards of 75% of the population who received about 40% or so of total household income in Japan, were able to save little or nothing in the form of money savings from personal income.[60] Middle-class families receiving about 2,000 yen during the year saved 10 to 20%. And among upper income groups the percentage was of course much higher. To judge by comparisons among income classes, wage earners with yearly incomes ranging between 650 and 2,000 yen show an average savings propensity of 0.10. Their marginal propensity was around 0.22. In other words, an increase of 100 yen in family income brought an increase of only about 78 yen in family expenditure.

Simultaneous household budget statistics, however, can hardly be applied to interpret the historical consumption function.[61] They only reflect the spending habits of families with different amounts of income at a given community standard of living. Over a long period of time ideas change as to what constitutes poverty, comfort, and luxury. With the industrialization and urbanization of Japan, and introduction of other Western influences, these changes in outlook and norms were substantial throughout large groups of the Japanese population. Where income exceeds the requirements of any *accepted* standard of comfort the savings ratio is apt to increase. But if the standard itself advances along with a historical growth of income, the community ratio of savings to income may fail to increase, may even fall.

There is little doubt that the secular growth of income per capita

[60] As regards farmers, however, see Chapter 8, notes 25 and 26.

[61] See William Fellner, *Monetary Policies and Full Employment*, Berkeley, 1946, pp. 59ff.; also James S. Duesenberry, "Income-Consumption Relations and Their Implications," in *Income, Employment and Public Policy, Essays in Honor of Alvin H. Hansen*, New York, 1948, pp. 77-78.

in prewar Japan did bring with it a material rise in consumption standards. Beside the indirect testimony of national income data, certain evidence is cited in Chapter 3. Food supplies became more ample and varied; clothing improved in quantity and variety; many people came to enjoy better housing and better medical care; literacy brought widespread use of newspapers, books, and periodicals; other phases of living—travel, electric lighting, communications, commerical amusements, household equipment, etc.—all testify to a slow growth of consumer outlay per capita.

This was partially necessitated—and partially nullified so far as any real gain in well-being is concerned—by the demands of city life, which required additional outlays for travel, recreation, and daily existence. It also received impetus from the characteristic Japanese fondness for new fashions and gadgets typified in baseball, cameras, and fountain pens. Among the more prosperous professional and business classes, in fact, the introduction of Westernisms imposed a dual strain on the pocketbook. For they took on new habits of clothing, housing, and recreation without at the same time discarding the obligation to maintain traditional Japanese standards of comfort and social obligation.

As a matter of fact, there is a necessary interdependence between the secular growth of income, technical progress, and consumer outlay. The expansion of production in Japan owed its stimulus in part to the release of consumption from feudal restraints and the new desires and needs which developed as the country was opened to modern influence. These changes were accelerated by urbanization and industrialization, which fostered easy communication and created new living needs. Advances in technology and production called for, and depended upon, better education and public health and other activities of government. These services further expanded consumer outlay. Only as the latter grew could the profitability of new investment be maintained so as to balance investment and savings at a rising level of income.

Thus the secular growth of the Japanese economy required the growth of consumption no less than that of investment. And at the same time it made it possible. Foreign markets offered Japan no escape from this necessity, important as they were to the growth of the economy. And in fact the bulk of the increasing national output was consumed at home. Nor is the statement contradicted by the fact that a far more than proportionate share of the fruits of progress was consistently appropriated by the big industrialists, financiers, landlords, and other members of the well-to-do propertied class.

Whether in actuality savings grew more rapidly than income

through the prewar decades is uncertain. In the United States, where income per capita more than doubled from 1869 to 1929, Simon Kuznets' data fail to show any tendency for the savings ratio to rise.[62] After 1900 it actually drifts downward. Colin Clark concludes from comparisons among many Western countries that aggregate savings tend to remain a constant proportion of national income—around 10%—though with many irregularities.[63] Quite possibly the historical pattern of Japan differs from that of America or Britain, at least in modern times. One would suppose that the national savings ratio increased materially through the early stages of industrialization, from 1880 to 1910. It was during this period that the centralized pattern of financial and political controls was fashioned to build the foundations of the State. Thereafter the momentum of economic growth, sustained through the thirties, suggests perhaps a secular rise, hardly a decline, in the rate of capital formation actually achieved.

More than this, the historical response of Japanese consumers to rising incomes through these years might be expected to show a different pattern from that observable elsewhere. What have become virtual necessities in the West are still undreamed-of luxuries in the East. How quickly they enter the scale of wants and with what intensity depend on many circumstances of tradition, education, and environment. The value placed by a Japanese upon better provision of present comforts—indeed, his whole definition of comforts—is different from that prevailing in the West. The propensity to save at any particular level of per capita income is apt to be much greater than the average Westerner would think possible in terms of his own scale of values. Among upper income groups it may well exceed that in most countries of Asia.

The simplicity of Japanese living standards has often been the subject of comment. For the mass of the people, of course, this has been little more than grim necessity. But it has probably been further reinforced by social traditions that tended to retard the rise in consumer expectations which elsewhere have accompanied economic development in modern times. And it has extended as well to middle-class families well above the poverty line by Japanese standards. For an explanation one must look to Japan's cultural background, including not only the age-old acceptance of poverty but also the cultivation of nonmaterial values and personal frugality enforced by group discipline. Only this will make intelligible to the Westerner the comparative contentment of a Japanese family with a rice-fish-vegetable diet, a house of wood and paper and mats, and a general lack of

[62] *National Product since 1869*, New York, 1946, pp. 118-20.
[63] *Conditions of Economic Progress*, 2d edn., London, 1951, pp. 504-08.

those appurtenances and material diversions which figure so importantly in Western life. While foreign-style products had entered considerably into urban living standards after World War I, the change is easily exaggerated. They consisted in good part of certain specific appliances, or details of decoration, convenience, and amusement, rather than any fundamental departure from the traditional mode of Japanese family life.[64]

By comparison with the value standards prevailing among many other peoples, perhaps most of them, social position and prestige in Japan are less dependent on display of material wealth. In this respect Japanese society is comparatively democratic, however hierarchical and authoritarian in other respects. The well-to-do classes of modern Japan, although living on a plane far above the masses, have generally failed to exhibit those tendencies to extravagant, conspicuous consumption found among the sheiks and city notables of the modern Arab world, the elite of Latin America, the Indian princes, or for that matter, the *daimyō* of ancient Japan.[65] Their extravagances in prewar times were more likely to run to *objets d'art* than to yachts and polo ponies. One saw rich Indians on the Riviera, but not rich Japanese. And, as noted above, they put their wealth largely into securities rather than gold or diamonds or land. The work habits, the frugality, and even the sense of "calling" displayed by many Japanese businessmen have sometimes recalled to Western observers the rationalistic Protestant ethic which contributed so powerfully to the rise of modern capitalism in Europe.[66]

Whatever the social evil of extreme concentration of wealth in

[64] See Emil Lederer, *Japan in Transition*, New Haven, 1938, p. 66.

[65] Of feudal Japan around 1700, James Murdoch writes as follows (*A History of Japan*, vol. III, London: Routledge and Kegan Paul, 1926):

"Neither the Shogun, nor his favorites, nor the Daimyo, nor the Samurai were hoarding money. On the contrary, they were spending it lavishly with both hands . . ." (pp. 206-07).

"Few Samurai thought either of hoarding or investing money; such practices were not in consonance with the traditional way, or ways, of the warrior. The increasing . . . revenues of most Samurai householders were promptly and right royally disbursed. A century or even half a century before the Samurai's superfluous funds would undoubtedly have been spent on weapons or war-harness for himself, or trappings for his charger. But armour was scarcely even donned nowadays, and to so much as trim the mane of a steed or pare its hoofs was nothing short of a felony punishable by transportation. Accordingly, the money now went on finer clothes for the master himself, or on richer robes and girdles and hair-pins for his wife and concubines and daughters, while the menials in his household were augmented in number. . . . Tea-house parties, with crowds of dancing-girls as waitresses, were great functions in Yedo. . . . The chief ambition of each [clan seneschal] was not to be outdone in luxurious and ostentatious display by the representative of any other clan" (pp. 201-02).

[66] While noting this oft-cited parallel, I would not wish to press it very far. Nor have I sufficient knowledge of the Japanese business class to define precisely the limits and qualifications appropriate to the statements in this paragraph.

the hands of the *zaibatsu*, therefore, it was not that they wasted their substance in riotous living or salted it away in unproductive hoards. The urge to power and prestige in an industrializing society, the close relations between the business and political elites, the tradition of clan unity and discipline, the emphasis on modified primogeniture carried over in Japanese law from feudal times—all worked to perpetuate the great fortunes and to encourage the reinvestment of a large share of upper-class income in the creation of new capital assets for the Japanese economy.

Still other circumstances encouraged voluntary private saving as incomes rose from the subsistence level. First was the system of taxation developed in prewar Japan, which included a variety of taxes widely dispersed in their incidence on the population. Until the turn of the century both national and local governments financed themselves largely with real estate taxes paid by the rural population in the main. As such revenues fell progressively short of providing the necessary funds, they were supplemented increasingly with (a) levies on consumption, in the form of excise taxes and profits from fiscal monopolies on tobacco and salt, and (b) miscellaneous business taxes which also bore more heavily on small and medium incomes. Real estate and consumption taxes alone furnished as much as 80% of all tax revenues in 1893. From 1913 on they still provided around 50%. After World War I the central government came to rely increasingly on progressive taxes applied to personal and corporate income. Even then the tendency both in the law and in its application was to deal leniently with large property incomes, the source of a large share of the country's savings. Meanwhile the remainder of the tax system continued to be heavily regressive. We return to this subject in Chapter 10.

Second, Japan lagged far behind most industrial countries in the public provision of social security and consumer services, except elementary education. Apart from the case of agricultural subsidies during the interwar years, the State Treasury was never regarded seriously as an instrument for equalizing the distribution of income. Nor was it employed extensively to provide cheap credit to small businessmen to offset the disabilities they suffered in the commercial money market. As a result, the inequalities and insecurities inherent in the economic situation were allowed to develop largely unchecked by political action. Personal security continued to depend mainly on family thrift; in no other way could one provide for the future.

These motivations operated with particular effectiveness among millions of small industrialists, tradesmen, and farmers. Nearly one in three persons gainfully occupied in prewar Japan was an enterpriser of some sort, either a small employer, or an independent who worked, usually precariously, on his own. This was true in all non-agricultural pursuits, taken together, no less than in farming. (See above, Table 17.) It is a commonplace that the incentives to saving are apt to be keener among a people where entrepreneurial responsibility is thus widely distributed, as compared with one made up largely of wage earners employed by large corporations or the government.

Third, in many Oriental countries large expenditures are traditionally made for funerals, weddings, caste observances, and other religious or social obligations of a formal character. Such expenditures are commonly a heavy drain on village income. Although they may at the same time be an incentive to production, they diminish the supply of savings for capital improvements. In Japan they have not been absent. But they seem to have been less significant than in India, for example, and to have given way fairly readily under the impact of modernization.[67]

Finally, a considerable fraction of savings and investment came to be institutionalized in the hands of big banks, insurance and trust companies, and the great industrial and trading combines. These private institutions were joined and reinforced by the great semiofficial banks in mobilizing liquid funds for investment. Such concentration of control had at least two important consequences for the rate of saving and the use to which savings were put. In the absence of a public security market the large banks were closely linked with operating companies whose capital needs they financed, both short- and long-term. Yet like the industrial combines themselves, they tended to maintain highly diversified pools of investment which only occasionally got them in trouble through excesses of speculation. They played a strategic role, therefore, in attracting the savings of investors, large and small, and channelling them into industrial and commercial investment, including equities. To borrow a phrase used by C. F. Remer in another connection, they were engaged in "borrowing rentier and lending entrepreneur."

[67] In rural districts, however, they have continued to be of importance down to modern times. J. W. Robertson Scott writes in *The Foundations of Japan*, London, 1922, pp. 138-39, that in Toyama a peasant with a balance of 100 yen at the end of the year had to pay 30 to 40 yen to the temple. The marriage of a daughter usually involved heavy expenditures, and if there were two or three a farmer might have to borrow substantially for the purpose. Official surveys of farm family budgets in the thirties found that 4 to 5% of total household expenditures were devoted to ceremonial expenses such as those for weddings and funerals. In more prosperous years it ran to 5 to 10%. One of the recommendations of the Food and Population Commission (1927-30) was "to encourage abandonment of formalism in social life which encourages superfluous expenditures and discourages saving." For statistical details see *Japan Statistical Year-Book, 1949*, cited, pp. 226-29.

This pattern of financing, whatever its shortcomings, must have served to enlarge considerably the volume of savings available for industrialization in a country inexperienced in such fields.

Within the big banks and combines, moreover, profits were immense in good times, and control over their disposition heavily concentrated. This control could be used either to plough back a large share of earnings, or alternatively in hard times to pay dividends out of capital. Corporate profits on paid-up capital tended to fluctuate between 5 and 15% in most of the interwar years, while dividends were more stable in the vicinity of 6 to 9%. For 1930 corporate savings have been estimated at 204 million yen, or 24% of corporate profits (net of taxes and intercorporate dividends). In 1937 they rose to 756 million yen, or 37% of net profits.[68] These sums are less than 5% of national income in the aggregate. As a fraction of aggregate savings, however, they may have run to 20 to 40%, and their share of the total must have risen steadily with the spread of the corporate form of organization.

How much the rate of capital accumulation in Japan was affected by institutional savings one cannot be sure. Their effects were perhaps less significant here than in a country where the securities of big corporations are more widely distributed among small investors. For in Japan equity ownership as well as control was concentrated in the well-to-do class, either directly or through banks and holding companies. This class would have invested a relatively high proportion of its corporate earnings even if the latter had all been paid out. In other words, it was the prevailing inequality of incomes rather than corporate organization as such which made for large savings from such incomes. However, the big holding companies, banks, and operating concerns may well have chosen to plough back a somewhat larger share of their earnings than would have been reinvested had financial control been more decentralized. Moreover, their very size enhanced their profits, and further enriched their owners, through the bargaining advantages it gave them over smaller competitors and wage earners.

The foregoing paragraphs sketch some of the factors influencing the relations between income, savings, and consumption in prewar Japan. They suggest how it came about that productive capital was accumulated at what seems to have been a fairly rapid rate, and by rather orderly processes, even while the population grew

[68] *National Income of Japan*, cited, p. 187. To compare profit-savings ratios in Japan and other countries is difficult, owing to variations in accounting practices with respect to depreciation, etc. Also, Japanese firms paid heavy bonuses to top executives out of declared profits. Total business savings were much larger in good times than corporate savings, of course, for they included the savings of millions of small entrepreneurs.

apace and the level of average income remained low. Without prolonged inquiry into this little-explored subject it is impossible to measure these functional relationships in statistical terms. One remains in doubt as to what the savings-income ratio actually was at any time, or how it responded to the growth of income. The evidence suggests, however, that the ratio of savings to disposable income rose somewhat as economic development proceeded and remained at a high level, relative to that in other parts of Asia, through most of the half century or more preceding World War II.

Continuing Scarcity of Capital. This impression of a high rate of saving through much of the prewar era is not in conflict with the fact that the supply of Japanese capital as well as natural resources continued to be relatively scarce, judged by Western standards. The latter is evidenced in various ways—in the high price of land and its intensive cultivation by hand labor, in the slow process of mechanization except in a few manufacturing industries, in the tendency to run machinery long hours at high speeds and long after it would have been thrown on the scrap heap in the United States. It is also borne out by the costs of borrowing liquid funds in the money market for most industrial, commercial, and agricultural purposes. Economic progress brought a fairly persistent decline in money rates, but we would now regard them as very high.

A few examples of the cost of borrowing will illustrate this point. Early in the Meiji period (1877) a law was passed to curb usury. It declared unenforceable interest rates above 20% on all loans of less than 100 yen, above 15% on loans of 100 to 1,000 yen, and above 12% on loans over 1,000 yen. In the main this law seems to have remained a dead letter for some years. On secured loans of 5,000 to 10,000 yen the prevailing rate was 12% in Tokyo during 1879-81 and in excess of 20% in Fukuoka.[69] On small loans it was much higher, especially in agriculture. After the turn of the century the average rate on secured loans above 5,000 yen dropped to 10% or less, but again the small borrower had to pay much more. As late as 1920 the chief need of the agricultural village was still said to be for capital at less than a rate of 20%.

Meantime, of course, the costs of borrowing by large business concerns and by the government fell to much lower levels. During the decade 1921-30, for example, government bond yields ranged from 5.47 to 5.98%, corporate debenture yields from 6.42 to 8.97%, and the Bank of Japan's discount rate on commercial bills from 5.11 to 8.03%. Even these rates ran 2 to 4% above com-

[69] Mayet, *op.cit.*, pp. 110-16. Detailed tables of Tokyo and Osaka money rates will be found in Tōyō Keizai Shimpō-sha *Meiji Taishō Kokusei Sōran*, Tokyo, 1927, pp. 100ff.

parable borrowing costs in the United States.[70] They reflected the tight money market of the postwar decade in some degree, and were substantially lowered when the collapse of the yen ushered in the easy money policy of the thirties.

Borrowing costs for farmers and small businessmen continued to be much higher. In 1929 new agricultural loans were still being contracted at an average rate of 9.2%. On the total outstanding farm debt of 5 billion yen, most of it incurred in earlier years, interest charges were even steeper. A 1932 survey placed the average rate at 10.2%, but 28% of the total farm debt was being carried at rates of 12% or more.[71] Even charges amounting to 20% or more were not uncommon. Small merchants and industrialists paid comparable rates, often with still higher risk premiums. For example, the cost of short-term industrial loans in Tokyo during 1930 still averaged 15%. A proposal put forward at this time to lend government funds to small businessmen at 15% on ten-year contracts was demanded as a measure of "relief."[72] Short-term consumer credit, of course, was even more costly. The hard-pressed peasant or worker might be able to borrow from a friend, or from a mutual-aid society. But more often he had to turn to a local pawnshop, a landlord, or a moneylender. Here his actual costs might run as high as 100% or more on an annual basis.

The larger business concerns typically relied on borrowed money (debentures and bank loans) to the extent of at least 20 to 30% of their total capital.[73] Smaller concerns borrowed still more heavily, sometimes from banks but more often from big manufacturers or merchants with whom they did business. Market rates of interest were therefore an important factor in production costs. Taking the discount rates of the Bank of Japan and the Bank of England on commercial bills as somewhat indicative of the difference between the Tokyo and London money markets, we find that the borrowers from the Bank of Japan had to pay more than double the British rate between 1890 and 1910. They still paid over 50% more in the decade 1926-35. (Table 24.)

Such comparisons, of course, reflect differences in the risk and liquidity of loans, and variations in the supply of money balances as against the demand for them. There is reason, too, to think that

[70] Harold G. Moulton, *Japan, An Economic and Financial Appraisal,* Washington, 1931, pp. 430-31.

[71] *National Income of Japan,* cited, pp. 162-64.

[72] John E. Orchard, *Japan's Economic Position,* New York, 1930, p. 244.

[73] This figure is from a Mitsubishi survey of over 300 companies (excluding insurance firms and stock exchanges) in the early thirties (*Japanese Trade and Industry,* cited, p. 107). A similar survey by the Bank of Japan in 1939 showed 311 major companies dependent on bank loans and debentures for 30% of their total resources.

Japanese interest rates would have dropped more quickly had it not been for the sheer force of habit and custom carried down from times when rates were still higher. More important, however, was the fact that prospective earnings on new capital continued to be large, despite the growth in national wealth. As the stock of capital grew, the most immediate and urgent requirements of industrialization were met—for example, railways and basic improvements in the land. But the continued growth of population, tech-

Table 24. *Bank of Japan and Bank of England*
Discount Rates on Commercial Bills, 1886-1935[a]

Annual Average	Bank of Japan	Bank of England
1886-90	6.13	3.56
1891-95	6.53	2.61
1896-1900	7.52	3.22
1901-05	7.23	3.42
1906-10	6.46	3.81
1911-15	6.35	4.21
1916-20	6.35	5.55
1921-25	7.92	4.37
1926-30	5.88	4.61
1931-35	4.39	2.67

a *Oriental Economist*, vol. III, no. 5, May 1936, p. 282.

nical progress, and the widening of markets tended to keep up the anticipated yield of new investments, and therefore the demand for investment funds. Capital continued to be relatively scarce as a productive agent.

Another reason for the continued shortage of capital, no doubt, was the large expenditure of successive governments on war, armament, and colonial development. At times such military and strategic outlays cut heavily into Japan's margin of current income over consumption requirements.

For reasons already noted, it is difficult to say how much of a net drain such military expenditures imposed on the civilian economy of Japan. Their effect is often exaggerated. From 1926-35, for example, Army and Navy expenditures averaged 637 million yen a year, or 5% of national income, during a decade which witnessed the Manchurian Incident. Additional expenditures indirectly for military and strategic purposes would still leave the figure well under 10%, and this seems to have held true through most of the preceding decades. The total contributions of the central government to the various colonial governments (including the Kwantung Leased Territory) did not exceed 322 million yen for the entire period from 1910 to 1929.[74] Nor did state subsidies to steel, shipbuilding, and other strategic industries involve large amounts, though they often meant the difference between profit and loss to the owners. (See Chapter 10.)

In war years, of course, military costs soared to far larger proportions. They reached an all-time peak of 51% of gross national product in 1944, according to one estimate.[75] In the earlier wars, as previously observed, they were also substantial. But it is not unlikely that deficit financing of war costs in these more limited conflicts stimulated the fuller and more efficient utilization of Japanese resources to the point where there was little if any sacrifice of the civilian economy.[76] At this time, in any case, the tax structure was such that a good deal of the tax burden fell on consumption rather than savings.

The actual effects of sustained military expenditure on productive capital formation, however, especially in certain sectors of particular importance, may well have been more unfavorable than these broad statements would indicate. In the early period Japan's military prowess, as demonstrated in the wars with China and Russia, won her international recognition, and helped open up the London capital market to Japanese borrowing. This borrowing, mainly for war purposes, stimulated capital formation at home and augmented her total resources. But Japan's credit position soon deteriorated as a result of the financial difficulties which shortly ensued. And in subsequent decades—notably in the thirties—the high level of military expenditure, together with the foreign policy it served, was hardly calculated to inspire international confidence in the credit of either Japan's government or her private corporations. Domestically, also, it is likely that tax revenues for military purposes, as well as public borrowings, came increasingly from the margin of incomes otherwise available for private investment, rather than consumption.[77]

However this may be, there is no doubt that heavy commitments

[74] As compiled by the Bank of Japan. Moulton, *op.cit.*, p. 232. This does not include Japanese Army and Navy expenditure, or certain other outlays connected with colonial activity. Takahashi's estimate of 651 million yen is cited above (page 53) as the amount spent by Japan upon the "protection" of Korea and other grants and payment obligations assumed in this colony from 1907 to 1931.

[75] United States Strategic Bombing Survey, *The Effects of Strategic Bombing on Japan's War Economy*, Washington, 1946, p. 16. This includes private capital outlays in munitions industries but excludes war expenditures overseas, except for pay of armed forces.

[76] Real income would have grown still more rapidly, of course, had the State applied its taxing and borrowing powers on a similar scale to purposes which were economically more productive.

[77] Especially with the increase in the later decades in the proportion of tax revenue secured through income and business profits taxes. (Table 43.)

to military expenditure, even in the interwar periods, left comparatively little in the Imperial Treasury for public improvements of the sort which only the government could be expected to undertake. The lagging development of Hokkaido, the northern island, as a frontier for agricultural settlement is a case in point. From 1895 on the Army and Navy continuously absorbed as much as 40% or more of central government expenditures.[78] When general administrative requirements and debt service were also provided for, little remained for public works or social welfare. More broadly, the whole policy of military expansion, with its emphasis on colonies and war-essential industries, attracted private capital and skilled labor from pursuits where they were already scarce, and where they would have contributed far more to the growth of national income and wealth. A constant feature of the Japanese scene throughout these decades was the dearth of public funds for agricultural and other internal improvements, and for housing, health, and sanitation. Yet all the time large sums were being lavished on the armed forces and on imperialist adventures abroad.

Finally, the perennial shortage of capital in small-scale industry and agriculture reflected special institutional obstacles to the flow of private investment funds into these fields, compared with the more modern sectors of the economy. Higher interest rates here are insufficient alone to demonstrate this, of course, for loans to small businessmen and farmers are apt to involve greater risks and handling costs. It should also be remarked that the number of banking offices relative to the population—one index of accessibility—became moderately high. From 1926 to 1936 the number of head and branch offices declined from 7,858 to 6,415, but there was still

[78] Outlays on the Army and Navy in the General Account constituted the following percentages of total national government expenditures (for the years 1888-1933, computed by S. Hijikata in "Die Zusammenhange zwischen Staatshaushalt und Industrialisierung in Japan," *Weltwirtschaftliches Archiv*, vol. 46, part 1, July 1937, p. 212):

	Total Expenditures (millions of yen)	Army and Navy (percent)		Total Expenditures (millions of yen)	Army and Navy (percent)
1888	82	28.0	1918	1,017	36.2
1893	85	27.0	1923	1,521	32.8
1898	220	51.2	1928	1,815	28.5
1903	250	33.2	1933	2,255	38.7
1908	636	33.5	1938	3,288	35.5
1913	574	33.4			

To the above Army and Navy expenditures should be added military pensions and a large share of interest on the national debt, also chargeable to military purposes. This would raise the total military outlay to 40 to 50% of the national budget through the period 1895-1935.

one office to every 11,000 people.[79] However, the concentration of banking controls in the hands of large financial interests, and the solicitude of the government for these interests, conferred financial advantages on them well beyond what would probably have represented an economic allocation of resources.

In modern Japan the banking system has supplied the major portion of funds invested in modern enterprise and in government securities.[80] With the bank failures and mergers of the twenties small business became increasingly dependent on big financial institutions closely affiliated with the big industrial concerns. This gave the large firms a financial advantage which was often decisive, especially during periods of hard times. Centralized control over the supply of capital in the hands of big business and the State helped no doubt to perpetuate the dearth of credit for small businessmen, keeping interest rates for them at high levels and exerting a corresponding pressure on wages and working conditions.

As for agriculture, State economic policy from the beginning was directed primarily at the promotion of industry and commerce, rather than the interests of the farmer. If the village was perennially starved for capital, this was partly the reason.[81] Only after 1920 was this shortage relieved in some degree by tax reforms, agricultural subsidy, and the organization of a nation-wide network of rural cooperatives. The whole fiscal policy of the Meiji governments, beginning with the Land Tax Reform of 1873, might be characterized as designed to extract the maximum amount of revenue from agriculture to defray the expenses of the State and to forward the industrial and military ambitions of its ruling groups.[82]

[79] C. C. Liang gives figures for other countries as follows: United States (1950), 7,740; India (1949), 65,200; China (1947), 94,100. Economic Commission for Asia and the Far East, Committee on Industry and Trade, *Mobilization of Rural Savings with Special Reference to the Far East*, New York: United Nations Economic and Social Council, E/CN.11/I&T/WP.1/L.5, October 15, 1951, p. 22.

[80] Financial institutions held 66% of the 23.5 billion yen of government and domestic corporate securities outstanding in March 1928, according to an estimate of the Bank of Japan. Foreign investors held 10%, and other Japanese business concerns a part of the remainder. Moulton, *op.cit.*, p. 427.

[81] It is worth recalling, however, that this problem of rural credit has been universal in Asia, and not peculiar to Japan. Commercial banks cater mainly to the needs of the more prosperous urban class engaged in trade and industry. Except where cooperatives have been organized on a large scale the credit business of rural areas is still handled mostly by moneylenders and small unorganized banks. In India, for example, there are said to be some 300,000 moneylenders who generally charge 12 to 50% on loans, and sometimes as much as 300 to 400%. Economic Commission for Asia and the Far East, Committee on Industry and Trade, *Mobilization of Domestic Capital through Financial Institutions of the ECAFE Region*, New York: United Nations Economic and Social Council, E.CN.11/I&T/40, January 3, 1951, chap. 5.

[82] Examining the sources of funds for the founding of modern capitalism in Japan, Y. Horie concludes as follows: "The creation of capital by the Meiji Government as

It is fair to add that agriculture was necessarily the main source of capital and tax income during the early period. Japan's long-run interests probably required levying an initial tribute on the farmer to foster industrialization and national defense. Later decades saw some abatement of this discriminatory policy as wealth and income grew in other fields. However, the continuing disabilities of the peasant, including the shortage of cheap credit, remained a conspicuous feature of the Japanese scene long after a flourishing industry had been established and the country's political independence had been assured. There was now far less justification, on grounds either of social justice or of sound economic policy. (See Chapter 10.)

Investment and Economic Progress

Important as were the social institutions and financial mechanisms which helped to enlarge the supply and lower the cost of investment funds, the more dynamic impulse to capital formation in Japan is to be sought on the demand side. Here we return to the point emphasized at the outset of the discussion of savings. If wealth has been created far more extensively in modern Japan than in Tokugawa Japan, the change was not primarily in traditional impulses to thrift, in the existence of great wealthy families, or in the taxing powers of the State. Rather, it lay in the whole conjuncture of circumstances which created new opportunities for and incentives to productive investment and enterprise after the Restoration. Through both State and private enterprise—increasingly the latter—a stream of resources was consequently attracted into the business of acquiring new capital assets, either by making them at home or by buying them abroad.

Hoarding and Investment. There is no need to repeat again all that has been said concerning the various stimuli which came into play after 1868 to generate an active process of capital formation. A long wave of expansion, with periodic surges and recessions, was set in motion by the change in objective circumstances and the psychological response of the nation and its leaders. These circumstances, together with the new freedom and security of property ownership, evidently created a new state of profit expectations—a confidence in investment gain—which was effective through wide sectors of the economy in breaking this bottleneck of economic development.

well as the accumulation of wealth by the feudal lords and the accumulation of funds for commercial and loan purposes by the *chonin* was at the expense of the agricultural class." "An Outline of the Rise of Modern Capitalism in Japan," *Kyoto University Economic Review,* vol. XI, no. 1, July 1936, p. 106.

In this connection one particular change deserves emphasis, as it represents an all-important departure from the investment practices of traditional agrarian societies. The appearance of new and sufficiently attractive opportunities for productive enterprise served gradually to break down the traditional preference, characteristic of these societies, for hoarding wealth such as land or precious metals rather than investing in the creation of new capital assets.

This change is often misunderstood, through a confusion between financial investment which involves merely buying up existing assets, and investment spending upon newly produced assets (capital formation). It is the latter, of course, with which we have been concerned in this chapter. Throughout most of Asia, and in traditional Japan, the problem of capital is not that it is absorbed or "tied up" in agricultural land, as is sometimes said. Rather it is simply not produced except at a very slow rate, in the form of either improved land or anything else. The reason has something to do with the premium placed on landownership. In a densely settled agrarian economy of the preindustrial variety, land rent is sustained at a high level by the pressure of population and the weak bargaining position of the small tenant. It is not easily reduced by increasing the supply of land. As compared with other producer goods, land affords still other advantages to its owner: high political and social prestige attaching to the landed class; a relatively safe and stable return; ease of disposal (liquidity) if necessity arises; and related opportunities for gain through combining the functions of landlord, tax collector, moneylender, etc.[83] The same values are found in varying degrees in hoards of precious metals and treasures of art.

The resulting preference for landholding (or money hoards) sets a high standard of yield which funds must return if they are to be invested in producing new capital assets for industrial or commercial enterprise. But opportunities of sufficient attractiveness in such a society are apt to be severely restricted by the limitation of the market, by a stagnant technology, and by the lack of security and status in nonagricultural pursuits. By the time all the costs and risks of new business ventures are reckoned under such conditions, the anticipated net return is apt to be too meager to bring forth any large amount of investment funds. New investment is therefore discouraged except where high profits can be anticipated over a

[83] So pervasive are these privileges and powers conferred by land holding that the term "feudal" or "semifeudal" is often applied to the agrarian systems of Japan, China, and other Far Eastern countries. To use the term this way only obscures the true character of feudalism, as it once existed in Europe and parts of the Far East. But it does emphasize the essential point that the advantages of control over land and its produce are not to be measured merely in terms of rents reckoned on a capitalistic basis.

short period, as in the quick turnover of certain types of trading ventures. For such reasons as this Keynes remarks that "in certain historic environments" the preference for landownership may have been a heavy drag on economic progress.[84]

Thus traditional China has been described as a "land-rent-centered" society. Landownership and public office were the avenues to economic security and social prestige. They were the keys to gentry status. This fact, plus the absence of legal security for business enterprise, hampered the growth of commercial and industrial enterprise. In feudal Japan, landownership was a less absolute and exclusive property right, and the preference for landholding was perhaps less highly developed. More accurately, the preference took different forms and found more restricted expression among those classes with some surplus of income potentially available for investment. The power and income of the nobility rested on feudal status, which was associated with hereditary control over the revenue from land. Merchants, on the other hand, were largely barred from seeking the security and prestige of landlordism as it flourished in China. Even so, it was characteristic of the last century of Tokugawa rule that land investment (as well as gold and silver) attracted a large share of the funds accumulated by the rising merchant class, who circumvented feudal prohibitions by reclaiming waste land or acquiring *de facto* ownership through foreclosure on debts.[85]

---

[84] "That the world after several millennia of steady individual saving, is so poor as it is in accumulated capital-assets, is to be explained, in my opinion, neither by the improvident propensities of mankind, nor even by the destruction of war, but by the high liquidity-premiums formerly attaching to the ownership of land and now attaching to money. I differ in this from the older view as expressed by Marshall with an unusual dogmatic force in his *Principles of Economics*, p. 581:—'Everyone is aware that the accumulation of wealth is held in check, and the rate of interest so far sustained, by the preference which the great mass of humanity have for present over deferred gratifications, or, in other words, by their unwillingness to "wait." ' " *The General Theory of Employment, Interest and Money*, cited, p. 242.

[85] The whole subject of capital formation in traditional Oriental societies is yet to be investigated with the tools of modern economics. No doubt it played a less dynamic role than in modern industrial societies. For one thing, savings and investment in a subsistence economy are small in relation to income. Also, there was no problem of balancing investment and saving decisions in the case of a farmer maintaining or improving his own land, or a government requisitioning grain to support workers conscripted for the *corvée*.

Nevertheless the problem of fluctuations in investment, both private and public, seems to have been present in some degree. At all times a high premium attached to landownership as a means of economic security and symbol of social prestige. This exerted a persistent drag on the formation of capital and expansion of incomes in commerce and industry. In addition, when hard times brought heavy distress sales of land by impoverished peasants, funds were likely to be drained out of productive pursuits in even greater amounts. For example, merchants were apt to use their capital accumulated in business enterprise to purchase land from former owners who now required the proceeds for consumption purposes.

One wonders if there is some analogy between the role of public works activity

This premium upon landholding lingered on in the modern period. It reflected the intense desire of millions of small peasants to own their own farms, and avoid the crushing burden of high rents charged against the produce of a farm already too small to support a family in comfort. Landownership might or might not bring a large return on the investment. High rents are not to be confused with high investment yields to the owner. So high were land prices in prewar Japan that even rents running to 30 to 40% of the total crop might yield less than 5% on invested capital.[86] However, the Japanese system of land tenure gave the landlord relative security with little entrepreneurial responsibility. He could also hope for capital gains as population and development increased land values. And his position as a village proprietor opened up supplementary opportunities for profit through local moneylending, trade, and industrial activity.

With the industrialization and commercialization of the economy, the premium on land was progressively diminished by the attractions and increasing familiarity of other types of investment. And as the inclination weakened to hold wealth in the form of land, or other liquid assets, funds were made available on more favorable terms to produce new capital goods for use in expanding and diversifying productive activity. This was not a matter of the attracting into new employments of capital previously "locked up" in agriculture;

---

in the traditional Chinese economy and that of public spending in modern industrial economies. That such activity was essential to maintaining the physical productivity of agriculture is clear. Did it also have multiplied effects on income, consumption, and savings through associated changes induced in stocks of grain, the supply and circulation of money, and general commercial activities? If so, this might offer an additional reason why the neglect of public works was characteristically a symptom of economic decay, political unrest, and a gathering dynastic crisis.

[86] Nasu, *op.cit.*, pp. 128-31. Direct comparisons between investments in land and, say, Kanegafuchi Spinning Company stock are made difficult by differences in risk, taxes, etc. It appears, however, that land prices remained high, relative to yields (net of uncertainty). One authority, Shiro Kawata, wrote as follows in 1933: "The current market value of agricultural land is usually at a much higher level than its equitable price level, which is estimated by capitalizing the money returns from that price of land on the basis of the prevailing rate of interest. This phenomenon is peculiar to a country like Japan where agricultural industry is characterized by the preponderance of small-scale tenancy, the bargaining of farmers in small tracts of land, and the consequent urgent demand for farm land which far exceeds its supply. Such a tendency is still further exaggerated by the keen desire of tenant-farmers, prompted either by actual need or by sheer pride and ostentation, to possess farm land at any cost and with utter disregard for sound economy." "Price Standardization in Government Control of Rice," *Journal of the Osaka University of Commerce*, no. 1, September ·1933, p. 20.

The following comparison of annual yields on various kinds of investment in Japan during the years 1921-36 is given by figures of the Hypothec Bank of Japan: farm land, 5.4 to 7%; company shares, 4.9 to 9.4%; company debentures, 4.5 to 8.4%; loans to individuals on the security of immovables, 10.1 to 11.5%. *Japanese Agricultural Land Statistics*, cited, pp. 51-52.

rather, it facilitated the growth of the *total* capital stock of the country.[87]

A Dynamic Economy. A fresh study of business cycles in prewar Japan is needed to illuminate more clearly the dynamics of her economic growth. With the appearance of more or less periodic fluctuations in business conditions toward the end of the nineteenth century the Japanese found themselves concerned with the problem of all capitalist economies—the importance for equilibrium of a continuous flow of investment expenditure adequate to balance savings at rising levels of employment and income.

What rate of expansion in income (output) was required to keep the market economy running in high gear, given the technology and saving habits existent at any time, we do not know. Whatever the "required" rate, it appears broadly to have been approached in practice through a good deal of the prewar era, to judge from the rarity of severe depressions and periods of stagnation. The stimuli, as previously noted, arose from the rapid gains in population, technology, and foreign trade; the government's tax incentives, subsidies, and war spending; and other factors sustaining profit expectations at a high level in relation to the cost of securing funds. The resulting investment decisions served in turn to expand incomes and to make these expectations (in the aggregate) come true.

If growth was sustained with few serious interruptions over half a century or more, as the production curves indicate, one factor of special importance was probably the volume and character of the nation's foreign trade. In the first place, exports expanded steadily for seventy years, reinforcing the demand for industrial products in the home market. (See Chapter 6.) It operated to prolong upswings in business activity and to shorten the downswings where they originated in domestic dislocations. Second, since an increasing share of the earnings of exports were returned abroad to pay for imported materials and equipment used in their manufacture —25%, more or less, in the interwar years—the volume of those earnings could expand correspondingly further without generating inflationary cost increases within Japan. Third, because Japan met so many of her requirements for producers' goods overseas, a rise in money incomes and prices generated from whatever source was dampened by the "leakage" of expenditures on im-

[87] Of modern Japan, Talcott Parsons has remarked: "A certain prestige seems to attach to landownership as compared to other sources of income, but by no means a decisive one when compared to China or 'county' England. On the whole, owners of rural land tend to merge with the larger middle class of people of business and professional status, which, though much smaller and weaker, is very similar to our own in basic social characteristics." Douglas G. Haring, ed., *Japan's Prospect*, Cambridge, Mass., 1946, p. 91.

ports. Finally, because Japanese industry was geared to an elastic world market for such supplies, it could probably avoid more easily some of the bottlenecks and cost dislocations which are apt to appear in an industrial structure based more narrowly on its own capacity in this respect.[88] The limiting factors in Japan were more largely her capacity to finance imports, and her inelastic supply of technical and administrative skills.

The corollary of this dependence on foreign trade, however, was the sensitivity of the Japanese economy to the conditions of foreign demand. In the later decades 25% or more of its industrial output was regularly exported. (See Chapter 7.) Especially striking was its vulnerability to fluctuations in the American silk market, which was only partially mitigated by the growing demand for cotton goods in Asia. The trade balance was a matter of constant concern. Discount rates in Tokyo moved closely in relation to the import/export ratio after 1900, and a rise in the trade deficit was usually a symptom of approaching crisis.

Despite the problem of the balance of payments—indeed, as the chief cause of it—a chronic tendency toward monetary inflation seems to have persisted through much of the period from 1868 to 1920, reappearing again in the thirties. Only in the eighties, and again between 1920 and 1932, was the secular upward drift in Japanese wholesale prices arrested. (See Table 25.) This, too, is a feature of Japan's economic growth deserving more careful study. A cursory review of the data suggests a chronic tendency for the rate of private investment and government spending to exceed the amounts required to utilize productive resources to the full at the existing level of technology. This was encouraged not only by a series of wars and incessant armament expenditure, but also by what seems to have been a general bias in favor of easy money and credit expansion on the part of big business and the State.

One economist, Tokuzo Fukuda, remarked in 1926 on the "irrational" faith of the Japanese in the benefits of inflation.[89] He attributes it to the prosperity induced by paper money issues during 1877-80 and the war booms of 1894-95, 1904-05, and 1915-19. The extremes of fiat currency were ended by the Matsukata reforms leading to the adoption of the gold standard in 1897. However,

[88] This point is suggested by Shigeto Tsuru at the conclusion of his interesting study of the *Development of Capitalism and Business Cycles in Japan,* unpublished ms, Widener Library, Harvard University. See also his "Economic Fluctuations in Japan, 1868-1903," *The Review of Economic Statistics,* vol. xxiii, no. 4, November 1941, pp. 176-89.

[89] "La 'Cyclicité' de la Vie Economique et de la Politique Economique Eclairée par l'Example de l'Evolution Japonaise de 1868 à 1925 dans ses Rapports avec l'Etranger," *Journal des Economistes,* 1926, pp. 16-17.

the State continued to pursue fiscal and monetary policies which made the protection of the foreign balance and the accumulation of specie objects of constant concern. During the next two decades successive doses of inflation were administered with the help of the Chinese indemnity, foreign borrowings, and the export boom of

Table 25. *Index of Wholesale Prices in Japan Proper,*
1870-1938[a]
(1910-14 = 100)

1870-74	45	1905-09	96
1875-79	48	1910-14	100
1880-84	48	1915-19	164
1885-89	47	1920-24	221
1890-94	54	1925-29	185
1895-99	70	1930-34	134
1900-1904	79	1935-38	171

a For 1870-99, unweighted arithmetic average of wholesale price relatives of fifteen commodities, based on 1868 (Asahi Shimbun-sha, *Nippon Keizai Tōkei Sōkan,* Tokyo, 1930, p. 1108); 1900-1938, Bank of Japan wholesale price index (Bank of Japan, *Economic Statistics of Japan,* Tokyo, passim, and Tōyō Keizai Shimpō-sha, *Keizai Nenkan* [1939], Tokyo, 1939, p. 19). The Bank of Japan index is also a simple unweighted average of monthly price relatives of fifty-six commodities in Tokyo, based on October 1900. Here the two indices are spliced together in the period 1900-1904 and recomputed with 1910-14 as 100. Needless to say, this gives only a very crude measure of the central tendency of price changes, especially before 1900.

1915-19. These piled up reserves of precious metals and foreign credits which lasted until the mid-twenties. The difficulties which thereupon ensued—at the time Tokuda was writing—were hardly calculated to diminish faith in monetary expansion. The process was soon renewed with the aid of drastic depreciation of the yen.

Through these decades, in short, the demand for funds for investment and war spending chronically exceeded the sums made available from existing incomes through voluntary savings and taxation. Given the acquiescent attitude of the authorities toward credit expansion, the result was a more or less persistent tendency to inflation, which periodically got out of hand and culminated in a slump. On the whole, however, the boom periods predominated. They were often wasteful, producing speculative excesses and distortions. By chronically inflating profit margins, moreover, they relieved producers of the incentive otherwise present to improve methods and cut costs. Yet, looking at the troubled experience of other countries in this field, one is inclined to conclude that the monetary mechanism was employed fairly successfully in prewar Japan to speed the transition to industrialism, to build the power of the State, and to accelerate the growth of real income and productive capacity. To this point we return again in Chapter 10.

Lessons of Japan's Experience. In current discussions of industrialization in Asia no problem looms larger than that of finding the necessary capital. Often it appears that a poverty-stricken nation with industrial ambitions cannot possibly provide most of the capital required for such purposes, especially when its population grows rapidly and yet expects immediate gains in living standards. If its needs are to be met, therefore, foreign loans and gifts must be found on a massive scale. They may be expected to cover not merely the cost of machinery imported from abroad but even a large part of the whole cost of financing economic development. As foreign capital is difficult to attract in quantity, however, and piles up repayment charges, this line of reasoning ends in a dilemma.

The Japanese experience in retrospect is encouraging in its technical successes, while confirming the importance of the whole political and cultural setting of economic development. In this restricted sense it lends support to Colin Clark's advice that "we must not fall into the old-fashioned error of regarding the accumulation of capital as the limiting factor in economic progress."

It shows, first of all, that the modernization of technology (in the widest sense), in an environment of expanding opportunities, is paramount, and itself tends to stimulate the creation of increasing amounts of man-made capital, even in a country poor in land and mineral wealth.

Second, it demonstrates that if other conditions are favorable, substantial progress can be made in the early stages of industrialization with comparatively modest amounts of new capital, produced mainly with domestic labor and materials. Except in large-scale public works, transport, and a few basic industries, Japanese investment proceeded by small unit increments with cumulative results. If this process did not take effect more rapidly in rising productivity and income per capita, the chief deterrent was the relentless increase of population.

Third, it confirms the experience of other countries in showing that the provision of credit to the peasant and the small industrialist is a problem of special difficulty and importance, requiring the creation of cooperative and public institutions specifically adapted to this purpose. Particularly is this true when population grows rapidly, piling up a great surplus in rural areas. "In all countries where farming is in the hands of small producers," remarks R. H. Tawney, "the fundamental problem of rural society is not that of wages, but of credit."

Fourth, the Japanese offer the precedent of one Far Eastern

nation which carried through a far-reaching program of industrialization without heavy and continuous borrowing abroad, and yet
with a significant rise in living standards over several decades. This
is not to imply, of course, that foreign assistance cannot speed the
process, and reduce the sacrifices and deferments of consumer gains
that would otherwise be required. In the initial stage, particularly,
overseas aid can provide a significant stimulus.

For the process of capital formation to go forward at a rapid rate,
however, certain essential conditions must be present. They are
important whether economic development is to proceed under private
or public auspices, or some combination of the two.

One is the stimulus of new opportunities and incentives to economic growth and structural change. In the case of Japan these were
both economic and political, centering to an unusual degree in her
expanding relations with the outside world. A second condition is a
framework of political order, legal security, and public administration favorable to the growth of economic enterprise, and particularly
to risk taking in new types of undertakings.

Both circumstances were present in Japan. Together they encouraged both the bureaucrat and the businessman, each in his
respective sphere, to anticipate attractive returns on new investment. Through the financial institutions that developed they drew
large resources into capital creation. Active investment spending
raised the levels of income and savings, immediately through the
monetary stimulus and ultimately through additions to productive
capacity. The process worked in cumulative fashion, though with
far less revolutionary consequences in rural life than in the great
urban complexes of modern industry, commerce, and finance.

Finally, this analysis has emphasized those political and social
arrangements which imposed restraints of various kinds upon the
consumption of current income, and made it possible to allocate
substantial resources to capital formation. One strategic component
of savings, in this sense, was the tax revenue collected by the State
and devoted to public works, armament output, and loans and subsidies to private business. Other increments of savings were forced
by investment and armament expenditure which failed to bring
about a commensurate rise in output and diverted resources from
consumption through the mechanism of price inflation. More important over the period as a whole was the "voluntary" component
of savings, i.e., the disposable income which individuals and firms
would have withheld from consumption even if it could have been
spent on consumer goods and services without bringing price increases. Various factors cited earlier enabled the Japanese to finance
a large stream of investment outlays with such savings. Most im-

portant were the social traditions and institutional controls which distributed income and wealth quite unequally, yet preserved a stable social order and a strong emphasis on personal frugality.

This combination of circumstances built up a savings-investment process which carried industrialization steadily forward. Moreover, it was initiated and sustained without resort to totalitarian controls over economic life. The fiscal needs of the government were met without stifling the developing spirit of enterprise. Currency disorders were kept within manageable bounds after the early misadventures. And increasingly after 1880 the major responsibility for investment decisions, except for military concerns, was left to private initiative under the general surveillance of the State. (See Chapter 10.)

In a more egalitarian setting, and with a more insistent, public demand for dramatic improvement of living standards, the formation of capital could hardly have proceeded so rapidly in a country as backward and impoverished as Meiji Japan, unless the State had intervened far more extensively and coercively to mobilize resources for the purpose. Considerable use was made of the more coercive instrumentalities of government as it was. Had the main reliance of economic development been on them, given the capacities of the Japanese bureaucracy, one wonders whether innovation and growth would have proceeded as rapidly or efficiently as they did. It may also be questioned whether, in the light of Japan's political tradition, she would have been either more democratic or more peaceable. On the other hand, the entire system rested on a grossly unequal distribution of wealth and power which was itself technologically inefficient in some respects and wholly opposed to human and democratic values.

One may hope that elsewhere the potential contradictions in these objectives may be reconciled more successfully than in prewar Japan. And indeed it may be doubted whether most other Oriental peoples will so patiently tolerate a similar concentration of economic privilege, where it does not carry with it a more direct responsibility to the nation. For Japanese capitalism displayed an all too callous disregard for the immediate well-being of the worker in the factory and the field. It perpetuated evils like child labor and tenant oppression long after the remedies were at hand.

Recognizing this fact, one should also acknowledge that the Japanese pattern of capital accumulation, and the institutions which made it possible, had their constructive features. If they failed lamentably to solve the problem of distributive justice, they were nevertheless remarkably successful in creating new income and wealth in ever increasing amounts. No doubt they would have been even more successful had the owning class taken a more enlightened view of the technical as well as social benefits to be derived from better living and working conditions for the common people. But a more egalitarian system would not necessarily have enlarged economic opportunity for the masses, whatever its levelling effects. It would have had to perform equally successfully the tasks of technological innovation and capital accumulation, unless sacrifices on this score had been offset by greater restraints on population growth and on imperialist adventures abroad. Where an economic system is so limited in its productive capacity as to condemn the mass of people to a life of grinding poverty, ignorance, and disease, whatever the pattern of distribution, these tasks are basic to almost all aspects of social progress.

CHAPTER 6

FOREIGN TRADE AND ECONOMIC GROWTH—I

Japan's Rise as a Trading Nation

NO aspect of modern Japan is more dramatic than the revolutionary growth in her foreign commerce after 1868. From a state of economic isolation hardly paralleled in the annals of other civilized peoples, this island nation emerged in seventy-five years to become one of the great trading empires of the world. If Japan was more profoundly altered during the century after 1850 than during the preceding millennium, the root cause was the opening of the country to Western influence, in which economic enterprise played such a conspicuous role.

In 1850 there was virtually no Japanese merchant marine, no mercantile establishment abroad, hardly even any awareness among Japanese of the commercial and industrial revolutions then transforming the West. Trade with the rest of the world, even Japan's immediate neighbors, had for two centuries been confined to a tiny trickle. Individual Japanese had been forbidden to go abroad on pain of death. No ship of more than 50 tons' capacity could be built in Japan. In their effort to seal off all disruptive influence from the outside, Tokugawa Iemitsu and his heirs had acted with Draconian effectiveness. Once flourishing maritime contacts with China and southern Asia were largely suspended. The arts of shipbuilding and navigation decayed. Only through the small Dutch and Chinese colony at Nagasaki did Japan continue after 1639 to maintain a limited trade in metals and luxury wares. Here the Dutch, limited to one ship a year, were cooped up under restrictions and surveillance which Karl Thunberg, a Swedish botanist employed by the Dutch East India Company, likened to being "buried alive."

Among a people whose island character had pushed them naturally toward maritime enterprise in earlier times, and whose history had long demonstrated a receptivity to foreign influence, it is astonishing that this state of affairs could have been enforced for over 200 years.[1]

---

[1] A Japanese economist in 1708 made a statement reminiscent of the Manchu Emperor Ch'ien Lung's famous dictum: "With the exception of medicines, we can dispense with everything that is brought us from abroad. The stuffs and other foreign commodities are of no real benefit to us. All the gold, silver, and copper extracted [for export] from the mines during the reign of Ogosho-Sama, and since his time, is gone, and, what is still more to be regretted, for things we could do well

No less astonishing, against this immediate background, is the transformation of modern times. Energies long pent up in a seclusionist Japan now found their release in the politics and the technology of the new age. It was as though the Japanese had set out to telescope within the space of three generations the whole commercial and industrial development which had occupied three crowded centuries in the West. At the end of this period, and before the shattering blows of World War II, Japan had built a far-flung network of trade ranking fifth among those of all nations. Ships flying the Rising Sun were a familiar sight in the great ports of the world. Japanese businessmen now supplied a major share of the factory goods consumed in Asia. Elsewhere, they made steady inroads on the established markets of older industrial competitors. And whether it was American cotton, Malayan rubber, or Egyptian phosphate, Japan had now become one of the largest customers for raw materials entering world trade.

For Japan herself foreign commerce proved to be the key unlocking the door of economic opportunity. Initially it provided a highway over which new impulses and a new technology came in to revolutionize much of her economic life. Later it enabled her to draw increasingly on the world's industrial resources to compensate for her own basic deficiencies. As a result she came to acquire a degree of dependence on the world economy exceeded by that of few other nations in modern times.

This dependence on overseas markets and materials reached far beyond the limits of Japan's own territories and possessions, despite the extension of her rule over some 30 million neighboring people. The price of her new wealth and well-being was thus a basic political insecurity arising from dependence on distant peoples and resources she could not hope to conquer. For her imperial-minded militarists, however, such dependence was no more acceptable than had been her undeveloped military and industrial potential of fifty years earlier. To escape from this contradiction between modern technology and nationalism, they risked everything in a violent attempt to carve out a new and self-sufficient empire in East Asia.

The result is now history. War wrecked the commercial foundations of Japanese industrialism, devastating the very areas especially important to Japan's own livelihood. The postwar generation thus inherited the painful task of rebuilding those foundations anew. Unfortunately it faced conditions now far less favorable, thanks in no small measure to Japanese aggression itself.

Internal v. External Expansion. Since overseas trade has played

without." Quoted by A. F. Thomas and Soji Koyama, *Commercial History of Japan*, Tokyo, 1936, pp. 130-31.

such a cardinal role in Japan's economic development, it may seem surprising that more specific treatment of this aspect has been reserved for such a late stage of our analysis. In the historical narrative of Chapters 1 and 2, it is true, Japan's changing economic relations with the outside world were fitted into their appropriate place. Subsequently, too, they have received some attention as they were linked with changes in the industrial arts, the growth of markets, new incentives to investment, and the redirection of Japanese labor and capital into industrial employment. However, they have yet to be brought into any sort of central focus.

The reason is one of perspective on the over-all patterns of economic growth. Much of the Western literature on Japan gives a false impression of her economic development by undue preoccupation with foreign trade and its associated activities. This is natural, if only because it is here that Japanese industrialization has impinged directly on the economic life of the rest of the world. Here, too, it has been most intimately related to the expansion of political empire overseas, as foreign trade and investment became the pretext and the instrument for imperialist ventures. The rise of textile, pottery, and machinery exports, the growth of the Japanese market for foreign cotton and industrial equipment, the spread of overseas shipping and banking activities, the connection between business and political aggression in China—such facts as these have most concerned the foreign observer.

This emphasis has been reinforced often by a doctrinaire view as to what was really happening inside Japan. According to this view, the dominant tendency in Japanese economic development after 1893 was the mushrooming of industries producing for the foreign market; other sectors of the economy remained little affected by new impulses and opportunities. This circumstance, one is told, reflected the social and political structure of the country, which concentrated wealth and power in the hands of the favored few. Lack of mass purchasing power at home thus left no profitable alternative open to Japanese capitalists but to press forward in search of overseas markets where they could employ their expanding resources. It also drove them inexorably to seek the support of a compliant State in seizing new opportunities by military conquest. The whole historical process served to earn handsome profits for the *zaibatsu*, it is conceded. It also built up the foundations of military power. But little gain is said to have accrued to the hard-pressed peasant or worker.[2]

[2] This interpretation of Japanese trade expansion is almost a commonplace of Western political writing on Japan. Earlier (page 149), a passage was quoted from a special issue of *Fortune* on Japan to the effect that "her industrialization is

From such an analysis it would follow that other countries embarking on economic development in order to raise living standards would do well not to emulate the Japanese pattern. Instead they should seek to create a prosperous home market by a more diversified and all-embracing program of modernization. The lessons of Japanese experience are essentially negative, one would conclude, so far as any genuine contribution to human welfare is concerned.

It would be foolish to ignore certain elements of truth in this picture. Few countries undergoing industrialization have had heavier dependence on overseas markets or arrived at it more rapidly than Japan. Basically this reflected factors of population, resources, and trading opportunities which would have conditioned Japan's economic development, whatever her political and social system. However, the prevailing social system certainly influenced the composition of trade, as well as the scale of foreign borrowing and lending. For example, income inequalities, reinforced by governmental tariff policy, served to restrict imports of Western consumer goods in favor of raw materials and machinery. The concentration of control in large-scale banking and business may itself have increased the *relative* magnitude of Japan's international economic activities, because it created more readily the kind of contacts, cooperation, skills, and capital which were especially needed in such activities. One may argue that it led to a somewhat disproportionate allocation of Japanese resources to the cultivation of foreign markets, with corresponding neglect of avenues of home investment which would have been socially more productive and beneficial for the people.

Certainly overseas trading opportunities attracted large amounts of capital into export employment as Japanese industry matured. They contributed thereby to the high rate of investment which seems to have characterized the Japanese economy through much of this period. To this extent they limited the immediate gains in consumption. From the beginning, too, Japanese foreign policy

---

an industrialization which must sell its goods abroad since her domestic market is incapable of buying her industrial products."

The "motor force" of Japanese industrialization after 1890, according to this view, was the drive of Japanese capitalism for foreign markets, at the expense of continuing poverty at home. E. H. Norman, among others, accepts this argument in his classic *Japan's Emergence as a Modern State*, New York, 1940. The growth of the home market in Meiji Japan stimulated industrialization, he says, particularly military industry. But this market remained "relatively narrow" as a result of high rent and taxes, low wages, and other factors restricting purchasing power. Citing the entry of Japanese cotton goods into competition for the China market in the 1890's, he concludes (pp. 165-66): "This one example shows how Japanese industry, partly under the pressure of foreign competition and partly because of the insufficient purchasing power of the home market, had no alternative but to look to the foreign market as the guarantee of future expansion and progress."

emphasized the necessity of trade expansion, even if the actual course of empire building served as much to hamper and distort this growth as to foster it. The political insecurities associated with this pattern of development were one of the factors contributing to those military risks and commitments which ultimately led Japan down the path of disaster.

With full allowance for such considerations, however, the idea that the drive for foreign markets was *the* motor force of Japanese industrialization is nothing but a literary invention. It has little relationship to the facts. The true place of foreign trade in the dynamics of Japanese development is the subject of this chapter and the one which follows. But already it must be evident that the process of economic growth was at once more pervasive and more complex than any such simple thesis would suggest. The initial stimuli, and the new techniques, came largely from abroad. In this sense the Industrial Revolution in Japan was the creation of foreign trade. But the national response was positive and pervasive, working throughout the economy to produce changes which affected all sectors in varying degrees. It was precisely because this was so, and because it brought a steady rise in productivity and wealth, that imports and exports also grew. A country gains in foreign trade, other things being equal, as its national income grows. Poverty makes poor customers and inefficient suppliers.

If Japan's overseas market expanded, so too did her home market. The latter remained at all times far larger in scale. Changes in domestic tastes and habits, and in the investment requirements of home industries, reacted upon employment and income to a much greater degree than did foreign demand for Japanese goods. Some of Japan's imports went into the processing of manufactures for export; but the greater part were consumed at home. Machine production and mechanized transport were certainly not confined to industries selling abroad, although conspicuous there. Agriculture lagged behind in the process of growth, as we have seen. Yet even here steady growth took place through the first half century, providing foodstuffs, raw materials, and buying power to support the expansion of industry.

Japan's whole internal development was profoundly influenced, in fact was made possible, by the mounting exchange of goods and services with the outside world. But equally it was this general process of national growth which gave substance and momentum to the expansion of foreign trade. To suppose that a country can build a great overseas commerce in manufactures on the foundations of an economy otherwise unreconstructed and stagnant is to ignore all the lessons of history.

Not only were external and internal development closely related, but in economic terms they were two aspects of the same process. Specialization might lead to expanding circuits of exchange between Japan and Australia, or between Nagoya and Sendai, or, as was actually the case, some combination of the two. Machine methods of producing cotton goods migrated from Lancashire and Massachusetts to Osaka. So they migrated, too, from Osaka to outlying villages, and for reasons essentially the same. Similarly, it was access to North China coal and iron as well as Kyushu coal which attracted the metallurgical industry to Fukuoka Prefecture, at the western entrance to the Inland Sea. One hears much of Japan's international balance of payments, but a region such as the Yawata-Tobata industrial area, just like Japan as a whole, faces the necessity of balancing its imports and exports when it exports steel and other products to pay for iron ore, shipping services, or rolling mills.

Japan has been described as "a neat case" of national economic development. Yet in many respects hers was a unique case of international development, in which foreign influence and foreign trade played a major role. Actually the processes of growth were a complex interaction of the two. Herein lies the explanation of her rapid advance; also, of the difficulties into which she plunged herself when, after 1938, she sought to break away from the ties that bound her to the world economy.

If foreign trade is essentially nothing but an extension of the web of economic organization and activity across national frontiers, it nevertheless presents problems requiring special consideration. These center mainly around various barriers, other than mere transport costs, which restrict the international movement of goods, services, and the factors of production. They are social as well as political. Between Japan and the United States, for example, there are far greater differences in tastes and living habits than between Tokyo and the most remote regions of Hokkaido. This fact alone limits Japan's exchange of goods and services across the Pacific as compared with her internal trade.

Other differences are no less important. The textile mills of Osaka were fed with a stream of cheap labor flowing in from outlying farm districts. But any comparable movement of Japanese workers to the United States, or of Chinese to Japan, was blocked by political as well as economic obstacles. Foreign capital moved more freely into Japan at times, just as Japanese capital went to the colonies. Yet here too, far more than within the islands, free movement has been impeded by factors of risk and unfamiliarity— also political resistance.

These restrictions upon international mobility have perpetuated radical differences in the relative capital endowments, skills, and living standards of Japan and the West. Similarly Japan's own industrial advance after 1890 opened up a widening technological gap between herself and neighboring countries of Asia—a gap only slightly narrowed by the migration of Japanese businessmen and capital to these regions. Such differences in resources, human aptitudes, and demands largely determined the composition and direction of Japan's overseas trade.

Most importantly, of course, the political factor gives a special stamp and a peculiar importance to a country's international economic relations. All historical interpretations and policy judgments must recognize the special concerns which surround international dealings in a world of nation-states. It was Japan's good fortune that the foundations of her modern development were laid in an era when the world economy as a whole was expanding, and still organized on liberal principles for the most part. She herself pursued a fairly liberal trade policy for seventy years, except where her colonies and strategic industries were involved. Yet no small island nation, similarly dependent on overseas trade, could have failed to display constant solicitude over its international economic position. Least of all was this likely in the case of a people among whom the sense of national identity and of national destiny was so deeply implanted. Economic opportunity abroad was essential to both national power and well-being. The political issues associated with Japan's external economic relations were a constant preoccupation of her statesmen, and greatly influenced the course of development.

Japan's entry into the world economy is the subject of this chapter and the one which follows. Their purpose is to appraise the quantitative importance of overseas commerce in Japanese economic life, and its role in the dynamics of economic development. In choosing where to place the emphasis one is forced to be somewhat selective. Comparatively little attention is paid to the mechanism of financial equilibrium in the balance of payments as it operated from year to year, for example. Little is added to the analysis of foreign borrowing and the balance of payments given in Chapter 5. Similarly, the temptation is resisted to embroider the theory of international trade by refinements and case illustrations from the experience of Japan. The whole subject of Japanese business enterprise in the colonies likewise receives only casual discussion, save as it affected the economy of the home islands. These subjects all deserve more careful study than they have yet received, but are largely left aside here in order that we may focus on the broader contributions of overseas trade to the secular growth of the country.

Secular Growth of Overseas Trade. The first point to establish is the sustained and rapid expansion of Japan's overseas commerce from 1868 to 1938. Table 26 gives certain over-all measurements, disregarding the earliest years, when trade was still very small in amount. Most significant are the curves of physical growth, which take account of all external trade, whether with foreign countries or Japanese colonies.[3]

Several characteristics of this growth deserve attention. One is the persistent upward climb of both imports and exports. From 1880 to 1913 each increases eightfold in volume. On the average they doubled every decade, with a geometric rate of annual growth averaging about 7.5%. This was twice the growth rate of world imports as a whole during the period. It was also twice the rate maintained by Britain during the nineteenth century. The initial processes of modernization were now in full swing, as Japan fitted herself into the web of international trade. Impelled by a growing need for raw materials and machinery from abroad, the Japanese took full advantage of the general expansion taking place in the world economy at the time, and the liberal commercial policies which prevailed.

World War I afforded fresh windfall opportunities to extend Japanese exports overseas. They appeared both in belligerent countries and in neutral markets vacated by belligerents. The two colo-

[3] The terms "Japan" and "Japan Proper" are used interchangeably in the discussion of foreign trade in this book to designate the following area: the four home islands of Honshu, Kyushu, Hokkaido, and Shikoku; Okinawa after 1878; Karafuto (South Sakhalin) after 1904; and minor adjacent islands. They exclude other parts of the prewar Japanese Empire.

The terms "overseas trade" and "external trade" refer to the trade of Japan Proper, as defined above, *including* its trade with other regions of the Empire. (Where the distinction between foreign and colonial trade is immaterial, the term "foreign trade" may also be used in this sense.) This is contrary to the usual prewar practice, in both official statistics and the general literature. It adds considerably to one's statistical labors thus to combine Japan's trade with foreign countries and her trade with colonies at every point. However, the result is to give a more complete and accurate picture of Japan's real overseas dependence, and to afford a better basis for postwar comparisons.

Minor errors arise from the use of official statistics to compare prewar overseas trade, thus defined, with domestic production. In the production statistics of Japan Proper, Karafuto and Nanyo (Pacific islands mandate) are normally excluded. Only in a few items like coal, phosphates, fish, and lumber and pulp is it worth while to correct the discrepancy, however. The trade of both areas with foreign countries was negligible. Their trade with Japan was as follows in 1929 and 1937 (in millions of yen):

	IMPORTS FROM JAPAN		EXPORTS TO JAPAN	
	1929	*1937*	*1929*	*1937*
Karafuto	46.6	59.1	56.4	121.1
Nanyo	6.5	22.0	8.2	37.9

Table 26. *Growth of Trade of Japan Proper with Foreign*
Countries, Korea, and Formosa, 1885-1938[a]

ANNUAL AVERAGE	TOTAL VALUES[b] (MILLIONS OF YEN)		Balance of Trade	PRICE INDICES[c] (1910-14 = 100)		Imports ÷ Exports	QUANTUM INDICES[c] (1910-14 = 100)	
	Imports	Exports		Imports	Exports		Imports	Exports
1885-89	47	55	+8	47	57	82	16	16
1890-94	84	86	+2	53	66	80	25	21
1895-99	206	163	—43	69	87	79	46	31
1900-1904	308	274	—34	83	99	84	58	46
1905-09	468	413	—55	83	111	75	87	61
1910-14	650	606	—44	100	100	100	100	100
1915-19	1,423	1,663	+240	176	163	108	124	168
1920-24	2,440	1,915	—525	198	222	89	190	142
1925-29	2,849	2,494	—355	181	187	97	242	217
1930-34	2,212	2,058	—154	124	105	118	277	327
1935-38	3,868	3,772	—96	173	124	140	347	505

a Trade statistics for prewar Japan are available for all years after 1868. Beginning with 1885 they may be regarded as fairly reliable, except for the undervaluation of exports noted below. They are found in various reports of the Department of Finance, particularly the annual trade returns of the Bureau of Customs and Bureau of Revenue. The trade of Korea and Formosa under Japanese rule was reported separately by the Governments-General of the two colonies. As a matter of convenience the pre-1934 figures given here, and elsewhere in this study to a large degree, are taken from *The Foreign Trade of Japan: A Statistical Survey*, published by the Oriental Economist, Tokyo, 1935.

As officially defined, the foreign commerce of Japan Proper is the trade of the home islands (including Okinawa since 1879, South Sakhalin since 1905) with all overseas areas except the following (beginning in the years indicated): Formosa (1896), South Sakhalin (1905), Korea (1910), and Nanyo (1928). To combine the colonial and foreign trade of Japan one is forced to use the trade statistics of the colonies; for example, Formosa's exports to the Empire are regarded as Japanese imports from Formosa. This introduces minor discrepancies in valuation and timing, as well as small amounts of intercolonial trade.

b Import and export values were recorded in gold and silver yen prior to 1888; from 1888 to 1897 they were in silver yen. Japan adopted the gold standard in October 1897, with the yen valued at 11.574074 grains of gold ($0.49845). It fluctuated around this parity in relation to gold currencies until 1932, when it depreciated to a level of U.S. 28 to 29 cents.

The import and export figures used here and elsewhere in this study exclude gold and silver, "special" goods, and exports for ships' use (after 1900). Import values are prices at the port of origin before 1899. Thereafter they include cost, insurance, and freight. For the earlier years, therefore, about 15% should be added to arrive at c.i.f. value. Export values prior to 1904 represent market price at the port of clearance; from 1904 to 1911 they include packing charges; after 1911 they are f.o.b.

Students of Japanese foreign trade have voiced the opinion that exports have been consistently undervalued relative to imports. J. Inouye, discussing the matter in *Problems of the Japanese Exchange, 1914-26*, London, 1931, pp. 205-06, cites an opinion of the Department of Finance that exports were being undervalued to the extent of 4%. Margaret S. Gordon reviews the evidence and concludes that the annual discrepancy was less than 100 million yen before 1914, and 100 to 200 million thereafter. E. B. Schumpeter, ed., *The Industrialization of Japan and Manchukuo, 1930-1940*, New York, 1940, pp. 912-16.

c Price indices prior to 1930 are those of the Oriental Economist, *op.cit.*, pp. 699, 701. These indices are appropriately constructed; they are aggregates of prices weighted by given-year

quantities, the whole period being covered by splicing together three indices separately calculated for 1873-92, 1893-1903, and 1904-34. However, they relate only to articles in trade
with *foreign* countries for which quantity data are available—80 to 90% of such imports and
exports over the entire period. For lack of any more inclusive indices, they are used here
to deflate Japan's total imports and exports, including trade with Korea and Formosa, in
order to provide quantum indices. This procedure implies, none too accurately, that price
movements in overseas trade not covered by the Oriental Economist indices—30% or so of the
total in the later years—were parallel to those in the trade covered.

The resulting quantum as well as price indices are extended here from 1930 through 1938
with price indices and deflated trade values given by the U.S. Department of State in *The
Place of Foreign Trade in the Japanese Economy*, Washington, 1946, vol. II, tables 16, 24.

nies, Korea and Formosa, now also began to assume a new importance, as Japanese business enterprise developed their resources
and Japanese tariffs reserved their markets for home manufactures.
After the Armistice came a period of financial disorder, intensified
by the great earthquake of 1923. Yet neither was more than a
moderating influence on the continued growth of trade. The technical progress of the period paved the way for another upward surge
of commercial expansion when the yen collapsed in 1931. This was
checked only in the late thirties, and not until widespread alarums
had been spread abroad among Japan's industrial competitors by
the inroads of her goods in their established markets.

Actually the trade boom of 1932-37 was only a further intensification of what had been going on for a long time. It differed mainly
in the facts that (1) Japanese commerce was now a world-wide enterprise, and (2) the dislocation of exchanges, costs, and prices during
the depression gave the Japanese trade drive a sudden and concentrated impact, particularly in textile markets, just when unemployment was widespread in the West. Though it now created new
political frictions, the trading expansion which began in Meiji times
had continued steadily ever since, with little abatement. Four limited
wars, the ups and downs of the price level, the earthquake, and
other dislocations served only temporarily to deflect the quantum
indices from their secular upward drift. Now growth was accelerated;
now retarded. Meanwhile the composition of both imports and
exports underwent radical change. But the underlying forces of
development, both in Japan and in the world economy, steadily expanded the exchange of goods across Japan's national frontiers,
so long as the political and economic framework within which those
forces operated remained substantially unimpaired. The first great
setback came only when this framework was progressively undermined and destroyed by the war preparations and war making of
Japan and her Axis partners.

As a second characteristic of this commercial expansion, one
would expect to find that exports growing at such a rate would

absorb an increasing share of Japanese national product. Equally it is plausible that imports would constitute an increasing share of national income. This appears to be borne out by Prof. Yuzo Yamada's estimates of national income, when compared with the trade values of Table 26. In current yen the ratio of overseas trade to the estimated net value of all goods and services produced in Japan Proper is given in Table 27.

Table 27. *Overseas Trade of Japan Proper as a Percentage of Net National Product (Yamada Estimates), 1885-1938*[a]

ANNUAL AVERAGE	NET NATIONAL PRODUCT (MILLIONS OF YEN)	PERCENT OF NATIONAL PRODUCT	
		Exports	*Imports*
1885-89	937	5.9	5.1
1890-94	1,359	6.3	6.2
1895-99	1,962	8.3	10.5
1900-1904	2,565	10.7	12.0
1905-09	3,106	13.2	15.1
1910-14	4,104	14.8	15.8
1915-19	7,623	21.8	18.8
1920-24	12,627	15.2	19.3
1925-29	13,621	18.3	20.9
1930-34	12,029	17.1	18.4
1935-38	18,377	20.5	21.0

a Based on overseas trade values of Table 26. National product estimates are from Yuzo Yamada, *Nihon Kokumin Shotoku Suikei Shiryō*, Tokyo, 1951, pp. 114-17. Yamada's estimates are discussed above, pages 134ff.

Beginning almost from zero in 1860, both imports and exports had reached 10% of net national product by the turn of the century, if Yamada's estimate of the latter is at all close to the mark. The next decade raised them to about 15%, a substantial share. Through most of the interwar years the ratios fluctuated between 15% and 20%.

Japanese production of goods and services for the domestic market thus appears to have grown nearly as rapidly in value after 1918 as goods exported to foreign and Empire markets. Partly this was because of the relative decline in export (especially silk) prices from 1925 to 1931, and the lag in their subsequent recovery. At market values the output absorbed at home seems to have about kept pace with exports. And at all times it preponderated by a ratio of nearly 4:1. However, exports now played a critical role, not only in financing needed imports, but in linking fluctuations in Japanese business activity with those of the outside world.

Imports of merchandise appear likewise to have constituted about 20% of national income from 1912 to 1937. This indicates a fairly high degree of dependence in monetary terms, though not an exceptional one. It was about comparable with that of the United Kingdom, Germany, or Sweden at the time—far above the American figure, but well below an extreme case like that of Denmark.[4]

Japan's average propensity to import was now as high as it was because of (a) her specialized endowment in skills and resources, (b) her easy maritime access to markets and supplies abroad, and (c) her advances in productivity and buying power. It would have been even higher if per capita income had not still remained low by Western standards; also, if tariffs as well as peculiarities of Japanese taste and consumer habits had not operated further to limit trade with other countries.[5] Even so, few nations have become more fundamentally dependent on the world market for the essentials of national existence. Japan's purchases overseas in the main are not marginal items of consumption like coffee, or materials and equipment which she can produce herself at only slightly higher cost. They are food and industrial supplies vital to the whole structure of her living standards, equipment industries, and military potential.

A third characteristic of trade expansion observable in Table 26 is the rough parallelism between the growth of imports and that of exports. Until the currency depreciation of 1931 this applies broadly to their volume as well as their value. Such a parallelism is to be anticipated, especially in value totals. For exports served as Japan's principal means of payment for imports, while imports were the chief gain realized from the sale of exports. Fluctuations occurred in the trade balance from year to year, of course. They were associated with foreign borrowings and repayments, colonial investment, ship earnings and other service transactions in the balance of payments. Especially notable were the trade surplus created by Japan's export boom during World War I; then the

---

[4] Tse Chun Chang, "International Comparison of Demand for Imports," *The Review of Economic Studies*, vol. XIII (2), no. 34, 1945-46, p. 54.

[5] The average propensity to import may also have been restricted in Japan by the prevailing inequality in the distribution of income; this point is indeterminate. Such inequality has had the effect at any time of reducing imports of food and other consumer goods. On the other hand, it probably contributed historically to a high rate of capital formation which built up national income through industrialization and drew large imports from overseas. How a more even distribution of income would have affected this process of development is an issue involving many imponderables, political and economic. Suffice to say that the relationships are far more complex than is implied in the familiar cliché that Japan developed a heavy dependence on foreign trade because the buying power of the masses was repressed by institutional restraints, and Japanese industrialists therefore had to sell their goods abroad.

large deficits of the postwar years, financed by liquidating the credits and gold previously accumulated. For the period as a whole, however, Japan's international payments were overwhelmingly on commodity account; and the commodity accounts were not far from balancing. Unlike the great creditor and debtor nations of modern times, Japan has promptly collected the proceeds of her exports in the form of current imports for the most part. Likewise, she has paid for her swelling imports mainly with current exports, many of them actually manufactured from these imports.

If Japanese imports and exports were fairly closely balanced through most of the prewar decades, this does not mean that they exchanged on constant, unvarying terms. Despite their near equivalence in value (especially if exports of shipping services are added in) the volume of exports appears to have advanced more persistently than that of imports after 1914. The physical growth of imports shows some tendency to taper off after 1900, and again in the twenties. Exports, in contrast, follow an upward geometric progression which is virtually a straight line. In the five-year averages of Table 26 the only marked deviations are the hump of 1915-19 and the slump of 1920-24. From 1910-14 to 1935-38 imports increased at a geometric rate of 5.2% a year. The figure for exports is 6.7%.[6]

This suggests a fourth characteristic of Japan's prewar trading history. There appears to have been some tendency toward a deterioration in the terms of trade. It is true that the Oriental Economist price indices employed here are not very adequate for the entire range of overseas (including colonial) trade. (Table 26, note c.) Moreover, long-term comparisons of this sort have no clear meaning when both imports and exports changed so greatly in character from 1885 to 1935. However, the indices, if we take them at face value, point to a fairly stable ratio between the general levels of import and export prices from 1880 to 1909 (following an earlier decline in the ratio, between 1876 and 1880). Thereafter, the ratio rises; that is, more exports had to be shipped abroad to pay for a given volume of imports. From 1909 to 1918 the import price index nearly tripled, while export prices rose only 85%. Again, from 1931 to 1936 the former rose 70% and the latter only 24%. During most of the last thirty years, in other words, Japan

6 The Oriental Economist, *The Foreign Trade of Japan: A Statistical Survey*, Tokyo, 1935, pp. 33-39, fits parabolic curves fairly successfully to its quantum indices for Japanese trade with foreign countries from 1873 to 1934. A tapering off is evident in both imports and exports. When trade with the colonies is added, however, and the period extended through 1938, the conclusion hardly applies, especially in the case of exports.

was exchanging exports for imports on terms which seem to have been progressively less favorable.

Whether these barter terms of trade, calculated merely from prices, have any real significance over a period of years is questionable. So great were the technical advances in Japan's export industries that one doubts whether the "real cost" of her imports actually increased as the price indices suggest. The contrary is more likely. Indeed, one reason why the terms appear to move unfavorably was simply the reduction in the unit cost of her exports in labor and capital. But certainly a sharp deterioration is evident during World War I. It appears again when raw silk prices collapsed in the Great Depression. The result was to qualify seriously the immediate gains in real income which accrued from the industrial and trading booms of these two periods. It meant that foreign buyers of Japanese goods in Asia, the United States, and elsewhere shared largely in the consumer benefits from rising technical efficiency and continuing low wages in Japan.

Dynamic Role of Commerce. Examining more closely the role of foreign commerce in Japanese economic development, one may distinguish three levels or types of influence.

First, the opening of Japan to international trade after 1859 provided one of the main channels, and a whole new set of stimuli, for the introduction of modern science, machine technology, and business organization. This was its primary consequence, from which all others followed.

Most important, a swelling stream of imports formed a broad highway of learning from the advanced industrial nations of the West. Even items of trivial monetary value, like books and scientific apparatus could be of the highest strategic importance for the process of modernization. Further, the development of export markets on a large scale had certain catalytic effects. Beside paying for essential purchases abroad, Japan's growing export trade stimulated new investment in productive enterprise. It provided added opportunities and incentives for applying the new skills of machine manufacture and large-scale organization in industrial life. And it concentrated people in urban, industrial employments in and around port cities where they were more readily exposed to the new influences. Finally, continuing dependence on raw materials from overseas, together with a competitive export business, seems to have mitigated the dangers of monopolistic restriction and technical stagnation which were latent in the oligarchic business and political structure of the country. (See above, pages 233-34.)

The secret of Japan's rapid economic advance is probably to be found in no small degree in the dynamic role thus played by foreign trade as a stimulus to change and growth. In this respect her poverty in natural resources was an asset, not a liability, so long as the world situation permitted her to meet her deficiencies abroad. This chapter deals largely with these various aspects of international trade as the *activator of change* within the Japanese economy.

The second contribution of foreign trade to Japan's economic development went hand in hand with the first. Access to world markets enabled her to use her developing skills and resources to build up an economy drawing heavily on overseas supplies of commodities which she could not produce more cheaply herself. These she paid for with exports in which she found a competitive advantage. Her continuing backwardness in certain branches of engineering and, even more, her growing deficiency in the raw materials of industrialism made this a matter of peculiar importance. For example, her major industry, the textile industry, was built on four clothing fibers of which only raw silk was produced at home in appreciable quantities. Similarly, less than 20% of the iron and steel materials used in domestic consumption during the interwar years came from her own ore and scrap. The same thing was true of many other minerals and tropical products. Even domestic food supplies fell short of requirements by a growing margin.

In short, the world economy of 1868-1938 enabled Japan to reap the fruits of international specialization on a large and increasing scale. Perhaps no other country benefited so greatly from the system of relatively free and multilateral trade which prevailed over most of the globe through this period. For her import needs and her export opportunities were confined to no particular region. They required a global organization of trading activities combining the markets and materials of both Asia and the West. Multilateralism added tremendously to the productivity of the new industrial technology in Japan. It advanced the whole process of modernization and growth far beyond what would otherwise have been possible. To appreciate this truth one need only observe how greatly Japan's postwar recovery is complicated, and her future clouded, by the spread of bilateralism and trade controls.

A third consequence of developing overseas trade was the tying of the Japanese economy increasingly to fluctuations in world prosperity. This was both a stabilizing and an unstabilizing factor. On the one hand, economic disturbances originating within the country tended often to be checked by a counter-balancing response in foreign trade. A crop failure at home, for instance, became less serious than in Tokugawa times because of ready access to overseas rice and wheat. On the other hand, the level of world trading activity and prices came to exert a major influence on changes in income, capital formation, and consumer expenditure in Japan. In particular, as long as the American market continued to absorb huge quantities of silk at remunerative prices, the Japanese economy "hung by a silken thread." When this market was ruined by the depression of 1929-32, and the growing competition of synthetic fibers, Japan was plunged into a series of disorders and readjustments which had repercussions all over the globe. This aspect of Japan's international ties is dealt with only perfunctorily here, since full treatment would require a detailed study of her balance of payments and monetary history.

The ultimate consequences for Japan of her entry into the world economy ramified in all directions, of course. Among the Japanese themselves entirely new ways of social living developed out of the new impulses set in motion. Twice as many people now crowded together on the home islands than had lived there in previous history. A quarter of them lived in cities of over 100,000. Commercial expansion raised the merchant class to a new position of power in Japanese society. This brought a new alignment of class interests and political forces. Abroad, too, Japan's outlook was decisively affected by the network of economic cooperation and conflict which now characterized her status as an industrial world power. These broad political and social repercussions, however, must likewise be regarded as largely outside the bounds of this study.

Trade as a Highway of Learning

The Meiji Renovation, as Sir George Sansom observes, was in a real sense "an explosion from within." But what made it a revolutionary movement in technology and economic organization was the whole set of new stimuli which flowed in over the highways of communication now opened to the West. Commodore Matthew C. Perry stands as a figure of great symbolic significance in Japan, far more than among his own people.

International trade has served in modern times as the bearer of the Industrial Revolution around the world. This is indeed its classic role. There is no Western nation that does not owe much to borrowings of technology from the outside, made possible through the opportunities and contacts of commerce. Thus the Italian cities which led the Renaissance drew heavily on Byzantine and Arab culture imbibed through the Tyrrhenian trade. England assumed the industrial leadership of eighteenth century Europe only with the aid of skills first acquired from Flemish weavers, German metallurgists, and French machine-tool designers. In the nineteenth century she in turn exported the new technology of steam and steel and joint-stock finance to remake the Western world. The Far East in more recent times has provided still further examples. Japan in particular has occupied a dual position, first as the borrower of the industrial arts from the West, and more recently as the transmitter to her neighbors.

Catalytic Role of Imports. This process of learning did not begin in Japan with the Meiji Restoration. Despite the rigid seclusion enforced by the Tokugawa regime after 1639, the Japanese had retained a peephole on the outside world through the trade and residence of the Dutch at Deshima. Many an enterprising *daimyō*, *samurai*, and merchant had gone to school with the Dutch, displaying long before Perry the traditional eagerness of this island people for practical arts from abroad. Already, for instance, Matsudaira Yoshinaga, the adopted son of the *daimyō* of Echizen, had introduced into Fukui a gun factory, a cannon foundry, a powder mill, language study, vaccination, even a medical school. Despite the watchful eye of Edo, the feudal lord of Satsuma had even smuggled twenty-seven young men off to Europe, some of them later to become high officials of the Meiji regime. Such contacts were cramped and confined at best, however, until the conclusion of the new treaties with the Western powers in 1858. They are interesting chiefly as they testify to the discernment of a few restless spirits who sensed that Tokugawa Japan had reached an economic and political impasse from which it could be rescued only by the new learning. With the opening of Japanese ports to overseas trade these sentiments broadened into a national movement.

Western manufactures now began to be imported in a swelling stream. Japanese silk and tea soon found a growing market in Europe and America. Hundreds of foreigners came to Japan—as technical experts hired by the new government, as foreign traders, as missionaries and educators. A Japanese artist, first employed by the Mitsuis to paint a portrait of Perry, was later dispatched to study ships and machinery abroad. Others followed by the score, either as individuals or on government missions. They studied British textiles and metallurgy, American railways, French law, German military science. A Japanese Minister attended the World's Fair in Vienna "to expose the native works of the Empire." The Great Northern commenced to lay the first cable to Shanghai and Vladivostok in 1871; in 1874 Japan signed the Universal Postal Convention; in the following year Mitsubishi interests opened the first packet service to China; in 1880 the Yokohama Specie Bank was founded to finance foreign trade.

All such channels and opportunities of contact were eagerly exploited save one. Aware of political events elsewhere in Asia, the early Meiji leaders frowned on direct foreign investment in Japanese mining, industry, or agriculture. Even a German farmer who had established a model farm in Hokkaido at the invitation of the Shogunate was immediately bought out by the new regime.[7] Foreigners were restricted by law from owning land or operating mines. Although this did not bar them from participating in Japanese companies so engaged, such investments appeared none too secure under Japanese law.

There were other deterrents to Western business enterprise in Meiji Japan, of course. No great extractive industries could be developed to serve Western markets, as in the case of Indian tea, Sumatran rubber, Argentine beef, or Rhodesian copper. (Insofar as Japan's poverty in natural resources reduced the threat of Western imperialism, it was not an unqualified liability!) Western entry into Japanese industry was likewise handicapped by cultural distance—differences in language, consumer habits, law, and administration. Before 1897 foreign capital was also discouraged by currency instability as Japan passed through her experiments with paper, bimetallism, and silver. Such deterrents existed in China and India as well. But in Japan there was no regime of Western political control, or of settlements and concessions, to lessen their effect. And the official policy of the government was virtually to exclude foreign business investment, except in trading activity. It only modified this policy after it felt itself to be securely on its feet and abolished the regime of extraterritoriality in 1899.

After the turn of the century the suspicion of foreign business enterprise was relaxed. In fact, the new gold standard was adopted partly to attract Western capital. The Japanese borrowed heavily abroad during the next decade, and again on a more modest scale in the twenties. Mostly, it is true, this took the form of selling national and local bond issues in Western money markets, and secondarily the debentures of semiofficial companies and electric utilities. (Chapter 5.) In addition, however, small amounts of foreign equity investment found their way into the equipment industries. Here they played a strategic role in technological borrowing out of all importance to their size. For example, the General Electric Company acquired an interest in the Tokyo Electric Light Company in 1905. Through this connection the latter introduced the Mazda lamp in Japan. Armstrong-Vickers, a British concern, put up 45% of the capital of Nippon Seiko (Japan Steel), which was pioneering new metallurgical processes. Later, in the twenties, numerous foreign manufacturing concerns, most of them American, established branch plants in Japan. Or they acquired minority interests

[7] J. J. Rein, *The Industries of Japan*, New York, 1899, p. 20.

in Japanese firms through the offer of patent rights, equipment, or engineering skills. They went into the manufacture and distribution of electrical goods (Siemens, General Electric, Westinghouse), automobiles (Ford, General Motors), and other products like glass, aluminum, petroleum, sewing machines, film, and phonographs.

Even so, the scale of this participation was decidedly limited when one considers the whole array of Japanese banking, manufacturing, mining, and public utility enterprise. Total foreign business investment in Japan has been estimated at only 70 million yen in 1913, and no more than 200 million yen in 1933. (Above, pages 258-60.) Quantitatively it was negligible. Except in the handling and financing of overseas trade in the early decades, one cannot fail to be impressed with the meager contribution of foreign business enterprise *in Japan* to the industrialization process. It was confined largely to certain equipment industries, and even here the resources of the great combines together with the pervasive influence of the government often made it difficult for the foreign businessman to operate effectively. Foreign entrepreneurship was far less significant than in the industrial development of France, of Argentina, of many countries of the West. Still more striking is the contrast with colonial regions like the Philippines or India; or with China, where modern industrial enterprise was so largely concentrated in the foreign settlements and concessions under Western and Japanese management.

This contrast between Japan and the rest of Asia only underlines the feat of borrowing on which the Japanese embarked in 1868. As once before, when they imported the arts and institutions of T'ang China beginning in the seventh century, the process was selective in its purpose and uneven in its tempo and effect. Much was modified; much rejected altogether. But in the industrial arts it was a genuine commitment to learning. The boy Emperor bespoke high policy in 1868, and not ceremonial verbiage, when on assuming the throne he was made to proclaim that "intellect and learning should be sought for throughout the world, in order to establish the foundations of the Empire." One historian describes the Japanese temper of the time as "a craze for Occidental civilization . . . almost a pathological phenomenon."[8] If pathological, it had its roots deep in national tradition. And it was nourished by dreams of power and material well-being, as well as sober realization that only through modernization could Japan hope to preserve her independence in the world into which she had suddenly emerged.

The goods which now began to arrive in Western ships were many of them less important for their own utility than for the

[8] Chitoshi Yanaga, *Japan since Perry*, New York, 1949, p. 129.

demands they stimulated and the technical knowledge they conveyed. There is something symbolic in the copy of *Webster's Dictionary* brought home from the United States in 1860 by a young Japanese, Fukuzawa Yukichi. Beginning his career with the study of English, he went on to found Keio University and to become one of the leaders in the Enlightenment. Similarly, imports of English cotton fabrics and engine boilers had a catalytic effect far beyond their intrinsic value. Whereas the Dutch at Deshima had imported mainly handicraft goods and tropical produce from Asia— silks and sandalwood, spices, drugs, and hides—Japanese purchases now turned toward the machine manufactures of the West. In 1875 Europe and the United States supplied over 70% of Japan's 30 million yen of imports; Britain alone furnished 30%. Half of the total was made up of cotton and woolen goods. Much of the remainder was virtually a sample list of Western factory goods—pig iron, nails, pipes and wire, kerosene, refined sugar, arms and ammunition, books, dyes, shoes, clocks and scientific instruments, etc.

These cargoes were made up of things, but they were also transmitters of ideas. Some were products better suited to satisfy long-standing needs. Cheap cotton goods woven from machine-spun yarns, for example, soon proved themselves superior to native hempen cloth. Fine goods from Lancashire astonished the Japanese no less than calicoes and muslins from India had delighted the English two centuries before. Here, as around the world, machine-made textiles made their way steadily against handicraft products, first in the case of yarns and later in that of woven goods.[9]

Other imports served entirely new requirements. Modern office buildings and factories could not be built of wood and paper; they called for glass, cement, and steel—acquired through bringing in either the products themselves or the method of producing them. Some of the least valuable imports were the most strategic. Foreign flour and sugar might improve upper-class diets. Foreign rice might even relieve a crop famine, as for the first time in 1870. Kerosene lamps might lengthen the day by several hours. But a few steam engines served to unlock for Japan the secret of great concentrations of mechanical power independent of climate and terrain.

---

[9] The following story is told of the lord of Satsuma: "One day Nariakira asked his immediate councillors: 'Of all things western what do you dread most?' They all replied by referring to cannons and warships. Nariakira shook his head and said: 'No. It is cotton cloth. Unless we begin preparing now, we shall soon be all dependent on westerners for our clothings.'" (Shigeto Tsuru, *Development of Capitalism and Business Cycles in Japan*, unpublished MS, Harvard University, Widener Library.) In actuality Japan did in time become almost wholly dependent on clothing fibers from overseas, but not piece goods. By 1930, 95% of the textile raw materials consumed by the nation consisted of imported cotton, wool, and rayon pulp. See below, Table 33.

Together with domestic coal, fortunately present in abundance, they made it possible to move steadily from the spinning wheel to the automatic ring spindle, from the cart to the railway, from the blacksmith's forge to the rolling mill. And how estimate the significance for industrialization of precision instruments like the clock and the lathe? So, too, with imports of machinery for printing books and newspapers; of steel plate and artillery weapons; of new seeds and insecticides; of the marine turbine, the dry cell, the gas engine. Annual imports of machinery, instruments, and vehicles amounted in value to only 6 million yen in 1889-93. They were only 39 million yen in 1909-13, and 120 million yen in 1929-33. In none of these periods did they reach even 10% of Japan's total imports. Yet this gives no measure of the transformation they wrought.[10]

In the early years factory goods from overseas caused some displacement of domestic handicrafts, especially textiles. Cotton cloth and yarn made up a third of total imports during the first Meiji decade. Here, as elsewhere, these machine-made goods rapidly invaded the traditional market for homspun yarn and hand-woven fabrics. Imported sugar, indigo, and raw cotton likewise came in to replace native production in increasing degree. In certain localities severe hardships were worked on peasant families and artisans dependent on these ancient trades.

On the whole, however, the destructive impact of imported foreign manufactures on the traditional handicrafts seems to have been neither very pronounced, nor very widespread. It was slight by comparison with the inroads made in later years by Japan's own developing factory industries. Consumer tastes in Japan and the West were quite different in the main; markets were still localized; and most Western manufactures were well beyond the buying power of the masses. More severe at the time were the economic dislocations resulting from the breakup of the old political regime. When

---

10 During the nineteenth century the United Kingdom supplied the bulk of this equipment. With the turn of the century she was joined by Germany and the United States. After World War I the United States became the principal supplier of machinery as well as automotive equipment. The totals are as follows:

Annual Average	*Total*	*Machinery*	*Autos and Parts* *(millions of yen)*	*Instruments, Tools, Ships, Firearms, Watches, and Clocks*
1889-93	5.7	2.8	—	2.9
1909-13	38.8	26.1	0.5	12.2
1929-33	120.5	78.2	20.0	22.3

This comprises Group xvi of the official import classification, with the addition of office machines, tools, and ball bearings from Group xv. "Machinery" includes locomotives, engines, motors, dynamos, etc.

the flow of feudal revenues from the countryside to the town aristocrats was terminated, this cut away the livelihood of many a tradesman and artisan. The swordmakers and armorsmiths of Kyoto, for
example, had to turn to other copper and iron wares. Other disturbances accompanied the drain of specie abroad, which complicated the already tangled finances of the *Bakufu* and later added
to the monetary problems of the new government.

Soon new small industries sprang up on every side to copy foreign
goods—soap, matches, shoes, umbrellas, and the like. "The foreign
mania raged everywhere," says an official report, "and everything
was manufactured in imitation of foreign articles." Many were essentially handicraft industries, some providing new occupations for
declassed *samurai*. Here what counted was not any massive change
in production technique, but the spread of minor improvements like
the steel cutting tool, the thermometer, a new chemical pigment,
or the small steam engine and water wheel.

Other new ventures were larger in scale and more ambitious from
the start. As we have seen, the government actively fostered such
developments, furnishing capital, foreign experts, and technical
schools, and generally pioneering the Western-style factories. It
established the model silk filature at Tomioka; it bought 20,000
spindles from England to introduce machine spinning; it started
up the production of cement, glass, and foreign paper; it developed
new mines and shipyards; it encouraged plants which sprang up to
manufacture sugar, tobacco products, beer, paint, machinery,
matches, and artificial fertilizer. Significantly the first government
bonds issued for public sale, in 1878, were to finance new industrial enterprise.

Thus imports from the factories of Europe and the United
States, while displacing certain older trades, introduced novel wants
and techniques which in time built new industries. Industrialization
was further assisted by continued purchase from abroad of those
materials and types of equipment which were necessary to the operation of such industries but still beyond Japan's technical capacities.
The expansive effects of manufactured imports far exceeded their
competitive displacement, if we look at Japanese industry as a
whole.

This expansive stimulus is especially noteworthy in view of the
lack of tariff protection throughout the Meiji era. Until 1899
Japan's import tariff was limited to 5% by treaties with the Western
powers. Only thereafter was it raised selectively on numerous products. Even then the metallurgical and military industries continued
to rely heavily on government buying and other types of official
patronage. On the other hand, the new cotton industry displayed

very early the ability to stand on its own feet. Especially where coarse, low-quality goods were concerned, it quickly won a competitive position. Already by 1885 more cotton cloth was being produced than imported. With factory techniques already highly elaborated, and readily assimilable, the cotton industry was established far more readily in Japan than in England, even though the early British manufacturers were given a virtual monopoly of the home market by an embargo placed on imports of printed cottons from the East after 1700.[11] Numerous other, smaller Japanese industries likewise demonstrated a marked resilience in the face of foreign competition, especially where they were able to make simple improvements in equipment and marketing organization. Cheap skilled labor, together with the individuality and variety of domestic consumer tastes, enabled them to survive and even expand, just as many German handicrafts were able to withstand the competition of machine-made goods well into the nineteenth century.

One reason for the speed with which Japan turned to capitalistic techniques was the fact that modern devices for transport could be imported almost immediately along with machinery and large-scale methods for factory production. Earlier, in England, France, and the United States, the Industrial Revolution had to pass through two stages of transport. The first was the era of roads and canals; the second the era of railway and steamship. This delayed its start and protracted its advance. The turnpikes and canals built between 1750 and 1850 were a great improvement in themselves, serving to extend the market in a manner essential to the rise of the factory system. But they were as nothing compared with the widening of horizons and the cheapening of freight costs which followed from the introduction of the steam engine, the screw propeller, and the iron rail.

The Japan of 1868 was a society in which wheeled vehicles of any description were uncommon. It was not even in the "horse and buggy" stage. Even the lowly ricksha was a significant innovation of the first few years. Yet in a generation or two the Japanese were

---

[11] The difference is illustrated by a passage from an English *Parliamentary History* of the time, quoted by Paul Mantoux: "As the law now stands, no printed cotton, other than the manufacture of Britain, can be worn in this Kingdom. The wear of all others is forbidden by positive statute. The cotton therefore enjoys a monopoly over the whole island; the law admits no rival to it." *The Industrial Revolution in the Eighteenth Century*, New York, 1928, p. 262. Some smuggling of Indian prints seems nevertheless to have continued through the eighteenth century in response to the insistent demand. G. Von Schulze-Gaevernitz describes the founding of a "Patriotic Society" in Edinburgh in 1775, with the purpose of urging men to boycott ladies so depraved as to wear cottons from India. *The Cotton Trade in England and on the Continent*, London, 1895, p. 21. Japanese protectionism never reached such patriotic heights.

able to reorganize much of their life on an entirely new framework of mobility provided by a national network of railways and steam shipping. This in turn was linked with the outside world by means of ocean fleets which afforded the inestimable asset of cheap water transport directly to and from Japan's tidewater industrial centers. Machine technology thus came in to provide the tools for rapid unification of the home market and its ready extension abroad. This mobility created great cities at the nodes and terminals of commerce. It knit the country together in a complex web of specialization and exchange.

Absorption of Western Technology. In stressing the catalytic effect of imports of goods, we attribute perhaps too much importance to inanimate things as carriers of ideas, as compared with influences of a more personal character. The various types of cultural contact between Japan and the West were not separable. They were woven together in a complex pattern of assimilation.

Foreign travel and study by Japanese nationals certainly played a major role. Here, as in technical education generally, the government took an active hand. In a day when technical aid to undeveloped countries has become a subject for concerted international action, it is well also to recall the contribution of the Western expert and educator in Meiji Japan. Basil Hall Chamberlain calls them "the creator of the New Japan." This is a gross exaggeration. But already by 1876, according to Griffis, some 400 foreigners had been engaged in government service. British technicians built pilot factories and trained the Navy. German advisers helped to draft the Constitution and staffed the new medical schools. A French jurist was responsible for the criminal code. Americans took a hand in everything from agricultural science to seismology. Particularly in the frontier settlement of Hokkaido, experts and teachers from the United States, led by a former U.S. Commissioner of Agriculture, left an imprint visible even today. Early imports of Western manufactures into Japan were in part simply the tools and materials of this educational process, as for example when an American geologist, Raphael Pumpelly, introduced the use of explosives in a northern lead mine.

Much recent experience in other countries shows that it is not enough to land machinery and equipment at the ports of preindustrial countries, even if political conditions are favorable for their use. Without extensive technical advice such as the Japanese secured in one way or another, these cargoes may easily rust away like so much junk. The unusual feature of Japan's experience was not her failure to draw heavily on such assistance, but the speed with which she was able to dispense with it over wide areas of technology.

Not unrepresentative was the case of shipping. When Japan's premier shipping company, the Nippon Yusen Kaisha, was organized in 1884, it employed 174 foreigners in operating its modest fleet of 74 steamers aggregating 60,000 tons. During the Sino-Japanese War the number of foreign officers rose to 224. Thereafter it declined, as the Japanese themselves learned the science and business of navigation. By 1920 not a single foreign officer was employed on a Japanese vessel.

Nor should the historical role of the Western trader be overlooked. It was the foreign merchant who pioneered the early overseas trade of modern Japan, just as foreign banks provided much of the financing, and foreign shipping lines carried most of the cargoes down to the eve of World War I. As late as 1885 only 9% of Japan's export trade was in Japanese hands. Even that was largely trade with China and Korea. British firms predominated until after the turn of the century. Thereafter Americans took over a larger proportion of the dwindling share still handled by foreign trading houses. As the Japanese gained in knowledge of Western markets and in the skills of large-scale trading and finance they steadily replaced the foreigner. By 1913 the bulk of overseas commerce was handled by Japanese firms, and half of it already moved in Japanese ships.

The import-export merchant is sometimes regarded as a rather passive link in the international exchange of goods, placing and filling orders which come his way. As the airplane and telecommunications have multiplied direct and speedy contacts between buyers and sellers this has become more largely true. But in times reaching back to the Hansards and before, and in new and unfamiliar markets even in modern days, the successful merchant has played a more positive and dynamic role.

Consider, for example, the trading firm of Frazar and Company, which has carried on a business for three generations in the Far East.[12] Capt. George Frazar, a New England Yankee, took his first ship from Boston to Canton in 1834, buying silk and tea in exchange for New England manufactures. His son, Everett Frazar, set up business in Shanghai in 1856, and later founded Frazar and Company, Yokohama. There the firm traded continuously from 1867 to 1941, first under Everett and later under his son, Everett Welles.

Frazar and Company (Sale and Frazar from 1902 to 1927) introduced a series of products into Japan which reads like a roster of American engineering achievements during the period. In 1887 it sold the Japanese their first electric light plant, a 100-h.p.

12 "Yankee Traders," *Fortune*, November 1945, pp. 132ff.

affair made by Thomas A. Edison and installed in the Imperial Palace. In 1891 it supplied Tokyo's first streetcars; later the first phonograph. Long the agent for Baldwin locomotives, E. W. Frazar met a rush order for 100 British-type locomotives to be used in Manchuria during the Russo-Japanese War, completing delivery in the record time of six months. He was given the Ford agency for Japan in 1909. To encourage business, he established a taxi company as well as a drivers' school. The school furnished a driver with each car. In 1912 he arranged for the first demonstration of a Curtiss flying boat for the Navy, and sold the plane with which Japanese naval aviation was begun. About the same time he became interested in possibilities of fish canning in Japan. This led to the development of the salmon-canning industry, which for years gave the firm a prosperous business in importing tin plate and canning equipment and exporting tinned goods to Europe and the United States. In one line after another, business died away as American manufacturers went into direct distribution, or the Japanese learned to copy the product and supply their own needs. Success therefore called for initiative and imagination, and a high degree of flexibility in seeking out new opportunities.

Fortunately for Japan this was an era in which machinery and technique were made available freely by the advanced industrial nations. The old embargoes once maintained by the town guilds and nation-states of Europe had long since been swept away by the new principles of liberal commercial policy. The triumph of Cobdenism in England, for example, was signalized in 1843 by the removal of the last vestiges of restraint upon exports of British machinery. Anyone who could make use of the secrets of Manchester or Bridgeport or Lyons was free to acquire them. All he needed was the means to pay or the credit to borrow. Indeed they might be thrust upon him by aggressive salesmen reaching out for new markets. The chief political and legal restrictions were those surrounding certain military secrets, and those embodied in international patent and copyright conventions which Japan first signed in 1899. That the latter imposed no effective obstacle to Japanese copying of foreign designs was a constant complaint of manufacturers abroad.[13]

Thus the Japanese could tap the most advanced technology of the West wherever it might serve their needs. Within the limits

[13] The change in postwar international policy and practice, even on the part of the nation most resistant to State control, is illustrated by Japan's own postwar experience in placing equipment orders in the United States. Orders for $25 million of steel-making and -finishing equipment to modernize the Japanese industry were held up in 1952 until given an official priority by U.S. government control agencies.

of their buying power they could import capital, producer goods, and technical services in whatever combination they saw fit. Among the Western nations business came first. Any misgiving as to the ultimate repercussions on established industries or national interests of building up Japan was overridden in any case by the principle of common interest in world economic development.

Not until after 1937, when the renewed aggression of the Japanese Army in China began clearly to threaten the whole structure of peace in the Far East, was this attitude substantially modified. Even then, despite the dependence of Japan's war machine on equipment and materials supplied by the West, hopes of political appeasement and a laissez-faire tradition served to confine America and Britain largely to ineffectual measures of moral pressure and unofficial boycott, until their own armament demands began in 1940 to absorb all available output. Japan thus entered the war with an aircraft industry 50% equipped with foreign-built tools, and staffed with technicians trained in American plants and engineering schools. It was the planes produced by this industry which first laid waste to China, and later killed American fighting men by the thousand.[14]

This laissez-faire philosophy seems anachronistic today, as the forces set loose in the world, so stimulated by Japanese militarism itself, have returned us to the bitter divisions, alliances, and mercantilistic practices of the seventeenth century. Even during the prewar decade it was clearly in disregard of the interests of the Western democracies and the peoples of the Far East, including the Japanese themselves. It must be recognized, however, as an essential feature of that century in world affairs which, while it culminated in two destructive world wars, also produced a most extraordinary unfolding of productive powers around the globe.

The sequence of steps in Japan's technological borrowing and assimilation after 1868 was what one would expect. As regards material things, there was first the imported product; then the copy, usually inferior in quality; then the slow improvement which came with experience. Meanwhile imports were apt to shift to finer grades

[14] The U.S. Strategic Bombing Survey offers this rueful comment: "For assistance other than financial, the Japanese aircraft industry owed more to the United States than it did to its own government. It is sad, but true, that United States fighter and bomber pilots fought against aircraft whose origins could be traced back to United States drafting boards. Many Jap engines and propellers came from American designs which had been sold under license in prewar years. Many top Jap aeronautical engineers could claim degrees from Massachusetts Institute of Technology, Stanford, and California Tech. Their best production men had served apprenticeships with Curtis, Douglas, Boeing, or Lockheed. Here and there, war-time German influence was evident, especially in the jet- and rocket-powered types that never became operational, but it can be fairly stated that the Jap fought the war with aircraft on which the strongest influences in design were American." *The Japanese Aircraft Industry*, Washington, 1947, p. 4.

and specialties, or perhaps to be replaced entirely. The Japanese imitation, whether a fabric or a tool or a chemical, tended often to be shoddy. Usually, too, it was made with great waste of labor, judged by Western standards. Sometimes this reflected ineptness and inexperience, or, in the case of something like the automobile, the lack of a market sufficiently large to support an industry requiring massive investment.

Often, however, what the Westerner judged inferior was economically efficient, in that it represented an adaptation to Japanese conditions. Such conditions included a perennial shortage of capital and advanced managerial skills; also a level of buying power both at home and in neighboring Far Eastern markets which put products of Western quality quite beyond the reach of the people. This sometimes led, for example, to the use of materials which would be rejected as worthless in the West, as in the weaving of blankets out of old rags. Technical progress tended naturally to follow the line of least resistance. It adapted itself to the nature of the market, the level of skills, and available resources.

Many stories have been told of blind imitation by the Japanese —from the factory with the sawtooth roof facing the wrong way for the light, to the tailor who copied the Western suit of clothes even to the patch on the pants. They recall the older tale that even Hideyoshi wore a rosary and a crucifix in the fashion of his times. At the other extreme is the brilliant success of the Toyoda automatic loom. In 1929 rights to the manufacture and European sale of this Japanese loom were acquired by Platt Brothers, of Oldham, England. Japanese experts were dispatched to instruct the Platt engineers in its construction. Here the Industrial Revolution came full circle. For in cotton textiles it began with the tastes developed in England by the purchase of muslins and prints from India. Then came the rise of Lancashire to world preeminence in the century after 1750; its subsequent displacement in Asiatic markets by indigenous factory products manufactured with British machinery; and now the invasion of Western markets by Japanese cotton goods and even textile machinery.

The Toyoda loom was exceptional, of course. And even this achievement depended on machine-making tools and materials from abroad. More revealing over a broad field was the pitting of Japanese and American technologies against each other in the Pacific war. Japanese equipment often showed itself ingeniously adapted to the requirements of jungle warfare. Certain items like the Zero fighter plane were highly creditable engineering achievements. Yet in aircraft, as noted above, Japan entered the war with machinery and experience largely acquired directly from abroad in the preceding years. Even then she was one and a half to two years behind other countries in aeronautical research, and another year behind in its application on the production line.[15]

In other advanced engineering sciences, also, Japan still had much to learn. For example, her electrical industry produced excellent equipment for power generation and industrial machinery, but was backward in radio and radar. In general her machine-tool industry was unable to compete in products of high quality and specialized design. Right up to the war high-class precision tools had to be bought from foreign toolmakers. It is significant that the boom in the Japanese machinery and equipment industries during the thirties also brought a boom in machinery imports, until they were closed off by hostilities. Domestic output now provided a wide range of staple, standard types, and far exceeded imports in gross value. But the latter still supplied a critical technological deficit which was particularly important in the equipment industries themselves.

Japan's war performance was impressive enough, as it was. She lost the struggle less from engineering backwardness than because of the limited scale of her material resources. (One reinforced the other, of course.) Nevertheless, the war again confirmed her technological lag behind the West, even in armaments, which had long been given top priority. Elsewhere in the equipment industries the gap was often still wider. Thus the need for borrowing did not cease in 1913 or 1930. It has been a continuous feature of modern Japan in her relations with the advanced industrial nations. In 1950 one of Japan's most serious postwar problems was the widespread obsolescence of her industrial plant resulting in part from her ten years' isolation from the drafting rooms and laboratories of the West.

For this reason Japan's economic contacts with Europe and the United States have been much more vital to her industrialization than the trade values alone would suggest. Without continued access to the pools of science and engineering concentrated in the West her trade with Asia could never have reached large proportions. Indeed her whole industrial development would have languished, if it had ever gotten under way at all.

From the standpoint of her Western competitors, on the other hand, the record shows that their high wage levels and marketing costs continued to be offset in many lines by superior efficiency in labor, equipment, and business enterprise. Japan gained on the West, as the borrowing and absorption of technical skills narrowed competitive differences in manufacturing costs. But she continued

[15] *ibid.*, p. 90.

to offer a profitable market for industrial equipment, and of course a much larger, steadily growing market for industrial materials of all sorts. The Japanese case supplies no conclusive answer to the question whether, on economic grounds alone, the dispersion of industrial techniques around the world serves to reduce or increase the importance of international trade in relation to total world production.

The Growth of Exports. One familiar contribution of international trade to economic development is thus dramatically illustrated in the case of Japan. It afforded a ready avenue for the introduction of new wants and new techniques from the advanced industrial nations of the West. All newly developing countries have borrowed heavily in this fashion, and Japan differs from others mainly in the speed and scale of her assimilation.

More positively, foreign trade may serve also to *activate* technological change. For growing exports may generate new income and employment, and stimulate the application of modern science, machinery, and administrative skills in the industries affected. Such innovations in traditional ways of doing things require not only knowledge of new methods, but also the impulse to change. The stimulus must be strong enough to break the cake of custom and to induce individuals in considerable numbers to venture into new and untried activities. In Meiji Japan this impulse drew its strength from various sources, both economic and political. Indeed, it was gathering strength long before the arrival of Perry. A fresh incentive was added after 1858, however, in the profitable opportunities which soon developed for the export of Japanese goods to foreign markets. To seize and develop these opportunities required the modernization of transport, finance, and marketing organization, as well as production methods within Japan. Since exports were essential to finance the imports required for national defense and development, the fostering of these changes became an important object of State policy and received strong encouragement from the government.

Earlier, in Chapter 4, the growth of market demand and technological change in Japan were discussed in relation to each other. The distinguishing feature of modern capitalism is production for the market. Only as a large and steady outlet can be developed for manufactures of more or less standardized design does it become economical to concentrate production in large establishments, to introduce machinery, and otherwise to apply capitalistic methods.

Export markets offer no peculiar advantage in this respect, except perhaps as competition abroad may be more severe than at home, leading to improved methods and lowered costs. As a matter of fact, they are likely to be attended with added risks and difficulties. Usually profit expectations must be especially high in order to attract investment. The two premier industrial powers of the modern world—the United States and the Soviet Union—have developed great industries with only slight dependence on markets outside their territorial frontiers. Where a country is small, however, or too poor to afford a market large enough to support an industry at optimum size, the stimulus to technical progress coming from expansion abroad may play an important role. And even where the internal market is potentially large, the successful cultivation of an export trade may hasten its development. It will pay for needed imports, and help to foster the accumulation of capital and technical skills.

The direct effect of a developing foreign market on industrial technology depends upon the size and character of the foreign demand, as well as the economic setting and technical characteristics of the industry itself. No simple generalization will hold true. For example, the world demand for French luxury wares which embody the traditions of fine workmanship long prized by the French themselves has tended to preserve the handicraft techniques and small-scale organization of large sectors of their industry. Similarly, in the modern Far East the opening up of world trading contacts through improved transport and marketing systems has created a large export trade in products like wool rugs, bristles, and linen embroideries with little alteration in traditional methods of production. On the other hand, the effects upon technology will be quite different where the latent export opportunity requires far-reaching changes if it is to be exploited, and where conditions are ripe for such changes.

England is the classic case where industries with important export branches pioneered the Industrial Revolution in no small degree. This occurred first in the woolen industry, and after 1750 in cotton, textiles, pottery, and iron manufactures. It was no accident that the triumph of the factory system during the years 1750-1800 coincided with a 200% increase in the tonnage of merchant shipping clearing English ports. Lancashire grew with Liverpool. Yet British exports played a strategic role in the industrial changes of the period not so much because they were large in volume, relative to those of France and Holland, as because they came to comprise staple goods of mass consumption which were adaptable to machine manufacture. Products like cotton cloth, wrought iron, and Wedgwood's "useful" (as distinguished from "ornamental") pottery were in growing demand at home, as the revolution in British agriculture, transport, and industry widened the domestic market.

The technical improvements thus stimulated led also to a growing export business in Europe and the colonies. Export opportunities in turn reinforced the expansion of the home market, and advanced steadily in importance through the nineteenth century.

In Japan similar tendencies set in following the Meiji Restoration. The consequences for the modernization and growth of Japanese industry are worthy of study. It must be confessed that no simple and clear-cut conclusions can be reached, since the effects of growing foreign and domestic markets are not readily distinguishable. For most Japanese industries the export market played a subordinate role throughout the prewar decades. Also, it tended to absorb goods not essentially dissimilar in character from those widely consumed at home. The pattern varied widely from industry to industry, however, and the total impact of world demand in intensifying the rate of Japanese industrialization was highly significant.

First, we shall characterize briefly the early growth of exports, and more particularly the quantitative importance they came to assume in relation to national output. Having gained some perspective in this regard, one is in a better position to judge the significance of the foreign market in Japan's industrial progress. The problem—and it is not a simple one—is to make this significance clear, without exaggerating the role of trade in the total process of Japanese development.

The Expanding Foreign Market. With the forcing of Japan's closed door, and the opening of a number of ports under the treaties of 1858, her export trade entered upon a period of expansion which continued almost without interruption for eighty years. Through the Meiji era (1868-1911) shipments overseas doubled in volume, more or less, during each decade. It must be remembered, however, that they began almost at zero. By the turn of the century they had already reached an annual value of 200 million yen—a sizable amount though still only a small part of total Japanese production.

As one would expect, exports consisted at first of a variety of foodstuffs and industrial materials. Mostly they came from traditional occupations employing relatively simple handicraft methods. Among them were tea, dried fish, and seaweed; copper, gold, silver, and coal from newly developed mines; camphor, sulphur, and vegetable wax; and wood and straw products like matches, braids, and matting. By far the largest item, however, was raw silk. This one item accounted for 40% of the value of all Japan's exports during the first quarter century of the Meiji period, 1868-93.

These miscellaneous foods and materials found an export market chiefly in China and other nearby countries of Asia. The important exceptions were silk, tea, mats, and straw braids, which went mainly to Europe and the United States. In the West, too, were sold a wide variety of handicraft wares in which Japanese artisans had long excelled—silk textiles, pottery, lacquerware, fans, umbrellas, etc. Naturally enough, exports were chiefly things widely used in Japan as well. For such products the materials were at hand and the skills well developed. Japan's experience in this regard was quite like that of many other countries, especially those which lack the resources to develop great surpluses of minerals or farm products for export.

Production methods in most of these trades were little influenced at first by the opening of a foreign market. The export business tended to be confined to particular regions accessible to the principal ports. Moreover, the products of the craft industries of Kyoto or Tokyo depended for their appeal on individual design and workmanship. They continued to be fashioned in small shops by traditional methods.

In the mining of coal and copper, where exports added to the stimulus of expanding domestic requirements, output could not keep pace with demand without the modernization of equipment and skills. The mere introduction of mechanical water pumps to replace hand bailing in the copper mines, for example, was a revolutionary advance in this 1,000-year-old industry. It paved the way for much larger exports of unfabricated copper. More generally, however, because of the nature of the products as well as the lack of capital and knowledge, Japan's early export industries relied largely upon handicraft processes long familiar to her farmers and artisans. She had no extensive, undeveloped areas of land, or rich oil fields and mineral deposits, to exploit for export purposes on a large scale. Nor was the creation of great factory industries to be accomplished in a generation.

More important was the early influence of a developing foreign market upon commercial organization, and indirectly upon transport and finance. It was particularly in the export branches of certain industries that a trend appeared toward a larger scale of organization. This might be the small factory replacing the workshop. More often it was first the rise of the wholesale merchant to a position of increasing responsibility. When Japanese ports were first opened, exports of even small quantities of tea, copper, or silk created severe shortages and a steep rise in prices. The supply was quite inelastic, being geared to localized markets. The first requirement was to widen the marketing area. This led in turn to expansion and improvement of output.

The foreign market in particular required orders in bulk, standardization of quality, and certainty of delivery. To establish the necessary contacts called for knowledge and capital as well as initiative. It is interesting to note that foreign merchants, who dominated the Japanese tea trade for forty years or more, early developed the practice of employing thousands of workers to recure the tea in port cities before shipment abroad. This was hardly typical; but in Japan, as earlier in the West, the natural tendency was for the merchant to extend his control into the realm of production. There he came to furnish materials, to finance the process, and to take delivery of the commodity for distribution through successive stages of marketing. This development had already occurred in response to the growth of domestic commerce in Tokugawa times; now it received a fresh impetus. Some industries passed on to large-scale factory organization in later decades. Many of them, even in the export trade, remained organized predominantly along workshop lines. (See Chapter 4.)

The raw silk industry is the outstanding case of a traditional Japanese industry transformed in scale, and to a lesser extent in production methods, by the opening of a foreign market. Aided by the building of the Suez Canal, and the sudden outbreak of silkworm disease in France and Italy, Japanese silk won a foothold in both Europe and the United States during the seventies. Its supply was readily expansible. It required chiefly an abundant supply of seasonal farm labor, and did not compete seriously for land with rice and other food crops. The demand in the West for silk yarn rose steadily, first for the weaving of fabrics, and later for knitting full-fashioned hosiery.

The growth of the silk trade was almost uninterrupted for the next half century. To satisfy the demands of American weaving and hosiery mills for uniform, high-grade yarn, however, it was necessary to improve the quality of the product, from the silkworm egg on through to the bale of silk. In sericulture this meant the introduction of scientific methods of breeding and disease control; in reeling it stimulated the shift to large filatures equipped with machinery; in marketing it led to large-scale organization in the collection and sale of cocoons and raw silk.

The success of Japanese merchants and filature-owners in these technical improvements, assisted as they were by the government, enabled Japanese silk to triumph in competition with silk from China, the traditional home of the industry. Clearly the foreign market afforded the chief impetus to technological change in this instance. It absorbed at least half of Japan's annual output throughout the prewar decades, usually as much as 65 to 80%. And it exerted steady pressure in favor of the application of science, machinery, and modern business enterprise.

In contrast to silk, most of Japan's early factory products of Western style were sold in the home market. This was true, for example, of cotton yarn, paper, ships, machinery, cement, glass, beer, and flour. Originating as rather poor imitations of foreign goods, these products were too inferior in quality and limited in quantity to interest the foreign buyer. Initially most of them required a good deal of State assistance and patronage even to enable them to survive Western competition in the Japanese market.

By 1895 the new cotton industry was firmly established, and cotton yarn began to be sold abroad, mainly in China and adjacent regions. Exports of coarse cotton cloth, as well as other miscellaneous manufactures, soon followed in growing amounts. It was the expanding domestic market, however, which continued through the Meiji era to afford the chief stimulus to industrial growth. Here the framework of a national economy established in the earlier decades was now further enlarged by population increase, and by improvements in agriculture, transport, and commercial organization. An inflationary stimulus was added by two successful wars and a rising level of armament expenditure. Even in cotton textiles, where Japanese exports tripled in volume from 1900 to 1913, nearly half of the total increase in production went into home consumption. (See page 31.)

On these industrial foundations there now developed an export trade in cheap manufactures which grew steadily in volume, diversity, and geographical reach through the years. Especially powerful was the thrust of Japanese goods into new markets during the years 1915-19, when Europe's energies were absorbed in war. Again after 1931 came a second spurt, following the collapse of the yen in the Great Depression. Textiles continued through these decades to furnish the bulk of Japan's exports, both to Asia and to the West. In 1933, as in 1913, they accounted for nearly 60% of all shipments to foreign countries, Korea, and Formosa. By this latter date, however, Japan was also selling abroad substantial amounts of metal goods and machinery; foodstuffs like flour, refined sugar, and canned fish; chemicals and drugs; and miscellaneous consumer goods made of wood, paper, rubber, celluloid, etc.

Taken altogether, Japanese exports of manufactures far outstripped those of most other industrial nations in *rate of growth* over the first three decades of the century. Indeed, world exports of manufactured goods increase only 20% in physical volume from 1901-05 to 1931-35. By comparison Japan's rose 600% in volume, although in value they still comprised no more than one sixteenth of the world total at the end of the period.[16] Tables 29 and 30, below, show the rapid growth in manufactures relative to other exports, and the resulting shift in the composition of the Japanese export trade.

Exports and National Output. To explore at length the direct influence of a growing foreign market upon various sectors of the Japanese economy would plunge one into the details of scores of industries. In no two was the pattern the same. Even within a single industry wide differences prevailed in the importance of exports, and the influence of foreign demand on technology. We shall conclude this chapter with a brief characterization of Japan's prewar position, in over-all terms, leaving to the chapter which follows some further discussion of particular industries.

In merely quantitative terms, prewar Japan remained less dependent on foreign markets than is often supposed.[17] Overseas commerce, vital as it might be in supplying certain essentials of economic life, absorbed a comparatively small fraction of Japanese production as a whole in payment. This was especially true in the early decades, of course. But it remained true through a half century of industrial and commercial development, after Japanese goods and traders had become a familiar sight all over the world.

The total value of merchandise exports in relation to Japan's national output of goods and services has been noted earlier in this chapter. By 1910 it had reached 15%, so far as one can judge by the statistics. Thereafter export values rose more rapidly in boom times, and slumped more rapidly in depression. On the average they maintained a ratio a little under 1:5. From 1910 to 1938 the figure is actually 18%. This was three times the comparable ratio for the United States in the interwar years. It was similar to that for Britain and other industrial nations heavily dependent on world commerce.

---

[16] Data from League of Nations, *Industrialization and Foreign Trade*, Geneva, 1945, app. B, tables VII, IX, XI. "Manufactures" are defined according to the International "Brussels" Classification of 1913, Group IV. They include textile yarns, but exclude certain other semimanufactures as well as manufactured foodstuffs. As trade tabulations according to the Brussels system are not available except for a limited period, mainly the late 1920's and 1930's, the League had to use national classifications for other years, assuming that the fairly stable relationship of these national figures to those for the Brussels Group in the later years prevailed earlier as well. The method used to eliminate price variations was also quite crude, so that the comparisons given above are only approximate at best. As the League excludes Japanese trade with Korea and Formosa, I have increased its figure for Japanese exports of manufactures in 1931-35 by 25% to cover shipments to the colonies.

[17] The reader should be reminded that the trade statistics cited here refer generally to the overseas trade of Japan Proper (including Karafuto), and include her trade with Korea, Formosa, and the Kwantung Leased Territory as well as trade with foreign countries.

Interestingly enough, no upward trend is clearly discernible after 1915. Though the national product estimates are none too reliable, they at least give no evidence of any substantial increase in the export/output value ratio. Probably a larger share of commodity output came to be exported. But this appears to have been largely offset by the growing importance of nonexportable services in Japanese economic life.

These exports, moreover, did not all represent a net sum of values created in Japan out of Japanese labor and resources and producing net receipts to the full amount when sold abroad. Some 20 to 30% of their gross value now represented (1) imported materials reexported in the form of processed manufactures, or (2) exports which were otherwise offset by imports of the same or similar commodities. For example, as much as 60% or more of the manufacturing cost of typical cotton cloth exports represented imported raw cotton. Only the balance provided foreign exchange to pay for other imports available for domestic use. Again, while Japan exported some coal, lumber, and fish and vegetable oils, she also imported these products (usually different types) for home consumption. Any true picture of the *net* share of exports in her national output must take account of these intricate interrelationships between commodities moving in and out of the country.

Fortunately this laborious task has been accomplished for the years 1930-38 in a valuable study to which frequent reference has already been made. This is *The Place of Foreign Trade in the Japanese Economy*, begun in the U.S. Office of Strategic Services and completed in the Department of State under the direction of Arthur B. Hersey. Here the statistics of Japan's trade with foreign countries, Korea, and Formosa are first combined, item by item, and then related in various ways to the structure of production and consumption in the country. A principal objective is to make the distinction mentioned above, i.e., to distinguish export values which embody or offset related imports from those "originated" values which are created within Japan. The line cannot be drawn sharply in the case of many raw materials. It can hardly be drawn at all in the case of machinery and equipment used in export industries. But the principal materials can be allocated sufficiently to illuminate this important and little-understood aspect of Japan's trading dependence.

Table 28 classifies Japan's exports in 1930 according to these principles. Gross exports to foreign and Empire markets totalled 1,828 million yen. Nearly one quarter, however, represented the value of imports embodied in export manufactures, or imports substantially similar to certain exports. Net receipts ("originated" ex-

Table 28. *Gross and "Originated" Exports of Japan Proper to Foreign Countries, Korea, and Formosa, 1930*[a]

| | GROSS EXPORTS (MILLIONS OF YEN) | | | EXPORTS OFFSET BY IMPORTS | IMPORTS USED IN EXPORTS | ORIGINATED EXPORTS, COLS. 1—(4+5) |
	Total (1)	*To Foreign Countries* (2)	*To Korea and Formosa* (3)	(4)	(5)	(6)
All exports	1,828	1,435	393	161	296	1,371
Agricultural produce and fish[b]	109	67	42	59	—	50
Products of industries using mainly domestic materials[c]	825	720	105	90	19	716
Raw silk	423	423	—	28	—	396
Silk manufactures	78	73	5[d]	—	—	78
Agricultural products, processed[e]	75	60	15	6	17	52
Minerals, metals and manufactures[f]	136	107	28	26	—	110
Chemicals	66	33	32	13	2	51
Other[g]	47	22	25	17	—	30
Products of industries dependent mainly on imported materials[c]	894	648	246	12	277	605
Cotton[h]	385	325	60	4	172	210
Other textiles[h]	165	117	48	—	19	146
Metal manufactures and machinery[i]	150	66	84	—	18	132
Paper	47	33	14	4	6[j]	37
Foodstuffs (sugar and flour)	58	42	16	2	43	13
Other[k]	89	65	24	2	19	68

a Compiled from U.S. Department of State, *The Place of Foreign Trade in the Japanese Economy*, Washington, 1946, vol. I, passim; vol. II, tables 17-23. Gross export totals by classes here differ slightly from those in this report, vol. II, tables 18, 20, in that nonferrous metals other than semifinished copper are shifted here from the class of domestic-material industry to import-dependent industry. Included are all exports of Japan Proper (including Okinawa and Karafuto), except for trade with the Pacific islands mandate and all reexports. Korean and Formosan trade is from the trade returns of the colonies themselves, which introduces a slight element of noncomparability. Intercolonial trade is excluded from the colonial trade statistics, but not commodities in transit through Japan between foreign countries and colonies.

b Gross exports of wheat, beans, and rice (30 million yen) were entirely offset by imports, which exceeded exports. Exports of tobacco were largely offset, and fish exports (other than canned fish) to the extent of 25 out of 34 million yen. Originated exports were chiefly (in millions of yen): fish, 9; tea, 9; vegetables, fruits, and nuts, 14. Fresh and salt fish exports to Korea are excluded.

c For a definition of this class, see text.

d Omits small shipments of silk textiles to Formosa, which are included with other textiles.

e Canned foodstuffs and beverages account for 37 million yen of originated exports. Excluded from the table are fish exports directly from Japanese canneries in Kamchatka. Gross exports of vegetable and fish oils, fats, and waxes totalled 32 million yen but over half is deducted here to allow for imports of oilseeds and fish oils offset by exports or used in exports.

f Originated exports are mainly (in millions of yen): pottery and glass, 46; copper products, 22; electric lamps, 8; and cement and other nonmetallic mineral products. Coal exports of 26 million yen, largely to Korea, are entirely offset by imports of similar type.

g Originated exports are mainly miscellaneous wood products other than paper, totalling 27 million yen. As lumber imports exceeded exports, all lumber exports plus the lumber equivalent of exports of matches, veneers, and shooks have been offset against imports, to the amount of 17 million yen.

h For textile goods of mixed fibers the division between cotton, rayon, and other fibers is only approximate. Imported materials used in noncotton textile exports were (in millions of yen): rayon pulp and salt for rayon, 4; wool, 8; other fibers, 7. Originated exports of noncotton textiles were (in millions of yen): rayon, 46; wool, 2; flax, hemp, and other fibers, 98.

i Gross exports included 68 million yen of machinery, vehicles, clocks, and scientific instruments, and 82 million yen of other metal manufactures. Domestic production of ores and metals was insufficient for domestic requirements; therefore, these exports are regarded as dependent on imported materials, the deduction for the latter being divided about equally between iron and steel, and other metals and ores. See Table 32, note d.

j Paper pulp.

k Originated exports comprise a variety of manufactures of imported materials, including rubber products (11 million yen), oil products (7 million yen), and manufactures of leather, paper, celluloid, bristles, ivory, etc. They are probably overvalued because of failure to allow fully for imported materials.

ports) were thus no more than 1,371 million yen. Actually they were even less, for no deduction from gross exports is made for imported machinery and equipment, or fuel, or certain lesser raw materials used up in export industries. Only the principal imported materials are deducted in each case. (For further details on this classification of imports, see Table 32, below.)

Import-dependent industries furnished net export receipts to the amount of about 600 million yen, or nearly half of the total. These were industries whose chief raw material was imported in quantities at least equal to the quantities used in exports. The balance of the receipts came from industries which relied mainly on home-produced materials, or they were from largely unprocessed home products like tea and fish. (Of course, even these domestic industries were apt to require imported equipment, oil products, metals, or other foreign materials in some degree.)

One comparison stands out very strikingly here. Cotton goods nearly equal raw silk in gross export value by this time. But net export receipts from cotton goods are scarcely one half of the receipts from raw silk, after the cost of imported raw cotton is deducted. This originated export value, i.e., the value added by manufacture, is a much more significant measure of their true contribution both to

Japanese national income and to financing the import requirements of the home market.

For the years 1930, 1936, and 1938 Japan's net export receipts on commodity account may be compared with the total net value of goods and services produced within the country as follows:[18]

	1930	*1936*	*1938*
	MILLIONS OF YEN		
Net national product	10,224	15,779	20,682
Merchandise exports			
Gross value	1,828	3,508	3,909
Net receipts	1,371	2,427	3,048
	PERCENT		
Net export receipts ÷ national product	13.4	15.4	14.7

If the years 1927-36 be taken as fairly representative of Japan's prewar peacetime economy, it appears that about 15% of the net value of her domestic output was normally exported to foreign and Empire markets *in the form of commodities*. Exports averaged about 2,400 million yen over the ten-year period. Net export receipts probably came to approximately 1,800 million yen, after allowance for the share of total export values which embodied or offset imported materials. Net receipts from commodity exports were thus about one seventh of net national product, which averaged 12,000 million yen according to the best estimates available.

In addition, some of the services currently performed with Japanese labor and capital were "exported." They took the form mainly of foreign purchases of shipping space and insurance provided by Japanese concerns, and services purchased in Japan by tourists, diplomats, and other nonresidents of the home islands. Minor amounts of home-produced goods were also sold to nonresidents in Japan and foreign shipping companies, although they were not classified as exports in the trade returns. These categories of "exports" cannot be estimated statistically. For the international accounts of Japan prior to 1939 are not available except on all-Empire basis and do not record transactions between the home islands and the colonies.[19]

[18] Export values are taken from U.S. Department of State, *The Place of Foreign Trade in the Japanese Economy*, Washington, 1946, vol. I, p. 18. For net national product I have used the estimates of the Department of State in *National Income of Japan*, Washington, 1945, p. 86. They run 5 to 10% below those of Yamada cited earlier.

[19] A balance of payments for Japan Proper in 1936 was published by the International Monetary Fund in *Balance of Payments Yearbook, 1938, 1946, 1947*, Wash-

The likelihood is that all such sales to nonresidents of Japan Proper during the decade 1927-36 would be adequately covered if the sum of 450 million yen were added to the 1,800 million yen already given for annual net receipts from recorded commodity exports.[20]

We may conclude that the total value of goods and services originated in Japan Proper and exported to foreign countries and Empire markets averaged annually no more than 2,250 million yen in the period 1927-36. This was a little less than 20% of her entire net national output of all types. Probably this ratio may be taken as representative of the over-all dependence on foreign and Empire markets attained by Japan in prewar, peacetime days. For every yen of goods and services produced and sold overseas (or to nonresidents in Japan) over 4 yen's worth was produced and sold at home to residents of the home islands.

The export production ratio of 20% for the prewar Japanese economy as a whole conceals wide variations, of course, among particular industries and occupations. Moreover, it relates only to the

---

ington, 1949, pp. 244-45. However, this fails to give an adequate accounting of current invisible transactions between Japan and the colonies. Evidently the all-Empire debits and credits were merely adjusted by adding the *net* balances for investment income, tourist expenditures, and other net remittances between Japan and Korea and Formosa. These net balances, moreover, are crude estimates—by Frank M. Tamagna, as published in *The Place of Foreign Trade in the Japanese Economy*, cited, vol. II, pp. 121-23. They may contain a wide margin of error.

[20] Total inpayments in the international accounts of the Japanese Empire on the score of freight and insurance services, tourist and missionary expenditures, government receipts, and other current invisibles (excluding investment income) averaged 469 million yen a year from 1927 to 1936. (E. B. Schumpeter, ed., *The Industrialization of Japan and Manchukuo, 1930-1940*, New York, 1940, appendix, table IA.) To arrive at sales to foreigners of services produced in Japan Proper, or produced by concerns domiciled in Japan, various corrections must be made. For example, the above figure includes over 100 million yen of marine freight and insurance receipts on imports into Japan which were carried on Japanese ships and insured by Japanese companies. These services were actually paid for by *Japanese*, not foreigners. They are included as a credit in the balance of payments only to offset their inclusion as a debit item in the commodity account, i.e., as an element in the cost of merchandise imports, which are valued on a c.i.f. basis. The above total also includes a small share of services contributed by individuals and companies domiciled in the colonies. Probably the actual receipts in Japan Proper from what might be regarded as home-produced services sold to nonresident foreigners did not exceed 300 million yen a year.

Japan's receipts from the export of services to the colonies were probably smaller. Certainly this was true of freights and insurance on her exports. The value of Japanese goods carried to the colonies in Japanese ships was little more than a third of the value of the goods they carried abroad, and the haul was much shorter. In any case, the value of exports to the colonies as given above is the delivered value. It already includes freight and insurance. Concerning other services sold to persons domiciled in the colonies we are very much in the dark. In arriving at the above figure of 450 million yen they have been put arbitrarily at no more than 150 million yen.

later years when industrialization was already well advanced. Chapter 7 therefore examines more closely the position in each major sector of economic activity. This will give a clearer impression of the extent to which the stimulus and opportunity for modernization and growth came directly from the foreign market, and were now associated with the overseas demand for Japanese production.

CHAPTER 7

FOREIGN TRADE AND ECONOMIC GROWTH—II

WHILE no aspect of modern Japan has been more commonplace than her dependence on overseas trade, a good deal of misunderstanding yet exists concerning the precise extent and character of this dependence in prewar years. More often than not the importance in Japanese development of the foreign market—particularly the Asiatic market—is exaggerated.

For this reason the present chapter is devoted to the somewhat laborious task of characterizing more fully the role of overseas trade in the prewar economic development of Japan. Here we pass on from the function of imports as a carrier of modern technology, and the over-all significance of exports, to more specific measurements of trade in relation to output and consumption. The reader not concerned with these details may wish to proceed directly to the concluding section. Here is stressed the critical importance for Japan of the circumstance that she was able to industrialize within the framework of an expanding world economy organized on the basis of global, multilateral trade.

Export Dependence and Stimulus

The Service Industries: Shipping. In Japan, as in all countries, the service occupations have always been geared mainly to the domestic market, except as they are required for the production and movement of commodities in foreign trade. They include a wide variety of functions: land and water transport, telecommunications, banking, wholesale and retail trade, hotels and restaurants, the private professions, and various government activities. Together they accounted for as much as 40 to 50% of Japan's prewar production, when the latter is apportioned among different industrial categories in terms of the market values placed on their net outputs. (Table 38, below.)

Indirectly, many of these service trades depended importantly on overseas commerce. The export industries and the whole import-export business required the services of railways, lawyers and accountants, banks, shipping and trading firms. In certain fields the early stimulus to introducing new techniques was directly associated with foreign trade. For example, one of Japan's premier banks, the Yokohama Specie Bank, founded in 1880, was developed mainly to handle foreign exchange operations overseas. In the raw silk industry it was the American and European demand which gave the chief impetus to the improving commercial organization, and storage and transport facilities. And the home demand for almost all such services fluctuated with general business conditions in Japan as affected by commodity exports. But most services by their very nature could not be exported directly in any large degree. They were marketed at home. The same thing was true of the construction industry, whether it built ports, factories, or dwellings. Here, as in most of the service trades, the foreign market only indirectly exerted a significant influence on the growth of output and the modernization of technology.

The shipping industry was the chief exception to this rule. Immediately following the Meiji Restoration, the Japanese government took steps to lay the foundations for a modern merchant marine as an instrument of military and commercial policy. After a series of initial ventures the way was paved for rapid development with the formation in 1884-85 of the State-sponsored Nippon Yusen Kaisha and Osaka Shoshen Kaisha, destined to become two of the great shipping firms of the world. Each war which followed gave a fresh impetus to expansion, and demonstrated the military importance of a merchant fleet. Meanwhile the growth of Japanese trade steadily enlarged the opportunity for profitable peacetime operations.

Beginning at first on the near seas routes, Japanese steamship lines rapidly extended the range of their activities. In home waters, with the aid of foreign officers and the shipbuilders from the Clyde, they progressively displaced the small junks and other sailing craft which carried most of the coastal traffic in the early decades. (See above, page 106.) Abroad, too, they forged ahead until, following the shipping boom of World War I, Japan emerged in fourth place among the world's maritime nations. Henceforth her mercantile marine carried two thirds or more of her own overseas trade. It bid for an increasing share of the traffic on every major shipping route around the globe except the North Atlantic. By the end of 1936, it comprised a registered merchant fleet of 4,988,000 gross tons.[1] Some 2,964,000 tons comprised ocean-going steam and motor vessels of 3,000 tons or more. While financial assistance from the government had contributed to Japan's rise as a maritime power,

---

[1] Vessels of over 20 gross tons, all types, registered in Japan Proper. This does not include (a) vessels registered in Korea, Formosa, and Manchukuo, 370,860 tons; or (b) unregistered vessels of 5 to 20 tons in the Empire, 681,000 tons. Imperial Cabinet, Bureau of Statistics, *Nippon Teikoku Tōkei Nenkan*, no. 58, Tokyo, 1939, pp. 217-18. For an index of the growth of the total shipping tonnage of Japan Proper from 1885 to 1938, see above, Table 5.

geographic and economic advantages lay at the root of her success in international competition. Even without subsidies, Japanese costs in merchant ship construction and operation were now among the lowest in the world. (Government encouragements to shipping are discussed more fully in Chapter 10.)

In paying her way abroad Japan came to depend heavily on her overseas shipping industry. Shipping services sold to foreigners (outside the Empire) averaged 127 million yen a year in gross receipts from 1927 to 1936. This put the merchant marine well up in the rank of export industries. In addition, Japanese ships assisted still further in foreign trade by carrying 63% of the imports purchased by Japan from foreign countries (as compared with 73% of her exports). They also carried virtually all of her colonial trade. Net shipping receipts from abroad in the Empire's international balance of payments, i.e., the surplus of inpayments over outpayments, alone financed its average annual merchandise trade deficit of 131 million yen through this period.[2] They came close to doing so for the entire interwar period. (See Table 21, above.)

What part of the gross receipts of the Japanese merchant marine now came from the sale of its services in foreign countries and colonies is impossible to say. In any case this would fail to reflect its real dependence on overseas trade and travel. For the latter included the carrying of imports purchased by Japanese, as well as of Japanese passengers.

In actual cargo tonnage hauled, the shipping industry remained largely a home industry. One of Japan's great economic assets was the fact that she would rely on cheap, water transport for so much of her internal movement of bulky commodities; her railways concentrated mainly on short-haul freight and passengers. Of all the water-borne cargo entering the ports of the home islands during the years 1930-37, only about 27% (by weight) represented foreign

[2] "Shipping services sold to foreigners (outside the Empire)" include freight receipts on Japanese exports carried to foreign countries in Japanese vessels, receipts on goods carried between foreign countries, receipts from foreign passengers, and receipts from foreign charterage of Japanese vessels. They exclude receipts on Japanese imports carried in Japanese ships and foreign ship expenditures in Japanese ports, and carry no deduction for the expenditures of Japanese shipping companies in foreign countries. "Net shipping receipts" in the balance of payments include all such shipping transactions, as this is the significant figure in relation to the merchandise trade deficit. Even freight receipts on imports are properly included here, although paid by Japanese, since they also appear in the c.i.f. valuation of imports and increase the recorded trade deficit by so much. The term "Japanese" in this footnote refers to the Empire, including Korea, Formosa, and Nanyo (the Mandated Islands). Balance of payments data are from E. B. Schumpeter, ed., *The Industrialization of Japan and Manchukuo, 1930-1940*, New York, 1940, appendix, tables IA and III. Figures on the carrying trade are from Department of Finance, *Financial and Economic Annual of Japan*, no. 38 (1938), Tokyo, 1939, pp. 174-75.

and colonial trade. Three out of every four tons was moving from one Japanese port to another. The overseas share of outbound cargoes was even smaller, about 14%. Total cargoes entering and clearing Japanese ports during 1930-37 were distributed as follows (annual average, in millions of metric tons) :[3]

	Total	Foreign	Colonial	Coastwise and Interisland
In all vessels	193.5	32.7	8.3	152.4
In Japanese vessels	183.6	31.2		152.4

Foreign and colonial trade, however, was a good deal more important for the Japanese shipping industry than is indicated by its 21% share of total cargo tonnage. For overseas shipping involved longer and faster hauls, and higher receipts per ton of goods and passengers. It occupied much more than a fifth of the entire merchant marine, especially the bigger and more modern ships.

In 1933-34, for example, Japan's merchant fleet totalled 4,-680,000 gross tons of vessels 20 tons or larger. About 1,500,000 tons was employed in coastwise shipping, nearly half of it small sailing and auxiliary vessels. Another 1,500,000 tons, approximately, was engaged in near seas traffic with Korea, Formosa, and the Soviet Far East, and along the China coast. These ships were mostly ocean-going tramps and liners of 2,000 tons or more. The remainder, about 1,700,000 tons of still larger vessels, was engaged in the distant carrying trade with southern Asia, Australia, Europe, and the Americas.[4] By 1933, in other words, these ocean routes occupied over one third of Japan's mercantile fleet, as compared with

[3] Cargo tonnage carried by vessels of all nationalities is based on estimates of the U.S. Department of State in *Japan's Shipping and Shipbuilding Position, 1928-36,* Washington, 1948, pp. 9-10, 27. These estimates assume the ratio of intra-Empire and foreign trade tonnage to have been the same in 1930-34 as in 1934-37. Foreign trade is converted from weight-volume to metric tons at 2,380 lbs. per weight-volume ton. The share of Japanese vessels in the weight-volume tonnage of foreign and colonial trade during 1928-37 is given by the U.S. Tariff Commission in *The Shipping Industry of Japan,* Washington, 1945, p. 5. Here it is assumed to be the same in metric tons during 1930-37. Coastwise trade was monopolized by Japanese firms.

[4] Coastwise shipping tonnage in 1933-34 is estimated at 1,430,000 to 1,480,000 tons in *Japan's Shipping and Shipbuilding Position, 1928-36,* cited, p. 14. This included 680,000 tons of powered vessels over 100 tons; 650,000 tons in other, non-full-powered ships; and 100,000 to 150,000 tons of shipping space allocated from vessels engaged chiefly in trade with the Asiatic continent. If one accepts these estimates, it is possible from other data to compute roughly the tonnage used elsewhere. I have allocated to near seas foreign and colonial traffic some 350,000 tons of shipping space from vessels passing through the near seas en route to or from more distant regions.

no more than one sixth in 1913, and none at all in 1893. Its dispersion was now about at its prewar peak. After 1936 it was concentrated progressively in near seas areas, with the development of Yen Bloc trade and the disruption of normal commercial activities by war inflation and controls.

Finally, it should be emphasized that the chief impetus to the modernization of shipping and shipbuilding technology, aside from naval construction, came in the overseas trade. On the longer ocean routes Japanese operators met the sharpest competition from foreign liners, tramps, and tankers. And it was here that the subsidies given annually by the Japanese government for strategic and commercial reasons operated with greatest effect. Subventions granted under the laws of 1896 and thereafter placed a premium on the construction and operation of new vessels of the larger and faster types. Often they made the difference between profit and loss for the big concerns. The practice was to place new ships on the overseas routes and to relegate older ones to the near seas, if not to scrap them altogether. By 1936 Japan owned the third largest merchant fleet in the world. More important, her fleet boasted an unusually high proportion of fast motor vessels of the most modern design.

Thus, among all the service industries, it was in shipping that technological advances were particularly associated with commercial expansion overseas, despite their continuing importance in internal transport as well.

The Extractive Industries. A second major category of economic life in Japan has been the extractive industries: agriculture, forestry, fishing, and mining. These occupations, even as late as 1930, continued to provide 20% of the entire national product, and as much as 40% of all gainful employment. (See Chapter 9.) Earlier, of course, their share was much greater.

Here again, as in most service trades, direct dependence on prewar export markets was never very great. In other words, few such primary products were shipped overseas from Japan in relatively unprocessed form. Home producers contributed large quantities of industrial materials entering into manufactures which were sold abroad. They also fed the workers in export industries to a large extent. But even this share of the market was small in relation to the entire domestic demand for rice, vegetables, and fish. The same thing was true of coal and lumber, and of most other raw materials coming from the farms, forests, mines, and fisheries of the country.

It was of great significance, of course, that Japan's modest endowment in natural resources barred her from the pattern of economic development followed by many other nations. In countries more richly endowed or more sparsely settled, the initial stage has commonly been the creation of great primary industries serving the world market. These extractive industries provide a growing stream of income to pay for imports of machinery and other goods. Their export revenues help to service the foreign loans which may finance the development process in part. And they are likely in time to create new demands and indigenous capital resources for the growth of more diversified industrial activity. This was the familiar pattern in the new lands of the Western hemisphere as they were opened up to colonization and development during the eighteenth and nineteenth centuries. More recently, in a totally different setting, it has been the story of tropical Asia, with its huge exports of rubber, tin, oil, and foodstuffs.

When Japan was opened to the West, however, her islands were even then densely populated. If the historical estimates are at all accurate, she already had nearly as many people in relation to her cultivated land as has Great Britain, Belgium, or Holland today. In 1880 the Japanese figure was close to 2,150 per square mile. For Britain in 1940 it was 2,300, and for the United States only 245. Already Japan had twice as many people for her total land area as Europe on the eve of the Industrial Revolution. The comparison in arable land would be even less favorable.

Thus no great agricultural frontier beckoned the Japanese when they stood on the threshold of modern development. Assiduous efforts to extend the cultivated area over the next sixty years brought no more than a 33% increase. Meanwhile the population doubled. Through this period little of Japan's good farm land or fishery resources could be turned to export purposes without requiring large imports of more expensive food, or preventing an improvement in dietary standards. Nor were there great mineral deposits and forests which could be exploited to supply any wide margin of output over and above the growing needs of the Japanese themselves. In fact, as industrialization proceeded, it brought increasing dependence on foreign metals and fuels, and even lumber.

Domestic production of food and industrial materials did not fail to grow, as we have seen. (Chapter 3.) The statistics suggest that food production at least doubled over fifty years. Raw material output more than trebled. This expansion played a vital part in Japan's industrialization and economic growth. But Japanese farmers, fishermen, and mining concerns found their expanding market primarily in the needs of their own country as its population flocked into industrial and commercial pursuits. Even that part of their output which was shipped abroad took the form mainly of processed goods which advanced steadily in degree of fabrication as Japanese industry matured.

Had Japan been situated in closer proximity to the great industrialized nations of the West, her pattern of growth and structural change after 1868 would probably have been somewhat different. Both the pressure to industrialize, and the opportunity to do so, might have been somewhat diminished. She would have enjoyed more favorable access to large external markets for her coal, marine products, and high-value farm crops. Western consumer manufactures might also have competed more strongly in Japan than was the case, delaying the progress of industry. The course of events would have been different, too, if the Japanese as a people had been less ambitious to advance their material well-being and national power; or if, like other peoples of Asia, they had fallen under the domination of a foreign power interested mainly in developing the country as a supplier of raw materials and an industrial market.

As it was, industrialization brought a concentration of export goods progressively in the field of manufactures. Meanwhile imports moved steadily in the other direction. Before 1890 finished manufactures comprised nearly one half of Japan's entire purchases from foreign countries, and less than 10% of her exports to them. (Table 29.) Thereafter the balance swung increasingly toward imports of raw materials in exchange for exports of finished goods. After 1930 two thirds of her imports were raw foodstuffs and materials. Over one half of her exports were finished manufactures, and most of the remainder were semiprocessed goods. Actually, the structural shift was even greater, for Table 29 excludes trade with the Japanese colonies. It therefore omits nearly one quarter of Japan's overseas commerce. Most of this, too, was the exchange of factory products for foodstuffs and industrial materials.

Further evidence of this shift in the character of Japan's foreign trade after the turn of the century is found in Table 30. Here are reproduced the Oriental Economist indices of the physical volume of imports and exports by classes, summarized in five-year averages.

The divergence of various classes of goods in their rate of growth, as shown in Table 30, is what one would expect from the preceding table. Among imports from foreign countries it is raw and semiprocessed materials which advance most rapidly. And if colonial trade had been included, foodstuffs would also have registered a sharp increase. (In 1930 Korea and Formosa furnished 64% of Japan's total food imports.) Among exports it is finished manufactures which grow by leaps and bounds, followed by partly manufactured goods (chiefly raw silk).

Table 30 further reveals that the shift in Japanese imports and exports proceeded mainly by differential rates of growth in various classes, rather than the replacement of one by another. This is not

Table 29. Trade of Japan Proper with Foreign Countries, Classified by Stage of Production, 1868-1938[a]
(percentage shares)

Annual Average	All Classes[b]	Raw Products		Manufactures		
		INDUSTRIAL MATERIALS	FOODSTUFFS	FOODSTUFFS	INDUSTRIAL PRODUCTS Partly Manufactured	INDUSTRIAL PRODUCTS Wholly Manufactured
			EXPORTS			
1868-72	100.0	23.1	25.4		40.8	1.9
1878-82	100.0	11.6	37.1		40.4	7.2
1888-92	100.0	11.3	23.3		46.2	15.5
1895-99	100.0	10.7	14.3		45.9	26.0
1905-09	100.0	9.3	11.7		45.2	31.7
1910-14	100.0	8.4	4.3	6.5	50.1	29.6
1915-19	100.0	5.4	4.4	5.5	44.1	38.2
1920-24	100.0	6.0	2.5	4.0	45.3	40.9
1925-29	100.0	5.9	2.4	4.9	43.9	40.9
1930-34	100.0	4.1	2.4	5.9	32.4	52.1
1935-38	100.0	4.3	1.8	6.8	26.0	58.6
			IMPORTS			
1868-72	100.0	4.1	29.0		20.2	44.5
1878-82	100.0	3.5	14.8		29.9	48.6
1888-92	100.0	12.3	21.1		25.7	39.4
1895-99	100.0	25.9	22.5		17.7	32.0
1905-09	100.0	36.2	16.7		18.7	27.3
1910-14	100.0	49.4	8.0	4.3	18.2	19.6
1915-19	100.0	55.4	5.5	2.8	24.9	10.6
1920-24	100.0	48.5	8.3	4.6	19.8	18.0
1925-29	100.0	55.6	10.2	3.9	15.5	14.2
1930-34	100.0	58.2	8.1	2.8	15.9	14.2
1935-38	100.0	56.0	5.7	1.9	23.9	12.4

a Percentages for 1868-92 are from Kichihiko Taniguchi, "Strukturwandlungen des Japanischen Aussenhandels im Laufe des Industrialisierungsprozess," *Weltwirtschaftliches Archiv*, vol. 46, part 1, July 1937, pp. 241-42; those thereafter from data in Imperial Cabinet, Bureau of Statistics, *Nippon Teikoku Tōkei Nenkan*, passim, Tokyo.

Raw foodstuffs are mostly cereals, beans, and unprocessed marine products. Wheat flour, tea, refined sugar, beer, and canned fish are grouped with manufactured foods. Raw materials comprise such commodities as cotton, wool, coal, crude oil and minerals, rubber, oil cake, and lumber. Materials partly manufactured range from simply processed products like vegetable oils, straw braids, and hides to more highly fabricated goods, such as textile yarns, industrial chemicals, and iron and steel semimanufactures. Wholly manufactured industrial products ("finished manufactures" in the Japanese classification) include textile fabrics and clothing; vehicles and machinery; pottery, glass, and lamps; paper, brushes, toys, etc.

b Includes unclassifiable goods amounting to 3% or less of imports and exports in most years.

Table 30. *Trade of Japan Proper with Foreign Countries:*
Growth in Physical Volume, by Classes, 1903-34[a]
(indices; 1910-14 = 100)

		Raw Products		Manufactures		
					INDUSTRIAL PRODUCTS	
					Partly	Wholly
Annual	*All*	INDUSTRIAL	FOOD-	FOOD-	*Manu-*	*Manu-*
Average	*Classes*[b]	MATERIALS	STUFFS	STUFFS	*factured*	*factured*
			EXPORTS			
1903-04	57	75	78	79	52	59
1905-09	67	84	75	96	54	67
1910-14	100	100	100	100	100	100
1915-19	173	103	171	174	136	215
1920-24	138	46	75	99	133	190
1925-29	211	55	99	232	197	316
1930-34	283	41	137	380	209	450
1934	368	40	158	496	229	620
			IMPORTS			
1903-04	73	45	175	131	65	82
1905-09	92	65	111	104	88	160
1910-14	100	100	100	100	100	100
1915-19	119	149	99	91	106	35
1920-24	178	190	208	168	188	102
1925-29	217	253	277	204	226	91
1930-34	229	282	231	90	241	59
1934	245	314	206	69	310	64

a The indices for the various individual classes are from the Oriental Economist, *Foreign Trade of Japan: A Statistical Survey*, Tokyo, 1935, pp. 699-700. Each index is computed from the annual aggregate of quantities of individual items weighted by their prices in 1928. (For one year, 1903, it would appear from the Oriental Economist's explanation, on prefatory page 43, that the weights are prices from an earlier period.) Here the indices are given in five-year averages, with 1910-14 as 100.

The types of commodities grouped in each class are described in Table 29, note a. All commodities are included for which quantity data are available. For imports and exports as a whole they comprised 88% of the value of trade in 1903 and 84% in 1933. Whether the coverage is as extensive in each individual class is not known. Probably it is less complete for manufactures, where quantities of many items were not reported in the official statistics. In any case the indices give no more than a broad indication of physical growth, because of changes in the character of imports and exports and price relationships over thirty years.

b The index for "all classes" is not that of the Oriental Economist, which relates only to imports and exports for which quantity data are available. Instead, I have first computed relatives for the total value of all imports and all exports (except in trade with colonies) and then deflated each series by the corresponding import and export price indices of the Oriental Economist. This gives a somewhat more accurate measure of the volume trend of imports and exports as a whole. It assumes, however, that the prices of items for which quantity data are not available tended to vary with the prices of items for which the quantities are known, since the price indices are computed only from the latter. The corresponding values of the Oriental Economist index in 1934 are 309 for exports and 259 for imports.

entirely true. There appears to have been an absolute decline in exports of raw materials and imports of manufactures. Except for foodstuffs, however, it is doubtful if Japanese purchases of finished manufactures abroad actually declined in the aggregate. Here this kind of index is particularly unreliable, for it fails to cover many items for which quantities were not reported. It also fails to reflect improvements in quality and type, especially in the case of machinery and vehicles, which were major components of import manufactures after World War I.

The extent and character of Japan's dependence on overseas markets can be shown more concretely by a direct comparison of commodity production and exports. In the extractive industries, first of all, it is clear that the home market predominated heavily. After World War I the export share was about as large as it ever had been—larger if one includes all domestic foodstuffs and materials shipped abroad in manufactured form. Yet it was of minor importance, except in the case of a few specialties. The position was briefly as follows:

1. *Agriculture.* During the years 1928-36 Japan's exports of foodstuffs to foreign countries and colonies, whether in raw or processed form, took only 7% of her total production measured in calories.[5] The bulk of this was not farm crops, but canned fish. And it was heavily overbalanced by food imports, especially rice, sugar, and soybeans. The ratio of exports (in all forms) to domestic output was less than 4% for most farm products, including rice, barley, potatoes, vegetables, meat, and dairy products. For tobacco and beans it was 5 to 10%. Two other large export foods were sugar and wheat flour. The former began to figure appreciably in the list of Japanese exports after 1905, and the latter after 1925. In the case of sugar, however, refined exports were greatly exceeded by crude imports from Formosa and the Netherlands Indies (which were also much greater than Japan's own production). To a lesser extent imports of wheat from Australia, the United States, and Canada were likewise milled for reexport as flour. Thus it was Japan's sugar refineries and flour mills, rather than her farmers, that benefited from overseas trade in this respect.

The two most important export products of Japanese agriculture were silk cocoons and tea. Silk cocoons, it is true, cannot be regarded strictly as the product of an "extractive" industry. Nor were they exported in quantity until converted into yarn by the silk filatures. But it seems best to treat them here as a farm export crop, since cocoon growing normally comprised 70% of the cost of

[5] For details see U.S. Department of State, *Japan's Food, Beverage, and Tobacco Position, 1928-36*, Washington, 1948, pp. 44-46.

raw silk, and was a farm occupation directly associated with the growing of mulberry leaves for silkworm feeding. As already described, sericulture was geared predominantly to the foreign market. It was the American demand for raw silk, and Japan's success in ousting competitors from the market, which were responsible mainly for the eightfold increase in cocoon output from 1880 to 1930. Through this whole period two thirds or more of the annual production of raw silk was exported. Smaller amounts were also sold abroad in the form of woven textiles. Here, more than anywhere else, foreign trade was of direct importance to the Japanese countryside. Mulberries, cocoons, and silk reeling provided supplementary cash income to millions of peasant families. Here, too, the requirements of the world market exerted constant pressure on the Japanese sericulturist to improve and standardize his product, even though the work continued to be carried on mainly by handicraft methods in the home.

Tea ranked with silk as an export in the early Meiji years. Yet it failed subsequently to achieve the same spectacular growth. For sixty years exports maintained a fairly constant level of around 20,000 tons, except for a slump during the twenties. To supply this foreign market, while satisfying Japan's own requirements, the annual output rose from about 30,000 metric tons in 1891-1900 to 48,000 tons in 1931-40. About half of the total tea plantings, and nearly all of the export crop, came to be centered in the one prefecture of Shizuoka. Here climate and terrain were especially favorable. The acreage planted to tea in all Japan actually shrank 30% in this period, while average yields increased 140% in response to better plant selection, disease control, heavy fertilization, etc.[6]

The primary phases of producing and curing tea in the country districts were never thoroughly modernized. To secure large amounts of uniform quality for export, the tea leaves had to be refired, cleaned, and sorted by the larger wholesalers or the American export firms which continued to handle much of the business. This was one reason for the failure of the trade to prosper more largely. Tea maintained its place in the farm economy mainly because the Japanese themselves were a tea-drinking people and because it did not compete heavily for scarce resources. Like the mulberry leaves fed to silkworms, tea plants could be grown on hillsides and upland areas ill suited to rice. Moreover, tea, like silk cocoons, required a

[6] See Supreme Commander for the Allied Powers, GHQ, Natural Resources Section, Report No. 125, *Tea in Japan*, Tokyo, 1949, p. 43. Experiments in Shizuoka during 1929-32 showed that the yield in tea leaves from plots fertilized with nitrogen increased 42 to 74% as compared with the yield from plots which received none.

good deal of seasonal hand labor which could be provided cheaply by the farmer and his family without seriously interfering with the growing of food or other productive employment. The Japanese thus continued as the fourth or fifth largest tea-producing nation, but never achieved the supremacy in the world's tea trade which they held in silk.

2. *Fishing.* Japan is also one of the great fishing nations of the world. Before World War II her total catch was double that of the United States. It amounted to over a fifth of the entire catch of the world.[7] Equally, the Japanese are the world's greatest eaters of marine products, which supply more than four fifths of their protein. Over 90% of their annual prewar output was therefore regularly consumed at home, rather than sold abroad.

In the early Meiji decades there developed a small but useful export of dried and salted fish to China. After World War I the introduction of canning and refrigeration processes, accompanied by large-scale business organization, gave rise to a flourishing export trade in canned crab, salmon, trout, tuna, and sardines. This was associated with the extension of offshore fisheries, and especially of Japanese fishing activity in the more distant waters of the Okhotsk and Bering seas. It was the export demand, in fact, which prompted the introduction by big integrated concerns of the ocean-going factory vessels and refrigerator ships essential for such operations.[8] Foreign markets took 90% or more of the crab, salmon, and trout which were caught in or near Soviet territorial waters and processed in factory ships or in canneries located on Kamchatka.

Yet the fishing industry as a whole, with its myriads of small fishermen along the Japanese coast, remained far more important to Japan as a source of food and employment than as a source of foreign exchange. And the principal stimulus to its growth came from the increasing numbers and improved diet of the Japanese people themselves. At its prewar peak in the middle thirties the export trade took less than 10% of Japan's total catch. Aside from the 50 to 75 million yen of exchange which it provided each year, its chief significance lay in the impetus given to the large-scale, capitalistic techniques in overseas fishing, and the political friction

---

[7] In 1935-36 the world's fish catch is estimated at 16.8 million metric tons. Japan Proper accounted for 3.7 million tons in the two-year average, and Korea and Karafuto for another 1.8 million tons. U.S. Department of State, *The Japanese Fishing Industry, 1928-39, and Prospects for 1953*, Washington, 1948, p. 21. Somewhat higher figures for Japan, which include seaweed and are computed with different conversion factors, will be found in Supreme Commander for the Allied Powers, GHQ, Natural Resources Section, Report No. 95, *Japanese Fisheries Production, 1908-46*, Tokyo, 1947.

[8] Tokyo Association for Liberty of Trading, *The Economic Development of the Japanese Fishing Industry*, Tokyo, 1937, passim.

which such operations generated in Alaska, the Soviet Far East, and certain regions to the south.[9]

3. *Mining.* Exports were of more importance in the early development of modern mining in Japan. In the case of coal, Japan's chief mineral resource, her producers soon found a profitable market for a part of their growing output in nearby China. During the 1890's nearly a third of the tonnage of Japanese coal was regularly exported. Additional amounts went into ship bunkers. In 1913 shipments to foreign countries, Korea, and Formosa reached their all-time peak of 3.5 million tons—one sixth of total production. (Table 31.) Thereafter, as Japan's own requirements for industrial fuel and power expanded, coal exports dwindled in importance. In fact, she now shifted to an import basis, owing to the increasing dependence of her metallurgical industry on coking coal from North China. Coal furnished well over half of her entire consumption of fuel and power. (See Table 4, above.)

The coal industry thus ceased in the interwar period to have any large stake in the foreign market, except indirectly as it supplied fuel for other export industries and shipping. Its profits now depended rather on the restriction of imports, especially from Manchuria. The third ranking coal producer of the world, Japan produced and consumed over half as much coal in 1936 as all the rest of Asia put together (excluding the USSR).[10] In the rest of Asia (1937) about 0.07 metric tons were consumed per capita; in Japan, 6.4 tons. To meet her deficiency in high-quality supplies, especially coking coal, she drew widely from surrounding areas—Karafuto (South Sakhalin), Manchuria, North China, Korea, and French Indo-China.

Copper, Japan's second most important mineral, was developed much more largely as an export in the early years. This ancient Japanese industry had long attracted the interest of foreign merchants. The ready market abroad prompted the rapid introduction

[9] The State Department report cited above gives data from which are derived the following annual average production and trade of Japan Proper in fish and shellfish during 1928-36 (in fresh fish equivalent, thousands of metric tons):

Production	*3,396*
Coastal and inland	2,432
Offshore	715
Overseas	249
Trade with foreign countries and colonies	
Exports	253
Imports	288

[10] U.S. Department of State, *Energy Resources of the World,* Washington, 1949, pp. 37, 44. Consumption equals production plus net imports.

Table 31. *Production, Exports, and Imports of Coal and Copper Japan Proper, Selected Years, 1897-1936*[a]

| | Value of Production (millions of yen) | | | Volume of Production, Exports, and Imports | | | | | |
| | | | | COAL (millions of metric tons) | | | REFINED COPPER (thousands of metric tons) | | |
	ALL MINING	COAL	REFINED COPPER	Production	Exports	Imports	Production	Exports	Imports
1897	34.2	20.7	8.0	5.2	1.6	0.1	20.4	14.1	0.2
1913	146.8	71.0	42.0	21.3	3.5	0.7	66.5	42.9	2.0
1928	195.5	254.5	55.3	33.9	2.5	3.1	68.2	3.0	20.4
1936	589.4	305.5	66.6	41.8	1.9	6.3	78.0	12.4	53.3

[a] Production figures used here are those of the Ministry of Commerce and Industry, as given for 1897 and 1913 in Asahi Shimbunsha, *Nippon Keizai Tōkei Sōkan*, Tokyo, 1930, pp. 768-70, 1221-22, and for 1928 and 1936 in the Ministry's *Shōkōshō Tōkeihyō* (1936), Tokyo, 1937, table 38. Import and export data include trade with Japan's colonies. For the later years they are from the Oriental Economist's *Foreign Trade of Japan: A Statistical Survey*, Tokyo, 1935. For the later years coal figures are from Supreme Commander for the Allied Powers, GHQ, Natural Resources Section, Report No. 21, *The Coal Industry of Japan in Recent Years*, Tokyo, 1946, p. 7; and copper data are from NRS Report No. 44, *Mineral Resources of Japan (1925-45)*, Tokyo, 1946, p. 52. Refined copper output came almost wholly from domestic ore in 1897 and 1913. In 1928 and 1936 production from new domestic ore was about 60,000 and 66,000 tons respectively, the balance representing scrap and imported ore, concentrates, etc. NRS Report No. 106, *Copper in Japan*, Tokyo, 1948, pp. 36-44. Not included here is foreign trade in copper, brass, and bronze manufactures, except for copper shapes.

of modern mining methods after 1868. Japan soon rose to second position among the world's copper producers. Particularly she supplied most of the Oriental market for coin metal. Before World War I she exported 60% of her output, most of it in unfabricated form. (Table 31.) A good deal of the early stimulus to modernization and growth came directly from this export opportunity.

Again, as in the case of coal, copper exports dwindled in significance after 1918. Domestic fabrication and use increased, while abroad new ore deposits were opened in Africa and Chile to meet the world's requirements. Through the interwar period Japanese copper mines supplied little more than enough to meet the country's peacetime needs. Foreign trade was a balancing factor: large exports were revived again during the depression of 1929-32, whereas in years of high industrial activity imports exceeded exports by a growing margin. Unfabricated copper exports continued to absorb 20% of Japanese refinery output during the years 1928-36. But twice as much copper was now imported from the Western hemisphere, despite transport costs and the tariff now in force.

In other metals the story was similar, except that Japan's deficiency was typically much greater.[11] Even gold was produced in amounts only sufficient for the arts and industry. Monetary needs had to be met mainly abroad.

4. *Forestry.* Finally, mention should be made of Japan's "natural ornament"—her forests. Along with arable land, coal, fisheries, and water power they constitute one of her chief natural resources, although their annual yield is comparatively slight in terms of net value product. Japan compares with Sweden, the most heavily wooded country of Europe, in the richness of her timber supplies. Some 55% of her entire land area is forested, a figure twice as large as that for California, which is about the same size.

In feudal times these mountain forests remained in their primitive state. Only after the Restoration did they come under systematic exploitation. At first there was serious overcutting, until a system of protection began to be evolved after 1890 on the large tracts owned by the State and the Imperial Household. Reforestation is reported to have increased the forested area by 10% or more from 1915 to 1935. Even then, domestic supplies of lumber and pulpwood failed to keep pace with the demand. After World War I Japan became increasingly dependent on the forests of Karafuto

11 One other mineral produced in abundance in Japan is sulphur. Before the war Japan was the third ranking sulphur producer of the world, exporting about one third of her output. Although an essential raw material of sulfuric acid, perhaps the most important industrial chemical, it was of minor importance in terms of money value.

(South Sakhalin). She also was forced to import from abroad, especially softwoods from the American and Canadian Northwest. In the years 1828-36 production in Japan Proper averaged about 6,700 million board ft. Karafuto supplied 1,800 million ft., and foreign countries, Korea, and Formosa over 1,000 million ft.[12] Lumber and pulpwood comprised about half of the forest yield of Japan Proper in money value. Some 30% was fuel wood, and 20% was grass, bamboo, and miscellaneous products.[13]

As with Japan's other natural resource industries, this growing utilization of forest products took place almost wholly within the home islands. For her economic life was heavily dependent on wood. Housing and furniture were built almost entirely of lumber; charcoal remained the principal household fuel; and industrial development created large requirements for building construction, mine timbers, railway ties, etc. The paper industry alone grew to consume nearly 10% of the entire lumber and pulpwood output of Japan and Karafuto.

Exports of lumber and wood manufactures never attained sizable proportions in prewar Japan. They reached their all-time peak during the decade before World War II, when large amounts of construction materials were shipped to Manchuria, Korea, and Formosa. Yet lumber exports averaged only about 350 million board ft. during the years 1928-36, or 4% of production in Japan Proper and Karafuto. Other exports of wood in the form of paper, box shooks, matches, pencils, etc. added no more than 2%.[14] Meanwhile imports of lumber from foreign countries, Korea, and Formosa were three times exports. Also, more pulp and paper (taken together in pulp equivalent) were imported than were sold abroad. In short, while the foreign market stimulated the rise of particular wood-using industries like those producing paper, matches, pencils,

---

[12] Excluding firewood. Annual estimates given in *The Place of Foreign Trade in the Japanese Economy*, cited, vol. I, p. 301. See also U.S. Tariff Commission, *Japanese Trade Studies, Special Industry Analysis No. 23, Lumber*, Washington, 1945.

[13] According to the value of output in 1929-33, as given in the weights of the Nagoya index of production. "Hompō Genshi Seisambutsu no Seisan Sūryō," Nagoya Chamber of Commerce and Industry, *Nagoya Keizai Tōkei Geppō*, vol. VIII, no. 4, May 1936, supplement.

[14] Lumber exports are given in *The Place of Foreign Trade in the Japanese Economy*, cited, vol. I, p. 301. According to the same source (p. 303), some 800 to 1,000 million board ft. of domestic lumber (8 to 9% of total output) went into making pulp during the middle thirties. Most of this pulp was used for the manufacture of paper, of which about one sixth was sold abroad during 1928-36. Other miscellaneous exports of wood manufactures amounted to only one third of lumber exports in value and probably no more than 10% in wood content. (*Japanese Trade Studies: Lumber*, cited, p. 18.)

and rayon, it was a negligible factor in the growth of Japan's forestry and lumber industry as a whole.

Taken as a group, the extractive industries thus display a rather consistent pattern. Except in the case of a few products, the main stimulus to their growth was found in the developing internal market almost from the beginning. Silk, tea, and a few manufactured foodstuffs provided important earnings of foreign exchange, particularly in the early decades. Silk in particular persisted as a major export commodity for sixty years. Copper mining and coal mining, too, developed initially in part to serve the requirements of nearby Far Eastern countries. However, along with domestic production of other minerals, food, and forest products, they also fell progressively short of meeting Japan's own needs. After World War I they came to be based even more predominantly on the home market, except as coal was an industrial fuel widely used in export industries as well.

To measure these changing relationships in any exact fashion over the entire period is virtually impossible in view of the shortcomings of Japanese statistics. It would be a tedious affair in any event. In the foregoing paragraphs, therefore, attention has been focussed on the years 1928-36. These years of depression and boom give average export/production ratios which are fairly representative of the interwar period. In only few instances, moreover, were they exceeded in earlier decades.

To summarize: While silk and tea continued to be shipped abroad in substantial amounts, the export ratio for most farm products was less than 4%. For fish it reached 7%, mainly because of foreign sales of the fish caught and canned in northern waters. The food ratio as a whole is raised to 7%, too, when sugar and flour exports are included. For lumber and pulp it was no more than 6%, and for all forest products hardly 3%. These export percentages, it will be recalled, include shipments to foreign countries and colonies of all such primary products even in processed form (except where they are minor components of export manufactures). They also include considerable amounts of sugar and wheat imported from abroad and subsequently reexported after refining. In the case of minerals, imports now bulked so large as to make export/production ratios of little significance, though they were still very small.

The reasons why Japan exported so little of her primary production, either in raw or manufactured form, deserve reemphasis. One reason was her comparative poverty in arable land and minerals per capita. But it is hardly enough to say this. Her extractive industries grew substantially over a half century, as we have seen. In fact, her per capita output of fish, forest products, coal, and grains was large relative to that of most other Asiatic nations. Equally important was the rise of domestic demand for such products which accompanied the growth of population and industrial development. Japan's own requirement absorbed her entire food output, and more. It also took most of those industrial materials which she could still produce at home in competition with (or with protection from) overseas supplies. In view of the scale of expansion witnessed in her extractive industries generally, this fact alone is significant evidence of the over-all growth of the Japanese economy.

Manufacturing for the Export Market. It is in the realm of manufacturing industry, of course, that the world market has been of greatest importance to Japan. Sometimes, indeed, the growth of Japanese industry from Meiji times is attributed mainly to the expansion of overseas demand. This is a misconception, as emphasized earlier, and fails to offer any intelligible explanation of the substance and breadth of Japanese economic development. Our first task, therefore, will be to place Japan's prewar export trade in proper perspective as regards its quantitative significance. This will afford some basis for evaluating the role of the foreign market in contributing to her industrial modernization and growth.

To relate production and export quantities in any inclusive fashion presents numerous difficulties, even more than in the extractive industries. Many gaps and ambiguities are found in the Japanese statistics. And in any case there are hundreds, even thousands, of products each distinct from the others in some degree. One is forced to group them in broad categories in terms of money values. Yet the more they are combined the more the aggregate ratio of exports to production conceals wide variations among branches even of a single industry. Moreover, where materials pass through several stages of manufacture their values get reported several times, so that gross production values cannot be added together without duplication. A bale of cotton yarn appears in cotton textile output both as yarn and as cloth; a ton of iron is valued as pig iron, steel ingot, and then perhaps as printing machinery. On the other hand, if production aggregates are measured by net value added by manufacture, to eliminate double counting, then complicated adjustments must be made in export values to put them on a comparable basis.

In the following paragraphs an effort is made to cope with these difficulties in rough fashion so as to arrive at certain broad export/production ratios, mostly for the decade 1928-37. They indicate at least the general magnitude of exports in relation to industrial production over a period which included years of both depression and prosperity, the latter extending through the trade boom of the thirties. In few items was the overseas market more important in earlier decades. More commonly it was appreciably smaller.

To begin with, it would appear that some 25 to 35% of the entire product of Japanese manufacturing was sold abroad in foreign and Empire markets during the years 1928-37. This is a very rough estimate, which covers both factory and workshop industry but excludes the building trades. Very likely the correct percentage is nearer the higher than the lower limit.[15] For the preceding decade, 1919-28, it was probably not far different.

If as much as one third of all Japanese manufactures were being marketed abroad during the interwar years this is indeed a substantial share. In all probability it is larger than that for any other important industrial nation at the time, even the United Kingdom.[16]

[15] Gross manufacturing output in factory and workshop industry (excluding construction) was valued at 8,187 million yen in 1930, according to the Cabinet Bureau of Statistics. (Japan Economic Federation, *National Income of Japan, 1930-1939*, Tokyo, 1939, p. 59.) Exports of industrial products, defined in more or less comparable fashion, came to 1,700 to 1,750 million yen. (*The Place of Foreign Trade in the Japanese Economy*, cited, vol. II, tables 17-23.) This includes shipments to Korea and Formosa. In the gross output figure, however, there is a good deal of double counting of values of materials in successive stages of production. Such duplication is only slightly offset by the fact that exports are f.o.b., while production is valued at the factory. The real ratio of exports to production was probably in the neighborhood of 30% in 1930. It was somewhat higher during the years immediately preceding, as export values fell more rapidly than production values during the late twenties. From 1930 to 1936 it remained fairly constant. The figure of 25 to 35%, given above, is probably not wide of the mark.

Another approach yields somewhat similar results for mining and manufacturing taken together (excluding foodstuffs). To the total value of *net* output in manufacturing (excluding foodstuffs), as given in national income statistics, are added (1) the estimated value of industrial materials produced in agriculture, forestry, and fishing, which were mostly processed by Japanese industry, and (2) the value of all raw materials and semimanufactures (excluding foodstuffs) imported from foreign countries and colonies in the same years for industrial use. With a further allowance for transport merchandising and other services reckoned in sales prices, total gross output on this calculation comes to 5.0 to 5.5 billion yen in 1930 and 9.5 to 10.5 billion yen in 1936. Exports of manufactures and semimanufactures (excluding foodstuffs), adjusted to a similar valuation at the factory, may be estimated at about 1.6 billion yen in 1930 and 3.2 billion yen in 1936. This gives an export ratio in the neighborhood of 30% or more in both years.

Both these estimates are obviously very crude, though perhaps adequate for present purposes. They are probably nearer the truth than the often-quoted figures of the Mitsubishi Economic Research Bureau (*Japanese Trade and Industry, Present and Future*, London, 1936, p. 494). Here the export/production ratio for all industry is computed as 23.7% in 1929, 18.2% in 1931, and 20.5% in 1933. It would appear, however, that exports to the Japanese colonies are disregarded, and that there is double counting of materials in arriving at production totals. Also, workshop output does not seem to have been adequately allowed for.

[16] The United Nations Economic Commission for Europe has calculated industrial export/production ratios for seven leading manufacturing nations of Europe during 1938. (*Economic Bulletin for Europe*, vol. II, no. 1, first quarter, 1950, pp. 33ff.) With allowance for the difference in method of estimation, it would

It was heavily weighted, however, by two items which bulked much larger in foreign trade than in total manufacturing industry. The first was raw silk, of which Japan has long been the world's premier exporter. The second was cotton piece goods, in which she passed the United Kingdom as an exporter in 1933.

Together raw silk and cotton fabrics accounted for no more than 15 to 20% of gross manufacturing output (eliminating double counting) in the period 1928-36. In the early years their share was somewhat higher; from 1930 on, with the fall of textile prices and the ensuing boom in metals, machinery, and chemicals, it was to become even smaller. Yet they contributed over one third of all industrial exports to foreign countries and Japanese colonies during these years, and a similar proportion in earlier decades. Nearly 75% of Japan's raw silk output was sold abroad during this period. Virtually all of it went to the United States. Overseas markets likewise took 55% of the cotton cloth woven in Japan, and about the same percentage of all cotton manufactures (net, by weight).[17] For a comparison one may cite the British cotton and woolen industries, which exported 73% and 47% of their output, respectively, in 1930.[18]

Apart from raw silk and cotton cloth, the export ratio for Japanese industry was much lower in the aggregate during the interwar years. Probably it was no more than 15 to 20% in 1930. The new rayon industry which mushroomed in the thirties was geared heavily to foreign sales. But the woolen and silk-weaving trades continued to produce over three quarters of their goods for the domestic market. And the nontextile industries as a whole sold at least 4 yen of goods at home for every 1 yen's worth sold abroad. Yet they accounted for as much as 75% or more of total net product in manufacturing in 1930. In later years their preponderance was still greater. (See pages 455-61.)

This average export ratio of 15 to 20% for nontextile production conceals wide variations among particular industries, of course. The pottery trade, to cite one large component, disposed of 50% of its product overseas during most of the period 1928-36. Foreign and Empire markets likewise came to absorb 30 to 50% of the

appear that none of these countries was as dependent as prewar Japan upon foreign markets for the disposal of its manufactures.

[17] Quantity figures for exports of cotton yarn, cloth, and other manufactures identified as cotton goods, all combined in equivalent yarn weight, are given in U.S. Department of State, *The Japanese Textile Industry, 1928-36*, Washington, 1947, vol. ii, tables 4, 8.

[18] Alfred E. Kahn, *Great Britain in the World Economy*, New York, 1946, pp. 68-69. In 1907 as much as 84% of Britain's cotton textile production was exported. Among the Japanese textile industries, only raw silk ever approached this figure.

output of numerous other industries during the trade boom of the thirties. Mostly they were industries already producing extensively for home consumption: e.g., wheat flour, rubber goods, bicycles, enamelled ironware, and canned foodstuffs. In cement Japan was likewise the leading supplier of Far Eastern markets. She sold overseas about a fifth of her 1936 production of nearly 6 million tons.

On the other hand, the engineering trades as a group, including machinery, industrial equipment, vehicles, clocks, and scientific instruments, exported less than 10% of their output in 1930 and little more than 15% in 1936.[19] Moreover, in contrast to textiles and other consumer goods, this capital equipment went largely to the protected markets of Korea, Formosa, and occupied China. Shipments grew as they did only because of heavy programs of capital construction and military expenditure, in which Japanese suppliers enjoyed a preferred position. The advancing maturity of Japan's engineering industries is evidenced, nevertheless, in their strengthened competitive position. Naturally this improvement was most marked in those branches where the home market itself was large. The competitive strength of Japanese shipbuilders by this time is remarked upon elsewhere. The electrical equipment industry had grown under the tutelage of American manufacturing firms until it was in a strong position in all but a few subsidized lines like heavy turbogenerators and telephone apparatus. In textile machinery Japan had now rid herself of her long-standing dependence on British and Continental firms. By 1936 this was a 100-million-yen industry exporting 20 to 30% of its output to China, India, and Empire areas.

Still other major industries in Japan remained almost wholly confined to the domestic market. This was naturally true of the printing trades, and of electrical and gas utilities. The chemical industry, now beginning to reach major proportions, also exported comparatively little in the aggregate. Only in particular items like

19 Exports of machinery, vehicles, etc. to foreign countries, Korea, and Formosa are added together, and corrected by deducting rubber tires and adding electric wire and lamps to make them more comparable with production totals. This gives exports of approximately 80 million yen in 1930 and 300 million in 1936. Production of such items in government plants is estimated by assuming that it stands in the same proportion to private factory output as does government plant to private factory employment—35% in 1930 and 10% in 1936. Total gross output in the two years is thus placed at 940 and 1,890 million yen respectively. (All figures are from Ministry of Commerce and Industry, *Kōjō Tōkeihyō* [1930, 1936].) If we disregard any net addition to output from home workshops (plants of less than five workers) and assume that double counting of production values in factory statistics is offset by the higher f.o.b. valuations placed on exports, the export/output ratio was about 8% in 1930 and 16% in 1936. These calculations, and the assumptions which must be made in the absence of data, give a fair indication of the difficulty of computing accurate export/production ratios throughout the Japanese economy.

ammonium sulfate and dyestuffs did overseas markets take as much as 20% during the years 1928-37. So, too, with a vast range of small-scale industries producing variegated household goods, clothing, and foodstuffs for the Japanese population.[20]

These export/production ratios for the decade 1928-37 may be taken as broadly representative of the relationships which prevailed throughout the interwar years. In most industries they were typically lower in the early twenties. They reached their peak at the height of the trade boom in 1936-37. To carry them back through still earlier decades is impossible, except for a few staple products. But they were substantially lower through most of the Meiji period and only advanced as Japanese industry expanded and matured after the turn of the century.

As a final point of evidence it is of interest to compare the Nagoya index of manufacturing output (as reproduced and extended in Table 8) with the Oriental Economist indices of the volume of manufactured exports to foreign countries (Table 30). The latter may be summarized by combining manufactured foodstuffs and other wholly and partly manufactured goods, each weighted with the actual values exported during 1920-29.[21] The results are as follows:

	Manufacturing Production	Exports of Manufactures to Foreign Countries
1905-09	69	61
1910-14	100	100
1915-19	160	173
1920-24	217	157
1925-29	313	252
1930-34	377	326

Surprisingly, the index of manufacturing output advances more rapidly after World War I than the export index. More accurately, the volume of exports declines in the early postwar years, when the difficulties of financial readjustment were reinforced by the Great Earthquake of 1923; then it moves rapidly ahead with the technical advances of the late twenties and the depreciation of the yen in 1931. However, shipments to Empire markets are excluded from this export index. If added, they would cause it to rise from 100 in

---

20 These generalizations are based on production and export values as given in official statistics. The U.S. Tariff Commission's *Japanese Trade Studies*, Washington, 1945, affords a convenient secondary source of data on the decade 1928-37, especially as exports to foreign countries and Empire markets are combined, item by item.

21 The weights employed are as follows: manufactured foodstuffs, 5; other partly manufactured products, 50; other wholly manufactured products, 45.

1910-14 to at least 375 in 1930-34.[22] No close comparison of the
two series is warranted, in any case, for each is open to various
criticisms. About all one can say is that their behavior also fails
to bear out the notion that Japanese industry developed mainly to
serve a foreign market, or that it found its major stimulus in export
opportunities.

The home demand for Japanese manufactures thus absorbed continuously most of the output of industry, as well as primary products
and services. It developed *pari passu* with the expansion of overseas
trade. Their relative importance varied widely from industry to industry, as we have seen, and even among branches of a single industry. In two large trades, silk and cotton goods, especially, exports were of major importance, absorbing over half of Japan's
entire output after 1900. And elsewhere, in a number of industries,
the proportion of exports to total production actually ran higher
than the percentage given above, if account is taken of all materials,
equipment, and services used to manufacture export goods. Steel
products and machinery manufactured in Japan, for example, were
purchased extensively by other industries engaged in export business. Domestic sales of Japanese chemicals were in part sales to
textile and pottery firms marketing their goods abroad. So, too,
with coal, electric power, shipping, and railway services.

Once foreign commerce grew to such large proportions, the fortunes of the export trade made the difference between prosperity
and depression in Japan. Indeed, from a very early date the commercialized sector of the economy was sensitive to fluctuations in
world prices, incomes, and trading activity. As time passed this became increasingly true of the entire national economy. But Japanese industry depended no less on the prosperity of home agriculture, on the buying power of masses of workers and small businessmen, on the maintenance of domestic investment at high levels. In
sheer quantitative terms, it was here that it found its chief stimulus
to growth. If I have gone to tedious lengths in examining the statistics, it has been to demonstrate this truth which is so often overlooked if not denied. The home market also grew apace in prewar
Japan, and at all times absorbed the bulk of manufacturing output.

Exports and Industrial Technology. Aside from its quantitative
importance, what has been the influence of the foreign market on
technological change in Japanese industry? What historical effect
did it have on the acquisition of new skills, the adoption of new production techniques, the introduction of new business methods?

---

[22] This correction for colonial trade is made on the basis of the total values of
manufactured exports to foreign countries and to Korea and Formosa. In 1910-
14 the colonies took about 7% of all such exports, and in 1930-34, 25 to 30%.

One direct contribution of exports is obvious. They paid for imports of machinery, food, and materials which were essential to the modernization and expansion of industry. Some imported materials like raw cotton could have been produced more largely in Japan (at the expense of something else). In later years she also was technically able to provide a larger share of her machinery requirements as well. But the costs would have been greater, sometimes prohibitive. Instead she chose to buy abroad.

Through most of the prewar years such imports were financed almost entirely out of current exports, and not by foreign borrowing. Many countries have borrowed heavily abroad to finance industrialization, and today most Asiatic nations count heavily on external assistance in one form or another. It is worth noting that Japan paid for heavy imports of producer goods over a long period with little aid from the outside. Her success in doing this is to be explained partly by various circumstances which restricted imports of consumer goods to small proportions and conserved most of her foreign exchange earnings for this purpose. Shipping and other invisible services also played a part. But mostly it was made possible by the rapid expansion of industrial exports, notably raw silk and cotton goods, and later a broad range of manufactures. Silk and silk manufactures alone paid for nearly *one third* of Japan's entire purchases from foreign countries in the sixty years from 1870 to 1930.

Second, it was in the export trade that Japanese businessmen found some of the most profitable opportunities for new types of enterprise. This raised the general level of profit expectations, creating new incentives to invest. Capital and labor employed in export activity produced in turn a growing stream of money income to swell the volume of saving and spending in Japan. Expanding opportunities abroad thus made for a more dynamic process of capital formation, and a fuller utilization of Japanese resources, than would probably have occurred in a more self-contained pattern of growth. The general outlines of this process were sketched in Chapter 5. Here we need call attention only to the added stimulus given directly in the export industries, and indirectly throughout the Japanese economy, by the general rise in productivity resulting from industrial specialization in the world economy.

Third, by enlarging the scale of operations in various industries, especially those producing goods of uniform, standardized design, the export trade made possible certain economies of large-scale marketing, production, and finance. Where the domestic market is too small to permit realization of the full advantages of size, this is one familiar gain from expansion abroad—a gain usually shared by domestic consumers as well. If a country's national market is small, either because of a sparse population or because of poverty, this benefit may accrue over a wide range of manufactures. And even where it is of considerable size, there are always particular commodities and services which, because of their production technology or their limited demand, may be produced more efficiently with the addition of a foreign market. The combined market may support plants or firms of more nearly optimum size. More commonly, it may bring external economies associated with the growth of the industry as a whole.

Actually, in the case of prewar Japan, these advantages accruing from foreign trade were less than might be supposed in view of the poverty of her home market and the extent of her export business. For the economies of large-scale production are greatest in those industries where a large technical unit of production offers decisive advantages, or where the growth of the market permits a more efficient specialization and coordination of the various component processes of an industry. They are most conspicuous in such industries as fuel and power, metallurgy and machinery, and certain branches of chemicals. Thus Britain, Belgium, and Germany have all reaped important technological gains from a large export trade in such products, particularly specialized types for which their own demand is necessarily limited. The exports of prewar Japan, by contrast, were largely confined to nondurable consumer goods. As late as 1930 as much as 57% of all her exports to foreign countries and colonies were textiles. Another 13% were fish and agricultural products. The remainder were divided between minerals and metal goods, on the one hand, and cheap consumer wares made of wood, celluloid, paper, rubber, etc., on the other.

Most of these exports were produced in industries which also enjoyed a large home market. This was true, for example, of silk, cotton, and rayon piece goods; of flour, sugar, paper, and beer; and of metal products like bicycles and small electric motors. While generalization is not easy, it is safe to say that in most instances the mere addition of the export market brought no decisive gain in technical efficiency for the industry as a whole. In fact, one of the reasons for Japan's success in ousting European competitors from Asiatic markets for cheap cotton cloth and other low-grade manufactures was the very fact that these were broadly the things which the Japanese themselves purchased in large amounts.

In the main Japanese exports were also products of industries in which the optimum-size plant was medium or small. Establishments of less than 100 workers turned out most of the exported tableware, toys, rubber shoes, electric lamps, pencils, straw braids, brushes, hosiery, paper products, enamelware, and bicycles. They also produced a considerable share of the silk, cotton, and rayon piece goods. Partly this situation is explained by the dearth of capital and advanced managerial skills, which made the typical factory in Japan smaller than comparable plants in the West. (See Chapters 4 and 5.) Partly it reflected the fact that her comparative advantage in world markets tended to remain in those industries which, with a degree of modernization, could yet capitalize on her vast reservoir of cheap skilled labor. For example, this asset, organized in myriads of small workshops coordinated and financed by merchant-employers, enabled her to win a third of the world's international trade in toys during the thirties.

With certain exceptions, Japan's large-scale establishments and her great combines were relatively more prominent in sheltered industries dependent mainly on the domestic market. For example, they figured largely in mining, metallurgy, shipbuilding, printing, power, and industrial chemicals. In some degree this may have been because it was easier here to restrict competition and concentrate control than in the export field. But chiefly it was because those industries in which the economies of large-scale production are most pronounced were also those in which Japan remained at a disadvantage in foreign competition, owing to her deficiency in mineral resources, her dearth of capital and advanced technical skills, and her low standard of living. Within certain industries, notably textiles, the export branch tended to be larger in scale of production and more integrated than the domestic branch. But in other trades, as in ceramics, rubber goods, and electrical equipment, the reverse was true. It was the larger firms and factories which produced industrial porcelain, rubber tires, and standard electric lamps—chiefly for the home market. By contrast, exports of tableware, rubber shoes, and minature bulbs for flashlights and Christmas trees were produced mainly in small establishments.[23]

Thus Japanese industrial exports remained concentrated largely in fields where the home market was also large—usually much larger—and where the most efficient technical unit of production remained comparatively small in scale.

The industrial specialization fostered by the growth of export manufactures had, nevertheless, certain significant effects on production technology and the scale of economic organization. Without becoming involved in the details, one may distinguish the principal effects which were typical over a wide range of Japanese manufacturing.

---

[23] See T. Uyeda and associates, *The Small Industries of Japan*, New York, 1938, passim.

First, the export trade not only enlarged certain industries, but it promoted a greater regional concentration of production in the neighborhood of the great port cities of central Japan. This made for high land values, and it added to the capital required for public works and to other social costs of urbanization. But it must also have fostered various external economies associated with the growth of industry and its concentration at convenient points for transport and marketing. Economies of this type could be realized even when the technical unit of production remained quite small. Bicycle exports, for example, came mainly from Osaka. Here they were assembled from thirty or more component parts manufactured by small, independent industrialists in the environs. Osaka, too, was the center for producing enamelled ironware and exported 80% of its output. The production of matches, another small-scale industry, was concentrated in Kobe. Here foreign timber, paper, and chemicals could be readily imported, while labor was furnished by the wives and children of workers in other industries. Similarly, in the Nagoya region were congregated thousands of small pottery manufacturers and textile weavers. They were able thus to capitalize on a large pool of skilled workers, ready access to stocks of materials and equipment, and convenient marketing facilities. By 1938 the three great industrial centers of Tokyo, Osaka, and Nagoya, all major export centers, accounted for 30% of Japan's 3.2 million factory workers and 33% of the country's entire factory output. Yokohama, a small fishing village in Tokugawa times, had become a bustling emporium of 800,000 people.

Japan's excellent internal communications by sea and rail would have encouraged this pattern of regional agglomeration in any case. But an added impetus came from the development of export specialties suited to this type of organization. Greater division of labor, organized and coordinated within a framework of overhead controls provided by merchants, banks, and large factories, made these clusters of small producers more efficient than they otherwise could have been. It enabled them to withstand large factory competition in domestic and foreign markets to a surprising degree.

Exports and Standardization. The second influence of the foreign market on technological change in Japanese industry was connected with the *character* of the export demand. In general, as we have seen, Japan tended to export manufactures of the same general type as those used extensively by her own people. But there was one broad difference which prevailed over a wide range of products. Within many industries the foreign demand was directed toward goods of more uniform specification and standardized design than those produced for the home market.

To win foreign markets for processed foodstuffs and industrial materials, in the first place, the export trades had to be organized not only to handle relatively large orders, and to assure a regular flow of supplies, but also to bring about marked improvements in the quality and uniformity of shipments. In such items as raw silk, flour, tea, and vegetable oils the unreliability of Japanese products was a constant handicap. Often it was increased by sharp trading methods and low standards of commercial honesty. Only slowly and partially was this handicap overcome by the unremitting efforts of trade associations, industrial guilds, and the government itself.

As the scale of domestic commerce and industry expanded, the same tendency toward upgrading or downgrading on the basis of standard specifications appeared in production for the home market. But typically it took place earlier and more largely in the export branch of an industry. Especially was this true where the buyers were the more mechanized factory industries of the West. By comparison with the silk habutai weavers of Fukui, for example, the full-fashioned hosiery and broad-goods mills of New Jersey and Pennsylvania, with their automatic machinery, required silk yarn of more uniform size, of greater strength and elasticity. Export competition in such industries thus exerted a steady pressure in Japan toward technical improvements in manufacture, toward commercial honesty, and toward a more integrated, large-scale organization of the various stages from the raw material to the finished product.

There were other Japanese industries in which the export demand was also concentrated largely upon goods of more standardized construction and finish than those sold in the home market, but not necessarily of better quality—often the reverse. Exported silk fabrics, for example, were chiefly habutai, crepe, pongee, satin, and other wide materials of simple design. By contrast, fancy goods were woven mainly for Japanese use. Cotton exports first took the form of low-count yarns. Then they shifted increasingly to coarse sheetings, shirtings, drills, and T-cloths, largely in the gray. After World War I there was a marked trend toward bleached, dyed, and finished goods of greater variety; yet exports still contrasted with the variegated wide and narrow colored cloths worn by the Japanese.

The same contrast prevailed to a considerable extent in pottery, straw matting, wood and paper products, and a wide range of household goods. Japan was able to keep up a limited export trade in luxury wares of individual craftsmanship for which her artisans had long been famous. But there was little demand in Asia for such things, and the Western market was closely restricted by high tariffs. Her big export opportunity developed in cheap, low-grade consumer goods, notably coarse cotton cloth. Only slowly did it extend to more advanced manufactures. "Made in Japan" was apt to remain a synonym for crude and often shoddy wares, whether piece goods, pencils, or pots and pans.

At home, on the other hand, Japanese industry supplied virtually the entire market, from the cheapest goods to the finest luxury goods. And even products turned out for mass consumption in Japan have commonly been distinguished by great variety of design and appeal. Westerners have often remarked on the aesthetic element in Japanese living. It expresses itself in individuality of taste and abhorrence of standardization in matters of clothing and household decoration. As already noted, this difference between foreign and domestic demands was conspicuous in the cotton goods market. Here the Japanese themselves continued to demand a wide diversity of stencil-dyed toweling, *kasuri* woven of specially dyed yarns for children's wear, *kokura obiji* for women's sashes, and other striped and figured specialties less well suited to power weaving and large-scale finishing than the export staples. Over an increasing sphere of consumption this trait has been weakened in recent years. And, of course, it was never of importance in the markets for such products as flour, beer, books, and machinery. Nowhere, however, has the standardization of consumer taste which typically goes with the spread of machinery and mass production met with greater resistance than among the Japanese.

The contrast between the variety of consumer goods produced for home use, and the tendency of exports to concentrate more largely on items of more uniform quality and design, has made for a corresponding difference between the domestic and export branches of these industries with respect to their degree of mechanization and scale of organization. As among different industries we have seen that the rule does not necessarily hold. Sugar and foreign-style paper were manufactured for home consumption with more capitalistic methods than toys and tableware for export. Even within a single industry, the export sector might be more primitive, as in the case of the "town manufacturers" of miniature electric bulbs. But more commonly it was the export firms which tended to lead in the introduction of power machinery and factory organization. Here, too, within particular trades, one finds an earlier and more pronounced trend toward integration, both horizontal and vertical.

In such diverse industries as raw silk, tea, pottery, and bicycles, the export branch more readily passed from the handicraft to the merchant-employer and factory systems. Here there was stronger pressure to reduce the number of middlemen, and to develop more efficient arrangements for transportation and finance. Similarly, exports of silk, cotton, and rayon piece goods, being largely staple cloths of standard construction and simple finish, lent themselves more readily to power-loom weaving than the general run of fabrics consumed at home. They were also apt to be marketed through larger and more integrated organizations.

In the cotton industry, for example, it was the Chinese and Korean markets for heavy, coarse gray goods which drew the big spinners into the weaving trade after 1893, and led to the introduction of the large weaving shed equipped with automatic looms. These big spinning-weaving companies were closely linked with raw cotton importers, shipping companies, and export merchants. They formed the first successful cartel in Japan, the Japan Cotton Spinners' Association. They never succeeded in dominating the domestic market, however. All of the narrow fabrics and much of the wide material continued to be supplied by the smaller, specialist weavers, including medium-size independents and hosts of tiny workshops. During the interwar period the big firms even lost ground to the independents in the foreign field, as Japan's export opportunities shifted progressively toward lighter, colored cloths of more varied design and finish. In 1933 they produced only 28% of all home-consumed cotton fabrics, by yardage, and still less by value. Abroad they still accounted for as much as 55% of Japan's exports of 2 billion sq. yds.

This difference between the organization of production for the home and that for the foreign market owed something to the policies of the State. Through special encouragements to combinations of industrialists and traders in the export business, through commodity inspection and other technical aids, the government sought to promote "rationalization" in the interest of a stable and prosperous foreign trade.[24] Mainly, however, it is explained by other circumstances.

To recapitulate, trading activity in distant, overseas markets by its very nature was apt to call for larger orders, greater certainty of delivery, and more capital. This was true even where the comparison was with domestic activity organized on a national and not merely a neighborhood basis. Second, Japanese industrialists and merchants in direct contact with the outside world were likely to acquire more readily the technical and administrative skills necessary to large-scale production and selling, particularly in the earlier decades. Even the "capacity for organization," a trait of initiative in which the Japanese of all Oriental peoples seem to have been relatively well endowed, had to grow with experience. Bertil Ohlin refers to it as perhaps the scarcest of all the factors of pro-

[24] See Chapter 10.

duction. Foreign trade was one field in which lucrative opportunities soon developed for Japanese imitation and innovation in this respect. And finally the growth of manufacturing for export contributed still further to technological change by enlarging the scale of output in certain industries, particularly those turning out standardized types of goods easily suited to a more integrated and mechanized system of production.

In this latter regard it is well to note that the Asiatic market played a more strategic role than trade with the West. Japan's exports to the United States, Europe, and the British Dominions continued mainly to be materials and manufactures produced by relatively simple processes in which hand labor was the chief element of cost. Beside raw silk and silk textiles, they included such things as tableware, toys, perilla and rapeseed oil, tea, canned fish, and wood and straw products. The bulk of Japanese factory exports requiring more advanced and capitalistic methods of production, first cheap clothing materials and later a variety of other goods, found their market mainly in the East. (In part this was due to high tariffs in the West, and also to Japan's own preferential market in her colonies.) Trade with the West was immensely lucrative, especially before the decline of raw silk. It paid for much of the raw material and machinery which went into the development of Japanese industry. But the direct stimulus to more advanced processes of industrialization came more largely from the markets of the Orient, notably the Japanese home market, and secondarily that of Japan's neighbors.

The functional role of the export market in Japan's economic development may thus be summarized as follows: (1) exports paid for essential imports; (2) they contributed to the dynamics of income growth and capital formation; and (3) they fostered technological advance (a) by the contacts and industrial opportunities which they afforded and (b) by the enlarged scale of production which they made possible in certain industries. As argued above, too much importance should not be attributed to this last point, so far as prewar Japan is concerned. It was mainly nondurable consumer goods which she was able to sell abroad in large quantities. These were goods produced in industries in which for technical reasons the economies of mass production were limited, or they could be achieved in large part within the framework of Japan's own sizable market. Where this was not so, it was apt to be because the Japanese as consumers were reluctant to accept such gains at the expense of standardization of taste.

It may be that the decade 1935-45 marked a transition in this regard. For the technical strides made in Japanese engineering through the war years created new potentialities for Japan to emerge as an important postwar exporter of metal products, chemicals, and machinery, provided she can retool her industries and find the necessary trading opportunities.

If circumstances allow Japan to realize this potential, her capital goods industries may partially overcome their other major handicap in prewar years—the small size of the Japanese market to which they were largely confined. They may thus help to fill the void left by the decline of overseas demand for silk and cotton goods. In consumer goods as well, Japan's postwar trading opportunities are to be found increasingly in the more advanced manufactures embodying a larger component of capital investment and developed industrial skills.

Food Supply and Raw Materials

The foregoing analysis of the role of foreign trade in Japan's economic development has stressed first of all the historic function of trade as a highway of learning from the West, and as an activator of change. Over this highway, and partly in response to this stimulus, Japan imported the techniques of the Industrial Revolution, not in one great boa constrictor feat, but continuously and cumulatively over three quarters of a century. This she did largely through her own national efforts, and without benefit of large programs of foreign assistance, except as equipment and capital and know-how were supplied by private enterprise in the West on a commercial basis.

It was hardly less important, of course, that a nation with Japan's swelling population and limited natural endowment should be able also to draw increasingly on world supplies of industrial materials and foodstuffs. Only in this way could it nourish and sustain its industrial progress. This function of trade was secondary, or derivative from the first, in that ability to buy such supplies grew out of advancing technology. But it was equally an essential condition of growth after the turn of the century. Each reinforced the other, and together they worked a revolution in the industrial arts, with far-reaching consequences for both national power and national well-being.

Imports and Industrialization. So much has been written of Japan's growing dependence upon raw materials from abroad that only essential outlines need be sketched in here. It has been the price of industrialization, in the sense that it has involved the Japanese in the typical insecurities of a world-dependent, industrial state. Yet it has also been the means to industrialization, and its necessary outcome if Japan was to realize the gains in real income made possible by her entry into the modern world.

Several observations may be made first concerning the general course of Japan's import trade through the prewar decades. Having already summarized its historic growth in the preceding chapter we shall focus here mainly on the position toward the end of this period, after the patterns of industrialism were well established but before they began to be distorted by the war and armament expansion of the thirties.

1. It will be recalled, first of all, that Japanese purchases abroad grew rapidly and persistently in volume through every decade after 1860. (See Table 26, above.) Even after 1910 the indices maintain an annual rate of increase exceeding 5% down to the eve of World War II.

2. Merchandise imports were equal to about one fifth of the net value of goods and services produced in Japan Proper during the interwar years. (Table 27.) They may also be compared with gross national expenditure on goods and services for private consumption and investment, and government purposes. Such expenditures rose from 12.8 billion yen in 1930 to 18.1 billion yen in 1936, according to the figures of the Economic Stabilization Board.[25] Meanwhile commodity imports from foreign countries and colonies increased from 2.0 to 3.6 billion yen. They now amounted in value to 15 to 20% of national expenditure, as computed here. This reflects a heavy degree of international dependence, but one which is fairly characteristic of many of the world's great industrial and primary producing regions.

As observed in Chapter 6, a fairly stable relationship appears to have prevailed from 1914 to 1937 between imports, on the one hand, and national income or expenditure, on the other. Any study of the Japanese trade cycle would require close examination of this relationship in various categories of imports, as affected by technology and taste, investment activity, prices, tariffs, and other factors. Peculiarly important in the Japanese case is the dependence of exports on imported materials; far less than in the United States are imports a direct function of national consumer outlay.

The appearance of a rather stable Japanese propensity to import during the interwar years should be regarded as a more or less fortuitous result of many divergent influences, rather than a line of "normal" relationship. However, two factors operated to preserve a large degree of stability at the time. First, the volume of imports was closely associated with the level of activity in Japanese industry, which in turn largely influenced the level of national income.

[25] Bank of Japan, *Economic Statistics of Japan, 1951*, Tokyo, 1952, p. 369.

Second, periods of high income in Japan (relatively) were periods of high import prices as a rule. This was not because the Japanese import demand (in contrast to the American) was large enough itself to influence world commodity prices substantially. It was rather that foreign trade was so important for Japan that her business fluctuations tended to follow the general pattern of economic fluctuations in the countries with which she traded. This brought it about that periods of high incomes in Japan were apt to be periods of high incomes and high prices abroad. A notable exception was the Japanese economic recovery after 1931 in the midst of continuing world depression. Even then the yen prices of imports rose steeply as national income increased, owing to the depreciation of the currency. (Table 26, above.)

3. Japan continued to supply most of her import requirements from outside her own Empire. Korea was developed to furnish most of her imported rice; Formosa her sugar. Together they were the source of one quarter of her gross imports during the interwar years. Three quarters still came from foreign countries, however. Here Japan still procured virtually all of her external purchases of cotton and wool, of machinery, of coal, oil, and metals, as well as half of her food and fertilizer imports. Only after 1937 was a decisive effort made to shift to Empire (Yen Bloc) sources, and then with highly unsatisfactory results.

4. The process of industrialization, as we have seen, was vividly reflected in the changing composition of imports from foreign countries. Imports of industrial materials, whether raw or partly manufactured, grew inexorably decade by decade. (See Table 30.) Purchases of finished manufactures lagged far behind. By 1930-34, as a result, 58% of Japan's imports from foreign countries were industrial raw materials—twice the percentage of 1895-99. Some 11% were foodstuffs; and 16% were industrial semimanufactures. Wholly manufactured goods, averaging 230 million yen a year, were only 14% of the total. (See Table 29.) With the accompanying shift of her exports toward manufactures, Japan now typified the industrial nation closely geared to an exchange of overseas materials for the products of her own factories and workshops.

5. In one aspect of this change, however, Japan's experience was hardly similar to previous experience in the West. Industrializing countries have often maintained or even increased their aggregate purchases of manufactures as their own manufacturing capacity grew. Even industrial exporting nations have usually tended to be large importers of fabricated consumer and capital goods, except when such trade has been restricted by tariffs, exchange difficulties, and "cold wars." Some imports disappear as industrial capacity

matures, but their place is likely to be taken by new classes, finer grades, and more specialized types.

By contrast, Japan's imports of finished goods (excluding foodstuffs) actually declined in volume from 1903 to 1934, if the index of Table 30 gives a true measure. Whether any absolute shrinkage took place may be doubted; the index for this category is quite unsatisfactory. Clearly, however, imports of manufactures failed to grow appreciably even with the rise in incomes and diversification of demand which took place in the country. Foreign machinery and producers' equipment continued to play a strategic role, as emphasized earlier, in Chapter 6. Imports still equalled nearly 20% of the gross domestic output of such goods in 1930, and 10% as late as 1936. But consumer goods were never imported in quantities at all significant in the domestic market. Apart from food, they did not exceed 100 million yen in 1930, and much less than this in the earlier decades.

As Japan industrialized, her factories did not find much of their market through merely displacing consumer imports. Her experience in this regard has been different from that of India, for example. Nor, on the other hand, has Japanese industrialization created a large import demand for consumer goods (other than food), either from the West or from nearby countries.

While foreign exchange was largely devoted indirectly to consumer needs in prewar years, it was mainly in the form of industrial materials to be processed at home. Industrialization was thereby quickened, for overseas trade contributed more efficiently to capital formation without a large "leakage"—or benefit, depending on the viewpoint—in the form of consumer manufactures from abroad. But it has been less advantageous to older industrial nations not blessed like the United States with raw materials for export to Japan than has been the industrialization of countries like Canada or Belgium. Japanese competition in third markets was not softened by the corresponding growth of a profitable market in Japan itself, except for primary producers overseas. The migration of the factory system to Japan had an expansive effect on the American economy as a whole, and on the economy of the British Commonwealth including the Dominions, but hardly on that of New England or the United Kingdom.

Several circumstances explain this concentration on imports of food, raw materials, and equipment to the virtual exclusion of consumer manufactures. One was the Japanese tariff, which is characterized more fully in Chapter 10. During the interwar period rates were raised to 30 to 50%, even 100%, on a wide range of manufactures, ostensibly to conserve foreign exchange. If Japan had reason to complain of tariff restrictions in the West, the reverse was equally true.

Other limitations were basically more important than the tariff, however. From nearby Asiatic countries there was little the Japanese consumer wanted except food. So far as Western goods were concerned, incomes were generally too low and consumer habits only moderately changed by the process of Westernization, even among well-to-do people. The typical house was a simple affair of wood, paper, and matting. Clothing was mainly cheap cottons, supplemented by wool and silk. Tokyo department stores came to be filled with the factory-made gadgets so appealing to the Japanese, as well as Western-style articles of personal and household use. For the most part, however, home industries soon developed to supply such articles themselves, usually in cheaper and more satisfactory types. Durable consumer goods of complex design were out of reach of the Japanese pocketbook anyway. And finally, unlike India or Indonesia, Japan never acquired a large resident population of Westerners whose demands could be satisfied only with goods from their home countries. Thus consumer taste and purchasing power, as well as rapid industrialization fostered by a high rate of saving, combined to hold consumer manufactures to almost insignificant quantities in the import trade.

6. By contrast with manufactures, imports of raw materials grew steadily in response to the demands of both the domestic market and the export industry. The distinction between these two demands was taken up earlier in the discussion of gross exports and net export receipts. Again acknowledgement must be made of the work of Arthur B. Hersey and his colleagues in the report of the Department of State entitled *The Place of Foreign Trade in the Japanese Economy*, cited earlier. For 1930 and thereafter they reclassify all Japan's imports from overseas, distinguishing between imports which reflect actual consumption in Japan (in their original or processed form) and other imports. The latter are grouped somewhat arbitrarily into two categories (vol. I, p. xix): (1) imports used in exports, defined as "amounts . . . of the principal raw material [and a few subsidiary materials] used in each of a considerable number of exported commodities or commodity groups, to the extent that such raw material was imported"; and (2) imports offset by exports, defined as import quantities "against which there were equal quantities of the same or similar exports," but which were not actually used in exports. Only the residual imports, after deducting these categories, represent the net amounts going into home consumption (or changes in inventories).

Table 32 classifies Japan's import trade in 1930 according to this distinction between commodities retained for consumption in Japan, and those used in or offset by exports. It is the counterpart of Table 28, above, where "originated" export values are distinguished from those offset by imports. Both are worthy of close study if the essential character of Japanese foreign trade is to be understood.

Table 32. *Gross and Retained Imports of Japan Proper from Foreign Countries, Korea, and Formosa, 1930*[a]
(millions of yen)

	Gross Imports					Retained Imports Cols. 1−(4+5) (6)
	Total (1)	From Foreign Countries (2)	From Korea and Formosa (3)	Imports Offset by Exports (4)	Imports Used in Exports (5)	
Total imports	*2,006*	*1,545*	*461*	*161*	*296*	*1,549*
Food and						
fertilizer[b]	*697*	*346*	*351*	*72*	*44*	*579*
Food	534	192	342	55	43	435
Fertilizer and fodder	163	154	9	17	1	144
Metals and						
minerals	*315*	*293*	*22*	*26*	*20*	*269*
Fuel: coal and petroleum[c]	127	124	3	26	2	99
Iron and steel[d]	121	113	7	—	9	112
Other metals and minerals[e]	68	55	12	—	9	59
Other industrial materials and semi-finished products	*760*	*680*	*80*	*58*	*232*	*471*
Cotton, wool, rayon pulp[f]	465	457	8	4	184	276
Lumber and paper pulp[g]	62	59	3	17	6	39
Other materials[h]	234	164	69	37	42	156
Manufactures	*234*	*226*	*8*	*4*	—	*230*
Machinery, vehicles, instruments, and other metal manufactures[i]	141	141	—	—	—	141
Other manufactures[j]	93	85	8	4	—	89

a Compiled from U.S. Department of State, *The Place of Foreign Trade in the Japanese Economy*, Washington, 1946, vol. I, passim; vol. II, tables 1-16. Original data are from official foreign trade returns of Japan, Korea, and Formosa, with some reclassification. The figures relate to all imports of Japan Proper (including Okinawa and Karafuto), except for imports from the Mandated Islands. For Korea and Formosa data are from the trade returns of the colonies themselves. This introduces a slight element of noncomparability with data on Japan's foreign trade. Reexports and reimports of Japan Proper are excluded throughout, as is the trade of Korea and Formosa with each other. Transit trade through Japan between foreign countries and the colonies is included. For a definition of "imports offset by exports" and "imports used in exports" see the text.

b Retained imports include (in millions of yen): rice, 157; sugar, 142; other grains and beans, 83; fertilizer, 123; fodder, 21. Retained oils and oilseeds, whether for food or other uses, are placed entirely in "other" industrial materials. Imports used in exports are mainly unrefined sugar and wheat. Some 13 million yen of imports offset by exports are ammonium sulfate imports deducted to offset the nitrogen content of fertilizer exports. See Table 28, note b.

c Retained imports included (in millions of yen): petroleum products, 88; coal, 11. Imports offset by exports are coal; imports used in exports are oil.

d Iron and steel exports in 1930, including amounts used in exports of iron and steel manufactures, totalled 358,000 metric tons, or 12% of iron and steel imports (iron ore at 65% Fe content). This is prorated among imports of ore, pig, and scrap in proportion to the total imports of each, while imports of rolled steel are assumed arbitrarily to be wholly for domestic utilization.

e Excludes bullion and specie, and minor imports of nonmetallic minerals from Formosa. Retained imports included (in millions of yen): lead, 10; aluminum, 9; zinc, 7; tin, 4; and smaller amounts of cement, mercury, graphite, etc. Imports used in exports of metals and manufactures are estimated at 17% of the value of imports.

f Retained imports included (in millions of yen): raw cotton and yarn, 195; raw wool and yarn, 80; rayon pulp, 2. (These figures are approximate.) Raw cotton to the value of 4 million yen was reexported; imports used in exports were as follows (in millions of yen): cotton, 172; wool, 8; rayon pulp, 3.

g Retained imports were entirely lumber, after deduction of exports of lumber in various forms (17 million yen) and pulp imports used in paper exports (6 million yen).

h Retained imports included (in millions of yen): oils and oilseeds, 18; hides, leather, and tanning materials, 16; salt, soda ash, and caustic soda, 12; other chemicals, 23; dyes and pigments, 12; rubber, 11; commercial fibers, 11; miscellaneous, 53.

i Retained imports included (in millions of yen): machinery, instruments, watches, clocks, and firearms, 103; automobiles, cycles, and parts, 22; other metal manufactures, 16.

j Retained imports included (in millions of yen): textiles (other than yarn) and clothing, 27; paper, 13; and a residual for chemicals, drugs, glass, perfume, etc., 45.

Nearly one quarter of the total value of imports from foreign countries and colonies in 1930 was used in (or offset by) exports. This ratio was fairly typical of the whole interwar period. Among the overseas materials embodied in manufactured exports textile fibers predominated. Especially important was raw cotton. Here, too, are found sugar and wheat refined for export; about 12% of all iron and steel imports (Fe content); and similar shares of imported lumber, pulp, rubber, and other miscellaneous materials.

The export trades built upon imported materials were industries in which Japan had won a comparative advantage abroad with her cheap skills, effective organization, and propinquity to Asiatic markets. Or they manufactured overseas cotton, metals, etc., for sale in her colonies with the aid of Empire tariffs and other preferential advantages. Together these "import-dependent" export industries not only covered their own import needs, but furnished nearly half of the net exchange receipts ("originated exports" in Table 28) available in addition to meet other import requirements of the Japanese economy. Japan was thus becoming heavily dependent on her "workshop" role in international trade. By reexporting a part of her imported materials in the form of higher-value manufactures embodying Japanese labor and skills, she was steadily enlarging her capacity to buy abroad to satisfy her *own* needs as well.

Imports retained for consumption in Japan, so defined, amounted to 1,549 million yen in 1930. (Table 32.) In other words, about 75% of all the commodities purchased overseas were available for home consumption, after allowance for those which were used in exports, or offset by exports. (The latter are exemplified by coal imports from Korea matched by coal exports to Korea or elsewhere.) These retained imports furnished about 15% of the national income, the aggregate net flow of goods and services available from all sources in Japan to support the nation and add to its capital stock. Actually the figure is somewhat smaller. For the export deductions in Table 32 are confined mainly to the principal raw materials used in each export industry. By way of illustration, iron and steel imports are deducted insofar as they were exported in the form of sheets, wire, machinery, pots, and pans; but no allowance is made for steel going into plant and equipment to be devoted to making export chemicals or cotton goods. Nor is imported coal, or oil, or building materials used in export industries reckoned in; or imported machinery devoted to making export products.

To refine the import/income calculation further is hardly worth while, in any case. A complex machine depends for its operation on the correct functioning of all its interdependent parts, and this applies no less to an industrial economy. Most Japanese industries producing for the home market required some imported machinery and materials. In this sense their whole contribution to national income depended on the flow of such imports in greater or less degree. Cotton goods for the Japanese market were produced wholly with imported cotton; food grown on Japanese farms likewise depended heavily on imported fertilizer materials. Railways, shipping, and public utilities required imported metals and machinery. Foreign trade had become the foundation of Japan's entire industrial economy, far more than statistics of income/import relationships will show. Its drastic reduction, as in 1944-46, meant general paralysis.

The organic role which particular imports came to assume through the prewar decades can be made more explicit by looking more closely into Japan's quantitative dependence upon particular commodities from overseas to supply her essential requirements. A comprehensive summary of her supply position is presented in Table

33, again for the year 1930. It differs from most presentations of the subject in four respects: (1) it takes account of Empire trade, as well as trade with foreign countries; (2) it relates production and consumption to *net* imports, after deducting exports: (3) it combines materials in successive stages of processing—e.g., iron ore and metal; pulp and paper; wool fiber, yarn, and cloth—expressing them in basic material units; and (4) it places production from imported materials—e.g., fertilizers—under imports rather than domestic output. Allowance is made where possible for inventory changes in estimating apparent consumption.

Foodstuffs. Despite her need for industrial materials, Japan still devoted nearly 90% of her harvested acreage to growing food. Crop yields were among the highest in the world. Even so, an increasing share of the country's food supply now came from overseas in the form of rice and wheat, beans, sugar, fats, and oils. In some degree this might be attributed to inefficient farming practices; also the diversion of acreage to more profitable uses such as sericulture (mulberry farms) and building sites. Mainly, however, food imports were dictated by the over-all limitations of Japan's land resources. The latter were inadequate to provide for a growing population at improving dietary levels. From 1911 to 1927, for example, domestic food output barely kept pace with a 20% increase in population. Meanwhile food consumption per capita actually rose 16%. This was made possible only by a 277% increase in food imports.[26] By 1930 the nation was dependent on overseas sources for nearly one fifth of its total food supply (in brown rice equivalent).[27]

Table 33 shows Japan's position in 1930 as regards leading foodstuffs. Cereals, beans, and potatoes still supplied over 80% of the caloric intake of her people, now about 2,270 calories per capita. Of these major foods, imports now furnished about 13% (in grain equivalent). Rice imports came mainly from Korea and Formosa, colonies dominated and developed to serve Japanese interests. They supplied the types preferred by Japanese consumers and were exempt from the duty of 1 yen per 100 *kin* (132 lbs.) levied on foreign rice in the Japanese market. Soybeans and wheat were other major food imports. Manchurian beans, together with Korean fish oils, furnished a large share of Japan's entire fats and oils supply, 40% of which now came from overseas. Formosa was also the chief

---

[26] Calculations based on E. F. Penrose's indices of food production and imports in *Food Supply and Raw Materials in Japan*, Chicago, 1930, p. 73. These are geometric averages of quantity indices for individual items, weighted by annual average values, 1921-25.

[27] U.S. Department of State, *Japan's Food, Beverage, and Tobacco Position, 1928-36*, Washington, 1948, table 1.

source of sugar, thanks to stiff duties on shipments from the Netherlands Indies.[28]

In other foodstuffs the home islands were still virtually self-sufficient. Tea and fish were on an export basis, even though consumption per capita was high. Similarly Japan was a large producer of vegetables. This self-sufficiency, however, was relative to the existing diet. Food consumption was now higher than elsewhere in the Far East, except in Manchuria and Malaya. Yet the Japanese diet remained deficient in proteins, minerals, and vitamins. Partly this was due to unbalanced concentration on rice, a low-protein cereal whose chief virtue is that it economizes land. (An acre of Japanese rice land produced 55% more calories than land in wheat and 188% more than land in beans.) Partly it was due to excessive processing of rice and other foodstuffs which robbed them of vitamins.

Especially low was the intake of animal foods other than fish. Except for poultry and eggs, such products were consumed in negligible amounts, and mainly by prosperous people in the cities. Animal husbandry is a very expensive use of land in terms of caloric yield. Over half of Japan's farm families had no livestock at all. No great improvement could come except through imports; yet here meat and dairy products were significantly lacking, and feed concentrates were also expensive. Despite the abundance of fish, protein consumption was hardly two thirds of that in high-standard countries of the West.

Empire self-sufficiency in food, an important plank of national policy, thus implied actual diet deficiency. It posed a growing dilemma for those who saw in it an essential point of national security. In importing more and more of her food Japan was repeating the experience of every populous nation industrializing on a slender base of natural resources. As a matter of fact, her import deficit of 20% was still far below that of England, which had imported three quarters of her wheat and 40% of her meat from far more distant regions of the world in the decade before World War I. Nevertheless, it heightened the sense of insecurity which pervaded large elements of the population. More than anything else it made the "population problem"—certainly nothing new in Japanese history —a subject of public agitation for the first time in the twenties.

Industrial Materials and Fuel. The same expansionist pressures

[28] Noting that sugar was hardly consumed at all in rural districts, Kokichi Morimoto wrote at about this time: "Owing to a heavy protective tariff in the interests of native sugar, the price of sugar in Japan is scarcely exceeded anywhere in civilized countries." *The Efficiency Standard of Living in Japan,* Tokyo: Japan Council, Institute of Pacific Relations, 1931, p. 41.

Table 33. *Net Imports, Production, and Consumption of Leading Foodstuffs and Industrial Materials in Japan Proper, 1930*[a]
(thousands of metric tons, except as indicated)

	Net (Retained) Imports[b] (1)	Production (from Domestic Materials) (2)	Apparent Domestic Consumption[c] (3)	Percentage of Net Imports to Net Supply[d] (Cols. 1÷3)
Foodstuffs				
Rice[e]	1,127.4	8,710.4[f]	10,029.5	11.5
Other cereals[g]	255.1	3,067.9	3,323.0	7.7
Beans	703.0	461.1[f]	1,164.1	60.4
Sugar	768.4	98.8[f]	867.2	88.6
Fats and oils[h]	45.0	63.6	108.6	41.4
Tea	—9.0[i]	38.6	29.7	—
Fertilizers[j]				
Nitrogen content	127.0	502.0	629.0	20.2
Potash content	66.0	340.0	406.0	16.2
Phosphoric acid content	181.0	200.0	381.0	47.5
Fuels				
Coal	325.0	31,486.0	31,811.0	1.0
Petroleum (thousands of barrels)[k]	12,700.0	3,300.0	14,000.0	79.4
Metals and other minerals				
Iron and steel[l]	2,615.0	450.0	2,615.0	85.3
Copper	—29.6[i]	79.0	49.4	—
Lead	49.0	3.8	52.8	92.8
Zinc[m]	32.7	14.8	47.5	68.8
Tin	2.6	0.9	3.5	74.3
Aluminum	10.5	—	10.5	100.0
Cement	—565.7[l]	3,748.4	3,182.7	—
Salt	357.4	628.5	986.0	36.2
Textile materials				
Silk[n]	—30.4[i]	42.6	8.0	—
Cotton[o]	268.0	—	240.0	100.0
Wool[p]	29.4	—	32.3	100.0
Rayon pulp[q]	7.7	—	6.5	100.0
Other materials				
Lumber (millions of board feet)[r]	876.0	6,300.0	7,176.0	12.2
Paper pulp (and paper)[s]	—9.8[i]	625.5	615.7	—
Rubber[t]	20.0	—	20.0	100.0
Hides and skins[u]	18.0	6.0	24.0	75.0

a Compiled principally from U.S. Department of State, *The Place of Foreign Trade in the Japanese Economy*, Washington, 1946; and U.S. Foreign Economic Administration, *Japanese*

Trade Studies, Washington, 1945. Japan Proper, as defined here, includes the main islands, Okinawa, and Karafuto, but excludes all other parts of the Empire.

b Imports from foreign countries, Korea, and Formosa, minus exports to these areas. Net imports take account of imports and exports of food and materials as such, together with estimated trade in such items in other stages of processing (e.g., wheat and flour, metals and ores, fibers and yarns), expressed in material equivalents. Minor amounts embodied in imports and exports of certain finished manufactures are ignored. Domestic production from imported materials (e.g., fats and oils, iron and steel) is included under imports rather than under production.

c Production from domestic materials plus imports minus exports, adjusted in certain cases (indicated in notes) for changes in stocks where data are available.

d Ratio of net imports to the sum of production and net imports. The latter sum corresponds to apparent domestic consumption except in cases where changes in stocks are taken account of in estimating consumption. These cases are noted below.

e In brown rice equivalent. Consumption reflects a decline of 192,000 tons in stocks.

f Crop year beginning November 1929.

g Wheat trade includes flour in wheat equivalent; wheat production is for 1929-30 crop year; net wheat supply is one third of the total for "other cereals."

h Domestic output includes only production from domestic materials, mainly fish. Imports include fats and oils, chiefly fish oils from Korea, and oil-bearing materials (91,000 tons oil equivalent), mainly soybeans from China and Korea. Exports were both fish and vegetable oils, totalling 93,200 tons. Probably 75% or more of Japan's fat and oil consumption was for food; much of the remainder for soap and candles.

i Net export.

j Fertilizer supply of all types, as estimated by the Department of State. Domestic production was mainly manure, compost, and night soil, with lesser amounts of commercial fertilizers produced from domestic materials. Imports were chiefly oil cake, ammonium sulfate, phosphate rock (8% from Japan's Pacific island mandate), and potassium salts. Exports of 51,000 tons were largely ammonium sulfate and superphosphates.

k Estimated as follows (in millions of barrels): reported imports, 13.0; exports 0.3; domestic output, 2.0 plus 1.3 imported from Karafuto by the Navy; increase in stocks, 2.0. The Army and Navy used possibly 10%. (Department of State, *op.cit.*, vol. I, p. 228.)

l Total imports of 3.0 million tons include iron content of ore imports (1.5 million tons) plus pig iron, scrap, rolled and finished steel. Exports of iron and steel as such and of iron and steel used in machinery exports estimated at 358,000 tons. Domestic output includes iron content of domestic ores only (140,000 tons) plus 300,000 tons of domestic scrap used in steel production. Stocks of ore and scrap increased 450,000 tons (Fe content).

m Imports include domestic production of zinc (9,822 tons) from imported ore.

n Raw silk imports (including silk yield of cocoon imports from Korea), 2,710 tons; raw silk exports, 28,250 tons; silk content of piece goods exports, 4,899 tons; added to stocks of raw silk and fabrics, approximately 4,000 tons.

o In yarn equivalent. Imports of cotton fiber (net) and yarn, 505,400 tons; exports of yarn, cloth, etc., 237,400 tons; added to stocks of cotton and cotton goods, 28,000 tons.

p In yarn equivalent. Imports of raw wool and yarn, 32,400 tons; exports of woolen goods, 3,000 tons; stocks of wool and woolen goods reduced 2,900 tons.

q In rayon yarn equivalent. Imports of rayon pulp, 17,900 tons; exports of rayon goods, 10,200 tons; added to pulp stocks, 1,200 tons.

r Production includes all timber felled in the main islands and Karafuto, excluding firewood and pulpwood, the latter estimated roughly at 900 million ft. Exports of 230 million ft. do not include wood used in exports of veneer, match sticks and boxes, lacquer, and other wood manufactures.

s In pulp equivalent. Total imports of pulp, 58,900 tons; paper imports, 64,000 tons; paper exports, 133,000 tons.

t Two fifths of crude rubber imports (which totalled 33,000 tons) are deducted as a rough allowance for exports of rubber manufactures. (*ibid.*, vol. I, p. 316.)

u Imports and consumption are approximations, taking account of small imports and exports of leather on a hides basis.

were forcing Japan to ever greater reliance on industrial materials from overseas. Imports grew steadily in volume and variety, shifting from processed to unprocessed forms as Japanese industry matured. As remarked in Chapter 3, they did not so much replace as supplement the growing output of Japan's own farms, forests, and mines. Together overseas purchases and home output moved upward from decade to decade. But the former rapidly gained on the latter as industries multiplied and drew more and more of their materials from abroad.

These growth relationships are depicted in general terms in the following indices:[29]

	Manufacturing Output	Imports of Foreign Raw Materials and Semimanufactures	Domestic Output of Industrial Materials
1904	59	55	67
1910-14	100	100	100
1920-24	217	190	140
1934	460	319	184

By 1930 some three fifths of Japan's total import trade comprised industrial materials in raw and semimanufactured form. (Table 32.) Over two thirds of these materials, amounting in value to nearly 900 million yen, were retained in Japan to produce consumer goods and capital equipment for the home market. Retained imports are related to production and consumption in twenty-one leading classes in Table 33.[30]

In contrast to foodstuffs, only 10% of Japan's import requirements in industrial materials, raw or semiprocessed, were supplied by her colonies. (Karafuto is included as a part of Japan Proper.) Nor as yet were the resources of Northeast China soon to be seized by the Japanese Army of major significance. (The situation later in the thirties is remarked upon in Chapter 10.) Essentially Japan's

[29] Manufacturing output and domestic raw material production are measured by the indices of Tables 8 and 2, respectively, above. The import index combines the indices of Table 30 for raw materials and semimanufactures from foreign countries, weighting them in a 3:1 ratio corresponding to the values of imports in these categories during the years 1921-25. If materials from Korea and Formosa were included after 1910 the index would more nearly keep pace with the manufacturing index.

[30] "Retained" and "net" imports in Tables 32 and 33 are identical for most items. The principal differences are that paper exports of 4 million yen are deducted in Table 32 under manufactures rather than lumber and pulp; while on the other hand the latter category in Table 33 includes a deduction for exports of certain wood products which are disregarded in Table 32.

import trade was world trade. She purchased abroad in the cheapest market, gaining full advantage from cheap water transport which enabled her readily to resort to distant sources of supply. If foodstuffs came mainly from the colonies, industrial materials were drawn from the natural resources of North America, the Asiatic continent, and the Southwest Pacific. The United States furnished cotton, oil, metals, phosphates, lumber, hides, and skins. From China came cotton, coal, pig iron, hides, vegetable oils, and bean cake. Australia supplied wool; India, cotton and pig iron; and Southeast Asia, oil, rubber, iron ore, tin, and tropical fibers.

Textile fibers had long been the largest category of retained imports. The only clothing fiber produced at home was silk, and this was largely exported. Already, however, retained imports of metals and minerals rivalled textile materials in money value. (Table 32.) Of Japan's total iron and steel supply, 85% was imported in the form of ore, pig iron, scrap, and rolled and finished steel. Except for copper, the same home deficiency shows up in most other metals. It also prevailed in petroleum supplies, even with the output of Karafuto regarded as domestic. Coal imports were significant beyond the small fraction of total tonnage they supplied, of course. They furnished anthracite fuel and about one third of the coal used in making metallurgical coke for blast furnaces. If Table 33 were lengthened still further, it would only confirm Japan's striking dependence on the network of world trade for her essential mineral requirements.

The case of fertilizer imports is particularly noteworthy, in view of the food problem discussed above. Traditionally Japanese farmers had been compelled to rely almost wholly on green manure, compost, wood ashes, and night soil. The importance of night soil, in the absence of stock farming, is indicated in the remark of one agricultural expert: "The Japanese farmer, he keep five head of stock, his own family." As requirements grew, these self-supplied fertilizers were supplemented by fish meal and bean cake, both domestic and imported. After World War I chemical fertilizers came into increasing use to push crop yields still higher. In large degree the basic materials had to be imported from foreign countries. Table 33 shows imports providing 15 to 20% of Japan's total nitrogen and potash fertilizer, in all forms, and nearly half of her phosphates in 1930. However, for commercial fertilizers, which were much more expansible than the self-supplied varieties, the import shares were 45%, 40%, and 75% respectively.

Without such imports of chemical fertilizer, oil cake, and phosphate rock the Japanese would have been forced to import far greater amounts of food to raise their dietary levels. For the nation as a whole they economized precious foreign exchange. For the farmer they raised the ceiling which otherwise would have set even closer limits on any advance in productivity and income.

A New Demand for World Supplies. One final question may now be asked concerning the broad impact of Japanese industrialization on world markets for raw materials. Did her increasing purchases of such materials in raw and semifinished form represent a net addition to the world demand? Or did they represent mainly the displacement of British, European, and American manufactures of these materials by Japanese manufactures now sold in Japan and third markets? Did the growth of Japanese industry enlarge the aggregate world market for cotton, iron, rubber, etc? Or did it simply redirect the processing business from Western factories to Japan?

To answer this question in detail would take one into the ramifications of production and trade in many commodities and markets. In over-all terms, however, certain statistical conclusions can be drawn fairly readily for the period 1911-13 to 1928-30. The competitive dislocations in world markets after 1932 would modify them in some degree, but they hold in substance for the entire period from 1900 to 1935.

1. Japan's gross imports of industrial raw materials and semi-manufactures rose 140% in aggregate volume over this seventeen-year period, judging by the indices employed in Table 30. About 75% (by value) were retained within Japan for consumption in 1911-13 as well as in 1928-30. (This is a little higher than the figure for 1930 given in Table 32.) Already nearly one half of her raw cotton imports were being reexported in 1912 as yarn, cloth, and other cotton manufactures, mainly to Korea and China. (Above, page 31.) These exports were even then making substantial inroads on the markets of British and American competition and of native handicrafts in the Far East, and similar dislocations continued on a larger scale in later years, especially in the thirties. To this extent they shifted raw material demands from the industries of other countries to those of Japan. In the process they generated serious trade disputes and political friction.[31]

2. Most imported foreign materials, however, were retained for utilization in the Japanese islands. Such retained materials also grew about 140% in volume from 1911-13 to 1928-30. Adding in

[31] Low-priced Japanese goods also tended to enlarge the aggregate consumption of these products in foreign countries, by replacing more expensive Western goods. In some degree, too, they freed purchasing power to be spent on other products. These secondary effects make any real appraisal of the effect of Japanese competition on the older industries of the West a complicated calculation which—needless to say—rarely entered into the disputes and agitation of the thirties over Japanese trade.

the supplies secured from Korea and Formosa raises the aggregate growth to something like 150%. As no full deduction is made here for imported fuel and other commodities used in export industries, however, it would be safer to conclude that domestic utilization of industrial materials in consumer and capital goods for the home market was about 2.4 times as large at the end of the period as at the beginning.

3. This increase in retained imports was mostly a net gain in Japanese consumption of such materials from overseas. In no important degree was it merely the replacement of similar materials previously embodied in finished textiles, machinery, chemicals, etc. imported from the West. Imports of finished manufactures failed to grow largely in volume, as we have seen. They persisted mainly in restricted fields—high-priced consumer specialties, and complex types of machinery and equipment. But their raw material content was never large by comparison with Japanese purchases of crude and semifinished materials after 1910. For example, the metal content of machinery imports in any year was insignificant alongside the 2.6 million tons of iron embodied in retained imports of iron and steel products in 1930.

4. Clothing fiber imports are of special interest, because of their importance to the Japanese standard of living. Japanese consumption increased in the aggregate some 80 to 90% from 1911-13 to 1928-30, or 40 to 45% per person. As in the case of foodstuffs, this increase is attributable almost wholly to imports of raw materials from overseas. Cotton yarn consumption was about 140,000 metric tons a year in the earlier period, after allowing for exports of cotton goods. By 1928-30 it had reached 240,000 tons. Meanwhile the population grew from 50 to 64 million, so that per capita consumption rose from 6 to 8 lbs.[32] Silk, wool, and rayon now furnished about one sixth of clothing fiber consumption (by weight). Like cotton goods, wool and rayon goods were made wholly from imported materials.

As much as 95% of Japan's prewar clothing fibers thus came from overseas. Had she consumed her own raw silk, instead of exporting it, she would hardly have remedied this deficiency, except at a very much lower level of consumption. Not only were the

[32] The 1911-13 figure actually covers 1910-13. It is based on official data for cotton yarn output and for all imports and exports of yarn and manufactures. The yarn equivalent of exports of piece goods and other cotton goods is from U.S. Tariff Commission, *The Japanese Cotton Industry and Trade*, Washington, 1921, pp. 21, 23. Changes in inventories of cotton and cotton goods are allowed for in estimating 1928-30 consumption, or "net disappearance" (*The Place of Foreign Trade in the Japanese Economy*, cited, vol. I, pp. 278-80), but not the earlier figure.

amounts of silk relatively small, but when exported they paid in considerable degree for her cotton and wool. Only in the late thirties did Japan free herself from almost total dependence on foreign clothing fibers, by building up domestic output of rayon pulp to replace imports. The result was a drastic decline of clothing standards, both in quantity and quality.

5. Quantitatively, therefore, Japan's growing requirements for industrial materials from overseas was mainly a *new* demand for the primary products of world suppliers, growing out of her expanding *home* market. Abroad her export industries displaced competitive manufactures here and there, especially in cotton textiles. In such cases they enlarged the total demand for those particular raw materials only as they tapped new layers of demand for cheaper goods. However, over two thirds of her aggregate purchases through the prewar decades were utilized for domestic purposes, even after these export industries grew to sizable proportions. Here they represented mainly a net addition to world demand. The chief exception again was cotton textiles before 1913, when the Japanese industry had yet to occupy fully the home market. Yet even there the displacement of Western piece goods was small by comparison with the subsequent growth in the Japanese consumption of American and Indian cotton, or Australian wool.

While Japanese industrialization tended in some degree to shift the market for cotton, rubber, pig iron, and other materials from the factories of the West to the factories of the East, its main consequence has thus been to enlarge and diversify the aggregate market for such primary products and to expand the world economy. From a world standpoint the first consequence has been to some extent the price of the second. For the Japanese market itself was able to reach such proportions only as Japan developed buying power through making herself into a workshop fabricating overseas materials for sale abroad. The one aspect of her development has been essential to the other. How to accommodate the dislocations imposed upon older, established industries in the West has been— and will again be—one of the chief problems of economic statesmanship in the Pacific.

Multilateral Trade and Economic Opportunity

It remains to delineate one cardinal feature of Japan's prewar trading expansion. Only passing reference has been made thus far to its world-wide character, and to the mutual interdependence of those changing relationships which she developed with major regions of the globe.

Global Pattern of Commerce. The spread of Japanese trading activity around the world is illustrated in Table 34. Underlying the shifts portrayed here, of course, was a progressive specialization in the exchange of factory products for imports of food and industrial materials. The modest imports of early years were distributed over a wide range of manufactures and materials—mostly from Britain and China respectively. In payment, tea, silk, and various handicraft wares were shipped to the West. Nearby countries furnished a ready market for a few primary products like coal, rice, and copper. Before the turn of the century trade was distributed fairly evenly between Europe, Asia, and the United States, except that American producers of industrial materials and equipment had yet to win a significant share of the Japanese market.

Table 34. *Overseas Trade of Japan Proper, by Regions,*
1893, 1913, 1936[a]
(millions of yen)

	EXPORTS			IMPORTS		
	1893	*1913*	*1936*	*1893*	*1913*	*1936*
All countries	*88*	*716*	*3,585*	*86*	*795*	*3,641*
Asia	*27*	*360*	*2,263*	*37*	*413*	*1,937*
Japanese colonies:						
Korea and Formosa	—	84	892	—	65	877
China (including						
Manchuria and Hongkong)	23	218	716	25	93	398
India	2	30	259	9	173	372
Southeast Asia	—	24	302	1	81	238
United States	*28*	*189*	*603*	*6*	*122*	*847*
Europe	*28*	*147*	*308*	*40*	*220*	*330*
United Kingdom	5	33	147	28	123	73
British Dominions	*3*	*14*	*141*	—	*17*	*300*
Other	*2*	*6*	*270*	*3*	*23*	*227*

a See notes to Table 26 on the sources and characteristics of these trade statistics. In order to depict the over-all regional pattern, Japan's trade with the Kwantung Leased Territory, and with Manchukuo in 1936, is included here with China, though the former areas were virtually parts of the Japanese colonial empire. The Hongkong trade was partly transit trade with Southeast Asia, but is also classified here as trade with China. Hawaii, separately reported in the Japanese statistics, is included with the United States in 1913 and 1936.

The most noteworthy trend after 1893 was the emergence of Asia as Japan's primary trading area. This trend was accentuated, of course, by her seizure of Formosa and Korea, her acquisition of special rights in Manchuria, and the controlled development of these areas in the interest of Japanese profits and power. Empire trade grew much more rapidly than foreign trade during the interwar years, thanks to these circumstances. Here, with the proceeds of her exports and invisible earnings, Japan came to buy a large share of her imported rice, sugar, fats and oils, salt, coal, and iron. This colonial trade was less advantageous than might appear, because of the capital outlays and other burdens of empire. On the other hand, in purchasing such supplies the bargaining advantage was apt to be on the side of Japanese buyers; return payment in goods and services was shielded from foreign competition; and political control was assured—except in the event of a major war.

Elsewhere in Asia, beyond her encroaching political boundaries, Japan's overseas commerce grew at a less spectacular rate more consonant with her over-all economic expansion. Yet here too geographic and cultural propinquity helped to enlarge the trading opportunities which were latent in Japanese industrialization. Transport to and from the developing commercial centers along the littoral of East Asia was relatively fast and cheap. Business operations could be conducted much more easily from Yokohama than from London or New York. And Japanese goods found ready acceptance in markets where the level of incomes, consumer habits, and marketing arrangements were similar to those in Japan. In China, in India, and generally in the Far Eastern colonies they also met with lower tariff barriers than in the West. Such factors helped to compensate for the poverty of Asiatic markets. Even this poverty could work to the competitive advantage of Japanese exporters in underselling high-priced Western goods ill adapted to Asiatic living standards.

After the Sino-Japanese War coarse cotton yarns and fabrics made with cheap Japanese labor progressively invaded markets formerly occupied by American and European exporters in Korea and China. Later this occurred in southern Asia, as well. Soon, however, Japanese exporters too met growing competition from new factory industries on the mainland—partly through the overseas enterprise of Osaka spinners themselves. The continued search for markets compelled them accordingly to turn to goods which were of wider range and more advanced manufacture and yet could be produced more cheaply in Japan than by the high-wage industries of the West. The maturing of Japanese industry during and after World War I made possible this continued growth through diversification, though cheap piece goods and clothing continued to dominate the trade. This whole process of industrialization, accompanying and making possible Japan's shifting comparative advantage, drew steadily larger supplies of food and raw materials in turn from Eastern countries to Japan.

It is not surprising, therefore, to find that Asia accounted for half of Japan's entire overseas trade after 1913. China was her predominant market at first. But slowly the countries of southern Asia gained in importance. By 1936 this region bought nearly as much from Japan as the whole area of China, including Japanese-controlled Manchuria and the British colony of Hongkong. (See Table 34.) As a source of imports, too, China diminished greatly in relative importance during the interwar period, despite—partly because of—the depredations of the Kwantung Army. India had long furnished most of the short-staple cotton required by Japanese spinners. Now Southeast Asia found a growing market in Japan for oil, iron ore, rubber, vegetable fibers, and other tropical products. During the thirties southern Asia even began to approach the Japanese colonies in total trade with Japan. It might have outdistanced them had it not been for Japan's own system of imperial preference, coupled with mounting discrimination against Japanese goods in the Western-controlled colonies.

The Chinese mainland remained for Japan an important source of such essentials as coking coal, iron, cotton, salt, and soybeans. Its continental expanse of resources offered glittering vistas of a great and flourishing commerce if political relations could ever be established on a stable and harmonious basis. After 1931 grandiose plans were set out in Manchuria and North China to realize this ambition—under Japanese hegemony. In fact, however, all China still furnished only 10% of Japan's import requirements by 1936, as compared with 17% from southern Asia and 23% from the United States. The economic difficulties in attempting a solution to Japan's trade problem merely within this region, even aside from its military costs, became glaringly apparent in the turn to imperial self-sufficiency which marked the subsequent road to war.

The second noteworthy shift in Japan's trading orientation after 1900 was the receding importance of Europe, and the rise of the United States and the British Dominions.

To a unique degree Japan developed largely outside the orbit of European trade after 1913. The United Kingdom and continental Europe would take few Japanese manufactures. Their own exports of consumer goods to distant markets, notably textile fabrics, were competitive rather than complementary. Their industrial equipment met increasingly severe competition from Japanese as well as American producers. Europe thus played no role in Japan's rise as a trading nation comparable to its importance for the United States and other countries of the New World. In contrast to the Japanese figures of Table 34, some 75% or more of all United States exports found a market in Europe before 1900 and as much as 50% even in the twenties. America's great farm exports figured largely in this trade, to be sure. But Europe also took close to one third of all exports of finished manufactures from the United States between 1910 and 1935. Her share of such exports from Japan was almost negligible.

It was Japan's silk trade with the United States which accounted for most of her exports to non-Asiatic countries before 1930. At their 1925 peak, sales of raw silk in the American market reached 849 million yen. This was 37% of the value of all Japanese exports to foreign countries. Their share of net export receipts from foreign countries ("originated exports") was close to 50%. Only the American tariff, plus the generally shoddy quality of Japanese manufactures, prevented a much larger and diversified business in the United States.

On the other hand, the rich resources of the American continent, and the advanced capabilities of American industry, provided a variety of products required in ever growing amounts by industrializing Japan. Cotton was the principal item, followed by oil, steel, lumber, wheat, automobiles, and industrial equipment. Actually Japan took half of all United States exports to Asia in 1936—more than the entire continent of South America. Her armament boom now reinforced the tendency already created by peacetime industrialization. By comparison, her invasion of the American market with cheap and highly competitive cotton goods, toys, canned fish, etc. was quantitatively insignificant, despite the furor it aroused.[33] She likewise became a major purchaser of Australian wool and wheat, and of similar products from the other Dominions. In these lands, too, as in Latin America and the Middle East, Japanese textiles and other consumer goods made their way steadily wherever their progress was not blocked by tariff barriers and other trade restrictions.

Japan's Dual Outreach: East and West. Two further observations are important to an understanding of Japan's historical position in the network of world trade, and its contribution to her economic growth:

The first concerns an oft heard remark, almost a cliché. It is said that Japan owes much of her industrial success to the fact that she was first in the field among Far Eastern nations, able therefore to win a large market for factory goods in Asia. The lag in machine industry among her neighbors, coupled with the advantage she quickly won over her Western competitors, is believed to have conferred on her a trading opportunity which gave a unique impetus

---

[33] See the author's "American-Japanese Trade: Its Structure and Significance," *The Annals of the American Academy of Political Science*, vol. 215, May 1941, pp. 86-92; also *Trade and Trade Rivalry between the United States and Japan*, New York: American Council, Institute of Pacific Relations, 1936.

to her economic development, if indeed it was not the mainspring. Other Far Eastern countries, now industrially ambitious but later on the scene, appear to lack this advantageous head start in point of time.

This "early bird" thesis is open to two objections. First, it seems to say that Japan benefited from the continuing poverty and relative industrial stagnation of her neighbors. It implies, for example, that she would have been poorer, not richer, if China's economic development had proceeded more rapidly than it has. On economic grounds the proposition is dubious. One might better argue just the contrary. More probably Japan was handicapped, not aided, by the fact that East Asia remained the great "backward" area of the world. A more balanced and successful development of the entire Far East could hardly have worked to her economic disadvantage. Though it would have altered the particular pattern of her growth, it would probably have widened her total field of economic opportunity.

While the above objection is speculative, the second is a point of fact. To stress the importance of the Far Eastern market in this way obscures the global character of Japan's trading relationships, and indeed the all-round character of her development. Exports to all markets at their prewar peak took no more than 25 to 35% of Japanese manufacturing production. True, this is a large percentage, and a good deal of it is accounted for by the trade with East Asia. In the case of textiles other than raw silk, the Asiatic market absorbed two thirds or so of Japanese exports during 1928-37, and perhaps 35 to 40% of their entire output. By encouraging technological advance in these particular industries it played a strategic role—perhaps outweighing its quantitative importance in the total pattern of trade. Along with the growing domestic market for factory goods, it fostered the introduction of machinery and mass production, as well as modern banking, insurance, and shipping enterprise. Yet one should not overlook the significance equally of Japan's trading opportunities in the West.

The import-export trade with the United States, the British Commonwealth, and continental Europe generally equalled if it did not exceed in value her trade with Asia outside the colonies throughout the prewar decades. Equipment purchases here were essential to technical and industrial capital formation, even in the later years. By comparison with exports to Asia, shipments to the West of raw silk and other products like straw braids and vegetable oils produced a higher ratio of net export receipts (after deducting raw material import costs) to finance imports for home consumption. From 1870 to 1930 raw silk alone probably provided 40% at least of the total net exchange earnings from commodity exports to foreign countries which could be applied to buying food, materials, and machinery for domestic use.

Finally it is worth pointing out that Japanese products sold to the West came largely from agriculture and the small-scale trades. Thus they yielded income to those groups of the population in greatest need; they provided much employment in labor-intensive industry; their benefits were widely diffused. More than most factory exports to Asia, they helped to offset the heavy disadvantage of the peasant and small businessman in sharing the fruits of industrial progress.

Japan's trade with the West was never associated with empire expansion. Nor did it involve appreciable overseas investment and business enterprise, as did so much of her commerce in the Far East. It was conducted with nations which were politically independent—even quite hostile at times to her foreign policy—and technologically more mature. Yet it provided a large share of her essential raw materials, as well as critical items of equipment, and a still larger share of the export earnings with which she paid her way. Today the future of Japan may lie in the East. But if so it will be because of a general economic development in the region in which she can participate. In the past it has been her relations with the West, certainly in no lesser degree, which have nourished her economic growth. Proximity to the other countries of East Asia, with their relatively low incomes and technical backwardness, has not in itself been a great economic asset.

The second point deserving emphasis is the interdependence between Japan's commerce with the East and her commerce with the West. Modern Japan has faced both ways, in commerce as in culture. Table 34 reflects this ambivalent position in the world's trading network.

As the great silk producer, she resembled in one respect the primary producing countries of the Asiatic tropics and subtropics. On balance, prior to 1930, she exported heavily to the United States, and imported from Europe. Unlike these tropical countries generally, on the other hand, she imported heavily from southern Asia and the Dominions, and found her second principal market in China. Unlike them, too, she built up sizable earnings from overseas investment, shipping, and other services, which helped particularly to balance her accounts with Asia.

In this intricate web of transactions no single credit item can realistically be set off against any single debit. Nevertheless, Japan's midposition in the transition to industrialism is exemplified in the mutual dependence of these trading balances. For twenty-five years or more she was able to use the surplus proceeds both of raw silk exports to the United States and of sales of cotton manufactures and other factory goods in China to settle deficits arising from purchases of equipment in Europe and of raw materials in southern Asia and Australia.[34]

The collapse of silk prices in the late twenties induced a radical change in this position, without lessening at all Japan's multilateral dependence. Table 35 shows the shift in her regional trade balances between 1927 and 1936.

Table 35. *Regional Overseas Trade Balances of Japan Proper,*
1927, 1936[a]
(millions of yen)

	1927	1936
All countries	−329	−56
Asia	−175	+326
Korea and Formosa	−147	+15
China (including		
Manchuria and Hongkong)	+132	+318
India	−103	−113
Southeast Asia	−61	+64
United States	+167	−244
Europe	−240	−22
British Dominions	−87	−159
Other	+6	+43

a Department of Finance, *Financial and Economic Annual of Japan, 1937*, Tokyo, 1938, pp. 142-43.

The depreciation of the yen, following the decline of silk, ushered in a trading and industrial boom which pushed Japan still further toward the typical posture of a nation industrializing with scanty natural resources. Silk losses were more than replaced by a diversified export business in cotton and rayon goods and other manufactures. However, these goods went mainly to Asia, not the United States. Within her own spreading empire Japan poured resources into programs of development. Elsewhere her exporters reaped the windfall harvest of a depreciated yen. Meanwhile the whole expansion of arms and industry in the thirties drew increasing supplies of materials and equipment from the United States. The result was a dramatic overturn in the Japanese-American balance of trade. Japan's former dollar surplus gave way to a large deficit, which was partly caused (and paid for) by exchange surpluses accruing from the spread of her export manufactures in Asia and Africa.

34 See League of Nations, *The Network of World Trade*, Geneva, 1942, pp. 61-63, 83.

Fortunately the world's system of multilateral clearing was still largely in force at the time. It enabled Japan to turn a critical corner in her industrial transition, at the price of some exchange disorder, and a good deal of trade recrimination around the world. Implicit in her new trading position, however, was a latent instability. Many of her import requirements she could only meet economically in the United States. Given her limited American market, this meant in turn that she must be able to convert her export earnings elsewhere into dollars. Any break in the pattern of triangulation would plunge her into difficulties.

Already in 1936 this problem of bilateralism was beginning to present itself. A decade later, in postwar Japanese recovery, it was to assume critical proportions. The later, postwar phase resulted partly from the loss of her colonies, mainly from the general dollar shortage which most of the world shared with Japan. As it first appeared in the late thirties, it was of Japan's own making. War and conquest stepped up her import requirements from dollar and sterling areas. At the same time they crippled her exports to these regions, deflecting her resources increasingly to armament and to Yen Bloc exports. Here, in the expanding Empire, Japanese firms could monopolize the market, but their exports did not yield foreign exchange to finance imports from the outside world. The immediate result, as described in Chapter 2, was an exchange crisis which weakened her ability to get essential imports and put her in the strait jacket of a war economy after 1937. From the more far-reaching consequences of the whole policy, throughout the Far East, she is still struggling to extricate herself.

Economic Opportunity and National Security. Looking back over the seventy years from 1868 to 1938, one must conclude that Japan's great external opportunity arose not so much from her priority in Far Eastern industrialization, or her seizure of territory, as from the whole conjuncture of circumstances which enabled her to enter and trade peacefully in an expanding, relatively free, world economy.

This period witnessed a tremendous growth in the world's primary production, in both the tropics and the temperate zone. Food and industrial materials were poured out in ever increasing volume for the use of industrializing peoples able like the Japanese to export manufactures in exchange. Factory technique and capital migrated around the globe, largely free of political interference. The secrets of science and machinery were available to any peoples able to put them to effective use. War and political disorder periodically interrupted the peace of the Far East. But they dealt no shattering blows to economic life until Japan herself precipitated a global conflict in 1941.

In this historical context Japan developed the great network of commerce which is the subject of these chapters. Trading with the West, she specialized in products requiring cheap labor, plus a minimum of capital and special skills, exchanging them for primary produce, machinery, and equipment which she could not produce advantageously herself. Particularly important was her great farm-filature export, raw silk, which enjoyed a high income elasticity in the American market for half a century. Trading with the East, on the other hand, she built up an export business in factory goods which she could produce more efficiently than her neighbors, using them to buy food and industrial materials. Cheap water transport in all directions was an inestimable advantage. So, too, was the fact that, unlike a great continental nation, her demand upon world commodity supplies was not so great in size as to place her at a serious disadvantage in bartering her exports for them.

Japan's colonial empire was of some help in meeting her requirements, particularly for food. Far more important, however, was the relative freedom and efficiency of the world system of multilateral trade. Within wide limits it enabled her to buy and sell wherever her advantage lay, offsetting the resulting exchange balances with little or no regard to their pattern of distribution. Only with the weakening and breakdown of the system—in which Japanese aggression itself played a large part—did it become apparent how basic this was to the economic opportunity of the Japanese. Despite their meager physical resources it enabled them through their industry and enterprise to advance and prosper economically.

The tragedy of modern times is that such economic dependence breeds national insecurity. Among a people like the Japanese, anxieties on this score would be natural, whatever their political tradition. For they are a small island nation looking out on great continental neighbors both to the East and to the West. As it was, these anxieties were preyed upon by a militaristic leadership not only politically chauvinist but economically quite illiterate. At the very crest of their economic expansion, accordingly, the Japanese were coerced and cajoled into withdrawing from the world system and making instead a supreme bid for political hegemony in East Asia.

Ironically, this bid for empire was justified on the grounds of economic necessity. To be sure, the spread of economic nationalism in the thirties was putting brakes on further Japanese trade expansion for the moment, and clouding its outlook in the future. Yet Japan's real economic interest could only lie in combatting, not reinforcing, this inimical drift to trade restriction and bilateralism. It called at least for a prudent calculation of the chances of victory on the battlefield, and still more for a wider estimate as to whether the kind of world which would ensue would be one in which Japan could prosper. In both respects there was a disastrous failure of statesmanship.

CHAPTER 8

STRUCTURAL CHANGE:
THE REDIRECTION OF DEMAND

Income Growth and Structural Change

A familiar characteristic of economic development everywhere is the tendency, as the per capita income of a community grows, for people and productive resources to be transferred progressively out of agricultural pursuits into other types of employment. With advancing wealth and well-being, opportunities for gainful employment come to center more and more in manufacturing, commerce, and other service trades. Through the more rapid gains of these nonextractive industries the economy as a whole takes on a more balanced and diversified character.[1]

This differential growth may actually draw people out of agriculture, forestry, and fishing. More often, it only absorbs an increasing share of the growth in the working population; there is no absolute decline in agricultural employment. But in either case the so-called secondary and tertiary industries come to occupy a rising percentage of the labor force. They also provide a growing share of the national product. Indeed, this latter shift in the sources of national income is likely to proceed more rapidly than occupational redistribution itself. For the money value of output per worker in many of these newer trades is apt to be comparatively high, by virtue of greater mechanization, economies of large-scale production, or social restrictions of one sort or another upon the supply of equipment and skills of the necessary types. The historical rise in national income per capita therefore reflects two tendencies at work. One is the general advance in productivity fostered throughout the economy by technological advance. The other is the transfer of employment to pursuits with a higher net-value product. The growth of real income may also be advanced or retarded by a third circumstance: changes from one year to another in the terms on which a country

[1] The terms "extractive industries" and "primary industries" are used variously by different writers. In this study it has seemed most useful to group agriculture, forestry, fishing, and mining in this category, as being the occupations closely related to exploitation of Japan's natural resources. This classification is retained through the present chapter, although it will be evident that many statements referring to the shift of employment away from the extractive industries apply less to mining than to the other three, and especially agriculture. The secondary industries include manufacturing and construction; the tertiary industries commerce, finance, transport, communication, and professional and personal services.

trades its exports for its imports in exchanges with the outside world.

This process of structural change, of course, has been a conspicuous feature of modern Japan. Indeed, it is discernible, albeit at a slow pace, long before Japan was thrown open to the tides of Westernization. In preceding chapters we have observed its progress as a result of differential rates of growth in various sectors of the economy over the first fifty or sixty years of industrialization. It remains now to direct attention more specifically to the resulting shift in Japan's economic center of gravity.

Industrial Diversification. The fact that economic progress is typically accompanied by a redistribution of employment from agriculture to manufacturing and the services is a commonplace. Low-standard countries are usually countries whose people are largely occupied in farming, pastoral, forestry, and fishing pursuits. Before the Industrial Revolution even the more advanced countries of Europe probably had no less than 50% of their people in agriculture.[2] This was true of Germany as late as 1870. It has remained characteristic of Eastern Europe in modern times, and has been an important factor in the poverty, illiteracy, and rural backwardness of many parts of this region. The contrasting situation in much of Western Europe is symptomatic of the changes wrought by nineteenth century industrialization. It is illustrated by the following percentages of population remaining in agriculture and fishing during the interwar period: Netherlands (1930), 20.6%; Germany (1933), 28.9%; the United Kingdom (1931), 5.6%.[3] Similarly, while the total labor force of the United States grew from 29.1 million in 1900 to 54.2 million in 1940, the number of persons occupied in agriculture, forestry, and fishing actually declined from 11.3 to 9.4 million.[4] Most of the gain in total employment occurred in manufacturing and the service trades, especially the latter.

Throughout Asia today, excepting in Japan, the proportion of the working population in agriculture runs as high as 60 to 80%. In India the 1931 census showed 67.1% engaged in agriculture, forestry, and fishing.[5] Buck's sample studies of 1929-31 found 73% of China's male working population in agriculture, a third

---

[2] Abbott Payson Usher, *An Introduction to the Industrial History of England,* Boston, 1920, p. 259. In France at the beginning of the nineteenth century only one person in fifteen lived in a town of 20,000 or more inhabitants, while in Germany nearly 75% of the population was classified as rural. J. H. Clapham, *The Economic Development of France and Germany, 1815-1914,* Cambridge, 1923, pp. 54, 82.

[3] *Statistical Yearbook of the League of Nations, 1934/35,* Geneva, 1935, pp. 44-47.

[4] Solomon Fabricant, *Labor Savings in American Industry, 1899-1939,* New York: National Bureau of Economic Research, 1945, p. 30.

[5] *Statistical Yearbook of the League of Nations, 1934/35,* cited, p. 43.

or more of them with supplementary employment in other trades.[6] The experience of the rest of the world argues that any significant rise in income and productivity in Far Eastern countries will necessitate (and bring about) a transfer of workers out of agriculture, or at least the absorption of a growing share of the expanding population in industry, transport, trade, government, and the other services. Only in this way can these peoples free themselves from the pressure of population on land, and raise substantially the level of material well-being.

Colin Clark calls this principle of growth "Petty's Law," after the seventeenth century English economist who gave it one of its earliest formulations. Clark himself describes it as "the most important concomitant of economic progress, namely the movement of working population from agriculture to manufacture, and from manufacture to commerce and services." In his *Conditions of Economic Progress*[7] he examines it systematically, with a wealth of supporting detail drawn from different countries and historical periods. He has little difficulty in showing a rough but significant relationship between real income per capita and the percentage of workers in manufacturing and the services. This appears historically within countries, and as among countries during the years 1925-34. The higher the level of incomes, the smaller the share of the population in the extractive industries.

While this principle is almost a truism, it is a truism which is easily misinterpreted. From the fact that wealthy countries tend to have diversified structures of employment and income, there is a tendency sometimes to conclude that a similar transfer of resources away from agricultural employment in the peasant economies of Asia will necessarily reflect—even more, will itself bring about—a corresponding economic advance. This tendency appears, for example, in a good deal of the discussion of China's need for industrialization. Along with other considerations, it also underlies some of the attacks levelled against the prewar specialization of Southeast Asia in agricultural and mineral production for export. The way to progress is to put more people to work in industry; dependence upon agriculture is colonial and backward.

Before entering upon the Japanese case, it may be well to enter a broad caveat against any simple correlation between the growth of real income per capita and the degree of diversification ("bal-

---

[6] J. Lossing Buck, *Land Utilization in China*, Chicago, 1937, p. 372.

[7] See rev. edn., London, 1951, chap. 9. Although I have made little use of Clark's statistical data on Japan, I am much indebted to him for his stimulating and industrious explorations of growth and structural change in national economies around the world.

ance") in the employment of a country's resources. Several points are worth noting.

First, as discussed later, the structure of employment and income is influenced by a country's needs and opportunities in foreign trade. In themselves these may work either for or against the industrialization of employment. International specialization on the principle of comparative advantage should promote a growth of productivity and income, other things being equal. But the direction and rate of change in resource utilization depend on the nature of comparative advantage in the particular case. Denmark, for example, raised her standard of living by creating an intensive, capitalistic agriculture geared to a large export market in foodstuffs. In the case of Japan, on the other hand, the industrialization of a peasant population has been accelerated by favorable opportunities to produce cotton goods and other manufactures for world markets.[8]

Second, the *recorded* gain in employment and real income as manufacturing and the services grow is always specious in some degree. Especially is this true of a country emerging from a primitive state of economic organization. For one thing, as an index of welfare, income per head takes no account of the human and social costs of industrialism, or of the distribution of income among classes. But even apart from this, some of the apparent growth in productive activity is nothing more than the transfer of such activity from the self-sufficient family or village economy to the market place. Here it is apt to enter the country's statistical accounts as a net gain. Actually it may represent merely a greater commercialization of functions previously carried on in the home or the neighborhood. This fact complicates all long-term calculations of the trend of employment and income in Japan. Characteristically in Far Eastern countries there is a tendency to underestimate noncommercial production for home use.

Also, the growth of occupational and regional specialization, including the rise of cities, creates new requirements for transportation, banking institutions, public utilities, and social services. Some of these goods and services add nothing themselves to the level of material well-being except as they are essential to the new forms of production and the mode of life they necessitate. A picul of rice is not more nutritious because it has been transported a long distance. There is no real increase in income from the fact that urban congestion has to be offset by building and operating a subway

___

[8] Another qualification associated with foreign trade is the possibility that potential gains in per capita income associated with the industrialization of employment may be cancelled out by a deterioration in the barter terms of trade with the outside world.

system so that people can go about their business. Yet the expansion of such services is duly recorded in the national account as an advance in net production. For these reasons as well there is no necessary correlation between the recorded shift from primary to secondary and tertiary employment and economic progress in terms of real income.[9]

Finally, the notion that industrialization is necessarily the principal road to better living standards in Asia can easily lead to a neglect of the great potentialities of raising productivity in peasant farming. Even in the case of Japan this sector of growth provided a significant phase of economic development. Agricultural output appears at least to have doubled in the half century before World War II. (See Chapter 3.) So preponderant is agriculture in most underdeveloped countries that a gain of this magnitude raises real income as much as a manyfold gain in industrial production.

The redirection of employment toward manufacturing and services, while usually a necessary condition of economic advance, is by no means a *sufficient* condition. Except as it is the outgrowth of expansive stimuli which improve technology and raise incomes, in agriculture as well as in industry, it is likely to be impossible of achievement on any scale, owing to the lack of industrial markets and of food supply for the industrial labor force. And if industrialization is merely forced by the subsidy of home industries, through restricting imported goods or otherwise taxing the population, the result may well be a reduction rather than increase in real national income.[10]

[9] For these reasons, too, income comparisons between preindustrial and advanced countries commonly exaggerate the disparity in real income. For example, Simon Kuznets has attempted a rough revaluation of T. C. Liu's estimate of China's gross national product (in U.S. dollars) to make it more comparable with similar estimates for the United States. He makes larger allowances, first, for underenumeration of goods and services in the nonmarket sector, and, second, for a lower relative price level in China than is reflected in Liu's ratio of staple crop prices. Finally, he increases the Chinese figure to allow for greater elements of "grossness" in an advanced industrial economy—that is, the higher ratio of net product to the consumption of basic materials which arises from the more complex organization of the latter.

These adjustments raise Liu's estimate of gross national product in China (1931-36 average) from $16.7 to 26.5 billion. Kuznets believes this figure is still perhaps 20% too low for purposes of comparison. He concludes that China's per capita product was about U.S. $70. This would make it about one eighth, not one thirteenth, of the comparable figure for the United States, "Internation Comparisons of National Income," *Econometrica*, vol. 16, no. 1, January 1948, pp. 86-90.

[10] The importance for Japan's industrialization of her growing food and raw material output has been stressed in Chapter 3. Yet her comparatively small population and her ample foreign trade opportunities made this aspect less vital for her than it must be for China or India. Except as agricultural technique is improved, no large fraction of the population can be shifted out of farming into industry, nor

"Excessive emphasis on industry for industry's sake," says the International Bank for Reconstruction and Development, ". . . may leave an underdeveloped country with the symbol of development rather than the substance." Today the world abounds in "diversified" or "balanced" economies, where a good deal of industrial employment and investment opportunity have been gained only at the expense of total national productivity and wealth. In the main this was not the case with Japan's industrialization prior to 1938; but here too the creation by the State of numerous strategic industries brought dubious gains in the economic realm.

For a variety of reasons, therefore, it is misleading to say that the poverty of Asia will be relieved if x percentage of its working population can be shifted from agriculture to industrial pursuits. This type of statement has more validity for underdeveloped regions than elsewhere, it is true. The reason is that the transfer of peasant populations out of self-sufficient agriculture into more mechanized and urbanized occupations will itself expose them more rapidly to new economic incentives and educational advantages likely to raise their productive efficiency. The general level of technical skills may thus be improved more rapidly than otherwise would be the case. Especially is this true where the persistence of family and village ties provides a channel for the return flow of new ideas, skills, and capital to the countryside. Even so, such a transfer is only one condition of economic progress. It is apt to prove ineffectual unless other expansive forces are at work. The readiness of workers and investors to adapt themselves to changing opportunities, and the smoothness of the transition, are themselves important factors in growth. But the shifting pattern of resource utilization which accompanies real growth must be the result of technical progress, capital accumulation, and widening market opportunities.

In an analysis of Japan's historical experience, therefore, it has seemed best to deal first with these various factors in the growth of her productive powers (Chapters 3-7), and only then to ask what alterations they brought about in the structure of employment and income. This chapter considers the principal forces working to shift the balance of the Japanese economy increasingly toward manufacturing and various services. These are found primarily in the changing structure of domestic demand, reinforced by parallel changes in international demands affecting the volume and character of foreign trade. (The critical role of the State in accelerating the process is left largely to Chapter 10.) The effect of

---

can even the growth of the working population be absorbed in industry, without creating a formidable food import problem.

these shifts in spending patterns upon the utilization of resources is examined in Chapter 9. Here it will be evident that the redistribution of Japanese labor among various employments was influenced not only by the changing demand for goods and services, but also by technical and social factors controlling the relative supplies of different factors of production and the uses to which they were put.

Income Levels and Spending Habits. The basic reason for the redirection of productive activity, as economic development proceeds, is found in progressive changes which take place in what people want and can afford to buy with the growing income at their disposal. At very low levels of productivity and income, life is an unrelenting struggle to provide the bare necessities of physical existence. Little productive effort, or money income, can be devoted to the provision of comforts and luxuries. Still less is available for investment in the creation of new capital assets for future use. The bulk of it goes into food, mostly self-supplied.

An extreme case is that of the primitive Ainu of Japan. Their food consumption even on the most meager basis was once reported as absorbing 85 to 95% of their total expenditure.[11] More generally throughout Asia at least 60% of the economic activity of lower-income groups, who form the bulk of the population, is required to provide a simple vegetarian diet, from either home production or food purchased on the market. Clothing and housing absorb most of the remainder. Morimoto's sample budget studies in Japan during 1913-15, for example, show that food costs (including self-supplied food) amounted to 60% or more of the family budgets of tenant farmers and of urban workers at the level of "primary" poverty. Clothing and housing added another 15 to 20%, leaving only the slenderest margin for other amenities. Tenant farmers in Hokkaido devoted only 6.6% of their living expenses to "recreation," mostly in the form of smoking and pilgrimages.[12]

Other Far Eastern worker groups at similar levels of living have shown the same high percentage of family expenditure on food: 62% among Chinese handicraft workers in Tientsin (1930?);[13] 59% among farmers in North and East China (1922-

[11] Kokichi Morimoto, *The Standard of Living in Japan*, Baltimore, 1918, p. 18. A comparable instance is that of certain low-income families in Peiping, where Dr. Louise Morrow found food expenditure averaging 87% of total expenditure in 1923. Sidney D. Gamble, *How Chinese Families Live in Peiping*, New York, 1933, p. 322.

[12] *ibid.*, pp. 129, 142. Morimoto classifies these groups among the Japanese "poor," who, with incomes below 700 yen a year, could make no provision for comfort or luxury.

[13] Franklin L. Ho, *Industries*, Shanghai: China Institute of Pacific Relations, 1931, p. 47.

25) ;[14] and 58% among Indian working-class families in Ahmada-
bad (1926).[15] In the Near East, as well, food absorbs over 60% of
most family budgets.[16] Colin Clark's comparisons of national income during 1925-34 yield similar conclusions. Whereas only 11%
of income in the United States was spent on food and farm products,
the corresponding percentages were 70% for India, and 80% for
China.[17]

Under such conditions demand is directed overwhelmingly to
the products of extractive industries. Even clothing, shelter, and
fuel represent only small margins of value added to the products of
these industries by manufacture and transport. And such capital
construction as takes place is of a very simple character. It is
largely the maintenance and improvement of land, dwellings, and
inexpensive tools, accomplished in the spare time of families engaged mainly in farm cultivation. The concentration of population
and capital in agriculture and related occupations thus reflects a
parallel concentration of demand on primary goods. Moreover these
are typically consumed near the point of production and undergo
little processing before their final use. Charcoal, homespun cloth,
milled rice, mud and straw dwellings—these are the products of
local industry at its most primitive level.

As productivity and incomes rise, the structure of demand tends
to shift. Up to a certain point, it is true, any increments of income
may also be spent mainly on food. Thus Gamble found that food
expenditures, which absorbed over 60% of the budgets of the poorest
families in Peiping during 1926-27, tended to rise almost in proportion to income until the latter exceeded Ch. $40 a month.[18] This
higher food expenditure may afford a more adequate diet. Or it
may in part permit the substitution of preferred foods—as in the
historical shift from millet to rice in Japan.

Above a rather low level, however, family expenditures increase
more rapidly on clothing and housing of better and more varied
types, and still more on health, education, recreation, and other
comforts or luxuries. In historical terms, the income elasticities of

[14] J. Lossing Buck, *Chinese Farm Economy*, Shanghai, 1930, p. 386. In a summary
of sixty-nine Chinese family budget studies, L. K. Tao found the modal expenditure
on food to be 57.5%. *The Standard of Living of Chinese Workers*, Shanghai: China
Institute of Pacific Relations, 1931, pp. 8-9.

[15] "Recent Family Budget Inquiries," *International Labour Review*, vol. xxviii,
no. 5, November 1933, p. 654.

[16] Alfred Bonné, *The Economic Development of the Middle East*, New York,
1945, p. 73.

[17] "Economic Growth and Fluctuations," *Econometrica*, vol. 16, no. 1, January 1948,
p. 63. The percentages for China and India can be regarded as only the roughest of
approximations.

[18] *op.cit.*, p. 49.

demand for such goods and services are everywhere higher than those for food and other basic necessities. People are better able to satisfy long-felt wants; new needs and desires are multiplied; and a growing margin of labor, materials, or money income is available for capital improvements. It now becomes possible, too, for the state to appropriate a larger share of the national income to be spent on armaments and capital equipment. There is a corresponding decline in the proportion of resources spent on the bare necessities of life.

Countries or population groups with high incomes therefore devote a major share of their incomes to the diversified components of well-being as they may define them; also, perhaps, to armament and war. This in turn directs an increasing share of spending away from the extractive industries, the chief source of food and other simple necessities. Manufactured products themselves embody certain raw materials, of course. But the latter represent only a part of their total cost, commonly 20 to 60%. Moreover, this part is apt to decrease as processing becomes more advanced; as machinery and equipment grow in amount and complexity, with greater outlays for depreciation; and as the wider organization of markets necessitates increased transport and handling services to serve the more highly specialized economy. The service occupations, e.g., government and the private professions, also require certain materials and equipment. But their costs are usually only a part of the market value of such services. And the percentage of their value attributable in turn to primary production is still smaller, for they are apt to be highly fabricated.

A rise in incomes, therefore, tends to induce changes in the pattern of consumption and capital requirements which redirect employment progressively toward new and more diversified trades. And as the economy becomes more commercialized and urbanized, even the satisfaction of basic wants for food, clothing, and shelter requires that a growing part of the population be occupied in trade and transport, finance, manufacturing, public services, and the like. A city worker may spend no smaller fraction of his income on basic necessities than his farming cousins, and be no better off. Yet even the maintenance of this level of living under urban conditions will mean greater relative employment of productive resources in the secondary and tertiary industries.

National Expenditures in Prewar Japan. These principles are readily verified in the experience of Japan, so far as their general validity is concerned. Supporting evidence of one sort or another has been cited in the foregoing chapters. The actual measurement of the changing structure of national demand over a period of years, however, is another matter. The subject presents methodological problems of some complexity. It also requires an array of factual data such as are largely lacking for Japan prior to World War II. The statistical evidence is confined mainly to the later years, leaving one to draw such inferences as he may concerning the changes which had taken place in earlier decades.

An initial approach is to examine the components of gross national product or expenditure. Estimates of these national accounts for years beginning with 1930 have been published by the Economic Stabilization Board. Table 36 summarizes them for 1930, a

Table 36. *Gross National Expenditure in Japan Proper,*
1930, 1934, 1938 (Economic Stabilization Board)[a]
(billions of current yen)

	1930	1934	1938
Total expenditure at market prices	*12.8*	*15.0*	*26.3*
Personal consumption expenditure	*9.6*	*10.4*	*13.7*
Food	2.9	3.7	5.2
Housing (and furnishings)	1.3	1.4	1.6
Heat and light	0.5	0.5	0.7
Clothing	1.1	1.1	1.4
Other	3.8	3.7	4.8
Government expenditure on goods			
and services	*1.8*	*2.4*	*6.9*
National	1.0	1.7	6.2
Military	(0.4)	(0.9)	(5.0)
Local	0.7	0.7	0.7
Gross private domestic investment	*1.1*	*2.0*	*4.8*
Residential construction	0.3	0.3	0.4
Producers' plant and equipment	0.3	0.6	2.8
Net change in business			
inventories	0.6	1.1	1.6
Net foreign investment	*0.4*	*0.2*	*0.9*

a Estimates of the Economic Stabilization Board, taken here from Yuzo Yamada, *Nihon Kokumin Shotoku Suikei Shiryō*, Tokyo, 1951, pp. 21, 95-96, 106.

year of moderate depression, 1934, a year of substantial recovery, and 1938, when war mobilization was well under way. They can hardly be regarded as more than the roughest of approximations at best. But they present the major components of national expenditure in at least their general order of magnitude. These are (1) personal consumer outlay (including income in kind), (2) government purchases of goods and services, (3) gross private domestic investment, and (4) net foreign investment. Gross national product, less the net addition to business inventories (included in gross capital investment), is what the U.S. Department of Commerce calls "the consolidated sales of the economy." With an allowance for consumption of durable capital it becomes net national product.

Net foreign investment calls particularly for explanation. This is the net current payment of "the rest of the world" to Japan Proper, after offsetting all current outpayments against inpayments. The outside world was buying Japanese-produced goods and services, or making other remittances to Japan Proper for various purposes. Meanwhile Japanese businessmen, consumers, and the government were devoting some fraction of their expenditures to purchases and other remittances abroad. The balance of these current transactions with foreign countries and the colonies is net foreign investment. Fluctuating from year to year, it was a relatively small component of the national expenditure accounts through most of the prewar era. However, the gross volume of inpayments and outpayments grew to large proportions in the later decades. (See Chapter 6.) Thus the allocation of Japanese resources among various employments came to be influenced significantly by the size and character of these international exchanges, along with the outlays of businessmen, consumers, and the government on domestic goods and services.

Historically, important shifts also took place among the other major components of national expenditure, and in the composition of each.

Government purchases of goods and services, for example, tended to grow in importance as the State enlarged the scale of its activities. Its outlays for current goods and services, and investment in public enterprises, appear to have comprised 15% or so of gross national expenditure through the years 1918-37. (This excludes the operating expenses of government enterprises like the railways, electrical communications, and military industries, as well as government debt service, pensions, and other transfer payments.) Earlier they were a somewhat smaller share in all probability, while after 1937 they rose to a wartime peak of 50% in 1944.

State spending took the form mainly of wages and salaries paid to employees in the service of national and local agencies. The remainder consisted of purchases of materials and equipment for the armed forces, public works, education, and other activities. Military expenditure absorbed a quarter of the total through the twenties, and a rising percentage thereafter. In the actual process of industrialization, of course, government spending for both current and investment purposes was more significant than these yen outlays alone might suggest. (See Chapter 10.) Particularly before 1910, and again after 1937, Army and Navy orders for munitions and other war equipment (together with subsidies, tax rebates, and tariffs) were the props upon which many of Japan's heavy industries were built and upon which they depended largely for their profits.[19]

The growth of investment expenditure, private or public, meant a rising demand for newly produced machinery, construction materials, and other producer goods of domestic or foreign manufacture. Such capital outlays were devoted partly to offsetting the depreciation of existing capital assets. To maintain unimpaired this capital plant must have absorbed an increasing share of the country's productive activities with the growth in national wealth. The remainder of investment outlay went into increasing the stock of capital in amounts which varied widely from year to year. (See Chapter 5.)

Private domestic investment, like government expenditure, furnished a relatively small but probably increasing proportion of gross national expenditure. During the interwar years one may guess that it tended to range between 10% and 20% as a rule. The figures of the Economic Stabilization Board cited in Table 22 actually put it at 13% from 1930 through 1936, though reasons were given in Chapter 5 for mistrusting the whole computation. By its nature it exerted a dynamic influence on the level of Japanese employment and income, both short-term variations and long-term potential. A considerable share of capital outlay was devoted to construction activity, mainly land improvements and building structures. It provided in addition a growing market for the machinery and equipment industries, which, together with imports of capital goods, served also to enlarge Japan's industrial capacity. In this sense its strategic role in the structural changes under discussion here far outweighed its place in the national expenditure totals.

By far the largest component of the "consolidated sales of the Japanese economy" represented personal consumption expenditure. Most of the productive resources of the country continued to be devoted directly or indirectly to the consumer needs of the growing population. This was true of the later as well as the earlier decades of modern Japan, though perhaps in somewhat lesser degree. Be-

[19] Estimates of government outlays and other main components of national expenditure in five-year averages for the years 1918 and thereafter will be found in Yuzo Yamada, *Nihon Kokumin Shotoku Suikei Shiryō*, Tokyo, 1951, table 21. Professor Yamada also compiles a great deal of supporting detail for these years, and more fragmentary data on consumption, savings, and taxes back as far as 1887. To appraise this valuable work adequately, and to make full critical use of it, is an undertaking beyond the present study. Certain gaps and ambiguities are so evident, however, that only the most general significance can be attached to Professor Yamada's over-all statistical conclusions.

tween 1918 and 1937 private consumer outlay accounted for no less than 70% of gross national expenditure. Very likely the figure would run to 75% or more if a full accounting were made. Consumption requirements absorbed 70 to 90% of personal income through this period, according to Yamada's estimates. (*ibid.*, tables 18, 21.) Taxes (exclusive of indirect taxes) accounted for 7 to 9%. The remainder went into liquid savings—cash, bank deposits, and securities—in amounts which are estimated all the way from 25% of aggregate personal income in the prosperous year 1937 to very small (or negative) sums in years of depression.

Again the crudity of all such estimates must be acknowledged. It is difficult even to give any sharp definition to these concepts in the less commercialized sectors of the Japanese economy. The basic data are fragmentary and unreliable. There is no doubt, in any event, that personal consumption accounted for the bulk of national spending when the national accounts are consolidated as in Table 36. It still exceeded two thirds of gross national expenditure in 1936, despite the demands of the military and the boom in industrial construction. Not until 1941, under the impact of full-scale war preparations, did it first drop below one half.

Food expenditure, as one would expect, remained the largest item in consumption despite the rise in per capita income through the preceding decades. It took 35% of private consumer outlay from 1930 through 1938, according to these figures. This percentage is surprisingly low for a people still as poor as the Japanese. Beverages and tobacco are believed to be excluded, and one suspects that self-supplied foodstuffs may not be adequately allowed for. Household surveys used in constructing these accounts tend to understate family income and expenditure. Yet even if the correct figure was nearer 45% it had probably declined from the earlier levels, of 1880 or 1910. Yamada quotes one estimate for 1904 placing food outlays at 60% of national consumer expenditure. (*ibid.*, p. 95.) By contrast, the American people devoted only 30% of their consumer outlay to food in the mid-thirties, despite their higher dietary standard.[20]

[20] U.S. Department of Commerce, *National Income and Product Statistics of the United States, 1929-46*, Washington, 1947, pp. 41-44.

Foodstuffs absorbed 49.5% of total consumer expenditure in Japan during 1940, according to estimates of the Ministry of Finance. Detailed figures of such expenditures during the fiscal years 1940-44 appear in *Kokumin Shotoku Suikei*, Tokyo, 1947, and in English in U.S. Strategic Bombing Survey, *The Effects of Strategic Bombing on Japan's War Economy*, Washington, 1946, app. B. The Ministry estimates run consistently well above those of the Economic Stabilization Board, however. Total consumer expenditure is put at 26.7 billion yen in 1940 as against the Board's figure of 18.6 billion, while food outlays are 11.4 billion yen as compared with 7.1 billion yen. Not having the original publications I am unable to reconcile

Expenditures for clothing and for housing each now absorbed 10 to 15% of private consumer purchases, on the accounting of Table 36. Another 5% went into heat and light. Still another 10%, more or less, included here in "other" expenditures, were devoted to other industrial products: furnishings, medical supplies, recreational materials, etc. Here were found various items serving the luxury tastes of the more well-to-do classes, as well as the health and general well-being of larger numbers. As income grew to the point where it could provide more than the bare necessities, a considerable share of the margin went into better housing and clothing, electricity, soap and medicines, books and newspapers, and other commodities supplied mainly by the manufacturing and construction industries.

A conspicuous feature of the average Japanese consumer budget, however, as compared with that of the typical American family, is the slight importance of durable consumer goods. Small expenditures on furniture, automobiles, household equipment, etc. are of course a characteristic of a low material standard of living. They are also a factor of stability in an economy, for the demand for such items is apt to be highly sensitive to changes from year to year in consumer income. In Japan the metalworking industries in particular have remained geared much more largely to the market for producers' equipment.

A second contrast with American spending patterns is seen in the smaller place of consumer services, i.e., those commercialized outside the family relationship. House rents and other service outlays amounted to as much as 40% of consumer spending in the United States during the decade 1929-38. The Japanese figure can hardly have approached this level; probably it was no more than 25%. Some such conclusion is supported by family budget data given later in this chapter. Wage-earner families with an average income of 600 yen in 1926—above the median for the population as a whole—devoted 23% of their consumer outlay to services.

Even so, personal services performed outside the family must have gained in significance with the urbanization and commercialization of Japanese economic life. The following estimate of personal consumption expenditure during 1938, somewhat more detailed than Table 36, suggests the range and importance of those family outlays:[21]

the differences; nor does Professor Yamada do so. He himself uses the Board estimates in the work cited above.

[21] Estimates of the Economic Stabilization Board, given in United Nations, Statistical Office, *National Income Statistics, 1938-1948*, Lake Success, 1950, p. 107. Rent is believed to include imputed rent on owner-occupied dwellings.

	Millions of Yen	Percent
Personal consumption expenditure		
in Japan, 1938	13,703	100.0
Foodstuffs, beverages, tobacco	6,018	44.0
Housing and furnishings	1,644	12.0
Rent	(1,257)	(9.2)
Other	(387)	(2.8)
Heat and light	699	5.1
Clothing	1,360	9.9
Medical care	893	6.5
Education and amusement	855	6.2
Welfare, religious, and other		
organizations	1,103	8.1
Transportation	1,146	8.4
Overseas travel and remittances	—15	—

Beside housing, family expenditure on commercialized services included transportation (other than purchase and operation of vehicles); electrical and postal communications; the hotel, restaurant, and bathhouse business; medical care; recreation and amusements; private education, religious affairs, and other professional and domestic service. As one would expect, such services were much more important in the family spending of the urban wage and salaried class than among farmers. A full itemization would also include the tax-supported services of the State, of which public education was the most important civilian component in prewar Japan.

Here, then, in these expenditure patterns of the interwar period is some indication of the array of money outlays now directing the allocation of Japanese resources and productive activity after a half century of industrialization.

The actual impact of such spending by consumers, investors, and government agencies upon particular industries and occupations is not adequately measured in this fashion, of course. For this also involved the whole organization and technology of the Japanese economy. The demand for food and clothing, for example, was no longer so largely a demand for farm and handicraft labor in the locality where these products were consumed. To a far greater degree it was now a complex of demands for the products and services of various industries contributing to the production and movement of these goods through various stages to the point of consumption. Moreover, it was not wholly a demand for domestic goods and services. Partly it was spent on commodities from overseas, which enable foreign buyers in turn to purchase Japanese goods of quite different character. As a first approach to the subject, nevertheless, the national expenditure accounts explained above tell a good deal about the broad outlines of the demands operating to shape the structure of the Japanese economy toward the end of the prewar era.

Family Income and Expenditure. When one turns to the earlier decades for evidence concerning the historical changes in expenditure patterns which accompanied economic growth, the data become much more fragmentary. For great numbers of the population it might be safe to conclude that no radical alteration occurred from 1870 to 1930 in living and spending habits. Evidently these habits among the Japanese were more resistant to change than among most Western peoples reaching a similar stage of industrialism, owing to the speed of the transition and the force of tradition in Japanese society. Nevertheless, as described in earlier chapters, strong impulses were at work to redirect demand into new channels. They included the growth of national income, the new freedom of consumption and occupation, the tax and spending policies of the State, new institutions and incentives for saving, the crowding of millions of people into industrial employment and urban living, and the slow Westernization of consumer standards and modes of living in the cities.

Many details of this shifting pattern of consumption can be assembled, especially as regards the urban population. Except for a few staples of food and clothing, however, statistics of national consumption over several decades are generally lacking.

As an alternative approach, family budget studies likewise fail to offer direct measurements of trends in consumer spending and saving over a period of years. Numerous family budget surveys were made in Japan after 1920. But their findings cannot be compared in any satisfactory manner. They vary in reliability, scope, and method. Even where more or less identical groups were studied in successive years, their money expenditures were largely influenced by price changes. In particular the price of rice, the chief element in the Japanese worker's cost of living, was subject to wide vagaries. This alone heavily affected the margin of income available for other purposes. Year-to-year changes in the distribution of money expenditures therefore throw little light on long-term trends in spending habits.[22]

Something can be learned, however, from a comparison of the

[22] See, for example, Shiro Kawada's figures on the expenditures of Japanese farm families between 1922 and 1931. "The Income and Living Conditions of the Agrarian Population of Japan," *Journal of the Osaka University of Commerce*, no. 4, December 1936, pp. 19-26.

spending patterns of Japanese families at different levels of income within a single period. We may select for this purpose the well-known family budget inquiry of 1926-27. This year was fairly representative of the interwar years, i.e., the midperiod in Japan's transition from a primitive agrarian economy toward modern industrialism. And the study itself, an official investigation, covered 5,455 families of Japanese farmers, salaried workers, and wage earners. These families were widely distributed by place of residence, occupational employment, and income group. In Table 37 are summarized the findings for all families surveyed; also for three income groups at the bottom, in the middle, and near the top of the nine income classes included.

Before examining the relationships between income and expenditure at different income levels it is important to note where these family income groups fit into the Japanese income structure as a whole. How representative are they? While the precise distribution of household income in 1927 is not known, the rough estimates for 1930 presented in Table 23, above, give useful bearings.

First, well-to-do families at the apex of the country's income scale in 1927 are excluded from Table 37. Nearly all the families surveyed had an income of less than 2,400 yen in the year beginning September 1926.[23] By reference to the 1930 distribution of household income, one may hazard the guess that this income range probably took in over 95% of Japan's 12 million households in 1926-27.[24] It probably accounted for 65% or more of total household income, and a much larger fraction of total consumer expenditure. Thus the spending habits of Japanese families with less than 2,400 yen largely determined the structure of domestic consumer demand in the twenties. To this extent the sample is representative, although it omits an important margin of spending on luxury goods and services.

Second, from families in this income range the budget study selects only farmers, salaried workers, and wage earners. It thus excludes all independent businessmen except farm operators, or nearly 30% of the nonagricultural working population. (See Table 17, above.) The consumption habits of this group, however, probably did not differ radically from those of salaried workers and wage earners of the same income level. The chief difference was perhaps a higher propensity to save on the part of small industrialists and

[23] The upper limit in the case of farmers was a farm of no more than 2.45 acres. This gave approximately the same income limit and included nearly 95% of Japan's farm families. Asahi Shimbun-sha, *Nippon Keizai Tōkei Sōkan*, Tokyo, 1930, p. 688.

[24] National income in 1926-27 was 15% above 1930, according to S. Hijikata's estimates. "Saikin Waga Kuni Kokumin Shotoku," *Keizai-gaku Ronshū*, vol. VIII, July 1938, p. 810. Yamada's figures (*op.cit.*, table 18) give about the same result.

Table 37. Household Income and Expenditure of Farmers,
Wage Earners, and Salaried Workers in Japan, 1926-27[a]

| MONTHLY INCOME CLASSES | PERSONS PER HOUSEHOLD | MONTHLY AMOUNTS (YEN) | | | PERCENTAGE DISTRIBUTION OF EXPENDITURE | | | | | | | | |
		Total Income	Total Expenditure	Surplus or Deficit	Total	Food	House and Furnishings[b]	Clothing	Health and Sanitation	Travel and Communication[c]	Education and Child Care	Recreation and Social Life[d]	Other[e]
All households													
Farmers	5.83	96.2	96.4	-0.2	100.0	45.7	21.3	7.9	2.8	1.8	1.4	10.4	8.7
Wage earners	4.21	102.1	91.4	10.7	100.0	39.8	20.3	13.0	6.4	2.2	2.8	11.0	4.5
Salaried workers	4.17	137.2	124.3	12.8	100.0	32.7	22.9	13.8	6.2	3.1	3.2	13.5	4.6
Under 60 yen													
Farmers	4.33	47.1	59.8	-12.7	100.0	50.2	20.6	7.5	2.9	1.4	1.2	9.0	7.1
Wage earners	3.78	52.9	52.5	0.3	100.0	50.2	19.9	9.8	6.0	1.7	2.8	6.9	2.3
Salaried workers	3.25	53.3	54.1	-0.8	100.0	43.3	23.8	12.6	5.4	1.6	1.9	7.9	3.6
100-120 yen													
Farmers	6.31	109.8	107.7	2.2	100.0	45.3	21.4	8.0	2.5	1.8	1.4	10.6	8.9
Wage earners	4.23	109.3	97.9	11.4	100.0	38.1	21.1	13.1	6.5	2.2	2.8	11.4	4.6
Salaried workers	3.93	110.1	103.3	6.9	100.0	35.1	23.9	13.6	6.2	2.8	2.9	12.4	3.3
180-200 yen													
Farmers	6.56	189.9	139.3	50.6	100.0	36.8	23.6	8.8	4.2	1.9[f]	1.9[f]	15.4	8.3
Wage earners	4.68	188.8	154.5	34.3	100.0	31.8	20.3	15.8	5.8	2.8	2.6	14.0	7.2
Salaried workers	4.60	188.9	166.0	22.9	100.0	30.1	22.9	13.7	6.4	3.4	3.8	14.6	5.2

[a] Data compiled from Taijiro Matsuda, "The Family Budget Enquiry in Japan, 1926-1927," *Bulletin de l'Institut International de Statistique*, vol. xxv, part 2, Tokyo, 1931, pp. 284-301. Mr. Matsuda, chief statistician of the Cabinet Bureau of Statistics, presents the Bureau's survey of family budgets of 670 small farmers, 1,575 salaried workers (clerks, teachers, officials, etc.), and 3,210 wage earners in industry, mining, and transport in widely scattered localities. Budget accounts were organized and supervised for one year beginning September 1926. All households had two to seven persons, and none were engaged in business on their own account except farmers. For other details, see text.

[b] Housing, fuel, light, water supply, furniture, and furnishings.

[c] "Daily journeys," other business travel, transport, correspondence, and stationery.

[d] Gifts, entertainment, and other expenditures for "companionship," pleasure travel, and other cultural and recreational expense.

[e] Miscellaneous, including taxes and hired labor.

[f] For this income group Matsuda's figures show a sharp drop as compared with the corresponding percentages for lower-income farmers. As this seems improbable, the percentages for farmers in the 160-180-yen bracket are substituted here.

tradesmen, an important factor in small-scale capital accumulation.

Third, a more serious limitation is the fact that the number of families selected at different income levels below 2,400 yen is not at all representative of the actual distribution of the Japanese population within this income range. Most importantly, only 306 of the 5,455 families studied—less than 6%—had incomes of less than 720 yen during the year. For the entire Japanese population the proportion was nearer 75%. These millions of lower-income families, moreover, accounted for perhaps as much as 40% of total household income. This unrepresentative weighting results in an average income for all families in the study of over 100 yen a month—actually a middle-class income.

The distribution of expenditures for "all households" in each occupational group of Table 37 should be understood accordingly. It is in no sense an average for the population as a whole, or even for families receiving less than 2,400 yen.

More significant than this "all household" average is a comparison of expenditures by families in individual income classes. Here three are selected: (a) under 60 yen a month, (b) between 100 and and 120 yen, and (c) between 180 and 200 yen. Both money income and income in kind are included. Poor as it is, the lowest group still averages about 50 yen, a higher income than was enjoyed by over half of all Japanese families. The income classes up through the middle group represent another 20% or so of the total population. Families receiving over 120 yen comprised less than 5% of the total. The three classes thus range from middle- to upper-income families in Japan, excluding those at the peak.

Even within this restricted range the findings are of interest:

(1) At the lowest level of income there is no surplus of income over expenditure.[25] Indeed, in this particular twelve-month period, both farmers and salaried workers show a deficit. A surplus only appears in the higher groups, amounting to 15 to 20% of income in the 180-200-yen bracket. The earnings of families receiving less than 2,160 yen a year (180 yen a month) were devoted almost wholly to consumption needs. Only among relatively prosperous families—a minority of the population—could appreciable sums of money be withheld from consumption for investment.[26]

[25] For farmers in particular there are obvious difficulties in attempting (a) to account for income in kind (self-supplied commodities and services mainly), and (b) to separate business and family accounts. Most Japanese farmers keep no accounts on their own initiative, and at this time self-supplied commodities com•prised as much as 42% of the household budgets of agricultural families. Kawada, *op.cit.*, p. 18. These factors make for a fairly wide margin of error.

[26] In the case of farmers, however, the margin of family income over expenditure, as defined here, does not include all savings in the form of business income reinvested in fixed and working capital.

(2) Food expenditure, as a percentage of total expenditure, declines markedly as income increases. Among farmers and wage earners with less than 60 yen a month, food absorbs as much as 50% of the family budget. In the 180-200-yen class it is only about one third of total expenditure, and a still smaller fraction of total income. Yet the more prosperous families were 30 to 50% larger in size, which necessitated correspondingly larger food expenditures to maintain a given diet.[27] Although these upper-middle-class families spent two or three times as much as the poorest group on food, and enjoyed a more ample and diversified diet, they were still able to devote 70% or more of their total resources to other purposes.

(3) "Home" expenditure—housing, furnishings, fuel, light, and sanitation—shows no very significant variation in relation to total expenditure from lower income groups to upper. It tends to increase *pari passu* with total family outlay, varying around a level of 24 to 30%. Only at still higher levels of living than are depicted here would one presumably find its importance lessening.

(4) By contrast, clothing expenditure increases somewhat in relative importance from the lower to the higher income brackets (within each occupational group). Outlays for travel, education, recreation, and social life show a very substantial rise. This last group of items—mainly services—only absorbs 11.5% of the budgets of families with less than 60 yen a month. For those with 180 to 200 yen it comprises about 20%. The actual amounts spent increase four- or fivefold. It is this category of comfort and luxury, along with savings, to which the better-off families devoted most of their rising margin of income over food requirements. By any Western standard, of course, the amounts are still very small. And even then, some of this expenditure is business travel, while much of the remainder is "companionship," i.e., entertainment of friends, gifts, and ceremonial expenses. If the budget seems ample, it is only by comparison with the 6 yen or so expended on such amenities by the lowest income group.

(5) Finally, we may note certain differences between farmers and city workers. Naturally, these have grown in importance with the increasing urbanization of Japan. By this time 56% of the Japanese people resided in places of 5,000 or more, and 20% in

[27] Family size, converted to equivalent adult consumption units, is given as follows for wage earners and salaried workers (Matsuda, *op.cit.*, p. 290):

	Under 60 Yen	180-200 Yen
Wage earners	2.78	3.70
Salaried workers	2.36	3.56

places of over 50,000.[28] Food expenditures tend to be lower, and yet more diversified, among city workers than among farmers in the same income class. Partly this was because urban households were 20 to 30% smaller in size. On rice in particular the amount spent by city people in each class was very much less. Urban families, on the other hand, spent more on clothes, on travel, and on education and medical care.

A more detailed examination of Japanese family budgets shows a much wider range of differences between farm and city living than is depicted in Table 37. These differences reflect the physical necessities of urban life, as well as its social pressures and cultural opportunities. It was among city people particularly that new patterns of domestic life sprang up to enlarge the demand for Western-style goods and services. An industrial environment itself changes the pattern of consumer habits even within identical income classes. That the contrasts were not even greater in Japan is itself testimony to the tenacity of the old ways of living, and the ties which continued to link the city with the countryside.

Income Elasticity of Demand. The figures of Table 37 illustrate the influence of variations in incomes upon Japanese consumption habits within the middle range of incomes. Being confined to the percentage distribution of expenditures, however, they do not themselves give any quantitative measure of the response of family spending to changes in family buying power. This involves a determination of income elasticities of demand, i.e., the ratio between the percentage increase in such expenditures and the associated percentage increase in income. How much does food expenditure rise, for example, with a 1% growth in spending power, other factors remaining constant?

Family budget studies like the 1926-27 inquiry in Japan do not yield a conclusive answer for the country as a whole. But they do enable us to calculate income elasticities of demand for various items at the average level of income within segments of the population at the time of the inquiry. To throw further light on Japanese consumer behavior we shall select the group of 3,210 wage-earner families included in the Japanese budget inquiry of 1926-27.

Chart 2 depicts the average expenditures of these wage-earner families grouped in nine income classes.[29] They range from families receiving less than 60 yen a month (averaging 53 yen) to those receiving over 200 yen (averaging 231 yen). Expenditures are plotted along the vertical axis. They are divided into four cate-

[28] Imperial Cabinet, Bureau of Statistics, *Nippon Teikoku Tōkei Nenkan*, no. 57, Tokyo, 1939, p. 36. These figures are for 1925.
[29] Data from Matsuda, *op.cit.*, pp. 284-85, 290-93.

gories: (1) food; (2) clothing; (3) "home" expenditures (rent, house repairs, furnishings, water, fuel, and light); and (4) "other," including chiefly education, travel, gifts, and entertainment and other recreation. "Savings" are taken as the excess (or deficit) of total household consumption in relation to expenditures.

Chart 2. *Family Expenditures of Japanese Wage Earners, by Income Classes, 1926-27*

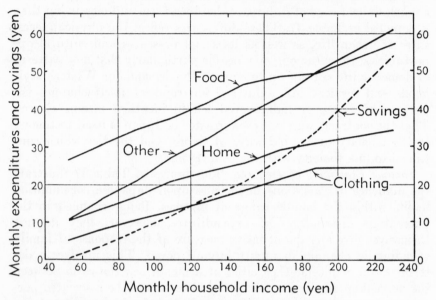

Source of data: Taijiro Matsuda, "The Family Budget Enquiry in Japan, 1926-1927," *Bulletin de l'Institut International de Statistique*, vol. xxv, part 2, Tokyo, 1931, pp. 284-85, 290-93. For details see text.

It will be noted, first, that the *amount* spent in each category grows as incomes rise above the level of 50 yen a month. Indeed, this is true of all twenty-four major items grouped in these categories. Only in relative terms does the demand for any item fail to increase.

In the second place, and more surprising, is the fact that there is a fairly definite *linear* relationship between income and particular expenditures as far up the income scale as the 160-180-yen bracket. The plotted points in each series tend to lie along a straight line. In other words, an increase in family income of a constant amount is associated with a rather constant increment of expenditure on food, on clothing, etc.

Food outlays, for example, increase about 4 yen for each 20-yen increase in income. "Other" expenditures have a steeper gradient, rising nearly 6 yen at each interval. The chief exception to this principle of straight-line growth is savings. These begin to rise by increasing amounts above the 150-yen income level. In the higher income brackets, above 180 yen, other expenditure groups begin also to show varying amounts of increment. Here the relationships generally tend to become curvilinear. Clearly no straight line can be fitted satisfactorily to the expenditure increments of the families of highly paid workers receiving 2,100 yen or more a year.

Examining a number of British and continental European family budget studies in similar fashion, R. G. D. Allen and A. L. Bowley discovered that this linear relationship between total income and expenditure on particular items tends to be characteristic of family groups which are homogeneous with respect to tastes, consumer habits, and prices paid for various goods and services.[30] This led them to reformulate Engel's law in more precise terms, as follows: "In a homogeneous group of families differing only in respect of income, the excess over (or defect from) the average of expenditures on any budget item bears a constant proportion to the excess over (or defect from) the average income." It appears that Japanese wage earners receiving between 600 and 2,160 yen a year in 1926-27 behaved more or less in conformity with this rule.[31]

From this fact it is possible within this income range to estimate average income elasticities of demand of wage-earner families included in the study, employing the methods developed by Allen and Bowley. For this purpose one requires two measurements for each expenditure series. The first is the percentage of income ($\bar{w}$) which the family of *average* income spends on each item. The average income of the wage-earner families in the study with incomes below 180 yen is 98.8 yen a month.[32] For each category of spending, $\bar{w}$ is therefore the ratio between average family expenditure and this average total income.

The second measurement expresses the gradient of a straight line fitted to each expenditure series. This constant, k, can be determined by the equation of the line of regression, $y = ke - c$, where y is the amount of money spent on a particular item at a level of expended income e, and c is a constant representing the point where the expenditure line crosses the vertical axis when the line is projected back

[30] *Family Expenditure*, London, 1935, p. 2.

[31] The degree of conformity is surprising, considering the wide range of incomes, employment, and residence represented in the 3,122 families of the study. Also, the size of the family increases with income, which tends to maintain expenditures on necessities above the level they would otherwise seek. The average number of persons per family, converted to adult consumption units, grows from 2.78 in the lowest income group to 3.75 in the 160-180-yen bracket. Matsuda, *op.cit.*, p. 290.

[32] This was well above the national average for Japan's 12 million households. Probably 90% received less than 100 yen a month in 1926-27.

to zero income.[33] With the values of k and $\bar{w}$ determined for each category of expenditure, the average income elasticity of demand for each is given by the formula $\bar{\eta} = \dfrac{k}{\bar{w}}$.

These measurements are as follows for this group of families of Japanese wage earners having incomes ranging from 635 to 2,160 yen during the year beginning September 1926:[34]

	Fraction of Total Income Devoted to Each Category at Average Income Level $\bar{w}$	Fraction of Increment of Income Devoted to Each Category k	Income Elasticity of Demand at Average Income Level $\bar{\eta}$
Food	0.36	0.20	0.6
Home	0.18	0.16	0.9
Clothing	0.12	0.14	1.1
Other expenditure	0.24	0.29	1.2
Savings	0.10	0.22	2.2

Several broad conclusions emerge:

1. The average family in this income range, receiving about 1,200 yen a year, spent over one third of its total income on food. It spent nearly another third on "home" and clothing, taken together. About one quarter was devoted to all other consumer needs. The balance it saved, about 10%. The variations around this average we have already noted in Table 37: the decline of relative expenditure on food as income grows, the sharp rise in the proportion of income saved, etc. (The values of $\bar{w}$ as computed here are not directly comparable with the percentages of Table 37, however; the former are in relation to total income, and the latter to total expenditure.)

2. Throughout this yearly income range of 635 to 2,160 yen, about 20% of any increment of buying power is spent on food. Clothing and home expenditure each take an additional 14 to 16%.

[33] Here this is done simply by fitting a line to the plotted points by inspection, selecting two pairs of observations for y and e in the middle income range, and solving for k.

[34] Actually the range of individual family incomes is higher than the limits given here. The highest and the lowest, however, are averaged in the highest and lowest income classes of Chart 2, and the values for $\bar{w}$, k, and $\bar{\eta}$ are computed from the seven class averages within the above range.

Colin Clark (op.cit., p. 385) gives similar data computed from Japanese family budgets a decade later, in 1936-37. They show still lower average and marginal propensities to consume food—0.331 and 0.138—and an average propensity to save as high as 0.122.

These three categories, composed largely of necessities, thus absorb one half of the increment of income from one level to another within this range of income. Also using the method of Allen and Bowley, Clark found the following values for *k* among nonfarm families in the United States with incomes of less than $3,000: food, 0.18; clothing, 0.09; and home expenditure, 0.25. Again these three categories total about 50%, albeit at a much higher level of consumption. By contrast, the value of *k* among North China farm families close to the subsistence level he found to be as high as 0.89.[35] Food expenditure absorbed nearly 90% of any increase in income.

Here again is presumptive evidence of the change which takes place as standards of living advance from the traditional poverty line of the Orient. By the mid-twenties Japanese wage earners at this relatively comfortable level were able to devote nearly 30% of any increment of income to miscellaneous expenditures—recreation, travel, child care, and additional items grouped under "other." This left an average of 22% for savings. If the savings figure seems high, it must be remembered that the amounts were still tiny and the proportion was lower among the poorer than among the more well-to-do families. Moreover, it cannot be assumed that *k* would have the same values at income levels below 600 yen a year, where over half the households of Japan were still to be found.

3. The income elasticities of demand in these categories are interesting. As one would expect, the lowest is for food. It has a value of 0.6 for the average Japanese family in this income range. In other words, an increase of 1% in total income from the average level is associated with an increment of 0.6% in food expenditure.

Among the North China farmers studied by Dittmer, Clark finds $\bar{\eta}$ to be 1.14 in the case of food.[36] Generally a high income elasticity of demand for food—greater than 1.0—is to be found among people on the margin of subsistence. The Japanese elasticity of 0.6 is not only well below this Chinese figure, but also somewhat lower than that found among Indian industrial workers in Cawnpore some years ago (0.9).[37] It is even lower than the corresponding figures for worker groups in Britain, Germany, and the United States in the twenties (0.7 to 0.9).[38] The latter comparison is surprising. If correct, it evidently reflects the habitual acceptance of a simple rice-

[35] *ibid.*, pp. 377, 384.

[36] *ibid.*, p. 384. Clark uses Dittmer's early study, of 1912-18, but notes the similarity of Buck's more inclusive figures for a later period, 1921-30.

[37] *ibid.*, p. 384.

[38] Allen and Bowley, *op.cit.*, pp. 32-33. Allen and Bowley give estimates of $\bar{\eta}$ in terms which are not strictly comparable with those given here, in that they are computed as the ratio between the percentage increase in expenditure on food, etc., and the percentage increase in total *expenditure*, not income.

vegetable-fish diet even by well-paid Japanese wage earners, and the correspondingly higher relative value placed on other types of expenditure and savings as income grows.

Turning to other categories of spending one finds that the income elasticities of demand for clothing and for housing and home furnishings are close to unity among Japanese workers at this average income level. In other words, a rise in income is associated with a more or less proportionate rise in expenditure here. For "other" expenditures $\bar{\eta}$ is likewise only 1.2. On the other hand, savings are highly elastic in response to a rise in income. Although the fraction of average income saved is low ($\bar{w} = 0.10$), the surplus of income over total expenditure grows at a rapid *rate*—more than twice as rapidly as income itself. A high elasticity here seems to be directly related to the comparably low income elasticity of demand for food.

This pattern of spending habits among Japanese wage earners is graphically summarized in Chart 3, again as suggested by Allen and Bowley. Family income is measured along the horizontal axis; expenditure along the vertical. As the two scales are identical, the 45° line is the line of total expenditure (including savings).

The categories of spending are arranged in Chart 3 in order of urgency, i.e., according to the value of c. (This order is inverse to their income elasticities of demand.) At the average level of family income XA, the expenditure on the several categories is plotted cumulatively on the vertical axis, beginning at the bottom with food (AF), which has the highest order of urgency. At any other level of income A_1, the corresponding expenditures may be computed from the values of k. The expenditure lines drawn through these points indicate the changing allocation of income as budgets grow. The amount actually spent on food, clothing, etc., at any level of income A_1, is given by the values A_1F_1, F_1H_1, H_1C_1, on the vertical scale. For Japanese wage-earner families with monthly incomes between 50 and 180 yen, the pattern exemplified in Chart 3 is remarkably consistent.

Historical Changes in Spending Habits. These relationships between the level of family income, on the one hand, and the pattern of expenditure, on the other, are helpful in understanding the changing structure of the Japanese economy, provided one does not attempt to read too much into them. Actually they only compare simultaneous spending habits of households at different levels of income in one year, given the standards of comfort and decency prevailing at the time. Accordingly, they do not necessarily portray historical shifts in consumer demands, or in the savings ratio, which accompanied the growth of national income over a period of years.

Chart 3. *Spending Pattern of Japanese Wage-Earner Families
with Monthly Incomes of 50 to 180 Yen, 1926-27*

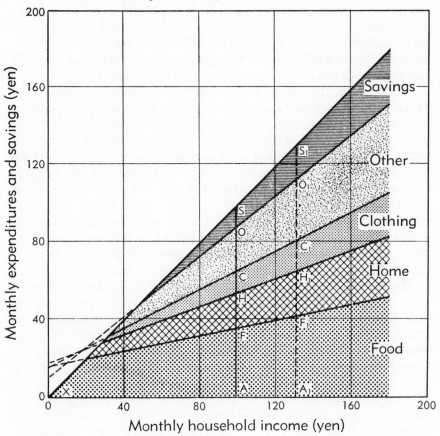

See text for sources and explanation.

They may give rather accurate clues through a short interval—for
example, from the hard times of 1931-32 to the relative prosperity
of 1936-37. As regards changes over several decades it would be
quite misleading to draw statistical conclusions from them.

The reason is that the desires and spending habits of a family
at any time are powerfully influenced by the existing plane of living and standard of living of the community. And these consumption standards are likely to change. If relatively prosperous Japanese families saved a sizable share of their income in 1927, for example, and relatively poor families little or none, this does not mean
that a historical rise in average incomes from the one level to the
other would bring with it this corresponding rise in savings. For
people's ideas of minimum comfort would be apt to undergo revision

in the meantime; also their needs and opportunities for security and economic independence through personal saving. The balance of choices between satisfying immediate wants and providing for the future would accordingly be modified. Certainly this has happened historically in Japan. Along with other changes, it makes quite uncertain how much the average propensity to save has actually increased with the rise in average income. (See Chapter 5.)

Similarly, in the realm of consumption, significant changes have taken place in modern Japan both in human wants and in opportunities for their satisfaction. Industrialization has opened up a wider range of choice; it has also imposed new necessities of living. Old culture traits have persisted with unusual tenacity, partly because of the speed of external modernization, partly because of measures of social compulsion and restraint which attended the process. Yet the notions prevalent in urban Japan after 1920 as to what constituted poverty, comfort, and luxury were far from identical with those of rural Japan in 1870. Even where old wants persisted there now became available to satisfy them a range of goods, particularly manufactures, far beyond what had existed earlier.

Modern armament is a conspicuous illustration. Equally one could cite schools, woolen clothing, paper and books, medical care, household lighting and metal wares, and scores of other examples. The growth of industrial cities led necessarily to progressive revisions of what constituted adequate clothing, shelter, and recreation, and such ideas filtered more slowly into the countryside. Wants that formerly were marginal moved into a more urgent category, perhaps at the expense even of adequate nutrition. This whole process is particularly complex in an Asiatic country like Japan where the urban population finds itself increasingly straddling two cultures, the old and the new.[39]

Simultaneous family budget studies from a particular period therefore leave us still with only inconclusive guides as to the real character of historical changes in expenditure patterns. The best that can be said is that they support the testimony of direct, though fragmentary, historical observations. (See Chapter 3.) This is particularly true if account is taken of income disposal among the well-to-do classes. The 1926-27 study detailed above fails to include the most prosperous families of Japan, who together received at least one third of total household income. Moreover, it excludes undistributed profits and other institutional income altogether, and fails to show how the State spent its tax revenues.

[39] For an interesting discussion of this development throughout East Asia see Bruno Lasker, *Standards and Planes of Living in the Far East,* New York: Institute of Pacific Relations, 1952.

Yet these were major sources of funds devoted to the import or construction of capital goods and armaments. Among upper income groups, also, consumer expenditure was concentrated much more heavily on manufactures and services catering to comfort and luxury requirements. New spending and saving habits had their most pronounced effects within these wealthier, more urbanized, more Westernized groups near the top of the income pyramid. This reinforced the tendencies observable on a more modest scale among the masses of the people.

There is no doubt, in short, that as productivity and income grew in Japan the demand for the net products of extractive industries, whether domestic or imported, tended to diminish in *relative* importance. Correspondingly, the relative demand for the net product of manufacturing grew steadily, and along with it the demand for a variety of commercialized services. This differential growth was the most powerful influence directing the employment of labor and capital increasingly away from primary production, and into manufacturing and service occupations. Food consumption rose appreciably. But the more rapid gains in spending are found in processed foods, personal and household furnishings, and such amenities as medical service, recreation, and travel, together with a wide range of government services, both civilian and military. By the end of the prewar era Japan was approaching a midposition between those nations, on the one hand, where productive effort had to be devoted largely to supplying the minimum essentials of life, and those nations whose productive capacity supplied a wide margin above such essentials.[40]

[40] As a crude indication of Japan's intermediate position the following estimates of consumer expenditure patterns in India, Japan, and the United States in 1938 are of interest:

	TOTAL PERSONAL CONSUMPTION EXPENDITURE, 1938 (PERCENTAGES)		
	India	*Japan*	*United States*
Total expenditure	*100.0*	*100.0*	*100.0*
Food, beverages, tobacco	66.3	44.0	32.0
Housing and furnishings	8.7	12.0	20.2
Clothing and accessories	11.2	9.9	12.2
Heat and light	2.1	5.1	4.1
Transport and communications	2.2	8.4	9.7
Health and personal care	⎫	6.5	6.4
Education and amusement	⎬ 9.6	6.2	6.2
Other	⎭	8.1	9.1

Sources: India (1938/39), R. C. Desai, "Consumer Expenditure in India, 1931-32 to 1940-41," *Journal of the Royal Statistical Society*, Series A (General), vol. cxi, part 4, 1948, pp. 261-308; Japan, estimates of Economic Stabilization Board reprinted in United Nations, Statistical Office, *National Income Statistics* (1938-48), Lake Success, 1950, p. 107; United States, *National Income and Product Statistics*

International Demand and Structural Change

Thus far changes in the structure of employment and income have been considered only as a response to changes in domestic income and demand. Except in a closed economy, however, they are also influenced by the type of specialization undertaken by a country in its international economic relations.

The distribution of resources among various employments, in other words, reflects both the home and the foreign demand for goods and services. The home demand, in turn, is influenced by the fact that a country can secure certain goods more advantageously abroad, paying for them by turning some of its labor and capital to production for the export market. It is therefore relieved of the necessity of meeting all its requirements directly out of whatever complement of resources it may happen to possess. Real income grows through specialization according to comparative advantage, and this has further reactions upon the country's demand for both imported and domestic products.

Specialization in Primary Production. The actual effects of foreign trade on the structure of employment naturally differ widely, depending on the circumstances. A region like Malaya, specializing in exports of tin and rubber and other agricultural products, might possibly achieve a considerable growth of production and real income with comparatively little transfer of employment to manufacturing and service occupations. As income expands through primary production for export, the increasing demand for industrial goods may be satisfied largely through imports, leaving productive resources concentrated mainly in the extractive industries.

In such a case it is conceivable even that primary production might account for a steadily increasing share of employment as economic development proceeds. This is unlikely, however. For one thing, most types of agricultural and mineral produce undergo some degree of processing before being exported. Other ancillary trades and local industries are also apt to be stimulated in conjunction with the production and marketing of primary products. Moreover, some manufactures in increasing demand cannot be profitably imported because of high transport costs, local market peculiarities, or other reasons. Most services must necessarily be performed at home. And there are few countries which have not applied some measure of government protection to home manufactures, where

---

of the United States, 1929-46, cited, pp. 41-44. The uncertainty of the data for India and Japan, and the difficulty of constructing comparable classifications, should discourage any precise comparison of these percentages.

they had the freedom to do so. Finally, the growth of agricultural output, and its specialization for the commercial market, almost certainly requires some improvement of techniques. This reduces the labor required per unit of output, releasing it for other purposes.

For these reasons the expansion of primary production and exports is apt to stimulate the rise of secondary and tertiary employments as well. Commonly their relative importance tends to increase. New Zealand, for example, employs hardly one quarter of her working force in primary industries, despite her large exports of foodstuffs and wool, and the ample diet of her people. Her high standard of living, and the efficiency of her labor in primary production, are reflected in the fact that the service trades occupy nearly half of her gainfully employed population. Under these conditions the successful development of the extractive industries under the stimulus of foreign demand brings in its wake a steady diversification of production in other directions as well.

While this is the general rule, it must be heavily qualified when applied to certain regions. The reasons are worth noting here, if only to bring the case of Japan into sharper relief.

In southern Asia, particularly, progress toward industrialization has been slow, despite substantial achievements in modernizing and expanding productive power in other spheres. Several factors have operated as deterrents. For one thing, social organization and incentives have not been conducive to the rapid acquisition of machine technology. And, of course, the policies of the prewar colonial powers centered principally on exploiting the great agricultural and mineral resources of their dependencies for which there was a growing demand in world markets. If they did not actively discourage industrialization, they did little to encourage it, being well content to leave the region dependent on imported manufactures, shipping, banking services, etc. Japan's own colonial territories are a notable example.

Two other circumstances in colonial Asia tended further to weaken the tendency toward diversification of economic activity which might otherwise be expected to follow upon modernization and development. One was the rapid growth of population which accompanied the expansion of primary production. As in Japan, population increase has applied a heavy drag on any rise in per capita incomes throughout this region. Thus the mass of peasant families remain unable to buy much for themselves beyond food and other simple necessities of life.

The other circumstance, not present in Japan, was the important role of foreign capital, foreign management, and immigrant labor in building up great industries producing sugar, rubber, petroleum, vegetable oils, etc. for export. This, too, restricted the rise of a home market for manufactures and services to the degree usually found in a more indigenous pattern of development. For it meant that a good share of the increment of income produced in the Indies or Malaya, for example, was transferred abroad as interest and dividends on foreign investments in estate agriculture, transport, and public services. Still other sums of current income have been remitted overseas in the form of gifts, leave pay, pensions, and investments by Western businessmen and civil servants, or by Chinese and Indian immigrants. This income may indirectly have given rise to a money demand for the products of the originating country even when transferred abroad, through the operations of the foreign exchange market. But such a demand was apt to be mainly for its primary staples exported to the metropolitan country or elsewhere. Furthermore, the spending of income retained in the region, as between domestic and overseas manufactures and services, has been weighted in favor of imports by the presence of a large, nonindigenous population, with its relatively high incomes, its alien tastes, and its business and family ties abroad.

The case of Indonesia before the war is instructive by way of illustration. Domestic national income at factor cost was placed by J. J. Polak at 2,815 million guilders in 1938.[41] Only 72% accrued to the 68,000,000 Indonesian people themselves on this reckoning. Some 275,000 Dutch and other resident Europeans received 363 million guilders (13%). Foreign Asiatics, chiefly 1,400,000 Chinese, earned 300 million (11%). An additional 100 million (before taxes) went to foreign corporations, and 41 million to government-owned enterprise.

In this dualistic economy the sector which was non-Indonesian in ownership and management was geared predominantly to the export of rubber, oil, tin, etc. to world markets. The proceeds of such exports served partly to transfer abroad the earnings of foreign enterprise, and more largely to pay for imports of various manufactures and services. This is brought out in the national income accounts for 1938 constructed by the Netherlands Bureau of Statistics, using revised data and slightly different concepts from those of Polak. Here factor incomes paid out (net geographic product) are estimated at 2,999 million guilders, of which two thirds was wage and salary payments to Indonesians. Net income of 233 million guilders was payable abroad on account of interest, dividends, profits, salaries, wages, and pensions (after offsetting receipts).

41 United Nations, Statistical Office, *National Income Statistics of Various Countries, 1938-1947*, Lake Success, 1948, pp. 73-74.

National income at factor cost was thus reduced to 2,766 million guilders.[42]

Moreover, the natural tendency of such an economy to import most of its advanced manufactures and technical services was reinforced in this case by the presence of the large European and Chinese minority, with its preference for items more readily imported than produced in the Indies. Beside the net outpayment mentioned above, the international transactions for 1938 show the entries given below in the right-hand column. All figures are in millions of guilders.

	PURCHASES OF GOODS AND SERVICES	
	From Enterprises within Indonesia	*From Abroad*
Indonesian residents	1,708	195
Indonesian enterprises	135	50
Non-Indonesian residents	447	140
Non-Indonesian enterprises	286	86
Government (purchases from business enterprises only)	134	53

	OTHER PAYMENTS ABROAD
Foreign investment by residents	21
Other income transferred by non-Indonesian residents	21
Redemption of government debt	40

The gross total of all such outpayments was as much as 860 million guilders. In other words, a very large share of the income produced in the islands was either remitted abroad as property and labor earnings, personal transfers, or debt service; or spent on consumer and capital goods and related services required from overseas. Offsetting these outpayments of course was a counterflow of inpayments of various kinds from the rest of the world. Mainly, however, the demand from abroad was for primary products, exports of which came to 678 million guilders.

The total income produced in Indonesia must have grown severalfold in the last half century of Dutch rule. Foreign capital, enter-

[42] United Nations, Statistical Office, *National Income Statistics, 1938-1948*, Lake Success, 1950, pp. 89-99. A more extreme case of colonial dependence is that of Northern Rhodesia, whose large mining industry has been built up wholly with foreign capital. Here Phyllis Deane found that 42% of total taxable income (income produced in Rhodesia plus income accruing to residents from abroad) was received by foreign companies and other nonresidents in 1938. Some 43% of taxable income was remitted abroad on behalf of the colonial government, foreign companies, and residents. P. Deane, *The Measurement of Colonial Incomes*, Cambridge, Eng., 1948, pp. 64-65.

prise, and skills contributed largely to this growth. And the greater part of the increment accrued, no doubt, to the Indonesian population. Unfortunately, however, this share appears to have been absorbed mainly in supporting larger numbers of people at a standard of living little above that of their forebears. From 1900 to 1940 the population of the islands nearly doubled. Of the margin of income, over and above subsistence requirements, a considerable share was claimed every year by remittances abroad, capital transfers, and expenditures on foreign manufactures and services.

Elsewhere, as economic development has proceeded, it is precisely this growing margin of buying power which has performed the critical function of redirecting labor and capital toward the secondary and tertiary employments. In Japan, for example, where development followed a much more autonomous pattern, it was spent mainly in the home market on a widening range of factory goods and services, either for consumption, or capital creation, or war. In Indonesia, and throughout the colonies of Asia generally, the large sums which went into outpayments of the types mentioned above served to stimulate still further the export of primary products which were in demand abroad, but not the production of varied manufactures for the domestic market. What was spent at home continued to be devoted overwhelmingly to the bare living requirements of the population, i.e., to the simplest types of food, clothing, and shelter.

It is not surprising, therefore, that only 300,000 people—1¼% of the gainfully employed—were engaged in modern factory industry in the Indies as late as 1939 despite the belated efforts of the Dutch authorities to encourage industrial development during the preceding decade. In addition, some 2,500,000 workers were found in small-scale industries, mostly handicrafts producing articles for local use.[43] The extractive industries still accounted for over 60% of the total production of the colony, while their share in total employment was even larger. One half of the entire import tonnage consisted of finished consumer goods.

Thus colonial policy, population growth, and the preeminent role of foreign capital and enterprise all combined to reinforce the principle of comparative advantage in preserving the agrarian character of the Indonesian economy. A similar pattern of development appeared in all the Eastern colonial territories, including notably those of Japan herself.

Industrial Specialization: The Case of Japan. The alternative type of international specialization is that of the country whose opportunities in foreign trade lie in the exchange of manufactured

---

[43] *The Economic Review of Indonesia,* vol. II, no. 8, August 1948, p. 120.

exports against food and raw material imports. Here the industrialization of employment, as economic development proceeds, outstrips the redirection of domestic demand. For labor and capital are attracted into manufacturing industries serving the export as well as the domestic market. Domestic food and raw materials may also be replaced increasingly with imported supplies, freeing resources for other uses.

Japan, of course, presents a striking case of this type of historical development. So long as she was closed to the outside world, her poverty in natural resources severely limited any shift away from primary reliance on a meager agriculture-and-fishing economy. During the period of Tokugawa isolation even a rapid improvement in industrial technology could have brought only limited industrialization. Certainly, without access to overseas raw materials and food, Japan would not have been able in modern times to feed and occupy a large urban population in industrial employment. Nor, with her people wholly dependent on limited natural resources, could productivity in farming have advanced to the point where farm purchasing power would have supplied a large market for industrial goods.

The role of foreign commerce in Japanese economic development has already been detailed in Chapters 6 and 7. Here it is only necessary to recall in brief how it sustained and reinforced the industrialization process after 1868.

International trade stimulated the rise of manufacturing pursuits in Japan in three respects. First, it brought in foodstuffs, materials, and equipment—and, above all, modern technology. These were all necessary to the development of industries serving the expanding domestic market for manufactured goods. Second, as the means of payment, it required the growth of industrial production for export, together with the related services necessary to the conduct of trade. Third, by raising per capita incomes in Japan through the gains of international specialization, it induced a further shift of home demand toward manufactures and services. The whole process was cumulative, of course. Growing foreign and domestic demand for Japanese industrial products called forth increasing supplies of suitable skills and equipment, while the resulting rise in productivity and income steadily widened the range of industrial markets.

What proportion of prewar Japanese industrial output was produced for the overseas market, what proportion for the home market, is not easy to say. In Chapter 7 the question is examined at some length, and with no very precise answer for the successive stages of Japanese development. In the early decades foreign demand played a relatively small role in quantitative terms. Never did it occupy more than a subsidiary place except in the market for raw silk, cotton goods, and a few minor items. However, by 1927-36, at the peak of Japan's prewar overseas dependence, foreign countries and her colonies took about one third of her industrial production in the aggregate. Since foreign trade also contributed indirectly to the growth of the *domestic* market for manufactures, and furnished materials to industries serving this market, it advanced the process of industrialization far beyond what a self-sufficient pattern of development could have made possible.

All countries entering the world market as manufacturing nations reveal these forces at work in varying degrees. By comparison with nations more abundantly endowed with natural resources, however, Japan had to carry further the resulting shift in industrial structure in order to maintain a given inflow of food and raw materials for domestic consumption. As described in Chapters 6 and 7, she had to export manufactures in sufficient amount not only to pay for such materials and equipment needed at home, but also to pay for those utilized in many of her chief export industries. In 1930, for example, some 25% of her imports were used in export manufactures, or offset by similar exports. To finance 100 million yen of imports for home consumption, she had to sell goods abroad to a value of 133 million yen. (See Tables 28 and 32.) This "workshop position," as the means to paying her way abroad, attracted capital and labor into industry and related occupations beyond the point where they otherwise would have been required.

Thus the growth of Japan's export trade, mainly in industrial products, reinforced the transfer of labor and resources induced by the rising home demand for manufactures. Meanwhile services were imported to only a slight extent—mainly shipping and certain financial services. By their very nature they were supplied mainly at home. Commodity imports, by contrast, rose to large proportions. But they shifted progressively from overseas manufactures to foodstuffs to feed her growing urban population and raw materials to sustain its industrial activities. This shift proceeded in response to the growth and increasing technical maturity of Japanese industries. It was reinforced by tariffs and subsidies to increase their preponderance in the home market for manufactures. Another factor limiting imports of manufactures, in favor of home production, was the wide disparity between Japan and the West in consumer taste and income levels. Traditional consumer habits were resistant to change in many respects, and domestic producers could cater to their peculiarities more readily than the factories of the West. By 1930, as a result, over 80% of Japan's imports from foreign countries and colonies were made up of food, fuel, and industrial materials. Only 12% were finished manufactures (excluding food). Among exports, however, the latter comprised nearly 50%, while other semifinished goods, notably raw silk, supplied most of the remainder.

In contrast to the experience of Britain as she industrialized, Japan's growing imports of primary products did not so much replace as supplement the output of her own farms, forests, fisheries, and mines. The extractive industries more than doubled their physical output in addition. (Table 3.) Even so, access to foreign supplies greatly facilitated and accentuated the shift of employment toward manufacturing and the service occupations. After 1900 most if not all of the millions of workers added to the Japanese labor force by population growth were absorbed in the nonextractive trades. Although agricultural output continued to grow, as described in Chapter 3, the farm population remained more or less constant.

The redirection of employment away from the primary industries was thus a response to combined changes in home demand and in the opportunities and necessities of foreign trade. All of these forces interacted as cause and effect with the growth of productivity and income within the country. The general direction of the shift was that common to all industrializing countries. But its specific rate and peculiarities reflected the special circumstances of Japan in the modern world.

It is therefore rather pointless to compare, as do some writers, the relative importance of industrial employment in Japan and that in a country like China or India, and draw inferences as to the degree of shift which must take place in China in order to achieve a corresponding level of real income per capita. For reasons outlined above, any Far Eastern country must experience some diversification of employment as the condition of economic progress. How far this need go, however, depends upon the resources and position of the particular country in relation to the world economy of the time. China and India, with their more diversified resources, could achieve a comparable level of real income with much less industrialization of their economies than Japan. This can only be regarded as a fortunate circumstance. It will minimize the internal adjustments otherwise required for economic development, as well as the strains imposed on the outside world.

One final observation may be made as regards income and industrialization. The market for Japanese manufactures was expanded by the rise of income and purchasing power, not only in Japan herself but also in the countries with which she was developing trade relations. In these areas the income elasticity of demand for Japanese goods depended on the competitive position of Japanese exporters as affected by many changing circumstances. But probably it was fairly high through the prewar decades, in both the silk market of the United States and the cotton goods markets of the East. Some qualification of this statement is required in one respect at least. To some degree a decline in purchasing power in Asiatic colonial markets, and in the West as well, tended to make cheap Japanese cotton cloth and other consumer wares more attractive relative to the higher-priced products of Western industries. This was a factor in the remarkable expansion of Japanese cotton textile exports during the depression years after 1929. In the main, however, Japanese industrialization has been aided by improvements in productivity and income throughout the Far East, and retarded by the failure of incomes to rise more rapidly.

Here again a popular impression runs contrary to the facts, as noted in Chapter 7. Much is made of Japan's priority in industrial development as the secret of her success. Because other Asiatic peoples failed to absorb machine technology as rapidly, it is said, Japan profited handsomely from the markets for factory goods which she was able to preempt after the turn of the century.

On balance it is much more likely that Japan was handicapped, not advantaged, by the lack of industrialization among her neighbors. The pressure of population growth left them in poverty which no amount of agricultural improvement alone could overcome. To this day the per capita market for manufactures, whether domestic or imported, remains extremely small through China and southern Asia. Even in Korea and Formosa, where foreign competition was excluded altogether, sales of Japanese factory goods were unimpressive. The lagging industrialization of other Far Eastern countries enabled Japan to capture a larger share of the Asiatic market for manufactured goods after 1895 than she might otherwise have had. The market itself remained undeveloped, however.

Had industrialization advanced more pervasively throughout the Far East, Japan would undoubtedly have had to shift out of the export market for coarse yarns and cotton goods more rapidly than she did. But if such industrial development had been of the expansive type, enlarging income and buying power rather than merely choking off imports, it would almost certainly have opened up markets for Japanese manufactures of much wider range and variety. There is little reason to doubt that Japan could have made the transition to a more diversified range of advanced manufactures with benefits to herself as well as to her Asiatic customers. This transition was already advanced, as a matter of fact, before war destroyed the structure of Japanese foreign trade.

Indeed, it was peculiarly to Japan's advantage, as we have seen, to move as rapidly as possible into exports of high-quality consumer goods and advanced types of machinery. Her poverty in natural resources gives her a special stake in developing export products which have a high value added by manufacture to the cost of imported materials. In this regard cheap cotton goods are a particularly poor line in which to specialize, once alternative opportunities can be created. An equivalent investment of resources in producing and exporting finer qualities of textiles and household wares, as well as industrial machinery and equipment manufactured from imported materials, offers a correspondingly higher net national return.

Such markets have been slow to develop in the Far East, for they depend upon higher incomes and purchasing power. And in the West they have been restricted from the beginning, so far as Japan is concerned, by tariffs on imported manufactures graduated according to the stage of processing. Had Asiatic demand for such goods expanded more rapidly, through the more pervasive modernization of economic life, Japan could have benefited correspondingly. Few Japanese statesmen saw this, and those who did were overborne by the industrialist's fear of competition and the militarist's desire for conquest. In this respect the ruling elements were tragically blind to their nation's interest. It should be added that American and British protectionists were equally neglectful of their own countries' stake in providing economic outlets for the Japanese in an expanding world economy.

For Japan today this problem remains, only exacerbated by the political and economic havoc of the war. Her economic future depends more than ever on the subordination of commercial rivalries and political antagonisms in East Asia to a larger, collective interest in the security and economic development of the whole region.

CHAPTER 9

STRUCTURAL CHANGE: EMPLOYMENT OF RESOURCES

FAR-REACHING changes in Japan's economic center of gravity resulted from the expansive forces described in preceding chapters. New patterns of resource utilization emerged in response to new patterns of domestic demand. They were reinforced by the winning of industrial markets abroad. Both these changes in turn were themselves elements in the interlocking processes which accompanied and made possible the general advance of technology, the accumulation of capital, and the growth of productivity and income. The whole development received a dynamic impulse from the opening of Japan to the West. It was spurred on by the power ambitions of the State. And its broad momentum came from the energies released in the new framework of enterprise established after the Restoration.

The structural changes which took place in the employment of Japan's productive resources over a half century or more have already been characterized in various aspects. Among them, for example, were the urbanization of employment, a larger and more capitalistic scale of organization, and the rise of production for export. It remains to examine more fully one major change: the altered balance of the major divisions of the economy as sources of income and employment.

Here again a familiar difficulty is encountered, namely, the lack of reliable statistical data, especially before 1920. Though one can speak with confidence of the general direction of change prior to World War I, it is only thereafter that a reasonably clear picture emerges. This chapter, therefore, is confined mainly to the interwar decades, 1920-40, with certain inferences as to the trend of earlier years. The general reader who does not care to be detained with these details is advised to pass on to the concluding section, "Mobility, Efficiency, Equality."

Structure of National Product

The best initial approach to an appraisal of the importance of various industries in sustaining a nation's livelihood is probably to be found in their contribution to the aggregate flow of goods and services, as valued in the market place.

We begin, therefore, with an inquiry into the changed structure of national income (or product) in prewar Japan. What was the value of goods and services produced in each major sector of the economy, at market prices, after deducting purchases of goods and services from other sectors, capital consumption charges, and business taxes? Put in slightly different terms, what were the total earnings paid to those residents who supplied the labor and capital employed in production, i.e., the sum of factor costs incurred? To arrive at net national product, as it is usually defined, certain additions would have to be made to income produced or distributed. For the general purposes of this study, however, these terms may be used more or less interchangeably, since prewar Japanese statistics in any case are inadequate for a precise computation of either sum.

Opinions will differ, of course, as to just what final significance attaches to these valuations of goods and services at the prices, wages, and interest rates which happen to prevail in the market. To appraise police protection, or the national defense establishment, by the same commercial standard as is used for beer and candy may seem to be a singular way to proceed. Similarly the rural farm as a way of life may be valued far beyond its production at prevailing prices. A good deal can be learned about economic structure, nevertheless, from a national income and product account set up in this fashion. It needs only to be borne in mind that existing consumer taste, business practice, government policies, a certain distribution of income, and other prevailing circumstances will cause such valuations to diverge considerably from socially more significant judgments.

Earlier, in Chapter 3, some attention was paid to estimates of Japanese national income by Prof. Yuzo Yamada. There our interest lay mainly in finding some over-all measure of economic growth from 1868 to 1938 which would summarize the evidence previously assembled on particular sectors of economic life.

The present chapter is concerned more specifically with structural changes taking place meantime in the distribution of national production among these sectors, especially the situation as it stood toward the close of the prewar period. Only in this way can certain basic features of the prewar Japanese economy be understood. For example, to evaluate the place of agriculture by noting that 50% of the working population was still chiefly engaged in farming, as is sometimes done, conveys a false impression of the extent to which agriculture still constituted the chief source of Japan's livelihood. Similarly, the impression that textiles preponderated heavily among prewar Japanese industries rests on figures of employment and gross value of production which fail to measure the actual shift of manufacturing income to the metalworking and other trades.[1]

---

[1] "Gross value of production" as the term is used in this chapter is not to be confused with gross national product. The former means simply the market value

Net Income Produced in Japan, 1930. The year 1930, at the mid-point between World War I and World War II, will be selected to portray the structure of Japanese production which had evolved out of fifty years of industrialization. This was a year of moderate depression, already becoming acute in agriculture. But it is not unrepresentative in most respects of the period which immediately preceded it or that which followed. Better than a later year like 1936 it shows Japan halfway in the transition to peacetime indus-trialism; and better than 1925 it reveals the accelerated shift to industry occasioned by the lag of agricultural oportunity. There are other practical reasons for its selection. It was a decennial cen-sus year, and one picked by the Japanese Cabinet Bureau of Sta-tistics for its first careful investigation of national income.

The CBS study of national income in 1930 is still the best inquiry of its sort for prewar Japan, despite its limitations. Moreover, the Bureau's figures were subsequently revised by the U.S. Office of Strategic Services. The latter corrected certain duplications and omissions, and reclassified industries in a more useful arrangement.

This revision was then projected through the years 1931-42 and published in preliminary form by the Department of State in *National Income of Japan*, mimeographed, Washington, 1945. My indebtedness to this valuable monograph has already been ac-knowledged in preceding chapters. To reproduce some of its sta-tistical findings here seems the more justified as the study itself is not widely available, and its form of presentation (a preliminary draft only) is ill suited to the general reader—indeed, is intelligible to the careful student only after working through a mass of sup-porting detail.

Table 38 presents the CBS estimate of Japanese national income produced in 1930, as adjusted in the American revision, and with certain minor corrections which I have added.[2]

---

of goods or services produced in an industry with no deduction for raw material costs or other expenses. As reported in the official statistics, it sometimes includes a good deal of double counting of values, as goods move from one stage of processing to another. Gross national product is identical with net national product (at market prices) except that no deduction from the value of production is made for deprecia-tion or depletion of capital.

[2] These latter corrections are as follows: (1) Cinema production (4 million yen) seems to be included inadvertently by the OSS both under manufacturing and under services. Here it is excluded from the latter. (2) The accounts of the postal savings system were divided by the OSS between finance and government. Here the former component (—23 million yen) is shifted to the government column. (3) Because of statistical difficulties the OSS entirely excluded from finance the net product of commercial banks. Here a minor fraction (19 million yen) is included under banking to reduce by so much the underestimate of income produced in finance. (See Table 38, note d.) The net changes in the OSS estimates are thus as follows (in millions of yen): private services, —4; government services, —23; finance, +42; total national income, +15.

Table 38. *Domestic National Income of Japan Proper,
by Industrial Origin, 1930*[a]

	Net Income Produced (millions of yen)	Percent
Total	10,239	100.0
Agriculture (and forestry)[b]	1,706	16.7
Fishing	186	1.8
Mining	216	2.0
Manufacturing[c]	2,800	27.3
Factory industry, private	1,809	17.6
Factory industry, government	116	1.1
Workshop industry	832	8.1
Other	43	0.4
Construction	468	4.6
Transport and communication	695	6.8
Railways	406	4.0
Government posts, telephone and telegraph	134	1.3
Other	155	1.5
Trade, wholesale and retail	1,707	16.7
Finance[d]	368	3.6
Banking	41	0.4
Insurance	67	0.7
Real estate (residential)	260	2.6
Other private services[e]	961	9.4
Professions	473	4.6
Catering and amusement	312	3.1
Domestic	198	1.9
(Minus tax deductions)	(−22)	
Other government services[f]	1,132	11.1

[a] Estimates of the Japanese Imperial Cabinet, Bureau of Statistics, as revised by the U.S. Office of Strategic Services, and published in U.S. Department of State, *National Income of Japan*, Washington, 1945, sect. A, and with minor corrections by the present author (see note 2 to text).

The principal revisions of the OSS are (1) to deduct certain charges for depreciation, depletion, and other costs ignored by the CBS from various industry totals and from aggregate national income (336 million yen); (2) to deduct all business (including business profits) taxes from production values, and part of agricultural taxes, as representing the contribution of government services (466 million yen); (3) to recompute government net product (see below); and (4) to eliminate double counting in the CBS handling of interest and dividends paid to banks.

[b] From gross market value of production (including self-supplied commodities) the CBS deducts fertilizer, fodder, and other materials used, plus depreciation as measured by tools and implements purchased. The OSS further deducts 177 million yen (53% of all taxes, including house taxes, paid by farm families) as representing the value of government services rendered. The CBS divides its total net product in agriculture (1,883 million yen) as follows (in millions of yen): private crop farming, 1,788; private livestock production, 15; private forestry, 35; public enterprise, 45.

[c] "Other" industry includes salt manufacture, movie production, newspaper and magazine publishing. Excluding these, private factories comprise all plants equipped

to employ five or more operatives; workshop industry comprises all other private manufacturing; and government industry comprises all publicly owned factories.

d The CBS figure for banking, trust, and finance companies is 163 million yen. This is a more reasonable estimate of labor incomes in banking plus earnings on bank capital than that given here. However, it includes interest and dividends paid to banks which are also included in the net value product of the paying industries. As such interest and dividends cannot be segregated out of the latter, double counting can only be avoided by reducing the net product of banking to a small residual. The latter is included here, together with the net income of finance and trust companies.

Real estate includes only residential rents paid out, minus maintenance costs. Business rents are not deducted elsewhere from gross value of product to arrive at net income.

e Net income in the professions includes (in millions of yen): religion, 101; medicine, 190; private education, 41; artists, lawyers, etc., 141. Catering and amusement include restaurants, 123; hotels, 53; barber shops and bathhouses, 94; amusements, 41.

f Government services represented in wages and salary payments are as follows (in millions of yen): pay of armed forces, 109; pensions and annuities, 146; public education, 233; local officials and police, 104; other civil service, 97. To this total is added an imputed return of 5% (466 million yen) on all government-owned property except that employed in enterprises included under other industries. A reduction of 23 million yen is then made to adjust the accounts of the postal savings system.

These figures should be used only with a clear idea of what they mean. Several characteristics may be noted:[3]

1. As a first approximation, Table 38 may be said to measure the net earnings of labor and capital employed in each major division of the Japanese economy—the sum of wages, salaries, interest, rent, and profits. The chief qualification of this statement, apart from the accuracy of the basic data, is as follows: Except in agriculture and "other private services," all business (including business profits) taxes are deducted from the income total of each division, as a rough measure of the services rendered by the government. In agriculture only about half of the taxes (including house taxes) paid by farm families are deducted, as a truer measure of these services. (See also the treatment of government services, finance, and real estate, Table 38, notes.)

2. Net income is calculated mainly by the gross-value-minus-cost method. From the market value of goods and services produced in each industry the following expenses are deducted: all raw materials, fuel, and energy consumed in the production process; estimated depreciation and depletion (the current consumption of durable producers' goods); and business taxes as described above. In trans-

3 Details in English concerning the CBS income study will be found in Japan Economic Federation, *National Income of Japan, 1930-1939*, Tokyo, 1939, and in S. Shiomi, "Japanese National Income in 1930," *Kyoto University Economic Review*, vol. IX, no. 2, December 1934, pp. 38-55, as well as in the Department of State monograph. The author has not had access to the original CBS publication, *Kokumin Shotoku Chōsa Hōkoku*, Tokyo, 1934.

port, communications, government service, and the private professions, however, net income is computed as the sum of wage and salary payments plus actual or imputed returns on capital. Excluded from the accounts entirely are changes in the value of existing assets, earnings from odd jobs and illegal pursuits, imputed income from owner-occupied dwellings and other durable consumer goods, and the activities of family members not directed to producing "marketable goods." The latter distinction, of course, sets up a rather arbitrary definition of income or net product. Statistically, as Pigou remarks, the national income is reduced if a man marries his housekeeper.

3. The estimates of Table 38 are confined to income produced within Japan Proper during 1930, i.e., domestic income. By definition this total is equal to (a) national consumption, plus (b) net domestic capital formation, plus (c) the net balance of trade in goods and services between Japan, on the one hand, and foreign countries and Japanese colonies, on the other. It differs from income accruing to the residents of Japan Proper in that the latter includes the net international balance in the flow of (a) property incomes, (b) wage remittances, and (c)noncommercial remittances like gifts. The CBS made a partial attempt to correct for these international transfers by deducting 63.6 million yen from income produced in Japan. This was to allow for the excess of interest, dividends, and profits paid to foreigners on investments in Japan over similar incomes received by residents of Japan from investments in foreign countries. But no corresponding data were available on similar transfers between Japan and her colonies, where Japanese investments were much larger. This correction is omitted here; indeed, it is inappropriate for estimating income originating in Japan. We may bear in mind, however, that net income accruing to residents of the country from overseas investments and remittances added a small margin of supplementary income to the total of Table 38.

Further definition of the concept of national income would carry us into refinements which are hardly necessary for present purposes. It might be noted, however, that the figures of Table 38 do not conform precisely to the definitions either of national income or of net national product which have lately won wide acceptance in the United States.[4] They exclude imputed rents on owner-occupied dwellings; they are net of depletion and the bulk of direct taxes on business profits; and they refer to income produced in Japan Proper rather than income accruing to the residents of the country.

[4] See U.S. Department of Commerce, *National Income and Product Statistics of the United States, 1929-46*, Washington, 1947; also Edward F. Denison, "Report on Tripartite Discussions of National Income Measurement," *Studies in Income and Wealth, Volume Ten*, New York, 1947, pp. 3-22.

More important are the inadequacies of the basic data upon which the estimates are built. For the difficulties of computing national income and product even in the United States are compounded in Japan by the inadequacies of statistical reporting. Especially is this true in the extensive noncommercialized sectors of the economy.[5] Where the household and the small unincorporated enterprise still predominate as the business unit, accounting practices are rudimentary if they exist at all. In agriculture, in home industry, and in most of the services it is necessary therefore to make many crude estimates of production values, current expenses, and factor incomes. How much food is produced and consumed on the farm without entering the national production statistics at all? In deducting costs of materials from gross production values, how distinguish between business and family expenses, or allocate costs and incomes among several different occupations carried on by a family in supplementary, part-time fashion? How estimate depreciation when even the accounting practices of large corporations are unreliable on this point?

The Cabinet Bureau of Statistics was aware of these difficulties. So far as possible it employed techniques to minimize them. Further refinements were then added by the U.S. Office of Strategic Services. The resulting figures for 1930 are undoubtedly the best estimate for any prewar year in Japan. Probably they are the best for any Far Eastern country in a prewar year. It should be borne in mind, nevertheless, that they contain a rather wide margin of error.

National Income by Industrial Origin. Proceeding now to examine the details of Table 38, one is struck with the comparatively minor role to which the extractive industries had sunk by this time. Formerly predominant as the source of national wealth and livelihood, by 1930 agriculture accounted for less than 20% of the production of Japan, measured by the earnings of labor and capital employed. Despite its expansion in preceding decades, it could no longer be considered the foundation of the Japanese economy in terms of current value of output. The income of the country now accrued mainly to the labor and capital employed in the processing and handling of goods, and other services of a private or governmental character.

The year 1930 was a year of depressed agricultural prices and incomes, to be sure. And comparisons of net income produced in dif-

[5] Actually, a sampling technique of field investigation was employed by the Cabinet Bureau of Statistics to collect the data necessary for estimating the ratio of net to gross product in agriculture and manufacturing. In agriculture 10,000 households were investigated, in small-scale industry 2,500 households, and in factory industry 700 plants.

ferent industries reflect not only the relative amounts of resources
employed, but also differences from one field to another in the
rates of return on capital and labor. A similar reckoning for 1925,
before the prices of rice, silk, and other primary products begin
their downward descent, would show net product in farming to have
been somewhat more important. This price decline, however, was an
initial stage in the whole series of events which accelerated Japan's
transition to industrialism in the next decade. In prewar Japan
agriculture was never to recoup its former position. Throughout
the decade 1930-39 the extractive industries continued to furnish
no more than 20% of net national product, in terms of the values
now placed on labor and capital in various employments.

The 1937 distribution of income, for example, compares as follows with that of 1930:

	1930		1937[a]	
	Billions of Yen	*Percent*	*Billions of Yen*	*Percent*
Total income produced	10.2	100	18.4	100
Agriculture, forestry, fishing, and mining	2.1	20	3.9	21
Manufacturing and construction	3.3	32	7.4	40
Services	4.9	48	7.1	39

[a] U.S. Department of State, *National Income of Japan*, Washington, 1945, p. 86.

Comparable figures for an earlier year, say, 1880, would certainly show agriculture in a much more predominant position. By
way of illustration, Yamada's estimates (above, Table 12) give
the following change in the distribution of net national product
from 1880 to 1935:

	1878-82	1908-12	1933-37
		(percentages)	
Total	100	100	100
Agriculture, forestry, fishing, and mining	38[a]	39	21
Manufacturing and construction	13	23	36
Services	49	38	43

[a] Agriculture and forestry only.

The extractive industries may well have been more important,
in the early years, and services (outside the family) less important,
than Yamada's figures suggest. For the years before 1910 his esti-

mates are very dubious, as noted in Chapter 3; moreover, the whole concept of national income accounting is difficult to apply to an economy still so largely precapitalistic in organization. Even if we raise the figure for primary production in 1878-82 by 10% to allow for fishing and mining, it still would be only 42%. This seems low. T. C. Liu's estimates for China during 1931-36 credit agriculture, forestry, and fishing with 60 to 75% of gross national product.[6] Industrial activity furnished 10% or so, and the service occupations the balance. J. J. Polak's figures for the Netherlands Indies in 1938, cited in Chapter 8, yield a similar conclusion. In India and the Philippines, likewise, agriculture still provides around 50% of national income. Yet already by 1880 Japanese manufacturing, transport, and commerce had apparently assumed more importance than is often thought. Even in late Tokugawa times a significant share of the population had come to make its living in the trade and handicrafts of castle towns and cities. In certain rural regions as well, these nonagricultural pursuits were an appreciable source of income for people ordinarily classed as farmers. Except in the most primitive household economy, indeed, manufacturing and the services are necessarily of considerable importance, even though carried on as rural by-employments to a large extent.

By 1930, at any rate, Japan's industrialization had advanced to the point where manufacturing outranked the extractive occupations by a wide margin of net product. The former accounted for about one third of the national total; the latter for about one fifth. During the next decade the share of industry advanced to 40% or more under the impetus afforded by foreign trade expansion and the rising level of armament expenditure. Partly the growing percentage of industrial income represents a rapid expansion of manufacturing production.[7] But it also reflects a shift in relative prices,

[6] *China's National Income, 1931-36*, Washington, 1946, pp. 12, 32-40.

[7] Changes in the physical volume of production in Japan are given as follows in official indices:

	1930	1937
Agriculture	100	105
Fishing	100	131
Mining	100	146
Manufacturing	100	197
Durable goods	100	264
Nondurable goods	100	163

Sources: Agriculture and fishing: indices of Ministry of Agriculture and Forestry (*Oriental Economist*, vol. vii, no. 7, July 1940, p. 414), adjusted to 1930 base by Nagoya indices ("Hompō Genshi Seisambutsu no Seisan Sūryō," *Nagoya Keizai Tōkei Geppō*, vol. viii, no. 4, May 1936, p. 60). Mining and manufacturing: indices of the Economic and Scientific Section, GHQ, Supreme Commander for the Allied Powers, Tokyo (Bank of Japan, *Economic Statistics of Japan, 1951*, p. 284).

profits, and wages favorable to industry—especially the capital goods and munitions industries. This enabled capital employed in these pursuits, and labor to a lesser extent, to claim an increasingly larger share of national income per unit of output.

More surprising is the importance of the various activities classified as service occupations. For industrialization is often conceived mainly in terms of the growing predominance of manufacturing activity. Yet wholesale and retail trade alone in Japan contributed a net product of 1.7 billion yen in 1930. This was as much as income produced in agriculture or in private factory industry. (It was largely value added to their product.) Another billion yen, 10% of national production, was represented by income produced in the private professions, domestic service, and the manifold activities grouped under catering and amusements. (Table 38, note e.) When government services are added in, this whole service division of the economy accounted for nearly 50% of net national product in 1930, and 40% in 1937.

Some of these nonmaterial services developed as ancillary trades to handle the financing and distribution of industrial and agricultural commodities. Functionally, therefore, they were an integral part of the new system of commodity production. As production processes became more capitalistic, and market organization increasingly complex, they naturally grew in importance. They also tended to become separated out as specialized occupations, being no longer performed so largely by the farmer or the industrialist himself.

Still other service occupations expanded in response to another tendency described in Chapter 8. With the rise in per capita incomes, an increasing share of Japanese consumer spending turned toward medical care, education, travel, and recreational interests requiring personal service. Probably governmental functions other than education also gained in importance, absorbing an increasing percentage of money incomes in the form of taxes. Such services cannot be imported or exported to any great degree. Their growth is therefore correlated closely with the growth and redirection of domestic consumer demand.

Government activities alone accounted for more than a quarter of the total value of all services, according to Table 38. Valued at factor cost (including an imputed return on property), they came to 1,132 million yen. Conceptually it may seem confusing to reckon the activities of the State on a par with those of the farmer or the merchant. There is a certain logic, however, in placing a market value on the contributions of the government to the civilian economy in the form of education, social services, public works, and the like. This is less true of the military services, but in 1930 their share was still relatively small.[8]

Here we are speaking only of the general functions of government, excluding State-owned railways, communications, and factories. The latter were quasi-commercial operations. Their costs were met more or less by the sale of goods and services, rather than by taxes. They are accordingly grouped more appropriately in their respective industrial categories. However, if we add them to other State services, the total share of national income originated by the government still amounts to no more than 15 to 18% in 1930. It was even less through most of the subsequent decade. Here is testimony again to the predominance of private ownership in prewar Japan.

This review of the major components of national production gives further evidence of Japan's midposition at this time in the transition to industrialism. By 1930 her economic structure was already quite diversified—certainly far more than in 1900 or 1870. In round figures, again, about one half of her total income now originated directly in commodity production. Here the balance was swinging steadily away from the extractive occupations toward manufacturing industry. Already the ratio in market values was 2:3; by the end of the decade it was still higher. The remainder of Japan's income was produced in a variety of services which together made up nearly 50% of net national product on this accounting. Over 25% originated in trade, transport, and finance. The balance of about 20% was divided equally between other private and government services.

All of these judgments, it should be emphasized, are confined to net product as valued at the prices prevailing in Japan for various goods and services. If women were forced to accept lower wages than men, if the State protected one industry and not another, if certain *zaibatsu*-controlled firms were able to earn monopoly profits—all such circumstances affect the value of net income as calculated here. The percentage claim of any industry on national income would have been different if income and opportunity had been more equally distributed. Business net product is therefore not identical with social net product as the latter may be defined for various purposes. Nor do changes in real national income necessarily measure changes in economic welfare. For the latter also involves considerations of equality, security, and the human costs of productive effort. These find no place in the above calculus of national income.

[8] Pay of the armed forces totalled only 109 million yen, or 20% of total government payrolls. See Table 38, note f. This is not a measure of military production as a share of total national product, of course. A part of the net product of other industrial sectors was also devoted to military purposes.

Net Product of Manufacturing Industry. Having placed Japanese manufacturing in the perspective of total national production, we may now examine briefly the relative balance among the principal manufacturing industries. Net income from production again offers a measure of the quantitative contribution of each industry to the total current flow of goods and services.

First, the major divisions of manufacturing may be distinguished by size of establishment and conditions of ownership. Three categories are given in Table 38: (a) private factories equipped to employ five or more operatives (1,809 million yen), (b) government-owned plants (116 million yen), and (c) a million or more "home" or workshop establishments too small to be classified as factories (832 million yen).

The characteristics of these three components of manufacturing were discussed in Chapter 3. By 1930 private factories produced the bulk of manufacturing income in Japan—65%. Workshop industry had long been slowly declining in importance. Yet it still accounted for as much as 30% of net income produced in manufacturing, and provided about 50% of all manufacturing employment. (See Chapter 4.) State-owned factories, by contrast, had ceased to play any significant role in quantitative terms. Their share was now a meager 4%, representing largely products for the armed forces and other government agencies. Together these three divisions of manufacturing originated some 2.8 billion of net income in 1930.[9] Already they furnished more than one quarter of the national income of Japan, a percentage which advanced even further in the industrial boom of the thirties.

The array of needs now served by manufacturing activity is better indicated by the altered balance among industries classified by types of products. Here again value added by manufacture serves as a measure of their respective contributions to national income. Unlike employment figures, it takes account of wide differences in labor productivity from industry to industry. And unlike gross production values, it is not distorted by differences in the value of raw materials processed, or by duplication of commodity values at different stages within a processing sequence.

Only for private factory industries are data available for calculating net product. Table 39 gives such estimates in approximate fashion for the year 1930. They are also given for 1936 to show the changes brought about by the industrial boom of the intervening years. In Japan, as in other leading industrial countries, factory

[9] Disregarding construction and three minor industries separately classified—salt manufacture, movie production, and newspaper and magazine publishing. See Table 38.

Table 39. *Gross and Net Value of Production in Private
Factory Industries of Japan Proper, 1930, 1936*[a]

| | 1930 | | | | 1936 | |
| | GROSS PRODUCT | | NET PRODUCT | | NET PRODUCT | |
	Millions of yen	*Percent*	*Millions of Yen*	*Percent*	*Millions of Yen*	*Percent*
All private factories	*6,200*	*100.0*	*1,954*	*100.0*	*3,633*	*100.0*
Textiles	2,174	35.0	407	20.8	521	14.3
Chemicals	902	14.5	357	18.4	911	25.1
Machinery, vehicles, etc.	695	11.2	330	16.9	822	22.6
Food products	954	15.4	282	14.4	247	6.8
Gas and electricity[b]	263	4.2	131	6.7	211	5.8
Metals and metal products[c]	501	8.1	126	6.4	469	12.9
Printing and binding	192	3.1	112	5.7	86	2.4
Ceramics	162	2.6	103	5.3	201	5.5
Wood products	163	2.6	44	2.5	74	2.0
Other	194	3.1	60	3.1	91	2.5

a Net product is computed for both years as follows (except for gas and electricity): (1) a first approximation was secured by substracting the value of raw materials and fuel consumed from gross value of production in each industry—all figures from Ministry of Commerce and Industry, *Kōjō Tōkeihyō* (1930 and 1936); (2) this provisional net product was then corrected for other deductible expenses by reference to the ratio between (a) raw material and fuel deductions as given by *Kōjō Tōkeihyō* and (b) total deductible expenses as computed for 1930 by the Cabinet Bureau of Statistics (Japan Economic Federation, *National Income of Japan, 1930-1939*, Tokyo, 1939, p. 59). In other words, minor expenses other than raw materials and fuel are assumed to preserve the same ratio to material and fuel costs in each industry in 1936 as existed in 1930. The error in this assumption does not materially affect the resulting figures for net product in 1936.

Total net product in 1930, as given here, differs slightly from "income produced" in Table 38. The latter is net of business taxes, and is based on CBS gross product figures which diverge somewhat from those of *Kōjō Tōkeihyō* used here in the case of food and metals.

b As given by the Japan Economic Federation, *op.cit.*, pp. 59, 63. The 1930 figures are those of the CBS; for 1936 they are computed from data on output and rates, assuming no change in the 1930 ratio of net to gross value of output.

c The rise in output of metals from 1930 to 1936, as given here, is evidently exaggerated by the shift meantime of the huge iron and steel output of the Imperial Iron Works from the category of government to private factories, as reported in *Kōjō Tōkeihyō*. In 1934 this State-operated company was merged with six private firms to form the Japan Iron Manufacturing Company. Though largely owned by the State, the new company was evidently classified henceforth as a private concern in the manufacturing statistics.

production falls into four main categories: metal manufactures, chemicals, clothing materials, and foodstuffs. Elsewhere (Table 14) is shown the parallel predominance of these four groups in Japan, Great Britain, Germany, and the United States.

Most surprising is the relatively small place now occupied by the textile industries as a group. For it was largely through silk and cotton goods that Japan was known to the outside world as a manufacturing nation before World War II.

In 1930 textiles still provided as much as 51% of private factory employment, and almost 40% of total manufacturing employment. Similarly, textile products accounted for 35% of the gross market value of all factory goods produced in Japan. Especially in the spinning trades, however, labor productivity and wage rates were low. And the 2.2 billion yen of products turned out by textile factories include a good deal of double counting. For instance, some cotton yarn produced in 1930 appears both as yarn and as an element in the value of cotton cloth woven in the same year. Actual net value added by manufacture is therefore only about 400 million yen, hardly one fifth of the gross value of production. (Table 39.) Textiles contributed no more than 21% of the total net product of private factory industry in 1930, as compared with over half of the total number of factory jobs.

It is a commonplace that the textile industries have pioneered the factory system around the world. In virtually every newly industrializing country they have tended to predominate. Japan was no exception to this rule, as we have seen. Yet the substantive importance of the textile trades as a source of manufacturing income both in Japan and elsewhere, is apt to be exaggerated, for the reasons given above.

For the early years, before World War I, no adequate estimates of net manufacturing product in Japan can be made. Even as early as 1914, however, textiles probably accounted for no more than 30% of the total income produced in all private *factories*.[10] This is a much lower percentage than is yielded by employment or gross production figures. Yet it is a more significant measure of the relative return to labor and capital employed in the textile trades, valued at market prices. As we have seen, the relative place of textiles declined markedly in the period ending in 1930. The intervening years witnessed a 150% increase in textile output, according to the Nagoya index. But other industries like chemicals, machinery, and electric power production advanced even more rapidly. (See Table 8.) The trend was clearly toward diversification of industry, with silk filatures and cotton factories losing their former primacy.

These calculations leave workshop industry out of account, to be

10 Assuming—rather inaccurately—that the ratios of gross to net product in textiles and total factory industry were the same in 1914 as in 1930. In the former year the gross value of textile goods produced in factories (plants with five or more workers) was 620 million yen, or 46% of total factory output (1,336 million yen). Asahi Shimbun-sha, *Nippon Keizai Tōkei Sōkan*, Tokyo, 1930, p. 724. Textiles accounted for as much as 63% of total employment in plants of ten or more workers. Tōyō Keizai Shimpō-sha, *Meiji Taishō Kokusei Sōran*, Tokyo, 1927, pp. 544-45.

sure. Here the weaving trades in particular continued to flourish. In 1930 textile establishments of less than five operatives evidently accounted for at least half as much value added to textile materials by manufacture as did the factories.[11] Including small silk-reelers as well as weavers, and allowing too for government factories producing woolen cloth for the Army and Navy, we may put total net product for all branches of textile manufacture at 600 to 650 million yen in 1930. Thus 1 out of every 4 or 5 yen of national income produced in manufacturing (2.8 billion yen) still originated in the processing of silk, cotton, wool, and other textile fibers.

Ranking now with the textile trades in importance were the industries producing chemicals and metal products of all sorts. Indeed, if the machinery and metallurgical industries are bracketed together as metal-processing trades, they already rival the textile industries in total net product by 1930. For this would include 456 million yen of net output produced in private factories (Table 39); at least 60 million yen in State-owned enterprise; and a further amount in small establishments of less than five operatives. The total must have been over 550 million yen in 1930, or 20% of total manufacturing income.[12]

Taking into view all Japanese industrial establishments, large and small, we may conclude that over 40% of the total net income produced in manufacturing activity at this time was divided more or less equally between textile products on the one hand, and metal

[11] This rests on the assumption that net/gross product ratios in small weaving establishments did not differ widely from those prevalent in factories weaving textiles. The gross value of woven goods produced in establishments of all sizes was as follows in 1930 (in millions of yen): cotton, 498; silk and mixtures, 425; wool and mixtures, 165; hemp, etc., 15; total, 1,102. Ministry of Commerce and Industry, *Shōkōshō Tōkeihyō* (1936), Tokyo, 1937, pp. 2-34. Factories accounted for 793 million yen of this total.

[12] No information is available on the various products turned out by government plants at this time. The figure of 60 million yen or more of net income for State factories producing metals, machinery, and vehicles rests on the assumption that these arsenals and plants accounted for no smaller (probably a larger) share of the net product of all government factories than of their employment. Employment during 1930 can be estimated roughly by averaging the year-end figures for 1929 and 1930. This gives the metallurgical and machinery plants 103,000 out of 224,000 workers, or 46%. Yasuji Koide, "Hompō Sangyō Kōzō no Hendo ni Kansuru Shiryō," *Nagoya Keizai Tōkei Geppō*, vol. viii, no. 9, October 1936, pp. 48-50.

For workshops of less than five operatives there are likewise no data on production of metal utensils, hardware and tools, electric lamps, bicycle parts, and other items classified as metal manufactures. Such information was first published in 1939, and it is not certain how complete the coverage was. The gross output of plants of less than five operatives was then recorded as amounting to only 2.5% of output in larger private plants, though their employees numbered 10%. Supreme Commander for the Allied Powers, GHQ, Economic and Scientific Section, *Number of Establishments, Employment, and Value of Products in Manufacturing Industries in Japan, 1929-1942*, Tokyo, 1947, table 2.

products and machinery on the other. This may seem surprisingly high. But it does not differ materially from the corresponding figures for Germany, Britain, or the United States. The balance between the two is only more heavily weighted in Japan on the side of textiles. Both groups of industries, it may be observed, were engaged largely in processing raw materials imported from abroad, rather than produced at home. Chemicals and manufactured foodstuffs came next in order of importance among factory industries. They were followed in turn by smaller industries producing gas and electricity, books, pottery, and wood manufactures. All of these latter industries relied mainly on domestic materials, though they still employed a good deal of Western machinery and equipment.

This was roughly Japan's industrial balance, then, on the eve of the Great Depression and the invasion of Manchuria. It reflected the stage of development now attained by Japanese manufacturing in response to the varied influences enumerated earlier in this study.

The ensuing decade brought far-reaching changes in the structure of industry. Japan embarked upon a period of feverish industrial expansion, first as a consequence of yen depreciation and reflation, then under the impact of large-scale military mobilization (Chapter 2). The later phases may be discounted as a violent dislocation of "normal" patterns of peacetime growth. But this should not blind us to the underlying forces raising the heavy industries to increasing prominence. The latter was more than a war phenomenon, though it was greatly intensified after 1937 by military spending on armaments, by a huge development program in Manchukuo, and by the resulting derangement of consumer goods markets both at home and abroad.

The figures for 1936, given in Table 39, show the growing ascendancy of the chemical and metal-processing industries by the middle of the decade.[13] After a five-year expansion of overseas trade, with the added stimulus of a nascent armament boom, these two categories of industry had come to provide 60% of net private factory output in Japan at current market prices. The textile industries, by contrast, had now dropped back into a decidedly secondary role, with only 14%. This had occurred despite the headlong expansion of Japanese cotton goods in markets all over the world. In industrial structure, as distinguished from foreign trade, Japan

[13] The actual increase in the net product of the Japanese metallurgical industries from 1930 to 1936, at (rising) yen prices, was nearer a twofold than a threefold gain. As noted in Table 39, the large iron and steel output of the former Imperial Iron Works was apparently shifted to the category of private production in the manufacturing statistics when in 1934 it was merged with other firms to form the Japan Iron Manufacturing Company.

had now clearly passed out of the characteristic early phase of industrialization, where textiles made from natural fibers are the mainstay of factory industry.

It should be emphasized again that these comparisons of net income produced in different industries are comparisons of money values at prevailing market prices in Japan. They are influenced not only by the amounts of capital and labor employed to process a given value of raw materials, but also by the rates of return which these factors of production were able to earn in particular employments. The machinery industries, for instance, required larger amounts of complicated equipment and highly paid labor per unit of output than the textile or woodworking industries. The entry of new firms into these trades was also more difficult. This served to raise their net/gross product ratios and their relative shares in national income.[14]

Year-to-year shifts in prices, market relations, and financial practices thus affected the trend of net income produced in different industries. The latter is an unreliable guide to changes in the physical volume of production. In the thirties the low level to which silk prices had fallen depressed the relative earnings of labor and capital in silk reeling. Much of this labor came from farm families who had nothing better to turn to for supplementary income. On the other hand, rising armament expenditures progressively boosted prices and profits as well as output in iron and steel manufactures. Producers of machinery and equipment expanded their scale of operations, but in addition they were able to claim a larger share of the national income in exchange for each unit of output. A part of the shift in the composition of net national product toward the equipment industries was simply a shift of this character. (Equally there was a shift in the division of the net proceeds of heavy industrial production as between capital and labor. This division moved markedly in favor of the capitalist, for wage rates in these industries during 1936-38 failed to rise significantly above their 1930 level.)

It may further be observed that a historical rise in net income originating in one sector of an economy does not necessarily mean a net gain in national income, even if it results from an increase in the physical output of that sector. For it is always possible to force an expansion of production in one industry at the expense of another. The gain in one field may represent simply a loss in the other,

[14] Earlier (page 183) it was observed that the prices of machinery and metal products, relative to those of textiles, were generally higher in Japan than in the West. Revalued at British or American prices then prevailing, the output of the metalworking industries would shrink in relative importance.

perhaps an absolute reduction in total real income. The official protection and subsidies extended to Japan's strategic industries from their birth served in some degree to draw labor and capital away from consumer goods industries, whose competitive position without such governmental aids was much stronger. Through the thirties, it is true, the decline of the consumer industries as a group was only a relative loss of position. From 1930 to 1936 the *Oriental Economist* index of investment goods production rose from 100 to 183. But the consumer goods index also advanced to 133.[15] Moreover, a good part of the former, as of the latter, was for civilian purposes. After 1940, however, war production (and blockade) brought a steep decline in civilian supply of almost all types. The output of investment goods in Japanese industry rose 171% from 1937 to 1944, while consumer goods output fell 66%. Meantime, agricultural production dropped 30%, as manpower and materials were diverted to military uses.[16]

The rise of the mining, metalworking, power, and chemical industries, whether described in terms of physical output or share of net national product, should be appraised in this light. Only in part did it represent a growth in the scale and maturity of Japanese industry in response to civilian needs, capabilities, and peacetime opportunities. In part it was a conscious redirection of the country's resources away from such manufactures as textiles, pottery, and foodstuffs, and toward those strategic industries considered vital as instruments of national expansion. In lesser degree the same thing may be said of the whole advance of factory industry and mining relative to agriculture and the small-scale trades.

The long-term trend toward the greater diversification of Japan's economy went much deeper than this. Too often it is interpreted largely in terms of the military goals of the State, to the neglect of other underlying forces of economic growth emphasized in this study. It would be a mistake, however, to overlook the persistent influence of national policy in shaping the course of events. From the days of the early Meiji statesmen, Japan's political ambitions gave a special twist and emphasis to her industrial development.

Structure of Employment

The structure of employment in prewar Japan, like the pattern of national income, shows the marked changes brought about by the expansive forces described in preceding chapters. By 1930 Japan was already well along the road to the industrialization of employment. With her population now at the full tide of growth,

---

[15] *Oriental Economist*, vol. VI, no. 10, October 1939, p. 692.
[16] *Economic Statistics of Japan, 1951*, cited, pp. 285-86, 288.

new job opportunities had to be sought—and were found—mainly
outside the traditional rural occupations which had previously
through the centuries been the foundation of her economic life.

Labor Force in Prewar Japan. The first national census of population and employment in Japan was taken in 1920. Prior to that
time neither the size of the labor force nor its distribution among
occupations can be measured with any accuracy. The increase in
the working population was discussed in Chapter 4, with the conclusion that it grew steadily with the increase in total population,
though very likely at a slower rate. The opinion was ventured that
it increased by perhaps no more than 65 to 75% from 1875 to
1935, as the total population doubled. However, the difficulties of
definition, as well as the inadequacy of statistics, make any such
estimate problematical.

Still more do these difficulties obscure the shifting pattern of
employment as among various occupations before 1920. In Chapters
3 and 4 reference was made to the oft quoted figures of Prof. S.
Hijikata, purporting to show the changing distribution of the labor
force by principal occupation through the Meiji decades. Linked
with the 1920 census, they show a redistribution after 1880 as
follows:[17]

	1880		1900		1920	
	Number (thousands)	*Percent*	*Number (thousands)*	*Percent*	*Number (thousands)*	*Percent*
Total gainfully occupied	*19,872*	*100.0*	*25,308*	*100.0*	*27,268*	*100.0*
Agriculture, fishing, and mining	16,100	81.0	17,477	69.0	15,110	55.4
Manufacturing and construction	1,267	6.4	3,281	13.0	5,300	19.4
Commerce and transport	1,277	6.4	2,566	10.1	4,225	15.5
Other private and public services[a]	657	3.3	1,050	4.1	1,442	5.3
Other	571	2.9	934	3.7	1,191	4.4

[a] Excluding domestic service.

Unfortunately, little confidence can be reposed in the pre-1920
figures, for reasons noted earlier. (See page 129.) One doubts very

[17] Hijikata's estimates for 1880 and 1900 are from Yamada, *op.cit.*, p. 152. The
1920 census figures (occupational classification) are quoted here from Imperial
Cabinet, Bureau of Statistics, *Rōdō Tōkei Yōran* (1930), Tokyo, 1930, pp. 3-4. To
the census total in the occupational classification I have added 642,000 domestics
(derived from the industrial classification), not otherwise included.

much that agriculture and fishing afforded the chief occupation of as many as 80% of the working population in 1880. Certainly their share of actual employment could not have been so large, even at this early date. Nor could the number of gainfully employed persons in other occupations have advanced subsequently by regular year-to-year increments, as Hijikata's figures require us to believe. But it is hardly worth speculating over the details. The main drift is clear, in any case. As economic development proceeded, it multiplied the opportunities for gainful employment outside the crowded field of agriculture. In part these opportunities developed as by-employments pursued by peasant families on the farm or in the neighboring town. In part they sprang up in the cities as Japan's industrial centers grew apace and drew millions of young people off the farms into urban livelihoods.

At the turn of the century three out of every five families in Japan were still engaged in farming, at least part-time, according to official reports. The figures are 5.4 million farm families out of a national total of 8.4 million families in 1903. Over the next thirty-five years the absolute number of agricultural families, as given by *Nōrinsho Tōkeihyō*, remains virtually stationary at about 5½ million. Actually, the official reports for these early years may exaggerate the population remaining on the farm, owing to deficiencies in the registration system. Moreover, there is no basis for estimating what share of the labor power of farming families was really being devoted to agricultural pursuits. This share may well have declined. Referring to the period around 1918, for example, J. W. Robertson Scott concludes that 5½ million families probably furnished no more than 10 million effective farm workers.[18]

In any event, Japan remained throughout the Meiji era a predominantly agricultural country. Farming continued to provide the largest share of the national income, and to afford the principal livelihood for over half of the country's population. Only slowly did it yield to the advance of the newer industries and service trades, where the more dynamic growth was taking place. More rapid transfer to nonagricultural pursuits was held in check by the swelling population, which brought intense competition in the industrial labor market and dammed up the existing farm population on the land.

Beginning in 1920, it is possible to gain a more accurate picture of the shifting pattern of employment.

Three nation-wide enumerations of the Japanese labor force were made, in 1920, 1930, and 1940. These censuses were comprehensive in scope, and fairly consistent in their industrial categories. How-

[18] *The Foundations of Japan*, London, 1922, p. 412.

ever, certain major ambiguities remain. People were asked simply whether they were gainfully occupied or not, and if so what their "principal" occupation was. Thus the figures include an immense but indeterminate amount of part-time employment, as well as some totally unemployed persons. We cannot be sure whether a rise or decline in the number reported as gainfully occupied in agriculture, for example, is anything but a more or less complete enumeration of part-time workers, especially women, children, and aged persons employed at home. Moreover, subsidiary and joint employments were still widely prevalent in Japan. For millions of peasant families supplementary nonagricultural pursuits were the chief source of cash income. Other millions of people combined handicraft industry with commerce, transport, or other services, one or the other being given as the chief occupation. The basket-maker, for example, might sell his product in the neighborhood; the food-vendor might prepare his own foodstuffs for sale. To place them in any single category is rather arbitrary, and fails to give a true measure of actual employment.

All this does not nullify the value of the census figures. To some extent the over- and underestimates in various industrial categories tend to cancel out. For example, the number of persons recorded in manufacturing includes many part-time workers who gave it as their chief occupation; but it excludes others who are classified elsewhere and yet followed it as a by-employment. There is no reason to assume that the two groups are equal, however, so the figures are a poor guide to the relative amount of labor actually expended in various pursuits. This situation is of course typical of all countries, East and West, where occupational division of labor is not yet highly specialized and economic life is still organized largely on a family basis. It may be recalled that Japanese farms were still operated almost entirely with family labor. Out of 14,687,000 persons principally occupied in agriculture and fishing in 1930, only 745,000 were nonfamily wage earners. Even in the remainder of the economy, family workers furnished nearly 20% of the total number of employed workers, excluding entrepreneurs. (See Table 17.)

With these limitations in mind, let us examine the major shifts which took place in the principal employments of Japan's working population after 1920. Table 40 groups the total labor force in certain broad industrial divisions between 1920 and 1940. The year 1940 was abnormal, of course. War mobilization was already well advanced. Heavy industry was booming under the stimulus of rising expenditures on munitions, war plants, and Manchurian development. The growing shortage of labor to man the war indus-

Table 40. *Population and Labor Force of Japan Proper, with Major Industrial Groupings, 1920-40*[a]

	1920		1930		1940	
	Number (thousands)	Percent	Number (thousands)	Percent	Number (thousands)	Percent
Total						
population	55,963	100.0	64,450	100.0	73,075	100.0
Civilian						
labor force	27,011	48.4	29,377	45.5	32,483	44.4
Armed forces[b]	250	0.4	243	0.4	1,694	2.3
Unoccupied	28,702	51.3	34,830	54.0	38,898	53.2
Total						
labor force	*27,261*	*100.0*	*29,620*	*100.0*	*34,177*	*100.0*
Male	16,987	62.3	19,030	64.2	21,424	62.6
Female	10,274	37.7	10,589	35.7	12,753	37.3
Civilian						
labor force	*27,011*	*100.0*	*29,377*	*100.0*	*32,483*	*100.0*
Extractive						
industries	15,272	56.6	15,014	51.1	14,983	46.1
Agriculture						
and fishing	(14,824)	(54.9)	(14,699)	(50.0)	(14,385)	(44.3)
Mining	(448)	(1.6)	(315)	(1.1)	(598)	(1.8)
Manufacturing and						
construction	5,139	19.0	5,876	20.0	8,132	25.0
Civilian services	6,542	24.2	8,415	28.7	9,150	28.3
Commerce, transportation, and communications	(4,614)	(17.1)	(5,851)	(19.9)	(6,246)	(19.2)
Government and the professions	(1,266)	(4.6)	(1,762)	(6.0)	(2,195)	(6.8)
Domestic	(662)	(2.4)	(802)	(2.7)	(709)	(2.2)
Other	59	0.2	71	0.2	218	0.7

a Census data for 1930 are from Imperial Cabinet, Bureau of Statistics, *Shōwa Go-nen Kokusei Chōsa Saishū Hōkokusho*, Tokyo, 1938, pp. 348-49; for 1920 and 1940 they are from Prime Minister's Office, Statistics Bureau, *Japan Statistical Year-Book, 1949*, Tokyo, 1949, pp. 68-71. The labor force classification is by the industry to which the person is attached (e.g., manufacturing), rather than by occupation (e.g., carpenter, salesman) as in the census figures quoted on page 462. Persons are classified by their chief employment, or if idle, where last employed. Excluded from each category are part-time workers whose chief employment lay elsewhere.

b The 1920 and 1930 totals exclude all components of the armed forces except officers and enlisted men, and all persons outside Japan Proper. These figures are taken from the census classification by occupation rather than that by industry. The 1940 total comprises all members of the armed forces whether in Japan or overseas. Most of the increase came after 1937, when the number was still only 634,000 at year-end.

tries as well as the armed forces had begun to produce serious bottlenecks in certain skills. Initial measures to conscript and allocate
industrial manpower had already been approved in 1938 and 1939.
These controls were still largely on paper, however. The civilian
employment situation in 1940 may still be viewed mainly as an
intensification of trends carrying back through the previous decade
and earlier.

Several conclusions may be drawn from Table 40:

1. The total labor force in Japan increased in twenty years from
27.3 to 34.2 million, or 25%. This was less than the rate of growth
in the total population (32%), but about the same as the increase
in the number of people in the ages fifteen to fifty-nine. (The 1940
figure includes young men absorbed into the armed forces overseas,
but excludes considerable numbers of civilians who also migrated
to the colonies and to occupied China in administrative, business,
and professional jobs created by expanding empire.)[19] Altogether
nearly half the population of Japan was gainfully employed at
the end as well as the beginning of the period. It was a relatively
young labor force, with 41% ranging between the ages of fifteen
and thirty in 1930. Nearly two thirds were males. In terms of actual
labor power, however, women and girls accounted for considerably
less than one third of the total. Part-time employment was much
more prevalent among them; perhaps also total unemployment on
the date of the census.

2. Agriculture remained the major source of gainful employment
(as opposed to net income) in prewar Japan. Together with the
related occupation of fishing, it continued to occupy over 40% of
the working population of the home islands. For civilian males the
proportion was 36% in 1940; for females 57%. The more interesting fact is its rapidly declining role, especially as a source of
male employment. The number of persons recorded in agriculture

---

[19] The role of emigration in the utilization of Japanese manpower during the
interwar years is examined in detail in a forthcoming study of Japanese population
by Irene B. Taeuber. My own impression, based on a much more cursory study
of the figures, is that prior to 1935, when military expansion and colonial development moved into higher gear, neither the armed forces nor net civilian emigration
overseas bulked large in the total employment situation, even for young men in
the most productive ages. As marginal outlets, of course, they could have had a
significance out of proportion to the numbers involved through relaxing the pressures
on the job market at home. (See above, pages 157-58.)

Yet the absorption of these men into the Army and Navy, or into overseas
civilian employment, can hardly be regarded as an economic safety valve for Japan
in reality unless the building of empire contributed to the preservation and growth
of her civilian economy. In point of fact, as it turned out, the intense activity of
the thirties directed to empire expansion represented a prodigious investment of
Japanese resources on which little return was ever collected except war and
disaster. (See Chapter 10.)

and fishing actually dropped 439,000 from 1920 to 1940. Meanwhile the labor force as a whole increased 6.9 million. Thus the entire net addition to the working population, after allowance for civilian in- and out-migration, found principal employment outside agriculture, in both the twenties and the thirties. Military mobilization in the latter decade took an additional 1.4 million men out of civilian jobs by 1940—over 1 million after 1937. Yet nonagricultural civilian employment within the home islands still absorbed 5.8 million, or 84% of the increase over 1920.

This stability of numbers engaged in farming is believed to have characterized the whole period after the turn of the century, as remarked earlier. The process of industrialization, despite its rapid rate, did not succeed in moving people off the farm, so rapid was the growth in total population. It failed therefore to increase significantly the ratio of land to agricultural workers. But it did provide some sort of livelihood in nonagricultural pursuits for the numbers added to the labor force, and at a slowly rising standard of living. This was no mean achievement in view of the 67% increase in the population after 1900. Possibly, too, those who remained on the farm were able to acquire an increasing margin of income from nonagricultural employments, at least until the decline of the raw silk trade after 1925. Nonfarm employment provided 15% of the earned net income of agricultural families in one sample survey of 1935. (See below, page 491.) A 1938 investigation revealed that only 46% of Japan's 5.4 million farm families were wholly engaged in agriculture, and another 30% "mainly" so. Some 24% gave farming as a subsidiary occupation.[20]

3. Actually the shift of *able-bodied* workers out of agriculture after 1930 was greater than the figures of Table 40 suggest. Especially was this true in the late thirties under the pressure of military conscription and the boom in war industries. From 1930 to 1940 employment increased 2.3 million in industry, and nearly 1 million in the professions. Meanwhile the armed forces also grew to unprecedented size. Mainly this was a demand for young men. It was supplied only by the transfer of 1,100,000 males from agriculture and of 400,000 from commerce. The former were replaced in large part by the wives and daughters of farm families who now had to perform an increasing share of farm labor. Eventually, however, this reserve of home labor proved inadequate, and the continued

[20] Supreme Commander for the Allied Powers, GHQ, Natural Resources Section, Report No. 101, *Japanese Agricultural Land Statistics*, Tokyo, 1948, p. 17. There are estimates showing that only one in three farm families in the eighties had any supplementary occupation, but it is impossible to judge their accuracy or comparability.

drain of men to the Army and the factories had adverse effects on farm output. Together with the shortage of fertilizer it brought an acute decline in food production in the late war years, just as food imports were virtually shut off by the Allied blockade.

Here is an illustration, parenthetically, of an important truth often overlooked in discussions of Oriental industrialization. As long as farming techniques remain primitive, there is no large surplus of labor in the densely populated countryside of Japan or of other Far Eastern countries, except in the slack seasons and for neighborhood by-employment. No large number of able-bodied workers can be taken off the farm without curtailing output, unless improvements in production methods to economize labor are simultaneously carried out. This was not possible in wartime Japan.[21]

4. Finally, the relative employment gains in Japanese manufacturing and the various service trades from 1920 to 1940 are of some interest. Industrial production grew more rapidly through this period than any other major component of economic activity in Japan. Its over-all increase approached 200% (Table 8). Yet the number of persons principally occupied in manufacturing and construction rose only 60%. Some 3 million workers were added to the industrial labor force, mainly after 1930. But the total working population of the country increased by more than twice this number. The balance were absorbed into commerce, transportation, and the professions, or were conscripted into the armed forces after the Manchurian incident in 1931.

In short, despite the growing manpower pool, technological advances in Japanese industry were so marked through this period that industrial employment lagged far behind production. Nor did the Army and Navy, or civilian emigration overseas, afford much relief from the pressure on the labor market until the late thirties. Even then colonial emigration took mainly civil servants, business and professional people; the net flow of civilian unskilled labor was inward from Korea, not outward. Agriculture having long been saturated, a large share of the new workers added each year to the labor force thus crowded into retail commerce, local transportation, and other urban services. These services naturally grew in importance with the development of the Japanese economy. And increasingly they emerged as specialized occupations where formerly they had been combined more largely with farming or craft industry. However, except in the more mechanized branches like railway transport, and the highly trained professions, productivity per worker remained very low throughout these trades. Here, as in

[21] *The Japanese Wartime Stanaard of Living and Utilization of Manpower*, cited, pp. 48ff.

agriculture, the pressure of population tended to perpetuate the primitive techniques and small-scale organization which had characterized these occupations traditionally.

In summary, the picture which emerges is one of marked transfer of employment away from agriculture, but with the rate of transfer, and the rise of productivity in both old and new occupations, held back by the relentless tide of population growth. A half century of industrial development had brought Japan to a midposition between the agrarianism of the traditional Far East and the advanced industrial specialization of a Britain or a Germany. At the close of the prewar era, upwards of half of her working population was still mainly engaged in agriculture, the absolute numbers little changed. The proportion was about that of Germany in 1890. But 25% now found their livelihood chiefly in industry. The balance, 25 to 30%, were employed in trade and transportation, together with a variety of private and governmental services.

Productivity and Employment. It is a commonplace that the industrialization of Asia involves much more than simply building factories and cities into which poverty-stricken peasants may escape from their overcrowded farms. In Japan employment opportunities were widened and diversified only as the outgrowth of a whole series of political, social, and economic changes. These made possible a slow rise in per capita production and incomes despite the parallel increase in the working population. The resulting rise in income and well-being could not have proceeded very far without industrialization, given Japan's deficiency in land and other natural resources. But the shift in employment away from the extractive industries, as suggested earlier, was a necessary condition of her development rather than its cause.[22]

In explanation of the direction and rate of this shift, emphasis was placed in Chapter 8 upon the redirection of demand for Japanese goods and services. As economic development proceeded, a rising proportion of Japanese incomes was spent upon consumer goods and services and capital equipment produced mainly in manufacturing, construction, and the service trades. The impact of this change in spending habits was reinforced in turn by the play of reciprocal demands in foreign trade. Here, too, Japan's changing import needs and her export opportunities in the world economy of this period turned her increasingly toward industrial specialization, as her manufacturing capabilities matured. Internal growth and external advantage thus combined to shift the balance of the Japanese

[22] This is not to deny, as remarked earlier, that industrialization and urbanization themselves greatly facilitate the introduction of new desires, new skills, and a new mobility in a traditionally static society, thus accelerating change at all levels.

economy away from primary production—a tendency accelerated by the pronounced bias of State policy in favor of industry in general and certain strategic industries in particular.

It remains to draw attention more explicitly to the fact that the actual distribution of Japan's labor force among various occupations reflected not merely the altered structure of demand but also the changes in the relative supply of various productive resources, their efficiency, and their cost.

This point has been discussed earlier in different context, but deserves reiteration here. For the demand for cotton goods or for coal is a demand for the joint services of several agents of production. These include a variety of natural resources, types and grades of machinery and equipment, labor and managerial skills. Physical and technical conditions usually set limits to the range of possible combinations, to be sure. Coal production requires mines. Steel billets can be produced in quantity only with large and expensive rolling mills. Medical services can hardly be provided without doctors. But most things can be created with fairly wide variations in the combination of particular types of labor and capital. To cite one familiar illustration, rice may be grown with intensive hand labor and close economy of land and mechanical equipment, as in Japan. Or it can be grown with extensive use of land and machinery, as in the United States.

Within certain physical limits the most efficient combinations— the technical coefficients—depend mainly upon the relative scarcity and prices of the factors of production. And the latter in turn reflect population, natural endowment, and all the social circumstances which determine the availability of capital in various forms and of labor in various grades, skills, and locations. Historically, therefore, the relative costs of the different productive factors in Japan have largely influenced the change in the employment of any particular agent which has resulted when consumer demand shifted increasingly from food to better housing and clothing, for example, or when foreign markets were widened for Japanese silk and cotton goods.

In preceding chapters, especially Chapter 4, a contrast has been drawn between the technical coefficients of production in Japan and in the wealthier nations of the West. The comparative scarcity of capital resources in Japan, both natural and man-made, has necessitated far greater reliance upon masses of unskilled and semi-skilled labor. Close economy has had to be practiced in the use of land, machinery, and the more advanced technical and managerial skills. This tendency appears in the hand cultivation of crops, in human transport, in "overstaffing" of factories and government offices, in the cheapness of unskilled personal services of all kinds. It has been sustained since 1868 by rapid population growth; also by such social institutions as the fragmented system of land tenure and a family structure which encourages the widespread employment of women and children. The early success of the Japanese textile industries in the face of long-established Western competition owed much to the abundance of low-wage labor of the requisite skills, which could be put to work with steadily improving equipment and techniques. Low wages also figured in the rise of other factory trades which were readily assimilated in this type of industrial environment.

More pertinent here than such international comparisons is the fact that within Japan itself there occurred broad historical shifts in the relative supply and price of various factors of production. This is reflected, for example, in the decline of interest rates relative to the earnings of labor. It is equally evident in the qualitative improvement which proceeded at varying rates in the different types of labor and capital techniques. The result of these differential changes was a corresponding change in the combination of industrial agents which it was economical to employ at any time in various productive uses. How many people came to be occupied in industry as compared with agriculture, for instance, depended upon the relative progress of mechanization in these fields no less than upon the shifts in home and foreign demand for their respective products.

All this is on a rather abstract level. Unfortunately, detailed verification throughout the Japanese economy is a thorny undertaking, full of pitfalls. Japanese statistics, as we have seen, hardly permit accurate comparisons of the productivity of labor and capital as between major industries. Nor are they adequate for measuring historical changes within many important sectors of production.

To suggest certain broad contrasts at a late stage in Japan's prewar development, there are placed side by side in Table 41 the distribution of the Japanese labor force, and that of net income produced, in the major divisions of the Japanese economy during 1930. Beside giving a more detailed breakdown of employment than was presented in Table 40, this also calls attention to the wide disparity in value of output per worker as among different fields.

In making any such comparisons between the number of workers and the net value of their output, one should bear in mind the nature and the limitations of the figures. Otherwise Table 41 can be seriously misinterpreted. The industrial categories of both tabulations are themselves closely comparable. The census classification of employment has been modified to bring it into conformity with the income classification used above. But the income calculation,

Table 41. *Labor Force and Income Produced in Japan Proper,*
by Industrial Divisions, 1930[a]

	LABOR FORCE BY CHIEF OCCUPATION		CONTRIBUTION TO NATIONAL INCOME
	Number (thousands)	*Percent*	*Percent*
Total	*29,620*	*100.0*	*100.0*
Agriculture (and forestry)	*14,131*	*47.7*	*16.7*
Fishing	*568*	*1.9*	*1.8*
Mining	*315*	*1.1*	*2.0*
Manufacturing[b]	*4,913*	*16.6*	*27.3*
Factory industry, private	1,983	6.7	17.6
Factory industry, government	153	0.5	1.1
Workshop industry (and other)	2,777	9.4	8.5
Construction	*963*	*3.2*	*4.6*
Transport and communications[c]	*1,159*	*3.9*	*6.8*
Railways	304	1.0	4.0
Electrical communications	215	0.7 ⎫	2.8
Other	640	2.2 ⎭	
Trade, wholesale and retail	*3,296*	*11.1*	*16.7*
Finance (and real estate)	*374*	*1.3*	*3.6*
Other private services	*2,676*	*9.0*	*9.4*
Professions	638	2.2	4.6
Catering, amusements, etc.	1,236	4.2	3.1
Domestic	802	2.7	1.9
Other government services[d]	*1,154*	*3.9*	*11.1*
Education	352	1.2	—
Armed forces	243	0.7	—
Other	558	1.9	—
Miscellaneous	*71*	*0.2*	—

a National income data from Table 38; labor force from Imperial Cabinet, Bureau of Statistics, *Shōwa Go-nen Kokusei Chōsa Saishu Hōkokusho*, Tokyo, 1938, pp. 348ff. As in Table 40, persons are classified according to their chief employment and in the industry to which they were attached. Part-time workers in any industry are excluded when their chief employment was elsewhere. Certain detailed industrial categories of the census have been shifted and recombined here to arrive at a classification roughly consistent with that used in the national income estimates of Table 38. Unemployed persons are classified where last employed. The census showed only 320,000 unemployed on October 1, 1930, but unofficial estimates run to 1,000,000 or more.

b The census total for manufacturing is subdivided here as follows: The number of private factory workers (i.e., in plants equipped to employ five or more operatives) is from Ministry of Commerce and Industry, *Kōjō Tōkeihyō* (1930), p. 12, with the addition of 40,000 entrepreneurs and 57,000 unemployed. (See U.S. Department of State, *National Income of Japan*, Washington, 1945, p. 128.) Government factory workers are tabulated from *Shōwa Go-nen Kokusei Chōsa Saishu Hōkokusho*, cited, pp. 349-51. Workshop industry is a residual which includes workers in 1,200,000 small establishments plus a small number engaged in salt manufacture, newspaper and magazine publishing, and the movie industry ("Other industry" in Table 38). As unemployment in factory industry is probably underestimated, it is likely that the factory totals are too low and the residual workshop figure too high. For further details, see above, pages 111-12.

c Census total plus 213,481 employed in government communications.

d The detailed census figures are used here to reclassify these service occupations, distinguishing for example between public and private education, medicine and public health. "Other government services" includes all national and local administration but omits employees of government-owned railways (232,499), bus lines (4,539), industry (153,348), and communications (213,481)—all of which appear elsewhere. The armed forces component is confined to officers and enlisted men. "Other" includes 33,492 persons in public revenue monopolies, some of whom belong more properly in government industry. The figures, however, do not permit a satisfactory breakdown.

as detailed earlier (Table 38), contains a measure of error as a valuation of the net earnings of labor and capital employed in each sector of the economy. And the labor force, to repeat, is distributed by principal occupation only, as reported by the census. Without corrections for wide variations in the amounts of part-time employment and unemployment no real estimate of output per head in various pursuits is possible.

Table 41 does tend, nevertheless, to support certain broad conclusions attested by more direct evidence. Net output per worker appears to be relatively high in factory industry when valued at prevailing market prices. Here 7% of Japan's labor force, as recorded by the census, produced 18% of the national income. It is also high in mining and railway transport, and in the skilled professions. It is low in workshop industry, in small-scale transport and domestic services, and most importantly in agriculture. These disparities remain even if a large allowance is made for more part-time employment (and unemployment) among the persons recorded in agriculture, small industries, retail trade, and other less capitalistic pursuits.

The main reasons for this disparity are obvious. Large factories, mines, and railways require a higher proportion of special skills and aptitudes which are scarce and difficult to acquire. They therefore command a higher rate of return. They also entail comparatively heavy outlays per worker on plant, equipment, patented processes, etc. Net product per worker reflected not only higher average wages and salary rates but also earnings on larger amounts of invested capital. Finally, these sectors of business enterprise, being less atomistic in structure, more difficult of entry, and more accessible to governmental favors, were apt to be pervaded by monopolistic influences which conferred higher rewards on entrepreneurship and investment.

Especially significant is the poor showing of agriculture. Net product in factory industry at market prices in 1930 was about 1,000 yen for each person chiefly occupied in this field. It was as high as 2,000 yen in chemical plants. In agriculture, however, net product *per farm operator* principally engaged in farming (and forestry) was less than 400 yen, if this computation of national income is at all close to the truth. Yet these 5 million farm operators together employed an additional 9.1 million persons reported as similarly engaged. The latter were part-time family workers to a large extent. Many probably contributed very little. But clearly, *per capita* output on a full-time basis would work out at even less than 400 yen in Japanese agriculture with these figures; especially as total agricultural product (1,706 million yen) includes the output of some 600,000 farm operators omitted from the above calculation because they reported farming as only a subsidiary occupation. Probably some product produced and consumed on the farm is omitted. On the other hand, no allowance is made for improvements in land and buildings or certain other minor costs properly deductible from gross output.[23]

Moreover, not all of this meager return could be kept by the farmer himself. The Cabinet Bureau of Statistics estimates the net output of these 5.6 million peasant families at 1,838 million yen in 1930, with no deduction of taxes, interest charges, or rent as an item of cost. (Public forestry is excluded here.) Table 38 (and 41) above deducts only 53% of the taxes paid by farmers as representing the contribution of the government to agricultural output. Actually, something like 700 million yen was paid over as rent, interest, and taxes to persons outside of agriculture, i.e., to absentee landlords, banks, and the government.[24] Only 64% of the earnings of agricultural labor and capital on this basis were retained by farm families. These figures may undertake the value of food and other necessities supplied directly on the farm.[25] But it is easy to see why

[23] Net product in industry is computed from Tables 38 and 41. The figures for employers principally occupied in agriculture and forestry (4,277,166) and for independents (729,324) are from *Kokusei Chōsa Saishū Hōkokusho* (1930), cited, p. 202. The Ministry of Agriculture and Forestry gives the total number of farm families as 5,599,670 in 1930, including those for whom farming was a subsidiary occupation. Imperial Cabinet, Bureau of Statistics, *Nippon Teikoku Tōkei Nenkan*, no. 51, Tokyo, 1932, p. 71.

[24] *National Income of Japan*, cited, pp. 161-71. Taxes accounted for 336 million yen; rent paid to absentee landlords is estimated to account for 173 million out of total rent payments of 463 million yen; and interest charges paid to persons outside of agriculture, 173 million out of 460 million yen of interest charges on agricultural debt.

[25] Yet they tend to be confirmed by other official farm surveys which purport to include all income in cash and kind. In the following year, 1931, a survey was made of 277 families whose farms (and probably incomes) were well above average size. Net family income from agriculture, after deducting rent and other expenses, was

the typical peasant family, and even more the millions of small tenant farmers, were under severe pressure to supplement their agricultural earnings with other industrial and commercial pursuits, carried on in the neighborhood or by sons and daughters who migrated to the city.

The year 1930 was a poor year for agriculture, it is true. Crops were generally good, but in the deflationary setting of the late twenties they drove farm prices down to ruinous levels. In 1930 the ratio of agricultural prices to those of industrial commodities bought by farmers was nearly 20% below its 1925 level.[26] As the above calculations of net product are market valuations, they reflect all the forces affecting the relative prices of goods and services. The agricultural depression of these years, followed by the industrial boom of the thirties, enabled industrial producers to claim an increasing share of the national income per unit of output.

Yet earlier, too, the average rates of return on capital, and on labor of comparable grades and skills, were probably lower in Japanese agriculture than in modern industry and transport. Net earnings on capital invested in agriculture tended to be depressed by a continuing premium on the ownership of land. (See pages 296-98.) And certainly common labor on the farm was poorly remunerated, being performed to a large extent by peasant families so situated that alternative employments were not readily available. Low productivity in monetary values is therefore partly a substandard rate of return to the agents of production in agriculture, by comparison with the more modern sectors of the economy. This circumstance, aggravated by the Great Depression, was at the root of the social discontents which the Army exploited in its anticapitalist, antidemocratic propaganda of the thirties.

The physical productivity of labor on Japanese farms also lagged markedly behind the advances scored in industry. A primitive level of technology was still evident on every hand, in the crowding of families on the land, the shortage of working capital, and the limited use of machinery and even of draft animals. (See above, pages 194-96.) Japan continued as late as the early thirties to employ as much as 40% of her *effective* (working) labor force in farming. Most of this labor went into the production of rice and

---

as follows: owner-operators, 478 yen; part-owners, 391 yen; tenants, 312 yen. Other sources of income added 163, 144, and 137 yen respectively in the three classes. Statistics Bureau, Prime Minister's Office, *Japan Statistical Year-Book, 1949*, Tokyo, 1941, pp. 224-25, 228-29. Details of a similar survey in 1935, when incomes had recovered somewhat from their depression lows, are given below, page 491.

26 Mitsubishi Economic Research Bureau, *Japanese Trade and Industry*, London, 1936, p. 170. For a further description of the plight of agriculture at this time, see above, page 63.

other high-calory cereals. Rice yields per acre were the highest in Asia. Yet even this concentration of labor power on agricultural foodstuffs yielded only a meager diet for Japan's 65 million people. Such improvements as were made in dietary standards after 1914 came about mainly through increasing imports from overseas, together with technological improvements in fishing.

On the other hand, earlier chapters have cautioned against the conclusion that physical productivity per agricultural worker did not in fact register significant advances in Japan after 1868. To repeat what has been said before, the physical volume of agricultural production probably rose at least 75% from 1895-99 to 1935-39, perhaps more. (Table 3.) Meanwhile the area under cultivation increased by only about 20%, and the number of farm families by perhaps no more than 10%, if that.[27] At the end of this period, in other words, the average peasant family operated a farm little larger than at the beginning. Yet it was able to produce at least 75% more food and raw materials, with no greater expenditure of labor, perhaps even less. Net product advanced more slowly owing to growing outlays for fertilizer and other deductible expenses.

Increasing agricultural yields were paralleled with more rapid gains in other extractive industries. Chapters 3 and 4 appraise the broad quantitative results, so far as the data permit. Even at a conservative estimate, food production probably doubled and raw material production more than tripled from 1895-99 to 1935-39. Meanwhile the country's population rose only 40%, from 42 to 71 million, and the labor force principally occupied in primary production appears not to have increased at all. The estimates quoted earlier suggest an actual decline from 17 to 15 million workers. Primary production, therefore, gained even more rapidly in relation to manpower in the extractive industries than in relation to the total population—especially before 1920. It provided a major share of the food, the industrial materials, and the markets which supported the entire increment in Japan's working population in nonagricultural employment.

The trend was in the right direction, in other words. If it failed to raise rural living standards more rapidly than it did, this was because of the headlong growth of population, the limit upon resources, and those other social and political obstacles which blocked a more thoroughgoing reconstruction of Japanese peasant life.

In manufacturing, technological progress was of course much more rapid. From such figures as are available it appears that output per manufacturing employee was increasing in the later decades

---

[27] This is a rough extrapolation of annual figures of farm population and cultivated area which actually go back only to 1903. See above, page 93, note.

at a rate which would double it every twenty to twenty-five years. The mechanization of industry is indicated in the rapid increase of horsepower per worker in factory industry—discussed in Chapters 3 and 4. Because mechanization advanced much more rapidly in manufacturing than in agriculture, the redirection of Japanese labor toward industrial pursuits proceeded more slowly than might be inferred from the increasing importance of industry as a source of national income.

The same contrasts are found, of course, among various individual industries making up the manufacturing total. Without entering upon historical comparisons, we may simply note the contrast at one point, again the year 1930, between the respective contributions of several major industries to net manufacturing product, on the one hand, and industrial employment, on the other. Here it is better to confine the comparison to private factories normally employing five or more operatives, rather than consider industry as a whole. This reduces the amount of part-time employment otherwise concealed in the employment figures. Table 42 gives employment in five principal industries in relation to net product during 1930.

Table 42. *Employment and Net Product in Selected Factory Industries of Japan Proper, 1930*[a]

| | NET PRODUCT | | EMPLOYMENT | |
	Amount (millions of yen)	Percent	Number of Workers (thousands)	Percent
All private factories, 1930	1,954	100.0	1,886	100.0
Textiles	407	20.8	964	51.3
Chemicals	357	18.4	70	3.7
Machinery, vehicles, etc.	330	16.9	205	10.9
Food products	282	14.4	164	8.7
Gas and electricity	131	6.7	11	0.6

a Net product figures are from Table 39, above; employment from Ministry of Commerce and Industry, *Kōjō Tōkeihyō* (1930), Tokyo, 1932, pp. 14-22. Employment figures are for the end of the year, and are therefore not strictly comparable with estimates of net product. Year-end employment was generally 5%, more or less, below the average for the year.

The differences in net product per worker extend from a little over 400 yen in textiles to more than 10,000 yen in gas and electricity. This is to be expected, of course. These industries vary widely in the amount of capital employed per worker, the relative skills of the wage earners and salaried workers engaged, and the level of profits. The shift from textiles to the metalworking and chemical industries in the prewar decade, like the shift from agriculture to industry generally, brought a less substantial gain in employment for Japanese workers than the production figures alone might suggest.

For the service trades, finally, it is difficult to draw any over-all conclusions as to the long-term trend of employment or productivity. Retail commerce of many varieties was so tied up with transport and workshop industry as a joint occupation that even the more recent census data are difficult to interpret. Moreover, the service occupations include everything from the highly skilled and well-paid professions like the law to the mass of small shopkeepers, street vendors, cart-pullers, and domestic servants whose net product on any calculation remained exceedingly low.

Those service occupations which continued to employ traditional, noncapitalistic techniques required increasing numbers of workers more or less in proportion as the demand for such services expanded. Indeed, Table 40 indicates that commerce, the professions, and the other services taken together absorbed nearly half of the entire increase in the civilian working population from 1920 to 1940—almost as many as industry. This testifies to the rising demand for these types of productive activity; also to the economic pressures which kept productivity and incomes at relatively low levels in many of these service trades. In these fields particularly is found a large amount of "disguised unemployment" among persons who are not actually out of work but lead a precarious poverty-stricken existence on the margins of the national economy.

In the case of transportation, however, one wonders whether "Petty's Law"—the movement of the working population from agriculture to industry and the services—applies at all. We do not know how much of the Japanese labor force was actually employed in moving goods and people from one place to another during the early Meiji period. According to Hijikata's figures, only 123,000 people, or 0.6% of the working population, were chiefly occupied in transportation in 1872. This grossly understates the actual importance of transport labor at this time, when goods were still carried largely on the backs of men. The next fifty years brought an enormous growth in the demand for freight and passenger haulage, as production expanded and became more specialized by regions, industries, and plants. So revolutionary was the shift from the bearer and cart to the railway and from the small sailing junk to the steamship, however, that the percentage of the labor force actually engaged in transport could easily have declined. The 1930 census shows only 943,000 people, or 3.2% of the working population, principally occupied in transportation, despite the tremendous increase in the mobility of goods and people.

Here is perhaps the most striking case of the replacement of human muscle with mechanical energy. With the aid of nothing more than a pole—and a strong constitution—a man can carry a 100-lb. load 20 miles a day. This gives a maximum of 320 metric-ton-miles a year. By comparison, the employees of the Japanese Imperial State Railways in 1930 handled traffic *per employee* amounting to 33,000 ton-miles of freight plus 61,000 passenger-miles.[28] Other forms of improved transport—carts, bicycles, and automotive vehicles—yield less spectacular contrasts. And, of course, one should not overlook the labor devoted to the construction and maintenance of the more costly forms of equipment, which extends all the way back to the coal mine and the blast furnace. Nevertheless, no aspect of economic life has surpassed large-scale transport in the degree to which the inventions of the past century have permitted a tremendous increase in productive activity with no corresponding requirement of human labor.

The shifting utilization of Japan's labor force, as industrialization proceeded, has thus reflected the uneven effects of technological advance in various sectors of economic life no less than the new patterns of demand for goods and services described in Chapter 8.

Mobility, Efficiency, Equality

Importance of Mobility. One final aspect of economic growth deserves emphasis. This is the importance of flexible adaptation of a country's labor force and capital resources to radical changes in demands and in technology. Without a high degree of mobility, new opportunities for economic gain are apt to be wasted. Also, gross inequalities arise in the distribution to different classes of the fruits of such progress as is achieved.

In the case of modern Japan, such changes were revolutionary in character. They required the training of masses of people in skills and work habits that had never existed before, and the investment of growing amounts of capital in totally new forms. As this was a continuing, dynamic process, it required the creation of a mechanism of adjustment which would work toward some sort of rough and moving equilibrium among various employments. It therefore meant the breakup of the old, static economic organization and rigid social structure of feudal Japan, and their replacement by a

[28] Traffic figures from Department of Finance, *Financial and Economic Annual of Japan*, no. 37, 1937, pp. 232-33; employment from *Kokusei Chōsa Saishū Hōkokusho* (1930), cited, p. 353.

new freedom of movement in response to the play of competitive forces.

Crucial to such changes was the creation of an enterprise system, which would give leadership and direction to this reorganization of the economy. Chapters 4 and 10 characterize the patterns which emerged in Japan, with their blend of State and private initiative, and of large- and small-scale organization. Here certain general comments may be offered on the more specific problem of mobility and friction in the redirection of productive resources. This problem was present in the case of capital as well as that of labor, but to a far lesser degree. It is the adaptation of labor supply to changing requirements which is apt to present special difficulties. Adam Smith remarks that "A man is of all sorts of luggage the most difficult to be transported."

Several kinds of mobility were involved in this process of diversification, specialization, and growth. One was greater geographical freedom of movement, e.g., the creation of a national market where people and goods could move about with increasing ease as a result of better transport and marketing facilities, wider knowledge, and the reduction of other political and social obstacles. Another was occupational mobility such that workers could seek new job opportunities and entrepreneurs could find the more productive uses for their capital and enterprise with a minimum of difficulty. This in turn necessitated a degree of social mobility which called for radical changes in the old feudal structure of classes and clans. As observed in Chapter 1, these new attitudes and tendencies were already discernible during the Tokugawa period, and even earlier. After the Meiji Restoration they received great impetus in the far-reaching reforms which destroyed the whole political and administrative basis of centralized feudalism. And increasingly they marked the advance of succeeding decades under the stimulus of the new incentives and the new technology which drove Japan forward along the path of economic development.

Testimony to this growing mobility has run all through preceding chapters of this study. It is reflected, for example, in the rapid and sustained increase in freight and passenger movement which marked every decade from 1880 to 1940. Even though over half of Japan's freight cargoes continued to move by water, her railways had grown to handle almost as much freight and passenger business in 1937 as the railways of all India, a continental area ten times her size and with five times her population. (Above, page 109.) Mobility appears, in a different form, in shifts in land use—to factory and urban sites, or to mulberries and tuber crops, and away from products like cotton and indigo which were replaced by imports.[29] It is evidenced likewise in the creation of financial institutions, security exchanges, and joint-stock companies, devices through which liquid capital was mobilized and made available for investment on a national basis. And most conspicuously, it is found in the extensive redistribution of Japan's working population, both geographically and occupationally.

On the other hand, there is also abundant evidence of continuing obstacles to a more efficient allocation of labor and capital among alternative uses. These included such circumstances as the unequal distribution of educational opportunity among the people, the cultural and technological lags of rural Japan, the technical and political factors which made certain industries the preserve of big financial cliques, the controls and subsidies applied by the State in the strategic realm, etc. The marked disparities which persisted in the earnings of labor in various employments testify to a highly imperfect utilization of the country's manpower to meet changing national needs and opportunities.

The over-all growth of population itself had restrictive effects on the transfer of labor. Though it swelled the absolute number of people annually seeking nonagricultural jobs, it actually retarded the *percentage* shift of the Japanese labor force out of the extractive industries. In its absence the rise in per capita purchasing power and the redirection of demand to new industries and service trades would presumably have gone further than it did. Greater supplies of domestic raw materials, and a larger share of the country's food supply, would also have been available. In less tangible ways the pressure of increasing numbers may have given a dynamic impulse to certain types of change, but on balance one doubts that it had this effect. (See pages 159ff.)

Population increase may be said to have eased the human costs of transfer in one respect. It brought onto the labor market every year large numbers of young, adaptable workers who could fill the requirements of the newer, urbanized trades without uprooting older people from their familiar tasks and surroundings. On the

[29] Many such shifts in land use brought a greater specialization of production by localities. Certain staple foods like rice, vegetables, and tea remained widely dispersed, but industrial crops and various food specialties tended to become more localized in response to production and marketing advantages. Shigeto Tsuru notes, for example, that as early as 1877-82 Osaka Prefecture was turning from indigo to sugar cane, Shizuoka from sugar cane to indigo, and Saitama from indigo to rice and tea. (*Development of Capitalism and Business Cycles in Japan*, unpublished MS, Harvard University, Widener Library, p. 166.) Within particular districts, moreover, better scientific knowledge led to more efficient allocation of land, particularly upland farms, to various uses. See Y. Yagi, "Horizontal and Vertical Differentiations in the Agricultural Production of Japan," *Kyoto University Economic Review*, vol. IX, no. 1, July 1934, pp. 33-60.

other hand, it actually went much further than this, and dammed up the peasant population of the farm so that there was little if any reduction of farm families even over several generations. Moreover, the population grew by natural increase most rapidly in the areas where economic opportunity grew least rapidly. Fertility was lowest in the metropolitan region of central Japan. It was higher generally through areas predominantly agricultural, and highest in the remote, mountainous prefectures of the Northeast.[30] This set up a differential rate of increase in rural regions which heightened the pressure for migration to the city, but preserved wide differences in income and productive efficiency.

Urbanization and Industrial Employment. The rise of great cities was the most striking outward feature of the population movement within Japan. Urbanization itself also extended social and occupational mobility still further by exposing vast numbers of people to the new ideas and new habits of living which went with city life.

Tokugawa Japan had known great cities, to be sure. The population of Edo (Tokyo) reached 1.4 million at the end of the eighteenth century, making it the largest city of the world. Such cities, however, were military and administrative centers to a large extent. They were the seats of the aristocracy and its army of retainers. Immense numbers of tradesmen and artisans were gathered together to cater to the wants of this class, as well as their own. They were said to comprise half the population of Edo. But the metropolitan community of this time rested essentially on the flow of feudal tribute from the peasantry to their rulers, and its concentration at key points. This community lived on rents and dues, like the European cities of the early Middle Ages. Of the rice imports of Osaka, a city of 400,000 people in 1780, some three quarters were sold on the market by *daimyō*, and only one quarter by farmers themselves.[31]

After 1868 the agglomeration of population which formed the modern cities of Japan was basically different. It represented much

---

[30] In 1930, for example, the gross reproduction rate was 1.57 in the city of Tokyo; 1.82 in all cities (incorporated municipalities generally with 30,000 people or more); 2.56 in noncity areas as a whole; and 3.05 in Aomori, the prefecture at the northern extremity of Honshu. Irene B. Taeuber and Frank W. Notestein, "The Changing Fertility of the Japanese," *Population Studies*, vol. I, no. 1, June 1947, pp. 17-23.

[31] Takao Tsuchiya, *An Economic History of Japan*, Tokyo, 1937, p. 196. Carl Bücher's remark concerning the movement of supplies to the residences of the feudal nobility in mediaeval Europe can be applied in considerable measure to Tokugawa Japan: "In all, however, there is lacking the characteristic feature of economic exchange, namely, the direct connection of each single service with its reciprocal service, and the freedom of action on the part of the individual units carrying on trade with one another." *Industrial Evolution*, tr. from 3rd German edn. by S. Morley Wickett, New York, 1912, p. 107.

more largely an economic growth based upon industrial specialization and exchange. It reflected the advantages arising from the concentration of industrial and commercial activity at locations which were strategic in relation to domestic and foreign markets and sources of raw materials, and the cumulative attraction of other industries and services in its wake. The city itself thus became a highly complex structure of specialized and interdependent activities, tied to the countryside in a two-way exchange of goods and services. It was this type of urban growth which J. H. Clapham had in mind when he described the growth of towns as "the best general test of industrialisation."

Urbanization was in full swing by the opening of the twentieth century. As with other aspects of Japanese demography, the statistics are rather unreliable before the first enumerative census of 1920. We know, however, that the new forces at work opened up swelling streams of migration within Japan. One agricultural area —the frontier of Hokkaido—received a large influx of new settlers. Its registered population grew from 348,000 in 1888 to 2,138,000 in 1918.[32] But the main drift was toward the cities. It appeared in the movement from villages to nearby towns and cities, in the movement from the more stagnant to the richer, industrializing prefectures, and especially in the great concentrations of the Tokyo-Yokohama and Osaka-Kobe-Kyoto regions. Most if not all of the increase in Japan's total population after 1900 is associated with the growth and increasing number of communities with more than 10,000 people.

After 1920 these movements continued, becoming susceptible now to better measurement. The "rural" population (in places of less than 10,000) remained stationary through the whole interwar period. It was 37.9 million in 1920 and only 37.5 million in 1935.[33] The entire increase in the country's population was thus concentrated in places of over 10,000. Existing towns and cities grew steadily in size, and their numbers multiplied through the incorporation of previously rural areas.

Again it was the influx of country people, as well as natural increase, which swelled the city populations. And, as in the United States during recent decades, it was the more prosperous countryside nearer the bustling cities of the industrial belt along the Inland Sea which furnished most of the migrants. Family contacts, knowledge of urban opportunities, and the costs of travel all made movement much easier here than from the poorer, less developed prefec-

[32] *Meiji Taishō Kokusei Sōran*, cited, p. 637; *Nippon Teikoku Tōkei Nenkan*, cited, no. 38, 1920, p. 27.

[33] *Nippon Teikoku Tōkei Nenkan*, cited, no. 58, p. 34.

tures to the northeast and southwest. Of every 100 people living in Japan in 1930, 63 still resided in the commune where they were born. But 21 had moved elsewhere in the same prefecture and 16 now resided in another prefecture.[34]

Even more phenomenal than the general drift to urbanization was the growth of big cities. In 1920 only 12% of the Japanese population lived in cities of over 100,000. By 1940 the proportion had risen to 30%.[35] At the peak of the city boom, from 1935 to 1940, virtually the entire increase in the country's population is found in these cities. Three quarters of it is confined to the Big Six— Tokyo, Osaka, Nagoya, Kyoto, Yokohama, and Kobe. Tokyo (population, 6,779,000) stood with London and New York as one of the largest cities of the world. Nearly 10% of the entire population of Japan now lived there, and another 10% in the other five.

The U.S. Strategic Bombing Survey estimates that, as World War II effected a still greater concentration of urban industry, the six cities named above furnished 50 to 75% of Japan's total production in five representative war industries.[36] Even before the war the industrial labor force was heavily concentrated in these urban centers and their satellite communities. The prefectures and metropolitan districts containing them accounted for 27% of the total Japanese population and labor force, but their share of the total number engaged in manufacturing was as high as 41%. Here also resided two thirds as many people engaged principally in transport, commerce, and the professions as in all forty-four of the remaining prefectures put together.[37] The cities of Tokyo and Osaka alone accounted for over 25% of all factory industry in 1938.

It should not be supposed, of course, that this historic surge from the country to the city was frictionless and fluid from the start, or that great masses of people moved eagerly to better wage opportunities in accordance with the classical canons of rational self-interest. On the whole, one is impressed with the speed and facility with which the Japanese accepted industrialism and urbanism, considering the highly localized and sedentary character of pre-Meiji peasant life. Seemingly there was less resistance and inertia here than in most other peasant economies beginning to industrialize. Even if this

[34] *Kokusei Chōsa Saishū Hōkokusho* (1930), cited, p. 73.

[35] *Japan Statistical Year-Book, 1949,* cited, pp. 42-43.

[36] Combat aircraft, electrical equipment, armament and vehicles, shipbuilding, and machinery and parts. This was one of several reasons why Japan proved so much more vulnerable to strategic bombing than Germany. In 1940 cities of over 800,000 accounted for only 12% of the German population, but for 23% of the Japanese. *The Effects of Air Attack on Japanese Urban Economy, Summary Report,* Washington, 1947, p. 1.

[37] *Kokusei Chōsa Saishū Hōkokusho* (1930), cited, pp. 10, 106-07, 120 of text.

be true, it was not without great difficulty and tremendous human costs that an industrial proletariat was created in Japan. People were pushed as well as pulled to the city. In the early phase it was perhaps the force of expulsion from the countryside as much as attraction to the city.

One sidelight was the difficulty of factory-owners in recruiting reliable and efficient labor. Peasant daughters, many of them under sixteen, furnished a large share of the early recruits. In 1896, for example, 261,000 out of 435,000 operatives in private plants employing ten or more workers were women.[38] Prisoners and vagrants were also extensively employed. The iron discipline, the poor working conditions, the false representations in hiring, the long hours—typically eleven, twelve, or more—all made for reluctance to enter factory industry even in this overpopulated country. The turnover of labor was constant, and labor piracy gave employers much difficulty. One investigator in the nineties concluded that half of the factory workers deserted every six months.[39] Labor costs were excessive, despite wage rates as low as 10 to 20 cents a day plus board and lodging.

To combat these difficulties, employers resorted extensively to contract recruiting, with various inducements which including not a little misrepresentation and some outright kidnapping. At its height there were as many as 50,000 persons engaged in recruitment.[40] Extensive use was also made of the dormitory system, by which workers—especially women—were housed and fed and largely confined to the factory premises. At its best this practice carried over the traditional paternalistic solicitude of the master for his employee; at its worst it was a system of virtual peonage. In all aspects of the industrial contract the scales were naturally weighted heavily on the side of the employer. His bargaining position was far stronger than that of the individual worker in terms of financial security, knowledge, and organization. And collective action by industrial workers was restrained from the beginning by harsh police repression of strikes, as well as by their general economic disabilities. Despite these circumstances—partly because of them—the scarcity

[38] *Nippon Keizai Tōkei Sōkan*, cited, p. 960. Forty years later, in 1936, 1,134,000 of Japan's 2,593,000 operatives in factories of five or more workers were still women, about one fifth of them under the age of sixteen and 73% in textile plants. *Kōjō Tōkeihyō*, cited, 1936, pp. 12-15. Factory employment of women is correlated fairly closely with the early predominance of the textile industries and their subsequent relative decline.

[39] Ernest Foxwell, "The Protection of Labour in Japan," *Economic Journal*, vol. xi, 1901, p. 110.

[40] S. Yoshisaka, "Labour Recruiting in Japan and its Control," *International Labour Review*, vol. xii, no. 4, October 1925, pp. 484-99.

of factory labor was a constant drag on Japan's early steps toward industrialization.

It is not surprising to find such conditions prevailing in Japanese industrial centers during the Meiji decades. In varying degrees they have been present wherever an agricultural population has first been exposed to the opportunities and hazards of modern industrialism. More surprising is their continuation well into the twentieth century after four decades of industrial experience. Yet one finds them perpetuated to a considerable degree in the Japan of the late twenties, and with only slow improvements through the thirties. Writing in 1930, John E. Orchard comments on the paradox that Japanese manufacturing industry still experienced so much difficulty in recruiting a satisfactory labor supply in a country with such an excess of population on the farm. Though textile spinners still spent 8 to 12% of what was paid out in direct wages upon recruitment, and though 40% or more of all factory workers were still housed in dormitories, he finds that ". . . the problem of securing labor is still acute. The recruited labor does not become permanently industrial. . . . It comes reluctantly, and the period of service is short. . . . Japanese labor not only has to be recruited to establish a mill but it must be recruited over and over, year after year, to keep the mill going."[41]

A government more solicitous for the welfare of its people would have taken steps long before Japan's did to abate many of the raw abuses of the sweatshop and the dormitory, of child labor and slum living, of long hours, widespread tuberculosis, and high accident rates.[42] In the interest of industrial efficiency alone, it was grossly neglectful to permit the continuation of conditions which made for a turnover of labor as high as 40 to 60% every year in factory industry as late as 1925.[43] Yet these evils flourished unchecked for decades in Osaka, Tokyo, and other developing industrial centers. Legislative proposals for improvement were stoutly opposed or emasculated in the interest of high profits. They were attacked under slogans praising the virtues of "liberty" and warning of the dangers

[41] *Japan's Economic Position*, New York, 1930, pp. 342-43.

[42] The excessive accident and sickness rates which so long characterized Japanese industry are well known. From 1920 to 1929, for example, an average of 846 miners were killed every year in the mines, and six times that number seriously maimed. In 1926 an official investigation was made of sickness cases among Japanese factory workers which required at least three days' treatment and absence from work. The rate in plants employing 500 or more workers was 284 per 1,000 workers. Respiratory and digestive diseases accounted for 22% and 23% of all cases, respectively. Tuberculosis claimed only 1.3%, but these were of course the more serious cases, as indicated by the fact that 88 out of each 1,000 cases were fatal. International Labour Office, *Industrial Labour in Japan*, Geneva, 1933, pp. 228, 243-47.

[43] Shuichi Harada, *Labor Conditions in Japan*, New York, 1928, p. 129.

of foreign competition. Characteristically, the Japanese were quick to jump to the latest cotton loom and steam turbine of the twentieth century. But when it came to social inventions to reduce the human costs of unregulated industrialism and slum cities, those in power chose to pass slowly through all the stages of indifference and neglect which characterized the Industrial Revolution earlier in the West. It was not until the late twenties—nearly half a century after the introduction of modern industry—that Japan began to acquire even the rudiments of State programs to safeguard factory labor and urban social welfare. (See Chapter 10.)

Thus, although cities grew apace, bringing radically new patterns of employment and living conditions, and although this was an essential condition of Japanese industrialization, the processes of movement and readjustment were achieved only at tremendous human costs. These gravely limited the economic efficiency of the new industrialism. They also created inequalities and injustices which placed a heavy strain on the social fabric of the nation.

Rural Diversification. If the transplanting of labor to the cities was one aspect of industrialization, another was the carrying into the countryside of improved techniques, business capital, and organization. In no small degree these were alternatives, and the industrialization of Japan reveals both tendencies at work. Despite the spectacular growth of cities—in part because of it—many an industry went to the small towns and villages in search of cheaper, more reliable labor, lower site rents, better procurement of materials, and other advantages. The movement of workers into new employments thus proceeded in rural Japan as well as in her growing industrial centers. The occupational shift went far beyond the relocation of people in cities.

One broad indication of this dispersion is found in the census distinction between "rural" communities and places officially designated at cities (incorporated areas generally with 30,000 or more people). Of 5.7 million persons chiefly occupied in manufacturing and construction in 1930, only 2.2 million resided in cities, thus defined. Nearly 3.5 million, or 61%, were in noncity areas. So, too, were more than half of the 4.5 million workers grouped under "commerce" and transport. For the noncity population, agriculture was by far the leading occupation, of course. It still afforded the chief employment for 60% of the gainfully occupied in rural areas. But industry, commerce, and transport together accounted for 28%, or nearly half as many.[44]

The occupational adjustment implied in these figures took place in a variety of ways. In part, it proceeded through the growth of

[44] *Kokusei Chōsa Saishū Hōkokusho* (1930), cited, p. 123.

new industrial and commercial activities to replace or supplement farming as the source of livelihood in the villages and small towns of Japan. More largely, it took the form of reorganizing and expanding nonagricultural pursuits long associated with peasant life. Many such pursuits were now developed on a more specialized basis with somewhat more capitalistic modes of production. Some persisted little changed in their traditional methods.

Whether the typical peasant family remaining on the farm actually devoted more or less of its time to gainful employment of a nonagricultural nature in 1935 than in 1885 is not easy to determine. Certain estimates given below would indicate that in 1935 such employment took about 20% of the working time of family adults. It is not to be assumed that this represented an increase from fifty years earlier, for such supplementary activities were widespread then, even if less commercialized. The tiny Japanese farm, and the fairly self-sufficient village, had long required a great variety of peasant pursuits. In a household economy undergoing gradual but only partial commercialization it is most difficult to apply definitions of gainful employment or income over a period of years with any consistency. Moreover, conditions varied widely throughout the country, so that generalizations are not too meaningful.

We know that various handicrafts and service occupations once combined with farming gave way in whole or in part to factory production, to commercial transport, and to specialized marketing arrangements. Sugar refining, the spinning of textile fibers, and paper making might be cited as examples. At the same time numerous other trades were reorganized or newly introduced on an extensive basis to take advantage of the idle labor of the peasant and his family, especially in the more accessible regions of rural Japan. These may have brought a net increase in the total amount of gainful activity carried on by the farm family where once there had been extensive underemployment through the slack seasons of the agricultural cycle. Certainly they increased cash income. The spread of commercial by-employments was also facilitated by improvements in agricultural techniques cutting down the amount of effort which the typical peasant family had formerly devoted to growing its own food supply. Thus the rise of rural industry, fostered on the one hand by severe population pressure on the farm, was yet assisted on the other by the modest secular increase in agricultural productivity. In the country as well as the city this helped to free labor for nonagricultural employment and provided the food to sustain it.

The most striking instance of a great industry built upon the foundations of rural labor was the raw silk industry. Here the expanding American silk market, linked to the Japanese countryside through the operations of large filatures, banks, and trading houses, came to provide a major source of supplementary income from cocoons for two out of every five peasant families in prewar Japan. Other local industries multiplied to serve the domestic market, either as household employments, neighborhood workshops, or factories dispersed through the countryside. Professor Uyeda distinguishes four kinds of occupational movements between agriculture and industry: (1) that of members of farm families who worked daily at home or in nearby plants (e.g., silkworm rearing, weaving) ; (2) that of others who took seasonal employment in adjacent towns (e.g., *sake* brewing, fish canning) ; (3) that of young people who migrated to the city for a few years of urban employment (e.g., girl spinning operatives) ; and (4) that of permanent migrants (most of the young men who left the farm).[45]

The attractive force of cheap peasant labor in the countryside was especially strong in the case of consumer goods industries which did not require large plants, complicated machinery, and access to pools of specialized skills such as were concentrated in the city. The electrical equipment industry, for example, remained heavily concentrated in the Kanto region around Tokyo, because of its special requirements for labor and materials. On the other hand, such a large-scale and mechanized industry as cotton spinning became rather widely dispersed. In 1930 less than half of Japan's cotton spindles were located in cities. Even in certain machinery and equipment industries, the manufacturing process was broken down into a series of stages, with much more extensive subcontracting of parts manufacture to small outlying shops than has been typical of similar industries in the West. Once established, such small plants were hard to eliminate from competition. Their costs were quite elastic, being composed so largely of the earnings of family workers who had nowhere else to turn for employment. For the large firm which they served, they secured the advantages of low-wage rural labor, plus a shifting of overhead and market risks to the small entrepreneur.[46]

---

[45] *The Growth of Population and Occupational Changes in Japan, 1920-1935*, Tokyo: Japanese Council, Institute of Pacific Relations, 1936, pp. 15-16. The term "urban peasants," as applied to Japan's city proletariat, is especially appropriate for the girl migrants enumerated above in class 3. Out of 150,000 operatives in Japanese cotton-spinning mills in 1930, 78% were women. Of the latter 67% were under twenty, most of them single girls housed in dormitories. One half had worked less than three years and three quarters less than five. Most of them returned eventually to the farm, having meanwhile used their slender savings to help out their families or accumulate a dowry.

[46] Even industries relying on imported raw materials do not necessarily find a

While labor conditions favored a dispersion of many industries widely through rural areas, the actual patterns of location in any instance were, of course, influenced by other factors. These included the accessibility of particular raw materials, special skills, markets, fuel, and power. The latter considerations tended in fact to concentrate the development of rural industries, if we exclude the mining and metallurgical industries of Kyushu and Hokkaido, in the more central plains regions of Japan near the main ports and population centers. By comparison, the more isolated interior and peripheral coastal regions tended to remain backward and undeveloped both industrially and agriculturally. Many such districts probably lost traditional by-employments as outside manufactures came in, without compensating gains. It is no accident that girl recruits for the spinning mills of Osaka and other textile centers came to be drawn mainly from the more mountainous and remote districts of Japan. In 1932, for example, 30% came from six prefectures in the southwestern island of Kyushu. Kagoshima alone, at the southern extremity, furnished 12%.[47] One recalls the recruitment of labor by the early English textile factories from the Irish tenant farms and the mountains of Scotland and Wales.

In such outlying districts peasant families found it especially difficult to supplement their meager farm livelihood with other local sources of cash income. It was here that population pressure was most severe. By way of illustration Uyeda cites the village of Ikazawa, located in the mountainous part of Niigata Prefecture, in north central Honshu. This village of 4,800 people in the early thirties was able to grow just about enough rice to feed itself. The cash income of its 773 families was confined to local earnings from the rearing of silkworms and from charcoal manufacture, together with remittances from 386 girls who had gone off to work for a period in cotton and silk mills. Cocoons yielded about 40,000 yen of net income to the village. Charcoal provided 20,000 yen, and the migrant daughters sent home another 20,000 yen. Ikazawa's cash income therefore amounted to little more than 100 yen per family,

---

port location most economical. Particularly those like textiles with low labor productivity and a large labor force may find it cheaper to locate in the food-producing countryside. For them the cost of transporting food to the cities, as an element in wages, may exceed the cost of moving raw materials from the port to the country. There remains, however, the advantage of locating a plant at the natural break in transport, i.e., the ship-rail terminal, together with other circumstances favoring urban concentrations of industry. No attempt is made here to study the location patterns of Japanese industry in all their ramifications, a large subject in itself.

[47] Teijiro Uyeda and Tokijiro Minoguchi, *Small-Scale Industries of Japan: The Cotton Industry*, Tokyo: Japanese Council, Institute of Pacific Relations, 1936, pp. 30-33.

a quarter of it from remittances and the remainder from two local craft industries.

A more general indication of the place of industrial and commercial by-employments in peasant life is difficult to give, even for a late prewar year, because of the unsatisfactory character of the statistics. We know that about half of Japan's 5½ million farm families had some such nonagricultural employment during the late thirties. For about one quarter of them it exceeded farming as a source of livelihood. Some light is thrown on its importance by sample surveys of farm accounts conducted annually by the Ministry of Agriculture and Forestry after 1931. The 1935 survey, for example, covering 288 families mostly operating 3- to 4-acre farms, shows the following utilization of labor:[48]

	Owner-Operators	Part-Owners	Tenants
Persons in family	*6.45*	*6.46*	*6.67*
Active persons over fourteen	3.67	3.79	3.74
Family working hours, in equivalent ten-hour man-days per year, excluding housekeeping duties	*735*	*759*	*756*
In agriculture	599	607	576
In by-employments	75	90	120
In other business	61	62	60

Agricultural labor on the family farm, including sericulture and stock breeding, evidently absorbed 80% of the working time of the active adults, men and women, outside housekeeping. Home industry, wage labor off the farm, and other pursuits occupied the balance. Labor hired from outside the family for agricultural operations averaged only 35 days (as reckoned above) for owner-operators, 32 days for part-owners, and 27 days for tenants.

The net income of these 288 families in cash and kind, after deducting rent, capital improvements, and operating expenses, was reported as follows for 1935 (in yen):[49]

	Owner-Operators	Part-Owners	Tenants
Net family income	*954*	*877*	*683*
From agriculture	765	702	503
From by-employments	134	131	143
From other sources (gifts, etc.)	54	44	37

[48] *Japan Statistical Year-Book, 1949*, cited, pp. 224-25. [49] *ibid.*, pp. 224-25, 228-29.

About 80% of net family income in cash and kind appears likewise to have been yielded by operation of the family farm itself. Whether this was typical of Japanese farming is uncertain. The farms surveyed average above the median size for the country as a whole. Much would depend in any event on their location and selection. Subsidiary occupations afforded rather less income than one would expect, especially as the figure for farm proprietors includes some income from property, and that for tenants some agricultural wages. The sample may not adequately represent the 20 to 25% of the country's farm families for whom agriculture was now actually a subsidiary occupation. About 15% or so of earned income, nevertheless, appears to have come from home industries, fishing, trade, transport, and other nonfarm employments in the neighborhood. Of the average family's net *cash* income they provided a much larger share—31% for owner-operators, 35% for part-owners, and 67% for tenant farmers.

Earlier, in Chapter 4, mention was made of the system of overhead controls by which myriads of tiny workshop enterprises, both rural and urban, were coordinated and linked with the market. Through merchant employers, banks, and large industries which they served, they were tied into the general structure of industry and trade in a bewildering variety of patterns. These connections and controls were the channels through which new techniques and capital were introduced; they gave small-scale industry much of its competitive strength. The wide distribution of electric power in Japan was likewise an asset. The basic factor, however, was low-wage labor.

Through a symbiosis of industry on agriculture, manpower in great amounts was recruited for industrial employment. It was grossly inefficient in most trades, of course, in the sense that per capita output was low. Equipment and working conditions were primitive. Hours ranged from twelve to fifteen or more a day; wages were commonly on a substandard family basis; and the small entrepreneur was often little more than the agent of the large firm which bought his product and perhaps supplied his materials and credit. Yet, if labor conditions were generally worse than in the factory, if the employer was at the mercy of the merchant capitalist, and children of their parents, there was nevertheless a degree of security as well as needed income in this diversified pattern of rural organization. Moreover, the discipline of work was far less exacting than in the large plant. The atmosphere remained freer and more informal, less disruptive of family life. And the entry and exit of small entrepreneurs was comparatively easy.

This whole amorphous mass of small-scale industries and trades, whether in villages, towns, or cities, thus served to bridge the gulf between the old and the new. Much publicity has attended the peasant girl entering the modern spinning mill with its automatic machinery, as the symbol of transition from farm to factory. Important as this was, it distracts attention from the more indirect and complex processes by which the transition in employment and skills was mainly effected. The small enterprise played a significant role in assimilating modern technology and accumulating industrial capital. With important exceptions like railways and metallurgy, the shift to more modern forms of industrial and commercial activity proceeded mainly through the medium of millions of these small establishments. Here the break with the past was less abrupt. Yet an essential link was provided with the organizational forms and work habits which were increasingly to dominate the future. It was this pattern of development which actually gave much of the real substance and momentum to Japan's economic growth.

Equally, it was the low level of incomes in this whole range of employments which exerted a heavy drag on factory wages in Japan. In a broad fashion, wage levels in modern Japanese industry have been geared to peasant incomes, reflecting the meager livelihood they too afforded. Thus the small wages for which peasant women were induced to work in cotton-spinning mills reflected the economic circumstances of the farm families from which they were drawn. K. Takahashi once calculated that the earnings of two of these girls tended to equal the income of a peasant family of three adult persons. But more generally the link with agricultural earning power ran through the miscellaneous small-scale trades, skilled and unskilled, which provided the chief employment opportunities for persons leaving the farm. Some male factory employees laid off in hard times might return to the countryside. Many more probably sought to eke out a livelihood in the small workshops, retail stores, and other service occupations which crowd the streets of every Japanese town and city. When factory employment failed to grow, as in the decade 1920-30, it is significant that most of the increase in the working population appears to have been soaked up in these small industries and services.

In this study no measurement is attempted of the historical trend of differing wage rates in Japan. Nor is it attempted to compare earnings in different occupations, or planes of living in different sections of the country. Such comparisons would greatly assist in judging the smoothness and effectiveness of adjustments to changing employment opportunities, and the obstacles that stood in the way. They are rendered very difficult, however, by the complexity of Japanese wage scales, the lack of reliable man-hour statistics, regional variations in the cost of living, the large amount of family and part-time labor, and the impossibility of separating the return on labor from the return on capital in agriculture and other sectors of the economy.

It is clear, in any case, that real wage rates in modern industry bore little relation to the marked advances in the productivity of factory labor over the years. (See pages 121-23, 143-45.) Instead, they were determined, with allowance for the premium on skills, by general conditions in Japan's perpetually crowded labor market. Here the growth of population applied relentless pressure. Technological improvements made Japanese labor steadily more efficient; but a large share of the gains accrued to others—partly to the industrial capitalist, but more largely to the domestic and foreign consumer. Industrial wage rates remained tied to the general level of wages in comparable urban employments, and ultimately to the plane of living of the peasant.

Questions for Further Study. Planners and administrators of economic development in other countries of Asia today might learn something from pondering Japan's whole experience in the difficult task of adapting a peasant people to the requirements of industrialization. No aspect of the problem is more important than this one of flexibility and mobility in redistributing a growing supply of productive agents in accordance with changing needs and opportunities.

Japan's physical environment, as it happened, dictated a pattern of development predominantly industrial. This called for an exceptional degree of geographic, occupational, and social mobility. Both her successes in certain respects and her failures in others deserve further study. Particularly one might look for lessons as to the mechanisms which tend to increase economic efficiency by smoothing and ordering such a transition, and the safeguards which will reduce its human costs. The discussion in the foregoing pages only points to certain more obvious features. A really thorough inquiry would require the combined talents of the sociologist, the engineer, and the geographer, no less than those of the economist and political scientist. It would be well worth doing.

Such a study would doubtless conclude that the geographic factor looms large in any comparison of Japan with great continental nations like China or India. Whatever limitations have been imposed on the Japanese by the fact that they were a small island nation, strategically located but with limited natural resources, this circumstance has accelerated the dynamics of modernization. The resulting emphasis on foreign trade and industrialization has intensified the structural changes required. But it has also facilitated them, by exposing people more readily to the new influences from abroad. Moreover, the approach to a national market for goods, labor, and capital has been greatly simplified by short land distances and good internal communications by sea. New techniques and employment opportunities have spread more quickly because most of the population lived in or not far from those regions of central Japan which developed great industrial and commercial centers.

Backward pockets of population have persisted down to the present day, of course. Especially are they found in the more remote prefectures to the north and southwest. Indeed, most of the farm population has remained at a continuing disadvantage in important respects. The attraction of people to the great areas of urban economic growth, and the expansive influences radiating from them, have been insufficient to equalize income and economic opportunity, even among comparable occupation groups throughout the country. Just how far this is true, and for what reasons, are complex questions requiring a good deal more investigation. It is apparent, in any case, that physical conditions alone have made the problem of such regional and occupational adjustments much easier than in the great hinterland of a country like China. To afford 500,000 Chinese villages a comparable degree of access to the outside world, merely in terms of physical communication, would require a prodigious effort many times that necessitated in Japan. By the same token, there has been less justification in Japan for the long persistence of the technological lags, the income inequalities, and the waste of both human and material resources symbolized in the gulf separating the small tenant farmer, for example, from the great *zaibatsu* enterprise.

Reflections of this sort take one quickly into the realm of social inheritance. Unfortunately, little effort has yet been made to apply the techniques of modern social science to a study of the interaction of social structure and motivation in Japan with the process of industrialization. Particularly intriguing is the speed with which the Japanese came to display a rather widespread spirit of innovation and enterprise in economic life, despite their inherited tradition of hierarchy, status, and conformity. Certain observations on this problem are offered in the next chapter, on "The State and Economic Enterprise." Given a spirit among the nation's political and social leaders that was technologically progressive on the whole, it may be that the Japanese propensity for teamwork and deference to leadership served to give order and direction to economic development, while at the same time it spread change rather than stifled it. These things are never simple, however, and such formulations only push the question a stage further.

One or two additional points are worth making here as regards the mobility and adaptability of the labor force. Modern Japan, first of all, has been relatively free of religious and caste barriers, by comparison with many other countries of Asia and the Near East. In India and the Arab world, for instance, such barriers have tenaciously obstructed the diffusion of knowledge, the migration of people into new regions and occupations, and the spread of new production techniques. In Japan, following on the changes already in progress during Tokugawa times, the political and legal restrictions of feudalism were thoroughly demolished after 1868. The Restoration leaders moved quickly to adapt law and politics to the requirements and opportunities of modern technology.

Since then the principal formal distinctions of class have been only two. One hereditary class, at the top of the social ladder, has been the Imperial Family and the new nobility created after the Restoration to preserve titular prestige. The other, at the bottom, is the *eta*, an outcast group of 1 to 3 million people probably descended from an ancient occupational caste once associated with animal slaughter. Other inherited class distinctions, of a more subtle character, have been much more widespread, especially in the village. Yet they are accompanied, as one student remarks, by "easy social relations in many important matters." Nothing has remained in Japan remotely comparable to the caste system of India, with its rituals and regulations which have served widely to stultify technical advance, dissipate savings, and stratify masses of people in a rigid pattern of occupations. The early Japanese leadership came largely from *samurai* ranks; but social mobility steadily increased as new talent arose from the middle class to take commanding positions in business, government, and the professions. Industrialization has tended to break down caste, here as elsewhere in the world, and has acquired fresh momentum in the process.

The Japanese family system, on the other hand, has continued to exercise a decisive influence in many ways. As a bulwark of the authoritarian principle, it has had much to do with the failure to develop a more liberal type of capitalism, i.e., with the persistence of oligarchic controls over wide areas of economic and political life. But the code of family obligation did not seriously deter entry into urban, industrial employment, despite the social tensions set up by the individualistic, competitive atmosphere of the latter. In some respects it even facilitated the process, for it preserved ties between the city migrant and the village which gave a degree of economic security to both, as well as providing a channel for diffusing new knowledge and attitudes through the countryside. Nor did the family spirit, strong as it was, prevent the successful creation of

larger institutional structures like the business corporation and the
Army, able to command loyal and efficient service. Traditionally it
had long been overlaid with a higher loyalty to the territorial feudal
overlord and the emperor. Otherwise, as in China, it might have
proved a greater obstacle to building a new framework of social
cooperation required for the successful application of capital and
labor in new industrial employments. Evidently the Japanese family
principle as it came down from the past has tended even to impart
cohesion and strength to other forms of corporate life in modern
times.

While social status has continued to rest significantly upon birth
and inherited position, increasingly the major barriers to vertical
and horizontal mobility have become essentially economic in character. These barriers to equality of opportunity have been associated with the inequality of wealth and income which has characterized modern capitalism almost everywhere, and certainly not least
in Japan. Once created, they tended to perpetuate themselves, block-
ing the road to greater freedom of movement in the new class structure which emerged. They have been reinforced by steady population growth, which has pumped in vast numbers of people at the
bottom of the pyramid, and by Japanese deference to authority,
which helped to entrench a privileged elite at the top. They have
served to maintain all the skills at a premium, so that gross disparities persist in the earnings and supply of various types of labor.
As in all densely populated, newly developing countries, there
has been a heavy oversupply of unskilled labor, which has been
economically wasteful and socially productive of hardship and unrest. The chief force working in a contrary direction has been the
slow diffusion of knowledge. Here the system of universal primary
education, begun early in the Meiji period, has served to spread
economic opportunity and to upgrade the general level of productive efficiency, so far as it has gone. But it has been all too inadequate.[50]

[50] Colin Clark (*op.cit.*, p. 460) gives figures to show that certain industrial skills
in Japan commanded a higher premium over the average wage level in the late
twenties than in more advanced countries like Switzerland and Belgium. This is
plausible, in that it is a general characteristic of newly industrializing countries.
Whether the historical trend in prewar Japan was toward greater uniformity or
disparity among wages rates is more conjectural. I have examined certain published wage data covering the period 1885 to 1935 to see whether wage rates for
various skilled occupations as a group rise or fall relative to the wages of common
labor. No very marked change occurs in either direction, though individual rates
vary markedly. In general the wages of skilled labor rise somewhat more rapidly,
suggesting that the premium on skills tended to increase under the pressure of
population. But the data are inadequate to support any firm conclusion, especially
as they are confined largely to the traditional skills (carpenters, stone masons,
mat-makers, etc.).

This brings one to the whole realm of State policy and action, obviously of pervasive importance in these matters. Already it must be clear that decisive contributions were made through the mechanisms of government to the creation of new economic opportunities, and the adaptation of the nation's resources to meet them. Especially noteworthy were the initial clearing away of feudal restrictions upon freedom of ownership, occupation, and residence after 1868; the construction of a new, national framework of economic enterprise; and the industrial bias of fiscal and financial policy. For the problems discussed in this chapter, the early inauguration of a system of public education was particularly important, as remarked above. Though the record here is not unimpressive, one wonders how much more economic progress might have been achieved had far greater efforts been made in this field. Equally evident are other deficiencies of State action, e.g., failure to curb the excessive human costs of city slums, to protect the industrial workers, and to make credit available more cheaply to the small peasant, industrialist, and tradesman. These questions, however, are better left to more extended discussion in a concluding chapter.

CHAPTER 10

THE STATE AND ECONOMIC ENTERPRISE

The Framework of Industrialization

THE history of Asia's attempts to industrialize teaches at least one hard-won lesson. No nation can simply import the Industrial Revolution from abroad, uncrate it like a piece of machinery, and set it in motion. Some of the skills, the equipment, and the money may come from the outside. External pressure may impose the necessity to remake traditional economies; foreign example may stimulate the ambition to raise productive power and economic well-being. But the real motive power of change must come from leadership and creative enterprise emerging from within. In former Secretary Acheson's phrase, the outside world can only supply "the missing component."

The truth is that the great bottleneck in economic development is usually not a dearth of capital resources, or even of skills. This may be serious at the outset. If it persists as a major obstacle, however, it is apt to be because of resistances encountered in constructing a social framework which will provide incentives and opportunity for human enterprise in new forms, thereby releasing the productive capabilities latent in most peoples of the world.

In the traditional East, as formerly in the West, the Industrial Revolution requires a revolution in social and political arrangements no less than in production technology. Steam and steel, joint-stock finance, and laboratory science can transform the economic life of any "backward" area. Yet they are only tools at best. Their successful application necessitates a whole pattern of pervasive, interlocking changes in traditional societies. They can only be put to work within a new social setting which entails a radical break with the past, led by elements in the society who will reject the sanctity of old ways and understand the social prerequisites of the new technology. The dream of K'ang Yu-wei, the Cantonese reformer of fifty years ago—"Chinese studies as the fundamental structure; Western studies for practical use"—has long since been dashed upon the rocks of reality.

The Problem of Enterprise. Perhaps the most critical problem for any people seeking to unlock the secrets of modern technology and apply them on a massive scale is how to organize the function of initiative and responsibility. In other words, how should the entrepreneurial function be allocated and directed so as to realize the maximum potentialities of growth?

Nations with high output levels may choose deliberately to cripple the exercise of this function for such purposes in order to realize other social goals—equality or security, for example. But peoples at the subsistence line can hardly do so without endangering advance in almost all sectors of national life. A greater production of goods and services is the condition of better public health, of literacy, of national security, of more stable and democratic governments. From economic histories of the West one sometimes gets the impression that the technical processes of division of labor, saving and investing, or creating new skills were impersonal forces which advanced under their own momentum and toward some predestined goal. Nothing could be further from the truth. Their dynamic impulse came from the energies and ambitions of the people and their leaders; they required myriads of human decisions; and they developed within a framework of social values and institutional controls which fostered them in certain respects while retarding them in others.

Of all the issues wrapped up in this problem of entrepreneurial responsibility, none is more basic than the role to be played by the state. For the state is the social grouping armed with a legal monopoly of coercive power. Or in Asia it is in the process of achieving that position. Its role can therefore be decisive. But it can be decisive in either a positive or a negative sense—by the things it does, or the things it refrains from doing. It may be a support to economic progress; it may be a drag.

In either case, the prospect of lifting the masses of Asia from the traditional poverty line, or of building economic power for other purposes, is apt to depend in very great measure on the role of government. What is to be the allocation of power and responsibility in the state? And what patterns of cooperation or conflict will it develop with other social groupings and individuals in the crucial tasks of innovation?

Watching the experiments now in process in Asia, one is impressed with a certain dilemma. In one form or another it appears in every country.

On the one hand, the option of free enterprise and private ownership, which has largely prevailed in the West, fails to provide in Asia an acceptable pattern of organization for rapid economic growth. The circumstances of the West which made it a great engine of material advance over 200 years are largely absent in the East. Moreover, most of these peoples are in a hurry. They are looking for short cuts. And as the price of material progress, they seem quite prepared to forgo certain political liberties which they have never known anyway in a meaningful sense.

On the other hand, the problem is hardly solved by turning over the whole task of economic development to the state. For if the traditions of private enterprise among Far Eastern peoples offer only a weak foundation for industrial and technical advance, so too with the traditions of Oriental bureaucracy. The truth is that many of the social and technological obstacles to modernization remain equally under public as well as private enterprise, with perhaps one or two added. They cannot be dispelled merely by doctrinal incantations, or by simply putting a man in the uniform of the state.

For all of these countries, each in its own way, this issue of the proper sphere of government in economic life is still being worked out in the hard course of experience. Economic progress is apt to be slow in the absence of dynamic leadership from the state. But equally one may not look uncritically to government as the all-powerful agency capable of effecting easy solutions on a massive scale. Any such approach merely glosses over the realities of government as practiced throughout most of Asia, as well as the true complexity of the problem. That problem is for each nation in its own context to determine the strategic responsibilities which the state can best handle, and to contrive that they be handled in such a way as to give real substance to the growth process through opportunities and incentives offered to increasing numbers of people in economic life.

The Case of Japan. Concerning this general issue, much can be learned from a study of Japan's experience during the first fifty years or so of her modernization.

For a century ago the Japanese were an Oriental nation of 30 million people also only on the threshold of modernization. In the main Japan exhibited the familiar features of Far Eastern agrarian economies: grinding poverty, intense pressure on the land, a tradition-bound technology, and a peasant population whose potential for growth was held in check only by widespread malnutrition, disease, and infanticide. Other factors hardly seemed more promising. Japan's endowment in industrial resources was meager. Her political tradition was feudal. And she had been artificially isolated from the commercial and industrial revolutions of the West by 250 years of enforced seclusion.

Yet the seventy-five years following the Restoration witnessed a growth of productive powers in Japan hardly surpassed in the annals of the West. From rigorous seclusion Japan emerged to become one of the chief industrial and trading countries of the

world. Her population multiplied rapidly, while yet supporting itself at a slowly rising level of well-being. Her industrial potential
remained well below that of the other Great Powers. When mobilized for war in 1941, however, it proved so formidable that the
United States, distracted as she was by the conflict with Hitler, required nearly four years and a prodigious military outlay to bring
Japan to her knees.

By any standard this was a remarkable technical performance.
It is curious, therefore, that more attention has not been paid to
the Japanese case in all the recent analysis and planning of economic development among her neighbors. For this there may be two
reasons. First, the literature on modern Japan has tended to stress
the militaristic and exploitative aspects of Japanese industrialism.
This has discouraged study of its more constructive features. Second,
Japan is often regarded as *sui generis,* so different in social heritage
and environment from other Far Eastern countries as to make difficult any transfer of lessons.

There is substance in both these points. But they can be exaggerated. Japan was dramatically successful in tackling the basic
factor in Asiatic poverty: low productivity per worker. Many of
the problems she surmounted in doing so are typical of those faced
by every people when they embark on the process. Some of the mis-
takes she made threaten to be repeated elsewhere. With all its
peculiarities, the experience of Japan in most respects is more relevant to the problem of industrializing other regions of East Asia
than that of any Western country.

In proceeding here to examine the role of the State in Japanese
economic development, it may be well to make three limiting definitions of the topic.

First, this discussion is confined mainly to actions and attitudes
expressed through the formal machinery of government. Only in
conclusion does it touch on the broader issue as to who controlled
the State, or the degree to which the political framework was part
of a larger social mechanism by which the dominant groups in
Japan imposed their will on the nation.

Second, it is concerned almost entirely with the policies of the
national regime, with the recognition that this fails at best to take
due account of elements of paternalism and control exercised informally but pervasively by local authorities in the towns and countryside.

Third, it concerns especially the influence of State policies on the
growth of real national income per capita in Japan, rather than
other values and consequences involved in industrialization, or other
objects of national policy, however important.

Japan offers a fascinating case for the testing of various hypotheses concerning the dynamics of economic growth.[1] In modern times she has been a frontier of cultural conflict and synthesis. Because she stood only on the rim of one great culture, the Chinese, she could more easily shake herself free from the accumulated rigidities of that culture, and borrow innovations in technique and organization from another which was now rising to world dominance. She owes much to the innovations of what Arnold Toynbee calls the "creative minority." Her development is equally a response to the challenge of physical environment—limited land resources but ready access to the sea. She has been powerfully influenced by wars, price movements, and other cultural and material factors.

Some of these circumstances are remarked upon here and there in this chapter, particularly in the concluding section on the "Momentum of Economic Growth." But the more one ponders the difference between the past century in Japan, on the one hand, and that in other Far Eastern countries like China or Thailand, on the other, the more elusive the question becomes. One becomes aware, too, of the danger that his judgments on issues like those discussed in the following pages will be colored by his own preconceptions and biases. A remark of Lionel Robbins' is apt in this connection:[2] "The causes of material progress, equally with the causes of intellectual progress, interact in so complex a manner that scientific generalizations about them are a matter of utmost difficulty. We neither possess the knowledge nor the capacity to elaborate laws of progress. We can only enumerate the causes hitherto observed and pass on to particular studies. It is no reproach to economists that they have been content to leave the devising of sweeping generalizations to poets, metaphysicians and amateur historians."

State Pioneering of Industry. The leaders of Meiji Japan, once authority was concentrated around the throne, proceeded with great energy and skill to lay the foundations for industrial development. A coalition of bureaucratic and mercantile interests, with the former in the ascendancy, they were urgently concerned to strengthen the new regime against pressing dangers, both external and internal. The bombardments of Shimonoseki and Kagoshima by American and British warships in 1862-63 had been a grim reminder of Japan's weakness in facing the West. The opposition of dissident clan leaders after 1868, as well as latent peasant unrest, argued no less cogently for a strong Army as a counterrevolutionary force

[1] See Joseph J. Spengler's interesting review of these hypotheses, "Theories of Socio-Economic Growth," in Universities–National Bureau Committee for Economic Research, *Problems in the Study of Economic Growth*, New York: National Bureau of Economic Research, 1949.

[2] "The Dynamics of Capitalism," *Economica*, vol. VI, no. 16, March 1926, p. 32.

at home. "Like Nehemiah," says Herbert Norman, "they had to build with sword in one hand and trowel in the other."[3]

These Meiji bureaucrats were strongly mercantilistic in philosophy. They sought to expand national power as the end of State policy, while keeping a firm grip themselves on the levers of control. Not without reason has Toshimichi Okubo, leader in industrial expansion, been called "the Colbert of Japan." Yet just as the Mercantilists of seventeenth century Europe drew on the precepts of economic policy fashioned earlier in towns and smaller territorial states, so Japan's post-Restoration statesmen applied on a national scale many of the practices developed earlier, in Tokugawa days, by the more progressive clans. Military strength and prestige remained, of course, in the forefront of their objectives. It was here they sought most eagerly the secrets of the West. Accordingly, they and their successors did not hesitate to sacrifice economic interests in the cause of State building. The "center of gravity," in Schmoller's phrase, now became the nation-state, occupied with consolidating its forces at home and preparing to enter the arena of competitive struggle abroad.

In the main, however, like their European counterparts, they seem to have regarded the pursuit of wealth and the pursuit of power as coordinate objectives, each reinforcing the other. *"Fukoku kyōhei"* was their slogan—"a rich country, a strong army." No doubt they often failed to realize points of contradiction between the two. Especially in later decades a clear choice had to be faced. For the logic of industrial development, sustained by world-wide trade, ran increasingly counter to the military ideal of a self-contained Empire. But at the outset, in any event, there was a good deal of sense in the general proposition. Industrialization would provide the sinews of military defense and centralized political control. Conversely, a powerful State could nurture economic development at home. And in foreign relations it would assure political independence and perhaps win other gains in the form of colonies, overseas markets, and investment opportunities.

This reasoning served to make industrialization a major concern of State policy in the Meiji "Renovation." Equally, it gave a pronounced bias in favor of power as distinguished from welfare objectives, wherever a conflict arose between the two.

Fortunately for the nation, nevertheless, the Meiji leaders conceived of their economic problem in broad terms. With remarkable perception, they seem to have realized from the beginning that industrialization is more than a matter of importing machinery and technical skills to be grafted into a society otherwise basically un-

[3] *Japan's Emergence as a Modern State*, New York, 1940, p. 102.

changed. To be sure, it was to be a revolution from the top, preserving the existing power structure in its essentials. It revealed little solicitude for the small peasant or the young factory hand. It was frankly antidemocratic in philosophy, reviving the reactionary symbols of the throne to tighten the grip of the new oligarchy at the center. Nevertheless, it set in motion a progressive transformation in Japanese society.

Its architects proceeded at once to demolish the archaic structure of the Tokugawa state. In its place they set about erecting a modern framework of law, political administration, and national defense. They saw that a revolution in transport, communications, and finance was required no less for economic development than for military power. And in general, unlike the contemporary rulers of Manchu China, they led in the movement to replace the classical learning with Western science and industrial arts. Most surprisingly, perhaps, they began very early to lay the foundations for a system of universal education, taking care to ensure that it would preserve and even strengthen the ancient core of authoritarian ideals symbolized in the emperor.

Japan thus embarked on the path of economic modernization with a centralized government which within a decade was seated firmly and aggressively in the saddle. Several other broad characteristics of this regime may be recalled.

First, the country succeeded in preserving its sovereign independence in the face of Western pressure. It had to accept the restriction of its import tariff to nominal rates, as well as the humiliation of extraterritoriality, until the unequal treaties of 1858 were terminated in 1899. For some years, too, the government was too weak to feel entirely secure at home, much less to make its writ run abroad. In contrast to most of Asia at this juncture, however, Japan was ruled by Japanese, with little qualification. Its ports, its industries, its currency were Japanese-controlled. The State discouraged foreign business enterprise within the country, and made little effort even to borrow abroad until after the victorious war with China. One cardinal circumstance, then, was that economic policy from the beginning was largely free of outside interference. It was nationalist in spirit and control.

Second, the Meiji oligarchy soon outwitted and dispersed all latent elements of serious opposition within Japan. It quickly mustered sufficient force to quell incipient peasant revolt, on the one hand, and *samurai* rebellion, on the other. If it warded off anything like the regime of foreign settlements and concessions in China, it also experienced nothing resembling the warlord period. As a unitary regime in a relatively small area with easy internal communications, it was likewise spared many of the problems inherent in countries larger in scale and less authoritarian in tradition.

Almost at once liberal parties arose to attack its policies and clamor for a share in government. These, too, it kept largely within bounds by police action and bribery, and by occasional concessions like the Constitution of 1889. Through the Meiji era the government remained an authoritarian, bureaucratic regime, presiding over a nation displaying marked cohesion and discipline, and with a Parliament (after 1890) capable of little more than obstructionist tactics. Within the limits of its resources, therefore, it was comparatively free to drive forward toward the goals of national development as conceived by its leaders. Behind-the-scenes struggles among elements of the ruling coalition were constantly in evidence, and sometimes overt clashes. But they were accommodated without radical changes in the structure of power, immediately by a judicious sharing of the spoils of office, and ultimately by invoking when necessary the prestige of the throne to silence dissident groups. Only after World War I were the State's targets blurred, and its energies distracted, by the appearance of new political forces and problems created by industrialism.

Third, the general dedication of economic policies to the building of national power has already been noted. As rapidly as the instruments of political action could be forged through the training and organization of a new bureaucracy they seem to have been directed fairly consistently to such ends. At the same time the regime never seems to have acquired delusions of its own omniscience or omnipotence in the economic realm. There was often confusion and hasty improvisation in deciding upon the actual course of action in pursuit of the general goal. The experiments with State pioneering of industry, with banking institutions, with railway financing, and with other ventures all show much trial and error through the nineteenth century. Probably this reflected a good deal of pulling and hauling within the government and its supporting groups. The *samurai*-bureaucrat and the merchant inherited authoritarian traditions of clan mercantilism and guild responsibility. On the other hand, they were visibly impressed by the liberal principles current in the West, or at any rate by the power and efficiency that accompanied them. They were eager to demonstrate Japan's modernity. In military affairs, law and administration, finance, and education the Japanese borrowed widely, and at first inconsistently. Rather quickly, however, they rejected the uncongenial and adapted the rest to their own circumstances and propensities.

Initially, it will be recalled, the State itself spearheaded the industrialization process by pioneering and financing new undertakings over a broad front. In the decade after 1868 it built and operated railways and telegraph lines. It opened new coal mines and agricultural experiment stations. It established iron foundries, shipyards, and machine shops. It imported foreign equipment and experts to mechanize silk reeling and cotton spinning. It set up model factories to manufacture cement, paper, and glass. Many new Western-style industries thus owed their start to government initiative. While public expenditures for such purposes were not large, if we exclude transport and communications, this leadership had a catalytic effect. For the State shouldered the early risks, reconnoitered the path of technical advance, and patronized many private ventures which followed on its heels.[4]

This phase of direct entrepreneurship passed rather quickly, however. In most industries it never went beyond the pilot venture. After 1882 the government relinquished its lead. Its hopes of revenue from its undertakings had been disappointed; it needed to conserve resources in order to stabilize its finances while yet embarking on ambitious naval and military spending; and it hoped to encourage private entrepreneurship by providing fresh opportunities for investment and experience. To share responsibility increasingly with private interests appeared to offer no threat to the political oligarchy. In fact, one of its problems was to find useful employment for restless *samurai*. The example of the West in the nineteenth century argued the merits of private enterprise. Most of the State's industrial properties, therefore, were soon disposed of at prices low enough to attract ready buyers. They went mainly to certain big capitalists enjoying official favor and capable of financing and operating them. The result was to endow the nascent *zaibatsu* with fresh opportunities to extend their activities. It consolidated still further the pattern of business oligarchy in close association with the government, which characterized large-scale industry and finance from the earliest days.

Thereafter State capitalism in the sense of public ownership

---

[4] The real motives of the Meiji leaders in this realm have been a matter of some controversy. Yasuzo Horie argues that in fact they were mixed, and changed as time went on. Initially the new regime simply inherited various mines, dockyards, and factories from the Tokugawa and clan governments. It soon began also to organize new undertakings. But its early purposes were not so much to stimulate industrial expansion as to serve more immediate ends: to forge military and administrative unity; to provide metal products and fuel for its own needs; to prevent unemployment among miners; to exclude foreign capital; even just to eliminate quarrels among private interests. After 1873 these military, financial, and political motives were reinforced by the wider objective of furnishing models for private industrial development. Particular objectives were to stop the gold drain by creating new exports, and to provide employment for idle *samurai*. "Government Industries in the Early Years of the Meiji Era," *Kyoto University Economic Review*, vol. xiv, no. 1, January 1939, pp. 67-87.

played a declining role in prewar Japan until its revival in the war economy of the late thirties. It was continued only on a much more selective basis. In 1896 the government established the Yawata Iron Works, largely for military reasons. This concern became the outstanding industrial enterprise operated by the State. It continued to dominate the steel industry.[5] In 1906 the government also nationalized all the trunk railways of the country—by far its largest operating investment. Soon it became the biggest stockholder in the South Manchuria Railway, which was taken over from Russia as a prize of war and made the chief instrument of Japanese enterprise in Manchuria. Subsequently it acquired part-ownership or special legal rights in other colonial development companies. At home it retained possession of the telephones and telegraphs and much of the forest domain. It continued also to operate certain Army and Navy undertakings, the mint, the Cabinet Printing Office, and the revenue monopolies in salt, tobacco, and camphor. More important, it exercised wide powers over the Japanese banking system through its control over the great special banks, even though its actual investment was not large. Local authorities also operated tramways, harbor services, and other ventures in "gas and water socialism."

These miscellaneous types of public enterprise never bulked large in the prewar Japanese economy in quantitative terms, whatever their importance in other respects. They went little beyond what was then regarded as the conventional sphere of public responsibility in most industrial countries. According to one estimate, the total value of investment in operating enterprise by the national government was about 4,500 million yen in 1934.[6] The Imperial Railways alone accounted for 3,682 million yen; the SMR and the Japan Iron Manufacturing Company for most of the remainder.

The census of national wealth in 1930 credited national and local governments in Japan with properties valued at only 18 billion yen. This was approximately one sixth of the total of 110 billion yen, about the same share as prevailed in the United States. (See above, page 238.) Most of it consisted of public land, forests, railways, and buildings. Governmental agencies of all sorts contributed no

---

[5] A number of private firms were subsequently encouraged to embark on iron and steel manufacture with the aid of subsidies, protective tariffs, and exemptions from income and business taxes for a period of years. But the Yawata Works continued until 1933 to turn out 60% of all the pig iron produced in Japan Proper and nearly half the steel. In 1934 the control of the government was extended still further by the merger of Yawata with six *zaibatsu* firms to form the Japan Iron Manufacturing Company. The new company was capitalized at 360 million yen, of which the government's share was 284 million. It accounted for upwards of half of the steel output of the home islands and almost all of the pig iron.

[6] M. Matsuo, "The Japanese State as Industrialist and Financier," *Far Eastern Survey*, vol. v, no. 11, May 25, 1936, p. 106.

larger a proportion of the current national output at this time, if one applies a market appraisal to all public services and undertakings. Valued at factor cost and with an imputed return on government property, they accounted for about 1,650 million yen, out of a domestic national product estimated at 10,239 million yen.[7] Nor were these public shares of wealth and income much larger in 1913, or even earlier. Figures of this sort are of limited significance, of course, but they do provide one useful perspective on the role of government in prewar Japan.

It was only after the outbreak of Sino-Japanese hostilities in 1937 that the State began extensively to invest and directly intervene in the control of industrial enterprise. In rapid succession scores of "national policy companies" were organized to expand the productive capacity of the Empire, particularly in war essentials. By the end of 1938 the Finance Ministry held shares in a dozen trading and industrial companies aggregating a billion yen. However, aside from the Japan Iron Manufacturing Company, these holdings were still chiefly in the SMR (400 million yen) and other semiofficial development companies formed to exploit the resources of Manchuria and North China. Even now the stimulation and control of Japan's war economy in its first phase were achieved less by direct public financing than by legislation giving the government sweeping control powers over private industry and trade.

Indirect Influences: Education. More significant than State investment and ownership in prewar Japan were the whole range of influences brought to bear through governmental action on the growth and direction of private enterprise after 1868.

These influences were selective in their intent, and in their effects. They reflected the aims and philosophy of those interest groups which were dominant in Japanese society. Though stamped throughout with a strong emphasis on national power, they tended to vary with the shifting outlooks and relative power positions of the military, the civilian bureaucracy, the political parties, and private business. They took effect through activities so varied in character as to be difficult to sum up in any consistent formula. They ranged all the way from routine services like crop reporting, aids to navigation, and patent protection, to programs of financial and technical assistance amounting to virtual partnership with private interests in certain key industries. Indeed, the full scope of political action bearing on Japan's economic development ran far beyond

[7] See Table 38, above. The principal items in government net product were the following (in millions of yen): government factories, 116; railways, 230; posts, telephones, and telegraph, 134; agricultural and forestry undertakings, 45; imputed return at 5% on government property, 466; and other government services (including armed forces' pay), 666.

what is ordinarily considered economic policy. As already emphasized, nothing was more basic to her industrial progress than the vigorous steps taken immediately after the Restoration to assure her national independence and to provide the framework of political and administrative unity. The whole course of subsequent development was shaped by Japan's success in this regard.

Second only to national unity and defense in its pervasive significance for industrialization was the attitude adopted at the outset toward education.

In traditional Japan formal learning had been largely the monopoly of the *samurai*. The only form of technical training was the apprentice system. The problem of modernization was first to establish a broad highway of contact with Western learning, and second to adapt and develop it on an indigenous basis. The government led in both tasks. It dispatched group missions and individual students in large numbers abroad to study Western science, administration, and the industrial arts. It hired hundreds of Western experts in almost every branch of technical skill from silkworm breeding to shipping and central banking. A Department of Education was created in 1871. Drawing on French models, it blueprinted a national system of education, with a primary school envisaged for every 600 children. Higher technical schools were organized in such fields as medicine, military science, navigation, agriculture, commerce, and fisheries. Tokyo Imperial University was developed as the training school for the civil service, and the leading center of university education and research.

Interestingly enough, the early Japanese educators like Fujimaro Tanaka, who became vice-minister of education in 1873, were strongly influenced by American ideas of democracy and utilitarianism in education.[8] Soon, however, the Meiji bureaucrats took alarm at this tendency. In the eighties official policy turned toward an increasing emphasis on nationalistic and authoritarian morals. As expounded in the Imperial Rescript on Education (1890), this philosophy of obedience and subservience to the State became firmly rooted in the curriculum. Cloaked in the trappings of Japanese mythology, it was revived and reached new heights during the recrudescence of blood-and-iron militarism after 1931. The Japanese are not the only people to have used State education to enforce social discipline within the established order, but they were pioneers in the more modern techniques of this form of regimentation.

It was remarkable, nevertheless, that Japan should move so quickly away from the philosophy of the Tokugawa ruling class, which was to keep the people steeped in ignorance, to a national

[8] See Chitoshi Yanaga, *Japan since Perry*, New York, 1949, chap. 7.

campaign against illiteracy. The interests of class and religion placed their stamp upon the curriculum; but they no longer blocked the road to popular enlightenment, as in so many countries of Asia and the West.[9] By the turn of the century substantial progress had been made toward a compulsory system of four-year (later six-year) primary education. Already 5 million children were receiving some rudiments of instruction at least, in 27,000 elementary schools. On this foundation was erected a tapering pyramid of technical and general education, at both secondary and higher levels. The latter was restricted in practice largely to boys from upper-income groups. Still there were now 15,000 students in forty-nine colleges and universities.

Elementary schools were operated almost entirely by local public bodies, usually with grants-in-aid. Private education was more important in the secondary field, and still more in higher learning. However, the Ministry of Education prescribed standards and maintained close surveillance throughout. Most of the technical schools in particular were public institutions. A great deal of short-term industrial training also took place in private factories, of course. But it was always limited by the turnover of labor. Almost everywhere this is apt to deter private employers from any large investment in the development of technical skills. In Japan, as in most countries, only the State found it advantageous to finance technical education on any scale. Along with the rest of the system of public instruction, it was constantly handicapped, so far as national government expenditures were concerned, by the priority given to military budgets. By 1903, nevertheless, some 240 technical schools of higher and lower grades had been organized. There were, in addition, the technical colleges of the universities, and 1,000 elementary "continuation schools" for part-time instruction in the simpler skills required for industry, commerce, agriculture, and fishing.

With all its limitations, both in scale and content, this system of general and technical education as it expanded was fundamental to industrial advance. In time Japan came to have a ratio of engineering students to the population said to be higher than in many industrial nations of Europe. In pure science, still more than in engineering, her universities and research institutes gained the re-

---

[9] It is sometimes forgotten how long the modernization and extension of education were delayed, even in Britain, by class interest and religious rivalry. Japan lacked the force of a great religious movement like the nonconformist movement to back the struggle toward this goal under State auspices. On the other hand, she was spared the handicap of a powerful established church which elsewhere has so often fought any encroachment on its monopoly of "voluntary education" while failing to provide adequate facilities itself. Not until 1876 was attendance at school made compulsory for children up to twelve in England, and not until 1890 was elementary education made generally available at public expense.

spect of the world. The mass of people never got beyond six years' schooling. But even this helped to diffuse the more modest technical skills widely among the population, especially in the towns and cities. And education encouraged an increasing degree of geographic, occupational, and social mobility among the people which was essential to the radical restructuring of the economy. Finally, by spreading economic opportunity without legal discrimination with respect to race, religion, or class, it was the chief force at work, however ineffectively, to combat the great inequalities so deeply rooted in Japanese society.[10] No other enterprise of the State paid handsomer dividends to the nation. The chief trouble was there was not enough.

A full assessment of the role of government in Japanese economic life would take account of policies of inaction as well as those of action. It was highly significant, as we have seen, that the Meiji governments showed little disposition to employ the powers of the State to redistribute income and wealth, to combat the concentration of control in finance and industry, or to shelter the peasant and worker from the rigors of competition. In the main, except for the diffusion of knowledge, their policies served rather to tip the scales the other way. No less significant was the attitude of the authorities toward the economic and social problem overshadowing all others—the relentless growth of population. Government bureaus and scientific institutions made considerable contributions to the advances in public health which steadily reduced the death rate. Birth control, however, was a subject on which Japan's political leaders were at least neutral and often frankly hostile. The practice of family limitation spread slowly through the cities in the later decades, but its open advocacy remained under legal penalties.

On some of these aspects of public policy a good deal has been said in earlier chapters of this volume. Others extend well beyond the bounds of this study. There are several features, though, which call for further discussion because of their pervasive effect on the whole industrialization process.

Money, Credit, and Fiscal Policies

Early Financial Expedients. Certain monetary and fiscal policies require further emphasis, first of all, because of the part which they played in nourishing the growth of Japanese capitalism through its

---

10 The most apparent discrimination in the use of public funds for education was on the basis of sex. The purpose of educating women, according to the minister of education in 1909, Baron Kikuchi Dairoku, was to equip them to be "good wives and wise mothers." Robert K. Hall, *Education for the New Japan*, New Haven, 1949, p. 419. Even under this traditional formula, however, a good deal was accomplished in the education of girls through the middle-school stage.

infancy. In Meiji Japan, as in all countries undertaking economic development, one crucial problem was to mobilize savings out of a mass of small incomes, by one means or another, and to generate a flow of investment funds into new forms of enterprise. Although government investment was itself a small part of the total, the whole process of capital formation was inevitably influenced by the State at almost every point.

A rising tempo of investment followed almost automatically from the new impulses and techniques which flowed into Japan, once she abandoned the policy of seclusion, threw off the old shackles on freedom of enterprise, and embarked on a new era of political unity, legal security, and technical advance. Such a development had long been latent in pre-Restoration Japan. It was now quick to manifest itself in the new climate of opportunity.

As described in Chapter 5, private capital formation was aided by wide inequalities in wealth and income; also by the resistance offered by traditional Japanese values to higher standards of material consumption. Yet the new circumstance was not either of these factors so much as new incentives and opportunities to use wealth in productive ways rather than to hoard or consume it. This process, however, required a steady growth of currency and credit to keep pace with the growth of production and its shift to a commercial basis. It called for new financial mechanisms to create and mobilize liquid purchasing power for private investment as well as State expenditure. And it could be accelerated by employing these mechanisms to inflate profit expectations so as to draw increasing resources into capital formation. In part such resources might previously have been idle, as in the case of mines, forests, or underemployed farm labor. In some degree they had to be drawn from labor and capital previously devoted to consumption. In large measure they were newly created in the process of growth.

The turbulent financial history of 1868 to 1881 reveals these processes at work. (See pages 245ff.) Only by large issues of paper money could the Meiji regime initially meet its requirements. As quickly as possible, however, it sought a more orderly solution. The land tax reform of 1873 created a State system of national revenue collected mainly from the agricultural class. Meanwhile, to augment the supply of liquid funds for public and private use, the authorities also encouraged the spread of joint-stock finance and private banking and note issue. The borrowing powers of the government were first employed on a large scale in the attempt to resolve the political problem of the displaced *samurai* by a mixture of conciliation and force. Over 200 million yen of public bonds were issued in commuting the feudal pensions of 400,000 families. Some of these bonds were used by nobility to found note-issuing banks, which led to a rapid increase in the supply of credit. Others afforded capital directly for small enterprises of all sorts that mushroomed in the inflation that followed.

These early financial expedients are difficult to assess in their effects on real capital formation. Initially, in all likelihood, the result was not so much to create new wealth as to redistribute spending on consumption from one class to another, and to concentrate the ownership of land and other existing assets. The government managed at any rate to meet its own most urgent political and administrative requirements through a critical period. At the same time, sizable pools of banking capital were created under the control of private financiers who began to seek outlets for their funds in new forms of large-scale enterprise. And a dynamic impulse was given to countless small undertakings in agriculture, commerce, and handicraft industry, some of which survived the deflation and depression of the eighties.

Most important, experience taught the need for a system of currency and banking which would be more ample and more stable than the early improvisations. This experience, together with further study of European practice, formed the basis for the far-reaching reforms undertaken by Count Matsukata after 1880 and carried out over the next two decades.

The Bank of Japan was now developed as a central bank of note issue and fiscal agent of the government. Other semiofficial banks were founded on government initiative to enlarge the credit system. They also served to extend the range of government control over the network of private banks which was growing apace. In a series of steps the currency was unified; the banking system was placed under a greater measure of Treasury supervision; and in 1897 Japan followed the example of most other countries in abandoning bimetallism after a long and unsatisfactory experience. She now adopted the gold standard, with the help of the sterling indemnity exacted from China as the price of defeat in 1895. Germany had used her war indemnity from France a generation earlier for a similar purpose. Western money markets were henceforth open to Japanese public borrowing, and large loans were contracted during the next fifteen years. (Chapter 5.) Japan's own banking system, although still inadequate in many respects, provided a fairly effective instrument for the development of modern industry and trade.

The Government in Banking. The key role played by the great quasi-public banks formed in the later Meiji years deserves special emphasis. Beside the Bank of Japan, they included particularly the

Yokohama Specie Bank, the Industrial Bank of Japan, the Hypothec Bank of Japan, and the Banks of Chosen and Taiwan.

These institutions functioned side by side, and often in close collaboration with the private banks, particularly the traditional Big Five—the First (Daiichi), Mitsui, Mitsubishi, Sumitomo, and Yasuda. Together they made for a powerful concentration of banking capital, and one which increased with the passage of time, as hundreds of smaller banks were gradually absorbed by the big private institutions in a series of financial crises. The importance of the government banks is indicated by the fact that their paid-up capital and reserves ranged between a fifth and a third of those of all special and ordinary (nonsavings) banks in Japan after 1900. Among the latter in turn, the share of the seven leading institutions in total paid-up capital, reserves, and deposits increased from 23% in 1905 to as much as 58% in 1941.[11]

The State itself provided very little of the share capital of the special banks. (The Imperial Household was a large stockholder in several, especially the Yokohama Specie Bank.) They secured their funds from private subscription to shares, from private deposits and debenture issues, and from public accounts. In each institution, however, the government appointed or approved the principal officers and directors. Under their statutes and bylaws, policies were also subject to continuous scrutiny and control by the Ministry of Finance. Another concentration of financial resources even more directly under the control of the Ministry was the huge fund of postal savings managed by its Deposits Bureau. From its inception in 1875 the postal savings system regularly received deposits far in excess of those received by the private savings banks. In 1934 it held 37.8 million accounts averaging 74 yen apiece. Its assets amounted to about one fifth of the entire assets of all other banks and insurance and trust companies.

Through its relationship to these institutions, as well as its participation in various "national policy companies" like the South Manchuria Railway and Oriental Development Company, the State was in a position to exert a large influence over the investment of private funds when it chose to do so. This was the more true since Japanese banks characteristically engaged in long-term financing of industry, agriculture, and real estate, as well as short-term commercial operations. No wide public market for securities ever developed; bank funds and business savings were the chief source of capital for industry and trade. The relation between the banks

11 These seven include the Big Five mentioned above; the One Hundredth Bank; after 1905 the Konoike Bank; and after 1941 the Sanwa, formed in 1933 by a merger of the Konoike with two other leading banks of Osaka.

and industrial concerns was thus unusually close, particularly in the case of the *zaibatsu* banks which were themselves part of the great combines.

The official banks served diverse purposes. One major purpose was to channel private funds into financing the government itself. Together with the Deposit Funds Management Bureau, they always held a sizable fraction of the public debt. The Bank of Japan, of course, performed the other usual functions of a central bank. While its powers over the money market were always somewhat limited, this was offset in some degree by official influence exerted through the other special banks. The Yokohama Specie Bank gave the country an efficient foreign exchange institution with branches all over the world. Operating in a field of vital importance to Japan, it functioned according to accepted banking principles, but with a large measure of public responsibility.

The Industrial and Hypothec banks conducted business in their respective spheres under strict control by the Ministry of Finance. The former was a mortgage as well as a banking institution, raising funds both at home and abroad for medium- and long-term financing of industrial enterprise. The latter became the center of a network of agricultural credit agencies sponsored by the government. They included the prefectural Agricultural and Industrial Banks; the Hokkaido Colonial Bank; and the Central Bank for Cooperative Associations, organized in 1923 as a "central chest" for thousands of cooperative credit societies which were formed under the laws of 1900 and 1917. Together these agencies furnished as much as a quarter of the funds borrowed by farmers in the later years. Most of the remainder came from local pawnshops, landlords, and merchants at much higher interest rates.

On a smaller scale the Industrial and Hypothec banks were also used after 1923 to extend low-interest loans to small traders and industrialists, with the aid of government guarantees and funds from the Deposits Bureau. Later, in the thirties, these lending institutions gained increasing importance in the industrial field as all sorts of "national policy companies" were launched to promote war industries. By 1939 the Deposits Bureau alone held 11% of all industrial debentures outstanding in Japan. All government banks and agencies together held as much as 20%.

In the realm of imperialist expansion and colonial development several of the public banks were long associated directly with special political objectives. Here severe losses to the government and the depositors sometimes occurred. For example, the Banks of Taiwan and Chosen played a major part in the development of their respective territories. They conducted all sorts of banking and currency operations for the Army and the colonial governments, beside financing Japanese business enterprise. "Development" is a euphemism for some of their activities. The Bank of Taiwan in particular had a long record of speculation and mismanagement, culminating in its failure in 1927. It was characteristic of the financial intrigue of the times that its collapse was allegedly precipitated by Mitsui and Mitsubishi, who called their loans to the overextended Bank in the effort to ruin Suzuki and Company, a rival sugar firm in whose speculations it was heavily involved. Also characteristic of the times was the response of the political parties in the Diet. They promptly voted 200 million yen to bail out the big creditors of the Bank, beside another 500 million yen to guarantee the Bank of Japan against losses incurred in emergency advances to other institutions to rescue them from ruin in the general collapse that impended.

The Bank of Chosen and the Industrial Bank of Japan were associated with the Bank of Taiwan in a long series of political maneuvers and financial manipulations in China. In 1915-18 they were the tool of Premier General Terauchi and the Japanese militarists in the unsavory Nishihara loans to Chinese politicians of the corrupt Anfu clique. Ostensibly given for railway construction, purchase of arms, and similar purposes, the real object of these loans was to follow up the Twenty-one Demands of 1915 with a further consolidation of Japanese influence in China. They were soon defaulted, and in the end the Japanese government had to acknowledge its responsibility by paying off the creditors to the tune of 156 million yen.

After 1931 the special banks were again freely employed as instruments of imperialism. The Industrial Bank invested heavily in Manchuria and North China, as well as in the numerous "national policy companies" floated at home. The Bank of Chosen served as fiscal agent for the Kwantung Army. It also financed a whole series of puppet regimes and companies on the continent. It was even so versatile as to engage in large-scale smuggling of silver, opium, and textiles in the Tientsin area, where the Japanese were trying to break down Chinese administrative authority in 1935-36.

These continental ventures form a colorful chapter in the history of the colonial banks. But they had little to do with Japanese economic development, except to dissipate valuable resources. The more constructive contributions of the special banks lay elsewhere.

Secular Expansion of Credit. To return to matters of more substantive importance for the Japanese economy, the fiscal operations of the government as well as its banking policies continued to provide an inflationary stimulus to growth even after the Matsukata reforms previously mentioned. Here the reader is referred to matters already discussed in Chapters 1, 2, and 5. Following the retrenchment of the eighties, government borrowing and spending were kept within more manageable bounds. Yet a steady rise in the public debt and note issue persisted over most of the next thirty years.

It is interesting that Japanese price indices show only three or four years between 1868 and 1900 when wholesale commodity prices failed to rise from the level of the preceding year. Again, from 1900 to 1920 only three such years are recorded. In fact, as remarked in Chapter 5, the secular rise in the price level only suffered two real interruptions in prewar Japan, once in the eighties and again between 1920 and 1932. (See Table 25, above.) The upward drift after the turn of the century characterized the whole world economy, to be sure. But in Japan it was reinforced by two factors. One was a chronic deficit in the government budget occasioned largely by the wars with China and Russia. The other was a general predilection for easy money which seems to have been shared alike by the government and the business community, and which helped to maintain private investment at a high level through much of the period 1893-1913. As already described, the government resorted at this time to large-scale borrowing abroad. This enabled the Bank of Japan further to expand the supply of credit, and—more important—it enlarged the real resources at Japan's disposal to meet the dual requirements of military spending and industrial development.

After 1915 came the windfall opportunities of the European war, generating a new wave of expansion in Japanese trade and industry. The collapse of 1920 ushered in a decade of financial disorders. Again the tendency was to stave off any radical deflationary readjustment. Government funds were used freely to shore up the credit structure and to meet the yawning gap in the balance of payments. This time the difficulty was more serious, and the remedy proved inadequate. It was succeeded by a brief trial of retrenchment and deflation, preparatory to a return to the gold standard. But this experiment, too, was ill fated, especially as it was attempted on the eve of a world depression. So, once more, recourse was had in the early thirties to mild doses of inflation, accompanied for the first time by drastic exchange depreciation. For another decade, almost, the civilian economy resumed its rapid growth, until it began to crumble under the strain of large-scale war.[12]

---

[12] This time, however, the growth in real national income was less impressive than the growth in national product, owing to the deterioration in the terms of trade occasioned by depreciation of the yen in 1931. As described in Chapter 2, import

To explore the financial history of prewar Japan at any length, of course, would introduce many complexities into this oversimplified outline. It may be sufficient, nevertheless, to draw attention to one essential feature of the growth of Japanese capitalism. The State continually drained large resources into armament and war; and it certainly failed to channel the flow of investment funds into many uses which would have had a high priority in terms of social welfare. But it did manage to provide, partly through design and partly through inadvertence, a monetary stimulus and mechanism by which large sums of purchasing power were placed in the hands of industrialists, merchants, and farmers able and willing to invest them in wealth-creating activities on a growing scale.

The secular expansion of currency and credit in prewar Japan was a rather disorderly process, to be sure. It was attended with the usual booms and depressions of a capitalistic economy. Some were induced by monetary mismanagement at home. Others grew out of external developments beyond Japan's control. Over the period as a whole, however, depressions were usually short-lived in prewar Japan. And, after the early experiences with paper money, runaway tendencies in boom periods which did not parallel similar price and income movements abroad tended to be held in check by difficulties which they invited in the balance of payments. In fact, the protection of gold reserves and foreign balances was a more or less continuous source of anxiety for the Treasury and Bank of Japan—a fact which testifies itself to the propensity to enlarge the supply of money whenever conditions permitted.

All in all, it would seem that Japan took over fairly successfully the intricate modern techniques of money and credit, where the responsibility of the State is so great. This is applying the standard, not of perfection, but of common experience at the time. In the main, Japanese governments refrained before 1937 from reckless abuse of their power to create credit. No less important, they avoided excessive regard for orthodox canons of "sound finance." The under-

---

prices rose sharply in relation to export prices during the ensuing trade boom. By 1936 the Japanese were exporting about one-third more goods to foreign countries to pay for their current imports than would have been required at the 1930 terms of exchange. These additional exports absorbed about one fifth of the 50% gain in national net product from 1930 to 1936.

The short-run gains from this experience in exchange depreciation and monetary reflation were nevertheless substantial, especially in view of the drastic readjustment which had to be made to the decline in the American silk market. The real difficulties came later as foreign governments moved to protect their markets against a flood of cheap Japanese manufactures; and still more when the Japanese military refused to call a halt to military spending, despite danger signals, and even assassinated the finance minister, prudent old Korekiyo Takahashi, to get him out of the way.

lying process of growth was a long tidal wave of technical innovation, as Japan took over and exploited the technology and trading opportunities opened up by contact with the West. New wants, new markets, new forms of production and organization were the impelling forces. Largely they were private and civilian in character, but the expansion in this realm was reinforced by continual government spending for armaments, which was especially significant in building the heavy industries. All this required a growing supply of new investment funds, renewed in cycle after cycle. In the field of money and credit, public policy helped to supply this need by a persistent bias in favor of monetary expansion.

At the same time certain other consequences arising from the predilection for easy money should not pass unnoticed.

One was the social cost of arbitrary redistributions of income occasioned by changes in the price level. The secular upward drift —a threefold increase from 1868 to 1938—meant that periodically great masses of people saw the buying power of their current incomes whittled away through price inflation generated by new investment and armament expenditure which was not matched by a corresponding increase in current output. This was part of the real cost of Japanese economic development. It was the mechanism by which a share of the capital was created. But even where it helped eventually to build the country's productive power, the future benefits were not shared among classes in proportion to the immediate deprivations. Characteristically, for example, the buying power of industrial wages failed to rise at all in the boom years 1915-19, but jumped 50% in the postwar depression of 1919-24. Similarly, the great expansion of industry and trade after 1931 brought only modest gains to the working class beyond the living standard they had already achieved in the twenties. A major share of the growth in national product went into industrial capital formation and armament, or accrued to foreign consumers of Japanese goods through the deterioration in Japan's terms of trade.[13]

Another consequence of the tendency to inflation, and the lax credit standards which invited it, was a chronic waste of capital resources. If it made funds available for wealth-creating activities, it also diverted them all too easily into speculation and ill-considered investment. It likewise relaxed the incentives otherwise present for technological improvements.

[13] On the other hand, inflation tended to benefit peasants generally by lightening the burden of farm debt and taxation. The deflation of 1881-85 worked great hardship on the small farmer, sharply increasing tenancy. Again, the depression of 1929-32 threw millions of peasants into virtual bankruptcy. The incidence of Japan's monetary policies on the fortunes of various classes requires more study than can be given it here, and depends a good deal on the time period which is considered.

The experience of the Japanese, no less than that of other peoples, shows that a degree of adversity impels a businessman to efficiency more often than easy profits on a rising market. For example, the depression of 1881-85 put through the wringer many an enterprise that had mushroomed in the inflation of the seventies. Those that managed to survive gained in maturity and efficiency as a result. Again, after 1926 the pressure of falling prices compelled various Japanese industries to make sweeping improvements in their managerial and technical operations. These gains explain in no small measure Japan's competitive successes in world markets during the thirties. Such periods were uncommon, however. Japanese businessmen and their bankers were apt to prefer the feather bed of cheap credit to the spur of sagging profit margins. They contrived through most of the prewar decades to have their way.

Meiji Taxation and Business Enterprise. A related field of State policy which bears importantly on economic development is taxation. This includes not only the scale and incidence of taxes levied by the government, but also the certainty with which they were collected, and ultimately the purposes for which they were used.

Among the early Meiji reforms none were more important than those which reorganized and enlarged the public revenue. Taxes on commercial and industrial enterprise now acquired a degree of regularity and predictability unknown in pre-Restoration Japan. Probably they were also lightened in the aggregate. In any case, arbitrary levies at the will of an arrogant political aristocracy became a thing of the past.

Initially, and for a generation or more, it was the peasant who continued to bear the main load, as he had under the *ancien régime*. The land tax reform of 1873, in effect, replaced the feudal dues he had previously borne with a money tax based on the assessed value of land. For twenty-five years this tax provided the national government with its chief source of revenue. Until 1882, indeed, it furnished over 80%. Also, local surtaxes on land, together with a house tax, were the chief source of prefectural and village income. Thus taxes on real estate actually furnished over half of all national and local revenue down to the turn of the century.

In 1882 an ambitious program to build an Imperial Navy was laid down. Arms expenditure rose almost uninterruptedly for the next thirty years as Japan passed successfully through the wars with China and Russia. Meanwhile the traditional taxes on land and *sake* fell increasingly short of meeting the fiscal need. While borrowing heavily to finance its outlays, the central government was forced to cast about for other sources of current revenue.

Surprisingly, as early as 1887 the Japanese imported from the

West the idea of a personal income tax. But the rate did not exceed 3% even on incomes over 30,000 yen; its yield proved negligible. In 1896 the authorities added a general tax on business turnover and capital, and in 1905 even a modest inheritance tax. In 1899 they also stiffened the income tax somewhat, applying it for the first time to company income. At the insistence of the wealthy House of Peers, however, bond interest and company profits were still exempted from the progressive rates of the personal income tax. They were taxed at only 2.0 and 2.5% respectively. Even then evasions were widespread.[14]

None of these early taxes on business income and property, excepting those on real estate, was heavy enough to yield much revenue. As late as 1913 they provided less than 15% of national tax collections. As a matter of fact, it was not until after World War I that the national levy on personal and corporate income came to yield much more than numerous petty stamp taxes on property transfers, patent medicines, legal documents, civil suits, etc.

The shift after 1893 in the structure of taxation, both national and local, is indicated broadly in Table 43. It was indirect taxes on consumer goods which largely financed the growing requirements of the national budget from 1880 to 1913. They took two forms: (a) excise taxes on liquor, sugar, soy, textiles, and a few other items, and (b) lucrative fiscal monopolies applied in 1898 and 1904 on the sale of two widely used products—tobacco and salt. If it is assumed that one half of customs duties were also collected on imports of consumer goods, consumer taxes provided the bulk of national tax revenues over and above the land tax. In 1893 their share was 79%; in 1903, 69%; and in 1913, 63%. Their increment in money yield over this twenty-year period was almost double that of all national taxes on income, capital, and business enterprise.

Meanwhile local taxes had also grown apace, to pay for mounting outlays on education and public works. Prefectural and municipal governments financed themselves with a hodgepodge of levies. Some of them were surtaxes on national land, income, and business taxes. Others were of a local variety. They amounted in all to 40 to 50% as much as national taxes after the turn of the century. As the central government shifted increasingly to taxation of urban business enterprise, local land and household taxes bore with especial weight on the rural population.

---

[14] For example, in the war boom year of 1905-06, only eighty persons reported taxable incomes of 50,000 to 100,000 yen, and only thirty persons incomes above 100,000 yen. The actual number must have been much greater. Japan Year Book Office, *The Japan Year Book*, Tokyo, 1906, p. 240.

Table 43. *Sources of National and Local Tax Revenue in
Japan Proper, 1893-1933*[a]

	1893-94		1913-14		1933-34	
	Millions of yen	Percent	Millions of yen	Percent	Millions of yen	Percent
Total tax revenue	107	100.0	660	100.0	1,567	100.0
National (including fiscal monopoly profits)	(72)	—	(470)	—	(1,002)	—
Prefectural, municipal, town, and village	(35)	—	(190)	—	(566)	—
Taxes on real estate[b]	66	61.4	131	19.8	282	18.0
Taxes on consumption[c]	22	20.4	210	31.9	493	31.5
Taxes on income, capital, business enterprise[d]	14	13.3	245	37.1	678	43.3
Customs duties	5	4.8	74	11.2	114	7.3

a Data from Tōyō Keizai Shimpō-sha, *Meiji Taishō Zaisei Shōran*, Tokyo, 1927; Japan, Department of Finance, *Financial and Economic Annual of Japan*; and Bank of Japan, *Economic Statistics of Japan*, passim. The distribution by type of taxes is only approximate.

b National and local land taxes, plus local house taxes.

c Chiefly national excise taxes on liquor, tobacco, and soy in 1893; national taxes on liquor, sugar, and textiles in 1913 and 1933; and net revenue in the General Budget from national fiscal monopolies on tobacco and salt. The tobacco monopoly replaced the tobacco excise tax in 1898. The salt monopoly was adopted in lieu of a tax on salt in 1904. Together with the less lucrative camphor monopoly, they yielded net revenue of 69 million yen in 1913 and 179 million yen in 1933. Certain minor taxes on consumption goods are excluded here, as well as all customs duties.

d Taxes on personal, business, and household income; the national succession tax; registration fees and stamp duties; and miscellaneous taxes on business enterprise in various fields. In aggregate yield these taxes were almost equally divided between national and local taxes in 1913 and 1933. National taxes in this category totalled 4 million yen in 1893, 111 million in 1913, and 336 million in 1933.

The incidence of this entire Meiji system of taxes, national and local, on savings and consumption is highly conjectural. In view of the nature and wide dispersion of taxes, however, they must have come out of consumption in considerable degree, and from slender margins of income which would otherwise have been saved by small farmers and petty businessmen.[15]

15 Horace Belshaw's characterization of taxation in underdeveloped countries is applicable to Japan at this juncture: "In under-developed countries, the great

Tax Policy in the Interwar Years. The currents of Japanese liberalism and democracy which reached their full tide in the decade after World War I naturally wrought certain changes in fiscal policy.

With armament spending cut back from its wartime levels, the government displayed more willingness to appropriate funds for agricultural relief and other social expenditure. For example, it spent considerable sums after 1921 in the effort to stabilize the price of rice through buying and selling operations. It assumed new responsibilities for public health, sanitation, labor exchanges, etc. It also effected minor revisions in the tax system designed to lighten somewhat the burden on small incomes. In 1926-27 the 10% tax on cotton fabrics and certain other excise taxes were abolished; the minimum exemptions from the income and inheritance taxes were raised; a special levy of 2% was imposed on interest from capital; and very small farm proprietors were freed from the land tax. The old business tax of 1896, imposed with little regard to ability to pay, was replaced by a tax of 2.6 to 3.6% on the net profits of companies and individual proprietors (in excess of 400 yen).

Yet, when it came to public expenditures, the Diets of this period displayed less interest in relieving agricultural distress or urban poverty than in appropriating huge funds to support the capital structures of the big banks and industrial concerns. Such institutions were apt to be closely affiliated with the political parties. This helped them to secure generous assistance from the public treasury in time of financial stress, as previously observed.

Tinkering with the tax structure likewise effected no basic change in social policy. It is significant that indirect taxes continued to supply 40% or more of the total national revenue, if monopoly profits on tobacco and salt are included. They weighed most heavily on the wage and salaried classes of the cities. In fact, so far as the city worker was concerned, they now offset the earlier discrimination against the farmer through the system of direct taxation.[16] The

relative importance of subsistence production and the relative small cash incomes among a large proportion of the people reduce the proportion of government revenue derived from direct taxation and increase that levied on objects which can be seen or transactions which can be interrupted. The cost of collection tends to be high and assessments tend to be more arbitrary. There is more scope for discrimination, and taxation tends to be heavily regressive. These conditions, together with comparatively immature fiscal administrations not only press heavily on living standards but also cause the fiscal systems to lack resiliency." "Economic Development in Asia, A Preliminary Approach," *Economia Internazionale,* vol. v, no. 4, November 1952, pp. 24-25.

[16] Hioye Ouchi, "Tax Burden on Salaried Men and Farmers as Revealed by the

small or medium-size business proprietor was still at an advantage, however. A 1929 study showed that his direct taxes were only half as high in relation to his income as those of the farmer in the same income bracket. This was about the same differential as had prevailed twenty years earlier. (See above, page 26.)

Large personal and corporate incomes continued to be subject to only mildly progressive levies until after 1937. The income tax had first gained importance during World War I. In the years which followed, it came to provide as much as 20% of national tax revenue. Under the revised law of 1920, in fact, rates were raised as high as 36% on incomes over 4 million yen. But virtually all interest, and 40% of corporate dividends and bonuses, were still immune from the progressive rates of the personal income tax. Interest (except the yield on national and savings bonds, which was entirely exempt) was separately taxed at only 4 to 5%. Applied to corporate profits, the basic rate was only 5%. Surtaxes on excess profits raised it no higher than 10% even when a firm made 30% on its invested capital. Moreover, loopholes and evasions were widespread, as a result of lax enforcement and fictitious bookkeeping. Whatever the legal rates, the taxes paid by Japanese corporations and well-to-do individuals always depended in no small degree on a process of individual negotiation, in which political influence and financial bargaining power carried a good deal of weight.

As late as 1933 all national taxes on personal income, business profits, and interest still yielded little more than the liquor tax alone (209 million yen). They provided less than half as much as all excise taxes plus fiscal monopoly revenue. Meanwhile, real estate and household taxes continued to be widely borne by the population; consumption taxes were heavily regressive; and various local and national taxes on business activity of different kinds had a broad incidence upon millions of small industrialists, tradesmen, and professional people. It was Jean-Baptiste Colbert, something of an expert in fiscal matters, who once remarked that "the art of taxation consists in plucking the largest amount of feathers with the least possible amount of hissing."

Looking back over the period as a whole, one may conclude that the over-all burden of taxation on the Japanese economy was kept at fairly moderate levels. Through the interwar period it ranged between 10% and 15% of the national income.[17] Earlier it may have

---

Official Survey of Their Livings," *Bulletin de l'Institut International de Statistique*, vol. xxv, part 2, Tokyo, 1931, pp. 372-92.

[17] For details on the years after 1930 see Chotaro Takahashi, "The Income Tax Burden: A Japanese Experiment," *The Annals of Hitotsubashi Academy*, no. 1, October 1950, pp. 61-63.

been higher, though probably not very much so. This ratio compared favorably with that prevailing in the United States at the time; it was well below that in many European countries. But it was kept at this level only by rigid economy in nonmilitary expenditure. It still represented a much heavier burden in reality for a people as poor as the Japanese, especially in view of the limited civilian services which they got in return.

The power to tax and spend was never used liberally by prewar Japanese governments as an engine for the more equitable distribution of wealth. As in most countries, the tax structure grew by the addition of layer on layer of miscellaneous imposts, with the development of new needs and potential sources of revenue. In the first decades, to repeat, the agriculturist carried the burden. Around the turn of the century this was shifted in increasing degree to the general public through consumption taxes. Only following World War I did corporate enterprise assume a major share of the load. After forty years of industrial progress the distribution by source of Japanese tax income as given in the table above was taking on the pattern shared by most industrial nations. Even then large property incomes continued to receive lenient treatment both in law and administration, particularly if they were derived from nonagricultural pursuits. Not until the tax reform of 1940, forced by the exigencies of war, was the whole system overhauled and the income tax put to work as an effective revenue instrument.[18]

[18] The structure of taxation in Japan in 1933-34, as given in Table 43, is compared with the structures in several European countries in the table below. The figures for the latter are roughly comparable, except that wherever possible customs duties on consumer goods are included under consumption taxes, whereas this is not done in the case of Japan. State revenue from public enterprise is excluded throughout, except for the surplus of fiscal monopolies, which is classed with taxes on consumption. European data are taken from "Changes in the Structure of Taxation in Europe," United Nations, *Economic Bulletin for Europe*, vol. 2, no. 3, third quarter, 1950, pp. 58-80.

| | PERCENT OF TAX REVENUE PROVIDED IN: | | | |
| | *Japan* | *United Kingdom* | *Sweden* | *Italy* |
TYPE OF TAX	*(1933-34)*	*(1928-29)*	*(1928-29)*	*(1928-29)*
Real estate	18	22	8	9
Consumption	32	30	26	40
Income, capital, and business enterprise	43	46	54	44
Foreign trade	7	1	12	7

One major difference between Japan and most countries of Western Europe (except France) at this time was that nearly half of central government taxes on "income, capital, and business enterprise" in Japan came from numerous small registration fees and stamp duties on property transfers, legal documents, etc., while in the latter countries they consisted largely of graduated taxes on personal incomes, inheritance, and corporate profits. The share of consumption taxes in Japan would be somewhat higher if customs duties on consumer imports were included.

In fairness one further observation should be made. A major obstacle to the national development of many Asiatic countries today is the refusal of their wealthy, propertied classes who hold political power either to pay taxes or to venture large savings in new enterprise. Plans for industrialization, land improvement, or educational reform in Iran and in the postwar Philippines, for example, have been crippled by inadequate tax revenues and private savings, without which foreign assistance can do little. Japan's prewar fiscal system, like her distribution of wealth and income, was highly undemocratic, judged by the liberal standard of modern times. Yet, just as the well-to-do class contributed aggressively to capital formation, so it was led by a mixture of coercion and consent to provide increasingly for the revenue requirements of the State.

Many circumstances enter into such differences. Clearly one of the most important was that modern Japan did not carry over into post-Restoration times a class of large land-owning families with an interest mainly in perpetuating the *status quo*, and the power to do so. Nor, on the other hand, was her process of modernization one in which the restructuring of values and political power took place at the center without much impact on the traditional outlook or the independence of masses of small gentry dominating the towns and the countryside. The very significance of the Restoration was that the keys to power passed largely to bureaucratic and mercantile interests with quite other purposes, and with the opportunity and capacity increasingly to give effect to them on a national scale. A look at the problem of economic development elsewhere only confirms the belief that in taxation as in many other matters this fact was crucial for Japan's subsequent economic growth.[19]

Tax Discrimination and Subsidies. The reader will observe that attention has been centered on the general structure of Japanese taxation, rather than tax discrimination in favor of particular industries. Tax immunities continued to be granted occasionally, as a rule for a limited period of years. Their chief purpose was to attract capital into desired fields of activity. Even as late as 1932, for example, a private concern might secure certain reductions or rebates in taxes if it engaged in mining or smelting iron, gold, silver, or lead; in overseas fishing; in reclaiming arable land; in operating a savings bank; or in exporting various products such as textile fabrics and refined sugar. But this practice appears to

---

[19] This is not to say that tax evasion was not fairly systematic and widespread. One recalls the charge, only half-humorous, that a Japanese corporation keeps three sets of books: one for the company itself; a second for the tax collector; and, when this is rejected, a third to be produced apologetically as the "true" picture. Nevertheless, by comparison with other countries in Asia, and many in the West, the Japanese record in such matters stands up surprisingly well.

have been employed rather sparingly as a device for industrial promotion.[20] The most important form of long-sustained discrimination as among industrial fields was the system of tariff duties on imports, which was highly discriminatory in its benefits. (See below.) Of a wider significance for the general growth of Japanese industry was the provision of a broad system of taxes which was fairly certain and impersonal in its administration—at least by Oriental standards—and which sought to minimize the deterrents to large-scale capital accumulation and business enterprise.

Much the same thing may be said of government subsidies to foster particular types of private enterprise. "Subsidy" is a word which can be defined broadly or narrowly. It applies to some of the funds made available by the Japanese government to the special banks, though these banks relied largely on private sources of funds except as the State came to their rescue in time of emergency. There was a considerable element of subsidy in the buying of Japanese products by government agencies in preference to imported goods. Expenditure on ports, highways, industrial research, and technical education had the character of public assistance to private enterprise. Still more was this true of the 185 million yen spent in the none too successful attempt to stabilize the price of rice from 1921 to 1932 through the buying and selling operations of the official Japan Rice Company.

In the more limited sphere of direct financial aid to nonagricultural enterprise, subsidies were used only sparingly through most of the prewar period. The outstanding case of subsidization was that of the shipping industry, which owed its early development and modernization to continuous subvention by the Japanese government. (See below.) Similarly, public grants and guarantees were employed to attract private capital into sugar refining, iron and steel manufacture, and the production of dyestuffs and other chemicals—the latter after British and American supplies were cut off during World War I. But these were rather exceptional. Until the practice of subsidy was generalized widely in the war economy of the late thirties, this type of aid was limited in scope and usually confined to a short period of years. It was much less important for Japanese industry as a whole than the broad foundation of credit and taxation provided by the State.[21]

[20] Tax exemptions and rebates were given more largely for other purposes. Instances are the tax immunity of the Imperial Household Treasury; the exemption of very small farm proprietors and businessmen from the land and business profits taxes after 1926; various exemptions granted to public bodies, foreign diplomats, and the military; the exemption of interest on national bonds from the income tax; etc.

[21] In the polemics over Japanese trade competition during the early thirties much was made of governmental subsidy as a factor in the cheapness of Japanese goods

Economic Foreign Policies

A national framework of political order and legal security, the direct pioneering of the industrial arts, public education, the expansion of money and credit, a tax structure favorable to large business enterprise yet meeting the essential requirements of the State—these were some of the ways in which the Japanese government fostered industrial progress through the decades after 1868.

The search for economic opportunity abroad was another broad area of State initiative and action. In its widest sense this includes all governmental policies directly affecting the movement of goods, ideas, capital, or persons across the national frontiers. In Japan as in all nations such activities linking the national economy with the outside world were a special concern of the State. For her these concerns were heightened by unusual dependence upon imports of technology and goods; also by the political insecurities of an island nation and the imperial ambitions of her rulers.

To review systematically all aspects of economic foreign policy at this point would repeat much that has been said in foregoing chapters. Instead, this section is focussed primarily on trade and tariff policies, shipping, and the broad significance of the overseas empire in the country's economic development. Before proceeding to these matters, however, one should note other facets of economic foreign policy largely omitted here.

First, the State naturally assumed major responsibility for creating the institutional framework of international economic contacts. Apart from diplomatic intercourse, the protection of persons and property, postal and cable communications, and other such routine functions, this involved particularly the creation and management of mechanisms relating Japan's financial system with world money markets. One of the most strategic sectors of govern-

---

sold abroad. Actually, direct subsidies to economic enterprise were far smaller than in the United States or many other countries at the time. The following summary of grants by the central government (local subsidies were largely for agriculture) is prepared from a table presented by G. C. Allen in E. B. Schumpeter, ed., *The Industrialization of Japan and Manchukuo, 1930-40*, New York, 1940, p. 734:

Average Annual Grants by the Central Government, 1931-36
(thousands of yen)

Agriculture	57,386	Railways	8,456
Trade	1,462	Shipping and shipbuilding	12,311
Industry and mining	6,202	Air services	1,847
Migration	4,563	Other	3,603
		Total	95,831

Over half of these subsidies were for agricultural public works and relief. Transport took most of the remainder. The grants to industry and mining went mostly to encourage the oil, iron, automotive, and chemical industries.

ment influence on economic development was clearly in the field of currency standards, foreign exchange, and banking operations conducted on behalf of State agencies or private enterprise. Previous chapters of this volume have narrated briefly Japan's early experiments with paper and bimetallism; the adoption of the gold standard in 1897; the development of the Bank of Japan and Yokohama Specie Bank to handle foreign banking operations; and the sequence of events which followed each other through the expansionist years after the turn of the century, the export boom of 1914-19, the troubled twenties, and the episode of currency depreciation which closed the prewar era. Enough has been said at least to highlight the principal phases of Japan's international financial history, and the institutional structure within which economic growth proceeded.

Second, the importance of technological borrowing from the West as a catalyst of industrial development has been emphasized. In Chapter 6 various aspects and channels of this borrowing have been noted. Here, too, the initiative of the State played a crucial role in the learning process during the early years, just as a half century later the hostility which it aroused abroad over its aggression in China served to choke off the stream of foreign borrowing through a decade of conflict and disorder.

Third, the migration of capital and labor across Japan's frontiers has been in some degree a substitute for merchandise trade, as a way of taking advantage of the resources and opportunities of the outside world. Little has been said in this study concerning movements of labor in and out of the country except to make clear their limited proportions. The extensive migration of Japanese businessmen, professionals, and other white-collar workers to Empire territories and China was closely associated, of course, with the overseas activities of the Japanese government and its armed forces. It had much to do with the growth of colonial trade. Otherwise it was more significant for Japan's political expansion in Asia than the over-all growth of her economy. (See above, pages 157-58 and 466.)

As for capital movements to and from Japan, there is no need to repeat here the analysis of Chapter 5. Foreign business investment in the Japanese islands was discouraged by the Meiji governments during the early decades because of its political risks. After the turn of the century it developed in a limited fashion, chiefly in the engineering, metallurgical, and electric power industries. Financially it amounted to little, though it helped to bring in advanced industrial technology. A more extensive counterflow of Japanese business capital to surrounding territories grew up in connection with the spread of Japanese trade and business enterprise. In the main, however, Japan probably would not have exported capital in any considerable amounts had it not been for State protection and encouragement in areas under heavy Japanese influence or control. Finally, the government played a paramount role in Japan's one venture in large-scale borrowing of *rentier* capital from the West. From 1897 to 1913 some 2 billion yen of loans were floated in Western money markets, largely on the credit of the State. The increased resources thus temporarily made available in the form of imports tided the country through a critical period of heavy war expenditure and capital formation. (See above, pages 253ff.)

Trade and Multilateralism. In the realm of overseas trade the State from the beginning gave active assistance to Japanese businessmen in search of trading opportunities. In part this took the conventional forms of export promotion wherever markets could be found for the growing range of Japanese manufactures. Export industries which could pay for necessary imports were an early and continuing concern of the government. Especially in the formative years it took an active hand in the study and development of foreign trade techniques, in exhibiting Japanese products abroad at expositions, and in the formation of chambers of commerce and commodity guilds for cooperative activity in this field. It also provided indispensable facilities. It created bureaus to inspect and certify the quality of export goods like tea and habutai silk. It established the Yokohama Specie Bank in 1880, and developed it as the chief source of funds for financing Japanese trade. It handed out generous subsidies year after year to develop and modernize the Japanese merchant marine as an important support to commercial as well as military expansion. And it proceeded, almost at once, to begin the conquest of a colonial empire within which Japanese businessmen were given more or less exclusive privileges of trade and investment.

Yet the most important contribution of the State to Japan's industrial growth in this whole realm of economic foreign policy was a negative one, in a sense. First by compulsion but later by voluntary choice, the Japanese government long adhered to the principle of multilateral, nondiscriminatory trade in her foreign (non-Empire) commerce.

The special value for Japan of this system of commerce was emphasized in Chapter 7. Fortunately it prevailed generally through the world during the first half century of her industrialization. As her industries grew she soon became heavily dependent on materials and equipment purchased all over the globe, and paid for likewise by exports to both Asia and the West. During 1929-30, for example, she had a credit surplus of as much as 175 million yen in trade with the United States, and 143 million yen in trade with China (including Hongkong and the Kwantung Leased Territory). Over half of her entire exports had long gone to these two countries alone. Surplus credits here enabled her to finance unfavorable trade balances of 233 million yen in Europe, 123 million yen in the rest of Asia, and similar deficits in other parts of the world where she bought industrial materials.

Japan was thus able to buy in the cheapest markets and to sell wherever she could get the best price. Her trade was somewhat limited by tariffs, her own included. But it was comparatively free of national discrimination and almost entirely unhampered by quantitative controls before 1933. The bilateral balances which developed were readily cleared in the world's money markets, within the limit of her total earnings and borrowings abroad.

During the first thirty years of her modernization, the principles of multilateralism and most-favored-nation treatment were forced upon Japan, in any case, by the treaties dictated by the foreign Powers in 1858. After winning her tariff freedom in 1899 she continued to adhere to them (except for the preferential position given her own colonies, and certain conventional tariff rates still bound by commercial treaties). In the general tariff revision of 1911 she adopted a single-line autonomous tariff. Apart from Imperial preference, equal treatment was extended to all countries with which she concluded most-favored-nation treaties. Little or no attempt was made to use the tariff as a bargaining weapon to force concessions from other countries. In return Japan enjoyed corresponding advantages throughout most of the trading world.

Only after 1933 did she begin to deviate importantly from these principles in dealings with foreign countries. Partly, of course, she was forced into bilateral bargaining and trade regulation by the spread of import quotas, import licensing, and tariff discrimination against Japanese goods all over the world. It was Japan herself, however, who contributed much to the revival of nationalism and violence which broke down the international economic order. The flooding of certain markets with cheap Japanese wares, after the yen fell from 49 cents to 29.4 cents, was bound to invite defensive barriers in countries ridden with depression and unemployment. Only belatedly did the Japanese government move to ward off the danger by encouraging export associations to undertake voluntary restrictions and price fixing on various export items. In 1934, under the Trade Protection Law, it also armed itself with power to retaliate against countries practicing discrimination. This power was soon used in trade disputes with Australia and Canada.

Meanwhile, far greater difficulties developed as the Japanese militarists pushed ahead with their plan to conquer and develop a self-contained "Coprosperity Sphere" in Asia. Little regard was shown for its consequences elsewhere. Among these consequences after 1937 were unrestrained inflation at home, a speedy crisis in the balance of payments, and the steady decline of civilian industry under the network of controls fastened upon industry and trade. Such a program of conquest—indeed, the whole bloc system of trade—was the antithesis of the type of economic foreign relations which had built the Japanese economy. It soon led to its destruction.

Quest for Empire. Long before, of course, Japan had embarked on a course of empire of which the Pacific war was perhaps the inevitable outcome.

As quickly as the new Meiji regime consolidated its position at home, and even before, its leaders began to experiment with force and diplomacy to extend the political frontiers of Japan. Through military victories over China and Russia, combined with adroit exploitation of rivalries among the other Powers, the Japanese won step by step an Empire of substantial dimensions. Already by 1910 the colonies nearly equalled the area of the home islands themselves. The growth of armament which accompanied the process, and the strategic gains which it conferred, enabled Japan a decade later to emerge from the Washington Conference as the predominant naval power of the western Pacific.

Formosa, Korea, southern Sakhalin, and other lesser acquisitions were developed as sources of food and raw materials. In return for rice, sugar, fish, and lumber, and coal, phosphates, and a few other minerals they took limited amounts of Japanese cotton goods and other manufactures. They accounted for 10% of the overseas trade of the home islands in 1911-13; and about 20% in 1928-30. The Kwantung Leased Territory became the base for exploiting the coal and iron resources of Manchuria under the aegis of the semiofficial South Manchuria Railway. In 1930, for example, Manchuria supplied about 6% (and Korea 8%) of Japan's total supplies of iron and steel materials of all sorts (Fe content), domestic and imported. Later, following the seizure of the whole territory in 1931-32, a tremendous investment was poured into the area in the hope of developing a great complex of basic industries secure from the hazards of foreign embargo or military blockade. Meanwhile, in China south of the Great Wall, Japanese businessmen went aggressively after trading and investment opportunities, using and being used by their government to create a politico-economic stake of growing proportions.[22]

[22] One illustration may be selected at random. In 1933 China used her newly won

The quest for empire in East Asia was impelled by no single motive, except as most Japanese were indoctrinated in varying degrees with a mystical faith in the Imperial Destiny. It drew support from various interest groups and for differing reasons. Its momentum and direction reflected the political struggle at home, as well as the resistance it met abroad. Economic gain was clearly one of the incentives—the one most frequently cited in justification after 1905. The world had to accustom itself to steady complaints of population pressure and poverty of resources in apology for blatant encroachments by the Japanese on their neighbors.[23]

As usual in the folklore of imperialism, so interwined were considerations of military power, economic advantage, national prestige, and "moral obligation" that even the honest testimony of the makers of Japanese policy is an unreliable guide to the facts. Nor does an objective analysis of the real interests at stake give one ready answers. David Hume once remarked that "though men be much governed by interest, yet even interest itself, and all human affairs, are entirely governed by *opinion.*"

Here was an area of State action, then, in which few opportunities were let slip. It is significant that the propensity for military expansion appeared as early as the seventies. This was long before industrialization had created any serious need for Asiatic markets or materials. Yet Japanese businessmen, while more prudent than their military compatriots, and more realistic about the economics of imperialism, were quick to exploit if not to create the opportunities which came their way. They were the more responsive when their government was prepared to underwrite the risk, as was not infrequently the case.

Economic imperialism thus became the handmaid of military aggression. Force, diplomacy, investment, trade, and migration were all employed in combination. They worked together for the greater

---

tariff autonomy to announce a new tariff schedule, with stronger protective features. Japanese diplomats and businessmen promptly made vigorous protests. Whether by coincidence or otherwise, the Japanese government soon made new demands on North China, pressed a fresh demand for repayment of the Nishihara loans, and dispatched gunboats and cruisers to Nanking in connection with an incident involving a Japanese vice-consul. When the new Chinese tariff was promulgated in 1934 it was found to reduce or leave unchanged many rates on imports of cotton goods and other items coming mainly from Japan, while raising them more generally in other categories. Meanwhile China's customs revenue in the north was being drastically reduced by huge smuggling operations connived at by the Japanese authorities.

23 "In Japan, as in Europe, increase of population was taken as an index of political power, and suggested expansion; later, when the limits of Japan's productive capacity became apparent, the population pressure served as the final reason for justifying any, even the boldest, venture." Emil Lederer, "Japan in World Economics," *Social Research*, vol. 4, no. 1, February 1937, p. 30.

glory of the emperor—for a while—and incidentally for the enrichment of certain business interests. The taxpayer patiently footed the bill.

It was only after 1931, with the conquest of Manchuria, that the Empire began to assume a major place in the total sphere of Japanese economic enterprise. The subject territories now acquired increasing prominence as an area of Japanese investment, trade, and white-collar employment. The focus of this overseas development was, of course, the new state of Manchukuo. The Kwantung Army took the initiative. Ambitious programs were set in motion to develop railways and ports; coal, iron, and light metals; hydroelectric resources, farm lands, and forests. Even cotton cultivation found its place among the five-year plans. Before the "Incident" Japanese investment in Manchuria was valued at 1,700 million yen, nearly half of it in the securities of the South Manchuria Railway Company and its subsidiaries.[24] This sum more than doubled during the next seven years,[25] reaching 3,600 million yen at the end of 1938. Investments in North China had risen meantime to about 600 million yen.[26] How much went simultaneously into Korea, Formosa, and the other colonies, or was accumulated out of existing enterprise there, is not known. (See above, page 261.) One estimate puts the net return of profits and interest from Korea and Formosa to Japan at 213 million yen a year from 1936 to 1939.[27]

Meanwhile the Empire served as an expanding job frontier, especially for white-collar workers. It attracted hundreds of thousands of Japanese males into civilian employment overseas, not to mention the soldiers required to garrison it and prepare for its

[24] The Foreign Affairs Association of Japan, *The Japan Year Book, 1939-40*, Tokyo, 1939, p. 1007. In the rest of China (including Hongkong) Japanese *business* investments came to only about 650 million yen. Nearly 30% consisted of textile mills, by which Japanese textile interests covered themselves to some extent against the loss of exports occasioned by developing Chinese competition in the cheaper grades of yarn and piece goods. See C. F. Remer, *Foreign Investments in China*, New York, 1933, pp. 470-95.

[25] The Japanese government's Bureau of Manchukuo Affairs estimated new Japanese investment in Manchuria at 1,950 million yen from 1932 through 1938. *Oriental Economist*, vol. vii, no. 3, March 1940, p. 153. There are various ambiguities in the figures, particularly as a measure of the outflow of capital from Japan Proper. Some funds originated locally, and others were never actually remitted as money balances or goods.

[26] According to a study of the South Manchuria Railway Company, translated and published by the Secretariat, Institute of Pacific Relations, *Industrial Japan*, New York, 1941, p. 215. Another estimate, by Hiroshi Higuchi, puts total Japanese investment in China Proper at 1,570 million yen on December 31, 1936, of which direct financing of business enterprise accounted for 840 million yen. *Contemporary Opinions on Current Topics*, no. 371, March 6, 1941, p. 4.

[27] U.S. Department of State, *The Place of Foreign Trade in the Japanese Economy*, Washington, 1946, vol. ii, pp. 122-23.

further extension. The grandiose scheme of the Overseas Ministry to colonize Manchuria with a million Japanese families never got beyond the experimental stage. By 1938, however, the Japanese population resident in all the overseas territories numbered almost 2 million people, of whom 600,000 had flocked to Manchuria.[28] Most of them were in business and professional pursuits.

Japan's external trade likewise reflected the boom in Empire areas. Korea, Formosa, and Manchuria absorbed 37% of her entire exports from 1933 to 1937. Largely they were cotton textiles, foodstuffs, chemicals, paper, and miscellaneous consumer wares. For the first time an important export outlet was also provided for Japanese iron and steel products, machinery, vehicles, and electrical goods. Construction activity in these areas, stimulated by internal inflation and by capital imports from Japan, reinforced the rapid development already taking place in Japanese heavy industry. Wherever political domination was secured, Japanese industrialists and traders automatically won a preferential position. Shipping companies enjoyed a virtual monopoly of intra-Empire trade. Even where political control was less than complete, *force majeure* might be employed to seize commercial or investment opportunities, as in the brazen, organized smuggling which went on in North China during 1933-37 under the euphemism of "special trade."

Some 29% of Japan's imports of goods were likewise furnished by Korea, Manchuria, and Formosa in the mid-thirties. The colonies had long been the chief source of her food imports. From them she now drew almost a quarter of her entire food supply.[29] Most important, the Empire furnished 15 to 20% of her total domestic and imported supply of rice, 75% of her sugar, and 12% of her fats and oils (mainly Korean fish oils and Manchurian beans). Here Japan also got 12% of her iron and steel supplies (in Fe content) and 10% of her coal. Karafuto was the source of about one fifth of her lumber and pulpwood. The list could be extended to include useful amounts of salt, phosphates, nonferrous metals, and many other minor items. (See Chapter 7.)

The truth is, however, that despite industrious efforts Japan was never able to satisfy from Empire sources, even including Manchuria, her chief overseas requirements for textile fibers, metals, petroleum, and fertilizers. In 1936 all the dependent areas together furnished no more than 15% of her total imports of industrial materials. And they supplied as much sugar and rice as they did only

28 Imperial Cabinet, Bureau of Statistics, *Nippon Teikoku Tōkei Nenkan*, no. 58, Tokyo, 1939, pp. 6-7, 60-61.

29 In brown rice equivalent. U.S. Department of State, *Japan's Food, Beverage and Tobacco Position*, Washington, 1948, tables 1-3.

because the Japanese government imposed discriminatory tariffs on purchases elsewhere. This is not to deny the natural wealth of these regions. For example, 40% of the Empire's prewar coal reserves were located in Manchuria, and another 14% in Karafuto and Korea. Nor can it be questioned that the opportunity afforded by conquest enabled Japanese enterprise to develop these resources and tie them into the economy of the home islands on a scale that would otherwise have been impossible. The real economic issue, putting aside moral considerations, is whether the gains were commensurate with the political risks and financial outlays which were the overhead of this pattern of overseas development.

Any such balance sheet of the economic gains and losses to Japan from imperial expansion is virtually impossible to construct. This is true even of the more modest Empire with which her Army and Navy were forced to content themselves before 1931. Still more is it true of Manchuria and the war in China. The bare facts of Japanese trade, investment, and employment in the colonies tell little of the real impact of political imperialism on her economic growth. They only describe the *de facto* dependence of the home islands on the Empire economy. They leave one to guess what commerce and enterprise might have developed in the absence of political control, or whether more productive employment for Japanese resources might not have been found elsewhere.

Much of the investment and trade in the Empire was beneficial economically to both the Japanese and the indigenous peoples. But some would have grown up anyway. And a good deal clearly represented a diversion of resources from more profitable channels through State subsidy, preferential tariffs, and coercion. Probably, equivalent supplies of Japanese-type rice could not have been developed elsewhere on as favorable terms; perhaps this is also true of coal, lumber, fish, and other products. The calculation of benefit would depend on how much of the over-all cost of the colonial establishment one threw into the balance. Certainly Japan's major trading stake lay in multilateral world trade. Her *economic* interest argued for combatting the rise of economic nationalism, not contributing to its spread.

Following armed conquest, of course, rich assets in the form of mines, railroads, factories, and trading opportunities could be gained by outright seizure. The Japanese are not the only people to show that this can sometimes be a lucrative business even in the complex world of modern industry. But how balance such short-term gains against the prolonged military effort involved in winning an empire? Or the losses to legitimate trade and investment which came from antagonizing first the neighboring peoples of East Asia and finally

the rest of the world.[30] If the logical outcome was to spread war
and destruction through China, and then through the entire Far
East, as indeed it was, then the verdict seems clear.

Very likely the whole program of empire building by prewar
Japanese governments contributed little to the secular growth of
the country's productive powers before 1938. Such contributions as
it made probably consisted chiefly in the general stimulus given to
industrialization by war and armament expenditure, noted earlier.
For this purpose government borrowing and spending alone, however, might better have been directed along more productive lines.
Mainly empire building increased national power, not economic
well-being. It was probably so intended by those military leaders
blessed with economic sophistication—were there any? One finds
it difficult to see what economic gains accrued which were substantial enough to offset the costs, even if no great war had resulted in the end. Like Germany before 1914, Japan probably
profited a good deal more from gaining access to the markets and
materials of other colonial empires (especially the British) without
having to shoulder the cost of developing and administering them.[31]

The Manchurian adventure in particular needs closer study, even
to see what its value was ultimately for Japan's war effort. Such
economic gains as it brought in the meantime were probably confined largely to the fillip given Japanese heavy industry by rising
State expenditure and private investment. But so far as this was
desirable it could have been achieved in other and more productive
ways, as remarked above. It represented in good part a tremendous
effort to build a military base on the continent which would be
securely under the control of the Army and which would free
Japan from dependence on foreign supplies of essential war materials. Much of the investment was questionable on economic
grounds, and would have been even if she had managed to retain
possession.[32] As it turned out, it was lost to the last penny, along

[30] Chinese boycotts of Japanese goods occurred sporadically from 1915 on, mainly
as a political protest against military aggression. After the Manchurian "Incident"
they became really serious. Japan's share of Chinese imports had risen from 14%
in 1904 to about 25% in the mid-twenties. From there is dropped to 14% in 1932,
in good measure because of the boycott. (C. F. Remer, *A Study of Chinese Boycotts*,
Baltimore, 1933, p. 235.) By 1936 many prominent businessmen in Japan were
discreetly urging a political settlement with China as the only way to revive profitable economic relations. But the Kwantung Army had other plans.

[31] This argument does not imply that serious dislocations would not result if
long-established economic relations within the Empire were destroyed by its breakup. Events after 1945 testify to the contrary.

[32] Here I may convict myself of the myopia about which Yosuke Matsuoka, architect of Japan's grandiose dreams in Manchuria, once complained. "The economists
of Europe and America," he once said, "are too anxious about money in the safe,
and are too little concerned with future developments. Such theories can not
be applied in the Orient." *Transpacific*, October 21, 1937, p. 17.

with the entire colonial stake which Japan had been seventy years in building.

This whole argument obviously rests on the premise that the Japanese were free to participate in a system of multilateral world trade, without undue fears for their national security in terms of access to overseas markets and raw materials. Such an approach may seem ingenuous today. Yet this system largely prevailed until the thirties. If it then progressively deteriorated, the Japanese could blame no one more than themselves. Actually their foreign trade expanded spectacularly until 1937; then it was crippled more by events in Japan than by those elsewhere. Meanwhile the spread of restrictions abroad was an ominous portent. In view of Japan's economic needs and her military capabilities, however, her real economic interest still lay in opposing the forces working in this direction, and making the best of them, not in reinforcing a tendency in the world so inimical to her future.

Tariff Protection. Much more straightforward in its effects, though also difficult to evaluate, was Japan's use of the protective tariff to foster industrialization.

Until 1899, resort to tariff protection was barred by the treaty agreements of 1858 and 1866 with the foreign Powers. The latter agreement bound Japanese import and export duties unilaterally at very low rates for the next thirty years. Even the recovery of tariff autonomy in the nineties still left treaty restrictions on the duties applying to many items. Rates were generally no higher than 10 to 15% until the general tariff revision of 1911.

The Meiji governments were thus compelled to rely more extensively than might otherwise have been the case on direct aids to new industries in the form of low-interest loans, dividend guarantees, bounties, and technical assistance. Doubtless this practice was not without its advantages. For direct subsidies of this sort are less likely to become indiscriminate and self-perpetuating than are disguised taxes on the public in the form of price-raising duties. The sheltered industry is more apt to be required sooner or later to justify continued aid. However this may be, it is interesting that early Japanese progress along the road of industrialization was made with little tariff protection from foreign competition. Even the whole range of alternative aids extended by the government was modest by comparison with the tariff walls and exchange controls which have become commonplace in other newly industrializing countries during more recent times.

After gaining her tariff independence in 1899 Japan embarked on a definite policy of industrial protection. Certain rates continued to be bound by convention until 1923, but general upward revisions were effected in 1911 and 1926. Particularly after World War I tariff policy became decidedly protectionist. High protection was extended to industries of strategic importance like iron and steel and dyestuffs.[33] It was applied as well to other factory trades which mushroomed during the war, and even to natural resource industries like lumber, tobacco, and copper.

Except in the strong export fields—notably silk and cotton goods —most of Japan's major industries were protectionist in sentiment. Her agricultural interests became no less so, as foreign and colonial competition came into the Japanese market. Confronted with this familiar issue of agricultural protection in an industrializing economy, the government followed a middle course. It admitted increasing amounts of colonial rice and sugar, while applying high duties on foreign foodstuffs for internal consumption. Cheap foreign rice, for example, had to pay a duty of 1 yen per 100 *kin*. The price of sugar was pushed higher in Japan than almost anywhere else in the world. Sometimes consumer groups were effective in resisting tariff increases. But this was apt to be true only where, as in the case of fertilizer materials, a well-organized body like the Imperial Agricultural Association could muster strong opposition in the Diet.

In the 1926 tariff revision the declared policy of the Minseito government was to grant little or no protection to scarce raw materials or to daily necessities. (Certain exceptions in practice have already been noted.) On the other hand, substantial aid was accorded to industries like the wool, rayon, machinery, and chemical industries regarded as having a promising future. It was also extended to others whose outlook was more problematical. Already under the tariff law of 1924 duties of 100% had been imposed on 123 items classed as luxuries. These were consumer goods which might otherwise have been purchased abroad by the urban middle class. When the more liberal Hamaguchi Cabinet assumed power in 1929 it proposed a lowering of rates on certain industries which it termed a "drag on industrial development." This move was largely abortive. With the onset of the depression the clamor from producing interests led instead to a steep upward revision. Despite the increased protection already afforded by the depreciation of the yen in 1931-32, rates were raised on chemicals, metal manufactures,

---

[33] When commenting on the League of Nations draft convention of 1925 for the abolition of import and export prohibitions and restrictions, Japan was at pains to reserve the right of a state to apply restrictions "to safeguard the maintenance of industries, the creation of which is or may be required by the vital interests of the State." League of Nations, *Abolition of Import and Export Prohibitions and Restrictions*, Geneva, 1927, p. 29.

lumber, foodstuffs, and other items. A surtax of 35% was also imposed on all other imports dutiable at specific rates.

Thus the 1924 and 1926 tariff schedules remained in force with upward modification through the next decade. Under the former a 100% duty was applied on about 100 items. They included (in 1930) vegetables and fruits; beer, soap, and perfume; certain leather and fur manufactures; shoes and many types of clothing and textile specialties; precious stones; mirrors, cutlery, watches, and clocks; phonographs, films, and toys. Under the 1926 act, duties ranging from 5 to 50% were applied on 647 classes of goods enumerated in the general tariff schedule. Where these were imposed on an ad valorem basis and not superseded by the 100% luxury tariff, they ran mostly from 30 to 50% on such items as piece goods, copper, metal manufactures, automobiles, musical instruments, and sporting goods. On cigars, cigarettes, and cut tobacco the duty was 355%. The infant rayon industry was given a duty of 27% in 1926; wheat farmers a duty of 40%. In 1927 and again in 1932 the iron and steel industry, already sheltered by tariffs and by certain exemptions from income and business taxes, received additional aid. After 1929 duties on lumber were raised several times at the behest of lumber interests. As a rule, however, the more advanced the stage of manufacture the greater the degree of protection. For example, tariffs on refined petroleum products were applied to encourage the home refining of imported crudes. Similarly, the progress of the textile industries toward finer weaves and finishes had long been encouraged by protection against British and French goods in such categories.

Tariff protection was further reinforced by the practice of government agencies in "buying Japanese" whenever possible. This administrative preference for home goods, common among most governments, was especially important to various branches of the Japanese metallurgical, equipment, and chemical industries because of the prominence of government agencies as buyers of such products. The historian of military industries in Japan, Ushisaburo Kobayashi, writes as follows of the system of indirect protection through home preference: "As soon as the system of military industry was put in order after the Restoration, the government issued instructions to the military and naval authorities to the following effect: The authorities should not refuse to use home products for materials required in military and naval industries merely on account of inconvenience or poor appearance even though they may be inferior in quality to foreign products, provided it did not lessen the accuracy and strength of manufactured materials. Home products should be used except when the prices of domestic and foreign articles differ so much that it incurs a great loss to the national finance when they are used in large quantities."[34]

The policy of preferential buying appears to have been followed consistently by the armed forces, though it did not deter them from making heavy purchases abroad where Japanese technology was markedly inferior. They themselves had a direct interest, of course, in building up domestic sources of finished munitions, equipment, and essential materials. This was insurance against war. The same policy was followed in considerable degree by the Imperial Railways and the Ministry of Communications. An important support was thus provided to Japanese manufacturers of steel ships, locomotives, trucks, aircraft, electrical apparatus, and a variety of chemicals and machinery. For years, too, the armed forces furnished the chief market for the woolen industry. In the aggregate, government orders never accounted for a large share of the total demand for factory goods in Japan. But they were a lucrative source of business for the metalworking and metal-using trades in particular. And they exerted a constant pressure toward qualitative improvements which would meet the specifications of competitive products available abroad.

The Japanese have complained bitterly, and with reason, concerning the high tariff walls erected in prewar years against Japanese manufactures abroad. In the United States, for example, as quickly as cheap manufactures from Japan offered any competitive threat to even a small segment of an American industry, they were apt to be shut off promptly.[35] Some Japanese apologists, in support of these complaints, have made much of Japan's own "free trade policy." They point out that less than half of Japan's imports during the interwar period were dutiable; moreover, that duties collected ranged only between 10 and 20% of the total value of imports. Such statistics prove nothing, of course. Where the demand for an item is elastic, a sharp tariff increase may virtually exclude it from the list of imports, thus reducing rather than increasing the ratio of dutiable imports to the total. It may also reduce rather than increase the ratio of duties collected to gross imports in the same manner. For example, if a country's tariff were so high as to prohibit all imports except one commodity, which was left on the free list, all imports entering the country would then be duty-free. One would hardly call this a low tariff!

---

[34] *Military Industries of Japan*, New York: Oxford, 1922, p. 167.
[35] See the author's *Trade and Trade Rivalry between the United States and Japan*, New York: Institute of Pacific Relations, 1936; Philip W. Wright, *The American Tariff and Oriental Trade*, New York, 1931; and numerous reports of the U.S. Tariff Commission on Japanese goods in the American market.

The fact is that Japan herself became strongly protectionist after 1922. Her own industrial tariff now invited comparison to that of nations ordinarily regarded as highly protectionist. In 1925, even before the upward revision of 1926, Japanese rates averaged 25 to 30% on manufactured goods. By comparison, even the "high" tariffs of Australia and the United States averaged no more than 35 to 40%.[36]

Many Japanese rates were wholly or partially ineffective, it is true, owing to the favorable position of Japanese producers in the domestic market. The main structure of Japanese industry as it developed after 1900 did not depend on government protection in large degree. However, tariffs and indirect preferences were employed to accelerate the development of a number of factory industries as they progressed through successive stages of technological maturity. Along with other governmental aids, they continued to sustain certain key industries, especially the sugar, chemical, and metalworking industries, at a level well beyond that which unrestricted foreign competition would have permitted. And high "luxury" duties, imposed originally to protect the balance of payments, served to shut out appreciable amounts of consumer goods which the Japanese public would otherwise have purchased abroad.

This last-mentioned point helps to explain one marked characteristic of the Japanese import trade in prewar years. Finished consumer goods (other than foodstuffs) were imported in amounts which seem surprisingly small in view of the rise in Japanese wealth and income. After the turn of the century they were consistently less than 10% of gross imports from foreign countries. After World War I they were hardly more than 5%. For this there were various reasons: e.g., the low living standards of the masses, the propensity to save among upper income groups, the cultural gap between consumer tastes in Japan and those in the West, the availability of cheaper factory goods at home. But the tariff was another restraint operating to keep out Western-style goods increasingly in demand by middle-class people. It operated similarly to limit foodstuffs from overseas, except from the colonies. Tariffs on consumer goods thus helped to reserve the home market largely for both the Japanese industrialist and the Japanese farmer, freeing foreign exchange resources for the purchase of machinery and industrial materials. In both fields tariffs on consumer goods weighed most directly on real wage rates in the cities. However, they probably hastened industrial capital formation in the process. They made it that much easier for Japan to industrialize rapidly with little resort to foreign borrow-

[36] League of Nations, *Tariff Level Indices*, Geneva, 1927, pp. 16-17.

ing, despite her heavy dependence on machinery and materials from abroad.

On balance there can be little doubt that protection in home and colonial markets helped to extend the range and diversity of Japanese manufacturing. The older industries—silk and cotton textiles, and small-scale consumer trades in great variety—needed little shelter from foreign competition over and above that provided by cultural differences and transport costs. But many newer industries requiring radical departures from traditional techniques and a large market for economical operation certainly benefited from tariff assistance, at least for a period of years. Where Japanese technology continued to lag, or the market was too small in any case, they continued to depend on government aid for survival. Other branches like the basic types of chemicals, electrical apparatus, and industrial machinery eventually reached a point of independence, particularly after the depreciation of the yen in 1931. In short, the classic "infant industry" argument found its justifications, even though the Japanese Diet—like other parliaments—was motivated largely by less technical considerations.

Whether the aggregate scale of industrial output was enlarged by the tariff is more problematical. In some degree it probably was, for the reason just mentioned. But industrial protection served in part merely to shift resources from one group of industries, especially the export industries, to fields which would otherwise have been supplied by imports.

It is still more difficult to say what contribution was made by the whole rather indiscriminate system of protection to the aggregate growth of Japanese national income, or its distribution. This would involve a close study of its results in a score of natural resource and manufacturing industries. When the tariffs on farm products, lumber, minerals, and manufactures are all taken into account, it would appear that in good part the effect of each was cancelled out by that of the others after 1922, except as all of them served to restrict specialization as between Japan and the rest of the world. In this latter regard they came in conflict with other measures being applied concurrently by the government to expand overseas commerce and shipping. These measures have attracted a good deal more attention. Considering the whole range of trade, shipping, and colonial policies together, however, one may question whether their net effect was not to curtail rather than expand overseas economic relations during the interwar period.

Shipping Subsidies. It remains to mention the field where State subsidy was employed with conspicuous success to create one of the great industries of modern Japan. An aptitude in maritime affairs came naturally to the Japanese, an island people, despite their long and enforced seclusion during the seventeenth and eighteenth centuries. It is remarkable, nevertheless, with what facility they took over the engineering technology and large-scale organization required for a modern merchant marine. To replace the small sailing junk with steam and steel was essential to the building of national power. From the early days, therefore, shipping and shipbuilding received the earnest attention of the Meiji authorities. Their attitude is reminiscent of the solicitude with which Britain built her merchant marine in the eighteenth century; even Adam Smith approved of the Navigation Acts.

The rise of modern Japan as a seafaring nation is sketched elsewhere in this study. (See Chapters 1 and 7.) Water transport is hardly less important for her in internal than in external commerce. The early growth of domestic trade after 1868 created an immediate demand for coastwise shipping. Even higher priority attached to the need for military transport in quelling internal disorders and embarking on foreign excursions, of which the first was the expedition to Formosa in 1874. Thereafter overseas shipping operations were steadily extended under the impetus of expanding foreign trade, the wars with China and Russia, and the unremitting patronage of the government. Already by 1913 Japan had become one of the world's important maritime nations. She now boasted a steam fleet of 1.5 million tons, most of it purchased abroad. Her own shipwards were still dependent on foreign materials and machinery. Yet they had now reached the point where they could turn out annually 50,000 tons of vessels of over 1,000 tons.

World War I provided a golden opportunity for further expansion. The Japanese merchant fleet almost doubled in size, as freight rates soared to fabulous levels. After the Armistice the world-wide surplus of tonnage arose to plague the shipping business in Japan, as elsewhere. Japanese operators managed nevertheless to retain a considerable part of their newly won gains. Their increased strength enabled them to secure a strong competitive position on certain key routes.

The case of the Japan-India trade, for example, is instructive. As far back as 1896 the Nippon Yusen Kaisha, backed by Japanese cotton-spinners, had forced its way into the Bombay-Japan shipping conference. The Peninsular & Oriental Steam Navigation Company, which then held 66% of the carrying trade, was forced to cede 18% to the Japanese. By 1913 the latter held 40% and the P & O 28%. The European war left the field to the Japanese. In 1921 a new agreement eliminated the continental European lines altogether and awarded 66% to the Japanese and 33% to the

British firm. In 1929 the Japanese share was again raised, to 80%, leaving the P & O only 20%.[37] Two thirds of all Japan's foreign trade was now carried in her own ships. Vessels flying the Japanese flag had become a familiar sight in the great ports of the world, and of course were the first-line auxiliary of the Imperial Navy.

It was in the early decades, before 1915, that State subventions were of particular importance to the growth of the Japanese merchant marine. Initially the Meiji governments tried a variety of expedients. They built and purchased vessels; they operated them themselves; they gave them outright or leased them to subsidized concerns like the Mitsubishi Company. By 1881 a decision appears to have been reached against government ownership, even in this strategic field. Instead, numerous small private concerns, most of them operating at a loss, were consolidated into several big companies with government backing. In 1884 the Osaka Shoshen Kaisha was formed and a year later the Nippon Yusen Kaisha. With continued guarantees and subsidies they extended shipping services from Vladivostok all the way to Bombay during the next decade. The NYK provided much of the tonnage requisitioned by the government for the war with China. With the help of over 200 foreign officers, it also operated additional ships purchased abroad by the government for the purpose.[38] Shortly afterward it pioneered the services to Europe, the United States, and Australia.

With the foundations now laid, the government decided on a more permanent and comprehensive program of shipping support. This was embodied in the navigation- and construction-bounty laws of 1896. State aids to Japanese shipping thereafter may be summarized as follows:

a. Foreign shipping companies, already barred from trade between the principal Japanese ports since 1894, were excluded altogether from the coastwise trade in 1911, unless on a continuous voyage from a foreign country. Similar laws were applied to the colonies. In foreign trade and travel as well, a good deal of business automatically accrued to Japanese companies through the administrative preference given them by government agencies. (Such pref-

[37] W. L. Hichens, "Anglo-Japanese Competition in the Shipping Trade," *International Affairs*, vol. xviii, no. 5, September-October, 1939, pp. 662-63. Not the least unsatisfactory aspect of the British position was the fact that they were forced to accept a schedule of rates negotiated between the Japanese shipping firms and the Japan Cotton Spinners' Association.

[38] Again in the war with Russia the NYK placed 400,000 tons of vessels at the disposal of the Army and Navy. Its official history points with pride to one of them, the *Shinano Maru*, a converted cruiser which first sighted the Russian Baltic fleet steaming toward Vladivostok and warned Admiral Togo in time for him to prepare for his decisive victory. Ten other NYK ships were blown up and sunk at the entrance to Port Arthur to block the channel.

erences must also have prevailed widely among trading and industrial firms affiliated with the big shipping operators, although some have denied this.)

b. Operating subsidies in the form of postal contracts and navigation bounties were awarded annually to Japanese companies under the laws of 1896 and 1909. Characteristically, navigation subsidies were restricted under the latter law to vessels of 3,000 tons and 15 knots or more, less than fifteen years old. A differential was set up in favor of newer, faster ships, especially if built in Japan and according to government specifications. The larger companies were thus helped to extend their ocean services and modernize their fleets. Jesse Saugstad gives figures purporting to show that from 1900 to 1914 government subsidies provided 77% of the total net earnings of all Japanese shipping companies with an authorized capital over 300,000 yen. Earnings totalled 158 million yen, of which subsidies furnished 122 million.[39] The war boom after 1915 eliminated the need for such subventions, although they were subsequently revived at an annual average of 11 to 12 million yen. In the later years they were a minor factor in the competitive strength of the Japanese firms. They went mostly to the NYK and OSK for services on the trans-Pacific and more distant routes.

c. Construction bounties were also paid in various forms to Japanese shipyards. From 1896 to 1917 they were offered by the government on ships of a certain minimum size. Higher rates were awarded for larger and speedier types and for those using Japanese equipment and materials. Customs duties were likewise remitted in 1906 on imported materials going into ship construction. As noted above, Japanese-built vessels were also favored in the award of navigation bounties after 1899.

Only small sums were used in these building subsidies, and they do not seem to have been very effective. It was the wartime shortage after 1914 which first boomed the industry. Launchings of steam vessels rose from 52,000 tons in 1909-13 to 646,000 tons in 1919. The earlier subsidy scheme was replaced in 1917 with measures to encourage the steel industry, mainly through bounties on the use of Japanese steel in ship construction. After the war, however, this failed to overcome other, adverse circumstances in the shipyards. The industry sank back into the doldrums, despite sporadic government measures to stimulate it with low-interest loans and other financial aids.

d. The spectacular advance in Japanese shipbuilding and fleet modernization came with the expansion of trade after 1931 and the

39 U.S. Bureau of Foreign and Domestic Commerce, Trade Promotion Series, No. 129, *Shipping and Shipbuilding Subsidies*, Washington, 1932, p. 326.

scrap-and-build programs adopted by the government in 1932. Some 11 million yen was spent on the first scheme, by which 2 tons of shipping over twenty-five years old had to be scrapped for every new ton built in Japan under subsidy. Subsidies were confined to ships of over 4,000 tons and with a speed of 13.5 knots or better. About 20% of the construction cost was paid by the government. This program, and the two which followed it in 1935 and 1936, led to the scrapping of some 500,000 tons of old shipping between 1932 and 1937. The old tonnage was replaced with forty-eight new ships of 300,000 tons. By 1937 Japan had a steam and motor fleet of 4 million tons, of which 3 million represented vessels over 3,000 tons. Half of these larger vessels were capable of 14 knots or better. With more tonnage under five years than any other national fleet, the Japanese merchant marine was thus handsomely refurbished to engage in world shipping competition, and to serve the Army and Navy in the great war which soon followed. (For further discussion of Japanese shipping in coastal and foreign trade, see pages 348-51.)

In summary, State subsidies and other encouragements helped significantly to found the Japanese shipping industry and carry it through its early period of growth. Without them the merchant marine could not possibly have doubled its tonnage each decade from 1880 to 1910, as it did. After that financial aids helped to enlarge the profits of the big operators, to force the pace of modernization, and to influence the design and the employment of vessels in accordance with considerations of national policy.

In the later years, however, Japanese costs in building and operating ships were below British and American costs. Cheap labor and advances in engineering now put Japan in a strong competitive position, especially after the fall of the yen.[40] Other advantages accrued from the concentration of control over the industry, and its close affiliation with related activities. The great Nippon Yusen Kaisha and Osaka Shoshen Kaisha alone grew to possess over a million tons of shipping between them. The Mitsubishi trust controlled the former, while Sumitomo had large interests in the latter. The Mitsuis had their own big steamship company. The big combines were equally prominent in shipbuilding; they also supplied shipbuilding materials and fuel; and they originated and financed much of the cargo carried in their vessels. These interlacing con-

---

[40] See U.S. Tariff Commission, *Japanese Trade Studies: The Shipping Industry of Japan*, Washington, 1945; also Imperial Shipping Committee, *British Shipping in the Orient*, London, 1939. The later concludes that the diesel cargo liners built in Japan under the scrap-and-build scheme in 1933-34 cost only half what they would have cost in the United Kingdom. Other Japanese advantages included building and operating subsidies, cheap capital for ship construction (3.7%), and operating costs for crew and provisions which were only half the British figure.

nections were a source of strength in world competition. They also facilitated the close control maintained by the government.

Japan's position at the crossroads of East Asiatic trade, combined with the factors enumerated above, thus enabled her to achieve a commanding position in the shipping of the Orient during the interwar period. Probably there were still a few ocean routes, distant or little used, where continued government subsidy to operators was warranted, even on economic grounds. But the chief justification which remained was the vital importance of a large and swift merchant marine as a weapon of national power. It must be added that this point was fully borne out in the Pacific war. Japan won and held a far-flung empire during 1941-44 largely by maritime power. Equally, once the Allied counteroffensive against her shipping began to close off the sea lanes upon which her economy depended she was doomed to defeat.

Group Interests and Public Policy:
Farmer, Worker, Businessman

Several other broad areas of public policy must enter into any survey of the role of the State in Japan's prewar economic development. By comparison with those already discussed, they are areas where in the main the government assumed only limited responsibilities and exercised little direct control. But its general attitude was nonetheless of great importance. One area was the organization of agriculture; a second was the protection of industrial labor; and the third the control of business organization and practice.

Agrarian Policies. A prominent feature of Europe's transition from mediaeval to modern times was the breakup of the old agrarian order and its replacement by new forms of proprietorship and new modes of production. The complex adjustments entailed in this change were long a major preoccupation of the developing national state. The statute books, the technological history, and the political struggles of Western Europe from 1500 to 1850 were taken up in no small measure with the emancipation of agriculture and the agriculturist from the bonds of feudalism and their adaptation to a new capitalistic order.

It may seem surprising that Japan's emergence from what is commonly described as "feudalism" should not have necessitated and brought about a similar transformation, or required a similar mass of legislation and regulation, in the realm of agriculture. The difference was not that European statesmen were solicitous for the well-being of the peasant, or concerned to assure their nation's food supply, while the Meiji leaders were indifferent. Nor was it that Japanese farming quickly sank to minor importance in the industrializing economy. On the contrary, as emphasized in earlier chapters, its expansion furnished much of the increment in national wealth and income for forty years, and much of the annual revenue going into new capital formation and military expenditure. Even after World War I, when its growth tapered off, it continued to provide the bulk of the country's food supply, while occupying nearly half of the working population.

This historical contrast takes one into broad issues which run well beyond the bounds of this study. For one thing, "feudalism" is a term better used to describe a pattern of political than one of economic organization. Even in political structure the term obscures wide differences among European societies, and still more between Japan and Europe, Tokugawa Japan, in particular, had achieved a fairly high degree of political centralization. And already by the eighteenth century the rise of internal commerce and handicrafts had developed to the point where the money economy had made heavy inroads on the old agrarian society.

Merchant capitalism would probably have advanced even more rapidly had it not been for two circumstances, among others. One was the fact that Tokugawa Japan, partly by the accident of geography and partly by the reactionary policy of seclusion, was cut off from the stimulus of commercial expansion afforded by international trade between peoples of diverse resources and cultures. For European peoples this was provided in the Mediterranean, Baltic, and North Sea regions, and later the New World. Another handicap probably was the fact that the Japanese feudal nobility and their retainers lived mainly in castle towns and cities, where their rice revenues drawn from the countryside sustained the merchant and artisan class. The latter found it more difficult as a result to emancipate itself from the old political and social order, with its contempt for mercantile pursuits, than its counterparts in mediaeval Europe. In Flanders during the late Middle Ages, for example, the town developed as the bastion of the rising independent bourgeoisie against the rural aristocracy.[41] In Japanese society the merchant remained in a more subordinate position, under close political control, until the nineteenth century.[42]

[41] Henri Pirenne, *Economic and Social History of Medieval Europe*, New York, undated, esp. chaps. 2, 6.

[42] By contrast with China, however, the merchants of Tokugawa Japan were barred from easy entry into the class which held prestige and power in the old order. Control over income from land, and access to a classical education, were not enough to win admission to an aristocracy of birth. Talent and capital tended more largely than 'in China to remain in mercantile pursuits, and to build up permanent commitments in this realm. Yet many a Tokugawa merchant and moneylender became a landowner and some even entered the *samurai* ranks by family adoption.

It is worth recalling that in eighteenth century France and England, too, a success-

More pertinent to our immediate concern, Japanese agriculture had long differed radically from that of Britain, northern France, and Germany in its organization. Neither widespread serfdom, nor the open-field system with its complex arrangement of common rights, nor joint and compulsory cultivation of the lord's demesne was characteristic of Japan.[43] Land was far more closely cultivated than in mediaeval Europe, where a peasant family required 30 acres or so to maintain itself. Terrain and climate, together with the greater density of the agricultural population, made for reliance on intensive rice growing by small farm operators. Labor and manure were supplied independently by the farmer and his family. Irrigation and roads might call for village cooperation and the local *corvée*, but not the close communalism of the European manor. By comparison with most of Europe there was little stock raising, for either food, clothing, or fertilizer. The sea was the source of animal protein. Cultivated land was fairly evenly divided among millions of small cultivators who held a qualified title to the soil— subject, of course, to heavy seignorial dues and other lesser obligations. The peasant of 1868 was bred in a tradition of self-reliant responsibility for managing his chief means of livelihood, the small family farm, even though his overlords might never have permitted him to retain more than a half of its produce for his own use.

When Japan entered the modern period, therefore, she was not confronted with either the necessity or the opportunity for a sweeping revolution in the techniques and organization of agriculture. This had both favorable and unfavorable aspects.

On the one hand, the heritage of peasant industry, family independence in farming, and village government was a real asset in making the transition to modern capitalism. It helped no doubt to mitigate those other traits of individual subordination and defer-

---

ful manufacturer often aspired to climb to gentry status. The elder Sir Robert Peel, for example, first made a fortune as a calico printer. On contributing £10,000 to the State in 1797, following an emergency appeal from Pitt, he was made a baron, and took as his motto *Industria*. His son went on to become the great Tory liberal who led the opposition to the Reform Bill of 1832, "that Magna Charta of the English middle class, which, in the realm of politics, crowned the industrial revolution." Paul Mantoux describes the England of 1700 in terms which, with certain modifications, could also be applied to premodern Japan and China: "Whilst the nobility [in China, the bureaucracy] was trying to get rich by trade, the merchant aristocracy was dreaming of that power and ascendancy which, in a country where the land system has long remained so traditional, is only acquired by the ownership of land." *The Industrial Revolution in the Eighteenth Century*, rev. edn., New York, 1928, p. 138.

[43] See the writings of K. Asakawa, for example, "Agriculture in Japanese History: A General Survey," *The Economic History Review*, vol. II, no. 1, January 1929, pp. 81-92.

ence to authority which might otherwise have had a much more stifling effect on economic initiative.

The Japanese were also spared the long, turbulent struggle which was required in Europe to abolish compulsory labor, common cultivation of the arable land, and common rights to pasture and wasteland. In northern France, it will be recalled, the separation of the demesne set in during the fourteenth century. The process was resisted and reversed in the eighteenth century, however, and not finally confirmed until the French Revolution. In Prussia the *corvée* survived until after 1850. In Meiji Japan, by comparison, it was comparatively easy to do away with the remnants of heritable subjection and bodily servitude, to abolish or continue common rights to forests, meadows, and fishing grounds, and to establish a system of proprietor and tenant farming based on private ownership. Landlord-tenant relationships, and the whole social structure of the village, retained the quasi-feudal stamp of tradition in many respects. But no complicated tangle of legal rights and obligations stood in the way of commercializing agriculture, or commuting farm rents and taxes to individual obligations fixed in money.

On the other hand, if the old system was not so rigid in Japan, neither were the pressures to change so great. The chief demand for agrarian reorganization of a limited type came from the young bureaucrats of the new Meiji regime. They wanted political unity under the emperor, and adequate fiscal revenue. This led almost at once to the abolition of the old territorial *han*, and the pensioning off of the aristocracy. One of their first concerns was to create a national system of land taxes paid in money. As a necessary concomitant of these changes they proclaimed freedom of occupation and domicile, and the full right of private property in land.[44] Such reforms effected little immediate improvement in the economic status

[44] Beginning in 1872, peasant cultivators themselves received title to most farm lands, except for those held by the Imperial Family, temples, and shrines. The farmer was also granted a new freedom to grow such crops as he wished, or, if he chose, to alienate his land in perpetuity and migrate to the city. In the case of mortgaged land, however, title was awarded to the mortgagee, usually a merchant. Elsewhere, too, the small peasant often lost out, either in the initial distribution, or subsequently through his inability to pay taxes and cope with the insecurities of a money economy. Very early it appears that 30% or more of the cultivated area was already under tenant farming. The necessity to pay taxes on other land under private ownership led to acquisition by the government of a large area of forest and meadow land once held by villages in common or by the nobility. Nobutaka Ike describes this also as "a not unimportant loss" to the peasant, who now had to buy fuel, building materials, and fodder. "Taxation and Land Ownership in the Westernization of Japan," *Journal of Economic History*, vol. vii, no. 2, November 1947, pp. 168-69. Since stock raising was of little importance, however, the Japanese countryside did not experience the long conflict over common meadows and pastures which, in R. H. Tawney's words, "kept European villages simmering for over a thousand years."

of the peasants, except for the more enterprising families of the upper stratum. Many were soon worse off, losing their security on the land and certain common rights previously enjoyed. An incipient agrarian movement for more radical change was easily suppressed, however. Within the village the more prosperous landowning households, whose superior status often carried back for generations, continued to retain a dominant position. Social differences came to depend more and more on property. But they were still reinforced by the head-and-branch family system and by semifeudal obligations of leadership and submission.

Even had the social structure been more brittle, so great was the density of the rural population relative to arable land and capital that little scope existed for the rise of capitalistic farming in Japan, as it appeared in England and the Low Countries once the encumbrances of feudalism were cleared away. Already in 1868 the total population numbered about 225 per square mile. This was more than twice the density prevailing in Europe prior to the Industrial Revolution. Moreover, hardly more than 15% of the land area of the Japanese islands can be regarded as cultivable. Most of it had long been tilled intensively by peasant families averaging no more than 2 to 3 acres apiece. Opportunities for new forms of enterprise, other than mere landlordism, had to be sought elsewhere in the main.

As a result the Meiji "Renovation" wrought remarkably little change in the life of the average peasant, or his system of cultivation. This did not deprive Japanese industry, as it subsequently developed, of a steady flow of labor from the villages. The crescendo of population growth took care of that. Nor did it prevent at least a doubling in agricultural output over the next half century. But it barred the road to any revolutionary advance in farm productivity, which would have required a sharp reduction of population on the land. It thus prolonged the poverty and self-sufficiency of rural life, and applied a persistent drag on industrial advance.

Within this limiting framework, post-Restoration governments took certain steps to raise agricultural output and adapt it to the changing needs of industrialization. Various technical aids and rural public works were fostered by the national government, and by local authorities as they gained in financial resources and experience. They helped to reclaim land, improved irrigation systems, and built roads and warehouses. In certain areas land was economized by readjusting and combining scattered farm strips more advantageously. Statutes were passed to encourage village fishing associations and agricultural cooperatives. After 1890 the State developed a network of agricultural experiment stations and other technical agencies which tackled problems of land management, insect control, better seeds, fertilizer practice, etc.[45] In certain lines impressive achievements were scored, as in silkworm breeding. Similarly, a program of scientific conservation was developed on Japanese forest lands, nearly 60% of which remained under the ownership of the crown and various public authorities.

No other public expenditure was more productive than this technical aid to agriculture, so far as it went. Small-scale but pervasive improvements in agriculture served to raise the physical productivity of labor on Japanese farms by 50 to 75% in the prewar era, despite the lack of mechanization, the persisting shortage of capital, and inefficient forms of land tenure. As argued in Chapter 3, this was of first importance for the whole industrialization and growth of the Japanese economy.

Beyond such technical aids and modest capital assistance, however, the fate of agriculture and the agriculturist was consigned pretty much to the play of private interest and market competition through the Meiji era. Once the initial reforms affecting landownership and taxation were carried through, the issues of land tenure and distributive justice in the countryside were largely left aside, despite their importance for technical modernization. The tax burden remained heavy in relation to services received. Usury flourished through the countryside. And little was done to stop the growth of tenancy by public action to furnish cheap credit or other protective measures. The inefficiencies of the land tenure system were perpetuated by the failure to require written contracts which would give the tenant security and compensate him for permanent improvements. Farm prices remained at the mercy of the weather and the operations of the "free" market, where the hard-pressed peasant was always at a bargaining disadvantage.

In contrast to this pattern of agricultural policies was the careful conservation of forestry resources under State management. Here of course the problem was radically different. Over two thirds of Japan's forests came into the ownership of the Imperial Household, the national government, and the local authorities. Relatively few people were dependent upon them for their principal livelihood, and protective management was essential if this great national resource was not to be quickly depleted.

A strict system of forest regulation had long been a feature of the Shogunate and the daimiates in Tokugawa days. The Restoration was followed by a period of administrative confusion and reck-

[45] See Supreme Commander for the Allied Powers, GHQ, Natural Resources Section Report No. 59, *The Agricultural Experiment Stations of Japan*, Tokyo, 1946.

less overcutting, especially on private lands. By 1890, however, the government was well started on a new program of conservation. Private forests continued to be overcut, but they comprised less than half the total and replacement of growth was rapid. From 1915 to 1936 the forested area was enlarged 13%. Nearly 60% of it remained under the ownership of the crown or various public authorities.

Japan's forests were more than three times her arable land, covering 55% of the country. Although their direct yield was small in money value, they were of immense significance for her national life. Intelligent care preserved them for timber and fuel, pulp supplies and camphor, even food products. It also protected farm lands against erosion and afforded invaluable hydroelectric resources. Finally, it perpetuated that feature of the landscape which, with the sea, lends such natural beauty to the Japanese islands.

Far more intractable, by comparison, were the social and technical problems of Japanese agriculture. After 1920 agrarian issues pressed insistently for attention. The early and easy gains in productivity had been realized. Colonial and foreign foodstuffs now began to press upon farm markets. The further progress of industrialization barely managed to absorb the increase in population in nonagricultural pursuits, leaving stagnant pools in the more remote areas. The rise of tenant disputes was a warning of gathering tension.

The Diets of the postwar decade, now increasingly sensitive to popular demands, were therefore compelled to concern themselves more actively with rural relief. They contented themselves, nevertheless, with a series of *ad hoc* measures which were palliatives at best. Food imports from noncolonial sources were restricted. Operations were begun in 1921 to modify fluctuations in the all-important price of rice through buying and selling operations by the Japan Rice Company. Modest gestures were likewise made to lighten farm taxes and ease tenant-landlord disputes. Most important, the organization of credit and marketing cooperatives was greatly extended under the revised law of 1917. Low-interest funds were provided on a considerable scale through the Hypothec Bank, a new Central Bank for Cooperative Associations formed in 1923, and related agencies. By 1935 two out of every three farm households were members of cooperatives. Similarly, although government support to the fisheries industry went mostly to aiding the big commercial firms extend their overseas activities, local fishing associations were now strengthened and encouraged to develop cooperative credit, purchasing, and marketing arrangements.

The collapse of farm prices after 1929 made the agricultural situation still more precarious. Millions of farm families suffered acute distress. In response, the government broadened its program to stabilize the price of rice and silk with public funds. It also made some effort to relieve the heavy burden of farm debt, to adjust tenant disputes, and otherwise to mitigate somewhat the plight of the small peasant. On the whole, however, no radical reorganization of Japanese agriculture was attempted, or even seriously contemplated. Even the further development of Hokkaido, Japan's own agricultural "frontier," lagged for want of funds. Nor was government money applied to farm relief on any scale, despite the solicitude proclaimed by the militarists who were now regaining power at the expense of the parties. Aid to the peasant was one of the slogans of General Araki, "that loud trombone of destiny." But he failed to produce much action. In time even the modest plans and programs of the depression years were set aside under the exigency of large-scale rearmament.

If living conditions nevertheless improved slowly in the villages during the thirties, it was largely due to the industrial boom which revived farm prices and attracted labor into industry on an unprecedented scale. (Above, pages 464ff.) Indeed, this might be said of the whole half century before the war. As between industrial development and "rural reconstruction" as we now conceive it, there is no question where the priority was placed by those in authority in prewar Japan. In terms of any final solution of Japan's farm problem they were basically correct. But even those measures of protection to the small peasant which would have helped and not hindered industrialization were largely neglected, where they called for interference with property rights or for large-scale public expenditure. Thus it was left to the Occupation regime in postwar Japan to make the first full-scale attack on this long-standing social problem.

Protection of Labor. In the protection of industrial labor, prewar Japanese governments were no less dilatory. By 1890 Japan had begun to repeat the ugly if now familiar history of the Industrial Revolution in the West. There was no regulation of hours or wages, or of child labor. There were no labor standards of any sort, except for general laws relating to property and contracts. Factory operatives commonly worked eleven to fourteen hours, day or night, and of course at a pittance. There were mostly girls, aged fourteen to twenty, hired from the countryside by practices which bordered often on seduction. Typically they were lodged in factory dormitories on a three-year contract. As many as 50% are said to have deserted within six months. Labor efficiency was correspondingly low. (See above, pages 485-87.) The old system of familial paternalism carried over into modern industry, with its reciprocal obligations of protection and subordination. But it soon lost most of its kindliness and humanity in the cold calculations of industrial capitalism.

Demands for workers' protective legislation by the State had arisen during the early Meiji years. In 1898 the government actually introduced a draft factory law into the Diet, after a reconnaissance of Western practice in such matters. But such proposals were the work of a handful of intellectuals and socially minded bureaucrats. The idea of spending money on enforcement aroused no enthusiasm among political leaders. They were absorbed in other objectives. The framework of administrative skills and knowledge was lacking, in any case. And any interference was actively resisted by businessmen and industrialists. The Civil Code of 1890 proclaimed "freedom of contract." It was said that the factory bill was contrary to the spirit of the Japanese family system; or, alternatively, that it threatened the new concepts of liberty and competition. Even the prohibition of child labor under ten was defeated. For another generation, as a result, one might see an eight-year-old girl operating machinery for long hours in a temperature of 100° or more.

It will be recalled that labor had practically no representation in the Diet at this time. Nor had labor organizations any legal status. For the times this is hardly surprising. Even in Germany trade unions were illegal before 1890, and in France their major disabilities were only removed in 1884. In Japan the Police Regulations of 1900 made it virtually a crime to agitate for a strike. The early growth of trade unionism thus met one of its severest obstacles in the stern suppression of any signs of radicalism. The first recorded strike occurred, significantly, when ricksha men in Tokyo organized a union to protest the introduction of streetcars in 1883. It was quickly put down when its leader was jailed on a criminal charge. In general there were few strikes until World War I, when the rising cost of living precipitated a series of demands for higher wages.

The first legislative enactments to regulate industrial labor were the Mining Act of 1905 and the Factory Act of 1911. Although introduced by the government they were not backed by any strong force of public opinion. Employer groups succeeded in postponing their actual enforcement until 1916. As finally applied to all mines and to factories with fifteen or more workers they imposed a legal limit of twelve hours of attendance (including one hour of rest) for women and for children under fifteen. The minimum age of entrance was set at twelve, except in the case of "light work." Here it might be reduced to ten. Other provisions covered holidays, maternity protection, and workmen's compensation. Despite long agitation, action on night labor was put off for another thirteen years in response to strenuous opposition from owners of textile mills.

The further progress of labor legislation in Japan owed much to the International Labor Organization, formed in 1919. Japan joined the Organization at the outset; in fact, she established the first permanent delegation. While insisting that Japanese industry required special latitude in labor matters, the government was sensitive to criticism abroad. It now moved cautiously to bring conditions in Japan into conformity with certain minimum standards advocated by the ILO.[46]

At home other forces pressed for reform. By 1925, when universal male suffrage went into effect, there were some 3 million workers in Japanese factories, mines, and large-scale transport. Through political parties and workers' organizations they were beginning to find their voice. Trade union membership advanced only slowly. It was handicapped by poverty; by the dispersion of small industrial plants; by the predominance of women factory operatives, most of them housed in company dormitories; and by factionalism among union leaders themselves. The unions could claim only 285,000 members in 1926. There were only 420,000 at their prewar peak a decade later. The Peace Preservation Act of 1925 set close limits upon their capabilities, and bills to give them full legal status were always killed in the Diet. Nevertheless, here was a growing force in the cities which helped both to extend the scope of protective legislation and to narrow the gap between the laws and their enforcement. Finally, beside the pressure of international opinion and the demands of labor, a slow process of education was at work among the big industrialists themselves. The more enlightened of them came to realize that better labor conditions did not necessarily mean higher costs, and that high turnover, accident, and disease rates might be a drain even on their own pocketbooks.

The decade beginning with 1921 thus brought significant advances. A Bureau of Social Affairs was set up in the Home Ministry to handle all matters relating to labor and social welfare. The Employment Exchanges Act of 1921 laid the basis for a national system of employment exchanges. A 1924 ordinance curbed some of the abuses in the recruitment of contract labor. The Health Insurance

---

[46] Here, as in other countries, the ILO made a valuable contribution merely by acquainting the Japanese with labor standards and regulatory practices elsewhere, and by making data on Japan available to the rest of the world. The summary of legislation given here is written largely from its excellent study *Industrial Labor in Japan*, Geneva, 1933.

Act of 1922 provided benefits after 1927 to all factory and mining workers in the event of sickness, accident, maternity, or death. A series of government inquiries gave a more adequate statistical foundation for legislative and administrative action in industrial matters.

In 1923 the Diet amended the Factory Act. As applied in 1926, its coverage was extended to all plants of ten or more operatives. Maximum working hours were cut from eleven to ten in the case of women and children, except that a large part of the textile industry was exempted until 1931. The minimum age of entrance into factories was raised to fourteen, although children of twelve or thirteen might still be employed if they had completed their elementary education. Employers' liability for accident benefits was also strengthened. In 1932 it was broadened to cover workers in construction, transport, and communication as well. Finally, the long-contested issue of night work was resolved with its prohibition for women and children in 1929. Later amendments and additions to these measures extended their scope here and there during the next few years, but made no sweeping changes.

It will be observed that this prewar labor legislation was confined mainly to the protection of women and juvenile workers. Japan followed the precedent of other industrializing countries in this regard. Only in underground mining labor were the hours of both men and women restricted by statute to ten a day in 1930. (By this time actual working hours in factory industry averaged only nine a day, 26.5 days a month.) Other, broader issues—factory wages, hours of work, collective bargaining, and social insurance (except for health and accident insurance)—had yet to become the subject of State action. Almost untouched also was the immense field of small-scale industry. Here the problems of regulation were far more different, though no less urgent. Moreover, enforcement of existing factory legislation lagged well behind the statutes, especially in the smaller undertakings covered by the Act.[47]

All this testifies to the limited advances yet made in safeguarding industrial labor, and the stubborn resistance from traditional influences and organized employer interests. Had the government been so minded, it could have moved long before it did to reduce the human costs of industrialization. "There is no twilight sleep," says T. S. Ashton of the Industrial Revolution in England, "to ease

---

[47] The remark of a British Commission reporting in 1866 on legislation to cover small workshops is applicable today throughout the Orient. "It is unhappily to a painful degree apparent through the whole of the evidence that against no persons do the children of both sexes need so much protection as against their parents." L. C. A. Knowles, *The Industrial and Commercial Revolutions in Great Britain during the Nineteenth Century*, London, 1921, p. 92.

the birth of a new form of society." Perhaps so, but it makes a difference if there is at least a sympathetic midwife in attendance.

Moreover, whatever apology may be made for the long neglect
of the social evils of factory industrialism and crowded urban living
in the early nineteenth century West, the same argument hardly
applies anywhere in the twentieth century. One of the reasons so
little was done before 1850 on the problems of sanitation and public
health in English and American cities was the lack of engineering
and medical science, as well as the techniques of the local public
authority. Similarly, adequate factory regulation required systematic industrial statistics, and the invention of proper techniques
of inspection and control. To introduce these things in any country
takes time. But today they can be quickly improvised, with foreign
assistance if necessary, where there is a will to do so. Particularly is
this true where, as in modern Japan, the central government is
empowered to intervene on a national scale, and need not defer to
a jealous regard for local independence, as in the early experience
of England and the United States.

In any event, Japan was now taking the first belated steps toward
recognizing the responsibilities of the State in this sphere of public
policy. Had the progress of 1921-36 been maintained for another
five years, her position would have invited comparison with that of
any other industrial nation facing similar economic handicaps. Unfortunately, a rapid retreat set in after 1937 from the gains of the
previous decade. The political reaction brought about by the resurgence of the military, and the exigencies of the war which followed, ended by sweeping away most of the structure of labor protection. After the war it had to be built anew.

Control of Business Organization and Practice. We come finally
to the policies of the State as regards the organization and control
of business enterprise. To what extent were the coercive powers of
government employed to shape the structure and behavior of industrial organization in prewar Japan?

This topic may be defined either narrowly or broadly. It raises
questions of public policy in relation to monopolistic combinations,
fair trade practices, the protection of the investor, etc. In the wider
sense it takes in the whole philosophy of governmental responsibility
in economic life. While many aspects of this broad field have already
been touched upon, it remains to characterize the extent to which
the Japanese invoked the political authority of the State more
specifically to regulate the pattern of business organization and
practice.

The early Meiji statesmen seem to have had no very considered
philosophy on the division of responsibility between public and

private enterprise, or on the usages of monopoly and competition in the latter field. Their early decisions were *ad hoc*, and stemmed from a variety of motives—military, political, and fiscal. From the beginning, however, public policy tended in practice toward the concentration of industrial and financial control, in the hands of either the government ministries themselves, or the business interests with whom the authorities were usually in close association. This was consistent with the old tradition of the clan bureaucrats and their relation to the Tokugawa merchants. It was dictated, further, by the haste to develop modern industry, particularly where it would strengthen military power.

Naturally, therefore, the Japanese turned to the German pattern in industrial policy, as in military organization. Although influenced by the currents of liberal thought flowing in from Britain and America, they had no comparable background of hostility to private monopoly or to government control per se. As in the Germany of Bismarck, both tradition and circumstance called for State leadership in developing the productive powers of the nation, for close cooperation between the State and big business, for intimate relationships between large-scale banking and industry, and for the encouragement of cooperative action and self-regulation on all fronts (except that of labor organization). Significantly, Kurt Singer remarks, it was a German economist of the Historical School who was called to the first chair of economics at Tokyo Imperial University.

In small-scale trade and industry the Meiji governments refrained perforce from wholesale intervention or control. Their chief concern lay elsewhere, except in one important respect. The early export trade was largely built on small-scale industries producing such commodities as silk products, tea, and straw mats. Here one problem soon became apparent. As markets widened these industries became increasingly competitive. Great numbers of small workshops, relying on irregular family labor, and remote from the market, made for a haphazard and unsystematic scheme of organization in which there was a chronic tendency to spoil the trade by turning out inferior goods. If exports were to prosper it was essential to improve and standardize the quality of such products.

A special incentive was thus given to a movement which was characteristic of the Japanese anyway. Through a series of laws enacted between 1884 and 1902 the authorities encouraged the formation of local chambers of commerce and guilds of industrialists and merchants for cooperative action. These trade associations were given legal status and tax immunities in order that they might engage in joint investigation, representation, and services like inspection. Although formed in large numbers, it should be added that such limited self-regulation as they achieved did not materially alter the atomistic structure of small-scale business, even in the export trade. This was modified only subsequently as a network of financial and marketing relationships developed through merchant-employers and wholesale traders linked the small producers, on the one hand, and with big banks, export-import firms, and factories, on the other.

Much more significant was the use of political authority to facilitate the growth of the great business combines which came to dominate large-scale corporate enterprise. A high concentration of control was inevitable in those industries requiring large investments and advanced technology, especially in the early years. For there were few places outside the government itself where the necessary capital and enterprise could be found. And the market would not support any extensive duplication of facilities. The first factories and mines were given every form of assistance by the government, where not actually operated by the State. Automatically they enjoyed a quasi-monopolistic position.

When the authorities abandoned the development of industry more largely to private enterprise after 1880 and adopted a selective policy of promotion, private capital became firmly established, and more competitive. But it was still difficult to attract funds into the more difficult and risky ventures unless there was a clear prospect of large returns. If development was to be rapid the hazards had to be reduced by government patronage and subsidy. It may be recalled that tariff protection was still ruled out of Japan's "unequal treaties." In such industries as shipping, railways, mining, and metallurgy, the fortunes of the new entrepreneurs continued to be influenced heavily by favors extended or withheld by the Army and Navy, other government ministries, and the official banks. Any ambitious and successful promoter was up to his ears in politics.

The big combines emerged toward the close of the nineteenth century as virtual partners of the State in establishing the industries essential to national power. Mining, metalworking, and large-scale transport all required large financial resources and advanced technical know-how. Even where a start could be made, they were often unable to grow unaided in the face of Western competition. They were built up under forced draft, nevertheless, by the awarding of exceptional privileges to those groups capable of commanding the necessary capital and skills. And as they prospered in one field, both their financial strength and their political influence enabled them to prosper in others.

Thus we find the process of industrial combination displaying very early its typical Japanese characteristics: It tended toward huge agglomerations of miscellaneous enterprise in a wide variety of fields, rather than independent monopolies in particular products. It was most pronounced in the heavy industries created under State patronage. And it gained a good deal of its momentum from the absorptive power of the big city banks, which were closely affiliated with the industrial combines, and also had close relations with the great semiofficial banks. (See Chapter 4.)

The *zaibatsu* grew to power as "instruments of national policy," in G. C. Allen's words. As their influence rose, they also became makers of national policy, sharing privilege and authority with the military and civilian bureaucrats and party politicians. So close indeed was the affiliation of the State and big business that it was sometimes difficult to tell where one left off and the other began. Increasingly the top figures in the big combines moved in and out of the government banks and the ministries handling economic affairs. They came to exercise great influence in the Diet through the political parties on which they lavished funds. They worked closely with the Army and Navy in the procurement of arms and equipment, and in financial imperialism overseas. They intermarried with the families of the peerage, ranking bureaucrats, politicians, admirals, and diplomats.[48]

For the execution of national policies involving economic matters the military and civilian bureaucracies were always forced sooner or later to turn to the combines for assistance. Even in Manchuria, where the Kwantung Army tried after 1931 to assert its independence by developing war industries on the pattern of State capitalism, it had eventually to come to terms with the newer and more responsive wing of the financial oligarchy. For the same reason the *zaibatsu* executives were able to retain major responsibilities for the general economic mobilization which came at the end of the decade. They were indispensable by virtue of their control over capital and over administrative and technical skills. For example,

[48] A striking example of such family relationships is that of Baron Hisaya Iwasaki, long head of the great Mitsubishi combine and heir of its founder. One of his sisters was married to Kijuro Shidehara, and another to Takaaki Kato, both of them distinguished diplomats and leading political figures of prewar Japan. A daughter and a niece were the wives respectively of Renzo Sawada and Viscount Nagakage Okabe, also in the diplomatic service. Another niece was married to Viscount Keizo Shibusawa, the "Nestor" of Japanese business, who headed the wealthy banking family of that name and held a long succession of important posts in government and finance. Two nephews married daughters of Teizaburo Sekiya, an ex-Vice-Minister of the Imperial Household, and Tetsujiro Shidachi, once president of the Industrial Bank of Japan. Finally, Baron Iwasaki's second son, Takaya, was married to a daughter of Seihin Ikeda, long the top executive of the Mitsui combine and occupant of many leading posts in the government as well. U.S. Department of State, *Report of the Mission on Japanese Combines*, Part I, Washington, 1946, p. 16.

the industrial control associations formed under the Mobilization Law of 1938 to coordinate each industry were headed commonly by an official from one of the combines, or by someone closely affiliated. While they may not have sought the war, may actually have dreaded it, they contributed immensely to its prosecution and reaped huge profits while it prospered.

It should be added that the owners and executives of the big banks, factories, and trading concerns never attained a decisive position in prewar Japanese politics. Probably this can be said even of their heyday, the 1920's. At the peak of their influence they were merely one wing of the ruling class, influential in economic affairs but insecure, and lacking the power to make the great political decisions shaping the destiny of the country. When the chips were down, following the military resurgence of the thirties, they found themselves at a fatal disadvantage in the struggle around the throne. What they wanted, how they saw the future of Japan, are not too clear. Actually, of course, they differed among themselves, itself a source of weakness. Most of them viewed with alarm the drift of political events after 1931, and particularly after 1936. Few if any welcomed the gathering crisis. However, neither wealth nor technical capacity in modern industry, when concentrated in the hands of a few, is any adequate weapon in politics against the determined use of military force and terror. In the end the *zaibatsu* were the victims of the system they helped to create.

Through the earlier decades, nevertheless, business interests both large and small were left comparatively free to develop most fields of industrial and commercial enterprise with little direct competition or regulation by the State. The policy which emerged after 1880 reflected the philosophy of liberalism then prevalent among the industrial nations of the West, as well as the financial exigencies of the government. It was also shaped by the interests and influence of the new business class in official circles.

Laissez faire is certainly not the term to apply, for it suggests a more negative, hands-off policy than ever prevailed in Japan—or, for that matter, the West.[49] The government retained certain levers of control, particularly through State banking and fiscal policy. And it continued its protective solicitude for the strategic industries and colonial development. Outside these restricted areas, however, business enterprise and business practice evolved without much direct control by the authorities. When the national government stepped in with its financial resources or its coercive powers it was more as a protector or partner of large-scale business than as a policeman or competitor. Even in this respect its direct intervention was

[49] *"Laissez faire* is quite literally the only untried utopia."—A. W. Macmahon.

confined to a relatively small (though strategic) segment of the total Japanese economy. Over the wider field its influence was pervasive but more indirect, being exercised through taxation and tariffs, credit management, technical education, labor legislation, and other policies discussed earlier.

The structure of private enterprise which emerged has been characterized more fully in Chapter 4. Here it is pertinent to emphasize that it was built on a legal foundation which guaranteed security for property rights and extended great freedom in their exercise. So far as the law was concerned, an investor or entrepreneur was free (until 1937) to enter almost any field of economic activity outside the few monopolized by the State. For the most part a firm could make such decisions as it chose with respect to prices, output, and market practices, either individually or in collusion with its rivals. (This is not to deny the more pervasive influence exerted informally by the Tokyo authorities in large-scale undertakings, or by local officials in their own bailiwicks.)

The significance of such legal freedom was enormously increased, of course, by extensive resort to the powerful tool of joint-stock finance. This device was taken over by the Japanese without the public distrust of concentrated business power which shaped the development of corporate law and its administration in Britain and America. More accurately, public fears that such power might be abused never became an effective restraining force in prewar Japanese politics or legislation. Instead, big business interests worked in close association with the bureaucrats and the parties to evolve a system of law which imposed as little restriction as possible on monopolistic practices in large-scale finance and industry. Absent from the spirit as well as the letter of the law was any philosophy of democratic control such as was long ago embodied in the antitrust laws and work of regulatory commissions in the United States. Virtually unlimited opportunity was thus given for the growth of industrial concentrations, so far as legislation was concerned. The only political influences working in a contrary direction before 1930 arose from the fact that intercombine rivalries carried over from business into politics. On occasion the balance of political privilege acquired by members of the business oligarchy might upset the balance of financial power. More often, probably, it tended to reinforce and perpetuate it.

To cite a few illustrations of the law,[50] no effective legal restriction was ever applied on intercorporate stockholdings or interlocking directorates. Exclusive sales agencies were another lawful device widely employed to build up vertical trusts in the great indus-

[50] Report of the Mission on Japanese Combines, cited, part 1, pp. 21-27, 56-59.

tries. A corporation could legally enter partnerships, secretly if it chose. It was also free to engage in almost any kind of activity with little regard to the ostensible purpose for which it was chartered. While the shareholders, typically a small number of individuals or concerns, had unlimited powers as a group, the individual share-holder enjoyed little protection under the Commercial Code, even against illegality and fraud.[51] The auditor, far from being a guard-ian of his interests, was more likely to be appointed by the insiders.

Moreover, the law was lax in its requirements for full and accurate information on company activities. This was true of articles of in-corporation, and no less of balance sheets and profit-and-loss state-ments. For example, the 1944 balance sheet of Yasuda Kogyo, a 40-million-yen company, could list a few items under such unen-lightening descriptions as "investments" and "receivables" and then lump the remaining 75% of the company's assets together as "other current assets"! Even stockholders had no right of access to cor-porate books except the yearly financial statement. Banks and other financial institutions were subject to stricter public surveillance and reporting requirements, especially after the bank panic of 1927. Characteristically, however, the Finance Ministry examined the pro-vincial banks much more frequently and closely than the *zaibatsu* banks, which were rarely scrutinized.

In short, the legal framework of modern industry and finance af-forded every facility for the exercise of "leadership" in structures of concentrated power, with little formal requirement, at least, as regards public accountability. No doubt it reflected in this respect habits of mind and practice long ingrained in the Japanese tradition.

War, Depression, and Industrial Controls. After World War I Japan shared in the world-wide tendency toward growing interven-tion by the State in economic life. Of this tendency many evidences have already been noted. Through labor legislation, tariff protec-tion, agricultural relief, and subsidies to banks, increasing use was made of the mechanisms of government to control and "stabilize" the economic system.

The drift toward more pervasive intervention was impelled by no single group interest. Nor was it directed toward any single pur-pose. Japan had emerged from the war as an industrial and trading nation of substantial proportions. She shared in the world-wide dis-locations which followed in the wake of the war. These were intensi-fied for her by the tremendous earthquake disaster of 1923. More fundamentally, she was now becoming heir to the typical social ills

51 Thomas L. Blakemore and Makoto Yazawa, "Japanese Commercial Code Re-visions Concerning Corporations," *The American Journal of Comparative Law*, vol. II, no. 1, January 1953, pp. 12-22.

and the popular demands which everywhere accompany industrialism. Small businessmen, workers, and peasants were exposed to the relentless crowding of population on the labor market. As the electorate widened and grew in political consciousness, it became more difficult to neglect the economic and social problems which earlier more authoritarian governments had been able to disregard. At the end of the decade came a severe depression. This intensified still further the pressure on the government to widen the scope of its responsibilities.

Prior to the slump of 1929-31 little attempt was made to introduce by political action any structural reforms in the organization of industry and trade. Now the shrinkage of markets and fall of prices sharpened the competitive struggle in industry. A number of cartels had already been formed in large-scale, capitalistic trades. They had enjoyed little success, however, in restricting production or controlling prices by voluntary action, except in a very few cases. (See above, page 230.) Among the mass of small industrialists and traders, competition was even more severe. Most of their labor was supplied by the family of the employer himself, or by hired workers who remained at work as long as they could contribute anything to their family budgets. The hard-pressed proprietor could stay in business by sweating his workers, or allowing his plant to depreciate. Voluntary agreements to impose any minimum standards of competition among these small firms were out of the question.

Out of this situation developed certain measures of government intervention. They began quite modestly as relief measures. They ended by being redirected toward the purpose of war mobilization and radically altering the structure of business enterprise after 1937.

The initial pressure for State action came from the big industrialists and financiers themselves. Its earliest form was a program to aid depression-ridden industries to improve their efficiency and lower costs. In 1930 a Bureau of Industrial Rationalization was set up for this purpose in the Ministry of Commerce and Industry. Its more far-reaching objectives were never realized. But it did assist the rapid gains in industrial efficiency achieved during these years under the pressure of falling prices. Also prompted by the slump was a move to give legal force to industrial agreements for the purpose of restricting competition in large-scale industry. The Major Industries Control Law of 1931 empowered the Commerce Minister to require all producers in certain designated trades to abide by agreements to allocate markets or control prices and production, wherever the scheme had been approved by two thirds of the firms in the industry.

Actually this Control Law never proved very effective.[52] By 1936, it is true, there were nearly fifty industrial cartels in Japan. Over half of them were in "major industries." In a few of them—notably cotton spinning, cement, paper, and beer—fairly tight controls over the market were enforced by agreements. These might be agreements to control output, fix prices, restrict imports, or operate joint selling syndicates. Elsewhere numerous attempts were made to arrive at similar restrictions. But they were usually frustrated, or soon broke down, because of fierce jealousies among rival groups and the recalcitrance of low-cost producers enjoying a competitive advantage. As prosperity returned after 1931, and industry resumed its expansion, the more successful firms lost interest in State-enforced agreements which only bolstered up the weak. Moreover, public groups protested that the government should use its power not to encourage monopoly but to protect the consumer. The Commerce Minister took little positive action in response to these protests except to issue a few warnings to price-fixing associations. On the other hand, little use was made of the compulsory feature of the Control Law to sanction cartel restrictions before 1937. Only in the cement industry was it invoked to enforce curtailment of output, and even there the proposal to enforce minimum prices was rejected.

Of greater interest today is Japan's experiment during the decade after 1925 with measures to support small producers and merchants in order to improve their competitive position.

In agriculture, as we have seen, the formation of rural cooperatives was now encouraged to provide the farmer with better facilities for credit, purchasing, and marketing operations. No comparable effort was devoted to strengthening the small industrialist or trader on the other hand. Prior to 1931 State intervention in this realm was still limited mainly to improving the quality of export goods. During the twenties the system of official inspection was somewhat extended, and certain guilds of exporters and manufacturers, organized under laws passed in 1925, were also designated to carry on compulsory inspection. But the individualistic traditions of these small trades, the perennial conflict between the small industrialist and the merchant, and the antagonism between the small merchant and the large stood in the way of effective cooperation, even for such limited purposes.

This continued to be true during the thirties to a large extent. However, two developments, one at home and the other in foreign

[52] See G. C. Allen's chapter on "The Development of Industrial Combinations" in *The Industrialization of Japan and Manchukuo, 1930-1940,* cited, pp. 680-718; also Keizo Fujita, "Cartels and Their Conflicts in Japan," *Journal of the Osaka University of Commerce,* no. III, December 1935, pp. 65-109.

trade, spurred the government to extend its efforts in behalf of the small businessman after 1930. The first was the general plight of the small industries, as falling prices intensified the pressures of competition. This created a growing popular resentment against the big financial and industrial interests, on which the Army radicals were quick to capitalize in their bid for power.

One legislative response was a series of measures to relieve and reorganize the silk industry, especially hard hit. These measures began with price-support subsidies and the collective organization of all branches of the industry to improve methods. After 1934 they were extended to include even subsidies to curtail mulberry acreage; also the licensing of all silk-reelers and -dealers with a view to reducing their numbers. Here, of course, the authorities were contending with an adverse trend in the world market for textile fibers. As it turned out, silk was never to regain its former position.

More generally, during the depression, the government stepped in to extend the organization of small industrialists and traders into manufacturers' guilds (*kōgyō kumiai*) and export guilds (*yushutsu kumiai*). They were strengthened with low-interest loans and small subsidies. They were encouraged to engage in joint purchase and sale, financing of members, and inspection and standardization of goods. In some cases they were urged to control output and prices. By 1937 over 700 manufacturers' guilds and 36 federations had been organized in trades producing textile fabrics, clothing, pottery, wood products, foodstuffs, metal goods, rubber wares, etc. In a few instances they were endowed with compulsory power to enforce the compliance of nonmembers with their regulations. But they had to rely in the main on voluntary methods, and this continued to be a grave source of weakness in these fiercely competitive trades. The revival of trade after 1932 improved their position; how much the guilds actually contributed to this end is open to doubt.[53]

The export guilds, like the manufacturers' guilds, were conceived originally as a medium for voluntary cooperation and joint facilities to aid the small businessman. After 1933, however, a second and unforeseen use for them arose in connection with the world-wide spread of discriminatory restrictions upon Japanese goods following the depreciation of the yen. Most of these goods were turned out by small industries like those mentioned above. Small merchants likewise played a part in their marketing. This made necessary

[53] For an excellent evaluation of this whole movement see the account by Allen, *op.cit.*, pp. 760ff. Details concerning a number of industries will be found in Teijiro Uyeda and associates, *The Small Industries of Japan*, New York, 1938.

some form of pervasive control machinery, either to administer quotas imposed abroad, or to forestall threatening restrictions.

The government turned to the export guilds to perform this control function. As the occasion arose they were endowed with legal authority to regulate the volume and price of exports under government supervision. It was largely in this realm, too, that certain manufacturers' guilds were given compulsory powers, often with confusing conflicts of jurisdiction. To cite one illustration, the British government proposed in 1933 to restrict the import of electric lamps from Japan. The Japanese thereupon organized a Federation of Electric Lamp Manufacturers' Associations to raise export prices in the hope of averting the action. Later, when the Board of Trade in London still insisted on a quota, the Japanese were forced to agree, and an Electric Lamp Exporters' Association for England was organized to administer and enforce the restriction upon the trade.

By 1937 there were ninety-four such export guilds in various industries. Some were country-wide and others regional. Forty-four of them were organized in relation to particular products, thirty-three in relation to particular markets, and seventeen on a combination of the two principles. Cumbersome as the machinery became, compulsory restrictions on the volume and price of goods were now being applied on 10% or more of Japan's total exports to foreign countries.

This whole episode in the organization, support, and control of small industrialists and traders has more than passing interest. For in one way or another the problem confronts all Far Eastern countries undergoing industrialization. In prewar Japan public policy was given a particular twist by the circumstances of the time. But it demonstrated both the possibilities and the difficulties in political action to strengthen small business enterprise.

In its original conception the experiment got far enough to indicate that government initiative backed by cheap credit might have accomplished a good deal through the techniques of association. Equally, it posed questions as to what the ultimate effects on Japan's industrial efficiency would be if the policy were carried to the point where radical alterations were made in the structure of production and marketing in the interest of the small industrialist. Long before this happened, however, the program was deflected from its initial purposes. First it was turned to the function of export control. And after the outbreak of Sino-Japanese hostilities in 1937, the whole network of industrial and trading associations became simply a part of the machinery by which the Japanese economy was mobilized for war.

From this point on, under the aegis of the militarists, Japan moved rapidly toward the "New Economic Structure," which was to give the State sweeping powers over economic enterprise in almost every sphere. Characteristically, the immediate impulse came from a balance of payments crisis provoked in 1937-38 by armament spending and Empire investment. This led the authorities into far-reaching restrictions not only upon foreign exchange transactions but upon all import-using industries—i.e., the whole industrial economy.

Free entry into business became a thing of the past with the passage in 1937 of the Emergency Funds Adjustment Law. Government approval was now required for any capital outlay in excess of 50,000 yen, or any new firm capitalized at over 200,000 yen. Petroleum and alcohol were added to the list of State monopolies. Other key industries like electric power, shipping, automobiles, and aircraft, as well as all essential materials, were placed under strict official control. In various strategic fields the government formed semimonopolistic "national policy companies." Elsewhere it encouraged consolidations and mergers of private concerns to force the pace of expansion. The Major Industries Control Law was revised in 1936 and 1937 to strengthen its coercive features. A year later came the General Mobilization Law, conferring virtually unlimited powers of regulation upon the government.

Japanese industry was now blanketed with a system of State-supported cartels in the form of control associations of every description. By 1941 there were said to be as many as 20,000 associations engaged in "controlling activity" with some degree of government authority. Private business fought a rear guard action against this encroachment upon its traditional sphere. Small producers were helpless to defend themselves, of course. Being engaged mainly in the production of consumer goods, they suffered heavily as a class. The big concerns made a good thing out of it where they could, and managed to retain major responsibilities in directing the whole apparatus of control. By the time of the Pearl Harbor attack, however, the structure of industrial organization and entrepreneurial responsibility on which the Japanese had built their industrial economy over fifty years was beginning to be altered almost beyond recognition. It was war that undermined its foundations.

Momentum of Economic Growth: Summary

Role of the State. Clearly the course of Japan's economic development after the Restoration was powerfully influenced by the militaristic and mercantilistic cast of her political institutions. Her heritage of feudalism, the ambitions of her new leaders, the kind of

world she now entered—all combined to project the State into a
prominent role and endow it with broad responsibilities in creating
the framework of industrialization.

As we have seen, the authority of the government was freely invoked in the early years to stimulate new investment and technological change, and to guide economic development in accordance
with national interests as conceived by those in power. Conceptions
of national interest were intermingled and identified with personal
and group interest of course, as they were in the Navigation Laws
of seventeenth century England or the Bonapartist reforms of nineteenth century France. A rapid succession of measures established
a milieu of law and administration and finance within which the
gestation of capitalism took place. Beyond this the government
itself actively shared the initiative in building systems of transport
and communication, establishing credit institutions, and even launching new factory enterprise. After the turn of the century, as it
receded more into the background, it still kept its grip on certain
levers of economic power. It used them to underwrite the established
order and to move its economic center of gravity increasingly toward
industrialism. Particularly it employed them to encourage those industries and activities which were strategic to Japan's war potential.
All this is readily demonstrated, and has been discussed at length in
the foregoing pages.

The more difficult problem is to evaluate the importance of political factors in the real substance and dynamics of Japan's economic growth over half a century. Particularly, what part did
social action through political mechanisms play in the crucial process of innovation by which Japan moved from the old to the new?
If industrialization multiplied the nation's productive powers four-
or fivefold, through what propelling force and by what instrumentalities was this achieved? The basic tools were modern science and
machinery. The opportunity for rapid economic advance was provided by opening the door to foreign trade and cultural contact. But
the task itself required sweeping changes in the organization of national life. It called for increasing specialization of functions, new
forms of social cooperation—above all, a new spirit of enterprise
in large sectors of the economy.

In interpreting this process, the historian can be misled by the
fact that its political features are more readily observed and recorded. Public decisions like the enactment of a statute or an investment by a State bank inevitably attract more attention than
bits of power machinery adopted by thousands of small weavers,
whatever their real significance. The vigorous initiative of the Meiji
oligarchy, and the pervasive influence of the State in subsequent

times, make it easy to exaggerate their substantive importance for the process of economic growth. From some accounts one might conclude that Japanese industrialization from 1868 to 1938 was largely the creation of a quasi-totalitarian state. The political authorities are pictured as bending their energies to the task with far-seeing unity of purpose and an almost unlimited grant of authority from a docile people. If great strides were made in assimilating machine technology, if capital accumulated rapidly, if output and markets grew apace, this is attributed in large measure to the driving political leadership of the State and the disciplined obedience of its population. In particular, war and armament are sometimes said to have given the chief impetus, and to have swallowed up most of the fruits.

Any such picture of Japan's economic development greatly oversimplifies and distorts the reality of events. For one thing, the Japanese State was by no means so monolithic or single-minded in its leadership as this would imply. Within the oligarchy no such unity of interest and outlook existed, except on the broad fundamentals of internal stability and overseas expansion. On the contrary, in many particulars of economic policy one finds sharp conflicts and rivalries among various factions of the military, the civilian bureaucracy, and business interests. Commonly decisions regarding a budget, a tariff, or a banking statute were reached by a process of political logrolling and compromise which was consistent with no single, calculated philosophy of national interest. Hesitation, indecision, stalemate are no less a part of the record.

Especially was this true after the turn of the century, with the gradual disappearance of the elder statesmen who had piloted Japan through the Restoration period. As the commercial classes grew in influence, and with them the political parties, the emphasis in national economic policy shifted increasingly from national power to wealth and well-being, at least for the propertied class. Perhaps it would be more accurate to say that elements of self-interest, always present in the Mercantilist policies of the clan oligarchs, became more confused and more contradictory as wider groups in the population came to share increasingly in political power. The military counterrevolution of the thirties reversed this trend for the time being. But even when it involved the nation in total war, it never succeeded in fashioning an all-powerful party ideology, apparatus, and discipline such as Hitler fastened upon Germany. Considering Japan's authoritarian traditions, one cannot fail to be impressed with the bitter divisions and deadlocks which persisted throughout the war crisis among elements of the armed forces, the career bureaucrats, and the industrialists. Still less is there reason to believe that Japanese political leadership in economic affairs was particularly coherent or far-seeing through much of the period after 1900.

What is more relevant here, a study of the whole process of economic growth in modern Japan leads to the conviction that the real drive and momentum lay in large measure outside the realm of national political ambition and State activity. At most the latter only accelerated a process of industrialization which was latent in the whole conjuncture of forces at work. The underlying motivations were doubtless complex, joining personal aspirations for economic betterment, nationalist sentiment, and other values which facilitated common action toward socially approved goals. At home were latent resources, both human and material, which only awaited development through the growth of knowledge and widening of personal opportunity. Abroad, the Japanese had the good fortune to enter the world economy at a time when they were able to gain relatively free access to the industrial technology and the materials in which they were deficient. In this setting they proceeded to build a new structure of industrial and commercial enterprise on the foundations already laid in Tokugawa times.

T. S. Ashton speaks of "those spontaneous forces of growth in society that arise from ordinary men and women and find expression in voluntary association, as well as in the State."[54] If we bear in mind the context of Japanese tradition, with its stress upon leadership, imitation, and teamwork, this is more suggestive of the process by which the modern Japanese economy was built than those formulations which put the emphasis on coercion and repression. Except in a few respects, some important and others quite marginal, it did not grow in response to the plans or dictates of the government. Political forces helped to create a favorable psychic milieu; the political mechanism was employed to provide certain important stimuli; and direct controls were applied at various points to serve political ends. But if economic expansion turned almost at once toward industrialization it was basically because Japan's resources, aptitudes, and opportunities drove her in this direction. If it was an orderly, organized process, it reflected less the coercive drive of the State than the Japanese capacity for consensus and cooperation. If it had real substance, it was because of the enterprise and energy of millions of small businessmen, farmers, and workers.

To be sure, the more advanced techniques of finance and industrial organization were pioneered by the big concerns in close association with the government. They developed new sources of fuel and power. They created a network of long-distance transport. They provided

---

[54] "Economic History and Theory," *Economica*, vol. XIII, no. 5, May 1946, p. 84.

a large share of industrial capital formation. No less important, they built up an overhead structure of commercial and credit or ganization which enabled myriads of small traders and industrialists to be linked together in coordinated but highly specialized patterns of activity geared to expanding markets. Nevertheless, without the exercise of personal initiative and entrepreneurial responsibility in increasingly pervasive fashion, and not merely at the top, the imperial ambitions of Japan's rulers would never have achieved any material foundation. They would have remained little more than the dreams voiced by Motoori Norinaga in the eighteenth century.

The sphere of actual State ownership was closely circumscribed after the experimental ventures of the early years. Aside from routine government services, indeed, State undertakings provided only a negligible share of the national product. Furthermore, the real economic growth of Japan took place chiefly in those areas of private activity which owed least to political subsidy and support. Vast sums were spent on conquering and developing the colonies, it is true, but this effort returned only a modest yield in trading or job opportunities. Particularly as a source of food the colonies were important; yet Japan's primary economic interests abroad lay outside the Empire. They were only placed in jeopardy by military expansionism.

Meanwhile, at home, those industries for which the government was always most solicitous, and where the *zaibatsu* were preeminent —the strategic industries—furnished only a small part of the growth in Japanese national income before 1935. Probably they served as an actual drag insofar as they were expanded after 1920 by political protection which attracted capital and skills from more productive employment. However this may be, they remained a small segment of the Japanese economy, despite their sheltered position. By way of illustration, the entire complex of mining, metallurgy, and machinery industries furnished no more than 8% of Japan's national product in 1930, and still less of her gainful employment. (See Chapter 9.)

Various exceptions may be made to this general argument, of course. Money values of production and trade are a poor guide to the importance of particular lines of enterprise, some of which are fundamental to a whole array of activities. The Japanese railways and electrical communications were of this character. They were either built by the government or soon nationalized. On the other hand, two other basic industries, coal and electric power, were developed mainly through private investment and enterprise, profiting of course from political favors whenever they could be secured. The rapid rise of the merchant marine owed much to the assistance lavishly given by the State. Yet even the shipping industry grew eventually to large proportions chiefly because underlying economic circumstances were favorable. (See above.)

Still more was this true of the broader fields of consumer industry, agriculture, and miscellaneous services which made up the great bulk of Japanese economic life. In the neighborhood and the village, no doubt, few major innovations in such trades were ever attempted without the consent and support of the local elders, who also controlled political life. Similarly in larger affairs the degree of informal control exercised by politically dominant groups went well beyond the laws on the statute books and the formal regulations of government ministries. By and large, however, through a wide range of small-scale industry, local commodity-handling trades, and personal services, even in a good deal of large-scale enterprise, one gets the impression of governmental indifference, certainly of inaction, so far as positive intervention through the formal mechanisms of the State is concerned.

One aspect of economic growth, associated as cause and effect with many others, was the secular expansion of market demands. This had two characteristics worth recalling in the present context. First, it occurred predominantly in the home market. Foreign and colonial markets at their prewar peak (1927-36) took no more than 25 to 35% of Japan's manufacturing output, and no more than 20% of her entire national product of all types. Nor—contrary to a widespread impression—did the overseas market for all goods and services, or even for manufactures alone, increase much more rapidly than the domestic market after 1910. Second, the national demand represented mainly the growing requirements of the civilian economy, expressed through private expenditures for goods and services. Private consumer outlay certainly accounted for at least 65% of gross national product, and private capital formation for most of the remainder. (Table 22.) Notwithstanding the catalytic effect of certain State expenditures this was true of the Meiji years; equally from 1911 to 1936.[55] In this realm of civilian enterprise occurred the great expansion of Japan's productive powers which carried the more marginal, strategic industries, as well as the whole cost of Japanese armament. Here was produced the real wealth which

[55] Evidence in support of these statements regarding income, employment, and foreign trade is presented in Chapters 5 to 8. It might be added that State activities of many kinds—e.g., the tax reform of 1873, the building of railways, the creation of a uniform currency, the promotion of exports—were especially important during the early years in fostering an increasing commercialization of the market and enlargement of its geographic scope. Nothing said above is intended to deny these strategic contributions, to which much space has already been devoted.

enabled the country, in addition, to support a growing population at a slowly rising standard of living.

The factor of war, with which State economic policy was so closely identified, has often been exaggerated as the mainspring of Japan's industrialization. The constructive achievement of Japanese militarism was to preserve the nation's independence, particularly in the early years. Thereafter military expenditures in the limited conflicts with China and Russia gave a fillip to economic expansion through the multiplied effects of State borrowing and spending on the whole economy. They reinforced the bias toward easy money and a high level of investment which was a marked characteristic of this period. In this respect they may actually have paid for themselves in good part, by stimulating fuller employment and technical progress even in civilian production.

Against these gains must be set the continual drain of armaments on Japan's limited capital resources, on her advanced machine skills, and especially on the government budget itself. From 1895 to 1935 some 40 to 50% of the national revenue was regularly spent on the Army and Navy, or on servicing loans incurred for military purposes. (Above, page 292.) This cut heavily into the governmental resources available for public works. It crippled education, farm relief, and other welfare expenditures which only a government could undertake. The dearth of public funds for such purposes was a persistent feature of the whole period. Moreover, the taxes which supported the military establishment probably came increasingly out of private income which would otherwise have been saved and invested. Even the foreign borrowings of the national government, which climbed 1,200 million yen in one decade, 1904-13 (Table 20), were devoted in large measure to military use, either directly or indirectly. So, too, was a large share of the 360 million yen indemnity secured from China just previously. A small fraction of these sums spent on reducing disease and accident rates in urban industry, for example, would have increased production efficiency as well as human well-being.

The drain of empire building went far to nullify the more constructive use of State power to mobilize savings for investment in productive enterprise. Fiscal and monetary measures employed for this latter purpose were especially important in the early years. At that time the private capital market was undeveloped. The problem in considerable degree was one of mobilizing surplus income from agriculture for industrial and commercial investment. Then, too, armament building could be justified much more easily as a measure of defense. After the turn of the century, however, Japan's economic advance owed little to her military expansion, unless we are to assume that otherwise the Japanese islands would have been placed under foreign subjection. Rather, the debt was the other way.

Significantly, the war which profited Japan the most was World War I, when she remained neutral in all but name. Had she again stayed on the side lines in World War II, she might once more have reaped fabulous gains. Instead, she wrecked her own economy and laid waste that very part of the world on which her prosperity depended. Professor Ashton, to quote him again, once suggested that the misery and unrest which attended the Industrial Revolution in England during the early nineteenth century were not so much the product of the factory system as of the Napoleonic wars. Under more peaceful conditions it would have been far easier to raise living standards as productivity advanced, to mitigate the evils of slums, and to reduce the insecurities to which industrialism exposed both the farm and city worker. Certainly this has been true of Japan.

The foregoing remarks, supported in more detail elsewhere in this study, all cast doubt on the thesis even in the case of Japan that the State was "the chief element in economic development" or the statesmen "the chief actors." Much the same opinion may be ventured with regard to the *zaibatsu*, especially in those undertakings which required continued patronage from the government because they were never able to stand on their own feet. The energies, the skills, and the ambitions which provided the real motor force of Japanese industrialization were much too pervasive and too diverse to be compressed into any such formula. They found expression through the activities of millions of small industrialists, tradesmen, technicians, farmers, and workers, as well as in the superstructure of big business. The economic modernization of Japan cannot be explained by "laws" of economic determinism, in which new modes of production follow one another in an inexorable sequence. But equally it went far beyond the activities of a few bold pioneers and organizers, whether statesmen, industrial magnates, or scientists. Also involved were myriads of small, unknown entrepreneurs who introduced and spread the new learning, and still larger numbers of humble workers who provided the growing pool of modern technological skills. This, too, called for initiative and adaptability.

Innovation and Enterprise. It would be interesting to know more about the social and technical processes by which such innovations were introduced and spread through Japanese economic life. They included new goods and new materials; new markets, modes of production, and organization; new wants, as well. Some were massive innovations like steam power, modern metallurgy, and the

joint-stock company. Others were modest adaptations and improvements in old ways, no less significant in their cumulative effect. The
actual dynamics of change and growth are an elusive subject, as
remarked above, but a few observations made here and there in
preceding chapters may be brought together at this point.

One cannot escape the conviction, first of all, that the comparative speed of Japan's economic modernization owed much to the
fact that both her geographic position and her particular complement of resources fitted her for the role of an industrial power with
extensive maritime trade.

Already by 1868 Japan was densely settled, with a population
of 2,000 per square mile of cultivated land. This is almost as many
as in the United Kingdom today. If she was to develop she had to
industrialize; her primary industries offered only limited opportunities for expansion. And if she was to industrialize, she had to trade,
especially as she lacked so many essential materials. Fortunately
the Japanese islands lay athwart what were destined to become the
main trade routes of the western Pacific. They were well situated
for extensive contacts with both Asia and the West. Overseas commerce, particularly with the United States and Europe, served as
a broad highway for the introduction of new stimuli and new techniques. These in turn pushed the nation still further along the road
to industrialization.

A related geographic factor of hardly less importance was the
configuration of the country. Japan is smaller than Sweden or
Siam. Most of the land area is within 100 miles of a port city which
has also tended to grow into an industrial center. Short land distances and interior communications by sea were a great advantage
in achieving political order and unity; also in fostering the easy
movement of goods and people within the framework of a growing
national market. They partly explain the remarkable surge of the
population to the cities which was such a conspicuous and essential
feature of industrialization. They also encouraged the dispersion of
many industries through the countryside, even industries heavily
dependent on imported materials and export markets. In such ways
they favored the diffusion of new wants and new knowledge far more
readily than is apt to be the case in a massive continental area like
India or China. And they spared Japan part of the immense capital
outlays required by such countries for land transport and water
control. For example, coal at tidewater and localized water supply
for irrigation were great advantages.

Finally, if the practices of industrial monopoly did not exert a
more baneful effect on Japanese economic development than they
did, this was due in part to competitive safeguards imposed by this

necessary dependence on foreign trade. At home there existed no raw material base comparable to the Ruhr on which to build powerful and restrictive monopolies in large-scale industry. Most Japanese industries had to rely in increasing degree on foreign materials if they were to grow. Moreover, the big combines were apt to find themselves on both sides of the fence, as importers as well as producers. A further restraint on market monopoly was the persisting need to import a good deal of machinery and equipment from Western manufacturers; also the importance for many industries of a highly competitive export business, which in turn handicapped efforts to control the domestic market.

After World War I the competitive stimulus of imports was weakened by the rise of Japan's tariff duties and the growing technical maturity of her industry. A number of large-scale trades, particularly those sheltered from foreign competition, were characterized by what was described earlier as a blend of jealous rivalry and mutual solidarity, of rugged independence and collusive agreement. Still, the continuing necessity of foreign trade, and its competitive character, operated as a check on the traditional Japanese propensity toward combination and group action. Otherwise the latter might have had a more stifling influence on technological progress.

Smallness and poverty in resources are hardly unmixed blessings, to be sure. Yet with nations as with individuals they may contribute powerfully to the dynamics of development. Japan's small size, her insular position off the coast of Asia, and her meager endowment in natural wealth per capita are often said to have created a national sense of inferiority and insufficiency which has made her people historically receptive to new ideas from abroad. However this may be, as a practical matter they aided the Japanese materially during the nineteenth century—first, in avoiding the full force of Western imperialism and preserving their political independence, and, second, in launching a program of rapid modernization. Among various patterns of economic development, circumstance directed them almost from the outset toward industrialization, urbanization, and trade, if in fact any far-reaching expansion of productive powers was to take place. This pattern is not without its disadvantages, and Japan has certainly not escaped the ills which attend it. It did serve, however, to maximize the inflow and permeation of science and industrial arts from the West at a rate not yet experienced by any other Asiatic nation.[56]

[56] England, too, in an earlier day and a quite different setting, reaped the advantages of island security and political unity; of easy access to a continent and the New World; of limited wars fought with the aid of subsidies and the balance

Physical factors alone, of course, do not explain the dynamics of growth. Many nations bear witness today to the fact that modern technology does not necessarily seed itself and take root in a backward, tradition-bound economy even where outside contacts bring it within easy reach.

It is true that Japan's industrialization was more largely a matter of transplanting and adapting to Japanese conditions the techniques already developed in the West than of making primary contributions to the world's stock of knowledge. Yet borrowing of this sort calls for more than rotelike absorption. It involves purpose, criticism, and a creative synthesis. It entails persistent trial and error, and the risking of fortunes both large and small, in a setting which offers rewards for success. New modes of production are apt to encounter subtle and powerful resistance. And this may take the form not only of political disorder, or indifference to material progress, but a deeper hostility to the habits of mind and social arrangements which these modes require. Even within a single country the degree of assimilation may be uneven among various regions and occupations. The case of Japan herself well illustrates this fact.

Like the other great societies of the East, Japan resisted certain aspects of Western culture, with its emphasis on individual self-assertion, competitive striving, and democratic expression. Inner values of the spirit have been tenaciously shielded from the disruptive penetration of Western ideals. But in the realm of the industrial arts, at least, too much has been made of the docility and conservatism of the Japanese. Here, within the limits of his environment and the opportunities which have come to hand, he appears to have displayed a ready willingness to abandon old ways, particularly where the acknowledged leaders of society pointed out the new. One recalls Sir George Sansom's remark, with reference to an earlier historical period in Japan, that the notion of the "unchanging East" is "a very dubious dictum."

As a sidelight on this question, it is interesting to note how the commercial spirit of the "new Japan" at the turn of the century

---

of power; of tidewater coal; of a climate salubrious for the cotton textile industry, the pioneer of the Industrial Revolution; and of a long succession of technical borrowings through the migration of technical skills from Germany, France, and the Low Countries. These circumstances help to explain the paradox, which is no less applicable to Japan, described by Barbara Ward as follows: "Knowing what we know today about the advantages to industrialization of large internal markets . . . and of secure access to raw materials, we should not have picked an island off the coast of Europe as the most favorable spot for beginning the industrial experiment. Geography would always set limits to the growth of a large internal market . . . [and] few of the raw materials necessary to modern industry can be found within Britain's frontiers." *The West at Bay*, New York, 1948, p. 23.

struck one American observer, coming himself from a country engaged in feverish economic expansion. Japanese industrial competition was already beginning to attract the attention of American businessmen. Accordingly the U.S. National Association of Manufacturers dispatched an investigator, Robert P. Porter, to look around. Porter was impressed by what he saw. He returned from his reconnaissance prophesying that the changes begun in "this energetic little island" would ultimately revolutionize the whole of Asia just as English enterprise had once remade the Atlantic world.

The reason, he thought, was to be found in the energy and ambition of the Japanese, which he described as follows:

"Commercial and industrial questions are now almost as popular subjects of treatment, both in the press and by public speakers, as the most urgent political questions whether foreign or domestic. Among them are such matters as the extension of existing steam routes, the results of treaty revision on trade, insurance, establishment of technical and commercial schools, the training of officers and men for the mercantile marine, improvement of chambers of commerce and of the existing system of trade guilds, the despatch of commissioners to study commercial conditions abroad, placing Japanese in commercial houses and factories in foreign countries in order to learn thoroughly their system of business, the establishment of a floating exhibition of Japanese products, the effects on the trade of Japan of the opening of the Siberian Railway and Nicaragua Canal, when Japan may become one of the greatest commercial centers of the world.

"There never was a people so completely absorbed in industrial and commercial questions as the Japanese at this period in their history. Emperor and Prime Minister, the Cabinet, Members of the Imperial Diet and minor officials are all imbued with the progress and future greatness of Japan in manufactures, in commerce, and as the dominating nation of this part of the world. At public dinners, on official occasions of all sorts, the drift of remarks is, what can be done to help the material progress of Japan. The vernacular papers have taken this up, and enterprises of all sorts are exploited with the vim and vigor displayed in the building of our own country."[57]

One may discount Porter's rather uncritical enthusiasm, based as it was on limited contacts and observations. Certainly he was not talking of the Japanese village, or even the masses of young people now beginning to swarm to the cities. Even in manufacturing he conceded that a quarter century of progress had carried Japan little beyond the handicraft stage where Britain and America

[57] *Commerce and Industries of Japan,* Philadelphia: NAM, 1898, p. 7.

stood in 1800. Yet this willingness to venture and to learn, if not to pioneer at least to imitate, in a climate of opportunity which makes it pay, is certainly an essential condition of economic development. That it appeared first at the top of Japanese society is not surprising. What impresses one is the degree to which it spread subsequently through a broad stratum of the population.

It was of great importance, of course, that a considerable segment of Japan's ruling class manifested a spirit of enterprise and adaptability at an early stage of her contact with the West. In contrast to the gentry and aristocracies of most other Asiatic nations, and many of their own compatriots, numerous young *samurai* grasped eagerly at the potentialities of Western learning. They were already restive in the chaotic state of affairs under the Shogunate. Already a good many had virtually been declassed and driven into farming and trade. Despite the antimercantile tradition of their class, it was they who began to display a spirit of capitalistic enterprise in manufacturing and commerce long before the overthrow of the old regime. In this they were joined by the many rich peasants of the central and western regions, and the new merchant class emerging in the port cities. From these elements were recruited the new bureaucrats, businessmen, and technicians who led the way in exploiting the new technology, in economic life as well as government. The common class roots of many leaders in the two fields facilitated the close interrelationships stressed earlier in this chapter.[58]

Only later, as experience accumulated and knowledge became more widely diffused, did increasing numbers of commoner families begin to respond to the new forces in such a way as to give breadth and depth to the process of modernization. Certain economic gains followed quickly and almost automatically from the new freedom

[58] "The section of the *samurai* class that did not take an active part in politics entered the business world. Many of these failed miserably in their new ventures, but the capitalist spirit which they displayed in trying their hands at company enterprises did much to arouse public interest in such enterprises. The general sentiment among the *samurai* in those days was that if new occupations must be chosen, they should turn to novel industries and undertakings not yet tried by *chonin* or farmers. Prince Iwakura was quite right when he declared that the *samurai* class alone had the capitalist spirit." Yasuzo Horie, "An Outline of the Rise of Modern Capitalism in Japan," *Kyoto University Economic Review*, vol. XI, no. 1, July 1936, p. 112.

It has often been remarked, on the other hand, that the leading *chōnin* of the Tokugawa era failed as a rule to make a successful transition to positions of prominence in the new order. Their generally conservative outlook and their close ties with the old nobility stood in the way. This exemplifies what is perhaps almost a law of economic evolution. The leading industrialists of nineteenth century England, too, were not in the main the successors of the merchant manufacturers of the eighteenth century. For example, the woolen masters of Norfolk and Devonshire were unable to change their ways. So it was very largely throughout Europe.

of occupation, the extension of cultivation, the reforms in currency and taxation, the improvement in transport, etc. However, beyond the façade of State-sponsored industries hastily erected in the early years, it took time for the process of innovation and imitation to reach back into traditional Japanese society. One great retarding factor was the quick response of population increase, which so discouraged advances in productivity by more capitalistic methods. Many traditional occupations seemed unaltered in their essentials even after fifty years. In particular, Japanese farming as a way of life changed very little, despite scientific improvements in agriculture which the experts have described as "a chemical and botanical revolution."

Throughout this whole process of growth emphasis must be placed on what seem today very modest improvements: the ricksha and the bicycle; the rodent-proof warehouse; elementary sanitation; better seeds and more fertilizer; the kerosene and then the electric lamp; a simple power loom; the gas engine in the fishing boat; the divorce of personal from business accounts; the principle of limited liability. Big and dramatic innovations like railways and great banks and holding companies might provide the scaffolding. But the structure itself was built, brick upon brick, by myriads of individual experiments and commitments. Inevitably this was a slow process, as it will be throughout Asia.

The system of enterprise through which Japanese development was organized and directed has been referred to above as predominantly one of private ownership and market competition. There are many qualifications to this statement, of course. Yet in the actual conduct of business operations little capital was invested in new undertakings except on the basis of private profit expectations. Losses were mainly a private responsibility, except in comparatively few trades. The innumerable decisions regarding what to produce, how to produce it, where and how to sell it, were left primarily to private initiative, subject only to various political inducements and controls.

Within this system it is significant that as late as the year 1930 one in every three persons gainfully employed in Japan was still in some sense an entrepreneur, carrying some risk and responsibility for business enterprise. (Table 17.) Even in manufacturing, plants of less than 100 workers, most of them separately owned, still accounted for at least one half of total output and two thirds of total employment. (See page 203.) Despite all the limitations upon the independence and the resources of the small businessman which prevailed, this meant a vast number of establishments within which new products and new ways of getting things done might be tried out. It put to work a strong incentive to save, which everywhere tends to be more powerful among small businessmen than among wage earners or large capitalists. It divided the risks in tiny parcels, with a cumulative gain from successful innovations. Much of the most productive investment and modernization of techniques took place in these medium- and small-scale sectors of the economy.

To speak of private enterprise and competition as characteristic of the prewar Japanese economy is not to deny the inward differences between the system as it developed here and its prototypes in the West. If competition was keen, its forms were influenced by age-old traditions of hierarchy and group solidarity. If enterprise was privately owned, the individual entrepreneur yet conducted his affairs in a context of Japanese ideals and institutions, with its own set of family obligations, paternalistic controls, and other social incentives and restraints. No people have ever organized economic life on the basis of unrestrained individualism, and certainly not the Japanese.

The small industrialist or trader, as well as the farmer, continued to operate essentially a family enterprise, utilizing family labor and drawing little distinction between family and business affairs. His independence in external relations was closely limited by mental horizon as well as meager financial resources. Where he was integrated into a larger framework of production and trade, he was apt to be heavily dependent on a larger merchant, factory, or bank. These circumstances are not peculiar to small-scale enterprise in Japan, of course. What is striking about the Japanese case is the amount of growth and technical improvement which nevertheless took place in many such trades. Perhaps the outstanding reason is the one already remarked upon. The Japanese were peculiarly successful in organizing and extending complex systems of production and marketing within which numerous small establishments came to perform highly specialized functions and were yet linked together in a flexible and far-reaching pattern of social cooperation. Geography favored such arrangements through providing good interior communications and easy contacts between the port cities and much of the countryside. But the Japanese themselves would appear to have inherited a flair for such patterns of group action.

The financiers and executives who built Japan's large-scale industries displayed marked capacity in performing the classic functions of capitalistic innovation. Yet here as well, it may be remarked that Japanese businessmen often seemed cautious in asserting the spirit of self-reliant venture. The corporation manager, like the political bureaucrat, was prone to take shelter in group responsibility. There were few rugged "captains of industry" even in the early days; corporate action came naturally to the Japanese. The great combines employed all the latest financial devices for concentrating business power, but their prominence in modern Japan was itself an expression of old traditions of authority and teamwork. So, too, were their close and mutually dependent relations with the government.

The opportunities of industrialization enabled successful enterprises to reap handsome, quasi-monopolistic rewards, for private capital would venture into new and risky fields only where large profits could be anticipated. Even then, the tendency was to insure against risks wherever possible by restraining competition and securing the patronage of the State in one form or another. A British observer of Japanese business at the close of the Meiji era had this to say: "Men look to the Government for aid, and having received it try to stifle competition. Success depends more on manoeuvering for privilege than on a steady persevering struggle against obstacles. As a natural sequence the supply of active, resourceful, self-reliant men of affairs does not keep pace with the demand, hence the timidity of capital and the cry for more and still more Government assistance."[59]

All this is not surprising, in view of Japan's authoritarian background, her intense nationalism and the difficulty which any people face in moving out of a static, traditional economy into new and untried fields. More surprising is the speed with which the Japanese moved to take over the organization and the skills necessary to modern industrialism. For example, while other peoples in Asia have shown no less aptitude for mechanical skills, the Japanese, aided by geographic circumstance, accomplished with unsual facility the great occupational and regional shifts in population which were no less important for industrialization. (See Chapter 9.) Considering the age-old emphasis on status and conformity, and the attachment of the peasant family to the soil, one might have looked for much more inertia, if not active resistance, when it came to new modes of activity which put a premium on personal initiative and dynamic change.

It appears, too, that the Japanese experienced less difficulty than most Oriental peoples in building and operating large-scale administrative structures which would make effective use of the new skills and energies in modern business and government. Elsewhere in Asia, such structures have degenerated all too often into nightmares of nepotism, corruption, and administrative disorder. Japanese society, like Chinese society, was traditionally oriented on a

[59] Charles V. Sale, "Some Statistics of Japan," *Journal of the Royal Statistical Society*, vol. LXXIV, no. 5, April 1911, p. 472.

family basis in considerable degree. But not in the same exclusive, atomistic fashion. The family obligation was qualified by, and ideally subordinate to, higher loyalties to one's overlord, and ultimately to the emperor. This helped not only to forge a new political unity after 1868, with the almost bloodless surrender by the feudal nobility of its traditional prerogatives, but also to create other new forms of social cooperation which functioned fairly efficiently.[60]

In the military realm, most vividly perhaps, one sees how Japan's feudal heritage helped her to take over modern patterns of large-scale administration. The modern Japanese Army has had its cliques and internal political intrigues. Yet it is interesting how quickly the Japanese created a centralized structure of command and general staff, based on German models, a modern system of technical training, and a practice of assigning new young officers on the basis of merit to responsible posts of command and administration. Their success in this regard, and the utter failure of the Chinese mandarinate under Li Hung-chang, gave Japan an easy victory over China in 1894-95. The same traits applied in the business world, in more qualified fashion, contributed greatly to the growth and efficiency of large financial and industrial organizations. They facilitated the adoption of joint-stock enterprise and the factory system. And they gave a degree of cohesion and order to the whole process of political and economic development which is one of the most striking features of modern Japan.

Yet respect for hierarchy, group discipline, and teamwork will not alone create modern industrialism. They may serve only to stifle it. One should beware of exaggerating this feature of Japanese modernization. It was an asset only insofar as it was accompanied by, and did not stultify, the ambition to advance through adopting new ways, and the willingness to adventure along new paths pioneered by leaders. Since it is so commonly stressed in accounts of Japanese industrialization, I have chosen rather to emphasize the factors of innovation and enterprise. Only slowly and unevenly did new value standards and technical capacities mature, of course. And they remained heavily qualified among the great mass of the people, especially in the more remote rural areas, away from the urban centers of change. Yet it was this process, advancing bit by bit through a wide range of occupations, which gave mass and momentum to Japan's economic advance.

The State and Economic Growth: Conclusions. The dynamics of Japan's economic development thus involved numerous elements of

60 See Marion J. Levy, "Contrasting Factors in the Modernization of China and Japan," *Economic Development and Cultural Change*, vol. II, no. 3, October 1953, pp. 161-97.

social organization, geographic circumstance, and historical setting. Many of them are not difficult to observe in operation. But to evaluate and integrate all of them in a comprehensive theory of economic growth which really gets at the root of the matter is hardly to be attempted in the present state of knowledge. Perhaps, to quote Lionel Robbins again, it is better left to poets and metaphysicians.

One aspect of the matter in particular, the role of political forces operating through agencies of the State, has been examined in this chapter. The outlook, the energies, and the authority of the Meiji leaders were clearly of immense significance, leaving a deep imprint on the subsequent course of economic development.

Yet the picture which emerges does not show the State in the central planning and directing role often ascribed to it, so far as the principal areas of economic growth are concerned. Especially is this true of the period after 1890, when the great expansion took place. Certainly no sufficient explanation of Japan's industrial development can be found merely in the thesis that her political tradition endowed her with an authoritarian military caste which engineered the modernization and industrialization of their country as the means to national power.[61] The existence of a strong central government infused with imperial ambitions served in some respects to stimulate and facilitate the process; in other respects it operated as a decided drag; in still other respects it had little direct influence on what took place.

The truly signal contributions to economic growth which were made through the political mechanism were, first, to ward off foreign subjection and assure the nation's political unity and order; second, to clear away the whole complex of political obstacles to freedom of ownership, occupation, and movement; and third, to carry through a series of architectural reforms in law, education, taxation, currency, etc. which created a setting favorable to the emergence of new forms of productive enterprise. In the realm of industrial development, particularly, the government furnished more direct encouragements and even actual entrepreneurship during the earlier years. Yet its influences exerted here through the prewar decades were inconsistent and discriminatory in their total effect, so far as real economic growth was concerned.

While the Meiji State was absolutist in politics, it was not totalitarian. Its policies widened steadily the range of personal freedom and opportunity in economic life. Such opportunity remained closely

[61] Nevertheless, for an interesting comparison between Japan and China in this respect see Hu Shih, "The Modernization of China and Japan: A Comparative Study in Cultural Conflict," *China Quarterly*, vol. 5, no. 4, winter number, supplement, 1940, pp. 773-80.

circumscribed for most people, and freedom was all too often the freedom to be exploited by the moneylender and the landlord. On the other hand, the State never substituted political rewards and punishments for private incentives to material gain. It enlarged the sphere of private ownership rather than government collectivization. It replaced a harsh and oppressive rule by feudal aristocrats with something which approached increasingly the modern standards of constitutional rule by law. The Japanese adopted Western technology much more readily than ideas of personal freedom; the latter remain heavily qualified to this day. Probably, too, the dependence of one on the other is less unconditional in the twentieth century than in the pioneering days before 1850. Yet it is significant that the Industrial Revolution in Japan, as in most of the West, was generated by such innovations as the abolition of heritable servitude, legal equality before the law, free choice of occupation and residence, and the construction of a new framework of security and opportunity within which private enterprise could develop.

Notwithstanding other, less constructive aspects of State policy, this framework made possible the building of a new national market for goods and capital, linked with the outside world through expanding trade. It encouraged that internal mobility of people among jobs and places which was so essential to economic growth and structural change. It provided a climate favorable to the cumulative advance of new investment and technical change. Other features of State encouragement and regulation reviewed earlier in this chapter were important in their respective spheres, of course. No one would say of Japan, as of nineteenth century Britain, that her industrial development "owed practically nothing to State aid."[62] But where State action contributed to the expansion of Japan's productive powers, and did not merely warp it in particular directions, or redistribute its benefits among classes, it served mainly to hasten and facilitate a process the chief motive force of which lay elsewhere.

The case of Japan is nevertheless significant, perhaps unique in Asia, in that political and social leadership throughout this period of transition was exercised by certain dominant groups who remained firmly in the saddle and were technologically progressive on the whole. These groups maintained their ascendency, accommodated their differences, and pursued their aims through a variety of social institutions and controls. Of these the political hierarchy was only one, although perhaps the most important.

Here, paradoxically, we may have the reason why direct State

[62] L. C. A. Knowles, *The Industrial and Commercial Revolutions in Great Britain during the Nineteenth Century*, London, 1921, p. 171.

intervention in economic life was rather limited through most of the prewar period, judged by modern standards. Given the temper of Japan's leaders, their control over wealth, and the strength of the Japanese social fabric, it was unnecessary to rely on State coercion extensively to mobilize resources for industrialization. Moreover, while different elements of the ruling coalition—for example, the military and the *zaibatsu*—often had divergent interests, they found it possible for a long time to harmonize their differences in a political regime with limited economic responsibilities; and no popular movement arose with sufficient power to wrest control and impose a different pattern.

Commenting on this point, Robert E. Ward raises more explicitly "the question whether or not reasonably effective national economic planning and the satisfactory implementation of large-scale developmental programs require the same degree of overt positive State participation in Japan—or perhaps in any major Oriental society—that the achievement of comparable results would necessitate in a Western society." He continues: "Making due allowance for the imperfection of the following categories, is it still not possible, in a Japanese cultural context characterized by a relatively homogeneous and continuous ruling class, a tradition of collective action and responsibility and some general pragmatic agreement that industrialization and economic development are desirable, that such informal oligarchic solidarity would of itself prove capable of achieving many of the results reflected by Japan's present stage of economic development? Such societies perhaps have more 'built-in social controls' than do more individualistically-structured ones. If so, this may somewhat explain the surprising moderation of the Japanese government in terms of formal participation in or the imposition of extensive controls on the national economy prior to the 1930's."[63]

It may well have been these circumstances which made Japan as responsive as she was to the liberal principles of economic organization current in the nineteenth century West, and enabled the system of private enterprise to prevail in such large degree for half a century. Significantly, it was only as internal tensions mounted after 1925, and as international tensions gathered throughout the world, that the State moved increasingly to take over direct control and management of the Japanese economy.

How far these circumstances prevail elsewhere today in Asia—or in postwar Japan itself—is less clear. As regards capital forma-

[63] Comments on this chapter submitted to the Conference on Economic Growth in Selected Countries, April 25-27, 1952, sponsored by the Social Science Research Council.

tion, for example, it may be doubted whether private initiative can do the job, or will be allowed to do it, in anything like the same degree. Many of the peoples of Asia are developing a set of social expectations and immediate demands such that they will probably be unwilling to tolerate the great inequalities of private property and income so patiently borne by the Japanese. Equally important, where income continues to be as unequally distributed as it is in, say, the Philippines, there is little evidence that the well-to-do class is disposed so largely as it was in prewar Japan to save and invest its money in creating new capital assets for productive enterprise.

A greater spirit of egalitarianism among the people, and a lack of entrepreneurial spirit among the owning class, where they prevail, will impel greater reliance on the State to mobilize capital and assume the risks and responsibilities of economic development, if it is to take place on any scale. Also, the tradition of private enterprise is greatly weakened, where it has not been discarded altogether, in the West. Moreover, the internal cleavage and balance of forces in most countries of Asia are such as to create a more violent struggle for political power than in pre-1931 Japan. These factors accentuate still further the tendency to State intervention in economic life as a weapon for enforcing the will of the group which manages to seize control of the apparatus of government. Finally, international tension and insecurity in the East, no less than the West, work in the same direction.

So far as this holds true, the pattern of organization and entrepreneurship which produced such rapid economic growth in Japan can hardly be duplicated elsewhere in Asia. Whether this is for better or worse remains to be seen. From the standpoint of democracy and well-being, one would hope that some of the human costs and social injustices of the Japanese experience could be avoided. The dilemma appears to lie in the urgent demands being made on new, untried governments to produce large and impressive results, when these governments are so lacking in the very skills and standards of large-scale, responsible administration which the job requires. Perhaps, as in Japan, once a pattern of order and growth is established, an initial period of State leadership and control will give way later to a larger measure of private enterprise, with some dependable demarcation of their respective spheres. The tasks required of the State are crucial in all these countries. Yet it is hard to see how their economic development can be either rapid or sustained without the release of the spring of private initiative.

In any case the lessons of Japan are worth pondering. In two respects they are a warning. Unless population growth can be held in check, the mere increase in numbers will absorb much of the gain of development. And unless political institutions can be created to harness productive power to welfare goals, still more of the gain may be dissipated in war and conquest.

But there is also a more constructive lesson in Japan's experience. It testifies to the potential of one Asiatic people at least for assimilating the skills necessary to economic progress, once a framework and atmosphere are provided to give full play to their productive energies. If the history of modern Japan argues for vigorous leadership in economic development, it is a tribute no less to the capacities of the common people.

INDEX